Crusade and Christendom

CRUSADE AND CHRISTENDOM

Annotated Documents in Translation
from Innocent III to the Fall of Acre, 1187–1291

Edited by

Jessalynn Bird, Edward Peters,
and James M. Powell

PENN

UNIVERSITY OF PENNSYLVANIA PRESS

PHILADELPHIA

Published by
University of Pennsylvania Press
Philadelphia, Pennsylvania 19104-4112
www.upenn.edu/pennpress

Printed in the United States of America on acid-free paper
10 9 8 7 6 5 4 3 2 1

Library of Congress Cataloging-in-Publication Data
Crusade and Christendom : annotated documents in translation
from Innocent III to the fall of Acre, 1187–1291 / edited by
Jessalynn Bird, Edward Peters, and James M. Powell. — 1st ed.
    p. cm. — (The Middle Ages series)
Includes bibliographical references and index.
Includes source materials translated into English.
ISBN 978-0-8122-4478-6 (hardcover : alk. paper)
    1. Crusades—Sources.   2. Church history—Middle Ages,
600–1500—Sources.   3. Christianity and culture—History—
Middle Ages, 600–1500—Sources.   4. Innocent III, Pope,
1160 or 61–1216.   I. Bird, Jessalynn Lea.   II. Peters, Edward,
1936–.   III. Powell, James M.   IV. Series: Middle Ages series.
D151.C765   2013
909.07—dc23
                                                    2012025735

*This book is dedicated to the memory of
our dear friend and collaborator
James M. Powell (1930–2011)*

Contents

Editors' Note

In 1971 Edward Peters published *Christian Society and the Crusades, 1198–1229*, a modest volume of historical documents in English translation intended to make available to students a number of widely scattered source materials and a brief survey of scholarship to date, dealing with the crusade movements of a particularly important period in both crusade and wider European history. The volume drew heavily on the distinguished and pioneering series *Translations and Reprints from the Original Sources of European History*, originally under the aegis of Dana C. Munro, the founder of crusade history in the United States. In the decades since the original publication, the amount of translated source materials and new scholarship has grown enormously, and perspectives on both the thirteenth-century crusades and the character of Christendom in the period have greatly changed. Two excellent and wide-ranging collections of scholarly articles that represent many aspects of the most recent scholarship are Andrew Jotischky, ed., *The Crusades*, vols. 3 and 4, Critical Concepts in Historical Studies (London, 2008), and Thomas F. Madden, James L. Naus, and Vincent Ryan, eds., *Crusades—Medieval Worlds in Conflict* (Farnham UK-Burlington VT, 2010).

In February 1991, James M. Powell, whose own 1986 study *The Anatomy of a Crusade* was a major part of the new scholarship, asked Peters if he planned to revise *Christian Society*. Peters decided that he would, since much of the more recent material is also often widely scattered and many important texts remained untranslated, but would Jim collaborate? Powell graciously agreed. In 2001 our friend Jessalynn Bird, a young American scholar of the period, completed her D.Phil. thesis at Oxford on James of Vitry and the School of Peter the Chanter, and it seemed logical to invite Bird, whose work then and since substantially complements that of Powell and others, to collaborate with us on the revision. She has done heroic work—many of the newly translated documents of the thirteenth century have been hers.

It has taken more than a decade to assemble the new version, and in the course of that decade the project became an entirely new book with much of a heavily revised older book inside it. The period has been redated to 1198–1291 (with one important item dating from 1187), from the beginning of the pontificate of Innocent III (1198–1216) to the fall of Acre (1291). The number of texts in translation and the range of topics addressed have greatly increased. It is no longer a revision or even a second edition. We have retained most of the translations in the earlier volume, but have reduced the number of texts on the Fourth Crusade by Munro and, in the case of the chronicle of the Fifth Crusade (1217–1221) of Oliver of Paderborn, originally translated and independently published

by Joseph J. Gavigan and the University of Pennsylvania Press, have revised the
text and scholarly apparatus.

Because of the scope and length of the book, we have not been able to cite
scholarly literature in languages other than English, except in a very few cases. But
we have attempted to indicate the locations of printed English translations of both
the texts we have included and other related texts from the late twelfth to the end
of the late thirteenth centuries.

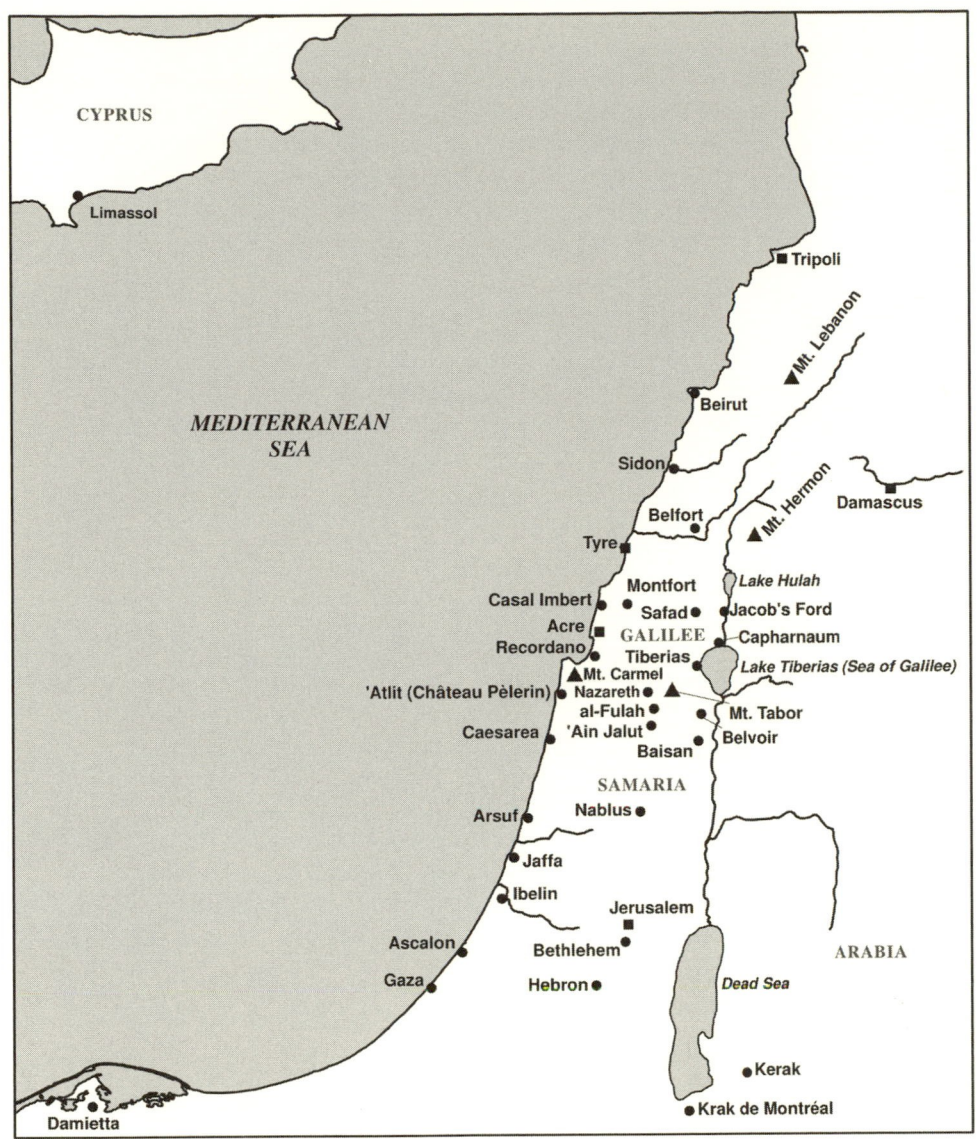

Map 1. The Latin Kingdom of Jerusalem in the Thirteenth Century

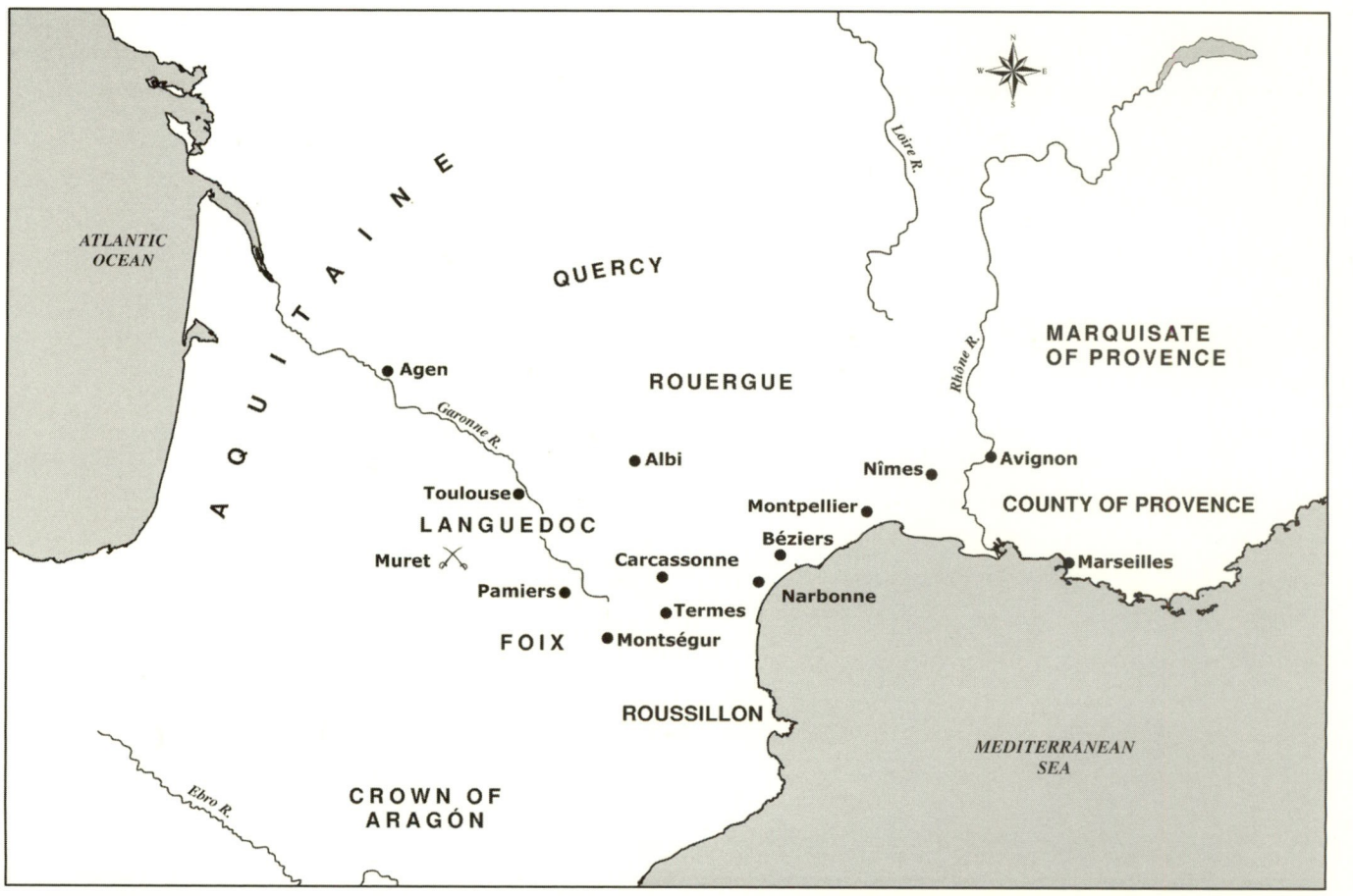

Map 2. Areas of the Albigensian Crusade and the Inquisition in Southern France

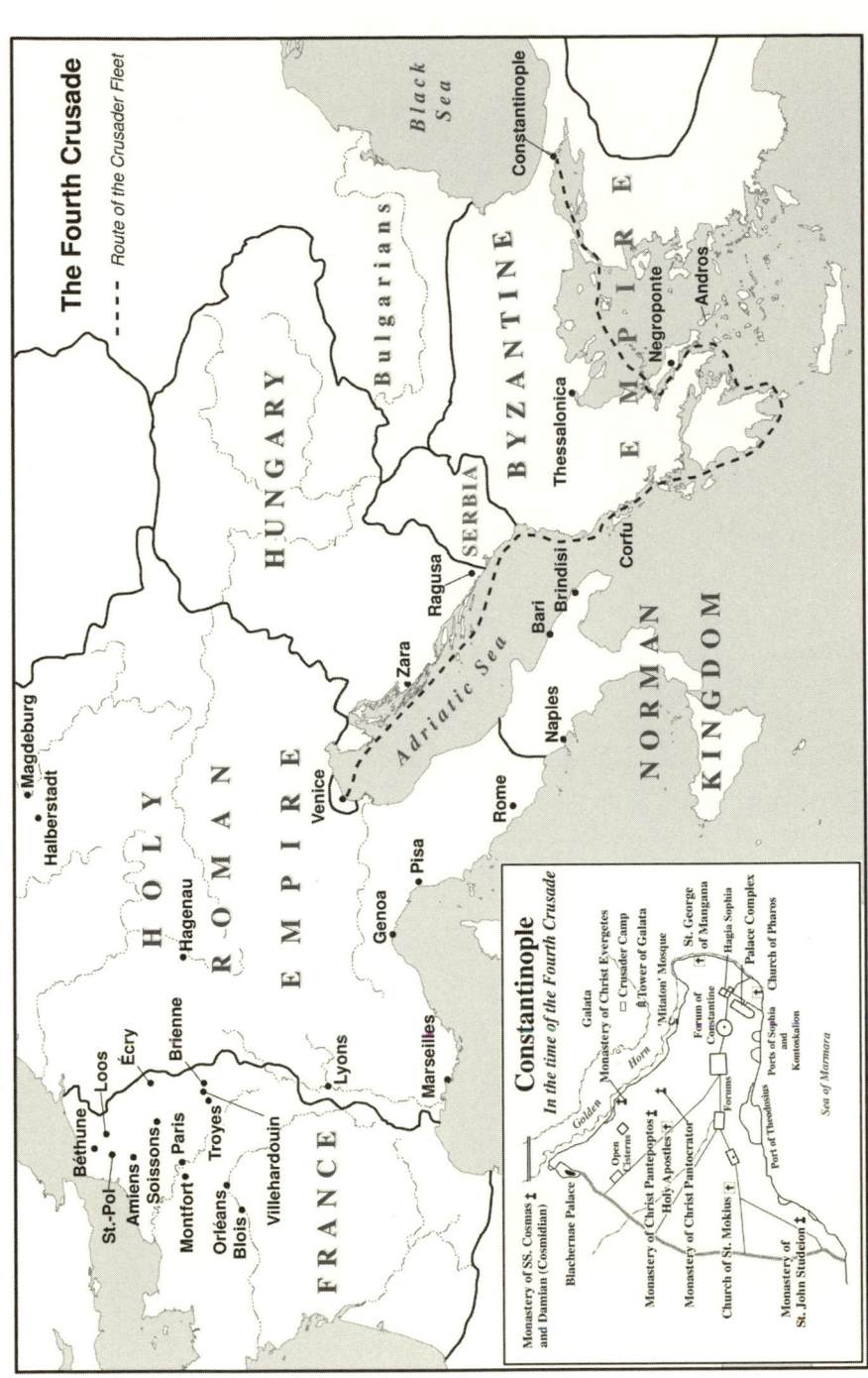

Map 3. The Fourth Crusade's Route to Constantinople

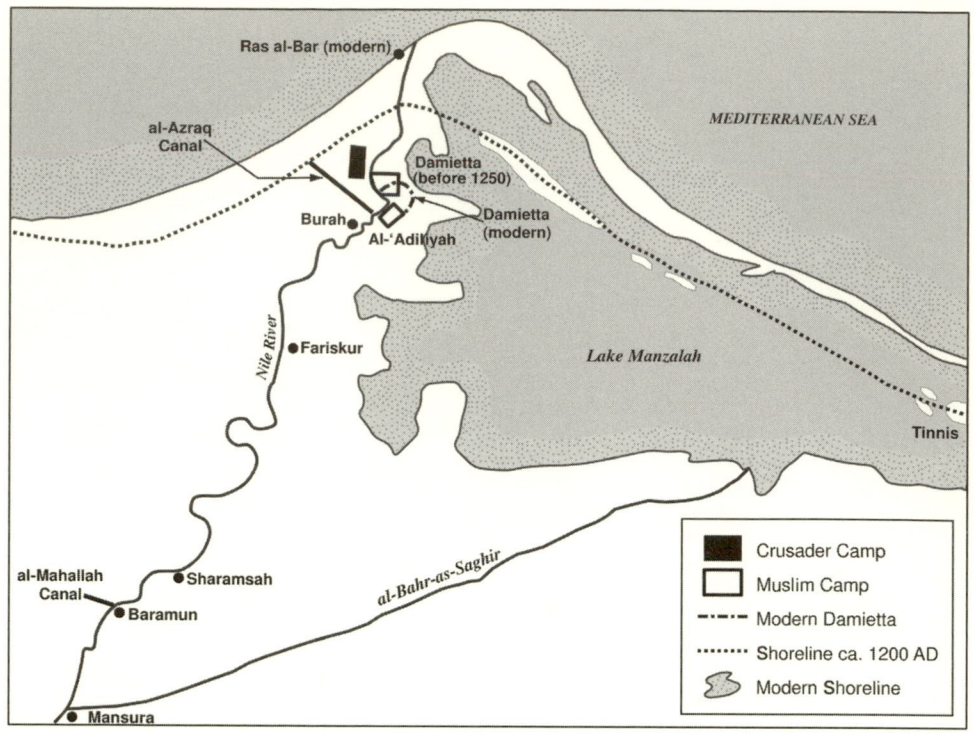

Map 4. The Damietta Region of Egypt

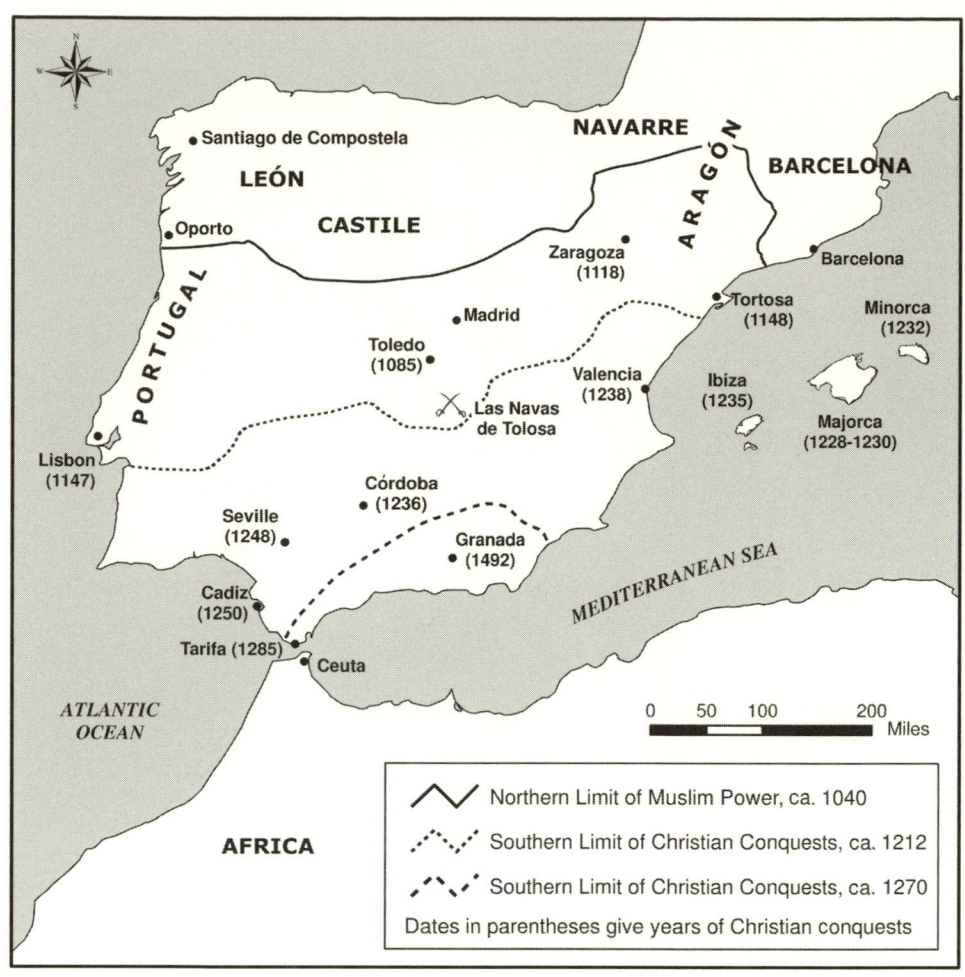

Map 5. Progress of the Reconquista in Iberia

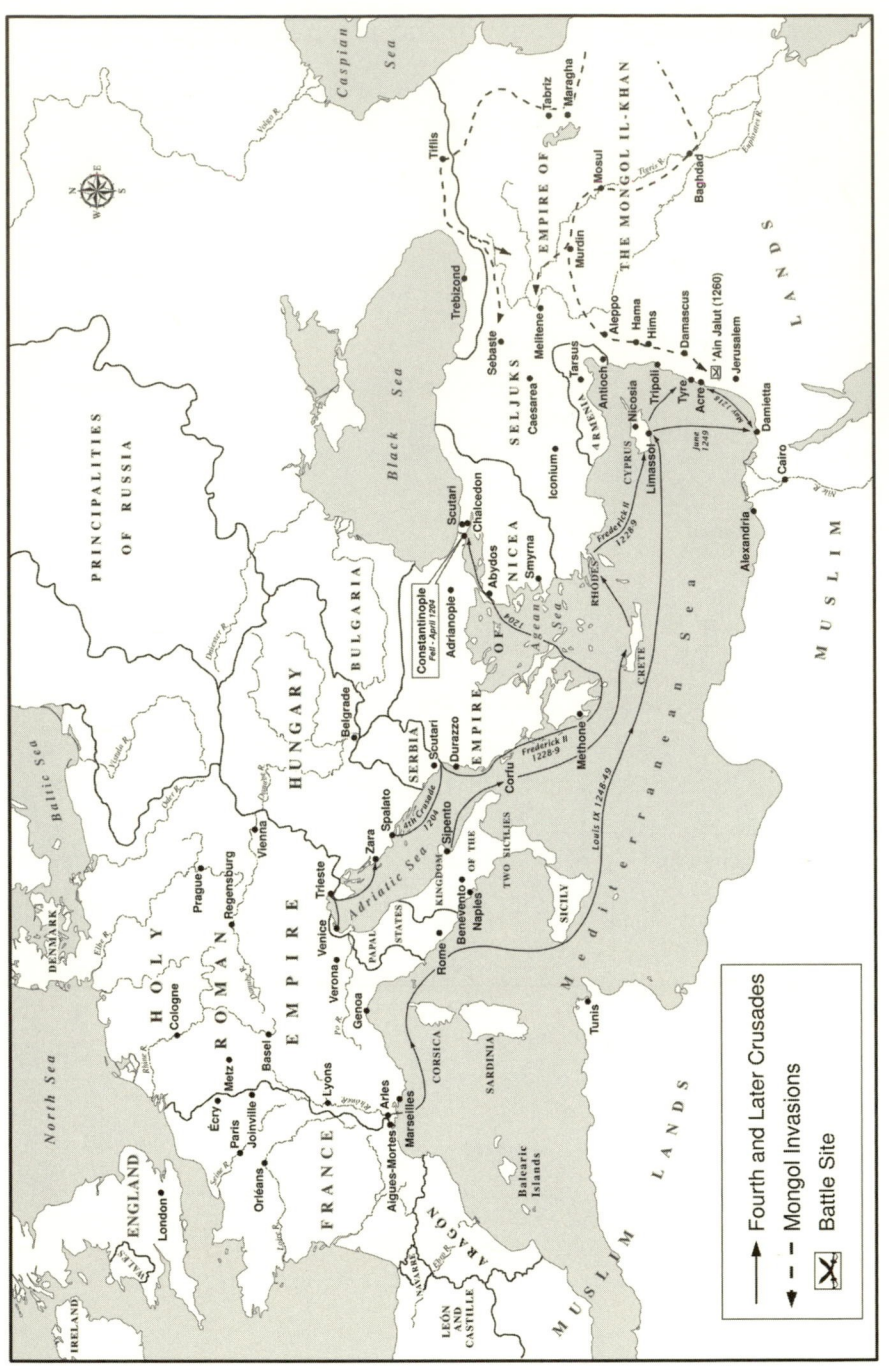

Map 6. The Mediterranean Region

Note on Abbreviations and Translation

Abbreviations

Pressutti — P. Pressutti, ed., *Regesta Honorii papae III*, 2 vols. (Rome, 1888–1895).

RHGF — *Recueil des historiens des Gaules et de la France*, ed. Martin Bouquet et al., 24 vols. (Paris, 1738–1904).

MGH SS — *Monumenta germaniae historica: Scriptores*, ed. G. H. Pertz, T. Mommsen, et al. 32 vols. (Hannover-Leipzig, 1826–1934).

MGH SS rer. Germ. — *Monumenta germaniae historica: Scriptores rerum Germanicarum. Nova series.*

PL — *Patrologiae Latinae cursus completus*, ed. J.-P. Migne, 222 vols., numbered 221 (Paris, 1844–1903).

Scriptural Abbreviations

Because different versions of scriptural citation are in use now and were in use in the period treated by this book, we have used a compromise system of citation laid out here. Editors' translations here are based on St. Jerome's Vulgate Latin translation from Hebrew, of which several different versions circulated in the schools and churches of the thirteenth century. Other translators of scriptural texts in this volume have cited other translations, for example, the King James Bible, the Douai-Rheims, or more modern ones. We have made no effort to systematize all citations, but the following list of abbreviations ought to identify a particular book of scripture without much difficulty.

Hebrew Scripture

Gn — Genesis
Ex — Exodus
Lv — Leviticus
Nm — Numbers
Dt — Deuteronomy
Jo — Joshua

Jgs	Judges
Ru	Ruth
1 Sm	1 Samuel (Some references combine Samuel and Kings as 1–4 Kings)
2 Sm	2 Samuel
1 Kgs	1 Kings
2 Kgs	2 Kings
1 Chr	1 Chronicles
2 Chr	2 Chronicles
Ezr	Ezra (In Greek and Early Christian lists, 1 and 2 Esdras)
Neh	Nehemiah
Est	Esther
Jb	Job
Ps	Psalms

Although most books are readily identifiable across the range of these translations, a particularly difficult point is the numbering of Psalms in different versions. The Vulgate version combines Psalms 9 and 10 of the Hebrew Bible. From Psalm 10 to Psalm 146 the Psalm number is one digit lower in the Vulgate than in the Hebrew and most (including Anglican) modern versions. Psalms 146 and 147 in the Vulgate are Psalm 147 in the Hebrew Bible. In all versions Psalms 148–150 are numbered the same.

Prv	Proverbs
Eccl	Ecclesiastes
Sg	Song of Solomon
Ws	Wisdom
Ecclus	Ecclesiasticus
Is	Isaiah
Jer	Jeremiah
Lam	Lamentations
Bar	Baruch
Ez	Ezekiel
Dn	Daniel
Hos	Hosea
Jl	Joel
Am	Amos
Ob	Obadiah
Jon	Jonah
Mi	Micah
Na	Nahum
Hb	Habakkuk
Zep	Zephania
Hg	Haggai
Zec	Zecharia

Mal	Malachi
1 Mc	1 Maccabees
2 Mc	2 Maccabees

New Testament

Mt	Matthew
Mk	Mark
Lk	Luke
Jn	John
Acts	Acts of the Apostles
Rom	Romans
1 Cor	1 Corinthians
2 Cor	2 Corinthians
Gal	Galatians
Eph	Ephesians
Phil	Philippians
Col	Colossians
1 Thes	1 Thessalonians
2 Thes	2 Thessalonians
1 Tm	1 Timothy
2 Tm	2 Timothy
Ti	Titus
Phlm	Philemon
Heb	Hebrews
Jas	James
1 Pt	1 Peter
2 Pt	2 Peter
1 Jn	1 John
2 Jn	2 John
3 Jn	3 John
Jude	Jude
Apoc	Revelation/Apocalypse

Apocrypha

For the apocryphal books, many cited in our period, see Bruce M. Metzger, ed., *The Apocrypha of the Old Testament* (rev. ed., Oxford, 1977), and J. K. Elliott, *The Apocryphal New Testament* (Oxford, 1993).

Forms of Citation

The numbering of chapters in the books of scripture began in the schools of Paris in the early thirteenth century. The numbering of verses within chapters did not occur until the sixteenth century. Therefore, the insertion of chapter and verse numbers throughout this book is derived from general modern usage with the variations noted above for Hebrew, Latin, and modern vernacular versions of scripture. In a few manuscripts (identified in the headnotes) the scribe will identify only a chapter of a scriptural book (a practice that was becoming more and more common). In such cases the editors have added the modern verse number(s) in square brackets.

Principles of translation and editing

The editors have made all translations as readable as possible, often revising older work, breaking up long paragraphs into shorter ones, and offering texts revised for modern usage in order to enhance clarity. In some cases we have omitted overly elaborate editorial apparatus in favor of shorter and updated material. In all our work we have remained faithful to both the original language of the sources and the needs of the modern reader.

INTRODUCTION
Crusade and Christendom, 1187–1291

Beasts of many kinds are attempting to destroy the vineyard of the Lord of Sabaoth, and their onset has so far succeeded against it that over no small area thorns have sprung up instead of vines and (with grief we report it!) the vines themselves are variously infected and diseased, and instead of the grape they bring forth the wild grape [Is 6:4]. Therefore we invoke the testimony of Him, who is a faithful witness in the Heavens [Apoc 1:5], that of all the desires of our heart we long chiefly for two in this life, namely, that we may work successfully to recover the Holy Land and to reform the Universal Church, both of which call for attention so immediate as to preclude further apathy or delay unless at the risk of great and serious danger.[1]

In his letter *Vineam Domini* of April 1213, laced with familiar biblical citations and echoes of others, Pope Innocent III (b. ca. 1160, r. 1198–1216) called for a general council of the Latin Church, vividly depicting the dangers facing universal Christendom and what he perceived to be the two most pressing and closely related tasks before it. To be sure, the first fifteen years of Innocent's pontificate had not neglected these problems, and the young pope had sent hundreds of letters concerning the threatened state of Christendom—letters that had urged, begged, cajoled, entreated, and thundered against the enemies of the church (seen as the entire Christian community), of peace, and of moral reform. In 1215 Innocent took two major steps to achieve the goals that he desired most. The Fourth Lateran Council, announced by the letter *Vineam Domini*, convened in Rome in November 1215. Its task was to build upon the work of earlier church councils and popes, as well as the more recent work of twelfth-century theologians and canon lawyers, toward the definition of dogma and law in the face of the need to reform the universal church, to achieve at last "the extirpation of vices and the

1. Translation cited from C. R. Cheney and W. H. Semple, eds., *Selected Letters of Pope Innocent III Concerning England (1198–1216)* (London, 1953), 144–145. The letter was circulated widely throughout western Europe. Papal letters are usually referred to by their opening Latin words and their locations in published collections, as well as date and place of issue. On the letter and the project, see Alberto Melloni, "*Vineam Domini*—10 April 1213: Summoning Lateran IV," in John C. Moore, ed., *Pope Innocent III and His World* (Brookfield VT, 1999), 63–73. The Moore volume is a superb collection of studies of Innocent III and the range of issues during his pontificate. On Innocent and the Muslim world, see 317–376. The image of heretics as foxes destroying the vineyard of the church was extensively developed by Saint Bernard of Clairvaux in his Sermon 65 on the Song of Songs (Sg 2:15) in 1144. Innocent III was greatly influenced by the works of Saint Bernard. Here Innocent uses the image more broadly to characterize all the ills besetting the church.

implanting of virtues, for correcting excesses, and reforming customs, eliminating heresies and strengthening faith, for quieting discords and establishing peace, for restraining oppressions and favoring liberty, for inducing Christian princes and peoples to aid and support the Holy Land."[2] Innocent gave the recipients of *Vineam Domini* two years of lead time in which to prepare for the great council, an advance notice unheard of until then. And Innocent himself promised to prepare carefully and thoroughly:

> Because it is not possible to convene the council for two years, we have decided in the meantime, with the help of prudent men, to investigate in the various provinces those matters that demand the attention of the apostolic supervision and to appoint suitable men as procurators of the business of the Holy Land so that, if the sacred council approves, we may personally take up the promotion of this business more effectively.[3]

"The business of the Holy Land," quite literally the *negotium terrae sanctae*, was of course the crusade, the *negotium crucis*, the "business of the cross." In Innocent's view the crusade, the "business of the cross," was inseparable from individual and collective moral reform on the part of Christian society.[4]

2. *Vineam Domini*, cited by James M. Powell, *The Anatomy of a Crusade, 1213–1221* (Philadelphia, 1986), 16. See also Brenda Bolton, "A Show with a Meaning: Innocent III's Approach to the Fourth Lateran Council, 1215," repr. in Brenda M. Bolton, *Innocent III: Studies on Papal Authority and Pastoral Care*, Collected Studies Series 490 (Aldershot, 1995), XI.
3. Powell, *Anatomy*, 15, from *Vineam Domini*. Powell's first chapter greatly illuminates these years. See also Parts III and IV below.
4. Innocent had no consistent term for "crusade," and the words "crusade" and "crusader" in the editorial material in the present volume and in some translated texts are used solely for the convenience of readers. Nor did Innocent recognize any numbering of expeditions. Crusade numbers in this volume are also used solely for the convenience of readers and refer only to particular campaigns. There is an extensive discussion of both problems in Giles Constable, *Crusaders and Crusading in the Twelfth Century* (Farnham UK-Burlington VT, 2008), Appendix A, "The Terminology of Crusading," 349–352, and Appendix B, "The Numbering of the Crusades," 353–356. On the different views of historians concerning the nature of crusade, the best discussion is also by Constable, "The Historiography of the Crusades," rev. in Constable, *Crusaders*, 3–43. See also Walker Reid Cosgrove, "*Crucesignatus*: A Refinement or Merely One More Term Among Many?" in Thomas F. Madden, James L. Naus, and Vincent Ryan, eds., *Crusades—Medieval Worlds in Conflict* (Farnham UK-Burlington VT, 2010), 95–107; Björn Weiler, "The *Negotium Terrae Sanctae* in the Political Discourse of Latin Christendom, 1215–1311," *Journal of Medieval History* 25 (2003), 1–36, repr. in Andrew Jotischky, ed., *The Crusades*, Critical Concepts in Historical Studies (London, 2008), vol. 3; Norman Housley, *Contesting the Crusades* (Malden MA-Oxford, 2006); Christopher Tyerman, *The Debate on the Crusades, 1099–2010: Issues in Historiography* (London-New York, 2012).

After the council ended, Innocent, as he had promised, drafted an elaborate and detailed appeal for yet another crusade, which he completed in December 1215 and appended to the canons of the council as canon 71, *Ad liberandam* (below, No. 16). Innocent had now taken up his second and closely related task, the planning of the Fifth Crusade, which was to set off in 1217, thereby, he hoped, bringing to completion his other great aim, the recovery of the Holy Land.

Innocent did not simply select these two goals out of a larger agenda. He firmly believed that God worked providentially in the world, that God had placed him on the throne of Saint Peter, and that the time was appropriate for these two great enterprises.[5] His early years in Rome, his studies at the schools of Paris, his work in papal service, his own experience of the loss of Jerusalem in 1187, the failure of the Third Crusade in 1189, and the growing urgency of moral reform all shaped his identification of those two aims and their interdependence.[6]

When Innocent was elected in January 1198, the crusading kingdom of Jerusalem had been reduced to a string of cities and towns along the Syrian coast from Tyre to Jaffa, as well as the island of Cyprus, whose lords and clergy continued to implore military aid from their fellow Christians in western Europe. The stunning victory of the armies of Saladin over those of the Latin Kingdom of Jerusalem at the Horns of Hattin on July 4, 1187, opened the way for further Muslim conquests, including that of the city of Jerusalem on October 20. The disheartening news reached Europe slowly. Not until late October did the news of Hattin reach the papal curia, where it elicited *Audita tremendi*, one of the most important papal letters in crusade history, one that drew upon a number of earlier papal letters and set the stage for later thirteenth-century crusade proclamations, expeditions, and crusading theory. Many other letters sent from the East also stressed the insult to Christ, to Christendom, and to every individual Christian believer, as well as the pollution of the holy places by infidels.[7] Both the circumstances surrounding the

5. Brenda Bolton, "Signposts from the Past: Reflections on Innocent III's Providential Path," in A. Sommerlechner, ed., *Innocenzo III: Urbs et Orbis*, 2 vols. (Rome, 2003), 1:21–55; John Doran, "In Whose Footsteps? The Role Models of Innocent III," in Sommerlechner, *Innocenzo III*, 1:56–73. On Christian apocalyptic senses of time and the crusade movement, see Brett Edward Whalen, *Dominion of God: Christendom and Apocalypse in the Middle Ages* (Cambridge MA-London, 2009).

6. For Innocent's life and pontificate, see John C. Moore, *Pope Innocent III (1160/61–1216): To Root Up and to Plant* (Leiden-Boston 2003; repr., Notre Dame, 2008); Leonard E. Boyle, "Innocent III's View of Himself as Pope," in Sommerlechner, *Innocenzo III: Urbs et Orbis*, 1:3–17; and Edward Peters, "Lotario dei Conti di Segni Becomes Pope Innocent III: The Man and the Pope," in Moore, *Pope Innocent III and His World*, 3–24; Brenda Bolton, ed. and trans., *Innocent III: Selected Documents on the Pontificate, 1198–1216* (Manchester-New York, forthcoming).

7. The best source is now Malcolm Barber and Keith Bate, *Letters from the East: Crusaders, Pilgrims and Settlers in the 12th–13th Centuries*, Crusade Texts in Translation 18 (Farnham UK-Burlington VT, 2010), with a list of other translations of letters into English, 173.

issuing of *Audita tremendi* and its substantial impact make the document an ideal starting point for this collection.

1. Pope Gregory VIII, *Audita tremendi*, October 29, 1187

The death of Pope Urban III on October 20, 1187, reportedly upon hearing the news of the slaughter at Hattin, resulted in the election of the elderly reform-minded papal chancellor Albert of Morra as Pope Gregory VIII on October 21. Within a week, Gregory, who himself died two months later, issued the letter *Audita tremendi*, not only the most impassioned plea for a crusade ever issued by a pope until then, but the fullest detailed account of crusaders' spiritual and temporal rewards and privileges to date. The letter was read aloud at the papal court—at the time in Ferrara, in northern Italy. Among those present may have been the young theology student Lotario dei Conti di Segni, later Pope Innocent III, who had just been (or was about to be) made a subdeacon by Gregory. If he was not actually present at the curia, Lotario certainly knew of the defeat very quickly. Peter of Blois, the Angevin cleric and literary figure, was certainly present and was greatly moved by the failure of the powerful and the needs and virtues of lesser folk.[8]

The letter circulated widely throughout Europe, inspiring the group of military expeditions that came to be known as the Third Crusade. But the impact of *Audita tremendi* long outlasted the Third Crusade itself. It inspired a new generation of moral theologians to consider the needs of the Holy Land and to link these to the moral regeneration of Christian Europe, one of the great themes of twelfth- and thirteenth-century history. Gregory's emphasis on the bloody circumstances of the defeat at Hattin, the loss of the True Cross, and the first cities taken by Saladin (the surrender of Jerusalem on October 2, 1187, was not yet known in the West when *Audita tremendi* was issued) frame his insistence that God's anger is the result of human sin, that penance is mandatory, not optional, and that a new expedition would be an opportunity for the salvation of Christian warriors.

In *Audita tremendi* Gregory clearly considers the Muslims to be pagans, not Christian heretics, as other Christian versions of Islam professed, since he believed that Muslims did not share the same God as the Jews and Christians. His critique of the Muslim enemy proceeds from a religious view of the crusade, but Gregory does not attack Islam in any detail—indicating that his primary concern is with the injury to and obligations of Christianity. He uses the term "Christians" in a way

8. On Innocent's probable presence, see John C. Moore, "Lotario dei Conti di Segni (Pope Innocent III) in the 1180s," *Archivum Historiae Pontificiae* 29 (1991), 255–258. On Peter of Blois, see Michael Markowski, "Peter of Blois and the Conception of the Third Crusade," in B. Z. Kedar, ed., *The Horns of Hattin* (Jerusalem-London, 1987), 261–269; and John D. Cotts, *The Clerical Dilemma: Peter of Blois and Literate Culture in the Twelfth Century* (Washington DC, 2009).

that apparently includes Eastern Christians. And he lays heavy blame on the sins of the Franks for the military disaster, a theme—known as *peccatis exigentibus*—that since the failure of the Second Crusade in 1147 had often been struck earlier in Christian history to explain military and other failures and became a cornerstone of later crusade preaching, by now virtually identifying the necessity of moral and spiritual reform with the crusade movement.[9]

> *On the identification of Christian sinfulness with crusade failure, see Christoph Maier, "Crisis, Liturgy and the Crusade in the Twelfth and Thirteenth Centuries,"* Journal of Ecclesiastical History *48 (1997), 628–657; and Giles Constable, "The Second Crusade as Seen by Contemporaries,"* Traditio *9 (1953), 213–79, repr. and rev. in Giles Constable,* Crusaders and Crusading in the Twelfth Century *(Farnham UK-Burlington VT, 2008), 229–300, with an extensive discussion of the views and influence of Saint Bernard of Clairvaux. The impact of* Audita tremendi *is extensively considered in Sylvia Schein,* Gateway to the Heavenly City: Crusader Jerusalem and the Catholic West (1099–1187) *(Aldershot UK-Burlington VT, 2005), 159–193; Penny J. Cole,* The Preaching of the Crusades to the Holy Land, 1095–1270 *(Cambridge MA, 1991), 63–79; and Brenda Bolton, "'Serpent in the Dust, Sparrow on the Housetop': Attitudes to Jerusalem and the Holy Land in the Circle of Pope Innocent III," in* R. N. Swanson, ed., The Holy Land, Holy Lands, and Christian History, *Studies in Church History 36 (Woodbridge UK-Rochester NY, 2000), 154–180.*
>
> *On popes and crusades before Innocent III, see I. S. Robinson,* The Papacy, 1073–1198: Continuity and Innovation *(Cambridge, 1990), 322–366; Colin Morris,* The Papal Monarchy: The Western Church from 1050 to 1250 *(Oxford, 1989), 134–153, 263–286, 417–451, 478–488; Jonathan Riley-Smith, "The Crusades, 1095–1198," in* The New Cambridge Medieval History, *7 vols. (Cambridge, 1995–2005), vol. 4, c. 1024–c. 1198, ed. David Luscombe and Jonathan Riley-Smith, part 1, 534–563; Jonathan P. Phillips,* The Crusades, 1095–1197 *(London, 2002); Peter W. Edbury, "Celestine III, the Crusade and the Latin East," in* John Doran and Damian J. Smith, eds., Pope Celestine III (1191–1198) *(Aldershot UK-Burlington VT, 2009), 129–143.* See also the works cited below, n. 21.

GREGORY, bishop, servant of the servants of God, to all Christ's faithful who receive this letter, greeting and apostolic benediction.

When we heard of the severity of the awesome judgment that the hand of God visited on the land of Jerusalem, we and our brothers were disturbed by such a great horror, afflicted by such sorrows, that we scarcely knew what to do or what we should do, save that the psalmist laments and says, "O God, the gentiles have invaded your inheritance, they have sullied your holy temple, they have laid waste Jerusalem; they have left the dead bodies of your saints as meat for the beasts of the earth

Source: PL 202, 1539–1542; trans. from Anton Chroust, Quellen zur Geschichte des Kreuzzuges Kaiser Friedrichs I, MGH SS rer. Ger. *n.s. 5 (Berlin, 1928), 6–10.*

9. The range of explanations for crusade failure developed particularly after the disputes concerning the failure of the Second Crusade in 1147. The range is characterized by Giles Constable, "The Second Crusade as Seen by Contemporaries," rev. in Constable, *Crusaders,* 229–300. See also the thirteenth-century material in Peter Jackson, *The Seventh Crusade 1244–1254: Sources and Documents* (Farnham UK-Burlington VT, 2009), 165–177; and texts below, Part X.

and food the birds of the air . . ." [Ps 78:1–2]. In fact, because of the conflict which the malice of [Christian] men has recently brought on the land by the inspiration of the devil, Saladin approached those parts with a host of armed troops. They were confronted by the king and the bishops, the Templars and the Hospitallers, the barons and the knights, with the people of the land, and with the Lord's cross (through which from memory and faith of the suffering of Christ, who hung there and redeemed the human race, was believed to be a sure safeguard and a desired defense against the attacks of the pagans), and after the battle was joined, our side was defeated and the Lord's cross was captured. The bishops were slaughtered, the king captured, and almost all our men were either put to the sword or taken prisoner. Very few are believed to have escaped. Also, the Templars and Hospitallers were beheaded in his [Saladin's] presence. With the army defeated, we do not think our letter can explain how they next invaded and seized every place so that only a few remained outside their power. Still, though we use the words of the prophet: "Who will give me water for my head and a font of tears for my eyes, and I will weep night and day for the death of my people" [Jer 9:1], we ought not despair now and decide to mistrust and believe that God is so angry with his people that in his anger with their commission of a multitude of sins he will not quickly pardon when he is pleased by their penance and, after tears and groans, will lead them to exaltation.

Indeed, whoever does not mourn at least in his heart in so great a cause for sorrow not only is ignorant of the Christian faith, which teaches us to join in all suffering, but of our very humanity. For from the magnitude of the dangers and their barbarous ferocity thirsting for the blood of Christians, and adding all their power in this cause to profane the holy and erase the name of God from that land, whoever thinks we should be silent should decide. Of course, when the prophets worked previously with total desire, later the apostles and their followers worked so that divine worship should be in that land and should spread from it to every part of the world by every means great and wonderful. God, through whom all things were made, who wished to take on flesh through his divine wisdom and his incomprehensible mercy and desired to achieve our salvation through the weakness of our flesh, hunger, thirst, the cross, death and resurrection, according to the words "And he has worked salvation in the midst of the land" [Ps 73:12] has himself decided to work for this end. Neither can tongue speak nor the senses understand what that land has now suffered, how much it has suffered for us and for all Christians, that we read it endured under its ancient population. Moreover, we ought not believe that these things happened because of the unjust act of the judge but rather by the iniquity of an unworthy people, since we read that at the time when the people were being converted to the Lord, "one thousand were persecuted and two were fleeing from ten thousand" [Dt 32:30]. On the contrary, however, the army of Sennacharib was overcome by an angelic force. But "that land also devoured its inhabitants" [Nm 13:33] and was not at peace for very long, nor could it restrain those who broke the law. Nor did it give teaching to those who would seek the heavenly Jerusalem, which they could not attain save through the exercise of good works and after many temptations. But they could long ago fear those things, when Arroasia [Edessa] and other land fell into the hands of the pagans [1144], and it was clearly foreseen if the people who remained had again done penance they would have pleased God whom they offended by their sins. For his anger is not quick, but he puts off the punishment, and gives time for repentance. But, finally, he does not lose his judgment in mercy, but exercises his protection for the punishment of sinners and for the surety of those to be saved.

We, therefore, should heed and be concerned about the sins not only of the inhabitants of that land but also of our own and those of the whole Christian people so that what is left of that land may not be lost and their power rage in other regions. For we hear from every direction of scandals and conflicts between kings and princes, among cities, so that we lament with the prophet and are able to say: "There is no truth, no knowledge of God in the land: lying, murder and adultery abound, and blood pursues blood" [Hos 4:1–2]. For this reason, everyone must understand and act accordingly, so that by atoning for our sins, we may be converted to the Lord by penance and works of piety and we may first alter in our lives the evil that we do. Then we can deal with the savagery and malice of our enemies. And, what they do not fear to try against God, we will not hesitate to do for God. Therefore, sons, consider how you came into this world and how all pass on, and thus you will pass on. Use the time for penitence and doing well insofar as it regards you, with thanks. Give yourselves, give after yourselves, because you, who cannot make even a gnat upon the land, have nothing of your own. We do not say, dismiss, but send us forth in the heavenly harvest which you have and deposit with him "upon whom the rust does not destroy, nor the worms, nor the thieves dig up and steal" [Mt 6:20]. Work for the recovery of that land in which for our salvation Truth has arisen from the land and did not disdain to carry the forked wood of the cross for us. Pay attention not to earthly profit and glory, but to the will of God who himself taught us to lay down our souls for our brothers. Give your riches to him, which whether willingly or unwillingly, you do not know to which greedy heirs they will be left. It is certainly not new, nor unusual, that that land is persecuted by a divine judgment that, after being beaten and corrected, it may obtain mercy. Of course, the Lord could preserve it by his will alone, but it is not for us to know why he would do this. Perhaps he wished to experience and bring to the notice of others if someone is understanding and seeking God, who having offered himself embraces the time of penance joyfully. He sacrifices himself for his brothers; though he may die young, still he accomplishes much. Heed how the Maccabees, afire with the divine zeal of the law experienced extreme dangers for the freedom of their brothers. They taught that not only riches but their persons should be sacrificed for their brothers, exhorting and saying to each other: "Gird yourselves and be powerful sons because it is better for us to die in battle than to witness the desecration of our nation and our saints" [1 Mc 3:58–59] Indeed, they were subject to one law; you by the incarnation of our Lord Jesus Christ have been led to the light of truth and instructed by the many examples of the saints. You should act without trepidation and do not fear to give away earthly possessions, which will last for such a short time, for those goods we are promised that "neither eye has seen nor ear has heard nor have they entered into the heart of man" [1 Cor 2:9], as the Apostle says: "That the sufferings of this time are not worthy to be compared to the future glory which will be revealed in us" [Rom 8:18].

We promise full remission of their sins and eternal life to those who take up the labor of this journey with a contrite heart and a humble spirit and depart in penitence of their sins and with true faith. Whether they survive or die, they should know that they, after they have made a true confession, will have the relaxation of the penance imposed, by the mercy of almighty God, by the authority of the apostles Peter and Paul, and ours. Their goods, from their reception of the cross, with their families, remain under the protection of the holy Roman Church, as well as the archbishops and bishops and other prelates. They should not face any legal challenge regarding the things they possess legally when they received the cross until their return or their death is known for certain, but they should also keep legally all their goods. Also, they may not be forced to pay interest if they have a loan. They should not travel in precious clothing, and with dogs or birds, or with others that display ostentation and luxury, but in modest garb and demeanor, they should do penance rather than affect vainglory. Dated at Ferrara on the fourth Calends of November [October 29, 1187], the sixth indiction.[10]

* * *

As grave as things looked, not all was lost. In August 1187, Conrad of Montferrat had commanded the successful defense of the city of Tyre, a crucial port that remained in Christian hands until 1291 and served as a bridgehead for later expeditions. Conrad was aided by the arrival of contingents from King William II of Sicily in 1188 and by fleets from Pisa and England in 1188 and 1190. Henry of Albano, Gregory VIII's legate, wrote to both Philip II Augustus of France (r. 1180–1223) and the emperor Frederick I Barbarossa (r. 1152–1190), urging them to take the cross. The patriarch of Antioch also wrote to Barbarossa and to Henry II of England (r. 1154–1189), who had been assigned a penitential pilgrimage in 1173 as penance for the murder of Thomas Becket in 1170 and was long interested in the crusade but prevented by local circumstances from actually departing.[11] But in January 1188 Henry finally did take up the cross, although illness and political difficulties prevented his departure, and he died in July 1189. His son and successor, Richard I (r. 1189–1199) took the crusade vow in November 1187—that is, within a month of *Audita tremendi*. Philip Augustus of France took up the cross in January 1188, and Frederick Barbarossa in March of the same year. Within five months of the issuing of *Audita tremendi*, the four most powerful rulers in the West had taken the crusade vow (including William II of Sicily, who died in 1189).

The other great military forces in the Holy Land and Europe were the military orders—the Knights of the Hospital of Saint John, the Knights Templar, and the Teutonic Knights—religious orders devoted to defending the sacred places and

10. Papal documents were dated according to the location of the pope when the document was issued (certainly not always in Rome), the part of the Roman month (divided into kalends, nones, and ides) to indicate the day of the month, and the year indicated by the indiction, by indicating in which year in a fifteen-year cycle (= indiction) a document is issued (here, the sixth year, but one would need an external reference to identify the starting year of the indiction).

11. Letters 41–48 in Barber and Bate, *Letters from the East*, deal with the communications in preparation for the Third Crusade. Crusade was considered a form of pilgrimage and might be undertaken voluntarily or assigned as penance for a serious offense, as in Henry II's case. See Brett Edward Whalen, *Pilgrimage in the Middle Ages: A Reader* (Toronto, 2011), as well as No. 35 on Richard of Cornwall's crusade (below, Part V), and No. 68, a liturgy for pilgrims and crusaders (cf. below, Nos. 4, 19, 50). Essential for thirteenth-century pilgrimage is Denys Pringle, *Pilgrimage to the East, 1187–1291*, Crusade Texts in Translation 23 (Farnham UK-Burlington VT, 2012).

their Christian inhabitants. Although a number of prominent members of the orders had been killed and some deliberately executed at Hattin, many survived. These forces, often operating independently of the kingdom of Jerusalem, had extended lines of communication with their convents in western Europe and served as financial facilitators for crusaders who could draw on Templar facilities in the East for funds they had deposited in Europe when they started out. The military orders were one of the great distinguishing features, besides crusading armies themselves, of the nature of military resources in the Holy Land.[12]

At the same time, popes and crusade preachers, inspired by the vibrant pastoral concerns of the moral theologians at Paris and proponents of moral reform elsewhere established new penitential liturgies, including fasts and public prayers, insertions of appropriate sections of the Psalms into the text of the Mass, and they searched out Scripture for crusade-appropriate examples.

The Third Crusade, the first major response to *Audita tremendi*, began with high hopes and great enthusiasm and was led by powerful kings with considerable resources. But it ended in internal conflict and very limited success.[13] Its leaders had either died or returned to more pressing affairs at home. Frederick I Barbarossa, the emperor of the Romans and the leader of the largest army ever fielded

12. On the orders, see Malcolm Barber, *The New Knighthood: A History of the Order of the Temple* (Cambridge UK-New York, 1994); Malcolm Barber and Keith Bate, ed. and trans., *The Templars: Selected Sources* (Manchester UK-New York, 2002); Helen Nicholson, *The Knights Templar: A New History* (Stroud UK, 2001); Helen Nicholson, *The Knights Hospitaller* (Woodbridge UK-Rochester NY, 2001); Alan Forey, *The Military Orders from the Twelfth to the Early Fourteenth Centuries* (Toronto, 1992); Alan Forey, *Military Orders and Crusades* (Aldershot UK-Brookfield VT, 1994); Malcolm Barber et al., eds., *The Military Orders*, 4 vols. (Aldershot UK-Brookfield VT, 1994–2008); Helen Nicholson, ed., *On the Margins of Crusading: The Military Orders, the Papacy, and the Christian World* (Farnham UK-Burlington VT, 2011); William Urban, *The Teutonic Knights* (London, 2003); Zsolt Hunyadi and Josef Laslovsky, eds., *The Military Orders: Expanding the Frontiers of Medieval Latin Christianity* (Budapest, 2001); Giles Constable, "The Military Orders," rev. in Constable, *Crusaders*, 165–182; Kelly DeVries and Robert Douglas Smith, *Medieval Military Technology*, 2d ed. (Toronto, 2012).

13. The sources for the Third Crusade available in English include Peter Edbury, trans., *The Conquest of Jerusalem and the Third Crusade* (Aldershot UK-Brookfield VT, 1996); Helen Nicholson, trans., *Chronicle of the Third Crusade: A Translation of the* Itinerarium Peregrinorum et Gesta Regis Ricardi (Aldershot UK-Brookfield VT, 1997); G. A. Loud, trans., *The Crusade of Frederick Barbarossa: The History of the Emperor Frederick and Related Texts* (Farnham UK-Burlington VT, 2010); Marianne Ailes and Malcolm Barber, eds., *The History of the Holy War: Ambroise's* Estoire de la guerre sainte, trans. Marianne Ailes (Woodbridge UK-Rochester NY, 2003). An independent history written in Old French and called by its editors the *Chronique d'Ernoul et de Bernard le Trésorier* covered the period from the First Crusade to 1229 and became the basis for continuations of the history of William of Tyre. These texts are being edited by Peter Edbury at Cardiff University. A series of brief chronological entries called the *Annales de Terre Sainte* were incorporated in later narratives (see below, No. 72). See Peter Edbury, "A New Text of *Annales de Terre Sainte*," in Iris Shagrir, Ronnie Ellenblum, and Jonathan Riley-Smith, eds., In Laudem Hierosolymitani: *Studies in Crusades and Medieval Culture in Honour of Benjamin Z. Kedar* (Aldershot UK-Burlington VT, 2007), 145–161.

in Europe until then, drowned in northern Syria in 1189, leaving the imperial throne to his son Henry VI. His leaderless army broke up, and its disorganized contingents returned to Germany and Italy. Richard I Lionheart, king of England, both an excellent strategist and a courageous battle leader, captured the island of Cyprus, and later left the Holy Land after securing the key coastal cities of Jaffa and Acre in July, 1191 and agreeing to a three-year truce with Saladin in October 1192. The fiction of Richard as a courageous but slow-witted leader is the product of romantic novelists (for example, Sir Walter Scott's *The Talisman*) and modern moviemakers.

But Richard was captured by his personal enemy the duke of Austria while en route home and held from December 1192 until February 1194—in complete violation of his status as a crusader as laid out in *Audita tremendi*—for an enormous ransom. King Philip II Augustus of France, having quarreled with Richard of England and fallen seriously ill, left the Holy Land in July 1191 and exploited Richard's captivity by encroaching upon the English king's possessions in France, continuing a conflict that had begun half a century earlier and lasted much later.

The enormous costs in men and matériel, as well as peoples' fear of God's immanent wrath, did not, however, dampen Christendom's crusading ardor. The Holy Land and the Christians in it remained in dire peril, and their fellow Christians remained obliged to help them. The two popes who reigned between Gregory VIII and Innocent III—Clement III (1187–1191) and Celestine III (1191–1198)—were both old men, but, like Gregory VIII, they too were devout reformers, had long been involved in crusade movements, and they continued the reforms laid out in *Audita tremendi*. Clement III had worked closely with Frederick Barbarossa on the preparations for the Third Crusade, and Celestine's bull *Misericors et miserator* of July 1195, among other letters, issued crusading calls and privileges that elaborated on and fine-tuned the spiritual rewards—and responsibilities—of taking the cross.[14] But Celestine III had little time and few resources to call on or organize a large new crusade so soon after the bitter experience of the Third Crusade and the ongoing conflict between Richard I and Philip II Augustus.

It was in this context of pastoral, political, and crusade history that the thirty-seven-year-old Lotario dei Conti di Segni was elected pope to succeed Celestine III on January 9, 1198. Lotario had been made a deacon by his relative Clement III in 1190 and was already the cardinal deacon of Saints Sergius and Bacchus, but he was not yet a priest when elected pope. He acquired the jurisdictional power of

---

14. On Celestine and crusade, see the study by Peter W. Edbury cited above, in the headnote to *Audita tremendi*; and below, No. 9. He had been a papal legate in Iberia and was much concerned with the wars against Muslims as crusades. See Joseph O'Callaghan, *Reconquest and Crusade in Medieval Spain* (Philadelphia, 2003), 155–176; and Peter Linehan, *Spain, 1157–1300: A Partible Inheritance* (Malden MA-Oxford, 2008); and Jennifer Price, "Alfonso I and the Memory of the First Crusade: Conquest and Crusade in the Kingdom of Aragón-Navarre," in Madden, Naus, and Ryan, *Crusades—Medieval Worlds in Conflict*, 75–94.

the pope upon election, but not the sacramental authority until he was ordained priest on February 21, 1198, and bishop the following day.

What had crusade come to mean in the course of Lotario/Innocent's lifetime? Not only popes and their emissaries, but also itinerant preachers, chroniclers, letter-writers, poets, and crusade propagandists and laypeople continued to lament the distress of the Christians in Outremer, "the lands beyond the sea," and to remember the heroic achievements of the first crusaders. By the end of the twelfth century a number of chronicle accounts of earlier expeditions to the East, particularly the First Crusade, circulated, as did the general history by William of Tyre with continuations.[15] There existed also a body of poetic literature in both Latin and several European vernacular languages circulated throughout Europe, both commemorating crusading achievements—historical and mythical—and sharply criticizing a number of aspects of crusade. Sometimes this literature accentuated individual themes in crusade history, one of them vengeance for offenses to Christ and Christianity.[16] Such works as *The Vengeance of Our Savior*, *The Song of Antioch*, *The History of Charlemagne and Roland*, and the crusade cycles, as well as several dozen French crusade songs, German lyrics, and thirty-five poems in Occitan known as *sirventes*—satirical political verses—surely contributed to a general heightened awareness of the crusade idea, in however imaginative a form they used.[17]

The new and various crusades also incited new criticism, some of it harsh in the extreme, and verse often proved an effective vehicle for indignation. The Provençal poet Guillem Figueira savagely denounced both the Fourth and the Albigensian Crusades:

> Deceitful Rome, avarice ensnares you, so that you shear
> the wool of your sheep too much. May the Holy Ghost,
> who takes on human flesh, hear my prayer and break your beak,
> O Rome! You will never have a truce with me because you
> are false and perfidious with us and with the Greeks. You do

15. Emily Atwater Babcock and A. C. Krey, ed. and trans., *A History of Deeds Done Beyond the Sea, by William, Archbishop of Tyre*, 2 vols. (New York, 1943); Peter W. Edbury and John Gordon Rowe, *William of Tyre, Historian of the Latin East* (Cambridge, 1988); Edbury, *Conquest of Jerusalem*; Guillaume de Tyr, *Chronique*, ed. R. B. C. Huygens (Turnhout, 1986); Janet Shirley, ed. and trans., *Crusader Syria in the Thirteenth Century: The Rothelin Continuation of the History of William of Tyre with Part of the Eracles or Acre Text* (Aldershot UK-Brookfield VT, 1999). On the independent Old French history and continuations of William of Tyre's history, see n. 13 above.

16. Susanna A. Throop, *Crusading as an Act of Vengeance, 1096–1216* (Farnham UK-Burlington VT, 2011). Throop discusses the theme in both literature and in papal and other documentary sources.

17. *The* Chanson d'Antioche: *An Old French Account of the First Crusade*, trans. Susan Edgington and Carol Sweetenham (Farnham UK-Burlington VT, 2011). Further translations of the literature in *Joinville and Villehardouin: Chronicles of the Crusades*, trans. with intro. and notes by Caroline Smith (London-New York, 2008), xxii–xxiii, 336–345; Jackson, *The Seventh Crusade*, 18–20; and below Nos. 33 and 56.

little harm to the Saracens, but you massacre Greeks and Latins.
In hell-fire and ruin you have your seat, Rome.

Figueira also lashed out at the disaster of the Fifth Crusade:

Rome, you know well that your base cheating and folly caused
the loss of Damietta; Evil leader, Rome! God will strike you down
because you govern too falsely through money.
O Rome of evil race and evil compact![18]

Nor were poets the only users of vituperative language. The polemical propaganda
hurled at Frederick II by Gregory IX and hurled back by Frederick and his supporters was equally savage (see below, Part IV).

But vernacular poets could also carry crusade ideals effectively into circles of
the laity. Early in the thirteenth century the German poet Walter von der Vogelweide wrote a "Palestine song":

Now my life has found a purpose
    for my sinful eyes behold
that pure land and very country
of which glorious things are told.
    This has been my prayer of old:
    I have seen the place which God
        in a human form once trod.

Many a rich and splendid country
    have I seen, but of them all
you deserve the highest honour
where such wonders could befall.
That a maid to birth could bring
    one who was the angels' king—
    was not this a wondrous thing?

Christians, Jews and also heathen
claim this land as rightly theirs.
May God make our cause to triumph
    By the threefold name he bears.
All the world has come to fight,
    but to us belongs the right;
    God defend us by his might![19]

18. Cited in Palmer Throop, *Criticism of the Crusade: A Study of Public Opinion and Crusade Propaganda* (Amsterdam, 1940), 31–50. There is a more balanced view of crusade criticism in Elizabeth Siberry, *Criticism of Crusading, 1095–1274* (Oxford, 1985).

19. The translation is from Colin Morris's fine introduction to *The Holy Land, Holy Lands and Christian History*, ed. R. N. Swanson, Studies in Church History 36 (Wood-bridge, 2000), xvi. See also Colin Morris, *The Sepulchre of Christ and the Medieval West: From the Beginning to 1600* (Oxford-New York, 2005), 254–94; Walter von der Vogelweide,

Although critics abounded, they usually criticized one or another aspect of crusade preaching, recruiting, financing, direction, or local impact, not the idea of the crusade or the sanctity of the Holy Land, and their criticism was tempered by the linking of crusade, devotion, and a reforming spirituality that carried through the thirteenth century well into the fourteenth and fifteenth centuries. In this volume the poems of Thibaut of Champagne and Rutebeuf, as well as those cited just above, are samples of the new kinds of literature inspired by crusade.[20]

And temporal as well as spiritual leaders proposed new crusading efforts. The new emperor Henry VI, the son and successor of Frederick Barbarossa, sent a crusading army ahead to the Levant in 1196, which captured Sidon and Beirut during the summer of 1197. Henry was himself preparing to join his army in the East when he died unexpectedly at Messina in September 1197. The disintegration of his army in the East in March 1198 after the initial successes posed new problems in crusade recruiting as well as new political trouble in South Italy and Sicily. A year later, at a tournament at Écry in Champagne, a number of lay barons and knights spontaneously took up the cross, the beginning of what became the Fourth Crusade (below, No. 6).

The conviction that certain sites in Syria and Palestine associated with the life and ministry of Jesus, particularly the city of Jerusalem with the Church of the Holy Sepulcher and the True Cross, were of utmost sacral importance to Christians everywhere and that their loss was a sure sign of God's displeasure with Christian society pervaded nearly all levels of thought and was common across western Europe.[21] Visionaries, lawyers, calculating and idealistic rulers, and calculating and idealistic popes expressed again and again the view that only by regaining Jerusalem could Christian society be assured of divine favor. That they had not regained the holy places behind the vast forces of the kings of Europe in 1189–1191 meant that perhaps rank, wealth, and force alone were not sufficient for their task. And

---

The Single-Stanza Lyrics, trans. F. Goldin (London, 2003); and Colin Morris, "Propaganda for War: The Dissemination of the Crusading Ideal in the Twelfth Century," in W. Shiels, ed., *The Church and War*, Studies in Church History 20 (Oxford, 1983), 79–101.

20. There is a good discussion in Helen Nicholson, *Love, War and the Grail* (Leiden-Boston, 2001). See also D. A. Trotter, *Medieval French Literature and the Crusades (1100–1300)* (Geneva, 1988); William E. Jackson, *Ardent Complaints and Equivocal Piety: The Portrayal of the Crusader in Medieval German Poetry* (Lanham MD, 2003); Alan V. Murray, ed., *The Crusades: An Encyclopedia*. 4 vols. (Santa Barbara CA, 2006), vol. 4, nos. 5–7, pp. 1307–1314; R. L. Crocker, "Early Crusade Songs," in T. P. Murphy, ed., *The Holy War* (Columbus OH, 1976), 78–98; Norman Daniel, *Heroes and Saracens: An Interpretation of the "Chansons de Geste"* (Edinburgh, 1984); T. Montgomery, *Medieval Spanish Epic: Mythic Roots and Ritual Language* (University Park PA, 1998); and above, n. 17.

21. Martin Biddle, *The Church of the Holy Sepulchre* (New York, 2000); Morris, *Sepulchre of Christ and the Medieval West*; Schein, *Gateway to the Heavenly City*. On the cross, see Giles Constable, "The Cross of the Crusaders," in Constable, *Crusaders*, 45–91; and Barbara Baert, *A Heritage of Holy Wood: The Legend of the True Cross in Text and Image*, trans. Lee Preedy (Leiden-Boston, 2004). On pilgrimage to Jerusalem, see texts translated in Denys Pringle, *Pilgrimage to Jerusalem and the Holy Land, 1187–1291* (Farnham UK-Burlington VT, 2012); and Whalen, *Pilgrimage*.

Christian society faced other difficulties besides the loss of most of the kingdom of Jerusalem to the armies of Saladin.

Since the eleventh century, in the wake of burgeoning demographic and economic growth in western Europe and in the wake of the great movement of reform known as the Investiture Conflict, there had occurred a redrawing of the boundaries between lay and clerical status, extensive changes within the clerical orders themselves (not without fierce intraclerical disputes), a new and much more prominent position claimed by the bishops of Rome as popes (of whose authority the successes of earlier crusades were a conspicuous component), and great demands for the reform of the lay life, including new definitions of legitimate warfare, social conflict, commerce, and marriage—all of which were touched on by crusading.

Among those whom most of these reforms did not reach—or who disapproved of them—religious dissent and heterodox beliefs and practices had found expression, and a succession of twelfth-century bishops and popes and the busy local and general church councils of the later twelfth century had begun the long process of the more precise definition of dogma that was to alienate yet others of the faithful. The problems of dissent and heresy—and the corresponding forms of ecclesiastical discipline—in fact, seemed to loom no less large in 1198 than did the problems of the Holy Land.[22]

Nor did the dangers to orthodox belief and the integrity of the church and Christian society begin or end with religious dissent. The twelfth century witnessed an enormous growth of both theoretical and actual political power in the hands of the territorial monarchs of western and central Europe. The great struggle to free the church and churchmen from lay domination, which had begun with the Investiture Conflict in the late eleventh century, once again appeared to be headed toward defeat. Kings and lay lords encroached upon ecclesiastical offices and property—even on the status of the various ranks of the clergy, as witnessed, for example, by the conflict between Henry II of England and Thomas Becket, archbishop of Canterbury, or between King John of England (r. 1199–1216) and Innocent III, or between Philip II Augustus and Innocent.

Churchmen often found themselves with few defenses against these immediate local pressures, and even the great strengthening of the papal office during the twelfth century could not always alleviate the greatest threats. Popes and emperors

---

22. Generally, see John T. Gilchrist, "The Lord's War as the Proving Ground of Faith: Pope Innocent III and the Propagation of Violence (1198–1216)," in Maya Shatzmiller, ed., *Crusaders and Muslims in Twelfth-Century Syria* (Leiden, 1993), 65–83; and below, No. 7; Charles J. Reid, Jr., "The Rights of Self-Defence and Justified Warfare in the Writings of the Twelfth- and Thirteenth-Century Canonists," in Kenneth Pennington and Melodie Harris Eichbauer, eds., *Law as Profession and Practice in Medieval Europe: Essays in Honor of James A. Brundage* (Farnham UK-Burlington VT, 2011), 73–92; David Bachrach, *Religion and the Conduct of War, c. 300–c. 1215* (Woodbridge UK, 2003); Maureen Purcell, *Papal Crusading Policy: The Chief Instruments of Papal Crusading Policy and Crusade to the Holy Land from the Final Loss of Jerusalem to the Fall of Acre, 1244–1291* (Leiden, 1975). For a particularly important theme, see S. A. Throop, *Vengeance.*

clashed throughout the twelfth century over the problem of the Matildine lands in
north-central Italy—a key element in the problem of the formation of a papal state
centered on Rome and its surrounding territories. Late in the twelfth century several popes watched helplessly as Frederick Barbarossa married his son Henry VI to
Constance, aunt and heiress of the deceased William II of Sicily (d. 1189), potentially surrounding Rome and its bishop with imperially controlled lands. Within
Rome itself the long-running political dispute between several popes and the
nobles and senate of Rome was only resolved marginally in the pope's favor by
Clement III (1187–1191), the year after *Audita tremendi* was issued and
circulated.[23]

There are no better indexes of the difficulties facing the direction of Christian
society than the first few years of the registers of Innocent III. Innocent took
particular care with the registers of his letters, but the registers for 1201, 1203,
and 1204 have been lost, as have those for 1214–1216, although many of these
years have been partially reconstructed. Many letters are incorporated in the opening sections of the *Gesta Innocentii*, the richly informative account of the first ten
years of Innocent III's pontificate, designed to inform the curia of Innocent's
policies and perhaps written by Innocent's close associate Peter of Capua. Many
were also copied into the narrative historical accounts of late twelfth- and thirteenth-century chroniclers. In the midst of these difficulties on many fronts the
kind of aid to the papal cause that the crusade potentially offered was considerable.[24] In the kingdom of Sicily, for example, the powerful servants of the late
emperor Henry VI (d. September 1197), especially Markward of Anweiler, so dis-
regarded the pope's rights of lordship that one of Innocent's first acts was, in utter
desperation, to threaten to launch a crusade against him. In this case, the crusade
was a last, desperate measure on the part of a pope without other resources.[25]
Between 1198 and 1291, however, the crusade became the only instrument on
which the pope could rely for widespread support—to recover the Holy Land, to
combat the threat of heresy, to defeat threatening pagans in northern or eastern
Europe, or to defend the church in Italy and Sicily. In the process of turning

23. On Roman affairs, see Robinson, *The Papacy*, 3–32; Peter Partner, *The Lands of
St. Peter: The Papal State in the Middle Ages and the Early Renaissance* (Berkeley and Los
Angeles, 1972), 203–235.

24. See Moore, *To Root Up and to Plant*; and James M. Powell, ed. and trans., *The
Deeds of Pope Innocent III by an Anonymous Author* (Washington DC, 2004). On papal
authority and the crusades, generally, see Michel Balard, ed., *La Papauté et les croisades / The
Papacy and the Crusades*, Acts of the VII Congress of the Society for the Study of the Crusades and the Latin East, Avignon, August 27–31, 2008 (Farnham UK-Burlington VT,
2011); and Rebecca Rist, *The Papacy and Crusading in Europe, 1198–1245* (London, 2009);
see also the works cited above in the headnote to *Audita tremendi*; and Kenneth M. Setton,
The Papacy and the Levant, 1204–1571, vol. 1 (Philadelphia, 1976).

25. For a balanced discussion, see Norman Housley, "Crusades Against Christians:
Their Origins and Early Development, c. 1000–1216," repr. in Housley, *Crusading and
Warfare in Medieval and Renaissance Europe* (Aldershot UK-Burlington VT, 2001), I, with
further references; and see below, Part VIII.

the crusade from an exclusive focus on the Holy Land, popes and secular rulers transformed and expanded the crusade idea itself.[26]

It took much of the early twelfth century for the crusade idea to be formulated in both theology and law. The early twelfth-century canon lawyer Ivo, bishop of Chartres, knew what he was talking about when in frustration over a law case that involved crusaders' rights he called the First Crusade a *nova institutio*, new institution—since it did not seem to be consistent with the institutions and practices treated by conventional canon law until then, and its consequences caused a great deal of legal trouble.[27] Not only did the apparatus of crusade privileges create a new dimension of canon law, but the new role of the church in protecting the property of crusading laymen increasingly appeared to violate local law. Like Ivo of Chartres in the early twelfth century, thirteenth-century canon lawyers also had to puzzle out the other legal complexities of crusading: what was the status of the crusader's wife—or widow? Did a crusader need his spouse's permission to make the crusade vow? How could the physically unfit acquire the spiritual benefits of crusade? When and in what circumstances might crusade vows be commuted? How could crusade organizers walk the fine line of crusade financing without bringing down charges of avarice or simony on themselves? Indeed, crusade financing was one of the central problems of European history and law in the thirteenth century.

The experience of the First Crusade, particularly as a sign of divine favor in triumphing over overwhelming odds, influenced the legal conception of crusade and shaped the narratives produced after 1099. In 1145–1147, after Edessa fell to the Seljuk Turks, many of the themes of the First Crusade narratives were revived by Pope Eugenius III (1145–1154), supported by Cistercian preachers like Saint Bernard of Clairvaux, in the first papal letter calling for a crusade, *Quantum praedecessores* (1146).[28] The Cistercian involvement in crusading endured through the late twelfth century and exerted considerable influence on Innocent III, underlying much of Innocent III's moral view of the needs of Christian society.[29] During

---

26. Two excellent and concise studies of the consequences of these circumstances to the crusade idea are James A. Brundage, "Immortalizing the Crusades: Law and Institutions," in Benjamin Z. Kedar, Jonathan Riley-Smith, and Rudolf Hiestand, eds., *Montjoie: Studies in Honour of Hans Eberhard Mayer* (Aldershot, 1997), 251–260; and James M. Powell, "Church and Crusade: Frederick II and Louis IX," *Catholic Historical Review* 93 (2007), 251–264.

27. James A. Brundage, *Medieval Canon Law and the Crusader* (Madison WI, 1969), 115–190; Powell, *Anatomy*, chap. 2; Giles Constable, "The Place of the Crusader in Medieval Society," in Constable, *Crusaders*, 143–164; James A. Brundage, "Crusaders and Jurists: The Legal Consequences of Crusader Status," in *Le concile de Clermont de 1095 et l'appel à la Croisade: Actes du Colloque universitaire international de Clermont-Ferrand (23–26 juin 1995)* (Rome, 1997), 141–154.

28. R. Grosse, "Überlegungen zum Kreuzugeaufruf Eugens III von 1145/6. Mit einer Neueedition von JL 8876," *Francia* 18 (1991), 85–92; Constable, "The Second Crusade as Seen by Contemporaries."

29. On Saint Bernard's and general Cistercian influence on Lotario/Innocent, see Peters, "Lotario dei Conti di Segni," esp. 17–21; and Constable, "The Second Crusade."

the later twelfth century the apparatus of crusading privileges and the rite for taking the cross became more precise and institutionalized as their implications and potential shortcomings became clearer in a series of papal calls for crusades between Eugenius III and Lucius III (1181–1185). Alexander III (1159–1181) alone issued five calls for crusades.

Until the early thirteenth century, however, recruiting for the crusade had remained an ad hoc practice. By the end of the century there existed categorical terms to designate both the men who fought in the Holy Land—*crucesignati*, "those signed with the cross," crusaders—and the enterprise upon which they ventured—*croseria, passagium generale, passagium particulare, negotium crucis*, crusade. A growing body of juristic theology defined crusader status (including the vow and the liturgical rite for taking the cross [below, No. 4]) in the eyes and courts of the church, and the vocabulary of crusading preachers had been shaped by a half century of experience.[30]

The articulation of the crusade idea had made the crusade a distinctly papal affair. The twelfth and early thirteenth centuries were not, literally speaking, a century of "papal monarchy," but the increasingly authoritative tone of papal correspondence, the emergence of the papal court as a final court of appeals for spiritual affairs, and the papal place in the science of canon law all contributed to increase the spiritual preeminence that the reform papacy of the late eleventh century had begun. The crusade constituted one more distinctly papal privilege—and obligation.

Popes, however, might call crusades and commission preachers and legates to recruit for them, but they could not lead them, and they often failed to control those who did. Even the command and strategy of the First Crusade had slipped from the hands of Urban II (1088–1099) after the death of his legate Ademar of Le Puy into the hands of the barons who had led their armies to the East. Later crusades demonstrated the same thing; their actual planning and execution had to be carried out by lay lords. The Second Crusade had been led by King Conrad III and King Louis VII of France. The Third was led by Frederick Barbarossa, Richard Lionheart, and Philip Augustus. Even the brief crusade of Henry VI was an imperial project, conceived, directed, and executed by a lay ruler. But by 1200 it seemed that perhaps kings and emperors might not be the ideal leaders of crusades, that lesser nobles, who could be more readily guided by popes and their legates, might succeed where the quarreling royals had failed.

Innocent III was determined to retain control of the crusade in his own hands, but throughout the thirteenth century the crusade idea continued to be renegotiated within a dialogue among popes, preachers, influential crusaders, territorial princes with their own local concerns, and ordinary Christians with their own views of salvation. The fall of Jerusalem, the rise of a newly militant Muslim

---

30. For law, see Brundage, *Medieval Canon Law and the Crusader*. On preaching, see Cole, *Preaching of the Crusades to the Holy Land*; and Powell, *Anatomy*, chap. 3.

power under Saladin, as well as the political successes of later Ayyubids and especially Mamluks, the vast pastoral movement of moral reform, and many Christians' contempt for squabbling princes who neglected God's business in order to further their own all coincided with the pontificates of Innocent III and his successors.

Upon the death of Celestine III in January 1198, Lotario dei Conti di Segni was elected pope at about the age of thirty-seven, taking the papal name Innocent III. Lotario/Innocent was a Roman aristocrat, a successful student, first at the church schools in Rome and later those in northern France that were becoming the University of Paris, and a papal diplomat and administrator of a high order. He was also a gifted liturgist, preacher, a prelate driven by a high sense of pastoral responsibility, and a moral theologian committed to using the crusade idea as a means for all Christians, warriors or not, to engage in a common spiritual undertaking.

Innocent had also left a paper trail. His somber moral works *On the Misery of the Human Condition* and others had shown him to be an imaginative moralist, a peer of the brilliant and influential group of moral theologians in Paris, one very much committed to the devotional lives of clergy and laity alike. His voluminous papal correspondence meticulously preserved in his surviving official registers (as well as external evidence of the contents of several lost registers), his astute, if not quite professional legal decisions, and his firm assertion of papal authority even in times of crisis proved him a brilliant pope, one of the most interesting and influential popes the church has ever had.

And Innocent had new and powerful tools that he was more than willing to use. He readily promoted his former teachers and colleagues at Paris to high pastoral and administrative offices. He supported and benefited from the new learning of the schools on the techniques of penance and preaching. More often than not, he approved new religious orders devoted to the spiritual life of the growing cities and their diverse populations—most famously, the Order of Friars Minor founded by Francis of Assisi and the Order of Preachers founded by Domingo de Guzmán, the mendicant orders. He made it easier for repentant dissidents to return to the orthodox Christian fold. As the letter *Vineam Domini* had promised, Innocent had dug into the roots of a dramatically changing Christian society and laid out its ideal direction in the Fourth Lateran Council, whose canons shaped the doctrinal and devotional life of the Christian West for the next three centuries.

*   *   *

It is not surprising, then, that the crusade idea and reality took on a new, vigorous, and enduring life under Innocent and his successors. Several aspects of this life are the subject of the ten sections of this book.

Part I, "The Pope, Crusades, and Communities, 1198–1213," begins with the efforts of Innocent III to deal with the variety of difficulties that brought him to use the crusade in various communities and the universal community of Christians: the Greek East in the case of the Fourth Crusade, the south of France and the Albigensian Crusade, the Iberian Peninsula and the battle of Las Navas de Tolosa, France and the Rhineland, and the spontaneous communities generated by the "poor" and the *pueri*, "children"—that is, the poor and the disenfranchised who proclaimed themselves more worthy to regain the Holy Land than the rich and mighty who had repeatedly failed to do so. Their sentiments found sympathizers in the highest ranks of Innocent's curia and in the work of Peter of Blois. As early as 1108, and explicitly in 1146, a number of thinkers had argued for the application of the crusade privilege in the area of struggle between Christians and pagan Wends and later Prussians in northern Europe and along the Baltic coast. At the same time, the idea of a Christian reconquest—a *reconquista*—of the Muslim-dominated Iberian Peninsula also aligned itself with the crusade idea. We have tried to be as inclusive as possible in this volume, with a necessary focus on the northern Mediterranean and its immediate borderlands, and we have included where possible important sources translated from Arabic. We have not been able to deal with the important crusade/conversion movements in the Baltic and in Prussia and elsewhere in northern Europe, nor, aside from Las Navas de Tolosa in 1212, have we been able to deal with the complex Muslim-Christian frontier in the Iberian Peninsula.[31] Nor have we been able to do more than touch upon the complex and changing status of Jewish Europeans and the Jews and Christians of the East in the light of a changing reality of crusade and Christendom.[32]

By 1213 Innocent decided that much more collective work had to be undertaken, and his design and execution of the Fourth Lateran Council between 1213 and 1215, culminating in the vast reform program and the new crusade appeal is the subject of Part II, "Crusade and Council, 1213–1215."

Part III, "The Fifth Crusade, 1213–1221" deals with the Fifth Crusade as the direct outcome of the resolutions of the Fourth Lateran Council, directed, after Innocent's death at fifty-six in 1216, by his capable successor Honorius III

---

31. On the northern European crusades, see Eric Christiansen, *The Northern Crusades: The Baltic and the Catholic Frontier, 1100–1525* (Minneapolis, 1980); William Urban, *The Baltic Crusade*, 2d ed. (Chicago, 1994); Alan V. Murray, ed., *Crusade and Conversion on the Baltic Frontier, 1150–1500* (Aldershot UK-Burlington VT, 2001); Iben Fonnesberg-Schmidt, *The Popes and the Baltic Crusades, 1147–1254* (Leiden, 2007); Alan V. Murray, ed., *The Clash of Cultures on the Baltic Frontier* (Farnham UK-Burlington VT, 2009); Marek Tamm, Linda Kaljundi, and Carsten Selch Jensen, eds., *Crusading and Chronicle Writing on the Medieval Baltic Frontier* (Farnham UK-Burlington VT, 2011); *The Chronicle of Prussia by Nicolaus von Jeroschin*, trans. Mary Fischer (Farnham UK-Burlington VT, 2010); *The Chronicle of Henry of Livonia*, trans. James A. Brundage (Madison, 1961; repr. with new introduction, New York, 2003). On the Iberian Peninsula after Las Navas de Tolosa, see Joseph O'Callaghan, *The Gibraltar Crusade: Castile and the Battle for the Strait* (Philadelphia, 2011), esp. 187–188.

32. On one aspect, the status of religious minorities in Islamic and Christian societies, see James M. Powell, ed., *Muslims Under Latin Rule, 1100–1300* (Princeton NJ, 1990); and Bat Ye'or, *The Dhimmi: Jews and Christians Under Islam*, trans. David Littman (Rutherford NJ, 1985).

(1216–1227), whose own early service under Pope Clement III had associated him with the Third Crusade and Frederick Barbarossa, the memory of which remained sharp throughout Honorius's pontificate.

Part of Honorius's plan for the Fifth Crusade was its association with the emperor Frederick II (r. 1215–1250), son and successor of Henry VI, who, after many delays and controversies, finally departed on crusade in 1227. Part IV, "The Emperor's Crusade, 1227–1229," illustrates the different points of view, several extremely hostile, toward the crusading enterprise of the most interesting ruler of the thirteenth century.

In each of these cases, despite the most vigorous papal efforts, control of the crusade ended up in the hands of those leaders on the ground who were capable of leading armies. One of the key moments in thirteenth-century crusade history was the Barons' Crusade of 1234–1245, considered in Part V, in which the threats posed to the Latin Empire at Constantinople (accidentally installed by the Fourth Crusade) divided the crusade movement and revealed the competing ideas of Christian unity that might drive crusaders and popes further apart.

The advent of the Mongols posed yet another problem, this time that of a defensive crusade, not only to protect the Holy Land, but also to protect western Europe itself. The various reactions to the Mongol threat, as well as proposals for both allying with and crusading against them between 1246 and 1261, are considered in Part VI, "The Mongol Crusades, 1241–1262."

The first crusade of King Louis IX of France (r. 1226–1270), from 1248 to 1254 marked the second attempt after the Fifth Crusade to regain Jerusalem through an attack on Egypt. Part VII, "The Saint's Crusades, 1248–1270," considers Louis's expedition, which, like the Fifth Crusade, had considerable initial success, but was defeated by overwhelming force and crusader misjudgment. Louis died at the very beginning of his crusade of 1270. Louis's first crusade also generated the most remarkable set of sources of any thirteenth-century crusade, including the personal memoir of Jean de Joinville, Louis's companion on crusade.

The attempts on the part of popes after Honorius III to protect papal and other territories in Italy from Frederick II, his successors, and their heavy-handed servants led to a series of "political" crusades, the Italian crusades of 1241–1268, considered in Part VIII, which ended with the establishment of the papally allied house of Anjou on the throne of the kingdom of Sicily from 1264 until the end of the thirteenth century.

Thirteenth-century crusades were not simply a group of arbitrarily numbered military expeditions to recover the Holy Land and the term then carelessly used wherever a pope might decide to send them. A crusade enterprise of any significant size required papal direction and extensive planning, from recruiting to financing, military intelligence, and logistics. One of the most important changes in the Mediterranean expeditions of the thirteenth century was the shift to maritime transportation from Europe to the Middle East and the decline of the overland route. These crusades were also theaters of individual and collective thought and devotion, touching on many aspects of an individual life besides the military. Part IX,

"Living and Dying on Crusade," attempts to illustrate the actual experience of crusading at key moments: buying in advance (or scalping) places on a crusade ship; an enforceable contract of crusade service; a lawsuit against a ship's master for breach of contract; a single bishop's journey that reveals both the attractions and risks of sailing to the Levant; and the wills that crusaders, like modern soldiers, had to make out when they departed for a combat zone.

Although the thirteenth century also saw a growing missionary movement, such a movement never displaced the original goal of occupying the Holy Land. Therefore, Part X of this volume, "The Road to Acre, 1265–1291," deals with the new crusade proposals brought together at papal request and spontaneous inspiration on the eve of the Second Council of Lyons in 1274—illustrating the impact and legacy of the events from 1198 till 1274 on the idea of crusade and the means now required to achieve its goals. Like *Audita tremendi* and the Fourth Lateran Council, the Second Council of Lyons took up once again the extensive planning of yet new crusades. In the event, the resurgence of Muslim power in the hands of the new Mamluk sultans of Egypt and the lack of resources available from Europe led to the erosion of Christian-controlled territories as, one by one, these fell to Mamluk forces. The fall of Acre in 1291 marked the end of all Christian territories on the Levantine mainland. But it did not reject the idea of crusade itself that had been so transformed between 1198 and 1291 that it had become built into the fabric of the concept of Christendom.

From the pontificate of Innocent III to those of Gregory X (1271–1276) and Nicholas IV (1288–1292), the crusade idea became a component of Christian identity for combatants and noncombatants alike. Each stage of crusading was precisely defined and institutionalized—in spite of occasionally imprecise terminology, crusades could not be mistaken for anything else. Succeeding popes could make crusade plans with the aid of records and memory of earlier crusades. Gregory VIII's reaction to the defeat at Hattin greatly influenced Innocent III. Innocent III's responses to the Fourth Crusade, the Albigensian Crusade, Las Navas de Tolosa, and the Children's Crusade in turn influenced Honorius III, Gregory IX, Innocent IV, Alexander IV, and Gregory X. The canons of the Fourth Lateran Council were echoed at the First and Second Councils of Lyons in 1245 and 1274. From Innocent III on there existed networks of reformers whose service and memory spanned several crusade campaigns. James of Vitry, Oliver of Paderborn, and Conrad of Speyer were all educated at Paris, knew about Fulk of Neuilly's preaching of the Fourth Crusade, and personally preached the Albigensian Crusade, the Fifth Crusade, and the crusade of Frederick II. Many families and individuals preserved crusading memories and traditions, dispatching crusaders over several generations, like that of Jean de Joinville and many others. Participants in the Third Crusade, like Count Hugh of Saint-Pol, also turned up in the Fourth, and some in the Fifth. Much of the later theory of the just war and the laws of war stemmed from the experience of the Fourth Crusade, the Albigensian Crusade, papal letters, canonistic commentaries, and the vivid polemical language that was often used. The period 1198–1291 witnessed many momentous changes in western Europe.[33] The crusade was central, not peripheral in all of these. The experience of actual crusades paradoxically serves as a measure of both the awareness of universal Christendom and the many local interests and anxieties that continued to constitute it.

33. The best single-author survey written directly from the sources remains John Hine Mundy, *Europe in the High Middle Ages, 1150–1300*, 3d ed. (London-New York, 2000). Another useful perspective is that of Robert Bartlett, *The Making of Europe: Conquest, Colonization and Cultural Change, 950–1330* (Princeton NJ, 1993). See also the *New Cambridge Medieval History*, vols. 5 and esp. 6.

PART I

The Pope, Crusades, and Communities, 1198–1213

As Christoph Maier has observed, the thirteenth was "arguably the century with the most intense and varied crusading activity of the entire Middle Ages."[1] Of course the circumstances of earlier crusade activity in northern Europe and Iberia and the changing fortunes of the Latin Kingdom of Jerusalem in the twelfth century, as well as the powerful Cistercian devotional commitment to the idea of crusade surely suggested the adaptability of the idea of crusade across a broader spectrum of ecclesiastical concern than Jerusalem and the Holy Land alone. But such adaptability played out most dramatically in the years after 1198, when Innocent III and his handpicked, trained assistants created a network of crusade preachers, recruiters, financial managers, and inspired lay warriors to link the crusade to the state of Christian society in many different forms, creating what may be considered a crusade culture.

This section illustrates at the end of the twelfth and the beginning of the thirteenth century the astonishing versatility of the crusade in the hands of a talented, driven, and frequently frustrated pope whose long view was always on the Holy Land, but whose many other concerns elsewhere and whose conviction that crusade and the need of religious reform in individuals and institutions were intimately connected were crucial to his pontificate.

In spite of the troubles in central and southern Italy, the diplomatic and marital problems of Philip II Augustus, the disputed imperial election following the death of Henry VI in September 1197, the turmoil of the city-republics in Tuscany, and the increasing volume of legal matters and the rising costs of administration in the curia, Innocent's earliest papal letters were full of discussions of the plight of the Holy Land and of the need for a forthcoming crusade. Although Amalric of Jerusalem had signed a treaty with al-Adil of Damascus that was to last until 1203, the treaty did not cover Cairo, and there was some discussion of whether Alexandria was the intended target, an eventual gateway to Jerusalem. In 1198 Innocent began his preparations for a crusade, issuing the eloquent and lengthy letter *Post miserabile* in August. It rhetorically painted a vivid picture of Muslim taunts against Christian failures in the East, appointed two of his closest advisers, Peter of Capua, cardinal deacon of Santa Maria in Via Lata, and Soffredus, cardinal priest of Santa Prassede, as his legates in western Europe, "so that by word and example they might invite others to the service of the cross," and

---

1. Christoph Maier, review of Caroline Smith, *Crusading in the Age of Joinville*, *Speculum* 82 (2007), 485–486 at 485.

reminded Christians that the crusade was God's offering of a means to salvation, but that God's people had to make themselves morally worthy of that gift.[2] On November 5, 1198, Innocent commissioned the preacher Fulk of Neuilly both to preach himself and to help Peter of Capua to select and train other preachers.[3] In the same year, at a tournament at Écry a number of princes had voluntarily taken up the cross and begun their preparations for further recruiting and transportation by sea to the Holy Land (below, No. 6).

In his letter of 1199 to the Byzantine emperor Alexius III, *Multe nobis attulit* (below, No. 3), Innocent asked for more Byzantine aid to Christians in the Holy Land as well as for reunion between the divided Greek and Latin churches. Here, too, the crusade was linked to an overarching view of the nature and needs of Christian society.

Innocent also sent out letters to the great churches of Europe and their leaders, urging, and then commanding them to contribute a fortieth part of their income to the crusade effort—the first tax on clerical income. Innocent also proposed to contribute substantially out of his own strained finances, and he commanded that special money chests be placed in churches, so that when crusade sermons were preached, contributions of the laity could also be collected and applied to the needs of crusade, although their application caused a number of difficult problems. His letters specifically echoed the privileges laid out by Gregory VIII in *Audita tremendi*, and they indicate a growing awareness of the size and complexity of mounting such an expedition early in the thirteenth century.[4]

The problems of finance reflected one great difficulty of a crusade to the East. Another was that of overall management and command. Thibaut III of Champagne, one of the first princes to take the cross at Écry, died before he could set out. The remaining princes elected Boniface of Montferrat as their leader and appointed a committee to represent them in arranging transportation by sea from Venice. After the financing and logistical planning of the crusade and the signing of a binding contract with the Venetians, the crusaders found that they could not provide enough troops and money to satisfy that contract. Many crusaders had simply ignored the Venetian rendezvous and made their ways to Syria by themselves, while others had simply never started out. The Venetians, who for their part had suspended their entire maritime economy for a year in order to build the ships and lay in the supplies needed for what would have been the largest amphibious military campaign in European history, demanded full payment.

---

2. *Post miserabile* is also translated in Alfred J. Andrea, *Contemporary Sources for the Fourth Crusade* (Leiden-Boston, 2000), 9–19, there from the register version. Andrea's important collection translates nearly all of Innocent's letters concerning the Fourth Crusade. The description of the two legates is from Powell, *Deeds*, 61. On what is probably Innocent's own view of the range of difficulties he faced in 1198–1199, see Powell, *Deeds*, 7–77.

3. The letter to Fulk is translated in Andrea, *Contemporary Sources*, 19–21.

4. Two letters are translated in Andrea, *Contemporary Sources*, 24–32; and Powell, *Deeds*, 133–139 (specific reference to Gregory VIII, on 136).

Once it was clear that this was impossible, they offered an alternative—the crusaders might have their period of obligation extended if they assisted Venice in bringing to heel the city of Zara, in Dalmatia, a rebellious former ally of Venice at the time dependent on the kingdom of Hungary, whose ruler had taken the cross and was therefore technically protected against any military intrusion at home. At this point a number of crusaders, including Simon de Montfort, who later led the forces of the Albigensian Crusade (below, No. 7), left the army because they refused to attack a Christian city. After the capture of Zara, another diversion appeared in the person of Alexius IV, an exiled claimant to the imperial throne at Constantinople, whose father Isaac Angelus had been blinded and deposed by his brother, Alexius III. Alexius IV made substantial promises of aid for crusader-Venetian assistance in gaining the throne. When the crusaders and Venetians installed Alexius IV, the new emperor failed to fulfill his promises, and the forces that had placed him on his throne attacked and conquered the city in 1204.

The devastation caused by military conquest and several vast fires that destroyed much of the city appalled both Latin and Greek Christendom, including Innocent III, but it also presented an irresistible fait accompli to the pope—the reunion of the divided Greek and Latin churches. The Venetians and crusaders promptly elected a Latin emperor, Baldwin of Flanders, and divided the Eastern Roman Empire among themselves. By 1207 they had ceased to call themselves "crusaders" as they parceled out the spoils of conquest, although some of them then moved on to the Holy Land to join other crusaders. Innocent, horrified, infuriated, and undaunted, began plans for yet another crusade.

And he launched one, but not to the Holy Land. The highly intensified perception of religious dissent as heresy in the course of the twelfth century momentarily appeared just as pressing as the needs of Outremer and much closer to home. In some parts of western Europe, notably around the county of Toulouse, "heretics" appeared to have become almost a numerical majority. Innocent sent preachers, papal legates, and eminent monastic leaders, chiefly Cistercians, but also Premonstratensians, into the area, but response was generally indifferent or hostile, and local bishops appear not to have been of much use. The murder of the papal legate Peter of Castelnau in 1208 made the pope determine that stronger measures were needed. Since moral reform, orthodoxy and orthopraxy, and crusade were already firmly linked in his mind, in the same year Innocent offered full crusade privileges for the first time to those who would take up arms against the heretics, and the first crusade against Christians, the Albigensian Crusade, was launched (below, No. 7).

This crusade, too, slipped from papal control, and the bloodbath in southern France between 1209 and 1229 elicited expressions of horror not only from Christians elsewhere but from churchmen themselves. If the crusade crushed heresy in southern France, it did not crush it elsewhere, and the chief beneficiary of the enterprise was to be the king of France, who eventually gained, by a judicious exploitation of military force and legal authority, a large addition to his kingdom.

But the crusade against Christians was not the only new direction that the crusade took during this period.

In 1195 the Almohad caliph Ya'qub had inflicted a grievous defeat on the forces of King Alfonso VIII of Castile at the battle of Alarcos. So seriously did the pope consider the loss that in 1197 Pope Celestine III granted to warriors in Aquitaine the right to apply in Spain instead the vows they had taken to go on the Third Crusade but had not fulfilled. In 1210 the caliph took the strategically important castle of Salvatierra. These losses inspired Innocent III to proclaim yet another crusade, this time in Spain, accompanied by intercessory processions in Rome that were imitated elsewhere in Europe (below, No. 8). The plan drew in Peter II, king of Aragón, King Sancho VII of Navarre, and a large number of knights from Iberia and France.

In July 1212, while the Albigensian Crusade was well underway, Innocent III tried with limited success to suspend it in favor of the expedition in Iberia. The Christian rulers of Castile, Aragón, and Navarre and their combined forces encountered the Almohad army at Las Navas de Tolosa and, gambling on the outcome of a single pitched battle, routed the enemy and opened the route of reconquest into Andalusia (below, No. 9).

The intercessory processions that Innocent held in Rome and in northern Europe on the eve of Las Navas de Tolosa appealed widely to Christians throughout Europe. They also seem to have been identified with another idea that had taken shape after the disaster at Hattin. One of those present at the papal curia when *Audita tremendi* was read aloud was Peter of Blois, a scholar, moralist, and ecclesiastical administrator, who was struck by the spectacular failure of the great and powerful leaders at Hattin and became convinced that only through apostolic poverty and individual moral reform could the Holy Land be regained.[5] The failure of the Third Crusade certainly heightened this view. Peter, who had gone on the Third Crusade in the service of Baldwin, archbishop of Canterbury, wrote several works between 1187 and 1189 in which he laid out these ideas, claiming that only the poor and devout, not the proud and the mighty, could legitimately accomplish this task.

In 1212 and 1213 a number of the poor and devout took up these ideas, which were certainly not unique to Peter of Blois, and launched several militant processions toward the south of France and Italy, which came to be known as the Children's Crusade (below, No. 10).

By 1212 there had also been developed a formal liturgical rite for taking the cross (below, No. 4), sufficiently well known that even those who went on the Children's Crusade could voluntarily adopt it or a variation of it.

The number and variety of crusades and the communities in which they operated between 1198 and 1213 is utterly unlike those of any comparable period of

---

5. On Peter's ideas and other scholarship on his crusade experience, see John D. Cotts, *The Clerical Dilemma: Peter of Blois and Literate Culture in the Twelfth Century* (Washington DC, 2009), 218–230.

crusade activity. It suggests just how intensely the need for moral reform—individual and collective—could be made a precondition for a successful crusade, and, conversely, how the crusade itself could then be applied in entirely new situations and places. It also suggests how local interests and concerns always stood in tension with the broad views of the popes and the curia. Innocent III expressed pity for those who had gone on the hopeless Children's Crusade, and he echoed his friend Peter of Blois in lamenting that the rich and noble had been shamed by the poor and devout in performing God's business. And he decided that it was now time to place both of these issues before all of Christian society, East and West, which he did by calling for the Fourth Lateran Council in *Vineam Domini* in 1213.

2. Innocent III, *Post miserabile,* August 13, 1198

As the author of the *Gesta Innocentii,* the first volume of the register of Innocent's letters, and virtually all recent scholarship make abundantly clear, the first year of Innocent's pontificate was occupied with a number of major political and moral crises that compelled most of the pope's time and attention. Among these were the instability of the city of Rome and the papal territories and the problem of the divided and dangerous kingdom of Sicily in the wake of the death of Henry VI and the attempted takeover of the kingdom by Henry's powerful servants as well as the return of Henry's crusaders from the Holy Land in the spring of 1198. Moral reformers were greatly concerned with the venality of some of the clergy and the bitter legal disputes that often involved the highest ranks of churchmen, as they were with the marital problems of Philip Augustus of France, hostility between France and England, and unsettled relations with Eastern Christendom in the person of the emperor Alexius III, who had deposed his brother Isaac II Angelus and pursued Isaac's son Alexius IV. Innocent hoped and expected to be able to rely on archbishops and bishops, as well as the Cistercian monks and Premonstratensian canons to solve these problems; he regularly held consistories at the curia three times a week, began to reform the papal household and curia, and he also selected and appointed trusted individuals as legates.

But in the midst of these concerns, some of which lasted throughout his entire pontificate, Innocent never forgot the Holy Land and its greatly diminished condition, nor his and Christendom's obligations toward it. In chapter 46 the author of the *Gesta* states:

> Of all these things, he hoped most fervently to aid and recover the Holy Land, considering carefully how he could effectively fulfill this desire. Because some said that by delaying action the Roman Church was imposing serious and insupportable burdens on others, and, moreover, she was not ready to raise a finger for it, he chose two of his

brethren, namely, Soffredus, cardinal priest of Santa Prassede, and Peter, cardinal deacon of Santa Maria in Via Lata, on whom he imposed the sign of the cross, so that by word and example they might invite others to the service of the cross. He also ordered that all clerics in major and minor orders should pay one-fortieth of their ecclesiastical incomes in support of the Holy Land.[6]

Although the *Gesta* does not mention Innocent's first call to a major crusade, the letter *Post miserabile* of August 13–15, 1198, much of this paragraph is a summary of its text. But although *Post miserabile* was Innocent's first crusade proposal, it is not the first mention of his concerns for the Holy Land. In late February 1198, a month after his coronation and nearly two months after his election, Innocent sent to Aymeric, patriarch of Jerusalem (1194–1202), the letter *Rex regum*, announcing his election and his profound concern for the Holy Land. At the same time he wrote to the duke of Brabant, the landgrave of Thuringia, and others the letter *Quanta sit*, regarding his concerns over the prospect of the German crusaders leaving the Holy Land in the aftermath of the death of Henry VI. In August 1198 different versions of *Post miserabile* were sent from the papal chancery to different places in western Europe. The text translated here was sent to the archbishop of York, his prelates and other clerics, and to the local nobility of the ecclesiastical province of York. It was included in the chronicle of Roger Howden.

Roger Howden was a royal clerk from northern England (perhaps the source of his copy of *Post miserabile*) who had written brief accounts of the deeds of Henry II (1154–1189) and Richard I (1189–1199) and gone on the Third Crusade (1187–1192). When he returned, Roger wrote a more elaborate chronicle about the late twelfth century, in which he included earlier papal letters dealing with the Holy Land from Alexander III and Lucius III to Henry II, as well as letters from the patriarch of Antioch to Henry II in 1188, offering Henry the crown of the Latin Kingdom of Jerusalem. He also incorporated Henry's enthusiastic response to the patriarchs of Antioch and Jerusalem, as well as several letters from Terricus, the master of the Temple in Jerusalem, in 1187 to all Templars, informing them of the disaster at Hattin, and to Henry II for the same purpose.

Following the very long and sermonlike prologue, Innocent lays out a remarkably developed plan in *Post miserabile*. No kings are addressed, but ecclesiastical provinces and local nobles are to mobilize themselves and their armies for two years. Innocent appoints the cardinals Stephen (*recte* Soffredus) and Peter as legates for the crusade to Venice and to France and England respectively, absorbing their expenses himself. He sets the date of March 1199 for the assembling of forces, offers pardon of sins for different categories of crusade participants and supporters, takes their properties under ecclesiastical legal protection, and threatens severe legal penalties to all who disregard his rulings. He suspends payment of interest on crusader loans, including loans from Jews. He appoints two local

6. Powell, *Deeds*, 61–62; the whole chapter is important.

ecclesiastical figures at York, the unnamed prior of the house of Augustinian canons at Thurgarton and a certain Master Vacarius, to be assisted by one member of the Knights Templar and one of the Knights Hospitaller, to collect and protect the funds contributed. The present letter to York is dated at Rome, August 13, 1198. The copy in Innocent's register is addressed to the archbishop of Narbonne and others and is dated at Rieti, August 15, 1198. Some topics are treated in a different sequence in the two copies. The date/location discrepancy is interesting concerning chancery practice but not crucial (the curia was in fact at Rieti). Innocent here appears to have thought of Europe as divided into ecclesiastical provinces (which included both clergy and laity) as well as kingdoms.

Innocent has obviously given considerable thought to a new crusade and its ideal participants. His administrative arrangements laid out here are extremely detailed and coherent. But the letter confronted two problems that weakened its immediate impact. When he issued *Post miserabile* Innocent had been pope for only seven months and probably underestimated the kind and degree of cooperation he could expect from a wide range of prelates and nobles whom he left to organize themselves for the collective enterprise. Second, his date of March 1199 was far too early for the organization, financing, and departure of a crusade composed of components of ecclesiastical and lay territories whose leaders needed to devise a very large and complex military enterprise in mutual cooperation and without royal leadership and then connect with similar groups throughout Europe. Even Innocent's able legates could not compensate for local inadequacy.

Innocent also expanded the privileges for different levels of participation in the crusade, opening participation in spiritual benefits to a much broader segment of Christendom.[7] *Post miserabile* produced no crusade in March 1199, but Innocent had shown how he thought such a crusade ought eventually to be organized very early in his pontificate. And his interest in and concern for the Holy Land continued. In late December 1198 he sent the letter *Venientem ad nos* to King Amalric of Jerusalem (1194–1202) with a more fully developed plan for a crusade, and a few days later he issued *Graves orientalis terrae* in the same vein to the archbishops of Canterbury and York as well as to other prelates in western Europe.[8]

The text from the Gesta, *chap. 46, is from Powell,* Deeds, *61–63, discussed in Moore,* To Root Up and to Plant *44–47, 55–60; Christopher Cheney, Pope Innocent III and England,* Päpste und Papsttum, *Bd. 9 (Stuttgart, 1976), 239–270; Penny J. Cole, Preaching, 80–97; John Gillingham, "Roger Howden on Crusade," in D. O. Morgan, ed., Medieval Historical Writing in the Christian and Islamic Worlds (London, 1982), 60–75, repr. in Gillingham, Richard Coeur de Lion: Kingship, Chivalry and War in the Twelfth Century (London-Rio Grande OH, 1994). The copy of the letter from volume 1 of the register of Innocent III, translated by Andrea, Contemporary Sources, 9–19, was sent to the archbishop of Narbonne and others and correctly identifies one of the papal legates as Soffredus rather than, as here, Stephen. A number of letters from 1188 between the patriarchs of Jerusalem and Antioch and Terricus*

7. For both spiritual and temporal benefits, see Brundage, *Canon Law and the Crusader*, 139–190.

8. Trans. in Andrea, *Contemporary Sources*, 24–32.

and Henry II are translated in Barber and Bate, Letters, *nos. 46–47, 83–86; and others from the period in Dana C. Munro,* Letters of the Crusaders Written from the Holy Land, *vol. 1, no. 4, of* Translations and Reprints from the Original Sources of European History *(Philadelphia, 1896), 20–24. Letters from Innocent to England are calendared in C. R. Cheney and Mary G. Cheney, eds.,* The Letters of Pope Innocent III (1198–1216) Concerning England and Wales: A Calendar with an Appendix of Texts *(Oxford, 1967).*

INNOCENT, bishop, servant of the servants of God, to his venerable brothers the archbishop of York and his suffragans, and his dearly beloved sons, the abbots, priors, and other prelates of churches, and to the earls, barons, and all the people of the province of York, greetings and apostolic benediction.

After the wretched fall of the kingdom of Jerusalem, after the lamentable slaughter of the people of Christendom, after the deplorable invasion of that land on which the feet of Christ had stood, and where God, our king, had deigned to work our salvation in the midst of the earth [Ps 73:12], after the ignominious removal of the life-giving cross on which the salvation of the world had been hanged, and had thereby blotted out the signature of the old death [Col 2:14], the Apostolic See, alarmed at the awful recurrence of disasters so unfortunate, was struck with agonizing grief, exclaiming and bewailing to such a degree that, from her continual crying, her throat became hoarse [Ps 68:4]. And from excessive weeping, her eyes became dim. But in the true words of the prophet, "If we forget thee, O Jerusalem, let our right hand forget her cunning. If we do not remember thee let our tongue cleave to the roof of our mouth" [Ps 137:5–6]. Still the Apostolic See cries aloud, and she raises her voice like a trumpet, trying to arouse the nations of Christendom to fight the battles of Christ [Is 58:1], and to avenge the injuries done to him crucified, using the words of him who says, "All ye that pass by on the road, behold and see if there be any sorrow like unto my sorrow" [Lam 1:12]. For behold, our inheritance has gone to strangers, our houses to alien people [Lam 5:2], "The ways of Sion mourn, because none come to the solemn feasts . . . her adversaries now rule [Lam 1:4–5].

The sepulcher of the Lord, which the prophet foretold should be so glorious, has been profaned by the unrighteous and has thereby been made inglorious [Is 11:10]. Our glory, of which the Apostle speaks when

Source: William Stubbs, ed., Chronica magistri Rogeri de Houedene, *4 vols. (London, 1868–1871), 4:70–75. The paragraphing here has been emended in order to highlight distinct topics treated by Innocent and to indicate the extraordinary amount of administrative detail the document contains. Scriptural citations are indicated in brackets for readers' convenience.*

he says, "God forbid that I should glory save in the cross of Lord Jesus Christ" [Gal 6:14], is held in the hands of the enemy, and our Lord Jesus Christ, who, by dying for us, led our captivity captive, is driven in exile from his inheritance as though himself a captive [Eph 4:8].

In former days, when the ark of the Lord of Sabaoth abode in tents, Uriah [2 Sm 11:10–11] refused to enter his own house and withheld himself from the lawful embraces of his wife. But at the present day our princes, the glory of Israel having been transferred from its place, to our injury, give themselves up to adulterous embraces, thereby abusing their luxuries and their wealth. And, while they harass each other with inexorable hatred, while one is using all his efforts to take vengeance on another for injuries done, there is no one who is moved by the injuries of him crucified, nor considering that now our enemies are insulting us.[9]

[They are] saying [Ps 78:10; Dt 32:37; Lam 1:10]: "Where is your God [Ps 41:4, 11, 78:10], who can neither deliver himself nor you from our hands? Behold! Now we have profaned your sanctuaries. Behold! Now we have extended our hands to the things you most cherish and have, at the first attack, seized upon those places with the hand of violence. And whether you will or not, we hold possession of those places where you pretend that your superstition took its rise. Already we have weakened and broken asunder the lances of the Gauls, baffled the efforts of the English, crushed the strength of the Germans, and now for a second time subdued the haughty Spaniards. And though you thought to arouse all your might against us, hardly in any of your attempts did you succeed. Where, then, is your God? Let him arise now and help you, and let him be the protector of yourselves and of himself.

The Germans, indeed, who presumed that they should gain unheard-of triumphs over us, crossed the seas to our land with ardent spirits. And after they had taken the single fortified place of Beirut when no one was defending it, they would have woefully experienced our might, had not the opportunity of retreat come to the aid of themselves and their potentates, and their descendants would have forever mourned the slaughter we would have made of them. And as for your kings and princes whom we formerly drove out of the lands of the East, in order that they may

---

9. Innocent is here criticizing very specifically the adultery of Philip Augustus of France and other rulers who had violated the prohibited degrees of marriage, as well as the ongoing conflict between the kings of France and England. The references below to the Gauls, English, Germans, and Spaniards are very thinly veiled precise references to actual crusader losses. It is clearly Innocent speaking, not the rhetorical Muslim victors.

conceal their terror by putting on a show of daring, after returning to their skulking places—we will not dignify them by calling them kingdoms—they prefer to attack each other, rather than once more experience our strength and our might. What then remains except that you deserted those cut off by our avenging sword for your own purposes, and by running away claiming to restore peace to your territories? We should attack your territories for the purpose of destroying both your name and your memory."

How then, brothers and sons, are we to rebut the scorn of these insulters, in what terms shall we be able to answer them? When are we to see them on their part in pursuit of the truth, judging of what has reached our hearing based on specific information? For we have received letters from parts beyond the seas to the effect that when the Germans had reached Acre with their fleet, they seized the castle of Beirut, there being none to defend it, while the Saracens, making an assault upon Jaffa on the other side, gained possession of it by storm, and having slain so many thousands of Christians in it, leveled it to the ground. As for the Germans, hearing rumors of the death of the emperor [Henry VI], not waiting for the usual time of year for making the passage home, they embarked on board their ships for the purpose of returning home. At this the Saracens, who had collected a numerous army, raged with such violence against the Christians that it was not possible for the Christians to go out of their cities without great danger, nor yet to remain in them without fear. And too truly their sword has its horrors outside the cities and its anxious fears within them [Dt 32:25].[10]

Take, therefore, my sons, the spirit of fortitude, the shield of faith, and the helmet of salvation [Eph 6:16–17], putting your trust in God, not in numbers nor in your strength, but rather trusting in the power of God, to whom it is not difficult to save either with many or the few [1 Sm 14:6], and rush to the aid of him by whom you exist and live and have your being [Acts 17:28]. For on your behalf it was that "He made himself of no reputation and took upon him the form of a servant and was made in the likeness of men. And being found in fashion as a man, he humbled himself and became obedient unto death, even the death on the cross" [Phil 2:7–9]. And yet, while he is poor, you abound in wealth; while he

10. This is the process of the breaking up of the German crusade army of Henry VI described by the imaginary Muslim invective above. It seems that Innocent had an independent source on the process and the disorder and resentment it caused.

is put to flight, you are at rest and do not come to his aid while he is in want and exile. Who, then, in a case of such great emergency shall refuse to pay obedience to Jesus Christ? When he comes to stand before Christ's tribunal to be judged, what answer will he be able to make to him in defense of himself? If God has submitted himself to death for man, is man to hesitate to submit to death for God? "For the sufferings of the present time are not worthy to be compared with the glory which shall be revealed within us" [Rom 8:18]. Shall then the servant deny temporal riches to his lord when his lord bestows on the servant riches that are eternal, "which eye hath not seen nor ear heard, neither has it entered into the heart of man" [Is 64:4; 1 Cor 2:9]? Therefore it is said that a man should "lay up treasures in heaven, where thieves do not break in nor steal, nor moth nor rust corrupt" [Mt 6:20].

Let each and all, then, prepare themselves so that in the next month of March [1199] each city by itself and, in like manner, each of the earls and barons should, according to their respective means, send a number of warriors to the defense of the land of the nativity of our Lord, to be supported by predetermined sums of money, and there to remain for two years at least. For although daily anxieties on behalf of all the churches are pressing upon us, nevertheless we especially conceive as one of our chief concerns our desire to apply every energy to the rescue of the lands of the East, lest if help should chance to be delayed, the wingless locust may devour what the locust leaves behind and the last state become worse than the first [Jl 1:4].

But so that we may not seem to lay grievous and insupportable burdens on the shoulders of other men and be unwilling with our finger to move them [Mt 23:4; Lk 11:46], saying so much and doing little or nothing at all, and inasmuch as he who both does and teaches is to be called great in the kingdom of heaven [Mt 5:19–20], in the example of him who began to both do and teach, to the end that we, who though unworthy as we are to act as his vicars on earth, may set a good example to others, we have determined, both in person and in deed to aid the Holy Land. We have appointed our dearly beloved son Stephen [Soffredus], cardinal priest of the title of Santa Prassede, and Peter, cardinal deacon of the title of Santa Maria in Via Lata, God-fearing men famous for their knowledge and probity, powerful in both word and deed [Lk 24:19], and whom, among our other brethren, we do especially love and esteem, as legates of the Apostolic See, humbly and devoutly to precede the army of the Lord, after having, with our own hand, placed upon them the sign of the cross. They are not to be supported by offerings given through charity, but at our own cost and that of our brethren, by whom also we have determined upon sending other available aid to the said land.

Wherefore, in the meantime, we have sent the said Peter, cardinal deacon and titular of Santa Maria in Via Lata, to our most dearly beloved sons in Christ, the most illustrious kings Philip, king of the Franks, and Richard, king of the English, for the purpose of effecting a reconciliation between them, or at least obtaining a truce for at least five years, and exhorting the people to obedience to him [Christ] crucified. Peter as legate of the Apostolic See we command to be honored by all and obedience to be humbly shown to his commands and enactments. Stephen [Soffredus], cardinal priest and titular of Santa Prassede, we are about to send to Venice to obtain help for the Holy Land. Moreover, by the common advice of our brethren we have resolved and strictly enjoin and command you, our brethren the archbishops and bishops and our dearly beloved sons the abbots and other prelates of churches, immediately to levy a certain number of soldiers, or instead of such a certain number, a fixed amount of money, in the next March, having due consideration of the means of each, for the purpose of attacking the barbarous tribes of the pagans, and preserving the inheritance of the Lord, which he obtained with his own blood.

But if any cleric, a thing which we cannot believe, shall dare to oppose an ordinance so pious and necessary, we have determined that he shall be punished as a transgressor of the sacred canons and command that he shall be suspended from his duties until such time as he shall have made satisfaction for having done so.

Wherefore, trusting in the mercy of God and in the authority of the blessed apostles Peter and Paul, and in that power of binding and loosing which God has bestowed upon us, unworthy as we are [Mt 16:19], in the case of those who, in their own persons and at their own expense, shall undergo the labors of this expedition, we do grant them plenary pardon for those sins for which they have done penance with voice and heart and promise them the blessing of everlasting salvation as the reward of the just.[11]

11. This unusual formula seems to mean that Innocent here emphasizes the need for both inner contrition and oral confession and the undertaking of the assigned penance. It may derive from Innocent's experience at the schools of Paris, in which contrition and confession were greatly emphasized.

To those who shall not have gone there in their own persons, but have only, according to their means and rank, sent fit and proper men to stay there for at least two years, and also to those who, although at the expense of others, shall in their own persons have undergone the labors of the pilgrimage which they have undertaken, we do also grant plenary pardon for their sins. We also state that all persons who shall give suitable aid to the Holy Land at their own cost, according to the amount of aid they give, and especially in proportion to the feelings of devotion they shall manifest, shall be partakers in this remission.

And in order that all persons may prepare more expeditiously and more securely for giving to the aid of the land of the nativity of our Lord, we take their property under the protection of Saint Peter and ourselves from the time they have assumed the cross. The same property is likewise to be under the protection of the archbishops, bishops, and other prelates of the church of God.

It is our command that until their death or return is determined with certainty, their property shall remain safe and untouched. And if any person shall presume to contravene this ordinance, he is to be forced by ecclesiastical censure to observe it. Therefore, let no one entirely withhold himself from this work, since it has not been begun by us, but by the apostles themselves, who collected among the nations that they might help their brethren who were laboring in Jerusalem [Acts 11:29, 24:17; Rom 15:25].

We also wish you not to despair of the divine mercy, however much the Lord may be offended by our sins. If you set out upon your pilgrimage with all humility of heart and body, as you ought to do, the Lord may effect that which he did not grant to your forefathers. Probably, our forefathers might have conspired together and would have said, "our own high hand and not the Lord has done all this" [Dt 32:27; 2 Sm 12:28]. And they would have ascribed the glory of the victory to themselves and not to the Lord. We also trust that the Lord will not in his wrath withhold his mercies, since when he is angered he does not forget to show mercy [Ps 76:10; Hb 3:2], admonishing and exhorting us, saying, "Turn unto me and I will turn unto you" [Zec 1:3].

We believe that you should walk in the law of the Lord, not following in the footsteps of those who, going after vanity, have become vain and given themselves up to riotous living and drunken revelries [Ps 118:1; Jer 44:10; Dt 21:10; Rom 13:13] and done things in parts beyond the sea which they would not dare to do in the land of their own birth without having to endure great infamy and considerable disgrace. Place your hopes of victory in him alone who does not forsake those who put their trust in him; abstain not only from what is unlawful, but also from many things that are lawful [Jgs 2:16–20]. He who overthrew the chariot of Pharaoh in the Red Sea [Ex 15:4] will render weak the bow of the strong and will sweep away from all your faces the enemies of the cross of Christ as if they were the very dirt of the streets [Pss 9:4 and 17:43]. He will not give the glory to us or to you, but to his own name, who is glorious in his saints [Dt 6:22], wondrous in his majesty, a worker of marvels, and, after tears and weeping, the giver of joy and gladness [Tb 3:22].

If any of those who go on the pilgrimage shall at the time be bound by oath to pay interest, we order, brother archbishops and bishops, that you command their creditors in their several dioceses, by force of ecclesiastical compulsion, entirely to absolve them from their oaths and cease to demand from them any further interest, with no appeal allowed. And if any one of their creditors shall compel them to pay interest, let him be compelled by you, by means of similar compulsion, to make restitution of the same, with no appeal allowed.

Also, you princes our sons, we do command Jews to be compelled by you and by means of the secular power to forgo all interest from such people. And until such remission shall have been made, we order every kind of communication with them in matters of trade or any other matters whatsoever to be stopped, and this rule to be held by all the faithful of Christ under sentence of excommunication.

Also, so as to carry out these commands in your province more expeditiously and more perfectly, we have thought it proper to depute to you our sons the prior of Thurgarton and Master Vacarius to announce the word of the Lord to the others. We invite our venerable brethren, your archbishop and his suffragans and the others, to the fulfillment of the apostolic mandate to promote the cause of the Lord so that you may both be partakers of this remission and that in this your devotion may more fully shine forth. Also, for the more laudable promotion of these things, you are to associate with yourselves in these affairs one of the brethren of the order of the Temple, also one of the brethren of the Hospital of Jerusalem, men of character and prudence.

Given at Saint Peter's at Rome, on the ides of August, in the first year of our pontificate [August 13, 1198].

3. Innocent III, *Multe nobis attulit,* 1199

From the very beginning of his pontificate, Innocent III turned his attention to the problem of the Holy Land. Within a few weeks of his election and coronation, in early February 1198, he wrote to the patriarch of Jerusalem and to the duke of Brabant and the landgrave of Thuringia, all of whom were already in the East on the crusade launched by the emperor Henry VI in 1196. His concerns were later reflected not only in dozens of his letters but in daily life at the papal curia, in his appointment of crusade legates and preachers, and in his imposition of a tax on clerical incomes.

Innocent also knew the importance of the cooperation of Constantinople in any crusading enterprise. He also knew that relations between Greek and Latin Christendom had been greatly strained in the wake of ecclesiological tension since the second half of the eleventh century that had created a schism between the two churches and in the course of the early crusade expeditions. Among his diplomatic efforts early in his pontificate was the letter *Multe nobis attulit,* sent on November 13, 1199, to Alexius III, the emperor at Constantinople (r. 1195–1203), urging the emperor to devote more of his energy and resources to the assistance of the Holy Land and to work for the reunion of the Greek and Latin churches. Scholars have disagreed about Innocent's early concern with crusading, but this letter clearly indicates his longtime desire for the unity of Eastern and Western Christendom. The slightly earlier letter from Innocent, *Post miserabile,* dated August 13, 1198 (above, No. 2), contained much stronger and impassioned language directed at Western leaders, but it too suggests a strong concern very early in the pontificate, particularly in the wake of the news of the collapse of the German crusade launched by Henry VI in 1196, which reached Innocent in early August 1198.

Other translations of Innocent's letters concerning crusades may be found in Powell, Deeds, 61–63, 77–231; and Andrea, Contemporary Sources. On the debates over the degree of Innocent's early concern, see Bolton, "Serpent in the Dust," 154–155; and Cole, Preaching, 80 n. 4. On the occasion of Multe nobis, see James M. Powell, "Innocent III and Alexius III: A Crusade Plan That Failed," reprinted in Powell, The Crusades, the Kingdom of Sicily, and the Mediterranean (Aldershot UK-Burlington, VT, 2007), VI. On the estimation of Innocent's devotion to the crusade by the author of the Gesta, see Powell, Deeds, 61–63.

To ALEXIUS, Illustrious Emperor of Constantinople. It has brought us a feeling of much exaltation that, just as we received letters from Your Imperial Excellency, Your Imperial Highness humbly received our legates and letters, and has responded kindly and devotedly on those matters that we recall we wrote concerning the unity of the church, even if not sufficiently and clearly. You have replied in writing that your empire has

Source: Gesta Innocentii Tertii, in *Powell,* Deeds, *77–81.*

heeded our exhortations and advice. For he, who is the origin of all power [Rom 13:1], according to the Apostle, the searcher of loyalties as well as hearts [Apoc 2:23], Jesus Christ, who holds the heart of princes in his hand [Apoc 3:7], who opens and no one closes [Prv 21:1], has opened the ears of your Serenity, and has breathed in a spirit of devotion to you, so that you might hear humbly and accept with a kindly spirit those things that have been written by us, though insufficient, his vicar and the successor of the prince of the apostles, in reply to the letters of Your Imperial Magnificence.

Although you might believe that we reproved Your Magnificence for your lack of support for the Holy Land, we have not, however, written to criticize but to advise. Although a reproving tone is not foreign to the pontifical office, as Paul said when writing to Timothy: "Preach the word, insist whether it is convenient or inconvenient, convince, reprimand, reprove in all patience and teaching" [2 Tm 4:2]. But we wonder why Your Imperial Prudence has apparently not yet given a sign of a commitment to the recovery of the Holy Land in your letters, because, as can clearly be seen from the detention of his land, that the Lord, who makes those confident of salvation from his mercy, not in the multitude, nor in the ark, but in his virtue, was not yet appeased regarding our sins. For you fear, as your letters show, that, if Your Imperial Serenity should wish to anticipate the time foreseen by God for the liberation of this land, you would lament to have labored in vain and you would be blamed by the Lord through the prophet, who said: "They made rulers, and not through me, they have ruled and not recognized me" [Hos 8:4]. It is true that we speak not so much to criticize as to instruct.

If you consider carefully and look to the truth, you might understand finally what must be understood in another way. For the giver of all good things, who gives to each according to his works, who is not pleased with forced service, has granted a free will to man so that, in matters where a human remedy can be found, he might not tempt the Lord. For it has been written: "You shall not tempt the Lord your God" [Mt 4:7; Lk 4:12]. It is, therefore, as a result of the necessity of the Christian people or rather of Jesus Christ, that both you and all those who have been washed in the waters of holy Baptism should use free will to aid the Crucified exile. If you wish to await the time unknown to men for the redemption of that land and do nothing by yourself, but leave everything to divine disposition, without your help the Lord's sepulcher could not be freed from the hands of the Saracens. Therefore, through negligence,

Your Imperial Magnificence would incur a divine offense, and as a result you would not win the favor of the Lord by your assistance.

For have you not understood the Lord's meaning? Are you not his counselor, so that you should, certain of the divine disposition, then first move your arms against the pagans and work for the liberation of the province of Jerusalem, since the Lord has given us the task to free the unhappy Christian people and his inheritance from the hands of the Saracens? Have you not read of "the depth of the riches of the wisdom and the knowledge of God, how incomprehensible are his judgments and how unsearchable his ways" [Rom 11:33]? Of course, if you understand the secrets of the divine mind, and you foresee by the hidden eye of revelation the liberation of the Lord's sepulcher, would there not be merit for you then to set out first to the Holy Land, to aid the Lord in carrying out his will, which cannot be either prevented or perpetuated by you? And those who think this way are forced to call the prophets foolish when they preached that they should do penance, and God foresaw that their sin was increased by their contempt; so, when Moses warned Pharaoh at God's command to free his people [Ex 5:1–2], his heart was so hardened that he was unwilling to free the people, and he was beaten. It would not even be according to the opinion of such individuals either to cease from vices or to attain virtues, but rather to stand for the divine will, which has foreseen how each individual will be lost or saved. Your Imperial Excellency has read, as we believe, or has heard, that, because of the sin of the Israelite people the Lord changed the forty days, within which it was promised that they would enter the Promised Land, into the same number of years, and, on the contrary, at the contrition and tears of Ezekiel, the Lord extended his life by fifteen years. From this we can clearly understand that the duration of the Saracens' persecution can also be shortened. We read in the Gospel concerning the persecution of Antichrist: "Unless those days were shortened, no human would have been saved" [Mt 24:22].

In addition, among other secret and unknowable causes of the invasion and detention of the Eastern Land, the Lord perhaps foresaw this in his mercy, so that, when they, after they left relatives and friends as well as all the goods they had and, following Christ, took up the saving sign of the cross in defense of that very land, they were crowned with martyrdom. Therefore, triumphant, the church rejoices and grows in heaven, for which reason the church militant seems to suffer and diminish. We are unwilling, however, to dwell longer on these matters, since the truth is apparent to those correctly paying attention and diligently searching. But Your Imperial Highness will thus aid the exiled Christ in order to avoid the criticism of detractors and to avoid hearing that Gospel charge of the Last Judgment against yourself: "I was a stranger, and you did not take me in, sick and in jail, and you did not come to me" [Mt 25:43].

But we rejoice that on the subject of the union of the church, for which we especially sent our letters and legates, just as we have received letters from you, you seem to have a ready concern and intend to work diligently for what we have written. For you have replied in your letters, to use your words, that it is the function of our Holiness according to earlier synodal practices to carry out the requisite doctrines. And thus, by the most holy action of our Holiness, which is with you, the church will not delay an agreement. Although the Apostolic See exists not so much as a result of a conciliar decree as it is the divine head and mother of all the churches, as should be clear to Your Highness from the content of the letter we sent to our Venerable Brother, John, the patriarch of Constantinople, and a copy of which we sent you, and, therefore, the patriarch should differ neither on account of the disparity of rites nor differences in doctrine, but should obey us kindly and devotedly as his head according to the ancient and canonical constitution, since matters which are certain must not be left in doubt.

Moreover, we have decided out of many ecclesiastical necessities, with the Lord as author, to summon a council and to celebrate a synodal meeting, at which, if summoned by us according to your promise, this will occur, since these matters that we have sought by our letters are doctrinal: namely, that the member should return to the head and the daughter to the mother. Obligated by due reverence and obedience to the Roman church, we will admit him kindly and joyfully as a most beloved brother and a special member of the church, establishing concerning other matters those that must be decided by the authority of the Apostolic See and the approval of the sacred council with the advice of him and our other brethren. Otherwise, since we ought not further support the scandal of the church, and we ought also to root out tares and chaff from the fields of the Lord, we cannot pretend but in the same council, if it is granted from above, to proceed in this matter with the counsel of our brethren.

We, therefore, advise Your Magnificence and exhort you with a greater concern and we enjoin you on the remission of sins that you should so work that the patriarch, either in person, or, if perhaps he is tied up for a good reason and is unable, through suitable procurators and some of the more important prelates of the churches, will attend the council at the appointed time, that he would subscribe to the obedience and reverence of the Apostolic See beforehand according to the constitution of the canons: if things should worsen, which we do not believe, we would be forced to proceed both against you, who can if you wish, carry out what we order, and against him and the Greek church.

On the other matters, we have, however, instructed our beloved son, John, our chaplain and familiar, the legate of the Apostolic See, an honest and discreet man, valued by us and our brethren for his religion, regarded for his honesty, and devoted to Your Serenity. We advise and exhort with greater concern that you should receive him kindly as a legate of the Apostolic See and that you honor and trust him in the matters that he shall propose to you on our behalf; you should know for certain that, if you desire our advice, when the storm has been stilled, tranquillity can come to you. Dated at the Lateran on the Ides of November [November 13].

4. Rite for Blessing Those Taking the Cross from the Late Twelfth-Century Lambrecht Pontifical

How did one become a crusader? And how did others know? From the Council of Clermont (1095) onward, crusaders typically sewed cloth crosses onto their clothing as the outward symbol of the legally and spiritually binding vows they took. The cross joined the other visible symbols of pilgrim status, the staff and the scrip. Yet, because of the intimate association of the crusade with the Jerusalem pilgrimage, a separate formal liturgy for taking the cross was slow to develop. Legally and spiritually, crusaders were to be classified as pilgrims, and there was originally no standard procedure or format for taking the cross. While some took the crusading vow moved by the spirit of revivalism that often occurred during sermons preached by local clerics or crusade recruiters, others did so in the more formal setting of a clerical or princely court or in private from a priest or chaplain.

However, as the crusade became increasingly institutionalized and the rights and obligations of crusaders increasingly defined, rites for departing pilgrims were adapted for the use of crusaders and inserted into local liturgical books. These ceremonies varied from region to region, and many, including Jean de Joinville, continued to take the cross and the pilgrims' staff and scrip in separate ceremonies (below, No. 50). One of the most detailed surviving rites for crusaders, preserved in the Lambrecht Pontifical, specifies that the mass of the Holy Cross should initiate the ceremony. The laity present are clearly not to be passive during the ceremony, but are to actively participate in singing the antiphons. This pontifical may have originated from an Italian port city familiar with shipping crusaders and other pilgrims, hence its somewhat unusual inclusion of a blessing for the crusaders' ship. The pontifical's late twelfth-century date means that this rite may well have been used for crusaders departing on crusades both during and well after the date that the rite was recorded.

Cecilia Gaposchkin, "From Pilgrimage to Crusade: Liturgy, Devotion, and Ideology, 1095–1300," Speculum (forthcoming); Jessalynn Bird, art. "Vow," in Murray, The Crusades, 4:1233–1237; Brundage, Medieval Canon Law and the Crusader, 30–114; Michael Markowski, "Crucesignatus: Its Origin and Early Usage," Journal of Medieval History 10 (1984), 157–165; James A. Brundage, " 'Cruce Signari': The Rite for Taking the Cross in England," Traditio 22 (1966), 289–310; Kenneth Pennington, "The Rite for Taking the Cross in the Twelfth Century," Traditio 30 (1974), 429–435; and the works cited above in the general introduction, n. 4.

The rite for receiving the sign of the holy cross for those setting out for Jerusalem

FIRST of all, the mass of the Holy Cross should be sung, just as it is set forth in the book of the sacraments,[12] and once it has been sung, those who are going to depart ought to prostrate themselves in the shape of the cross, and let them place their clothing and signs [of the cross] near the altar and let these psalms be sung: The Lord rules [Ps 22], May the Lord have mercy [Ps 66], Sing to the Lord [Pss 95:97; 149], The Lord has reigned [Ps 96]. Amen.

Savior of the world, save us whom you redeemed through the cross and [your] blood, we beseech you, our God, to aid us.

Kyrie. Christe. Kyrie.[13] Our Father.[14]

Prayers. Through the sign of the cross, free us, our God, from our enemies. O Christ, we worship you, and bless you, because through your cross you redeemed the world. This sign of the cross will be in heaven when the Lord shall come to judge. O Christ the Savior, save us through the power of [your] cross, you who saved Peter upon the sea, have mercy on us.

Bless O Lord, this sign of the holy cross that it might be a remedy to save the human race, and vouch through the invocation of your most holy name, that those who should take it up or wear it, might obtain

Source: Pennington, "The Rite for Taking the Cross," 433–435.

12. That is, a sacramentary, a liturgical book consulted by the priest or other celebrants.

13. This refers to the liturgical prayer in the canon of the Mass, the *Kyrie eleison*, "Lord, have mercy."

14. The prayer beginning "Our Father," the *Paternoster*, also in the canon of the Mass.

bodily health and protection for their souls. Through [Christ our Lord, etc.].

Another [prayer]. Creator and preserver of the human race, bestower of spiritual grace, granter of eternal salvation, send forth, O Lord, your spirit over this your creation, so that it [the spirit] might enable the progress of those who will have partaken of it toward eternal salvation, armed with heavenly defense. Through [Christ our Lord, etc.].

Another [prayer]. Lord of Abraham, Lord of Isaac, Lord of Jacob, O Lord who appeared to your servant Moses on Mount Sion, and led forth the sons of Israel from the land of Egypt, assigning to them an angel out of your love [for them], who would guard them by day and by night, we beseech you that you might deign to send your holy angel who might similarly watch over your servants and preserve them from harm from every diabolical attack. Through [Christ our Lord, etc.].

Another [prayer]. O Lord, Holy Father, Almighty and Eternal God, you who are leader of the saints and direct the paths of the righteous, direct the angel of peace with your servants, that he might lead them to their determined destinations. May their expedition[15] be agreeable such that no enemy ambushes them upon the way, let the approach of the wicked be far from them, and may the Holy Spirit deign to be present as their marshal. Through the same Lord [etc.].

Then let the signs [of the cross] be sprinkled with holy water and censed and be placed [upon their clothing with these words]: In the name of the Father and the Son and the Holy Spirit, receive the sign of the cross of Christ both in your hearts and upon your bodies that you might be preserved from all your enemies and from all the plots of the Devil himself.

Meanwhile, this antiphon should be sung by those standing around them: O glorious cross, O cross worthy of adoration, O precious wood and wondrous sign through which the Devil is vanquished and the world is redeemed through the blood of Christ.

When this is finished, let the priest say: [Let us] kneel and pray.

Let all the earth worship you, O Lord, and sing to you. Psalm: The Lord is our refuge [Ps 45], etc. Let us pray. Help O Lord, we beseech, your servants, that you might heed our prayers during misfortunes and prosperity, and that you might deign to frustrate the impious deeds of

---

15. The word here is *comitatus*, which could be translated as "company." It is commonly used in military contexts to designate a military expedition.

our adversaries through the banner of the holy cross, that we might be able to seize the port of salvation. Through [Christ Our Lord, etc.].

Lift up [etc.]. Afterward they themselves, if they are able to do so, ought to sing this antiphon. Sanctify us, O Lord, through the sign of the holy cross, that it might serve as a shield for us against the savage missiles of our enemies. Defend us, O Lord, through the holy wood [of the cross] and through the just price of your blood with which you redeemed us.

Ver[sicle]. We worship you, O Christ, and we bless you. Because through your cross [etc.]. O Lord, our God, save us and also protect with perpetual assistance, those whom you caused to rejoice through the holy cross, to his honor. Through [Christ our Lord, etc.].

The blessing for the ship. O Lord, be appeased by our supplications and send your holy angel from the highest heavens that he might deliver [from harm] this very ship with all sailing in it. Lead it to its intended destinations so that, once it has finished all of its business, you might deign to recall it again in [due] time to its own [home] with every cause for rejoicing.[16] Through [Christ our Lord, etc.].

The blessing upon the wallets and staffs. O God, come to my aid [Ps 69], in its entirety. Kyrie. Christe. Kyrie. Our Father [etc.]. I believe in God [etc.].[17] Through [Christ our Lord, etc.]. The Lord rules [Ps 22].

Prayers. Rise up, O Lord God, and let your hand be raised up, lest you forget in the end [cf. Ps 7:7]. Perfect my steps upon your paths, so that my footsteps are not moved [Ps 16:5]. Make wondrous your mercies, you who make safe those trusting in you. May he send us help from the sanctuary and defend us from Sion [Ps 19:3]. Lord, hear my prayer, and my outcry [Ps 101:1].

An oration. O Lord Jesus Christ, creator and redeemer of the world, you who commanded your blessed apostles to take up staffs when going out for such an important preaching, we earnestly request with humble devotion that you deign to bless these wallets and staffs in such a manner that those who are going to receive them as a token of their pilgrimage and for the sustaining of their bodies, might receive the fullness of your heavenly favor, so that they might obtain the defense of your blessing, and just as Aaron's staff, by flowering in the temple of the Lord [Nm 17], distinguished itself in its own rank from those of the rebellious Jews, so

16. *Omni gaudiorum effectu.* See the discussion on ship blessing in Part VII, No. 50, below.

17. This is the Apostles' or another similar creed, from *credo,* "I believe," also in the canon of the Mass.

also these your servants seeking, by this sign, the patronage of the blessed apostles Peter and Paul, you might absolve from all their sins, through which they will be crowned on the day of judgment, freed from the impious, standing on the right side of the Lord.

Another [prayer]. May the sign of God the Father and the Son and the Holy Spirit descend upon these staffs and upon these wallets which these persons want to carry as a token of their pilgrimage and help those who shall carry them to stand firm, safe and protected from all human and diabolical attacks. Through [Christ our Lord, etc.].

Another [prayer]. O Lord, you who assemble the scattered and guard those gathered, increase the faith and assurance of your servants, and grant in the future that through the intercession of the blessed Mary, Mother of God, and of the saints N.,[18] whose shrines these individuals desire to visit, and through the intervention of all the saints and of your elect, they might merit to receive the remission of all their sins in this world and the fellowship of all the blessed in the future. Through [Christ our Lord, etc.].

Antiphon. May the days of repentance come for us, for the redemption of sins, for the salvation of souls.

Antiphon. Let us commend ourselves to the power of God in diligent long-suffering through the weapons of righteousness.

Here the staffs are bestowed, while saying: In the name of our Lord Jesus Christ, take these staffs for sustenance during the journey and the labors of your pilgrimage upon the way, so that you might be able to overcome the troops of your enemies and reach the shrines of the apostles Peter and Paul and other saints to which you desire to hasten, so that, your journey completed, you might deserve to return to us unharmed, preserved by our Lord.

This prayer ought to be said over the wallets: In the name of our Lord Jesus Christ, receive these wallets as part of the garb[19] of your pilgrimage so that thoroughly emended and cleansed and saved, you might merit to reach the shrines of the apostles Peter and Paul and other saints which you desire to hasten to and so that, your journey accomplished, you might return to us unharmed, that he himself might deign to preserve you, he who when he was rich was made a pauper and destitute for our sake although we were sinners and unworthy, Jesus Christ, our Lord, who

18. The name or names (*Nomen, Nomina*) of the saint or saints whose shrines were to be visited was to be inserted here.

19. The word here is *habitum*, the same word used for the monastic habit.

with God the Father and the Holy Spirit lives and reigns, God through all the ages.

Prayers. May the God of our salvation make this journey prosperous for us [Ps 67:20].

Versicle. Direct us in the way of peace, O Lord [Ps 143:1]. Through [Christ our Lord, etc.]. Blessed be the Lord [cf. Lk 1:68–70].

Oration. Hear us O Lord our God, and deem worthy to direct the way of your servants toward the prosperity of your salvation, so that in every occurrence of worldly vicissitudes, they might be always protected by your assistance. Through [Christ our Lord, etc.].

Another [prayer]. O God of endless mercy and boundless majesty whom neither distance between places nor interval of time removes from those whom you watch over, help your servants who trust in you in every place, and through all the ways in which they will be traveling, consider them worthy of your being their leader and companion; so that no adversity may harm them, no difficulty hinder them, but rather everything be salutary, everything prosperous for them, so that under the power of your right hand, whatever they might strive after with righteous desire, they might attain with a speedy accomplishment. Through [Christ our Lord, etc.].

5. Letters of Innocent III to Hubert Walter on the Preaching and Financing of the Crusade, 1200–1201

During preparations for the Fourth Crusade, Innocent III approved the revivalist and reforming message that the popular preacher Fulk of Neuilly and others had linked to recruiting for the crusade and allowed Fulk to appoint co-preachers from various orders of monks and canons regular. Later, in preparation for the Fifth Crusade, Innocent directly appointed teams of individual preachers to organize recruiting in each region. Probably chosen according to the advice of the legate Robert Courson and other individuals known to Innocent, the teams often consisted of a blend of regular religious, often Cistercians and Premonstratensians, and clerics from local dioceses, and they were intended to organize special preaching tours in addition to the diocesan-based vernacular preaching of the crusade. Innocent's instructions to later crusade preachers reflect dilemmas that had emerged during the Fourth Crusade, including how to craft the image of the crusade preacher to reflect the moderation and humility needed to make their message credible while providing them with the resources to fulfill their duties and to manage the offerings made to them for the crusade to stamp out any suspicion of peculation. And legates and preachers wrote to Innocent concerning the problems they encountered.

Their queries shaped Innocent's policy toward vow redemptions and the funding of the crusade, although the consequences of both groups' decisions were often unforeseen, as the letters of Gervase of Prémontré (below, No. 18) illustrate. New crusade policies slowly emerged out of this dialogue. Although Innocent often referred the preachers back to the crusade bull *Quia maior*, translated below (below, No. 11), its interpretation remained clearly open to debate, and Innocent's declaration that everyone should be permitted to take the cross without being examined for the ability to fulfill the vow in person or husbands seeking their wives' permission marked a dramatic change in papal policy sparked in part by the consequences and precedent of populist recruiting by Fulk of Neuilly and his associates during the Fourth Crusade. The concept that all should be able to participate in the crusade through taking the cross, and thereby be able to share in the spiritual (and sometimes temporal) benefits of crusader status, later led to various crises involving funding for impecunious crusaders and the impact of large numbers of *crucesignati* with special legal and economic rights upon public order and the resources needed by various rulers.

An ecclesiastic who distinguished himself in royal service and became both justiciar of England and archbishop of Canterbury (1193–1205), Hubert Walter had been a key and highly effective participant in the Third Crusade and had witnessed the difficulties his predecessor as archbishop of Canterbury, Baldwin, had faced in organizing the crusade in England and maintaining the morale and morals of a crusading army overseas. After the end of the Third Crusade, in 1196 Hubert had asked Pope Celestine III what was to be the fate of those crusaders who had failed to fulfill their crusade vows, and he received instructions to force those who were able to go to do so, grant delays to others facing temporary impediments, and allow the infirm to fulfill their vows through sending substitutes at their own expense. Celestine also gave Hubert permission to initiate inquests into unfulfilled crusade vows in the archdiocese of York. Then acting as papal legate for England (1195–1198), Hubert had ordered an inquest into unfulfilled crusade vows with the object of using excommunication to force their fulfillment or formal dispensation.

When Innocent III declared preparations for what would become the Fourth Crusade, the English prelates were again urged to use excommunication to force laggard *crucesignati* to fulfill their vows and to preach the crusade. As archbishop of Canterbury, Hubert was to oversee crusade preparations in England, and he summoned a council for his province, which publicized the pope's orders and set a deadline for all those signed with the cross to depart. However, because of the festering conflict between the kings of England and France, Hubert was placed in a difficult position when it came to the commutation or deferral of the vows of individuals deemed essential to the crown.

The political unrest that followed the untimely death of Richard I in 1199 contributed to England's poor crusade recruiting. Collection of clerical and lay income taxes intended to subsidize crusaders was ineffectual, and the lack of moneyed leadership meant that many English *crucesignati* lacked the funds necessary to fulfill their vows. Hubert's experience as a bishop, royal administrator, tax collector, justiciar, and crusader made him acutely aware of the problems presented by those who took crusade vows and yet never fulfilled them. Hubert's queries for further definition elicited further clarification of which individuals could be dispensed from their vows and under which circumstances. Innocent III's two replies to Hubert's questions concerning crusade vows were quickly incorporated into decretal collections and influential handbooks for the teaching and practice of canon law, and they illustrate how in this period crusade recruitment and canon law were being profoundly shaped by the dialogue between Rome and individual ecclesiastics.

C. R. *Cheney*, Hubert Walter *(London, 1967), esp. 124–132; Christopher Tyerman*, England and the Crusades, 1095–1588 *(Chicago, 1988), 34–35, 63–64, 68–69, 74, 96–97, 171–172; Helen J. Nicholson, trans.,* The Chronicle of the Third Crusade *(Aldershot UK-Brookfield VT, 1997), 98, 119, 135–137, 147, 215, 230, 330, 377–379, 386.*

Letter of Innocent III to Hubert Walter, archbishop of Canterbury, 1200

You asked what you were to do about those who took the cross to help the Holy Land and who, because of infirmity or poverty or some other good reason, could not usefully fulfill their vow of pilgrimage; since you have been ordered by papal letter to compel those without distinction who have laid aside the cross they had taken up to resume the cross and carry out their pilgrimage, eschewing appeal and notwithstanding any indulgence they may have obtained from our predecessor. We reply to your enquiry thus: the weak and the poor go thither more to the disadvantage than to the advantage of the enterprise, since the former cannot fight and the latter are obliged to beg, unless they happen to be nobles or great men who are taking soldiers with them at their expense, or are craftsmen and farmers who can gain the necessities of life by their own labors and contribute to the support of the land (although it would not be opportune to enlist many such, having regard to the sparse resources of the land and its small population).

Therefore we think that a distinction should be made between those who are believed to have a temporary impediment and those whose impediment is lasting. Delay may be granted to the former; the latter must compound, and according to their means and the expenses they might have incurred, with allowance also for any labor expended, let them

Source: C. R. Cheney, Hubert Walter *(London, 1967), 127–129.*

send to the help of the Holy Land, performing by others what they cannot do themselves. We think another distinction also should be made: between those who pronounce a vow for the sake of defending the Holy Land and those on whom is enjoined the path of pilgrimage as satisfaction for their sins. As regards the former, more attention should be paid to the helping of the Holy Land, as regards the latter, more to the effort of making the journey, according to the object of the taker of the vow or the object of the penitent. Therefore if any taker of a vow is useless for fighting, although able to make the journey, it is better for him to redeem his vow than to incur expenses, and this should apply also to the penitent who is too delicate to make the pilgrimage enjoined on him; but it should not apply to the penitent who, although unable to fight, is able to travel. Careful discrimination must be used about these things, lest the salvation of souls or the profit of the Holy Land be endangered by anything done through favor or for money, or love or hate, or any other reason. Therefore we wish religious and reliable men to make provision for dispensation of this sort. But concerning women we think this ought to be observed: let those who do not wish to stay behind accompany their husbands if they are going; but others, unless they happen to be rich and able to take soldiers with them at their expense, should redeem the vow they have made, the rest being persuaded earnestly to provide for the help of the Holy Land according to their means.

You also asked what you ought to do about those who say they return from the Apostolic See and bring letters with unknown seals of cardinals concerning their absolution from a vow; since they ought not to have been easily believed about the impediments they alleged. We have decided to reply thus: when on occasion we grant apostolic letters to such people, we write to those who know best their persons and their circumstances, that they shall diligently look into the truth of the impediments alleged, and shall arrange for them what is best for the salvation of their souls and the help of the Holy Land, taking care (as stated above) that there is no deceit in the avoidance of the vow. When we do this, if it should appear that such persons have obtained the letters by suppressing the truth or stating falsehood, we wish the letters to be of no use to those who got them, whether the letters are from cardinals or from us, whether they are of dubious authenticity or are genuine; and we order that notwithstanding such letters the persons be compelled to perform or redeem their vow, eschewing appeal, as stated above.

Innocent III's reply to Hubert Walter's further queries, September 1201

YOU have diligently asked whether our statement there constitutes a general rule that prelates of all sorts everywhere are allowed to absolve their subjects [from the crusade vow] according to the form expressed there. We reply to this that although in our response the law is declared, to what sort of persons and to whom the execution of the law specially pertains is not explained. For the execution of the law pertains only to those who receive a special order from the Apostolic See about it. This also answers your further enquiry on the interpretation of the phrase about "religious men," which was: whether those only are there termed "religious men" who have taken the religious habit, of whom many are simple and ignorant of the law, or whether [these "religious men" are] the bishops, who, as they excel others in dignity, ought to be pre-eminently religious; for the execution of the law is the concern of neither unless it has been delegated to them by the Apostolic See.

Secondly, concerning what was said: "If any taker of a vow is useless for fighting, although able to make the journey, it is better for him to redeem his vow than to incur expenses," you asked whether this is to be taken in a general sense, including even nobles and great men energetic in counsel and able to bring with them many soldiers, or whether this term only embraces lesser folk. But if for a moment you cast your eye over our former responses you will find this problem settled in the course of our consultation, where we say: "the weak and the poor go thither more to the disadvantage than to the advantage of the enterprise"; although it might be put in another way, that those men are not useless for fighting who, while themselves unable to fight, help the fighters by giving mature counsel and supply by others what they lack themselves.

In the third place, you asked how to interpret the statement about women: "let those who do not wish to stay behind accompany their husbands if they are going; but others, unless they happen to be rich and able to take soldiers with them at their expense, should redeem the vow they have made." This last clause seems to speak only of those who have taken the vow; but what was written above: "let women who do not want to stay behind" etc. would seem to apply to those who attached themselves to the enterprise of the cross without being bound by any vow. You also say that some people take this to mean that in these circumstances men

Source: C. R. Cheney, Hubert Walter *(London, 1967), 129–130.*

may take the vow and fulfill it without the consent of their wives. To this we reply that in so great a crisis of Christendom, to avoid impeding help for the Holy Land, men may take this vow of pilgrimage and carry it out without their wives' consent; but their wives are to be carefully admonished to give consent.

Concerning clerics we reply that, since clerical duties render them inept for fighting, unless they are energetic in counsel or trained in the art of preaching or engaged in the service of great men, or else are so rich and powerful that they can bring others as soldiers with them at their expense, it is more expedient to allow them to compound than to oblige them to fulfill their vow, if need arises or if it seems useful. What we say concerns those who take vows, not those on whom the toil of pilgrimage is enjoined as penance.

6. Facets of the Fourth Crusade, 1202–1204

All of the sources and most of the scholarship on the history of the Fourth Crusade are available in English translation and listed below. The selections presented here are intended to offer several key moments in the process of the assembly, developing organization, and financial and political difficulties that the crusade encountered, certainly not even a synopsis of the entire crusade. They were made and translated by the founder of crusade history in the United States, Dana C. Munro, in a pamphlet entitled *The Fourth Crusade*, which appeared as volume 3, number 1, of the pioneering translation series *Translations and Reprints from the Original Sources of European History* in 1896. Munro's selection has never been surpassed as a compact set of extracts from different sources with quite distinctive, often conflicting perspectives from the major historical narratives. Not all of these are reproduced here.

Among the chroniclers, Villehardouin, marshal of Champagne, represents the view of more than one of the princes. Born around 1155, he was connected by birth and marriage to many of the nobility of Champagne, participated at the tournament at Écry in 1199, and was one of those who went to Venice to negotiate the contract for the transportation of the army of the Fourth Crusade. Having participated in the sieges of Zara and Constantinople, Villehardouin remained in the new Latin Empire and acquired estates in the Peloponnesus. He died around 1213. His point of view in the narrative is uniformly an aristocratic one, and his is the best account of at least the "official" attitude of the crusade leaders during their remarkable misadventures on the Adriatic and the Bosporus.

Nicetas Choniates was a Byzantine official and an eyewitness to many of the events described by others. His account of the conquest is rather a lament for the destruction of a great city.

Gunther of Pairis was a monk in the entourage of Abbot Martin of Pairis, a great Alsatian monastery near Basel, whose account of the crusade was written chiefly to authenticate the relics that the bishop brought back to Alsace.

The best English edition of the entire chronicle of Villehardouin is that by Caroline Smith, Joinville and Villehardouin: Chronicles of the Crusades *(London-New York, 2008). On the author, see Jeanette M. A. Beer,* Villehardouin: Epic Historian *(Geneva, 1968). A similar aristocratic viewpoint is that of Count Hugh of Saint-Pol, a veteran of both the Third and Fourth Crusades, in his letter to various European princes shortly after July 1203, translated in Andrea,* Contemporary Sources, *177–201. Another narrative from a similar social perspective is the* Devastatio Constantinopolitana, *translated in Andrea,* Contemporary Sources, *205– 221. The account of Nicetas is translated by Harry J. Magoulias,* O City of Byzantium: Annals of Niketas Choniates *(Detroit, 1984). The full translation of Gunther of Pairis is that of Alfred J. Andrea,* The Capture of Constantinople: The "Historia Constantinopolitana" of Gunther of Pairis *(Philadelphia, 1997). Other important sources not translated here are the account of Robert de Clari, a much lower ranking participant. The full translation of Robert's narrative is that of Edgar H. McNeal,* The Conquest of Constantinople *(New York, 1936, repr. 1966). There is a new English translation with the Old French text in Robert de Clari,* La conquête de Constantinople, *ed. Peter Noble (Edinburgh, 2005); narratives associated with relics (the* Anonymous of Soissons *and the* Deeds of the Bishops of Halberstadt*) are translated in Andrea,* Contemporary Sources, *223–238, 239–264. Eracles was the title of a vernacular French continuation of the great Latin history of the crusades up to 1184 by William of Tyre, part of which has been translated by Janet Shirley,* Crusader Syria in the Thirteenth Century *(Aldershot UK 1999), 121–143. With the exceptions of the first and last selections, the texts in this section have all been selected and translated by Dana Munro. On Munro and other American crusade historians, see Hans Eberhard Mayer, "America and the Crusades,"* Proceedings of the American Philosophical Society 125, no. 1 (1981), 38–45.

The best accounts of the Fourth Crusade are those of Donald E. Queller and Thomas F. Madden, The Fourth Crusade: The Conquest of Constantinople, *2d ed. (Philadelphia, 1999); and Jonathan Phillips,* The Fourth Crusade and the Sack of Constantinople *(London, 2004); Michael Angold,* The Fourth Crusade: Event and Context *(New York, 2003); Benjamin Arbel, Bernard Hamilton, and David Jacoby, eds.,* Latins and Greeks in the Eastern Mediterranean After 1204 *(London-Totowa NJ, 1989); Thomas F. Madden, ed.,* The Fourth Crusade: Event, Aftermath, and Perceptions; Papers from the Sixth Conference of the Society for the Study of the Crusades and the Latin East, Istanbul, Turkey, 25–29 August 2004 *(Aldershot UK-Burlington VT, 2008).*

The calling of the Fourth Crusade: The barons at Écry, November 1199 (Villehardouin)

ELEVEN hundred and ninety-seven years after the Incarnation of Our Lord Jesus Christ, when Innocent [III] was pope at Rome and Philip [II] king of France and Richard [I] king of England, there was in France a holy man who was called Fulk of Neuilly (this Neuilly is between Lagny-sur-Marne and Paris) who was a priest and held a parish in that town. And this Fulk of whom I speak began to preach across the Île-de-France

Source: Edward Peters, ed., Christian Society and the Crusades, 1198–1229 *(Philadelphia, 1971), 2–3.*

and the surrounding areas, and Our Lord performed many miracles through him.

Know also that the fame of this holy man spread as far as the court of the pope at Rome, and the pope sent to France and ordered this good man to preach the cross by papal authority.[20] Shortly after, the pope sent one of his cardinals, Master Pierre de Chappes,[21] a crusader, to offer an indulgence which I will describe to you: all those who crossed themselves and took up the service of God during one year of a military expedition would be acquitted of all the sins they had committed and of which they had confessed themselves. Because this indulgence was so great, the hearts of men were much moved, and many took up the cross because of the great indulgence.[22]

The year after Fulk began to preach, there was held a tournament in Champagne, at a chateau called Écry.[23] And by the grace of God it happened that Thibaut, count of Champagne and Brie, took the cross himself as did Count Louis of Blois and Chartres. And this was at the beginning of Advent. Know also that this Count Thibaut was a young man, no older than twenty-two years of age, and Louis was no older than twenty-seven. . . .

With these two counts there joined as crusaders many high barons of France: including Simon de Montfort[24] and Renaud de Montmirail. Great was the excitement across all lands when these great men took up the cross.

The tournament at Écry was a dramatic curtain-raiser, but the actual mobilization of a crusade army took some time, particularly since Thibaut of Champagne died and another prominent, respected noble, Boniface of Montferrat, had to be persuaded to accept the leadership. A committee of nobles, including Villehardouin, was appointed to negotiate for passage. They found a favorable response in Venice.

20. Innocent's letter of November 1198 to Fulk is translated in Andrea, *Contemporary Sources*, 19–21.

21. Peter of Capua, cardinal deacon of Santa Maria in Via Lata.

22. Earlier crusade indulgences were conditioned by the requirement of two years in the field.

23. Villehardouin should not be misread here. There is substantial evidence that Fulk was not present at Écry, but it also shows that Fulk was well known among the northern French aristocracy at whom the crusade appeal was aimed and that Villehardouin associated Fulk's preaching and papal commission with the Fourth Crusade.

24. Simon de Montfort later became the leader of the Albigensian Crusade.

The contract with the Venetians, April 1201 (Villehardouin)

"MY LORDS," said the doge, "we will tell you what we have decided, if we can get the Grand Council and the people of the country to agree to it; and you shall decide whether you can fulfill your part.

"We will furnish *huissiers* for carrying 4,500 horses and 9,000 esquires, and vessels for 4,500 knights and 20,000 foot soldiers.[25] The agreement shall be to furnish food for nine months for all these horses and men. This is the least that we will do, on condition that we are paid four marks per horse and two marks per man.

"And we will observe all these conditions which we explain to you, for one year, beginning the day we leave the harbor of Venice to fight in the service of God and of Christianity, wherever we may go. The sum of these payments indicated above amounts to 85,000 marks.

"And we will do still more: we will add fifty armed galleys, for the love of God; on the condition that as long as our alliance shall last, of every conquest of land or money that we make, by sea or land, we shall have one-half and you the other. Now deliberate whether you can fulfill these conditions."

The messengers went away, saying that they would talk it over and reply the next day. They consulted and discussed that night and then resolved to agree to it. The next day they went to the doge and said: "Sire, we are ready to make this agreement." The doge said that he would speak to his people and tell them the result.

It was explained in council that they would go to Babylon, because at Babylon they could do more injury to the Turks than anywhere else.[26] And in public it was announced that they would go across the sea. It was then Lent [March 1201], and on Saint John's day [December 27] the following year, the 1202nd year after the incarnation of Jesus Christ, the

Source: Dana Munro, Fourth Crusade, 3.

25. *Huissiers* were large transport vessels capable of carrying horses and men. See John H. Pryor, *Geography, Technology and War: Studies in the Maritime History of the Mediterranean, 649–1571* (Cambridge, 1988). On the increasingly important subject of logistics, see John H. Pryor, ed., *Logistics of Warfare in the Age of the Crusades: Proceedings of a Workshop Held at the Centre for Medieval Studies, University of Sydney, 30 September to 4 October 2002* (Aldershot, 2006).

26. Babylon was the name Christians used for Cairo and for Egypt generally throughout the period covered in this book. On the route, see John H. Pryor, "The Venetian Fleet for the Fourth Crusade and the Diversion of the Crusade to Constantinople," in Marcus Bull and Norman Housley, eds., *The Experience of Crusading*, vol. 1, *Western Approaches* (Cambridge, 2003), 103–123.

barons and pilgrims were to be at Venice and the vessels were to be ready on their arrival.

> *The destination of the crusaders' Venetian fleet was to be Egypt, although this was kept secret from the army itself. The attraction of Egypt as a key to Jerusalem had long been discussed, and the treaty with Damascus was to remain in force until 1203 and did not include Egypt. The Fifth Crusade later took the same route. Since not all crusaders joined the assembly at Venice, some leaving for the Holy Land from other Italian ports, or from Marseilles, Genoa, or even Flanders, those who did appear in Venice found themselves unable to pay the Venetians the contracted price for transportation. Of the 33,500 soldiers agreed upon in the contract, only around 12,000 appeared in Venice, although the full contracted amount still had to be paid, since Venice had virtually suspended its entire maritime commercial economy for a year in order to construct the immense fleet that the crusaders required.*
>
> *The stalemate was overcome when the Venetians offered to let the crusaders extend the time for payment if the crusaders aided the Venetians in capturing the city of Zara on the Adriatic, a formerly Venetian-dependent city now under the protection of the king of Hungary (who, to further confuse the issue, had also taken the cross himself, thus placing his property under the protection of the church).*

The Zarans were also Christians—could crusaders fight Christians? (Villehardouin)

THEN the abbot of Vaux of the order of Cîteaux rose and said to them: "Sirs, I forbid you, in the name of the pope at Rome, to attack this city; for the inhabitants are Christians and you are pilgrims."[27] When the doge heard this he was much irritated and troubled. He said to the counts and barons: "Sirs, this city was practically in my power, and your people have taken it from me; you had promised that you would aid me in conquering it; now I require you to do so."

Then the counts and the barons and those who belonged to their party held a conference and said: "Those who have prevented this agreement have committed a very great outrage, and it was not right for them to try to break up the army. Now we shall be disgraced, if we do not aid in capturing the city." They went to the doge and said to him: "Sire, we will aid you in capturing the city, in spite of those who wish to prevent it."

Accordingly the city was surrendered to the mercy of the doge of Venice, on condition that the lives of the inhabitants should be spared.

Source: Munro, Fourth Crusade, *7, 9–10.*

27. The Cistercian abbot Guy of the monastery of Vaux-de-Cernay later played a crucial role in the Albigensian Crusade.

The siege and capture of Zara outraged Pope Innocent III and alienated a substantial part of the crusading army, including Simon de Montfort, some of whom left the force and found other transportation to the Holy Land. Then, in December 1202, messengers arrived at Zara from the court of Philip of Swabia, brother of the late emperor Henry VI and candidate for the imperial crown. Philip informed the crusade leaders and the Venetians that Alexius Angelus, son of the deposed Byzantine emperor Isaac Angelus, and Philip's own brother-in-law, promised the crusaders that if they helped him regain the throne, he would place the empire and the Greek church under the Roman obedience, contribute 200,000 marks to the army, send an army to Egypt along with the crusaders and Venetians, and remain a staunch ally.

THERE it was hotly discussed, pro and con. The abbot of Vaux of the order of Cîteaux and the party that wanted to break up the army said they would not agree to it; it was fighting against Christians; they had not set out for this purpose, but they wanted to go to Syria.

The other party replied, "Good sirs, in Syria you can do nothing, you can see that clearly from those who have left us and gone to other ports. You know that it is through the land of Babylon or through Greece that the land of Outremer will be reconquered, if it is ever recovered. If we refuse this offer, we shall always be ashamed."

The army was in discord, just as you have heard. And do not wonder that the laymen could not agree; for the white monks of the order of Cîteaux in the army were also in discord. The abbot of Loos, who was a very holy and excellent man, and the other abbots who agreed with him preached to the people and cried out to them to have mercy, saying that, for God's sake, they ought to keep the army together and to make this agreement; "for it is the best means of recovering the land of Outremer." And the abbot of Vaux in his turn, and those who agreed with him, preached very frequently and said that that was all wrong; that they ought to go to the land of Syria and do what they could.

The crusaders and Venetians accepted Alexius's offer and sailed into Constantinople in May 1203. After several sieges of the city, the usurping emperor (Alexius III Angelus, brother of Isaac and uncle of Alexius IV) fled, and Alexius IV and Isaac were formally installed as emperors in July 1203. But Alexius was slow and reluctant to fulfill his agreement with the crusaders, and internal tensions within the city exploded in the large fire in the city in July 1203 and in a much more destructive fire in August 1203. Later riots heightened tensions, and finally the crusaders had to confront Alexius directly.

At the end of January 1204, a Byzantine noble, Murtzuphlus, overthrew Alexius IV, assumed the throne as Alexius V, and ordered the crusaders and Venetians to leave Constantinople. In February 1204, Murtzuphlus murdered Alexius IV, and, shortly after, open conflict broke out between the Byzantines and the crusaders. The crusaders' agreement about the future of Constantinople if it was conquered is known as the "March pact."

The compact of division, the "March pact," March 1204 (Villehardouin)

THEN the members of the host debated and consulted upon the best course to pursue. The discussion was long and stormy, but the following was the result of the deliberation. If God granted that they should capture the city, all the booty that was taken should be brought together and divided fairly, as was fitting. And if they captured the city, six men should be chosen from the Franks and six from the Venetians; these were to take the oath upon relics that they would elect as emperor him whom they should judge to be the most useful for the good of the land. And he whom they chose as emperor should have one-quarter of all the conquests both in the city and outside; and in addition he should have the palace of the Lion's Mouth and Blachernae. The other three-quarters should be divided into two parts, one-half for the Venetians and one-half for the crusaders. Then twelve from the wisest of the army of the pilgrims and twelve of the Venetians should be chosen to divide the fiefs and the offices among the men and to define the feudal service which each one owed to the emperor.

This compact was guaranteed and sworn to by both the Franks and the Venetians, with the condition that any one who wished could go away within one year from the end of March. Those who remained in the country must perform the service to the emperor, as it might be arranged. Then the compact was made and sworn to and all who should not keep it were excommunicated by the clergy.[28]

Account of the sack, April 1204 (Nicetas)

HOW shall I begin to tell of the deeds wrought by these nefarious men! Alas, the images, which ought to have been adored, were trodden under foot! Alas, the relics of the holy martyrs were thrown into unclean places! Then was seen what one shudders to hear, namely, the divine body and blood of Christ was spilled upon the ground or thrown about. They

Source for the compact: Munro, Fourth Crusade, 14–15.
Source for the account: Munro, Fourth Crusade, 15–16.
28. A fuller version is translated in Powell, *Deeds*, 163–166.

snatched the precious reliquaries, thrust into their bosoms the ornaments which these contained, and used the broken remnants for pans and drinking cups—precursors of Antichrist, authors and heralds of his nefarious deeds which we momentarily expect. Manifestly, indeed, by that race then, just as formerly, Christ was robbed and insulted and his garments were divided by lot; only one thing was lacking, that His side, pierced by a spear, should pour rivers of divine blood on the ground.

Nor can the violation of the Great Church [Hagia Sophia] be listened to with equanimity. For the sacred altar, formed of all kinds of precious materials and admired by the whole world, was broken into bits and distributed among the soldiers, as was all the other sacred wealth of so great and infinite splendor.

When the sacred vessels and utensils of unsurpassable art and grace and rare material, and the fine silver, wrought with gold, which encircled the screen of the tribunal and the ambo, of admirable workmanship, and the door, and many other ornaments, were to be borne away as booty, mules and saddled horses were led to the very sanctuary of the temple. Some of these, which were unable to keep their footing on the splendid and slippery pavement, were stabbed when they fell, so that the sacred pavement was polluted with blood and filth.

Nay, more, a certain harlot, a sharer in their guilt, a minister of the furies, a servant of the demons, a worker of incantations and poisonings, insulting Christ, sat in the patriarch's chair, singing an obscene song and dancing frequently. Nor, indeed, were these crimes committed and others left undone, on the ground that these were of lesser guilt, the others of greater. But with one consent all the most heinous sins and crimes were committed by all with equal zeal. Could those, who showed so great madness against God Himself, have spared the honorable matrons and maidens or the virgins consecrated to God?

Nothing was more difficult and laborious than to soften by prayers, to render benevolent, these wrathful barbarians, vomiting forth bile at every unpleasing word, so that nothing failed to inflame their fury. Whoever attempted it was derided as insane and a man of intemperate language. Often they drew their daggers against any one who opposed them at all or hindered their demands.

No one was without a share in the grief. In the alleys, in the streets, in the temples, complaints, weeping, lamentations, grief, the groaning of men, the shrieks of women, wounds, rape, captivity, the separation of those most closely united. Nobles wandered about ignominiously, those of venerable age in tears, the rich in poverty. Thus it was in the streets, on the corners, in the temple, in the dens, for no place remained unassailed or defended the suppliants. All places everywhere were filled full of all kinds of crime. Oh, immortal God, how great the afflictions of the men, how great the distress![29]

Abbot Martin's theft of relics, April–May 1204
(Gunther of Pairis)

WHILE the victors were rapidly plundering the conquered city, which was theirs by right of conquest, the abbot Martin began to cogitate about his own share of the booty, and lest he alone should remain empty-handed, while all the others became rich, he resolved to seize upon plunder with his own sacred hands. But, since he thought it not meet to handle any booty of worldly things with those sacred hands, he began to plan how he might secure some portion of the relics of the saints, of which he knew there was a great quantity in the city.

Accordingly, having a presentiment of some great result, he took with him one of his two chaplains and went to a church, which was held in great reverence because in it the mother of the most famous emperor Manuel had a noble grave, which seemed of importance to the Greeks, but ours held for naught. There a very great amount of money brought in from all the surrounding country was stored, and also precious relics which the vain hope of security had caused them [the Greeks] to bring in from the surrounding churches and monasteries. Those whom the Greeks had driven out had told us of this before the capture of the city. When many pilgrims broke into this church, and some were eagerly engaged in stealing gold and silver, others precious stones, Martin, thinking it unbecoming to commit sacrilege except in a holy cause, sought a more retired spot where the very sanctity of the place seemed to promise that what he desired might be found.

There he found an aged man of agreeable countenance, having a long and hoary beard, a priest, but very unlike our priests in his dress. Thinking him a layman, the abbot, though inwardly calm, threatened him with a very ferocious voice, saying: "Come, perfidious old man, show me the most powerful relics you have, or you shall die immediately." The latter, terrified by the sound rather than the words, since he heard but did

Source: Munro, Fourth Crusade, *16–18.*
    29. On the city, see Jonathan Harris, *Constantinople: Capital of Byzantium* (London, 2007).

not understand what was said and knowing that Martin could not speak Greek, began in the *Romana lingua*, of which he knew a little, to entreat Martin and by soft words to turn away the latter's wrath, which in truth did not exist. In reply, the abbot succeeded in getting out a few words of the same language, sufficient to make the old man understand what he wanted. The latter, observing Martin's face and dress, and thinking it more tolerable that a religious man should handle the sacred relics with fear and reverence, than that worldly men should, perchance, pollute them with their worldly hands, opened a chest bound with iron and showed the desired treasure, which was more grateful and pleasing to Martin than all the royal wealth of Greece. The abbot hastily and eagerly thrust in both hands and working quickly, filled with the fruits of the sacrilege both his own and his chaplain's bosom. He wisely concealed what seemed the most valuable and departed without opposition.

Moreover what and how worthy of veneration those relics which the holy robber appropriated were is told more fully at the end of this work. When he was hastening to his vessel, so stuffed full, if I may use the expression, those who knew and loved him, saw him from their ships as they were themselves hastening to the booty, and inquired joyfully whether he had stolen anything, or with what he was so loaded down as he walked. With a joyful countenance, as always, and with pleasant words, he said: "We have done well." To which they replied: "Thanks be to God."

List of relics stolen by Abbot Martin (Gunther of Pairis)

THEREFORE, "Blessed be the Lord God, who only doeth wondrous things," who in His unspeakable kindness and mercy has looked upon and made glorious his church at Pairis[30] through certain gifts of His grace, which He deigned to transmit to us through the venerable man, already so frequently mentioned, Abbot Martin. In the presence of these the church exults and by their protection any soul faithful to God is aided and assisted. In order that the readers' trust in these may be strengthened, we have determined to give a partial list.

First, of the highest importance and worthy of all veneration: A trace of the blood of our Lord Jesus Christ, which was shed for the redemption of all mankind.

Source: Munro, Fourth Crusade, *18–19.*

30. The monastery of Abbot Martin and Gunther at Pairis was not far from Basel, where Martin had preached a memorable crusade sermon in the cathedral in 1200. The reference seems to be to Ps 74:1.

Second, a piece of the cross of our Lord on which the Son of the Father, the new Adam, sacrificed for us, paid the debt of the old Adam.

Third, a not inconsiderable piece of Saint John [the Baptist], the forerunner of our Lord.

Fourth, the arm of Saint James, the Apostle, whose memory is venerated by the whole church.

There were also relics of the other saints, whose names are as follows:

Christopher, the martyr
George, the martyr
Theodore, the martyr
The foot of Saint Cosmas, the martyr
Part of the head of Cyprian, the martyr
Pantaleon, the martyr
A tooth of Saint Lawrence
Demetrius, the martyr
Stephen, the proto-martyr
Vincentius, Adjutus, Mauritius, and his companions
Crisantius and Darius, the martyrs
Gervasius and Protasius, the martyrs
Primus, the martyr
Sergius and Bacchus, the martyrs
Protus, the martyr
John and Paul, the martyrs

Also relics from the following: the place of the Nativity of our Lord; Calvary; our Lord's sepulcher; the stone rolled away; the place of our Lord's ascension; the stone on which John stood when he baptized the Lord; the spot where Christ raised Lazarus; the stone on which Christ was presented in the temple; the stone on which Jacob slept; the stone where Christ fasted; the stone where Christ prayed; the table on which Christ ate the supper; the place where He was captured; the place where the mother of our Lord died; His grave; the grave of Saint Peter, the apostle; the relics of the holy apostles Andrew and Philip; the place where the Lord gave the law to Moses; the holy patriarchs, Abraham, Isaac, and Jacob; Saint Nicholas, the bishop; Adelasius, the bishop; Agricius, the bishop; John Chrysostom; John, the almsgiver; the milk of the mother of our Lord; Margaret, the virgin; Perpetua, the virgin; Agatha, the virgin;

Agnes, the virgin; Lucia, the virgin; Cecilia, the virgin; Adelgundis and Euphemia, the virgins.

Written and sealed—in this year of our Lord's Incarnation, 1205, in the reign of Philip, king of the Romans, Innocent, supreme pontiff presiding over the holy Roman church—under the direction of the bishops Lutholdus of Basel and Henry of Strassburg.

With the conquest of Constantinople, the Latins elected Baldwin of Flanders as emperor, as per the March pact, crowned him on May 16, 1204, and set about organizing the Latin Empire. Innocent III, who had fulminated against the conquest of Zara, had also explicitly forbade them to go to Constantinople.[31] After the city fell, Baldwin communicated his version of the conquest to Innocent, and at first, before he learned the full extent of the destruction, Innocent considered the capture of Constantinople as a sign of God's will and a benefit to the crusading purpose.[32]

Not until mid-1205 does Innocent seem to have been informed of the full extent of the devastation of Constantinople and the horrors of the sacking of the city. At the same time, events in the Holy Land and the military defeat and death of Baldwin I at the hands of the Bulgars in April 1205 made it clear that the crusade was virtually at an end and that the Latin Empire of Constantinople added a new dimension to the problem of the Holy Land.

The crusade endangers the Holy Land: Innocent III reprimands his legate Peter, cardinal priest of the title of Saint Marcellus, July 12, 1205

WHEN we heard some time ago that you and our beloved son Soffredus, cardinal priest of Santa Prassede, legate of the Apostolic See, had left the province of Jerusalem during a period of much need, had arrived by ship in Constantinople, we wondered and were much disturbed, dreading the imminent danger to that land. And behold, what we feared has happened and what we were worried about has now come to pass. For in addition to the fact that with the death of the patriarch of Jerusalem, the church of Jerusalem was vacant, and there was a certain rivalry between Christians from the war that took place between our dearest son in Christ, the illustrious king of Armenia and the count of Tripoli over the principate of

Source: *Powell,* Deeds, *173–175.*

31. Andrea, *Contemporary Sources,* 39–45, 59–64.

32. Andrea, *Contemporary Sources,* 98–112. Innocent's remarkable letter detailing the differences between Greek and Latin Christianity is translated in Powell, *Deeds,* 170–172. Baldwin's long letter to Innocent is translated in Powell, *Deeds,* 156–163. Innocent's response is translated in *Deeds,* 166–170; and in Andrea, *Contemporary Sources,* 113–5. For the context of the letters, see Jonathan Harris, *Byzantium and the Crusades* (London-New York, 2003).

Antioch, afterward, due to the unforeseen death of Amalric, king of Jerusalem, of shining memory, and of his son, the kingdom of Jerusalem was almost entirely without government. And because you, who should rather have sought greater help there, and invited others to aid the same land both by word and example, of your own will went to Greece, not only pilgrims but also natives of the Holy Land went to Constantinople, following in your footsteps, with our brother the archbishop of Tyre, likewise in your train.

Therefore, with your departure, that land has remained destitute in men and arms, and its most recent situation was made worse than in its earlier state by your action, since all its friends departed from it in your company, and there was no one to console her from all those dear to her. For this reason, her enemies have gained the advantage, should they wish to break the truce, which also is said by some to have expired with the deaths of the king and his son. Therefore, we are quite disturbed and are rightfully angry with you that you both decided to leave the land that the Lord consecrated by his presence and in which our king long ago wonderfully worked the mystery of our redemption.

Although, of course, our venerable brother, the bishop of Vercelli, was postulated for the patriarchate of Jerusalem and we approved his postulation and ordered the *pallium* to be granted to him, still on account of his many occupations, he cannot quickly cross the sea. Therefore you should have paid heed to and considered carefully the reason for your delegation. Because we sent you not to seize the Empire of Constantinople, but to defend the rest of the Holy Land and to restore that which was lost, if the Lord should grant that it should be restored. Since we and our brothers provided adequately for your expenses, we sent you not to seize on temporal riches but to deserve eternal.

But when we also learned recently from your letter that you had absolved all the crusaders who delayed in defense of Constantinople from the preceding March to the next from their vow of pilgrimage and the burden of the cross, we could not fail to move against you, since you neither should nor could attempt such things in any way, whoever might suggest the contrary to you and however they might seduce your mind. For since they assumed the cross for this especially and principally and vowed particularly to the Lord their God that they would cross over the sea to aid the Holy Land and they later deviated from the path and obtained even until today an excess of temporal benefits, we leave to your judgment whether it was permissible for you to make such a change, nay, rather to pervert such a solemn and pious vow. For behold what we relate with grief and shame. By what we seemed to have profited until now, we are impoverished and by what we were made greater, we are rather reduced.

For how indeed is the Greek church, which has been afflicted to some degree by persecution, to be returned to ecclesiastical unity and devotion to the Apostolic See? They look upon the Latins as nothing but an example of perdition and works of darkness, so that now they rightly abhor them more than dogs. For those who are believed to seek not things for themselves but for Jesus Christ ought to use their swords against the pagans, but they are bloody with the blood of Christians, and they do not spare anyone because of religion, age, or sex, carrying out incests, adulteries, and fornications in the eyes of men and exposing both matrons and virgins dedicated to God to the filth of mercenaries. And it was not enough for them to exhaust imperial riches and seize the spoils of princes and minors, but they reached out their hands for the treasures of churches and what is worse for their possessions, seizing silver tablets from their altars and breaking them in pieces among themselves. They violated sacristies and carried off crosses and relics.

Besides, since it was impossible to hide what is believed among so many thousands of men, will the Saracens who, after the capture of Constantinople, were too beaten down by fear not realize that the crusaders will return to their own land after a year? Divine punishment will now begin to best their iniquities, and already rages against them, and will the Saracens not recover their courage and devour the lambs that you left as morsels to the wolves, if the right hand of God alone does not restore them [1 Sm 17:28]? Also, how could we in the future invite the peoples of the West to aid the Holy Land and defend the Empire of Constantinople when some will argue, even if it is not your fault but the result of your action, that the crusaders, having deserted their pilgrimage, are returning to their homes absolved, and those who despoiled the empire, having left it unfortified, desert it when they are stuffed with spoils? Let not the word of the Lord be bound on your tongue, and like mute dogs, may you be unable to bark, but say this publicly and protest before all so that the more they who found you negligent up to now may find you blaming the more in behalf of God and because of God.

Although Innocent III could not turn his back on the Latin Empire of Constantinople, by mid-1205 he had learned with bitter regret of the terrible cost of that enterprise and saw the utter failure of his crusade. And he had learned several very hard lessons, among them the great responsibility of papal direction and continuous monitoring of any future crusade and the necessity of financial and logistical support for a crusade. He applied these lessons to his next great crusade plan (below, Part II), but he also turned to other aspects of Christian society that seemed to pose problems even more pressing.

7. The Albigensian Crusade, 1209–1229

The Albigensian Crusade, launched by Innocent III in 1209, is conventionally regarded as the key moment in crusade history in which the crusade was turned against Christians, not, as at Zara and Constantinople in 1204, as a result of insufficient planning and organization, unforeseen circumstances, and political contingencies, but deliberately and with a full array of crusade features as these had become widely recognized and required during the second half of the twelfth century: papal declaration, preaching, recruiting, privileges, definition of crusader status, and protection of crusaders' property. The selections here are representative of slightly different and largely monastic viewpoints.

The subject of dissent and heresy in southern France has been exhaustively—and contentiously—studied. But there is little dispute about the mechanics of the Albigensian Crusade. Innocent III appealed to the king of France, Philip Augustus, for aid, but Philip was tied down in his conflict with King John of England and the emperor Otto IV. Innocent had launched preaching missions into the region, aiming to reform the local clergy, gain the aid of local nobles (at first by offering indulgences comparable to those of pilgrimages to Compostela and Rome), and preach the faith against dissenting doctrine. Earlier church councils, especially the Third Lateran Council of 1179, and popes, especially in the decretal *Ad abolendam* of Lucius III in 1184, had provided Innocent with formidable weapons against heresy. Increasingly, the new schools in the north of France, especially Paris, also provided new preaching techniques and methods of confession, adding a pastoral dimension to the problem of ecclesiastical discipline.

Innocent had sent legates into the south of France, especially the county of Toulouse, in 1198, and in 1203 replaced them with Peter of Castelnau, Ralph of Fontfroide, and Arnaud Amaury of Cîteaux. In 1204 Innocent offered full crusade privileges to Philip II. By 1206 Bishop Diego of Osma and his young canon Domingo de Guzmán had begun their preaching that later led to the formation of the Dominican Order.

Roger Wendover, chronicler at the monastery of Saint Albans in England, considered these circumstances from a certain distance and recorded events as news of them came to him, often in several different versions, and he included original documents whenever he had them. He was much less caught up in the intensity of the moment than was Caesarius. Caesarius of Heisterbach, more intimately connected to the vast Cistercian network and engaged in training young monks, offers a more vivid and arresting account of the crusade.

Roger Wendover began to write his chronicle at the monastery of Saint Albans around 1217 and continued until 1235, when he was succeeded by Matthew Paris. He died in 1236. Roger was uniquely well informed and, like Roger Howden, a sensible user of documentary evidence. His account of the Albigensian Crusade (and the Fourth Lateran Council of 1215, below, No. 15, as well as the crusade of Frederick II, below Part IV) reflects the point of view of a learned, able English monastic cleric who had access to important documentary sources and possessed the intellectual and literary ability to organize events and present a coherent narrative.

As a monk and novice-master at the Cistercian monastery of Heisterbach, Caesarius, a native of Cologne, traveled widely and gathered tales from many individuals. He used these in collections of sermons and edificatory stories intended to instruct novices at his monastery and perhaps also as preaching aids for his abbot Henry, who recruited for the Fifth Crusade and the crusade of Frederick II (below, Parts III and IV). Caesarius also benefited from the transmission of propaganda and news through the Cistercian monastic networks; many of the order's monks and abbots had become involved in antiheretical preaching and the Albigensian Crusade, including Arnaud Amaury, abbot of Cîteaux and long-serving papal legate.

Although Caesarius's account of the Albigensian Crusade was for a long time dismissed as the overwrought imaginings of an isolated and ill-informed monk, he has recently been rehabilitated as a precious source for attitudes toward heresy within clerical and Cistercian circles. Like many of his contemporaries, Caesarius was concerned about the spread of heresy not only in southern France, but also in northern France and Germany. He probably wrote the section translated below in 1220, during a series of military setbacks suffered by the crusaders in southern France. His vision of the heresy as but one of many allied dangers attacking Christendom and the famous words he attributes to Arnaud Amaury (although almost certainly fictitious) reflect contemporary preachers' and legates' attempts to justify the antiheretical crusade and present heresy as a real and insidious threat worthy of diverting resources from other crusading theaters (including the Iberian Peninsula and the Holy Land). Caesarius's portrait of heretics in southern France as heirs to ancient heresy and as unmitigated dualists possessed of a formal structure of beliefs also reflects the views of those involved in promoting the antiheretical effort.

The selections from Roger's chronicle in this volume are taken from J. A. Giles, trans., Roger of Wendover's Flowers of History, Comprising the History of England from the Descent of the Saxons to A.D. 1235, Formerly Ascribed to Matthew Paris, *2 vols.* (London, 1849). *The best discussions of Roger and his work are those of V. H. Galbraith,* Roger Wendover and Matthew Paris *(Glasgow, 1944); and Richard Vaughan,* Matthew Paris *(Cambridge, 1958).*

For Caesarius, see Jacques Berlioz, "Tuez-les tous, Dieu reconnaîtra les siens": Le massacre de Béziers (22 juillet 1209) et la croisade contre les Albigeois vus par Césaire de Heisterbach *(Portet-sur-Garonne, 1994); Jessalynn Bird, "Paris Masters and the Justification of the Albigensian Crusade,"* Crusades 6 *(2007), 117–155; Richard Kay,* The Council of Bourges, 1225: A Documentary History *(Aldershot UK, 2002); Beverly Mayne Kienzle,* Cistercians, Heresy and Crusade in Occitania, 1145–1229 *(Rochester NY, 2001).*

On the vast subject of heresy, particularly in the south of France, see Walter L. Wakefield, Heresy, Crusade and Inquisition in Southern France, 1100–1250 *(Berkeley and Los Angeles, 1974); and Malcolm Lambert,* Medieval Heresy: Popular Movements from the Gregorian Period to the Reformation *(Oxford, 1992); Laurence W. Marvin,* The Occitan War: A Military and Political History of the Albigensian Crusade, 1209–1218 *(Cambridge, 2008); Mark Gregory Pegg,* A Most Holy War: The Albigensian Crusade and the Battle for Christendom *(Oxford, 2007); Damian Smith,* Crusade, Heresy and Inquisition in the Lands of the Crown of Aragón, c. 1167–1276 *(Leiden, 2010); Catherine Léglu, Rebecca Rist, and Claire Taylor, eds. and trans.,* The Cathars and the Albigensian Crusade: A Sourcebook *(London-New York, 2012).*

On crusades against Christians, see Housley, "Crusades Against Christians." *On clerical participation in war generally, see Bachrach,* Religion and the Conduct of War. *On papal policy through the first half of the thirteenth century, Rist,* The Papacy and Crusading.

Original sources in English translation are Janet Shirley, ed. and trans., The Song of the Cathar Wars: A History of the Albigensian Crusade/ William of Tudela and an Anonymous Successor *(Aldershot UK-Brookfield VT, 1996); W. A. Sibly and M. D. Sibly, trans.,* The History of the Albigensian Crusade: Peter of les Vaux-de-Cernay's "Historia Albigensis" *(Woodbridge UK-Rochester NY, 1998); W. A. Sibly and M. D. Sibly, ed. and trans.,* The Chronicle of William of Puylaurens: The Albigensian Crusade and Its Aftermath *(Woodbridge UK-Rochester NY, 2003).*

The Albigensian Crusade from the chronicle of Roger of Wendover

The Albigensian heresy and the launching of the crusade, ca. 1165–1208

ABOUT that time the depravity of the heretics called Albigenses, who dwelt in Gascony, Arumnia, and Albi, gained such power in the parts about Toulouse, and in the kingdom of Aragón, that they not only practiced their impieties in secret as was done elsewhere, but preached their erroneous doctrine openly, and induced the simple and weak-minded to conform to them. The Albigenses are so called from the city of Albi, where that doctrine is said to have taken its rise. At length their perversity set the anger of God so completely at defiance, that they published the books of their doctrines among the lower orders, before the very eyes of the bishops and priests, and disgraced the chalices and sacred vessels in disrespect of the body and blood of Christ.

Source: Giles, Wendover's Flowers of History, *2:278–82 and 474–82; Peters,* Christian Society, *25–35, with new revisions.*

Pope Innocent was greatly grieved at hearing these things, and he immediately sent preachers into all the districts of the west, and enjoined the chiefs and other Christian people as a remission of their sins, that they should take the sign of the cross for the extirpation of this plague, and, opposing themselves to such disasters, should protect the Christian people by force of arms. He also added, by authority of the Apostolic See, that whoever undertook the business of overthrowing the heretics according to his injunction, should, like those who visited the Lord's sepulcher, be protected from all hostile attacks both in property and person. At this preaching such a multitude of crusaders assembled, as it is not to be believed could have assembled in our country.

Not only the preaching and anger at the heretics' insults triggered the crusade, but also the murder of Innocent's legate Peter of Castelnau by a supporter of Raymond VI of Toulouse in 1208. Innocent, furious, placed Arnaud Amaury in command of a volunteer force, which began to move down the Rhône valley in the early summer of 1209 and turned west toward Béziers.

Of the movements of the crusaders against the Albigensians, Béziers, July 1209

WHEN therefore they were all assembled and prepared for battle, the archbishop of Narbonne [Arnaud Amaury], the legate of the apostolic see in this expedition, and the chiefs of the army, namely the duke of Burgundy, the count of Nevers, and the count of Montfort, struck their camp and went to lay siege to the city of Béziers.[33] But before they got to it the lords of some of the castles, having little confidence in themselves, fled at the sight of their army. The knights and others who were left in charge of the said castles, went boldly as good catholics and surrendered themselves with their property, as well as the castles, to the army of the crusaders. On the eve of Saint Mary Magdalen [July 21, 1209] they surrendered the noble castle of Cermaine to a monk, since the lord of the castle, who also possessed several others of great strength, had taken to flight. They warned the citizens of Béziers, through the bishop of that city, under penalty of excommunication, to make choice of one of two alternatives; either to deliver the heretics and their property into the hands of the crusaders, or else to send them away from among them, otherwise, they would be excommunicated, and their blood was on their own heads.

33. Simon de Montfort had been in the army of the Fourth Crusade but left it in a dispute over the siege of Zara, proceeding to the Holy Land independently and then returning home. He is a major figure in the history of the Albigensian Crusade.

The heretics and their allies scornfully refused to accede to this, and mutually swore to defend the city; and, when they had pledged their faith, they hoped to be able for a long time to sustain the assaults of the crusaders. After the city was laid siege to, on the feast of Saint Mary Magdalen [July 22], the catholic barons considered how they could save those among them who were catholics, and made overtures for their liberation. But the rabble and low people, without waiting for the command or orders from the chiefs, made an assault on the city. And, to the astonishment of the Christians, when the cry to arms was raised, and the army of the faith was rushing in all directions to the assaults, those who were defending the walls inside threw down the book of the gospel from the city on them, blaspheming the name of the Lord, and deriding their assailants: "Behold," they said, "your law, we take no heed to it; yours it shall be." The soldiers of the faith, incensed by such blasphemy and provoked by their insults, in less than three hours' time crossed the fosse and scaled the walls, by the Lord's assistance.

Thus was the city taken, and on the same day it was sacked and burnt, a great slaughter of the infidels taking place as the punishment of God; but, under his protection, very few of the catholics were slain. After the lapse of a few days, when the report of the miracle was spread abroad, the Lord scattered before the face of the crusaders, as it were without their assistance, those who had blasphemed his name and his law, and at length the followers of this heretical depravity were so alarmed that they fled to the recesses of the mountains, and what may be believed, they left more than a hundred untenanted castles, between Béziers and Carcassonne, stocked with food and all kinds of stores, which they could not take with them in their flight.

Fugitives from Béziers had fled west to Carcassonne, where they were pursued by the crusader army, flushed with victory at Béziers.

The capture of the city and castle of Carcassonne, August 1–15, 1209

THE CRUSADERS, moving their camp from this place, arrived on the feast of Saint Peter *ad vincula*[34] at Carcassonne, a populous city, and till now glorying in its wickedness, abounding in riches, and well fortified. On the following day they made an assault, and within two or three hours they crossed the entrenchments and scaled the walls amid showers of missiles from the crossbows, and the blows of the lances and swords of its wicked

34. The feast of Saint Peter in Chains, August 1, also known in English as Lammas.

defenders. After this they set up their engines of war, and on the eighth day the greater suburb was taken after a great many of the enemy, who had incautiously exposed themselves, were slain, and the suburbs of the city, which seemed larger than the body of the town, were altogether destroyed. The enemy being thus confined in the narrow streets of the city, and suffering as well from their numbers as from want of provisions more than is credible, offered themselves and all of their property, together with the city to the crusaders, on condition of their lives being preserved out of mercy, and of being saved for at least one day.

After holding a council, therefore, the barons received the city almost as it were under compulsion; in the first place because, in men's opinion, it was deemed impregnable; for another reason because, if that city were altogether destroyed, there would not be found a nobleman or the army who would undertake the government of that country, as there would not be a place in the subdued land where he could reside. Therefore, that the land, which the Lord had delivered into the hands of his servants, might be preserved to his honor and the advantage of Christianity, the noble Simon de Montfort, earl of Leicester, was, by the common consent of prelates and barons, chosen as ruler of that country. Into his hands was delivered as a prisoner the noble Roger [Trencavel], formerly viscount and ruler of that country, together with the whole of the province, including about a hundred castles, which, within one month, the Lord deigned to restore to the catholic unity. Among these same castles were several of such strength that there would have been, in the opinion of men, but little cause to fear any army. After effecting this, the count of Nevers and a large part of the army returned home, while the illustrious duke of Burgundy and the rest of the nobles proceeded with their army to the extirpation of this heretical depravity, and after this they delivered into the hands of the earl Simon de Montfort several more castles which they took either by fair means or by threats.

The crusading army ripped through the county of Toulouse, besieging Toulouse as early as June 1211. The following text is an example of the kind of negotiations that were recorded as having taken place.

Messengers sent to Toulouse by the crusaders, 1213

As THE city of Toulouse had been reported to have been long tainted with this pestiferous sin, the barons sent special messengers, namely the bishop of Saintonge, the bishop of Foroli, the viscount of Saint Florentius, and the lord Accald de Roussillon, to the inhabitants of that city with letters from them, ordering them to deliver up to the armies of the crusaders the heretics of that city, and all their property. But if by chance they should say that they were not heretics; that those who were signified and expressed by name should come to them to make a plain declaration of their faith, according to Christian custom, before the whole army. Should they refuse to do this they would, by the same letters, excommunicate their chief officers and counselors, and place the whole town of Toulouse with its dependencies under an interdict.

Shortly before these negotiations, the kings of Castile and Aragón were preparing to launch their forces against local Muslim powers, and they won a spectacular victory at the battle of Las Navas de Tolosa in July 1212 (below, No. 9), a victory that greatly enhanced the prestige of Peter II of Aragón (1196–1213), who proposed to mediate between the contending forces. But the fortunes of war and politics swung back and forth for the next decade. At the battle of Muret in 1213, Peter himself was killed in combat with the crusaders' forces.[35] At the great Fourth Lateran Council of November 1215 (below, Part II), Simon de Montfort was made count of Toulouse, since Raymond VI had been excommunicated in 1211, but Simon died in a failed siege two years later, and his son failed to rally the northern forces. The direction of the crusade eventually fell into the hands of Louis VIII of France. After much discussion with the pope, Louis and the papal legate Romanus assembled an army twice the size of that of 1209, and by 1229 the south of France was pacified, if not in devotion (see Wendover's remark about self-interest and fear of the king of France below) then in subjection to the king of France. The Treaty of Paris of 1229 and the Council of Toulouse in the same year conventionally mark the end of the Albigensian Crusade. The following section summarizes the conquest of Toulouse in the years 1226–1229.

The destruction of Toulouse, 1226–1229

ABOUT the same time a crusade was preached throughout the French provinces in general by the Roman legate [now Romanus Frangipani, cardinal deacon of Saint Angelo], that all who could carry arms, should assume the cross against the count of Toulouse and his followers, who were said to be infected with the foul stain of heresy. At his preaching, a great number of prelates as well as laity assumed the cross, being induced to do so more by fear of the French king or to obtain favor with the legate, than by their zeal for justice. For it seemed to many to be a sin to attack a true Christian, especially as all were aware that, at the council lately held at Bourges [1225], the said count had with many entreaties begged of the legate to go to each one of the cities in his territory to

35. Damian Smith, "Peter II of Aragon, Innocent III, and the Albigensian Crusade," in Sommerlechner, *Innocenzo III: Urbs et Orbis,* 2:1049–1064.

inquire into the articles of their faith, and had declared that if he, the legate, should find the inhabitants of any city to hold opinions contrary to the catholic faith, he himself would exact full satisfaction from them. And if he found any city in a state of disobedience, he would, as far as lay in his power, compel that city and its inhabitants to make atonement; and as for himself he offered, if he had sinned in any way, which he did not remember to have done, to give full satisfaction to God and the holy church, as a faithful Christian; and if the legate wished it he would undergo a trial of his faith.

All these offers the legate refused, nor could this catholic count find any favor with him, without abandoning and forswearing his inheritance for himself and his heirs after him. The French king at the preaching of this legate assumed the cross, but would not proceed in the expedition unless he first obtained letters from the pope to the king of England, forbidding him, under penalty of excommunication, to annoy him, the French king, or to make war against him concerning any territory he at present held, whether justly or unjustly, as long as he was engaged in the service of the pope and the church of Rome, in exterminating the heretic Albigenses, and their abettor and accomplice the count of Toulouse, but should aid him with assistance and advice in forwarding the cause of the faith. After this the French king and the legate appointed our Lord's Ascension-Day for all those who had assumed the cross to assemble under penalty of excommunication, at Lyons, equipped with horses and arms, to follow them on the proposed expedition.

The pressure exerted by the legate Romanus, the Council of Bourges in 1225, the peacemaking efforts of Pope Honorius III, and crusade preachers all combined to inspire Louis VIII to take the cross and convene an army at Bourges in May 1226. The king and his army marched east toward Lyons and then sailed down the Rhône until they reached Avignon, in the marquisate of Provence, on June 7.

Of the siege of Avignon by Louis VIII, the French king, 1226

IN THE meantime our Lord's ascension arrived, on which day all the French crusaders had been ordered by the king and the legate to assemble without fail. The king, having made all the necessary preparations for the expedition at Lyons, proceeded on his journey with, as it seemed, an invincible army, followed by the legate, the archbishops, bishops, and other prelates of the churches. The army was computed to consist of about fifty thousand knights and horse soldiers, besides foot soldiers, who could hardly be counted. The legate then publicly excommunicated the

count of Toulouse and all his abettors, and laid all his territory under an
interdict. The king, as we have said, set out with shields and standards
glittering, and his march was so awful that it looked like an army of castles
in motion, and at length entered the province of the count of Toulouse.
On the eve of Whitsunday[36] they all reached Avignon, which was the first
city in the count's dominion that they came to, and they determined to
commence their attacks there, and thus to subdue the whole of the
count's territory with the inhabitants of it from beginning to end.

The king and the legate on their arrival there deceitfully asked leave
of the inhabitants to pass through the city, saying that they had come
there with peaceable intentions, and asked a passage through the city only
to make a shortcut in their march. The citizens, however, after deliberat-
ing on this request, put no faith in their assertions, and said that they
wanted to get into the city with treacherous intentions rather than to
make a shortcut. The king then becoming enraged, swore that he would
not leave the spot until he had taken the city, and immediately ordered
his engines to be arranged around the place and a fierce assault to be
made. A severe attack was then commenced, and petraries, crossbows,
and all other kinds of military weapons were now put in constant use. On
the other hand the city, till that time unattempted by hostile troops, was
well defended by trenches, walls, turrets, and ramparts outside, while
within it was well garrisoned with knights and thousands of soldiers, and
well supplied with horses, arms, collections of stones for missiles, engines
and barriers, and was well stored with provisions, and did not therefore
fear the assaults of the besiegers. The defenders of the city bravely hurled
on them stone for stone, weapon for weapon, spear for spear, and dart
for dart, inflicting deadly wounds on the besieging French.

Of the mortality and famine among the besiegers

AFTER the siege had been carried on for a length of time, the provisions
of the besiegers failed them and numbers of the troops died; for the count
of Toulouse, like a skillful soldier, had, before the arrival of the French,
removed out of their way all kinds of provisions, together with the old
men, women, children, and the horses and cattle, so that they were
deprived of all kinds of sustenance. And it was not only the men who
suffered, but also the horses and cattle of the army perished of hunger;
for the count had caused all the fields throughout the district to be

36. A moveable feast, the seventh Sunday after Easter: Pentecost.

plowed up, so that there was no supply of fodder for the cattle except for what had been brought from the French provinces. Therefore large bodies of troops were obliged to leave the camp to seek for provisions for the men and food for the horses, and on these excursions they took many towns which opposed them, and they often suffered great loss from attacks by the count of Toulouse, who with his troops laid in ambuscade for them. At this siege the French were exposed to death in many ways, from the epidemic disease which was raging dreadfully among their men and horses, from the deadly weapons and destructive stones of the besieged who bravely defended the city, and from the general famine which raged principally among the poorer classes, who had neither food nor money.

In addition to the other miseries, which assailed the army without intermission, there arose from the corpses of the men and horses, which were dying in all directions, a number of large black flies, which made their way inside the tents, pavilions, and awnings, and affected the provisions and the liquor; and being unable to drive them away from their cups and plates, they caused sudden death among them.

The king and the legate were in dismay, for if such a great and powerful expedition were to return with their purpose unaccomplished, the French as well as the Romans would incur much taunting. The chiefs of the army, then, to whom the delay seemed long on account of such numbers of deaths, begged the inferior ranks as well as their chiefs to attack the city; on this such a multitude of troops marched against the city that, in marching over a bridge which was built over the Rhône, the bridge was broken, either by the citizens, or by the weight of the troops who were fighting there, and about three thousand men were precipitated into the rapid stream. Then there arose a cry of exultation from the citizens, but dismay and confusion pervaded the French army. After this, the citizens, watching their opportunity, sallied from the city one day in great force when the French were sitting at table eating and drinking, and rushing on them when the French were unprepared for them, slew two thousand of the French, and then returned into the city without loss to themselves, and these sallies they continually made against them. The French king was in dismay, and ordered the slain to be thrown into the Rhône, to avoid the stench, for with such a number of dead bodies they had no other burial place. They then made a wide deep trench between them and the city, and the operations of the siege were carried out at a greater distance from it. The legate and the whole assembly of prelates during this time, having no other means of punishment, excommunicated the count of Toulouse, the citizens, and all the inhabitants of the province.

The death of Louis, the French king, November 8, 1226

AT THIS time, Louis, king of the French, to escape the pestilence which was committing great ravages in the camp, retired to a monastery called Montpensier, near the besieged town, to await the capture of the city. At that place Thibaut, count of Champagne, came to him, having been employed forty days in the siege, and, according to the French custom, asked leave to return home, and on the king's refusing his permission, he said that having served the forty days of duty he was not bound to nor would he stay any longer. The king then, roused to anger, declared with an oath that if the count went away in this way he would ravage his territory with fire and sword. The count then, as report goes, being in love with his [Louis's] queen, caused some poison to be administered to the king, and being urged on by the impulses of desire he could not abide longer delay. After the departure of the count, as he had said he would, the king was taken dangerously ill, and, the poison working its way to his vitals, he was reduced to the point of death; some, however, assert that he died not by poison, but of dysentery.

On the death of the king, Romanus, the legate of the apostolic see, who was present at the siege, and the prelates, his secret advisers, who were also there, concealed the death of the king until the city should be surrendered; for if the siege were to be now raised, a great reproach would be cast on them. The legate and the prelates, therefore, who were at the siege, pretended that the king was delayed by severe illness, but that in the opinion of his physicians he would soon be convalescent, and then exhorted the chiefs of the different battalions to attack the city with all their power. They preserved the king's body with large quantities of salt, and burying his entrails in the convent, they ordered his body to be wrapped in waxed linen and bulls' hides. It was then placed in safe custody in the convent, and the legate and the prelates then returned to the siege. However, finding that they gained no advantage, but were entirely failing owing to different misfortunes, the legate, by the advice of the elders in the camp, sent a message into the city asking them, on receipt of security, for safe-conduct to and from the city, to send twelve elders of the city to the legate as soon as possible to make terms of peace.

How the city of Avignon was taken by the French by treachery

AFTER hostages had been given for their safety, twelve citizens came out to a conference with the legate, when, after a long discussion about peace, he earnestly advised the citizens to surrender themselves, saving their persons, their property and possessions, and all their liberties, to the utmost extent that they had ever enjoyed them. To this the messengers replied that they would on no account surrender themselves to live under the dominion of the French, whose pride and fierce insolence they had often experienced. After much disputing on both sides, the legate at length asked permission to go into the city with the prelates who were present, to put the faith of the inhabitants to the test, declaring on oath that he had prolonged the siege only to provide for the safety of their souls; he also added that the cry of infidelity, which had gained power in the city, had reached the pope, and he therefore desired to know whether they supported this cry by their actions. The citizens then, trusting to the promises of the legate, and having no suspicions of treachery, after an oath had been taken on both sides, on the above-named condition, gave permission to the legate and the prelates to enter the city without any others, and in company with them.

But, as had been prearranged, as soon as the gates were open, the French treacherously and in disgraceful disregard of the oath which had been made by the legate, forced their way into the city and made prisoners of the inhabitants, and having thus treacherously gained a victory they destroyed the towers and walls of the noble place. The legate then consigned the city to the charge of the French, and raising the siege he ordered the body of the king to be carried to Paris by the priests assembled, to be buried among his ancestors as was the custom with kings. The king died, as they say, in the month of September, but they concealed his death for a month or more. Of those who went to the siege with the king, twenty-two thousand died at the place [Avignon], including those who were slain and drowned, as well as those who died of the pestilence or by natural death, and thus left great cause of tears and sorrow to their wives and children. Hence it seems clearly evident that an unjust war had been undertaken, of which covetousness was the cause rather than the wish to exterminate heresy.

Caesarius of Heisterbach's dialogue on the Albigensian Crusade

The dialogue by Caesarius of Heisterbach is a didactic literary work written by the schoolmaster of a monastery near Cologne to instruct his novices about their lives

and identities as monks and other relevant topics. In this case it is a dialogue between
a master and a novice on the Albigensians and the Albigensian Crusade.

IN THE time of Pope Innocent III, the predecessor of Honorius III, who
now holds the papal seat, while the schism which had come to be between
Philip and Otto, kings of the Romans,[37] as yet endured, through the envy
of the devil, the heresy of the Albigensians began to shoot up, or if I were
to speak more accurately, to bear fruit. Its vigor was so potent that all the
wheat of its people's faith seemed to be converted to the tares of error.
Abbots from our order were sent with certain bishops so that they might
uproot the tares with the hoe of catholic preaching. But resisted by the
enemy of mankind, who had sowed these tares, they achieved little
there.[38]

> NOVICE. What was their error?
> MONK. Some of their heresiarchs collected points from the
> teaching of Manichaeus, some of them borrowed from the
> errors which Origen is said to have written in his *Periarchon*,
> likewise many added [other beliefs] as well, which they had
> invented in their own hearts. Following Manichaeus, they
> believed in two principles, a good God and an evil God, that is
> the Devil, whom they claim created all corporal things, just as
> the good God created all souls.
> NOVICE. Moses established that God created both bodies and
> souls, saying: "God fashioned man," that is his body, "from the
> mud of the earth, and he breathed into his face the breath of
> life," that is the soul [Gn 2:7].
> MONK. If they accepted Moses and the prophets, they would
> not be heretics. They deny the resurrection of the body; they
> ridicule the idea that the living can supply any services whatso-
> ever for the dead; and they say that going to churches or praying
> in them does no good. In this, they are worse than the Jews and
> pagans, because they believe in these things. They mock bap-
> tism; they blaspheme the sacrament of the body and blood of
> Christ.

Source: *Caesarius of Heisterbach,* Dialogus miraculorum, *V.21, ed. Joseph Strange, 2*
vols. (Cologne, 1851), 1:300–303.
37. That is, Philip of Swabia and Otto of Brunswick, rival claimants to the German
region of the Holy Roman Empire.
38. The parable of the wheat and the tares (Mt 13:24–30) was a locus for discussions
regarding the use of force versus preaching in combating heresy.

NOVICE. But how can they endure such a great persecution by the faithful, if they look for nothing from this in terms of a future reward?

MONK. They claim that they await the glorification of the spirit. A certain monk associated with the abbots mentioned above, seeing a certain knight seated on a horse speaking with his plowman and appraising the knight as a heretic, as he in fact was, drawing nearer to him, said: "Tell me, good man, whose field is this?" And when he answered, "It is mine," he added, "And what do you do with its fruits?" He replied, "I and my family live from them, and in addition I give something to the poor." And when the monk said, "What good do you hope for from this almsgiving?" the knight answered with these words: "[I hope] that after death my spirit might continue in glory." Then the monk said: "In what manner will it continue?" The knight said: "According to its merits. If it lived well, and is deserving before God, after exiting my body, it will enter into the body of some future prince or king, or another illustrious person of this sort, in which it will take delight. If however, I have lived evilly, it will enter the body of a wretched pauper, in which it will endure tribulations." This fool believed, as do other Albigensians, that according to its merits, the soul would migrate through various bodies, even those of animals and serpents.

NOVICE. [Foul] pits of heresy!

MONK. Indeed, for the error of the Albigensians grew so very strong that within a short space of time it corrupted up to a thousand towns, and if it had not been cut down by the swords of the faithful, I think that it would have infected all of Europe. For in the year of Our Lord 1210, the cross was preached against the Albigensians in all of Germany and France,[39] and during the following year, Adolph III, count of Berg, William III, count of Jülich, and many others of various positions and ranks rose up against them.[40] Similar events took place in the

39. Caesarius uses the term *Francia*, which often meant those lands directly under the rule of the French king, that is, a large part of what is today northern France.

40. Adolph was the brother of Engelbert de Berg, who served as provost of Cologne when Caesarius of Heisterbach studied at its cathedral school. Engelbert participated in the Albigensian Crusade before later becoming archbishop of Cologne. After Engelbert's sudden assassination, Caesarius wrote his hagiographical biography.

kingdom of France, Normandy, and Poitou. The main preacher
and leader of all of these men was Arnaud, a Cistercian abbot,
afterward archbishop of Narbonne.[41]

Coming to a great city called Béziers, in which more than a
hundred thousand people were said to live, they laid siege to it.
Before their eyes the heretics urinated upon a volume of the
holy gospels, and flung it from the wall toward the Christians,
and shooting arrows after it shouted: "Behold your law,
wretches!" However, Christ, the begetter of [these] gospels, did
not leave the injury inflicted upon himself unavenged. For like
lions inflamed with zeal for the faith, some of his followers set
up ladders after the example of those of whom we read in the
book of Maccabees and intrepidly scaled the walls [1 Mc 5:30;
2 Mc 11:11]. Struck by a divine terror, the heretics drew back
and when the following wave of attackers opened the gates, they
took the city. Realizing from the confessions of those men that
catholic persons were mingled with the heretics, they said to
the abbot: "Lord, what ought we to do? We cannot distinguish
between the good and the wicked." Both the abbot and the rest
of the army's leaders worried that from an overwhelming fear of
death they would pretend to be catholics and then return to
their perfidy after the departure of these men. And he is said to
have said: "Kill them [all]. For the Lord will acknowledge his
own" [cf. 2 Tm 2:19]. And so innumerable people were slain in
that city.

There was another great city in that region, called *Pulchram-
vallem* after its setting, which was situated near Toulouse, which
they took by divine power.[42] And when its populace was examined, although everyone pledged their willingness to return to
the faith, four hundred and fifty, hardened by the devil, persisted
in their pertinacity. Of these, four hundred were burned in the
flames, the rest were hung from gallows. The same thing was
done in other cities and strongholds, the wretches hurling themselves to their deaths. In fact, the Toulousans, in dire straits,

41. That is, Arnaud Amaury, abbot of Cîteaux (1200), papal legate for the antiheretical effort in southern France (1204–1214), and archbishop of Narbonne (1212–1225).
42. Lavaur, according to Jacques Berlioz, "*Exemplum* et histoire: Césaire de Heisterbach (v. 1180–v. 1240) et la croisade albigeoise," *Bibliothèque de l'École des Chartes* 147
(1989), 49–86.

promised to make complete satisfaction, but deceitfully, as later became apparent. For after the leader and head of all the heretics, the perfidious count of Saint-Gilles,[43] was legally deprived of everything at the Lateran Council, that is, [all his] fiefs and allods, cities and castles, and the greater part of them had been occupied by right of war by Count Simon de Montfort, a catholic man, he moved to the city of Toulouse. And to this day, he has not ceased to attack and harass the faithful from it.

And this very year, as Lord Conrad of Urach, cardinal bishop of Porto and Santa Rufina,[44] who was sent as legate against the Albigensians, wrote to the Cistercian chapter, some of the powerful men of the city of Toulouse did a thing so dreadful in hatred of Christ and to the confounding of our faith, as ought to deservedly disturb even those very enemies of Christ. One man emptied his bowels next to the altar of the greater church, and wiped his unclean parts with the altar cloth. In fact, others adding madness to insanity, put a harlot upon the sacred altar, using her there in full sight of the Crucified. Afterward they tore down the sacred image itself, amputating its arms, proving themselves far worse than Herod's soldiers, who after Christ had died, did not shatter his legs, but spared them.[45]

Novice. Who would not be amazed at the great patience of God?

Monk. Indeed, he is long-suffering and recompenses the patient. For when, after their victory, the Damiettans tied a rope around the neck of a crucifix and dragged it though the streets, he later punished them so horribly in the neck and throat for that very reason.[46] And so I believe that he will by no means overlook these blasphemies.

---

43. That is, Raymond VI, count of Toulouse and Saint-Gilles.

44. The former abbot of the Cistercian monasteries of Villers, Clairvaux, and Cîteaux, Conrad was appointed legate for the Albigensian Crusade (1220–1223) by Honorius III.

45. This scatological anecdote was based on actual allegations brought before Raymond VI of Toulouse by Arnaud Amaury in his capacity as abbot of Grandselve. Although the offender was never punished, the story was re-aired as proof of Raymond VI's fostering of heresy at the Council of Lavaur (1213). Both this story and that of the harlot were recounted in a circular letter from the cardinal legate Conrad of Urach (formerly a Cistercian abbot), then responsible for promoting the Albigensian Crusade.

46. Caesarius refers to the plague that struck the Egyptian defenders of Damietta during the Fifth Crusade, an incident mentioned also by Oliver of Paderborn.

Before, as related above, the army of the Lord came against them, the Albigensians urged Miralimomelinus,[47] king of Morocco, to come to their aid. He arrived in Spain from Africa with such an unbelievable host, that he hoped he would be able to conquer all of Europe for himself. In fact he sent word to Pope Innocent III that he would stable his horses in the portico of the church of Saint Peter and fix his banner upon it. This was fulfilled in part, albeit in a different manner than he had planned. And because God crushes every arrogant person, in the same period, that is, in the year of grace 1212 . . . forty thousand fighters of his army were cut down. However, he transferred himself to Seville, where he died from grief. His princely banner was captured in battle and sent to Innocent III, and was hung in the aforementioned church to the glory of Christ.[48] Would that such things could be said of the Albigensians.

8. Innocent III and the Intercessory Processions of 1212

In a circular letter sent throughout Europe in 1212, Pope Innocent III urged prelates to organize processions along the model of one he had already held in Rome to earn divine favor for the Christian army opposing the Almohad offensive at what would become known as the battle of Las Navas de Tolosa (below, No. 9). To craft his new liturgical form of intercession for the crusade, Innocent appears to have drawn on the penitential resonances and liturgical form of the sevenfold litany of Gregory I (590–604), whom Innocent much admired, local processions held in honor of the feast of the Exaltation of the Holy Cross in Rome, and intercessory processions held for the Major Litany, where clergy and laity alike processed from sacred place to sacred place with banners, liturgical crosses, and relics in order to beseech divine aid for all Christendom. Although intercessory processions had long been invoked on a local basis to avert or alleviate natural disasters or human enemies, Innocent's appeal marks the first occasion on which such processions were to be held throughout Christendom on behalf of the crusade, and the concept appears to have contributed to the crusade of the *pueri* in 1212 (see below, No. 10). Inspired by the success, spiritual and military, of the new liturgical form

47. "Leader of the Faithful," a title applied to the caliph of Morocco. The Almohad government in Morocco was headed by Muhammad III al-Nasir (r. 1198–1213), whose father Yakub abu Yusuf al-Mansur had defeated Alfonso VIII of Castile at the battle of Alarcos in 1195.

48. For accounts of the battle of Las Navas de Tolosa, which attracted the attention of chroniclers all over Europe, see No. 9 below.

of participation in the crusade, Innocent later ordered similar processions to be held monthly throughout the Fifth Crusade (below, Part II, No. 11).

The processions and accompanying fasting, prayers, and almsgiving were believed to generate suffrages that funded the partial and plenary indulgences awarded to those who participated in the crusade through personal service or financial sacrifice. Wide-scale liturgical intercessions would be organized to support many future crusades and often provided a more accessible form of "crusading" than actual participation in a military expedition.

> *For liturgy and the crusades, see A. Linder,* Raising Arms: Liturgy in the Struggle to Liberate Jerusalem *(Brepols, 2002). For the specific context of the 1212 processions, see Christoph Maier, "Crisis, Liturgy and the Crusade in the Twelfth and Thirteenth Centuries,"* Journal of Ecclesiastical History *48 (1997), 628–657; Susan Twyman, "The* Romana Fraternitas *and Urban Processions at Rome in the Twelfth and Thirteenth Centuries," in Frances Andrews, Christoph Egger, and Constance M. Rousseau, eds.,* Pope, Church, and City: Essays in Honour of Brenda Bolton *(Leiden, 2004), 205–221; and the texts on Las Navas de Tolosa, below, No. 9. For the Children's Crusade, see Gary Dickson,* The Children's Crusade: Medieval History, Modern Mythistory *(Basingstoke UK-New York, 2008).*

IN THE name of the Father and the Son and the Holy Spirit. Amen. On the fourth day within the octave of Pentecost let a general procession of men and of women be held on behalf of the peace of the universal church and the Christian people, and particularly so that the Lord might be favorable toward those fighting in the war which is rumored to be presently waged between them and the Saracens in Spain, lest God abandon his inheritance to disgrace [Ps. 93:14], and the nations have dominion over them [Dt 15:6]. And let everyone universally be instructed to come to this procession, nor should anyone excuse himself from it except those who have mortal enemies.

Therefore at the height of the morning let the women gather at Santa Maria Maggiore while the clergy gather at the basilica of the Santi Apostoli and the laymen at Sant' Anastasia. And after they have gathered, let the bells of these churches be rung simultaneously and let all proceed to the Lateran *campus*[49] in this order. Let the cross of the Lord of Santa Maria Maggiore precede all the women. And the nuns ought to be alone and in the first part of the procession, while the rest of the women ought to proceed at the end, without gold and gems and silk garments, praying

Source: PL *216:698–699.*[50]

49. An open space in front of the Lateran Palace often used for public gatherings.

50. Many thanks to Brenda Bolton for generously sharing her vast knowledge of the geography of Rome and her preliminary translation of this letter, soon to appear in a sourcebook on Innocent III (see Introduction n. 6 above). Her assistance saved us from many embarrassing errors.

with devotion and humility, with weeping and wailing. And all who are able to ought to walk in bare feet; and let them come along the Via Merulana, and passing before the church of San Bartolomeo, let them come into the Lateran *campus* and station themselves before the *fellonia*,[51] remaining in silence.

In addition, let the cross of the fraternity precede the clergy.[52] And the monks and canons regular should be in the first part of the procession; while in the last part the rectors and other clerics ought to proceed in the aforementioned manner. And let them come through the Via Maggiore[53] and the arch of Basil[54] and before the palace of the cardinal bishop of Albano and there station themselves directly in the middle of the Lateran *campus*.

And let the cross of the Lord of the church of San Pietro precede the laymen, and after it the Hospitallers ought to follow first, and last of all the other laymen, marching just as was outlined above, and let them come past the basilica of Santi Giovanni e Paolo and in front of San Nicola in Formis[55] into the Lateran *campus* and station themselves in the other part of it.

Meanwhile, by all means let the Roman pontifex[56] with the bishops and cardinals and chaplains enter the basilica which is called the *Sancta Sanctorum*,[57] and there, after reverently taking up the wood of the life-giving cross, let him come in procession before the palace of the cardinal

51. This may to refer to an equestrian statue that stood before the Lateran Palace from the tenth century onward, which became a site where the bodies of executed criminals would be exposed to public view (and censure). Twyman sees this, rather, as a passageway near the Lateran Palace.

52. This refers to the *Romana Fraternitas,* an ecclesiastical organization, which, under the guidance of its rectors, played an important role in the life of the clergy of Rome, representing their interests, arbitrating disputes between churches in the city, enforcing papal rulings on ecclesiastical matters, and interesting itself in the reform and discipline of the clergy, including the selection of candidates for ecclesiastical offices. Innocent III appears to have been supportive of its role in the city, probably because it coincided with his own concern for ecclesiastical reform. The basilica church of Santi Apostoli served as the congregational center of the fraternity.

53. That is, the via dei Santi Quattro Coronati, which leads from the Colosseum to the Lateran Square.

54. The medieval name for the classical arch of Aqua Claudia, which appears to have acted as the entrance to the Lateran precinct.

55. Literally, Saint Nicholas near the arches (*formae*) of the old Roman aqueduct built by Nero.

56. That is, the pope.

57. That is, the chapel of Saint Lawrence [San Lorenzo] in the Lateran Palace, known as the "holy of holies." Innocent here draws upon the tradition of processions held for the feast of the Exaltation of the Holy Cross (September 14) in Rome, where the relic of the true cross and other holy objects associated with the life of Christ were taken in procession and displayed to crowds in the Lateran *campus* before mass was celebrated in the Lateran

bishop of Albano and let him deliver an exhortatory sermon to all the people while sitting on the steps.

Once the sermon is finished, just as the women arrived in procession, so they should proceed to the basilica of the Holy Cross[58] and there a cardinal priest ought to be present and should celebrate a mass for them while saying this prayer: "Omnipotent, sempiternal God, in whose hand are the rulers of all, etc." And then the women ought to return to their own homes in peace.

The Roman pontifex with the bishops and cardinals and chaplains ought to go down through the papal palace into the Lateran basilica. In fact, the clerics ought to enter it through the narthex and the laymen through the *borgo*,[59] and after mass has been celebrated with due veneration, he and everyone else ought to process to the Holy Cross in bare feet, such that the clerics precede him and the laymen follow after him, and once their prayers have been completed, each one ought to return to his own home.

Moreover, let everyone fast, such that no one except the infirm should eat fish or any kind of pottage, rather, those who can should be content with bread and water. Those who cannot do this ought certainly to drink their wine well watered; they may also eat herbs and fruit and vegetables in moderation. And let all open their hands and hearts to those in need, so that through prayer, fasting, and almsgiving, the mercy of the Creator might be rendered favorable toward the Christian people.

9. The Battle of Las Navas de Tolosa, 1212

The Iberian Peninsula had long been considered a special area of conflict because of the protracted struggle between Muslim and Christian forces. Papal privileges for participation in Iberian Christian military campaigns usually strongly resembled the privileges for those crusading in the East. In 1147 Pope Eugenius III issued the privilege *Divina dispensatione*, equating the campaigns in Iberia with those

---

basilica. This feast, which commemorated the emperor Heraclius's defeat of the Persian king Chosroes and his return of the relic of the true cross to Jerusalem, became quickly and deeply associated with crusading.

58. That is, the Basilica of Santa Croce in Gerusalemme, a church built for Constantine's mother, the empress Helena, in the grounds of the Sessorian Palace. Helen was commonly credited for discovering the relic of the True Cross in Jerusalem, a relic that figured importantly in crusading liturgy and propaganda.

59. An extension of the Lateran grounds east, west, and north of the square, dating from the fifth century.

against the Wends in northern Europe, and both with the crusade to the East. In 1155 the papal legate Cardinal Hyacinth Bobone (later Pope Celestine III, 1191–1198) called for a crusade at the Council of Valladolid. But political rivalries among Christians and the emergence of a powerful Almohad principality in the 1170s under the caliph Abu Yusuf Ya'qub al-Mansur I (1163–1184) prevented a significant response. In the wake of *Audita tremendi*, Pope Clement III (1187–1191) in 1188 equated the taking up of arms against Muslims in Spain with the same action in the Holy Land. In 1191 the new pope, Celestine III, paid particular attention to Iberia and the need for peacemaking among fractious local Christian rulers. The massive Christian defeat at Alarcos in 1195 got their attention.

The defeat of Christian forces at Alarcos by the Almohads under the caliph Abu Yusuf Ya'qub al-Mansur ("the Victorious," 1184–1199) led to a temporary reversal of the Christian position in the Iberian Peninsula. In response to this new threat, the kingdoms of León and Castile made peace, and a major campaign was declared against the infidel, soon formally elevated to the status of a crusade by Innocent III, who declared processions to be held in 1212 (above, No. 8) and temporarily suspended the Albigensian Crusade in preparation for the looming clash of forces in what would become known as the battle of Las Navas de Tolosa. Recruits from southern France and other regions, including a contingent temporarily diverted from the Albigensian Crusade, poured into the Iberian Peninsula to join armies mustered by the kings of Castile, Aragón, and Navarre. This vast muster presented the usual problems of provisioning, discipline, and outbreaks of violence against Jewish and Christian civilians. However the victory at Las Navas, rightly seen as a turning point in the relative power of Christian and Muslim forces, was soon broadcast in triumphal letters preserved in chronicles throughout Europe.

Joseph F. O'Callaghan, Reconquest and Crusade in Medieval Spain *(Philadelphia, 2003); Martín Alvira Cabrer, "'Le triomphe de la Croix: La bataille de Las Navas de Tolosa (16 juillet 1212)," in Laurent Albaret and Nicolas Gouzy, eds.,* Les grandes batailles méridionales: "Mieux vaut mort que vif vaincu" (1209–1271) *(Toulouse, 2005), 62–72; Damian J. Smith,* Innocent III and the Crown of Aragon: The Limits of Papal Authority *(Aldershot UK-Burlington VT, 2004); Damian Smith, "The Papacy, the Spanish Kingdoms and Las Navas de Tolosa,"* Anuario de Historia de la Iglesia 20 (2011), *157–178; Peter Linehan,* History and the Historians of Medieval Spain *(Oxford, 1993). On the problematic term and concept of* Reconquista, *see Adam J. Kosto, "Reconquest, Renaissance, and the Histories of Iberia, ca. 1000–1200," in Thomas F. X. Noble and John Van Engen, eds.,* European Transformations: The Long Twelfth Century *(Notre Dame IN, 2012), 93–116.*

An account of events leading up to the battle

THE STORY goes that in the city of Morocco there was a Saracen named Miramamolin[60] and he was a most mighty sovereign in treasure and peoples. And he held under his sway many great countries which spread from

Source: *Bernat Desclot,* Chronicle of the Reign of King Pedro III of Aragon, *trans. F. L. Critchlow, 2 vols. (Princeton NJ, 1928–1934), 1:31–32.*
    60. See above, No. 7, at n. 45.

Tripoli in Barbary as far as Tunis and Algiers and from Algiers to Ceuta and from Ceuta to Morocco. And he was ruler over all the land of Fez. . . . Moreover, he was heir in Spain to Seville and Córdoba and Jaén and Ubeda and to all the realm of Granada and of Murcia even as far as Valencia.

And this Saracen, Miramamolin, held a council with his wise men and told them that he had in mind to cross over into the land of Spain with all his hosts and to drive out the Christians from it, for it seemed to him that with his army he could conquer all of Christendom. And his counselors and chieftains agreed with that which he said and answered that he had spoken well and had made a good resolution, for there were more warriors in the fourth part of his dominions than in all the lands of the Christians. And so this Miramamolin made ready to cross over into Spain and sent his messengers throughout all his lands to all that knew how to wield arms, summoning them to cross over with him into Spain, for he desired to drive all the Christians out of Spain and to conquer all Rome.

And as soon as the peoples of the regions of Africa and of Organa and of Tunis and of all Barbary and of Spain learned these tidings of their lord's will, they counted their battles as already won and made ready to cross over into the land of Spain. And Miramamolin turned toward the land of Spain and from Tangiers, crossed the narrow sea and came to Seville. And there he tarried for the space of four years, for his armies were not yet assembled, nor could they all be made ready. And Miramamolin sent his envoys to the king of Castile and to the three kings of Spain, bidding them to hasten and depart from the land, or else he would wage war against them and all those who worshipped the cross.

And when the king of Castile and the other kings heard this message, they all foregathered in council and sent envoys to the pope and to the king of France and to the king of England and throughout Christendom to spread the tidings that Miramamolin had crossed over into Spain from Morocco with a multitude that no man could number and that he was about to wage war with all the Christians of the earth, to the end that they should give up their lands to him. When the pope had received and read the letters which the envoys had brought to him, he sent his cardinals and legates throughout all Christendom to make known this matter to all people and to absolve from their sins as many as would go forth to war.

An account from 'Abd al-Wahid al-Marrakushi's *History of the Almohads,* written in 1224

AFTER returning to Seville from this victory [at Salvatierra], the Amir Mu'minin[61] Abu 'Abd-Allah called up the people from the furthest reaches of the country and they assembled in great numbers. He left Seville at the beginning of 609 (June 1212) and marched to Jaén. He stayed there to make his arrangements and organize his troops. Alfonso—may God curse him—left Toledo with a vast army and proceeded to Cala-trava, which he besieged. The castle had been in Muslim hands since al-Mansur abu Yusuf (Ya'qub) conquered it following the great victory [of Alarcos]. The Muslims surrendered it to Alfonso after he had given them a safe-conduct. Thereupon, a large number of the Christians withdrew from Alfonso (may God curse him!) when he prevented them from killing the Muslims who were in the castle. They said, "You have only brought us along to help you conquer the country, and forbid us to plunder and kill the Muslims. We don't have any need of your company [if we're only going to act] in this way."

The battle of al'Iqab and the defeat of the Muslims

THE COMMANDER of the faithful left Jaén and encountered Alfonso at a place called al-'Iqab, near the castle called Hisn Salim. Alfonso drew up his army, arranged his men and launched a surprise attack on the Muslims, who were not prepared for battle. They were defeated and a great number of the Almohads were killed.

The main reason for this defeat was the divisions in the hearts of the Almohads. In the time of Abu Yusuf Ya'qub they drew their pay every four months without fail. But in the time of this Abu Abd-Allah, and especially during this particular campaign, their payment was in arrears. They attributed this to the viziers and rebelled in disgust. I have heard from several of them that they did not draw their swords nor train their spears, nor did they take any part in the preparations for battle. With this in mind, they fled at the first assault of the Franks.

This Abu Abd-Allah stood firm on that day like no king before him; were it not for his steadfastness the whole of that army would have been exterminated, either killed or captured. He then returned to Seville and

---

Source: Charles Melville and Ahmad Ubaydli, eds., Christians and Moors in Spain, *vol. 3,* Arabic Sources *(Warminster UK, 1992), 139–141.*

61. The title *amir al-mu'minin* (Latin: *Miramolinus*) or "commander of the faithful" was used by various Muslim rulers.

remained there until Ramadan (January 1213), when he crossed over to Marrakesh. . . . This great defeat of the Muslims took place on the Monday in mid Safar 609 (mid-July 1212).

Alfonso—God curse him!—pulled out of this place after he and his men had taken their fill of the chattels and possessions of the Muslims, and set off toward the towns of Bayyasa (Baeza) and Ubbadha (Ubeda). He found Baeza, or most of it, empty. He burnt its houses and destroyed its largest mosque. He then descended on Ubeda, where many of the defeated Muslims and the people of Baeza, as well as the town's own population, had collected. He invested it for thirteen days and then took it by force, killing and capturing and plundering. He and his men set aside as prisoners enough women and children to fill all the Christian territories. This was a greater blow to the Muslims than the defeat in battle.

A letter describing the success of Las Navas de Tolosa to Pope Innocent III, 1212

Probably drafted by a scribe of Archbishop Rodrigo Jiménez de Rada of Toledo, who accompanied Alfonso's army and had gone on a preaching tour in Italy, Provence, northern France, and the Rhineland to recruit for the campaign, this letter presents a carefully crafted image of the victory, attributing the defection of the majority of ultramontane forces to the heat and difficult terrain. The real reason for their defection appears to have been Alfonso of Castile's permitting the Muslim garrison at Calatrava to surrender and depart unharmed, a type of arrangement previously forbidden by Innocent III. The denial of booty and slaughter of nonbelievers to non-Iberian crusaders, many of them temporarily diverted from the Albigensian Crusade, led them to abandon the campaign in disgust, although Arnaud Amaury and others remained with the Iberian army.[62]

Peter II of Aragón later traded on his status as hero of Las Navas to convince Innocent III to temporarily cancel the indulgence for the Albigensian Crusade lest its demands hinder the progress of the campaigns in Spain and the new crusade Innocent was planning for the Holy Land. Peter even proposed that Raymond VII of Toulouse be permitted to reconcile himself to the church and clear himself of the taint of fostering heresy by going on crusade against the Muslims in Spain or the Holy Land. When Innocent's legates persuaded him that Peter had stretched the truth somewhat, Peter abandoned diplomacy and was killed when he opposed Simon de Montfort and his army in pitched battle at Muret in 1213.

Source: Colin Smith, ed., Christians and Moors in Spain, *vol. 2, 1195–1614 (Warminster UK, 1989), 14–25; PL 216:353.*

62. A complementary account of this campaign can be found in Joseph F. O'Callaghan, trans., *The Latin Chronicle of the Kings of Castile*, Medieval and Renaissance Texts and Studies 236 (Tempe AZ, 2002), 49–56.

To THE most Holy Father Innocent, Pope by the Grace of God, Alfonso, King of Castile and Toledo by the same, sends greetings, kissing your hands and feet. We know that your Holiness has not forgotten that we planned to do battle against the perfidy of the Saracens, and we reported to you humbly and devotedly by our messengers, begging your help in all things pertaining to a father and a lord, which help we recognize we have obtained in kindly and compassionate fashion from our loving Father.

For this reason we did not delay in sending our heralds (whom we thought most suitable for carrying this forward) out with our letters to certain parts of France, adding that we would provide, to the extent that could reasonably be sustained, the necessary costs of provisioning all those knights coming to join the campaign, and for all their serving-men to the degree that was fitting.

Hence it was that, when people heard of the remission of sins which you granted to those coming to join us, there arrived a vast number of knights from the regions beyond the Pyrenees, including the archbishops of Narbonne and Bordeaux and the bishop of Nantes. Those who came numbered up to two thousand knights with their squires, and up to ten thousand of their serving-men on horseback, with up to fifty thousand serving-men on foot, for all of whom we had to provide food. There came also our illustrious friends and relatives the kings of Aragón[63] and of Navarre in support and assistance of the catholic faith, with all their forces. We did not fail to provide for all of them, as we had promised through our heralds, while delaying for a time at Toledo as we waited for some of our men who were due to present themselves for the campaign, and it must be said that the costs for us and for our kingdom were extremely heavy on account of the huge numbers involved. We had to provide not only what we had promised, but also money and clothing, for almost everybody, both knights and serving-men, was in need. However, God, who gives increase to the fruits of justice, provided abundantly for us in accordance with the generosity of his grace, and gave us all that could be desired equitably and richly.

When both hosts were assembled, we set out on the road God has chosen for us, and coming to a certain fort named Malagn, amply defended, [we found that] the French, who had arrived there one day ahead of us, at once stormed and took it with God's help.

63. Peter II of Aragon.

Even though it had fallen to us to provide them generously with all necessities, they [the French] became too concerned with the difficulties of the terrain, which was empty and rather hot, and they wished to turn back and go home. At length, after much pressure from us and the king of Aragón, they continued as far as Calatrava, which was only some two leagues from the aforementioned fort, and we all—Castilians and Aragonese and French, each from his own side—began to attack it in God's name. The Saracens inside, realizing that they would not be able to hold off this army of God, negotiated about surrendering the place to us on condition that they should be allowed to leave unharmed, although without their belongings. We were unwilling to accept any such arrangement. The king of Aragón and the French held a council about it, and knew that the place was strongly fortified with walls and outer defenses, deep ditches and lofty towers, so that it could not be taken unless the walls were undermined and made to collapse; but this would be much to the detriment of the Friars of Salvatierra,[64] to whom it had earlier belonged, and could not be held [by them] in case of need. For this reason they most earnestly urged that the place be handed over to us whole and undamaged with the weapons and all the great stores of food that were in it, and that the Saracens should be allowed to leave empty-handed and without weapons.

So we, paying heed to their firm wishes in this matter, assented to their proposals, the conditions being that a half of all that there was inside should go the king of Aragón and the other half to the French, no part of it being retained by ourselves or our men. The French—still keen on the idea of going home, even though the Lord God was showing us grace and favor, and even though we were willing to go on providing them all with necessities in a generous way—driven as they were by the urge to go home, all together abandoned the cross, together with the archbishop of Bordeaux and the bishop of Nantes, even though there was certainly going to be a battle with the Saracens. And they all went off, except a very few who stayed on with the archbishop of Narbonne[65] and Tibaldo de Blazon, who was one of our liegemen, and also his men and certain other knights of Poitou. Those who remained, knights and serving-men,

---

64. This refers to the Order of Salvatierra, a native Iberian military order actively involved in the Reconquista.

65. That is, the Cistercian Arnaud Amaury, legate for the Albigensian Crusade. Here an ally of the Iberians, he vigorously opposed Peter II's interference in the Albigensian Crusade (1213).

amounted to scarcely one hundred and fifty; and of their foot soldiers, none at all remained.

Since the king of Aragón was waiting at Calatrava for certain knights of his and the king of Navarre, who had still not joined us, we set out with our men and arrived at a certain enemy castle called Alarcos. We took this castle, well-defended though it was, together with three others: Caracuel, Benevente, and Piedrabuena.

Going forward from there we reached Salvatierra, where the king of Aragón joined us, having brought only a small number of noble knights in his army, and the king of Navarre, who similarly was accompanied by a force of scarcely two hundred knights.

Since the sultan of the Saracens was close to us, we resolved not to attack Salvatierra, but, advancing toward the Saracen host, reached a mountain range which was impossible to cross except in certain places. Since on our side we were at the foot of the range, the Saracens advancing from the other side were able to occupy the crest, seeking to bar our passage. But our men went up bravely, because up to that time only a few Saracens had reached that area, and vigorously drove them off with God's help. And they took a fort called Ferral, which the Saracen ruler had built in order to bar our way.

Once this was taken, the army of the Lord was able to go on up to the mountain peaks in safety, but it was hard going because of the lack of water and the barrenness of the place. Seeing that they could not block that pass, the Saracens occupied another exceptionally narrow and difficult passage on the downward slope; indeed it was such that a thousand men could readily defend it against the greatest army on earth. At the far end of it lay the whole Saracen army with their tents already pitched.

Since we could not stay there because of the lack of water, nor advance because of the difficulty of the pass, certain of our men advised that we should go back down the mountain and look for another pass some distance away. But we, concerned for the danger to the faith and disgrace to our person, refused to accept this advice, preferring to die for the faith on the difficult terrain of the pass rather than seek an easier way or back down from an affair which concerned the faith, in whatsoever fashion it might be.

When we had thus strengthened our resolve, our barons—who were to strike the first blows in the battle—heard of the suggestion of a certain shepherd, whom God by his command sent to us, that in that very spot another relatively easy passage existed. In a certain place close to the enemy camp, although barren and dry, they pitched camp, since the Saracens did not know of this pass. When the Saracen army realized what was happening, they advanced in order to stop the camp being established. Our men, even though few, defended themselves bravely.

We and the kings of Aragón and Navarre waited, fully armed, with our men in the place where we had first halted, which was on the crest of the mountain, until the whole army of the Lord safely reached the spot where our advance patrols had marked out the camp. Thanks be to God, it happened that although the way was difficult and waterless, also rocky and wooded, we lost none of our men. This was Saturday, the fourteenth of July. Late that day the Saracens, observing that we had safely erected all our tents, drew up their battle lines and approached our camp, indulging in skirmishing rather as in a tournament, as a prelude to battle.

Very early the next day, a Sunday, the Saracens came up with their huge army arrayed in battle lines. Wishing to study the numbers of their men and their disposition and attitude and to find out how they behaved in all circumstances, we took advice from our expert and seasoned men, and resolved to wait until the following day, a Monday. In these circumstances, we posted cavalrymen and foot soldiers so that the enemy should not in any way be able to attack to the ends of our line, and this did not happen thanks to God's grace.

The following day, a Monday, we all armed and set out in God's name, in full array, to do battle with them for the catholic faith. The enemy occupied certain eminences, places very steep and difficult to climb because of the woods which lay between us and them, and some very deep gorges cut by streams, all of which presented a major impediment to us and greatly aided the enemy. Then indeed he by whom and in whom and through whom all things are miraculously done, directed his army against his enemies and our front ranks and some of the middle ranks cut down many lines of the enemy who were stationed on the lower eminences by the power of the Lord's cross.

When our men reached the last of their lines, consisting of a huge number of soldiers, among whom was the king of Carthage, desperate fighting ensued among the cavalrymen, infantrymen, and archers. Placed in terrible danger, our people were scarcely able to resist any longer. Realizing that the fighting was becoming altogether impossible for them, we then started a cavalry charge, preceded by the Lord's cross and our banner with the image of the Holy Virgin and her Son imposed upon our device. Since we had already resolved to die for the faith of Christ, as soon as we witnessed the shame being suffered by the cross of Christ and the image of his Mother when the Saracens assailed them with stones and arrows, we broke their line with its vast numbers of men, even though the Saracens resisted bravely in the battle and stood solidly around their lord.

Our Lord slew a great multitude of them with the sword of the cross. Then the sultan with a few of his men turned in flight. For a time others of the enemy bore the thrust of our attacks, but after the heavy loss of life, the rest soon turned and fled. We followed up the pursuit until nightfall and killed more in that rout than we had in battle. In this way the battle of the Lord was triumphantly won by God alone and through God alone. To God be the honor and the glory, who granted the victory of his cross through Jesus Christ our Lord.

The Saracen horsemen had numbered one hundred eighty-five thousand, as we afterward learned in a true account from certain servants of the sultan whom we took prisoner. The foot soldiers were innumerable. On their side there fell in battle one hundred thousand armed men, perhaps more, according to the estimates of the Saracens we later captured. Of the army of the Lord only some twenty or thirty Christians fell in our whole host—a fact not to be mentioned without the most fervent thanksgiving, and one scarcely to be believed, unless it be thought a miracle. What cause for joy and thanksgiving! Yet there is one cause for regret here: that so few in such a vast army went to Christ as martyrs.

In order to show how immense the enemy's numbers were, when our army rested for two days after the battle in the enemy camp, for all the fires which were needed to cook food and make bread and other things, no other wood was needed than that of the enemy arrows and spears which were lying about, and even then we burned scarcely half of them. Even though our army was running short of food and other supplies, because we had spent so long in bare and barren countryside, we found such an abundance of food and weapons, as also of warhorses and beasts of burden, that our men, by taking as many of them as they wished, still left more out of the huge number of animals than those they took.

On the third day we advanced to certain enemy fortresses—Vilches, Baos, and Tolosa—and captured them at once. Eventually we reached two towns, Baeza and Ubeda, the largest on this side of the sea except for Córdoba and Seville. We found Baeza already destroyed. A great number of people had fled from all the nearby settlements to Ubeda, because it was exceptionally strong both on account of its situation and on account of its defenses. Since the people knew that no other city of that size had been stormed or taken by the emperor or by any other Hispanic ruler, they thought they would be safe there. However, by God's grace we captured Ubeda in a short time, and, since we did not have enough people to settle it, we razed it to the ground. Some sixty thousand Saracens perished there; some we killed, others were taken as captives into the service of the Christians and of the monasteries which needed to be repaired in the border regions.

We ordered all this to be set down in writing for you, most Holy Father, earnestly offering all the thanks we can for the aid of all Christendom and humbly asking you whom God has chosen for the highest rank among his priests, to offer up a sacrifice with all praise to him for the salvation of our people.

In the papal registers the following prayer appears at the end of the letter, which was forwarded to many recipients in Europe.

PRAYER: Omnipotent and merciful God, you who resist the proud yet give grace to the humble, we announce to you with fitting proclamations of praise and faithful acts of thanksgiving that in renewing miracles of old, you granted a glorious victory over the faithless peoples to the Christian people, and we humbly beseech you that what you wondrously began you mercifully continue to the praise and glory of your holy name, which is devoutly called upon by us your servants. Through our Lord Jesus Christ, etc.

10. The Children's Crusade, 1212–1213

Although older histories viewed the crusade of the *pueri* as either an eschatological self-sacrifice perpetuated by children or an outbreak of mass hysteria, recent studies have suggested that the *pueri* were not necessarily all children. From the First Crusade onward, there was a continuous tradition of actual or attempted popular participation in the crusade, often sparked by itinerant preachers who stressed apostolic poverty. In the spring of 1212, a combination of intensive recruiting for various crusades since 1187 and the more immediate stimulus of processions instituted prior to the battle of Las Navas de Tolosa (above, Nos. 8 and 9) appears to have sparked movements in Germany and northern France that evolved into a popular crusade. Its adherents included men and women, children, mature adults, and the aged, who were described by chroniclers by terms including *pueri* (literally, "children," but figuratively, "the powerless"), the poor, and shepherds. These terms suggest that many of the participants were dependents, persons under the age of legal majority, or those too poor to set up their own households working as day laborers who interpreted crusade preachers' condemnations of the sinful and exhortations to sacrifice one's possessions for Christ in an act of voluntary poverty as meaning that since the powerful had failed to recover the Holy Land, the literally poor had been chosen by God to do so. The movement also expressed the frustration felt by many who had witnessed the failure of the Third and Fourth Crusades to retake Jerusalem and been denied personal participation in these expeditions due to their age, sex, or poverty and military leaders' fear of burdening the army with too many noncombatants. Traveling in processions with liturgical crosses and solemn songs, the *pueri* and their leaders proceeded to Italy, but the movement disintegrated when the pilgrims failed to find passage overseas. The excerpts from chronicles below reflect the attempts of contemporary and later chroniclers to explain the motivation and fate of its adherents. What is certain is that the popular enthusiasm of the crusade of the *pueri* influenced Innocent III's decision in 1213 to ensure that every member of Christendom could potentially participate in the crusade through traveling to the Holy Land in person, funding a substitute or making a monetary contribution, or participating in the monthly liturgical processions and daily masses intended to earn divine favor for the crusade.

Gary Dickson, The Children's Crusade: Medieval History, Modern Mythistory *(Basingstoke UK-New York, 2008); Peter Raedts, "The Children's Crusade of 1212,"* Journal of Medieval History *3 (1977), 279–323.*

An account of the French movement by an anonymous chronicler from Laon, writing before 1219

An English Premonstratensian canon living in France, the anonymous chronicler of Laon voraciously described the varied religious movements and political events of his time in his *Chronicon universale*, which ended in the year 1219. His is the only surviving contemporary account of the career of Stephen of Cloyes, the erstwhile leader of the French branch of the *pueri* movement.

THAT same year [1212], in the month of June, a certain boy [*puer*] named Stephen, a shepherd by profession, from a village called Cloyes near the town of Vendôme, used to claim that the Lord appeared to him in the guise of a poor pilgrim and accepted bread from him and entrusted to him letters to be carried to the king of the Franks. When this boy had come, together with shepherds of a similar age, nearly thirty thousand people flocked to him from various parts of France. While the same boy

Source: Anonymous of Laon, Chronica, *ed.* RHGF *18:715.*

tarried at Saint-Denis, the Lord used to accomplish many powerful things through him, as many testified. And there were also in many more places many other *pueri* whom vulgar mobs held in great reverence because they believed them to also be wonder workers. To these a host of *pueri* joined themselves, as if to advance to the holy boy Stephen under their leadership. All of them acknowledged him as their master and leader. Finally, after the king consulted with the masters of Paris regarding the mustering of the *pueri*, they returned to their own lands at his command, and so their youthful devotion was as easily curbed as it had been aroused. Yet it seemed to many that through such innocents assembled by their own will, the Lord would accomplish something great and new upon the earth, but it proved far otherwise.

An account of the German movement by a contemporary chronicler from the Cologne region

This anonymous chronicler from Cologne yields valuable insight into the composition of the Rhineland *pueri*, who appear to have attracted a wider range of ages and social groups to their ranks than the followers of Stephen of Cloyes. A bustling city, Cologne became a mustering point for the Rhineland *pueri* partly because it housed the prestigious pilgrimage shrine of the Three Kings, whose peregrinations in search of the infant Christ and association with the Holy Land meant that they were invoked as patron saints for pilgrims.

IN THIS very year [1212] there happened a thing wonderful enough and indeed greatly to be marveled at, because it was unheard of in this age. For around Easter and Pentecost, from every part of Germany and France, with no one exhorting or preaching, driven by I know not what spirit, many thousands of *pueri*, from six years of age to full manhood, went off against the will of their parents, relations, and friends. Some of them abandoned their plows or wagons which they were driving, others the flocks which they were grazing, or if they had anything else in their hands, they suddenly ran off, one after the other. And they signed themselves with crosses; and so in groups of twenty or fifty or a hundred, they began to travel toward Jerusalem with banners raised high.

Whenever they were asked by many by whose counsel or by whose exhortation they had set forth in this manner, particularly when not many

Source: Chronicae regiae Coloniensis continuatio prima (1175–1220), *ed. G. Waitz,* MGH SS *vol. 24 (Hannover-Leipzig, 1879), 17–18.*

years before now numerous kings, even more noblemen, and innumerable commoners had arrived in the Holy Land in a powerful host and with their business unaccomplished had turned back, and that they indeed were still of a youthful age and possessed neither strength nor power for having attempted this kind of exploit, they briefly responded: that in this they were submitting to divine command and for that reason they themselves would undertake with a willing and easy spirit whatever God wished to be accomplished by them. But when they had progressed a little on their journey, some were turned back at Metz, some at Piacenza, some in fact at Rome. Indeed others reached Marseilles, but whether they crossed the sea or not or what their final end was is uncertain; nonetheless one thing is certain, that from the many thousands who went forth, scarcely a few returned home.

Excerpt from a crusade appeal delivered in Paris circa 1213

While the anonymous chronicler from Laon claimed that the masters at Paris had advised Philip Augustus of France to send the *pueri* home (perhaps because their project lacked leadership and funding), the movement nonetheless resonated with many of the goals dear to the hearts of the Paris-trained reformers. The *pueri*'s emphasis on poverty (spiritual or literal) and on triumph through moral right rather than military right is echoed in many of the crusading appeals delivered by Paris masters circa 1213–1217. Preserved as jotted notes by anonymous copyists, these appeals demonstrate the intimate way in which the moral reform of Western society was believed to be essential to the success of the crusade, as essential as adequate funding and recruiting.

The following excerpt is found in a sermon that appears to have been delivered in Paris circa 1213. The sermon urges its audience to take the cross and to win victory through shunning pride, anger, murmuring, and lust (characteristic vices of the upper levels of society, although other levels also come in for their share of moral criticism) and instead embracing poverty, tribulation, humility, rejoicing, patience, and temperance (including moderation in possessions). Referring to the importance of liturgical intervention through invoking Old Testament examples, where, through the songs of the clergy the Israelites' enemies were defeated, the sermon warns that the time of the Antichrist appears to be approaching, and the world is entering its old age. Through the images of the greening tree and the dawn of the final age where triumph over the Antichrist's forces would come through spiritual men marked not by worldly power but inner poverty, the preacher appears to have sought to reclaim the Joachite and Sibylline imagery appropriated by the *pueri* and the recently condemned Amalrician heretics (1210). In a sermon clearly addressed to both ecclesiastics and laypersons, the preacher urges his audience to set an example by taking the cross so that others will follow them. He also warns them that it is God's power and perseverance and lack of internal division that will win the day rather than military might alone. Clearly the preacher was attempting to make sense of the *pueri* movement and channel some of its spiritual vigor into recruiting for what would become the Fifth Crusade.

Nicole Bériou, L'avènement des maîtres de la Parole, 2 vols. (Paris, 1998), 1:58–70, 94–96; 2:676.

HOWEVER, some will arise from the whole, that is, those signed with the cross, both true servants and sons of God. And it is probable that many will come. For when indeed the tree begins to become green[66] near the ground, this is the sign that the spouse will ascend the branches [cf Song 7:7–8]. The tree is the Christian people, the land is that place in which Christ was raised up for the faith, those nearer to this land are the innocent children [*parvuli*] who the other year were signed with the cross, after those, the poor laypersons and clerics who have already become green through taking the cross who are, as it were, closer to Christ. And so it is likely that these persons will be followed by other greater persons.

Albert, abbot of the Premonstratensian canonry of Stade

Born in the late twelfth century, Albert composed his annals from about 1232 to 1256, while abbot of the Premonstratensian canonry of Stade near Hamburg in northern Germany. His relatively neutral account of the *pueri* was composed a generation later, but may have been based on oral reports of eyewitnesses.

[1212]. AROUND the same time *pueri* from all the villages and cities of every province flocked with eager steps toward the overseas regions, without a rector, without a commander. And when it was asked of them to what end they so hastily proceeded, they answered: "To Jerusalem, to obtain the Holy Land." Many of them were confined by their relations, but in vain, because, after breaking out from their enclosures or walled rooms, they went into exile. When Pope Innocent III heard news of them, lamenting, he said: "These *pueri* put us to shame, because while

Source for crusade appeal: Paris, Bibliothèque Nationale, nouv. lat. acq. 999, fols. 233ra–234va, here fol. 234rb.

Source for Albert: Annales Stadensis, ed. I. M. Lappenberg, MGH SS, vol. 16 (Hannover-Leipzig, 1859), 355.

66. Literally *urescere*, which means "to burn" The scribe may have accidentally substituted "to burn" (*urescere*) for "to turn green" (*virescere*) by mentally associating the Sibylline and Joachite image of the greening tree with the burning bush given as a sign to Moses (Ex 3:2) that the Israelites would go out from Egypt to the promised land. Some chroniclers suggested that the *pueri* identified with the Israelites of the Old Testament to the extent that some believed they would cross the Mediterranean with dry feet as the Israelites had the Red Sea.

we sleep, they hasten to the recovery of the Holy Sepulcher." And yet what became of them remains unknown. But many returned [home], and when they were asked the reason for their journey, they said that they did not know. Furthermore, around the same time, naked women, saying nothing, used to run together through villages and cities.

An account from Trier

An anonymous author who probably belonged to the Benedictine monastery of Saint Eucharius contributed to the Trier chronicle from about 1190 to 1242. His account of the *pueri*, perhaps based on personal observation or eyewitness reports, sheds light on the genesis of the movement once it reached Trier and on its charismatic leader Nicholas. Probably mixing surmise with mythologizing, he speculates on the movement's demise with the benefit of hindsight.

[THERE occurred an event] wondrous and unheard of throughout the ages. For, as if by divine inspiration, *pueri* flocked from all the towns and villages of Germany,[67] and after gathering in each separate place, united into throngs and undertook the march toward Jerusalem as if they were going to take back the Holy Land. The head and leader of this undertaking was a certain Nicholas, a young man [*puer*] from Cologne, who bore over himself a symbol like a cross, which took the form of a thau,[68] which he used to assert was a sign of the sanctity and miraculousness he possessed. Nor was it easy to make out what kind of material or metal it was made of. And when the *pueri* came to Brindisi, the local bishop, suspecting deception, would not allow them to cross the sea. In fact, they were sold to the pagans by Nicholas's father, and so they were lured by the wickedness of demons, and because of this both the boy himself perished and his father met with a wicked end at Cologne. Moreover, most of the *pueri* perished, for those who had abundantly supplied those setting out gave nothing to those returning. After a few years the preaching of the cross arose and the people of God became fired up in aid of the Holy Land and rushed in throngs to take the cross in an extraordinary manner. And this resulted in a powerful expedition to the overseas regions. In this

---

Source: Gestorum Treverorum, continuatio *quarta*, ed. G. *Waitz*, MGH SS, *vol. 24 (Hannover-Leipzig, 1879), 398–399.*

67. The term used is *Teutonia*, which is often used to describe German-speaking regions that do not precisely conform to modern-day Germany.

68. This refers to a cross shaped like the Greek letter "t" or "thau." Preachers for the crusade commonly invoked Ez. 9:4, which described the spiritually elect being signed with a "thau," an image the *pueri* appear to have appropriated for themselves here.

expedition, George, count of Wied, brother of the archbishop of Trier, played a leading role.[69]

An account from the monastery of Marbach

Written perhaps after 1230, this account comes from a continuation added to the annals of Marbach, an Augustinian abbey in Alsace, a region through which the *pueri* passed. The annalist's hostile account nonetheless provides a valuable portrait of the movement's denouement.

AT THE same time, a certain vain expedition came to pass when *pueri* and foolish persons snatched up the sign of the cross without any discernment, motivated more by curiosity than concern for their salvation. For young men and girls of either sex, not only minors, but also adults, the married with the virgins, traveling with empty moneybags, used to proceed not only throughout all of *Alemannia* [Germany], but even through parts of Gaul and Burgundy. Nor could their relations or friends hold them back by any means, instead, they embraced that journey with single-minded exertions, to such an extent that far and wide through villages and fields, casting aside their tools and whatever they held in their hands at the time, they joined those passing through. And just as we are often and easily as a crowd ready to believe such novelties, there were many who judged that these things were done not from fickleness of mind, but through divine inspiration and from a certain piety, so that they used to aid them by giving them money, provisions, and necessities.

However, when clerics and certain other persons who were of more sound mind used to speak against them and condemned that journey as vain and useless, the laity used to vehemently oppose them, saying that the clergy were unbelievers and that they were opposing the undertaking out of envy and avarice rather than for the sake of truth and justice. But because every undertaking which is begun without weighty deliberation and without vigorous discussion cannot come to a good end, after this obtuse multitude reached the region of Italy they scattered and dispersed throughout its cities and towns, and many of them were engaged as male and female servants by the inhabitants. Others are said to have reached the sea and to have been lured off by sailors and mariners and transported

Source: Annales Marbacenses, *ed. H. Bloch, MGH SS, vol. 9 (Hannover-Leipzig, 1907)*, 82–83.

69. That is, the Fifth Crusade. For George of Wied's role in the Fifth Crusade, see Part III, Nos. 20 and 21 below.

to other provinces of distant lands. In fact, when a remnant arrived in Rome, they realized that they could make no progress seeing that they lacked the support of any authority, and in the end, understood that their work was worthless and unprofitable. Nonetheless, they by no means were absolved from the vow of the cross, with the exception of young people under the age of discretion and those weighed down by old age.[70]

And so, cheated and confounded, they began to head back, and those previously accustomed to traveling through the land in crowds and never without a song of encouragement among their ranks, now returned singly and in silence. Barefoot and starving, they were held in derision by everyone, because many virgins had been raped and had lost the flower of their virtue. In the same year an expedition of those signed with the cross was formed by the duke of Austria and certain other barons of the land and other men of various conditions, in aid of the count of Montfort for opposing the Albigensians, that is, the heretics from the land of Saint-Gilles, together with the *routiers* or *coterelli*, at the personal command and instigation of Pope Innocent III, who enjoined them to perform that journey for the remission of sins.[71]

Alberic of Trois-Fontaines views the *pueri* in retrospect

A well-informed and widely read monk of the French Cistercian monastery of Trois-Fontaines, Alberic wrote his chronicle between 1227 and 1241. It was later given minor additions by a monk from Neufmoûtier near Huy, a religious house whose founder was claimed to be Peter the Hermit, the leader of the popular elements of the First Crusade. The report of the Children's Crusade follows an account of recruiting for a crusade against the Albigensians that resulted in a large group of reinforcements going to aid Simon de Montfort in southern France in 1211/1212. Alberic's account illustrates the next generation's mythohistorical attempts to give meaning to the movement of the *pueri*, introducing two new archvillains to explain the disappearance of so many of its participants.

IN THIS year [1212] an expedition of children occurred, which gathered, wondrously enough, from every direction. At first they came from the

Source: Alberic of Trois-Fontaines, Chronica, ed. P. Scheffer-Boichorst, MGH SS, vol. 23 (Hannover-Leipzig, 1874), 893–894.

70. The annals of the Austrian abbey of Admont claimed that Nicholas fulfilled his vow during the Fifth Crusade, serving for two years before returning home unharmed (*MGH SS* 9:579–593, here p. 592).

71. Canon 27 of the Third Lateran Council (1179) had called on princes to suppress heresy and the ravages of roving bands of mercenaries (the *routiers* and *coterelli* in the text above) and the two became quickly associated in propaganda for the Albigensian crusades.

regions surrounding the village of Vendôme near Paris. And when they had reached about thirty thousand, they came to Marseilles, as if they were going to cross the sea to fight against the Saracens. However, the rogues and wicked men associated with them so corrupted the entire army that some perished upon the sea, others were sold, and only a few from so great a multitude returned home. The pope nonetheless commanded that thereafter everyone who had escaped from them should cross the sea in the same way as those who had taken the cross when they had reached the age of majority.

Now the betrayers of these children were merchants from Marseilles called Iron Hugh and William the Swine.[72] Since they were masters of ships, they ought to have conveyed them overseas without charging them, as they had promised them. And they filled seven very large ships with the *pueri,* and when they had traveled for two days upon the sea a tempest arose near the island of Saint Peter at the Rock,[73] which is called "the Recluses," and two ships went down and all the *pueri* in those two ships were drowned. And so it is said that after some years Pope Gregory IX had a church dedicated to the New Innocents built on the same island and installed twelve prebendaries. The bodies of the children which the sea cast up in that place are kept in that church and are displayed, still incorrupt, to pilgrims.

However, the betrayers brought the rest of the five ships to Bougie[74] and Alexandria[75] and there all the children were sold to merchants and Saracen rulers. The caliph bought four hundred of them, all clerics, as his portion, because in this manner he wanted to separate them from the others living among them. Yet he treated the priests and all the others very decently, as was his custom. This is the caliph of whom we related above that he studied in Paris in the habit of cleric so that he might dedicate himself fully to learning those things which are ours, and this man already had recently omitted to sacrifice bread to camels.

And so in the same year in which the *pueri* were enslaved, the rulers of the Saracens gathered at Baghdad and eighteen children were killed in

---

72. Alberic appears to have seized upon the names of two actual individuals to create his villainous merchants. Hugo Ferreus worked for the viscount of Marseilles, while William Porcus was a Genoese captain who served as one of Frederick II's admirals before his alienation from the emperor caused him to flee to Sicily in 1221. See Dickson, *Children's Crusade*, 145.

73. The island of San Pietro near Sardinia.

74. A port on the coast of the then-Muslim-ruled Algeria.

75. One of the primary ports of Egypt.

their presence, subjected to various kinds of martyrdom because they would by no means abandon the Christian faith. However, the remainder were diligently raised up in slavery. One of the aforementioned clerics whom the caliph had bought as his portion was present and saw this and faithfully recounted that he heard none whatsoever of the children apostatize from Christianity. And the two aforementioned betrayers, Iron Hugh and William the Swine, later came to the ruler of the Saracens in Sicily called Mirabellus and wanted to plot treason against the emperor Frederick with him. But the emperor triumphed over them, the Lord granting, and Mirabellus and his two sons and these two traitors were hanged upon the same gallows. And he who related this added that eighteen years after this expedition Mascemuch of Alexandria was still faithfully guarding seven hundred of the betrayed *pueri*, no longer children, but adults of more mature age.

A letter of Honorius III concerning a surviving *puer*, August 19, 1220

Precious evidence of one *puer* who survived to regret his crusade vow is recorded in the official registers of the letters of Pope Honorius III (1216–1227). Preparations for the Fifth Crusade meant that Otto was feeling pressure to either seek dispensation from or make good his unfulfilled crusade vow, which would have been considered binding if he had made it when he was fourteen years or older. Dispensation from crusade vows was typically reserved to the pope and his designated agents, and Otto appears to have sought the spiritual and financial help of the patriarch of Aquileia in making his petition to Rome. His name indicates that he may have been one of the surviving Rhineland *pueri* who journeyed to Italy and remained there after the movement disintegrated. He may well have been a cleric in minor orders or a student before taking his vow. Later documents describe an Otto who became a canon of and master of the scholars at Saint Felix before becoming an official under the patriarch of Aquileia. If this Otto was the same as the Otto of the petition, his dispensation paved the way for a successful church career.[76]

To THE patriarch of Aquileia and Henry, canon of Cividale del Friuli. Otto, a poor scholar, intimated to you in his petition that some time ago he imprudently assumed the cross with a host of other *pueri*, hoping that they could cross the sea with dry feet. For this reason he humbly supplicated you that since from that time he has put down the cross which he

Source: Vatican City, Archivio Segreto, Reg. Vat. 11, fol. 13r, Pressutti no. 2627.
76. Dickson, *Children's Crusade*, 121–123.

took up in this manner nor has he afterward resumed it, he fears in his conscience that for this reason we would deign to advise you that he be obliged to cross the sea. For this reason we commit to your discernment through a papal commission that if the aforesaid account is proved to be the truth, by our supporting authority you may render him freed and absolved from this kind of fear and labor as long as he is not bound to his original vow for another reason.

PART II
Crusade and Council, 1213–1215

The Fourth Lateran Council, first announced in the letter *Vineam Domini* of 1213, took place in the Lateran basilica and palace complex in Rome from November 11 to November 30, 1215. Not only did it represent the culmination of the work of the legislative councils of the twelfth century, but it incorporated the intellectual and scientific developments in the fields of theology and canon law that had taken place in the schools as well as the strong claims for papal authority that had grown up at the same time in both fields. The council also, as Innocent had said in *Vineam Domini*, attempted to fulfill the two great aims of his pontificate, the moral reform of the church and the recovery of the Holy Land.

It was an immensely large church council, including 71 primates, 412 bishops, 802 abbots and priors, and thousands of other clergy—a total of around 5,000 clerical personnel, including the primate of the Maronites, the troubadour-turned-bishop of Toulouse Fulk of Marseilles in the company of Saint Domingo de Guzmán, representatives of the patriarchs of Antioch and Alexandria, and representatives of Frederick II, the emperor Henry of Constantinople, and those of the kings of England, France, Aragón, Hungary, Cyprus, and Jerusalem. Only two bishops were to be left behind in each province, and every ecclesiastical community that was not attending had to send a delegate. The number of visitors was so great that the council was usually referred to simply as "the Great Council." The presence of the participants put a great material strain on the resources of the city of Rome and surrounding regions, since Rome itself had a population of only around 35,000 people in 1215. Innocent III also had to place a limit on the numbers of staff and servants each prelate might bring with him to Rome.

The council had much other business besides the decisions on dogma that it made. The problem of the Albigensian Crusade loomed large, since both Raymond VII of Toulouse and others involved were also present in Rome. So did the problem of the dispute between Otto IV and the young Frederick II over the empire. In the midst of the council Innocent III led a long and quite spectacular procession to reconsecrate the church of Santa Maria in Trastevere. These aspects and others made the council vividly memorable to those who had witnessed it and fascinating to those who read or heard their reports.

In this section we use two of Innocent III's three letters about the council from 1213, *Quia maior* (No. 11) and *Pium et sanctum* (No. 12), circulated widely to virtually all the spiritual and temporal leaders in Europe, as well as a recruiting sermon probably preached between 1213 and 1217 (No. 13), Innocent's responses to questions of his representatives on crusade matters (No. 14), Roger Wendover's short and secondhand but textually important account (No. 15), and canon 71, the crusade canon, of the Fourth Lateran Council, *Ad liberandam* (No. 16).

11. Innocent III, *Quia maior*, 1213

In April 1213, the papal curia drafted three letters setting forth the plans of Pope Innocent III for a new crusade and summoning a general council to be held in 1215. The longest of these letters, known as *Quia maior* from the opening words of its Latin text, was devoted to planning for the crusade. A second letter, *Pium et sanctum*, issued at the same time (No. 12 below) appointed preachers to work on behalf of the crusade, while *Vineam Domini* (discussed above, Introduction) announced the purpose and date of the council. Innocent devoted great care to the preparation for the crusade. His earlier experience with the Fourth Crusade and the troubles of the ongoing Albigensian Crusade made it all the more important that there should be detailed planning and continuing supervision. *Quia maior* was an effort to codify the experience that various popes had gleaned during the previous century. Yet, this document remained tentative in some of its features, leaving important questions to be settled at the council. For this reason, it should be read in conjunction with *Ad liberandam*, canon 71 of the Fourth Lateran Council (below, No. 16) and *Post miserabile* (above, No. 2).

BECAUSE there is now greater need than ever before to provide for the needs of the Holy Land, and from that assistance it is hoped that greater than ever benefit will result, behold, we cry out to you with a new summons. We cry out on behalf of him, made obedient to God the Father even to the death on the cross, who, while dying on the cross, called out in a loud voice, crying out that he might save us from the torture of eternal death [Mt 27:50; Lk 23:46]. And he cried out also for himself and said, "If anyone wishes to follow me, he should deny himself, and take up his cross and follow me" [Mt 16:24]. It was as if he said more clearly: He who wishes to follow me to the crown, let him hasten to the battle which now is proposed for the testing of all. For almighty God could, if he wished, defend that land entirely so that it would not be handed over to the hands of the enemy. He could also, if he wished, free it quite easily from the hands of the enemy, since nothing can resist his will [Rom 9:19].

But, since evil now abounds [Rom 5:20] and the charity of many has become cold [Mt 24:12], in order to arouse his faithful from the dream of death to a desire for life, God has proposed a task for them in which he can test their faith like gold in a furnace [1 Pt 1:7], presenting them

Source: PL, 216:817–821.

with an opportunity for salvation, indeed a reason for salvation so that those who strive mightily for him might be happily crowned by him, and those who are unwilling at a time of such necessity to become his servants will merit a just sentence of damnation on the final day of the last judgment. O how great a benefit will result from this cause; how many, converted to penitence, have handed themselves over by service of the Crucified for the liberation of the Holy Land, as if by suffering martyrdom they have obtained the crown of the glory [cf. 1 Pt 5:4; 1 Thes 2:19], who would perhaps have perished in their iniquities entangled in carnal desires and earthly seductions.

This is an old device of Jesus Christ that he deigned to renew in these days for the salvation of his faithful. For if some temporal king was deprived of his kingdom by his enemies, if his vassals did not only sacrifice their property but also their persons, would he not when he recovered his lost kingdom condemn them as unfaithful and devise unthinkable tortures against them, by which he might evilly ruin the evil men? Thus the King of kings, our Lord Jesus Christ, who brought body and soul and other goods to you, will condemn you for the vice of ingratitude and the crime of infidelity if you should fail to aid him with the result that he lost his kingdom that he bought with the price of his blood.

Know then that whoever denies aid to the Redeemer in this time of his need is culpably harsh and harshly culpable. For, also, insofar as, according to the divine command, he loves his neighbor as himself and for him [Lv 19:18; Mt 19:19], he knows that his brethren in faith and in the Christian name are imprisoned by the faithless Saracens in a cruel prison and endure the harsh yoke of slavery, he does not expend the efficacious work for their liberation, that the Lord spoke of in the Gospel. "Do to others whatever you wish them to do to you" [Mt 7:12]. Or perhaps you do not know that many thousands of Christians are held in prison and slavery by them and they suffer countless torments?

And, indeed, the Christian people possessed almost all the Saracen provinces until after the time of Saint Gregory.[1] But after that time, a certain son of perdition, the pseudo-prophet Muhammad, arose, and he seduced many away from the truth with carnal enticements and pleasures. Even though his perfidy has lasted until the present, still we trust in the Lord who has now made a good sign that the end of this beast, whose

---

1. Gregory I (590–604), whose writings greatly influenced Innocent III.

number, according to John's Apocalypse [Apoc 13:18], counts 666, of which now almost six hundred years are completed, approaches.[2]

Certainly, besides the earlier great and serious injuries heaped on our Redeemer for our offenses by the faithless Saracens, recently, to the confusion of the Christian name, they built a fortress on Mount Tabor, where Christ showed the nature of his future glorification to his disciples. By this, they think that they may be able to occupy the nearby city of Acre quite easily, and then, without any resistance, invade the rest of this land, since it is almost devoid of men and wealth. Therefore, dearly beloved sons, changing dissensions and fratricidal jealousies into treaties of peace and goodwill, let us gird ourselves to come to the aid of the Crucified, not hesitating to risk property and life for him who laid down his life and shed his blood for us; likewise certain and sure, that if you should be truly penitent, through this temporal labor, as if by a certain shortcut, you will arrive at eternal life.

For we, empowered by the mercy of almighty God and the apostles Peter and Paul, from that power which God gave to us, although unworthy, of binding and loosing, grant the full forgiveness of their sins to all, contrite in heart and having confessed orally, who undertake this labor in their own persons and at their own expense, and we promise an increase of eternal salvation in payment of the just. But, to those who do not make the journey in person, but send suitable men at their expense according to their ability and income, and to whose also who even at the expense of another, make the journey personally, we grant the full pardon of their sins. And we desire and concede that all who donate a suitable amount from their wealth for the support of the Holy Land may share in this remission according to the amount of their support and the depth of their devotion.

We also receive the persons and property of all who take the cross under the protection of Saint Peter and our own, and they are also under that of archbishops, bishops, and all prelates of the church. We decree that they and their goods should be maintained whole and safe until there is certainty about their return or their death. If anyone should act contrary to this, ecclesiastical censure should be levied without any appeal by the prelates of the church. If any about to set out owe loans, sworn by oath, at interest, we order their creditors to be forced by the same requirement

---

2. The apocalyptic theme was closely associated with the idea of crusade. See below, Parts IV and VI.

to remit the loans sworn to them and to stop the payment of interest. But if any creditors should force them to pay interest, we order them by the same instruction to pay it back. But we order that Jews to be forced to pay back their interest by the secular power, and, until they remit it, contact with all Christ's faithful, under penalty of excommunication, both in goods and other matters should be denied them.

But so that aid to the Holy Land may be more easily shared among several individuals, we ask each and all, through the Father, Son, and Holy Spirit, confessing one single truth, one eternal God, in place of Christ, for Christ, to divide among themselves by archbishops and bishops, abbots and priors, and the chapters of cathedrals and conventual churches, as well as cities, villas, and towns, a certain number of fighters with expenses necessary for three years according to their abilities. And if one cannot fulfill this, let several be joined together as one, because we hope that persons will not be lacking if there is sufficient funding. We ask that this be done by kings and princes, counts and barons, and other magnates, who perhaps cannot personally go to the aid of the Crucified. We seek naval help from maritime cities. So that we may not appear to be imposing heavy and unsupportable burdens, while we do little or nothing, we protest before God in truth that what we require others to do, we will ourselves be ready to do. We provide for the needs of the clergy for this business to be met so that, without opposition, they may be able to mortgage the income of their benefices for up to three years. Since aid for the Holy Land would be quite impeded and delayed if it should be necessary to examine each person for suitability and sufficient means to take on personally this kind of vow before taking the cross, we grant that, save for members of religious orders, whoever wishes may receive the sign of the cross, so that should urgent necessity or a clear benefit require it, the vow can be commuted or redeemed or deferred by apostolic mandate.

And for the same reason, we revoke the remission of sins and indulgences we granted up to this time for those setting out against the Moors in Spain or against the heretics in Provence, especially since they were granted for reasons that are now entirely in the past, and for a particular reason that has for the most part ceased. In both cases things have now prospered so that there is no urgent need. If required, we will take care to act in any immediate necessity. But we agree that remissions and indulgences of this kind should still be available to the men of Provence and Spain. Because corsairs and pirates put too great obstacles in the way by seizing and despoiling aid passing to and from the Holy Land, we bind them and their chief supporters and patrons with the chain of excommunication, forbidding under the menace of anathema anyone to have business with them in any contract involving sale or purchase, and ordering the rulers of cities and their possessions to recall them and hold their iniquity in check. Otherwise, since being unwilling to prevent evil men is nothing else but to favor them, and he suffers by suspicion of a secret association who is unable to oppose open villainy, we will take care to exercise ecclesiastical severity against their persons and lands, since such men are, no less than Saracens, enemies of the Christian name.

In addition, we renew the sentence of excommunication promulgated in the Lateran Council against those who trade with their galleys in arms, iron, and lumber with the Saracens, and those who are in charge of Saracen ships, and we consider that they should be deprived of their property and seized as slaves if they should be captured.[3] We order that in every maritime city this sentence should be renewed on Sundays and feast days. But since in the long run we should trust more in divine mercy than human power, we ought to struggle in this conflict not only with physical weapons but also with spiritual.

And so we decree and order that every month there should be a separate general procession of men, and, where possible, separate for women, in humility of mind and body, where word of the salvation-bringing cross is proposed with diligent exhortation to the people, with devout insistence of prayers asking that the merciful God should take away the opprobrium of this confusion, freeing from the hands of the pagans that land in which he established all the sacraments of our redemption, restoring it to the Christian people to the praise and glory of his holy name.[4] Fasting and alms should be joined to prayer in order that the prayer may fly more easily and quickly to the most pious ears of God, who hears us with mercy at the proper time. Every day during the solemnities of the mass, after the kiss of peace, when the offering for the sins of the world or the salvific host is consumed, all, both men and women, should prostrate themselves on the ground and the following psalm is to be sung in a high voice by the clerics: "O God, the gentiles have come into your

---

3. The reference is to the Third Lateran Council of 1179. See Olivia Remie Constable, "Clothing, Iron, and Timber: The Growth of Christian Anxiety About Islam in the Long Twelfth Century," in Noble and Van Engen, eds., *European Transformations*, 279–313.

4. These monthly processions grew out of the Roman processions of 1212 (see above, No. 8).

inheritance . . ." [Ps 78], and at the end, "Rise up, O God, and your enemies will scatter, and those who hate him will flee from his face" [Ps 68]. The celebrant will sing this prayer at the altar: "We humbly pray you, O God, who arrange all things with wonderful Providence, that, seizing the land that your only-begotten son has consecrated with his own blood from the hands of the enemies of the cross you restore it to Christian worship. Direct the vows of his constant faithful mercifully to its liberation in the road of eternal salvation. Amen."

Moreover, in those churches where the general procession is held, a concave trunk should be placed with three keys each in the charge of an honest priest, a devout layman, and a member of a religious order, in which clergy and laity, men and women, may put their alms to be used for the aid of the Holy Land according the decision of those to whom its care has been entrusted. Still, it is not necessary to make any decision on the usual and established process and transit or on the suitable time and place [for departure] until the army of the Lord is signed with the cross, but after considering all the circumstances, we will decide whatever we see to be proper from the counsel of prudent men. To carry out these affairs, we appoint our beloved sons, the abbots Eberhard of Salem and Peter, formerly of Neuburg, and C[onrad], the dean of Speyer, and the provost of Augsburg, men generally recognized to be of proven honesty and trust. And they may, on our authority, appoint acceptable men of foresight and honesty and decide whatever seems necessary for this business, carrying out faithfully and carefully those things they decide in individual dioceses through suitable men especially appointed for this purpose. For this reason, we admonish by asking you as a whole and we implore you in the Lord, commanding by apostolic letters and enjoining in the power of the Holy Spirit that you care for such men enjoying the legateship for Christ, ministering to their needs, that they may produce the desired fruit through you and in you.

12. Innocent III, *Pium et sanctum*, 1213

Following his general letter *Quia maior*, Innocent III sent the following letter, known as *Pium et sanctum*, around the middle of April 1213 to those he was appointing as crusade preachers. This letter was addressed to individuals whose work was already known to the papal curia, who had served, in many cases, as judges delegate. Many possessed considerable education. It is evident that the pope wished to use the two years prior to the meeting of the Fourth Lateran Council for a systematic program of crusade recruitment. His preachers reached all parts of western Europe. The copy translated here was sent to the immense ecclesiastical province of Mainz.

WE have conceived a plan for the aid of the Holy Land, and we have been working to bring it to fruition, as you can see clearly from our general letter. Since, therefore, we would obtain a fuller faith from your sincerity and care, and we consider you suitable to enjoy the office of legation for Christ in this case, we admonish, we request, and beseech your devotion in the Lord, commanding you strictly in advance by an apostolic letter and enjoining you in the remission of sins, that, on fire with zeal for the Christian faith, you should carry the word of the cross throughout the province of Mainz in heart and body, to avenge the injury of the Crucified. Just as is contained in our general letter, you should persuade the faithful with solicitous care and accurate solicitude, pursuing diligently and effectively all that you see contained in the same letter for the assistance of the Holy Land, of which we wish you to take careful note.

Moreover, so that in carrying out these tasks you may demonstrate that you carry the stigmata of Jesus Christ in your hearts, we strictly command that, rejecting every gift, you should not exceed on your travels the number of four or six persons in your company. Nor should you take anything except food and necessities from anyone, and you should consume these moderately and modestly. Also, you should keep modesty in these and other things so that nothing blameworthy may be found in you through which even a small offense to the gospel may be credited to you. You should promote with such desire and vigilance the cause of Christ that you may be a participant in the many and great goods we believe will come of it. If anything should be offered to you for the aid of the Holy Land, you should order it to be put carefully in some religious place. You should notify us of the details and result of your charge at the end of a year so that we may learn with whom you have worked in persons and in affairs dedicated to this salutary business, and we will reply to you with pleasure in what way you should proceed.

Source: PL 216:822.

13. An Anonymous Crusade-Recruiting Sermon, ca. 1213–1217

From the late twelfth to the mid-thirteenth century, networks of Paris-trained masters collaborated with members of the Cistercian, Premonstratensian, and, later, mendicant orders in the promotion of various reforming and pastoral programs and several crusades. The increasing institutionalization and intensification of crusade recruiting meant that, for the first time, manuals specifically designed for the crusade preacher began to be produced, and crusading sermons were recorded by Paris masters and their monastic and mendicant coworkers. Because these reformers viewed the crusade as an expression of religious devotion and penitence akin to life as a regular religious and the imitation of Christ accomplished by various saints, many crusading appeals were preserved in sermons for the Invention (Discovery) and Exaltation of the Cross, Easter, Laetare Sunday, and Ash Wednesday, for the feast days of various martyrs and confessors, and in homilies for the Lenten and Advent seasons. These moralists' fusion of reform and crusade and their conception of the crusade as a permanently available and valid quasi-regular lifestyle ensured that crusaders and pilgrims also earned a place in another new genre: sermon collections aimed at various specialized estates in society. The preservation of crusading appeals was also linked to the growth in the demand for and compilation of pastoral materials in Parisian, monastic, and mendicant circles and the renewed commissioning of individuals from them to preach various crusades, which created a similar demand for the preservation of crusading propaganda.

The sermon below appears to have been delivered by an unnamed preacher to a mixed urban audience in Paris during the transition from recruiting for the Albigensian Crusade to recruiting for the Fifth Crusade (ca. 1213–1217) and was preserved by canons from Saint-Victor in Paris who collaborated with Cistercians and Paris masters in organizing the Fourth, Albigensian, and Fifth Crusades. It is particularly valuable in that it was not reworked extensively for inclusion into a sermon collection meant for other purposes, but was preserved in a rough reporting format. Although the original notetaker has shortened many themes and stories to condensed versions, this sermon and others like it more closely represent crusading appeals as actually delivered than the complex smorgasbord of themes offered in numerous model crusading sermons, which their authors intended to be altered to fit the occasion and audience as desired. The preacher drew on many materials available to him, including scriptural commentaries, the lives of the saints, and anecdotes of miracles sent to Paris in written or oral form by Paris-trained masters and Cistercians preaching the Fifth and Albigensian Crusades, including James of Vitry, Robert Courson, Oliver of Paderborn, Fulk, bishop of Toulouse, Guy, abbot of Vaux-de-Cernay (later bishop of Carcassonne), and William of Pont-de-l'Arche, archdeacon of Paris.[5] The themes and arguments used by

5. For Oliver of Paderborn's and James of Vitry's letters, see the translation of Oliver's *Historia Damiatina* below, No. 21, and James of Vitry's account of his travels, below, No. 65.

the anonymous preacher closely resemble many of those used by James of Vitry and other preachers recruiting at the time, suggesting that successful images and material were recycled and shared. The sermon here is similar to another contemporary collection of reforming sermons delivered in Paris and preserved in Bibliothèque nationale (MS lat. nouv. acq. 999) in that it has not been reworked by later compilers of crusade sermons.

The scholarship on sermons is extensive. For our subject, see Jessalynn Bird, "Paris Masters"; Bird, "James of Vitry's Sermons to Pilgrims"; Christoph T. Maier, Crusade Propaganda and Ideology: Model Sermons for the Preaching of the Cross *(Cambridge, 2000); Christoph T. Maier,* Preaching the Crusades: Mendicant Friars and the Cross in the Thirteenth Century *(Cambridge, 1994); Cole,* Preaching; *Powell,* Anatomy, *51–65.*

Sermon on the commendation of the cross

BEHOLD, *I will send fishermen to you and they will fish you out and feed upon you* [Jer 16:16]. *Those who take to the sea in ships* [Ps 106:23]; today this is fulfilled among you [cf. Luke 4:21]. *The wisdom of this world is foolishness before God* [1 Cor 3:19]. Job [says]: *It cannot be found in the land of those living amidst delights* [Jb 28:13]. You teach such wisdom as that which [is absorbed] by someone nursing from the milk drawn from the breasts. Some old people still suckle from one of the devil's nurses, that is the flesh, which has two teats: lust and gluttony. Others suckle another nurse of the devil, that is the world, which has two breasts: pride and cupidity. *They speak against me, etc.* [Ps 118:23]. For whatever the Lord considered wisdom these kind of men [viewed as] foolishness, whenever he used to teach: beware *lest your hearts be weighed down by intoxication and drunkenness* [Lk 21:34]. The wisdom of this world is that a man should multiply his possessions by any means whatsoever. The apostle [says]: the wisdom of the flesh is death [cf. Rom 8:6–7]. The Lord's wisdom is most excellent, *the lord's lucid commands illuminate the eyes* [Ps 18:9]. The Lord's wisdom is [this]: to surrender what cannot be possessed for long in exchange for that which cannot be lost, to spurn riches, dignities, delights and embrace the contrary for the Lord's sake. Those who do such things are reckoned fools by the world.

This began in Noah's time. For when he was building the ark they used to call him a fool when he used to warn them. I say to you more than Noah that the Lord will not grant the world one hundred years before the end. And I say to you more: death will come upon you quickly

Source: Jessalynn Bird, "The Victorines, Peter the Chanter's Circle, and the Crusade: Two Unpublished Crusading Appeals in Paris, Bibliothèque Nationale, Ms. Latin 14470," Medieval Sermon Studies *48 (2004), 5–28, text on 25–28.*

and then this will be the end of the world for you. I forewarn you of the [coming] flood. Never were there so many dangers before the Flood as now: for at that time, neither taverns nor gluttony nor usury but the sin of luxury alone was the entire cause of the flood. After that sin, all were drowned because they exposed themselves to many in a wicked fashion. Therefore you ought to fear more, because a greater flood awaits you and you know that it will come [cf. Gn 6–9]. *Pray therefore to the Lord king, etc.* [cf. Lk 10:2; Mt 24:20; Zec 14:16–17]. Everyone considers whatever the Lord does a public privy and so the Lord does so many things against [them]. He addresses them in his ire: *I in turn will laugh at your ruin, when what you fear overtakes you* [Prv 1:26]. You betray me for money in this way and I will make a mockery of you. You fear poverty and baseness and wretchedness and will have them in full measure.

Behold I, etc. [Jer 16:16]. This world is a sea, so that this sea is great and spacious, etc. The sea [*mare*] is so named after its bitterness [*amaritudine*].[6] For there is nothing in this world except bitterness. The sea reeks and this world is foul. Before the Lord's countenance, the soul of the corrupt sinner stinks more than every corpse piled together at once would reek. Bitterness signifies the penalty for sin, the stench signifies sin. You cannot cross this sea unless you vomit up every sin. The sea, swelling to a great height, is raised up and signifies the swelling of pride which resembles an inflated bladder. The sea is stormy and signifies anger and tempestuous hatred. Concerning the woman who claimed that she was made a prostitute through the wickedness of her husband.[7] The sea is cloudy and signifies the sad state of the world by which death is wrought and the envy of those who are made downcast by their neighbors' successes. The sea, which receives all waters and yet is never sated, signifies cupidity. The foam of the sea signifies lust. The sea expels the dead but retains the living. So the lovers of the world do not care for those dead to the world, that is, good people, but retain those living for the world, so that usurers and people of this ilk inundate the sea. In this way there is now one inundation, because you live for the world. And if I returned after ten years, I would perchance find very few of you.

6. This image was prevalent in anti-vice sermons. The preacher probably obtained his etymology of the word "sea" (*mare*) from a collection of distinctions, one genre of pastoral aids produced in Paris for the use of preachers. See Alan of Lille, *Distinctiones dictionum theologicalium*, in *PL* 210:815a–d.

7. This tag seems to indicate a memorable *exemplum* or illustrative story.

Therefore the Lord sends prelates who ought to be fishers, and priests who do not look after their sheep. This sea has certain fish called dolphins who cavort before a storm. The gluttonous are of a similar nature, who are like a pig which has a mouth full of bran [even] when it is slaughtered. In addition it has infernal eels, that is, usurers who have so many . . . hiding places and are so slippery and wriggling that they cannot be held, neither through an oath nor another means. It also has whales, that is, princes who defend usury; these cannot be caught.[8] Formerly, the Lord stretched out many nets. One was the Cistercian order, another the Cluniac, and yet nearly all have fled from these and other nets, and the net of penance.[9] And for this reason those who are or have become fishers, are hunters. When the hunter blows the horn, the hounds ought to come with him and bark ferociously. Priests are hunting dogs, but they are mute and fat because they cannot run and are at peace with the wolves, that is, with armed robbers and similar people. The wretched priest who accepts the offering of a usurer is accursed and excommunicated because he communicates with an excommunicate.

There are seven kinds of wild beasts in this world. The lions of pride, such as knights and certain armed robbers, the serpents of envy, such as those who rejoice in another's sin. You wallow in the sins of your fathers, yet rejoice in the sin of priests. On the priest Martin.[10] The wild boar is the irascible. The wild ass is the despairing [*accidiosus*]. The foxes of cupidity are deceitful merchants. Concerning a certain man who used to say "I'll put them [that is, my coins] into my 'wicked profit,' calling his purse 'wicked profit.' "[11] Concerning the hawkers and the mongers, they are as many as they are varied. Concerning the hostelers who are traitors; a gluttonous bear who makes a larder of his belly.[12] For this reason the

8. For crusade recruiters' attempts to combat usury, see Jessalynn Bird, "Reform or Crusade? Anti-Usury and Crusade Preaching During the Pontifcate of Innocent III," in John C. Moore, ed., *Pope Innocent III and His World* (Aldershot UK-Brookfield VT, 1999), 165–185.

9. Many other preachers used this image, including James of Vitry and Caesarius of Heisterbach, whose abbot Henry preached several crusades with Oliver of Paderborn.

10. This appears to be an abbreviation for a well-known story about a priest named Martin.

11. The scribe appears to be referring to an *exemplum* (illustrative tale) that lampoons avaricious merchants. The quotation is composed partly of an Old French dialect, which Daron Burrows generously helped me to decipher.

12. These phrases appear to refer to *exempla* concerning the groups named, including hawkers and mongers (small-scale traders).

behemoth sleeps in damp places . . .[13] About the boy slain from the drunkard's stench, the pig of lust.[14]

On the types of lust. [To] the whore [*lecatrix*] who bares her breasts for fondling at any hour, if you die without penance and confession, you will perish without end. Understand wretched lecher, if there perhaps is anyone of this ilk or more, who perchance possess in themselves all these beasts or one or two of them (and one suffices for eternal damnation), I have a net of the lord pope which I hold out to you, that is, a pardon which the Lord sends into the land. If you understood this pardon as the bishops and archbishops do, you would run to it.[15] Pray therefore to the King of Paradise that he might illuminate your hearts.

There are seven nets. The first is the forgiveness of every sin. If Judas himself came to me, I would say to him, if you are penitent and confessed, take this way and you will be like a child who comes down from baptism.[16] All the great sinners are captured by this net. The second net is for the penitents, that is, the quittance of all penances through this way. Whereas the evil will burn in hell for as many years as there are drops of water in the sea, and only then will their punishment be revoked, if you are confessed and penitent and die with this pardon, you will suffer no infernal or purgatorial punishment but will be freed through this way. The fourth net is the kingdom of heaven. The fifth is the release from all other voyages.[17] The sixth concerns the relatives and wives and friends associated with you in your voyage, if they should die, because you can help them in this manner.[18] The seventh net is if you should die before you undertake this journey, provided you have a firm intention of going, you will

13. Cf. Jb 40:10, 16. This sentence ends with severe abbreviations, suggesting a quotation that we have been unable to identify. The association of these verses from Job with lust is common in theological and pastoral works, including Richard of Saint Victor, *Explicatio in Cantica canticorum*, PL 196:476d. The association of gluttony with lust was also commonplace.

14. This phrase appears to refer to diatribes against the drunkards and lustful. James of Vitry's sermons to the married raged against inebriated husbands who demanded the marital debt from their pregnant wives and caused them to miscarry, thus killing their unborn children. See Thomas Frederick Crane, ed., *The* Exempla *or Illustrative Stories from the* Sermones Vulgares *of Jacques de Vitry*, Publications of the Folklore Society 26 (London, 1890), 94–95, nos. 226 and 229.

15. That is, the full crusading indulgence.

16. That is, a child handed down from the baptismal font, newly cleansed of sin.

17. By this period, the crusade vow was held to outweigh and/or fulfill the obligations entailed in other pilgrimage vows.

18. The transfer of part or all of the benefits of the crusading indulgence to those who aided the crusader was based on current practice regarding vows of pilgrimage.

fly with this pardon to the Lord, because your desire will be reckoned to you as a done deed. He who takes the cross will cross over to the Lord through a shortcut and profitable way.

14. Innocent Responds to Queries by Conrad of Speyer, *Quod iuxta verbum*, September 1213

Many of the individuals whom Innocent III appointed to preach the Fifth Crusade were highly educated men who had either served effectively as judges delegate or proved their experience in spiritual and legal matters as leaders of important religious groups or houses. Conrad, dean of Speyer, was one of those individuals: from a prominent German family and educated in Paris, Conrad had already distinguished himself in preaching the Albigensian Crusade and would go on to become bishop of Hildesheim and imperial chancellor to Frederick II and continue to coordinate crusade efforts in Germany in that capacity. His queries to Innocent III regarding issues mentioned in *Quia maior* and *Pium et sanctum* elicited answers that reflected Innocent III's desire to prioritize the Holy Land crusade (while not entirely neglecting crusades in other regions) and the pope's willingness to change the very nature of crusade recruitment.

ACCORDING to the words of the apostle, you ought to take care not to [attempt] to discern the heights [Eph 3:18–20], but fear [to do so], and you with the prophet ought to realize your own imperfection, and nonetheless trust in him who gives abundantly to all [Jas 1:5]. Provided they are not importunate, he makes stammering tongues fluent [Is 32:4], and so, provided that you both humbly undertake the office of exhortation enjoined upon you and solicitously endeavor to fulfill it, he will commend your prudence. And because you will be advancing his own business most laudably, he will confer upon you fuller assurance. So then, having very favorably considered your inquiries, concerning those who, having taken up the sign of the cross, vowed to go against the heretics in Provence and have not yet fulfilled their vow, we respond that such persons ought assiduously to be persuaded to undertake the labor of the Jerusalem journey, since it is certain to be of greater merit. If perhaps they refuse to be induced to do this, they ought to be compelled to fulfill their [solemnly] spoken vow.[19]

Source: PL *216:904–905.*

19. Conrad had preached the antiheretical (Albigensian) crusade, but when Innocent canceled the indulgences offered for this crusade in 1213 in preparation for a crusade to the

Assuredly, concerning those who want to take the sign of the cross against the protests of their wives, whom you are uncertain whether because of this their resolution [to take the crusade vow] ought to be hindered, we are led to answer thus: that since the heavenly King ought to be greater than an earthly king, and it is well established that the objections of wives do not impede those called [to serve in] the army of an earthly king, it follows that those called to the army of the highest King and who wish to set out for it ought not to be impeded by the aforesaid occasion, since because of this the marital bond is not broken, but rather they are withdrawn for a time from conjugal cohabitation, which of necessity occurs frequently in many other cases.[20] On the other hand, what ought to be done concerning women and other persons who take the sign of the cross, and are not fitting or able to fulfill their vow, can be inferred clearly from the general letter, in which it is expressly stated that, with the exception of persons living under a religious rule, whoever wishes to may take the sign of the cross, such that when urgent necessity or evident usefulness should demand it, their vow may be commuted or redeemed or deferred by apostolic mandate.[21]

Certainly, because the Lord has summoned your colleague from the light [of this earth], according to your own request, we are led to substitute the abbot of Schönau in his stead: and so that your work might be able to become more productive, both to you and to the aforesaid abbot we grant that to arsonists and to those who laid violent hands upon clerics or other ecclesiastical persons, who wishing to take the sign of the cross, and having done fitting satisfaction for the injuries suffered, you might freely impose the benefit of absolution by our authority; unless perhaps the crimes of some of them might seem so weighty and grievous that they ought to be deservedly sent to the Apostolic See [for absolution].

Holy Land, Conrad and other recruiters were switched to the new crusade. He is here asking what to do about the vows of those who had originally intended to participate in the Albigensian Crusade, now possessed of a highly ambiguous status.

20. As did Innocent's previous letter to Hubert Walter (translated above, No. 5), this response of Innocent flew in the face of previous canon law, which required spouses to seek each other's consent before embarking on lengthy pilgrimages or on a crusade, because an absence of several years deprived the other spouse of conjugal rights and exposed her to the temptation of adultery.

21. That is, *Quia maior* (see No. 11 above).

15. Roger Wendover on the Fourth Lateran Council and the *Expeditio*

Roger Wendover was not present at Rome during the Fourth Lateran Council, but he was, as usual, fairly well informed about it, probably by someone who had been present and may have brought back early written accounts. His account of the council is particularly interesting because it preserves and mislocates a version of the *Expeditio*, canon 71 of the council, that is different from the full canon that exists in the record of the council (below, No. 16, *Ad liberandam*). His version of the text and circumstances of the crusade canon should be compared with the formal text of *Ad liberandam*. First, he identifies the text as the sermon by Innocent that opened the council, misdating the time of assembly a year earlier, and giving a much shorter version than the one that Innocent finally released as canon 71, conventionally, on December 14, 1215, and attached to the council's proceedings. He does not distinguish between different sessions of the council—the sixty articles were not read out until the third and final session on November 30. Stephan Kuttner and Antonio García y García suggest convincingly that Roger's text represents a preliminary stage of *Ad liberandam*.

Particularly important for its impression of the council is the narrative of a German cleric writing shortly after the council ended. See Stephan Kuttner and Antonio García y García, "A New Eyewitness Account of the Fourth Lateran Council," Traditio 20 (1964), 115–178. There is an English translation of the Latin text by Constantin Fasolt in Julius Kirshner and Karl F. Morrison, eds., Medieval Europe, *vol. 4 of* University of Chicago Readings in Western Civilization *(Chicago, 1986), 369–376. See also John W. Baldwin,* Masters, Princes, and Merchants: The Social Views of Peter the Chanter and His Circle, 2 vols. *(Princeton NJ, 1970), 1:315–343.*

Of the general council held by Pope Innocent at Rome

IN THE same year, namely, A.D. 1215, a sacred and general synod was held in the month of November, in the church of the Holy Savior at Rome, called Constantinian,[22] at which our lord pope Innocent, in the eighteenth year of his pontificate, presided, and which was attended by four hundred and twelve bishops. Among the principal of these were the two patriarchs of Constantinople and Jerusalem. The patriarch of Antioch could not come, being detained by serious illness, but he sent his vicar, the bishop of Antaradus;[23] the patriarch of Alexandria being under the dominion of the Saracens, did the best he could, sending a deacon, his cousin, in his place. There were seventy-seven primates and metropolitans

Source: Giles, Wendover's Flowers of History, *2:343–346.*
22. Saint John Lateran.
23. Tortosa.

present, more than eight hundred abbots and priors, and of the proxies
of archbishops, bishops, abbots, priors, and chapters who were absent,
the number is not known. There was also present a multitude of ambassadors from the emperor of Constantinople, the king of Sicily, who was
elected emperor of Rome,[24] the kings of France, England, Hungary, Jerusalem, Cyprus, Aragón, and other princes and nobles, and from cities
and other places. When all of these were assembled in the place above
mentioned, and, according to the custom of general councils, each was
placed according to his rank, the pope himself first delivered an exhortation, and then the sixty articles were recited in full council, which seemed
agreeable to some and tedious to others.

At length he commenced to preach concerning the business of the
cross, and the subjection of the Holy Land, adding as follows: "Moreover, that nothing be omitted in the matter of the cross of Christ, it is
our will and command, that patriarchs, archbishops, abbots, priors, and
others, who have the charge of spiritual matters, carefully set forth the
work of the cross to the people entrusted to their care; and in the name
of the Father, the Son, and the Holy Ghost, the one alone and eternal
God, supplicate kings, dukes, princes, marquises, earls, barons, and other
nobles, and also the commanders of cities, towns, and villages, if they
cannot go in person to the assistance of the Holy Land, to furnish a
suitable number of soldiers, with all supplies necessary for three years,
according to their means, in remission of their sins, as in the general letters is expressed; and it is also our will that those who build ships for this
purpose be partakers in this remission. But to those who refuse, if any be
so ungrateful, let it be on our behalf declared that they will for a certainty
account to us for this at the awful judgment of a rigorous Judge; considering, before they do refuse, with what chance of salvation they will be able
to appear before the only God and the only begotten Son of God, to
whose hands the Father has entrusted all things, if they refuse to serve the
Crucified One, in this their proper service, by whose gift they hold life,
by whose kindness they are supported, and by whose blood they have
been redeemed.

"And we, wishing to set an example to others, give and grant thirty
thousand pounds for this business, besides a fleet, which we will supply
to those who assume the cross from this city and the neighboring districts;
and we moreover assign for the accomplishment of this, three thousand

24. Frederick II—see below Parts III and IV.

marks of silver, which remain to us out of the alms of some of the true faith. And as we desire to have the other prelates of the churches, and also the clergy in general, as partakers both in the merit and the reward, it is our decree that all of them, both people and pastors, shall contribute for the assistance of the Holy Land the twentieth portion of their ecclesiastical profits for three years, except those who have assumed the cross or are about to assume it and set out for the Holy Land in person; and we and our brethren the cardinals of the holy church of Rome will pay a full tenth part of ours.

"It is also our order that all clerks or laymen, after assuming the cross, shall remain secure under our protection and that of Saint Peter; and also under the protection of the archbishops, bishops, and all the prelates of God's church, and that their property shall be so arranged, as to remain untouched and undisturbed until certain information is obtained of their death or their return. And if any of those who go on this crusade are bound by oath to the payment of usury, their creditors shall by ecclesiastic authority be compelled to forgive them their oath and to desist from exacting their usury; and we make the same decree with regard to the Jews by the secular authority, that they may be induced to do this. Moreover, be it known, that the prelates of churches who are careless in granting justice to crusaders, or their proxies, or their families, will meet with severe punishment. Moreover, by the advice of wise men, we determine that those who thus assume the cross, shall prepare themselves so as to assemble on the first of June next ensuing [June 1, 1216], and those who determine to cross by sea will assemble in the kingdom of Sicily, some at Brindisi, and others at Messina, at which place we also have determined, under God's favor, to be present, that by our assistance and counsel the Christian army may be duly regulated, and may set out with the blessing of God and the Apostolic See. And we, trusting to the mercy of an omnipotent God, and to the authority of the blessed apostles Peter and Paul, by virtue of that power which the Lord has granted to us, unworthy though we are, of binding and loosing, grant to all who should undertake this business in person and at their own expense, full pardon for their sins, for which they shall be truly contrite in heart, and of which they shall have made confession, and in the rewarding of the just we promise an increase of eternal salvation; and to those who do not come in person, but at their own expense send suitable persons according to their means, and also to those who come in person though at the expense of others, we likewise grant full pardon for their sins. And it is also our will that those should share in this forgiveness who out of their own property shall furnish proper supplies for the assistance of the said country, or who have rendered seasonable counsel and assistance on the aforesaid matters. And for all those who proceed on this expedition the holy and universal synod bestows the favor of its prayers and good wishes, to the end that they may better obtain eternal salvation. Amen."

16. The Fourth Lateran Council, Canon 71, *Ad liberandam*, 1215

Although the crusade, along with church (and individual) reform, was Innocent's great purpose in convoking the Fourth Lateran Council, the actual crusade privilege, designated as *Expeditio* in manuscripts and early printed editions of the canons of the council, was always located after canon 70 but was not numbered. Nor was *Ad liberandam* included with the other canons in later canon law collections, and only an excerpt appeared in the canon law collection *Liber extra* issued by Gregory IX in 1234, since it was considered to apply only to a unique event. Evidently, Innocent III worked on the text after the close of the council and issued it, at least according to an early editor of the canons, on December 14, 1215. Whatever its date, it had to be circulated widely and quickly, and it had to be identified with the council—at least three times in the text, Innocent indicates that a particular point has the support and approval of the council.

The best edition/translation of the canons of the Fourth Lateran Council is in Norman P. Tanner, S.J., ed., Decrees of the Ecumenical Councils, *vol. 1,* Nicaea I to Lateran V *(Washington DC, 1990), 227–271. See also Kuttner and García y García, "New Eyewitness Account." On the punishments that Innocent mentions for those who fail to fulfill their vows or attack crusaders' protected property—excommunication and interdict—see Elisabeth Vodola,* Excommunication in the Middle Ages *(Berkeley CA, 1986); Alexander Murray,* Excommunication and Conscience in the Middle Ages: The John Coffin Memorial Lecture *(London, 1991); and Peter D. Clarke,* The Interdict in the Thirteenth Century: A Question of Collective Guilt *(Oxford-New York, 2007).*

ASPIRING with ardent desire to liberate the Holy Land from the hands of the impious, by the counsel of prudent men who fully know the circumstances of times and places, the holy council approving: we decree that the crusaders [*crucesignati*] shall so prepare themselves that, at the Calends of the June following the next one [June 1, 1217], all who have arranged to cross by sea shall come together in the kingdom of Sicily; some, as shall

Source: Translation from E. F. Henderson, Select Historical Documents of the Middle Ages, *rev. ed. (London-New York, 1896), 337–344.*

be convenient and fitting, at Brindisi, and others at Messina and the places adjoining on both sides; where we have arranged then to be present in person if God wills it, in order that by our counsel and aid the Christian army may be usefully arranged, about to start with the divine and apostolic benediction.

And to the same end, those who have decided to go by land shall endeavor to make themselves ready; announcing this determination to us in the meantime, so that we may grant them for counsel and aid a suitable legate from our side [*legatus a latere*].

Priests, moreover, and other clergy who shall be in the Christian army, subordinates as well as prelates, shall diligently minister with prayer and exhortation, teaching them by word and example alike that they should always have the divine fear and love before their eyes, and that they should not do or say anything which might offend the divine majesty. Although at times they may lapse into sin, they shall soon rise again through true repentance; showing humility of heart and body, and observing moderation as well in their manner of living as in their clothing; altogether avoiding dissentions and rivalries; rancor and splenetic fury being entirely removed from them. So that, so armed with spiritual and material weapons, they may fight more confidently against the enemies of the faith; not presuming in their own power, but hoping in the divine virtue.

To the clergy themselves, moreover, we grant that they may retain their benefices intact for three years, just as if they were residing in their churches; and, if it shall be necessary, they may be allowed to place them in pledge for that time.

Therefore, lest this holy undertaking should happen to be impeded or delayed, we distinctly enjoin on all the prelates of the churches that, each in his own district, throughout their districts, they diligently move and induce those who have abandoned the cross to resume it to fulfill their vows to God, and for these and others who have been signed with the cross and who have hitherto been signed to compel them to fulfill their vows, if it shall be necessary through sentences of excommunication against their persons and of interdict against their lands, all backsliding being put an end to; those only being excepted who shall meet with some impediment on account of which, according to the ordinance of the Apostolic See, their vow may rightly be commuted or deferred.

Besides this, lest anything which pertains to the work of Jesus Christ[25] be omitted, we will and command that the patriarchs, archbishops,

---

25. *In negotio Iesu Christi*—that is, the crusade.

bishops, abbots, and others who have the care of souls shall passionately propound the word of the cross to those committed to them, exhorting through the Father and the Son and the Holy Spirit—the one sole true eternal God—the kings, dukes, princes, margraves, counts and barons and other magnates, also the communities of the cities, towns, and burghs, that those who do not in person go to the Holy Land shall donate a suitable number of warriors, with their necessary expenses for three years, according to their own wealth, for the remission of their sins—as has been expressed in our general letters, and as, for the greater assurance, we shall also express below. Of this remission we wish to be partakers not only those who furnish their own ships, but also those who on account of this work have striven to build new ships.

To those that refuse to go, if any by chance should be so ungrateful to our Lord God, the clergy shall firmly protest on behalf of the Apostolic See that they shall know that they are about to answer to us, at the final day of a strict investigation, before the tremendous judge. First considering, however, with what conscience or with what security they will be able to confess in the presence of Jesus Christ the only begotten son of God, into whose hands the Father gave all things [Jn 13:3], if they shall refuse in this matter, as if it were properly their own, to serve him who was crucified for sinners, by whose gift they live, by whose benefit they are sustained, nay, more, by whose blood they are redeemed [1 Pt 1:18–19].

Lest, however, we seem to impose heavy and unbearable burdens upon the shoulders of men, burdens to which we ourselves are unwilling to put a finger, like those who only say and do not do [Mt 23:3–4]; behold, we, from what we have been able to spare beyond our necessary and moderate expenses, do grant and give thirty thousand pounds to this work. And besides the cost of the transport from Rome and the neighboring places that we have granted, we assign in addition, for this same purpose, three thousand marks of silver which have remained over to us from the alms of some of the faithful, the rest having been faithfully distributed for the needs and uses of the aforesaid land, through the hand of the abbot of blessed memory, the patriarch of Jerusalem,[26] and the masters of the Templars and Hospitallers.

Desiring, moreover, to have the other prelates of the churches, as well as the whole clergy, as participators and sharers both in the merit and in the reward, we have decreed with the general approval of the council

26. Albertus de Castro, d. ca. 1213–1214.

that absolutely the entire clergy, subordinates as well as prelates, shall give the twentieth part of their ecclesiastical revenues for three years in aid of the Holy Land, through the hands of those who shall by the care of the pope be appointed for this purpose, certain monks only being excepted, who are rightly to be exempted from this taxation; likewise those who, having assumed or being about to assume the cross, are on the point of making the expedition.

We, also, and our brothers the cardinals of the holy Roman Church, shall pay fully one tenth of our ecclesiastical revenues; that is, twice as much as other clerics; and they shall all know that they are all bound faithfully to observe this under penalty of excommunication, so that those who in this matter shall knowingly commit fraud shall incur sentence of excommunication.

Since, indeed, those who with right judgment remain in the service of the divine Commander ought to rejoice in a special privilege: when the duration of the expedition exceeds one year in length, the crusaders shall be free from taxes and tallages and other burdens. Upon assuming the cross, we take their persons and goods under the protection of the blessed Peter and of ourselves, so that they shall remain under the care of the archbishops, bishops, and other prelates deputed for this purpose, so that, until most certain news shall have been obtained either of their death or of their return, their possessions shall remain intact and unassailed. And if anyone presume to the contrary he shall be restrained by ecclesiastical censure.

If any of those leaving on the expedition are bound by an oath to pay interest, we command, under the same penalty, that their creditors be compelled to remit the oath given them and desist from claiming interest. But if any one of their creditors shall compel them to pay interest, we command that, by a similar process, they shall be compelled to restore it. We command that Jews shall be compelled by the secular power to remit their interest, and, until they shall remit it, all intercourse with them on the part of all the followers of Christ shall be denied, under pain of excommunication. For those, moreover, who are unable to pay their debts to the Jews, the secular princes shall so provide, with useful delay, that they shall not incur the inconvenience of interest from the time when they started on their journey until most certain news is obtained of their death or their return. The Jews are compelled to add to the capital after having deducted their necessary expenses, the revenues which they in the meantime receive from the lands pledged to them toward the principal of the sum loaned, for such a benefice does not suffer much loss when it so delays the payment but does not cancel the debt. The prelates of the churches who shall be found negligent in rendering justice to the crusaders and their families shall know that they shall be severely punished.

Furthermore, since corsairs and pirates excessively impede the aiding of the Holy Land, taking and despoiling those who go to and return from it, we bind with the chain of anathema their helpers and those who favor them, forbidding, under threat of anathema, that anyone make common cause with them through any contract of buying or selling, and enjoining on the rectors of their cities and districts to recall and restrain them from this iniquity. Otherwise, since to be unwilling to disturb the wicked is nothing else than to encourage them, and since he who desists from opposing a manifest crime is not without suspicion of secret collusion, we will and command that, against their persons and lands, ecclesiastical severity shall be exercised by the prelates of the churches.

We also excommunicate and anathematize those false and impious Christians who, against Christ himself and the whole Christian people, carry arms, iron, and wood for ships to the Saracens. Also those who sell to them galleys or ships and who, in the pirate ships of the Saracens, keep watch or serve as helmsmen, or give them any aid, counsel, or favor with regard to their war machines or to anything else, to the harm of the Holy Land—we decree shall be punished with the loss of their own possessions and shall be the slaves of those who capture them. And we command that on Sundays and feast days, throughout all the maritime cities, this sentence shall be renewed, and to such people the lap of the church shall not be opened unless they shall send all that they have received from such damnable gains, and as much more of their own as aid to the aforesaid land, so that they may be punished with a penalty equal to the amount of their original fault. But if by chance they be insolvent, those guilty of such things shall be otherwise punished; that through their punishment others may be prevented from having the audacity to presume to act similarly.

We prohibit, moreover, all Christians, and under pain of anathema interdict them from sending across or taking their ships across to the lands of the Saracens who inhabit the oriental districts for four years, so that in this way greater means of transport may be prepared for those wishing to cross to the aid of the Holy Land. And the aforesaid Saracens may be deprived of the by no means small advantage which has as a rule accrued to them from this.

Although in different church councils tournaments have been generally forbidden under penalty, inasmuch as at this time the matter of the crusade [*crucis negotium*] is very much impeded by them, we, under pain of excommunication, do firmly forbid them to be carried on for the next three years.

Since, moreover, in order to carry on this matter it is most necessary that the princes and the people of Christ should mutually observe peace, the holy universal synod urging us, we do establish that, at least for four years, throughout the whole Christian world, a general peace shall be observed, so that, through the prelates of the churches, the contending parties shall be brought back to inviolably observe a full peace or a firm truce. And those who, by chance, shall scorn to acquiesce, shall be most sternly be compelled to do so through excommunication against their persons and interdict against their land, unless the maliciousness of the injuries shall be so great that the persons themselves should not have the benefit of such peace. But if by chance they despise the ecclesiastical censure, not without reason shall they fear lest through the authority of the church, the secular power shall be brought to bear against them as against disturbers of what pertains to the Crucified One.

We therefore, trusting in the mercy of almighty God and in the authority of the apostles Peter and Paul, from that power of binding and loosing which God conferred on us, although unworthy, do grant to all who shall undergo this labor in their own persons and at their own expense, full pardon of the sins of which in their heart they shall have freely repented, and which they shall have confessed, and, at the retribution of the just, we promise them an increase of eternal salvation. To those, moreover, who do not go thither in their own persons, but who only at their own expense, according to their wealth and quality, send suitable men; and to those likewise who, although at another's expense, go, nevertheless, in their own persons, we grant full pardon of their sins. Of this remission also we will and grant that, according to the quality of their aid and the depth of their devotion, all shall be partakers who shall suitably minister from their goods toward the aid of that same land, or who shall give timely counsel and aid. To all, moreover, who piously proceed in this work the general synod imparts in common the aid of all its benefits, that it may worthily help them to salvation.

Given at the Lateran, on the nineteenth day before the Calends of January [December 14] in the eighteenth year of our pontificate.

PART III
The Fifth Crusade, 1213–1221

The Fifth Crusade was the campaign envisioned in *Vineam Domini* in 1213, announced to the faithful and to crusade preachers in *Quia maior* and *Pium et sanctum*, also in 1213, and formally announced in *Ad liberandam* in 1215. A pope, not individual nobles and their willful and underfunded followers, as in the Fourth Crusade, nor an emperor, as in the crusade of 1197–1198, was to direct the vast enterprise. The crusade was also far more carefully planned and financed than earlier crusades. It revealed a greater degree of commitment on the part of participants, most from Italy but others from other parts of Europe, notably the lower Rhineland. In all, more than eight hundred individuals from all over Europe have been identified as having taken part. In July 1215 and again in 1220 the king-emperor Frederick II himself took the cross and promised extensive support from German lands and the kingdom of Sicily. It also reflects a new degree of lay spirituality on the part of its warriors, many of whom took to heart the idea of *imitatio Christi*, an "imitation of Christ," as a component of crusader identity. The crusade also emphasized the recent concept of Christian mission, the idea that Muslims might be converted if God so willed—during the course of the expedition, Saint Francis of Assisi preached to the sultan at Mansura, as dramatic an instance of mission as is conceivable.[1]

The Fifth Crusade took place in the immediate wake of several crusading disasters—the failed crusade of the emperor Henry VI, the Fourth Crusade, the Children's Crusade, and the still-controversial Albigensian Crusade. But it also reminded Christians of crusading triumphs—Las Navas de Tolosa and other successes in the Iberian Peninsula, the initial triumph of 1099, now familiarized in chronicles and histories like that of William of Tyre, the exploits of Godfrey of Bouillon and Richard I in vernacular verse narratives, and the visible survival of the Latin Kingdom of Jerusalem in coastal fortified, prosperous cities like Acre and in the kingdom of Cyprus. The explanation of failure—God's anger at the sins of Christian society—supported Innocent III's argument for universal Christian moral reform, a theme that ran through the Fifth and all other crusades of the thirteenth century, giving the crusade a central role in the life of the church. It also held out the idea of success if moral reform was carried through. And men could look to the heavens for signs if these could be read accurately predicting success or failure,

---

1. On this famous episode and its long history of interpretation, see John V. Tolan, *St. Francis and the Sultan: The Curious History of a Christian-Muslim Encounter* (Oxford, 2009). On the problem of conversion, see Benjamin Z. Kedar, *Crusade and Mission: European Approaches Toward the Muslims* (Princeton NJ, 1984); John V. Tolan, *Saracens: Islam in the Medieval European Imagination* (New York, 2002); John V. Tolan, *Sons of Ishmael: Muslims Through European Eyes in the Middle Ages* (Gainesville FL, 2008).

as in the signs and portents collected by Roger Wendover at Saint Albans (below, No. 17) and Oliver of Paderborn in Damietta (below, No. 21).

The communications network among bishops in place across Europe, papal legates moving from diocese to diocese on clearly defined routes, crusade preachers like James of Vitry and Oliver of Paderborn in geographically defined preaching tours, and the attention paid to all of these by Innocent III and his successors underlay crusade preparations in the years between 1215 and 1218. Their effectiveness is illustrated by the letters that some of them wrote to the popes and the papal responses. Examples are the letters of Gervase of Prémontré (below, No. 18), which reveal an astute awareness of the practical difficulties faced by crusade recruiters.

In several instances, local chronicles narrated the experience of crusaders from particular regions, like the Rhineland crusaders (No. 20). But the Fifth Crusade also found its own historian in Oliver of Paderborn, schoolmaster of the cathedral of Cologne and one of those most closely associated with the preaching and recruitment of the crusade even before 1213. Oliver's *Historia Damiatina* (*The Capture of Damietta*, No. 21) is an account written on the scene by an able and observant participant. Others on the Fifth Crusade also wrote letters back to Europe that further illuminate Oliver's narrative (No. 22). Crusade news also worked to establish conflict settlement back home, as in the report of the two recruiters in Marseilles in 1224 (No. 23).

Finally, Muslim accounts of the crusade also offer important perspectives on the Egyptian and Syrian Ayyubid triumph and the humiliation of the Christians (No. 24).

In some respects, the Fifth Crusade is the great turning point in crusade history. Launched on the basis of painful lessons learned in the past, adequately financed and commanded, supported both spiritually and materially by Christians in Europe, its failure challenged everything Innocent III and Honorius III had hoped for. But their hopes did not die; plans for yet another crusade, this time led by the emperor Frederick II (below, Part IV), began with the Treaty of San Germano in 1225 and continued apace, making Frederick's crusade in some ways the last phase of the Fifth Crusade, since the emperor's absence played a significant part, along with continuing logistical and military power, as issues in its frustrated outcome.

On the Fifth Crusade, the best study is Powell, Anatomy of a Crusade. *There are several letters in Barber and Bate,* Letters from the East. *Other untranslated sources include Reinhold Röhricht,* Quinti belli sacri scriptores minores *(Geneva, 1879), and Reinhold Röhricht,* Testimonia minora de quinto bello sacro *(Geneva, 1882).*

17. Signs and Portents: From the Chronicle of Roger Wendover, 1217

These brief selections offer a flavor of men's apprehensiveness and eagerness to answer the summons of Innocent's successor, Pope Honorius III (1216–1227). Twelfth- and thirteenth-century Christians recognized two sources of revelation,

Scripture and the book of nature. Natural phenomena could also point, even if uncertainly, toward some momentous event or transformation of the world. There is evidence that signs and portents were collected, sometimes used in sermons and letters to other crusade preachers and potential crusaders, and that people became familiar with them, even in places distant from those in which they had occurred. The events described here and collected by Roger Wendover are echoed in Oliver of Paderborn's *Capture of Damietta* (below, No. 21).

Of signs in the heavens by which the province of Cologne was incited to assist in the crusade, 1217

IN THE month of May in this year, on the sixth day before Whitsuntide, the province of Cologne was awakened to its duty to the Savior; for at the town of Bebon [Bedum] in Friesland there appeared in the sky the form of the cross in three places, one toward the north of a white color, another toward the south of the same form and color, and the third in the middle of a dark color, with the form of the crucifix, and the figure of a man suspended on it, with uplifted and extended arms, with nails driven through the feet and hands, and with the head bent down; this one was in the middle between the two others, on which latter did not appear the image of a human body; at another time and place too, namely, at a town of Friesland called Fuserhuse, there appeared near the sun a cross of a blue color, and more people saw this than those who had seen the former crosses: a third cross appeared at the town of Doctham [Dokkum], where Saint Boniface was crowned with martyrdom; at this place on the feast of the said martyr, many thousand men having collected together, a large white cross was visible, as though two planks were placed artificially across one another; this cross moved gradually from the north toward the east, and many thousands saw it.

How the inhabitants of Cologne and Friesland prepared to march to the Holy Land, 1218

ABOUT that time there was a great movement of the brave and warlike men in the provinces of Cologne and Friesland, for since the commencement of the preaching of the crusade after the general council, they had with great eagerness built three hundred ships and having embarked in them, to fulfill to the Lord their vows of pilgrimage, they set sail, and the greater part of them, with a large array of soldiers, had arrived at Lisbon, where a disagreement arose amongst them about laying siege to a strong

Source: Giles, Wendover's Flowers of History, *2:388–389, 404, ed. EP.*

castle called Alcazar de Sol, some being anxious to proceed, and others wishing to winter where they were; so the fleet was divided, and one part of it wintered at Gaeta and Sorrento and the other part under the command of two chiefs, namely, William, duke of Holland, and Gerard [George], count of Wied, laid siege to Alcazar de Sol. While they were still employed in the siege, a large force of Saracens was assembled against them, but the Christians bravely gave them battle, and, by the divine assistance, conquered the infidels. One king among the pagans was slain, and numbers of others were killed and made prisoners; the castle was at last taken by the Germans, and held by the Christians.

18. Gervase, Abbot of Prémontré, Letters to the Pope, 1216–1217

This and the following letter were written by Gervase, in his capacity as abbot of the monastery of Prémontré, the motherhouse of the of the Premonstratensian order (1204–1220), to Innocent III and his successor Honorius III (1216–1227). Gervase had heard *Vineam Domini* read aloud at the cathedral of Reims in 1213, attended the Fourth Lateran Council, sponsored the preaching of the Albigensian Crusade, knew Innocent III well, and was familiar with many of the individuals responsible for preaching and organizing the Fifth Crusade. His letters almost certainly reflect their reports (and complaints) from the field. Despite the detailed instructions laid out in *Ad liberandam*, Gervase notes many areas of confusion that have arisen concerning preparations for the crusade, including the extent of vow redemptions, the date and location where crusaders are required to depart, and how various funds collected for the crusade are to be used. His letters reveal that many had taken the cross expecting to participate personally in the crusade and to be subsidized from the various funds collected, but were now placed in a double bind. Deprived of leadership and funds, they faced excommunication and the revocation of their indulgence and crusading privileges if they did not depart at the date set by the Fourth Lateran Council. Gervase suggests the appointment of special agents to sort out the mess, overseen by a papal legate.

Honorius did appoint the agents, including Gervase among their number, and sent detailed instructions on the collection and distribution of the twentieth[2] to bishops throughout Europe. It was to be deposited in local religious houses with careful receipts kept and taken overseas by trustworthy laymen to fund crusaders from the area in which it was collected. The money collected in alms trunks[3]

2. The Fourth Lateran Council (1215) had imposed an income tax of one-twentieth of all possessions upon all ecclesiastics in Europe to fund the crusade, with the exception of certain religious orders vowed to poverty.

3. Innocent III had ordered the placement of wooden trunks for the collection of offerings for the crusade in every church organizing processions for the crusade.

was also to be distributed to local crusaders. In an ironic twist, Gervase and canons from Noyon and Châlons-sur-Marne were ordered to collaborate with the bishops of Châlons and Noyon in accomplishing the tasks listed above either in person or through agents appointed in consultation with local bishops. Gervase stubbornly clung to his associates' refusal to redeem the vows of the fit poor, dispensing only priests, clerks, and matrons "useless to the Holy Land," but he had troubles reconciling his independent commission with reserving penitential rights to bishops and their diocesan clergy. Rebuked by Simon of Tyre for not obtaining letters testimonial from bishops and cathedral chapters for vow redemptions, Gervase claimed that they had not attended the proceedings despite being asked, although he had obtained their general consent.

The archdeacon of Châlons was so intimidated by local antagonism that he delayed collecting vow redemptions until local mistrust subsided. He and others protected themselves from charges of peculation by ensuring that the money collected was placed in a local church or monastery for safekeeping, together with letters detailing the sums received from those dispensed in each deaconate and parish. However, varying factors often ensured that these funds were not available to humble crusaders, particularly later in the crusade, where money was sent abroad in response to petitions from the crusading army in the East and the demands of crusading fronts in Egypt, Spain, the Midi, Prussia, and Latin Romania. Popes would continue to struggle with developing systems for the collection of crusading funds and provision of vow redemptions that balanced efficiency with local knowledge of crusader's special circumstances. Future popes, particularly Gregory IX (1227–1241), turned to the mendicant orders, commissioning individuals to combine the roles of recruiter, dispenser, and tax collector. However, this solution threatened to alienate bishops and local clergy, who saw the friars as threats to their penitential jurisdiction and revenues.[4]

Jessalynn Bird, "Finance of Crusades" and "Vow," in Murray, The Crusades, 2:432–437 and 4:1232–1237; Jessalynn Bird, "Innocent III, Peter the Chanter's Circle, and the Crusade Indulgence: Theory, Implementation, and Aftermath," in Sommerlechner, Innocenzo III: Urbs et Orbis, 1:503–524; Frederick A. Cazel, Jr., "Financing the Crusades," in Kenneth M. Setton et al., eds., A History of the Crusades, 6 vols., 2d ed. (Madison WI, 1969–1989), 6:116–149; Powell, Anatomy of a Crusade; Maureen Purcell, Papal Crusading Policy: The Chief Instruments of Papal Crusading Policy and the Crusade to the Holy Land from the Final Loss of Jerusalem to the Fall of Acre, 1244–1291 (Leiden, 1975); Elizabeth Siberry, Criticism of Crusading, 1095–1274 (Oxford, 1985). A charter issued by Gervase is translated in Corliss Konwiser Slack, ed., Hugh Bernard Feiss, trans., Crusade Charters, 1138–1270, Medieval and Renaissance Texts and Studies 197 (Tempe AZ, 2001), 156–166, no. 26; see also C. R. Cheney, "Gervase, Abbot of Prémontré: A Medieval Letter-Writer," Bulletin of the John Rylands Library 33 (1950), 25–56, although Cheney's dating of some of the letters has been subsequently revised.

Source: *Gervase of Prémontré*, Epistolae, *in C. L. Hugo, ed., Sacrae antiquitatis monumenta historica, dogmatica, diplomatica (Étival, 1725), 1:3–8.*

4. See Matthew Paris's complaints regarding the friars published below, No. 36.

Gervase writes to Pope Innocent III, 1216

ZEAL for the aid of the Holy Land and the devotion in which I hold Your Holiness so consume me, that even if I were disposed, as it were, at death's door, I would not be able to remain silent. Certainly you recently sent into France the venerable in Christ father Simon, archbishop of Tyre, to whom you gave the power of promoting the word of the cross among the faithful of Christ and commuting the vows of humble persons, who either because of their infirmity or excessive poverty are useless for the aid of the Holy Land.[5] However, when the same archbishop was asked by many whether the magnates of France who had taken the cross ought to be granted permission to remain [at home] until a future year, he responded, "You ought to change nothing from the regulations of the general council[6] with respect to the greater or the lesser [crusaders]." And yet when he was questioned whether all ought to be forced to depart this year he responded that he neither had received nor knew of anyone else who had received from you any power for this [kind of] compulsion.

However, this same lord archbishop told me that immediately after the council of Melun [1216], which was solemnly celebrated at his arrival in France, he had written to you concerning those things which he had carried out with the lord king and other things concerning the business entrusted to him. But I did not take care to ask what he had written, believing that through him you were sufficiently informed concerning everything necessary to the business of the crusade; nor ought I to have chosen otherwise. Certainly because he did not make known to you those things which afterward broke out, he could not defend himself to your clemency at that time, and so I was led to intimate them to you briefly in this letter.

The masters of Paris assert that, since nothing was relaxed from the ordering of the general council, all who will not have departed this year both forfeit the privileges given to those signed with the cross and in addition are deprived of the remission from sins and indulgence, even if they return to the execution of their vow in the future. However as it happens the majority of the magnates will not depart [this year] and they

---

5. No vows had been commuted prior to the arrangements made by the Fourth Lateran Council (1215). Motivated perhaps by the reservations of the expedition's military leaders, its decrees had put an end to giving the cross to anyone who desired it and had supplemented the meager funding gathered through offerings through the imposition of a clerical income tax.

6. That is, *Ad liberandam*, translated above, No. 16.

do not care much about the assignations of the Parisians[7] because they do not dread being censured by either spiritual penalties by you or earthly penalties by secular lords. Lesser persons, however (that is burgesses and rustics, of whom there is a great number), are threatened with temporal penalties on occasion of these words. Because they say that immediately after the Nativity of Saint John the Baptist the nobles and powerful and even communes of the cities will take exactions and tallages from them as they did before they took the cross.[8]

So then, the lesser persons signed with the cross, who are not few in number, put into much bitterness and anguish of heart, answer that they are ready to stand by the apostolic regulations for their departure, if they will have been expressly declared to them, since they have prepared expenses for themselves and ardently long to fulfill their vow. But they add that they do not know how at all, or with whom they might depart, because, as far as human judgment extends, they are absolutely useless for the aid of the Holy Land unless they have knights from their own land and their own tongue[9] leading them.

Therefore, if it pleases you, Most Clement Father, you ought to speedily provide advice on these things, from whence solace for the desolate and aid for the oppressed might appear, lest the faithful of Christ, whom I saw take the sign of the cross with such great devotion and who are thus far ready to honor faithfully what they vowed without deception, fall into the pit of despair, if they should believe themselves to be bound to the vow of pilgrimage and nonetheless because of that delay to which necessity, not free will, led them, to have forfeited every privilege and indulgence of sins.

So then, I say and believe that many in this region perceive with me that it would be very advantageous for the business of the crusade if the Germans did not journey with the French, since we have never read that

7. That is, the masters at Paris.

8. Technically those who had taken the cross were exempt from all taxes and financial exactions. However, worried that he and his supporters would be denied important revenues and military service, the king of France had already limited crusaders' exemption from interest on loans, taxes, military service, and lawsuits. It would seem that he and other parties were arguing that those who did not immediately depart at the date set by the Fourth Lateran Council should forfeit all of their privileges as crusaders. On the complicated issue of crusader rights in this period, see Jessalynn Bird, "Crusaders' Rights Revisited: The Use and Abuse of Crusader Privileges in Early Thirteenth-Century France," in *Law and the Illicit in Medieval Europe*, ed. Ruth Mazo Karras, Joel Kaye, and E. Ann Matter (Philadelphia, 2008), 133–48.

9. That is, speaking their own language.

they were of the same mind in any solemn association. However, I and many believe that it would profit the business of the crusade if the duke of Burgundy and the duke of Louvain[10] and others, who seem to be of considerable authority in France and in the vicinity of France, whom thus far you have spared somewhat, were bound a little more tightly to undertake their journey in this coming year, such that the date for undertaking the journey is announced expressly under various penalties to both the greater and the lesser alike.

If it should please Your Holiness, you could write about all these things to the archbishops of Bourges, Reims, Rouen, Tours, and Sens and to their suffragans and even to more, if you wish, according to that which is revealed to Your Blessedness by the omnipotent Lord.

Nor if it pleases you, ought you to restrict the Franks to labor in traveling to the ports of Apulia and Sicily, but rather let them take ship wherever they wish and wherever they can more conveniently find a vessel.

Nor ought it to be hidden from you that a certain bishop among us, while sparing the nobles, has bound the lesser through threat of excommunication so that they depart, not in order as it is believed to promote the business, but rather so that he might empty their purses.[11] Since, therefore, it is known that this business particularly pertains to Your Holiness, there ought to be no one who takes procurations except legates present from your side, or a papal notary or any others whom you yourself personally expressly enjoin to be given procurations.

In addition, there are many in France excommunicated because they crossed into England with Lord Louis[12] (with whom I and others associate very dangerously). At the request of some of them I therefore suggest to and supplicate Your Holiness, that to whatever extent it should please you, you command the following solution, that for as many days as they spent in England, they should remain for the same number of days in the south of France for the defense of the Albigensian church, so that they might thus merit the grace of absolution. For you ought to know that many of them abstain from entering churches more from fear of God and

10. Formally, duke of Brabant. Louvain (today Leuven) was the chief city in Brabant.

11. The bishop was excommunicating crusaders who had failed to depart at the deadline set in order to extort monetary fines from those seeking absolution.

12. Gervase refers to the excommunication laid by Innocent III on the crown prince of France, Louis, and his supporters for invading the lands of John Lackland, the king of England, who had taken the cross at least partly for the legal protection it afforded him and his lands.

from reverence for his commands than from any diligence of their prelates. May Your Holiness remain strong in the Lord, so that God may preserve his church unharmed.

Gervase writes to Innocent's successor as pope, Honorius III, 1217

IF ZEAL for the holy Roman Church did not consume me and the rebukes of those reproaching her did not fall upon me as upon a son who loves his mother, I perhaps could dissemble with others and carelessly tolerate reproaches to so great a mother. Oh, if only every one of her members would take care to preserve her honor as much as they long to drink her milk. And it has been a long time since I last wrote, because, fearing to be accused of presumption, I postponed writing to Your Holiness, after the decease of your predecessor Lord Innocent of venerable memory. For I was expecting from day to day that according to the arrangements decreed at the general council [i.e., *Ad liberandam*] someone sent as a legate or messenger would arrive in the Gaulish regions to dispense those signed with the cross whom he saw to be useless to the Holy Land and would take care to regulate, with the speedy counsel of discreet men, the departure of both the greater and lesser. In fact, I was hoping that it would be particularly accomplished through the venerable man Master James [of Vitry], cleric of Acre, whose return to France for that very purpose I was awaiting day by day.[13]

But when I heard afterward that he had gone off to regions overseas and that you had written so much concerning the business of the cross of Christ to exalted persons to the north of the Alps, not knowing whether the pitiful flock of the Lord (who until then wore the cross no less devotedly than the nobles) would be overlooked in your letters, I resolved to intimate their numerous and manifold complaints to you who possess power over them.

For the lesser *milites*[14] and all the poor lament that, when at the admonition of those who are set over the church of God, they took the

---

13. James was instead approved as bishop-elect of Acre and departed to the East to prepare for the crusaders' arrival. For the complicated reasons behind Honorius III's rejection of James of Vitry as legate for France, see Bird, "Reform or Crusade?"; and Brenda Bolton, "Faithful to Whom? Jacques de Vitry and the French Bishops," *Revue Mabillon*, n.s. 9 (1998), 115–134. For James's journey, see below, No. 65.

14. The Latin term *miles* (pl. *milites*) possessed a variety of meanings, including "knight" or simply "soldier" or "warrior." Some scholars have chosen to translate it as "arms-bearer." See also Christopher Marshall, *Warfare in the Latin East, 1192–1291* (Cambridge, 1992).

sign of the cross, they were ready to deny themselves through all things and, at the time, to abandon all their possessions in order to transform the Holy Land back into its due condition. Now neither in the potentates of the world who do not care, nor in churchmen who when signing them with the cross promised money, counsel, and leadership do they find anyone who would be responsible for providing anything at all to those already signed with the cross, either counsel or solace, or even a complement of justice, when contrary to the privileges of pilgrimage, they were oppressed by the powerful.

Concerning this also they were not silent, that the money of the trunks which were placed in every single church and the twentieth from the clergy were rudely demanded by the Templars in some places, indeed in others by archbishops or bishops or their officials. And when complaints were made about what ought to be done after that, it was answered that it ought to be sent to N. However, when the name of N. resounded in their ears, few were found who did not rise up against the clergy, either through clandestine detractions or open rebukes. Recalling the fiftieth[15] collected a short time ago, which they had not seen expended for the use of the pilgrimage being organized at that time, they cried out, like rash men to whom an account was not rendered concerning everything which was being done, that current money had been absorbed by N.[16]

And because of this it happened that in many places the trunks were contemptuously thrown out of certain churches and the twentieth either was not collected entirely, or if it was collected, it was insufficient and of little benefit to the Holy Land. In fact, when the word of preaching for the relief of the Holy Land first came down from the holy Roman Church, everyone inferred that those who had taken the cross had been promised that the money which would be collected from every single region or province (whether through the trunks or through other means) would be paid out for the expenses of the poor who had taken the sign of the cross.

Moreover, when you wrote, as I said before, to certain noblemen, including the duke of Burgundy and Walter, lord of Avesnes, that they

15. This refers to the hotly contested imposition of a similar clerical income tax for the Fourth Crusade.

16. This may refer to Stephen of Nemours, bishop of Noyon, and/or his brother William, bishop of Meaux, who collected the trunk money, twentieth, and vow redemption money from their dioceses and sent half of it to Philip Augustus for the Albigensian Crusade and half directly to the Templar house in Paris, thus depriving local crusaders of subsidy.

ought to be ready to undertake the journey of their pilgrimage the following Easter and they wrote back to you requesting that you grant them, as it is said, a reprieve of one year: a confusion arose all over, because it was not known which of the two deadlines ought to be heeded.

Therefore, so that sound advice over all these things might be set before you, with a heavy heart acquired from necessity and not without having deliberated with certain men who are believed to know what may profit crusade preparations, I humbly and modestly suggest to Your Holiness, without prejudice to better counsel, that you grant to the aforesaid petitioners the delay in departure to the extent they seek.

Meanwhile, however, if you will not send a messenger or legate into France for the sake of preventing injury to the churches, you ought at least condescend to send letters at the right time, through which you might appoint agents [*ordinatores*] in every single province or diocese, to whom these four things could be entrusted. First, they could defend those who have taken the cross in their privileges. Second, they could dispense the useless from their vows. Third, they could gather together the money arising from the commutation of the vows, from the trunks, and from the twentieth (if it will have been collected) under the witness of competent men. Fourth, that it should certainly be their duty (if you wish to remove scandal) to distribute the collected money to warriors [*milites*] already signed with the cross, or yet to be signed, or even to others who are believed to be useful for promoting the business of the crusade. However, I know that, [even without] deducting all general expenses, the twentieth will be nearly impossible to pay by the [regular] religious and even by others with the single exception of those who have fixed incomes from which they live.[17]

In fact, for faithfully and discreetly carrying out the aforesaid [business] through themselves and through others, I believe the persons noted below to be suitable. . . .[18] In other provinces I know few men who I dare to recommend for carrying out this business, particularly when the Albigensian Crusade amply busies some of them in the occupied lands in the vicinity of the Albigensians.[19]

17. Gervase here claims that few monastic or canonical houses or secular clerics can pay the income tax of one-twentieth, which the Fourth Lateran Council (1215) imposed for three years (1215–1218) for the crusade.

18. Gervase here lists various individuals for various dioceses in France.

19. The Albigensian Crusade had been reinstituted because of the continued resistance faced by the occupying forces, and portions of the clerical tax instituted for the Fifth Crusade were soon diverted to the antiheretical crusade.

If therefore in these suggestions I should seem presumptuous to someone who does not pay sufficient heed to the evident neglect of this business and the disposition of the person making them, I humbly beg the pardon of your clemency, Most Blessed Father, understanding with the cognizance of a witness that in saying these things I preserve filial devotion toward a father and the disposition of fraternal charity toward my brothers and fellow servants. May Your Most Holy Paternity remain strong in the Lord, so that God may preserve his church unharmed.

19. James of Vitry's Sermon to Pilgrims

Once individuals had taken the cross, they had to be instructed in the behavior expected of them as soldiers of Christ and as pilgrims. James of Vitry included various exhortations suited to crusaders in material he later reworked for a collection of sermons addressed to various estates, including pilgrims and crusaders. We include here the second of two sermons in James's *sermones ad status*. This collection of sermons directed at people with specific functions or identities in society was written when James was a cardinal in the curia of Gregory IX (1229–1240). Unlike the *reportatio* format of recruiting sermons like that edited above (No. 13), the sermons to pilgrims in his collections do not reflect sermons as actually delivered. They were meant instead to present themes and material for the preacher to draw upon when crafting his own sermon. However, they do reflect James's experience as a recruiter, as bishop of Acre, and his preaching in the crusaders' camp during the Fifth Crusade. Many of the themes evident in the anonymous recruiting sermons are repeated in James's sermons to pilgrims, indicating that the material was shared and recirculated and that the message used to recruit crusaders was often repeated and adapted to lead them to the "ideal" fulfillment of their vow. In fact, James's two sermons for pilgrims present much advice geared toward crusaders, who were often spiritually and legally treated as a special subcategory of pilgrims, and material from his sermons was incorporated into later sermons addressed to crusaders written by Gilbert of Tournai and Humbert of Romans (below, Nos. 69 and 70). Most important, James's sermons provide insight into a relatively scantily researched area: how clerics played an invaluable role in crafting and maintaining the morale, identity, morals, and goals of crusading armies, in this instance, those of the Fifth Crusade (1213–1221).

Early thirteenth-century crusaders were often recruited and mustered in an atmosphere of revivalism that presented taking the crusader's cross as a mark of conversion equivalent to becoming a temporary regular religious. Becoming a *cruces-ignatus* implied the renunciation of the world (and its vices and ties) and the embrace of purgation through hardship on pilgrimage in imitation of Christ, the saints and the regular religious, whose intercessions and heavenly rewards *crucesignati* hoped to share. Individual and social reform was considered an essential part of crusade preparations but also of the life of the crusading army; sin ensured spiritual and military defeat; virtue, victory. Pilgrims were expected to be detached from their families, homelands, and possessions, to remain chaste (or celibate), to be humble in demeanor and clothing and generous in almsgiving. However, these values could conflict with the demands of life in a crusading army and the qualities valued by knightly, merchant, artisanal, and peasant society.

We can imagine James and other clergymen preaching advice similar to the material below at mustering points, ports where crusaders were gathering for departure, while traveling, and during the crusade campaign itself. Elected bishop of Acre, James embarked upon a reforming tour of cities of the Latin Kingdom of Jerusalem, particularly his new see of Acre, a notorious port city that served as the main entry point for pilgrims to the Holy Land yet was blamed by many for corrupting pilgrims and crusaders alike with its heady mix of various religions, taverns, and brothels.

As Oliver of Paderborn's chronicle and other surviving evidence illustrates, the advice of clergy and their attempts, in collaboration with the legate Pelagius, to restore military and spiritual discipline sometimes had a profound impact on the army's behavior, particularly after natural disasters or military reversals when divine favor was avidly sought in the search for survival and victory. Some of the specific images and advice included in James's sermons echo those found in contemporary letters and chronicles of the Fifth Crusade, suggesting that ecclesiastics attempted to redress crusaders' concerns that the military goal of their campaign, Egypt, had become severed from the spiritual goal of rescuing Jerusalem from enemy hands. Ecclesiastics lauded alternative holy places in Egypt and reassured the army that those who went to Jerusalem, if not in deed, then in desire and will, would obtain the crusade indulgence. Practical advice concerning the redistribution of material resources among crusaders and admonitions to fully fulfill one's vow and remain pure from sin in order to obtain the crusade indulgence also reflected sometimes acrimonious debates within the army as to what constituted the proper fulfillment of the crusade vow and attempts by Pelagius to fairly distribute the wealth of the captured city of Damietta and prevent resources from leaving the army along with departing crusaders.

Warnings against vices endemic to crusader camps reflect similar attempts to clamp down on gambling, prostitution, disorder, theft, sins of the tongue, and other forms of crime. Preachers also sought to reassure crusaders rattled by apparent strategic failure and natural disasters through urging the need for continual penitence and spiritual preparedness while stressing that God loved pilgrims and that divine consolation awaited those suffering and dying exiles who had forfeited everything for Christ.

The practice of dividing the books of Christian scripture into chapters had come into use in the schools of Paris virtually during James of Vitry's lifetime. Therefore, the manuscripts edited and translated here often indicate in the body of text the book and chapter number of scripture. Where this occurs, we have filled in the verse numbers (not in use until the sixteenth century) in brackets.

See Bird, "James of Vitry's Sermons"; Maier, Crusade Propaganda and Ideology.

[Sermon] to Pilgrims

THEME drawn from the last chapter of Zechariah. "The Lord will strike down all the peoples who do not go up to celebrate the feast of the tabernacles" [Zec 14:18]. . . . He celebrates the feast of the tabernacles who by girding himself up and struggling dwells in this world like a stranger and pilgrim. . . . And the last chapter of Zechariah says: "They will go up from year to year to Jerusalem so that they might adore the Lord, the King of Hosts, and celebrate the feast of the tabernacles and there will be those who will not go up from the households of the land to Jerusalem to adore the Lord, King of Hosts, and there will fall upon them not rain but disaster" [Zec 14:16–17]. Therefore everyone ought to go up to Jerusalem, because even if they are not able to go up from year to year in deed, then they ought to at least go up in desire and will: from the year of guilt to the year of grace, having earned the holy remission of sins, or from the year of grace into the year of glory, having received the reward of rejoicing, otherwise the rain of divine grace will not fall upon them, but rather the disaster of sin and guilt.

So then, in this feast the Israelites used to offer some of each of the year's fruits to the Lord [Lv 23:40]. And true pilgrims also take care to offer themselves, their own, and their possessions to the Lord: their own bodies by afflicting them for the Lord's sake; their own by departing from their wife and children, from relations and friends; their possessions by spending them on this journey in the Lord's service. And they offer spiritual sacrifices from all of their possessions, that is, the wheat of good works, the wine of ardent charity, the oil of joyfulness of mind, the fig of sweet piety and the apple, the odor of a good example and holy behavior.

So then, pilgrimage is called a feast in that we ought to labor with joy in the Lord's service. For it is said of the Maccabees that they used to fight Israel's battles with rejoicing [1 Mc 3:2] and the Egyptians said to Joseph: "May we find favor in the eyes of our Lord and we will serve the king joyfully" [Gn 47:25]. And in Leviticus 10[:19] we read that Aaron told Moses, "How can we please the lord with a mournful disposition?" Therefore you ought to observe this feast of pilgrimage with spiritual rejoicing, for whether you live or die you will belong to the Lord. If you live, it will be fortunate for you, because you will return with the treasure

Source: Douai, Bibliothèque municipale, MS 503, fols. 370v–374r; Trento, Biblioteca comunale, MS 1670 (F55), fols. 100rb–102va.

of an accomplished indulgence, absolved from all your sins. If in fact you die to this world in the Lord's service it is better for you because you will cross over to eternal joy. So then, whatever might happen to you, be it life or death, you ought to rejoice. Indeed, "for you, to live is Christ and to die is gain" [Phil 1:21].

In Leviticus 23[:26–36] it is said: "the day of propitiation was very sacred to the Lord." And for that very reason, this day is called the day of affliction and the day of expiation. For these three things coincided in that day. This is the feast of the pilgrims which is called the feast of affliction because they afflict their bodies for the sake of Christ, the feast of expiation because they are purged and expiated from all their sins. Because this happens from the Lord's great mercy it is called the feast of propitiation. For a great propitiation of the Lord is manifest in the remission of all sins and the granting of eternal life. According to the psalmist: "And in my old age abounding mercy" [Ps 91:11]. In the old age of the church, while the end of the world looms, the Lord proffers this great and fullest mercy to everyone. Therefore the feast of pilgrimage, that is, the feast of expiation, the feast of affliction, and the feast of propitiation is called a solemn feast very sacred to the Lord. Accordingly, it should be observed with a joyful attitude and with exultation because there is great rejoicing in heaven over one sinner doing penance.

For the Lord invites sinners to this feast of pilgrimage, saying through Jeremiah 46[:19]: "Pack your belongings for exile, daughter of the inhabitants of Egypt." The baggage of pilgrimage is the satchel of charity where we place all our works so that they might be done in charity and from it we also take what seems necessary for us and for our neighbors and the staff of the cross or holy hope, such that preserving trust in the Lord we hold onto long-suffering. For the staff of pilgrimage is broken by some of whom it is said in Ecclesiasticus 2[:16]: "Woe to those who throw away their support." However, Christ held onto the staff of the cross in his pilgrimage, upon which staff many dogs gnawed and still gnaw today, detracting from pilgrimage and contradicting the cross. According to Luke 2[:34]: "And in the sign which will be spoken against."[20] Certainly, the baggage of pilgrimage consists of a contrite heart and the confession of sins with which we go out from Egypt and migrate from vices to virtues.

---

20. See also James of Vitry's sermon 2.12 and Gilbert of Tournai's sermon 2.12 in Maier, *Crusade Propaganda*, 106–109 and 194–197.

In Ezekiel [12:3–4] . . . the prophet was commanded to go into exile by day before them so that he might provide a good example for others. Some, however, refuse to take the cross before a crowd even though the cross ought instead to be accepted openly and worn on the shoulders before everyone because of the example this sets. You ought to migrate from place to place, that is from virtue to virtue. For the pilgrim ought always to make progress for the better. You ought to carry out your packed possessions as if they were luggage for exile, that is, by removing bundles from your home. However, he who hoards bundles of riches and temporal things in his home does not demonstrate that he is going to go into exile, but rather the person who distributes his possessions to paupers or spends them in the Lord's service or at least distributes them to poor pilgrims and crusaders as we read of Cyrus in the second book of Ezra, that he commanded that all the others were to support whoever wanted to go to Jerusalem [Ezr 1:3–4].

Therefore it is time that we go up to the feast of the tabernacles. For today what the prophet says in Joel [2:21–22] is fulfilled before our eyes: "O land, do not be afraid, but be glad and rejoice because the Lord values what he has made . . . [and] just as the tree bore its own fruit, so also the fig and vineyard yielded their goodness." Indeed this is a reason for exultation and gladness because the wood of the cross bore its fruit which was made manifest in those signed with the cross, who expressly follow the Crucified so that they might obtain the indulgence of sins and the fruit of eternal salvation which will come to be through the grace of the Holy Spirit and the teaching of preachers. For the fig, that is, the sweetness of the Holy Spirit, and the vineyard, that is, the intoxicating teaching of the holy scriptures, yielded their goodness in these days which is clear from the conversion of sinners. Or the fig stands for the sermon soothing through promises, and the vineyard stands for the sermon stinging through warnings.

And this is what Isaiah says: "He will lift up the sign among the distant nations and will whistle for those at the ends of the earth" [Is 5:26]. Today the Lord lifts up the sign of the holy cross by inspiring and gathering the faithful from the entire world. And we ought not to put down the cross like those who suffer much for the sake of earthly things, but ought to raise it by laboring for eternal things. For you know that when a man carries a staff upright, a dog fears him and does not dare to draw near. However, when he drags the staff on the ground, the dog gnaws at it from behind. And for this reason we ought to lift up the staff of the cross against the infernal dogs who truly fear it and are confounded when for the sake of Christ the sign of the cross is raised up and fastened to the shoulders. For the Lord warns us to take up the cross, exhorts us so that we fight, and aids us so that we triumph. He watches over the struggling, aids those calling upon him,[21] and raises up the exhausted. How wretched are those who put down the cross or hide it, as do many who already for many years have taken the cross and then have concealed it, breaking their vow. Against them Parables 20 [Prv 20:25] says: "It is disaster for a man to devour holy things and afterwards to retract his vow."[22] For the Lord says: "Vow and render" [Ps 75:12]. The Devil says: "See that you promise: what harm is there in promises?"[23] To break a vow to the Lord is to mock him, and so Isaiah 28[:22] says: "Do not mock [God] lest your chains bind more tightly." And Malachi 2[:11] says: "Judah contaminated his sanctification." For when those who previously confessed and professed that they would perform this pilgrimage repent from the good which they began, they contaminate their sanctification.

In fact, this can be understood of certain pilgrims and crusaders who do not keep themselves from sins but in returning to their vomit befoul their pilgrimage [Prv 26:11]. For just as a horse with a lame hoof is useless, so a pilgrimage without perseverance to the end is rendered useless. Ezekiel 1[:10]. When the holy animals walked, they did not turn back. However, some do not observe the feast of the tabernacles, but of the taverns in which they intoxicate themselves. Seneca testifies: "Whatever is born in virtue, intemperance destroys."[24] In fact, a drunkard is not so much he who drinks wine as he who is drunk or absorbed by wine. For this reason Isaiah 28[:7] [says]: "Because of their drunkenness they are absorbed by wine." I saw many pilgrims who, fatigued from their journey, used to drink until they were dead drunk and others who, although they were not thirsty, when they saw their companions drinking, without any need to, began to drink lest perhaps they be cheated. Against this kind of incautious and drunken men Solomon says in Proverbs 23[:31–32]: "Do not gaze at wine when it turns golden yellow, when its color

21. This could alternatively read "the innocent."

22. Compare Oliver of Paderborn, *Historia Damiatina*, chap. 42, translated as the *Capture of Damietta* in No. 21 below.

23. Ovid, *Ars amatoria*, 1.443, in *The Art of Love and Other Poems*, ed. and trans. J. H. Mozley, 2d ed., Loeb Classical Library 232 (New York, 1935), 42–43.

24. Seneca, *Ad Lucilium epistolae morales*, ed. and trans. Richard M. Gummere, 3 vols. (London, 1925), 2:124–127, ep. 74, sect. 19.

sparkles in the glass. It goes down smoothly, but in the end it will bite like a snake and pour forth venom like a viper." For when they have become inebriated then their possessions will be stolen from them by evil tavern keepers or even by wicked companions. Certainly there is no love among hostelers. They live from theft. The guest is not safe from his host, nor the father-in-law from his brother's offspring. Friendship is also scarce. 2 Samuel 13[:28]. While drunk, Amnon was slain by his brother. Indeed many are slain by their brother, that is, by the body through drunkenness, since lust follows inebriation, according to the testimony of Ecclesiasticus 19[:2]. "Wine and women cause wise men to become apostates," that is, to depart from the way of the upright and "rebuke the prudent," that is, makes them worthy of blame. "After all, when she's drunk does Venus care about anything? She doesn't know the difference between head and crotch!"[25]

For you will find many prostitutes and wicked women in hospices who lie in wait for the incautious and maliciously repay their hosts like a mouse in the satchel, a serpent in the bosom, and a fire in the lap,[26] a thorn in the foot, a nail in the eye. In fact, it is safer to sleep among demons who can be put to flight with the sign of the cross than near this worst kind of women, who ambush drunkards. Judges 16[:1–19]. For when Samson slept among the Philistines, nothing bad happened to him, yet when he slumbered in Delilah's lap he lost his curls. So then, one ought to eat and drink to refresh the body, not to excess. . . .

In fact, above all things the pilgrim ought to guard himself from association with the perverse lest he be corrupted by the wicked's example or promptings. For you will meet many depraved people and reprobates on the way and even in the Holy Land. They change their homeland but not their behavior, they hasten across the sea, changing the skies above them but not their souls. For although the Holy Land ought to be a blessed paradise, such that through it paradise is designated in the holy scriptures, nonetheless in this kind of paradise there are many demons and most pernicious inhabitants. Jeremiah 13[:23]. For the Ethiopian does not change his skin even when he is among white [people]. Therefore it behooves you to diligently choose the company of the good, as

25. Juvenal, Satire 6, in *Juvenal and Persius*, ed. Susanna Morton Braund, Loeb Classical Library (Cambridge MA, 2004), pp. 260–261, lines 300–301.

26. Compare the Aesopian fable "About the man who put a serpent in his lap," related by James's contemporary, the similarly Paris-educated Odo of Cheriton. See John C. Jacobs, trans., *The Fables of Odo of Cheriton* (Syracuse NY, 1985), no. 88, pp. 136–137.

Solomon testifies in Parables 13 [Prv 13:20]. "He who walks with the wise will be wise; however, the companion of the foolish will become similar to them." And Ecclesiasticus 8[:18] says. "Do not set out on the road with a rash man," that is, with a fool who presumes too much in himself. In fact, sometimes many people are punished for the sake of one person's foolishness. And so he adds in chapter 8[:18]: "Lest perhaps his wicked deeds burden you." And in Apocalypse 18[:4]. "Go forth from there, my people," that is from Babylon or association with wicked men, "lest you be participants in its delights and lest you share in its disasters."[27] On the other hand, it is said of good fellowship in Ecclesiasticus 28 [sic]: "He who joins up with a person more respectable than himself takes a burden upon himself" [Ecclus 13:2], that is, the weight of fear by which we are restrained from sinning.

It is equally essential for pilgrims to refrain from disputes and litigation. For better to sustain a modest injury from your host or companion than harm one's soul by litigating, as [it says] in Ecclesiasticus 28[:10]: "Refrain from disputes and you will lessen sin," that is, both in yourself and in your neighbor who would sin by litigating with you. For this reason the same authority adds in chapter 28[:11]: "A man prone to anger incites disputes and a sinful person stirs up his friends and introduces enmity in the midst of those possessing peace," because this kind of man sows discord between brothers and destroys friendship between companions.

So then, since you are going to fight against the enemies of the Crucified, you ought not to fear because you have a just war and unjust adversaries, you possess a good conscience and they do not. There are more allies with you than with your adversaries because you fight with the aid of God, the angels, the saints, the suffrages of the church triumphant, and the prayers and merits of the church militant. For he who does not want to fall short in reaping ought not to fall short in sowing. In death you will acquire eternal life and your adversaries everlasting death. Therefore, be comforted and be strong, placing your hope not in man, but in God, not in the strength of a multitude, but in the mercy of the Savior.

Concerning those who trust in horses and worldly pomps, Isaiah 31[:1] says: "Woe to you who go down into Egypt for help, trusting in

27. Ironically, in letters written to individuals responsible for the promotion of the Fifth Crusade, James of Vitry depicted crusaders as hoping to rid themselves of their sins by going to the geographical Babylon (the name medieval people often used to refer to Egypt or the city of Cairo). See James of Vitry, *Lettres de Jacques de Vitry*, ed. R. B. C. Huygens (Leiden, 1960), here nos. 3–4, pp. 100, 102.

horses and putting your faith in chariots because there are many [of them] and in those riding on horses, because they are strong beyond measure and do not trust in the Holy One of Israel and do not look to the Lord." For you ought not to hope in the horses of worldly force, nor fix your goodwill in a horse's strength, because they slept when they mounted their horses, nor in the chariots of worldly pomp, that is, the Pharaoh's chariots. And so he adds in chapter 31[:33]: "Egypt [is] man and not God," that is, Egypt is a worldly and frail man and their horses are flesh and not spirit so that they will quickly fail them. And again in the person of such men, Isaiah 30[:16] says: "We will flee to [our] horses, therefore you will be put to flight"; as if to say, because you hope in horses, you will be put to flight by your enemies. "We will mount swift [horses], therefore those who pursue you will be more swift," that is, material enemies or demons.[28]

Therefore those who presume in their own military forces or go out to battle in mortal sin fall swiftly and easily. For this reason, in Joshua 7[:1–26] we read that Israel could not stand firm before its foes because she was polluted by the anathematized spoils from Jericho. In fact, we should fear the sins of Christians more than the Saracen forces. For our sins make them powerful. For this very reason when battle looms, you ought always to hasten to confession. According to that authority: "I opened my mouth and drew the spirit" [Ps 118:131]. I opened my mouth in confession and drew the spirit for the remission of sins. So then, after making confession and receiving the body of Christ and making your will, you can go out to do battle untroubled, assured of the crown of victory and eternal reward. Otherwise, if you go out unprepared, although you might shed blood for Christ's sake, it will not be of any benefit to you for eternal life. Proverbs 15[:8]: "The sacrifices of the impious are abominable." For it is written in Exodus 23[:18]: "Do not offer up the blood of your sacrifice upon leaven." To offer up upon leaven is to fight against the enemies of Christ in a state of mortal sin. And so Isidore [says]: "The sons of Israel were enslaved for many years because of their sins, but the converted were freed, because our sins grant power to our enemies."[29]

---

28. This passage bears marked similarity to a homily-like portion of James of Vitry's epistle 5. Written while he was in the crusader camp in Egypt, the letter reflects the kind of sermons he and other prelates in the army were probably delivering to crusaders before battle. See James of Vitry, *Lettres*, no. 5, pp. 117–118.

29. We have been unable to identify this citation.

For he who forfeits such great labors for the sake of a trifling carnal pleasure or any other sin is truly foolish and insane, like a farmer who labors throughout the year in his field and places the harvested crops on the fire. If, therefore, the devil should tempt you to sin you ought to reply to that insinuator, " 'Get thee behind me, Satan!' [Mt 16:23]. I deserted my wife and children for Christ, and although I do not comprehend that sweetness by which the native soil might hold everyone else and does not permit them to be unmindful of its own peculiar charm, nonetheless for the Lord's sake I conquered longing for my homeland and every fleshly affection. I spent much money in the Lord's service; I exposed myself to the perils of the sea and many other things. I do not want to lose all this for the sake of one base passion." For carnal pleasure is like a guest who after one day quickly passes on, leaving nothing for his host except dung.

For how very soon we will yearn for a support in this long life unless we possess assurance, for just as days and nights fly by quickly, so our pilgrimage swiftly heads toward death. No ship sails so violently or swiftly that it cannot be held back by any means. Yet our pilgrimage and our voyage to death cannot be checked nor does it ever rest. For this very reason the stubborn and obstinate who do not want to be signed with the cross for Christ's sake, whether or not they desire it, are pilgrims who every day make one day's journey toward death and into hell. However, these kinds of men remain mired in riches and pleasures and, yes, even in their own filthinesses, of whom Jeremiah 48[:11] says: "Moab was fruitful from her youth, resting on her own dregs [like wine]. She has not been poured from one vessel to another and she has not gone into exile. So her taste remains and her odor has not changed." She has not been poured from vessel to vessel, from the vessel of guilt to the vessel of grace. She has not gone into exile by wandering and laboring for Christ and so like a clouded wine she harbors a disgusting taste and foul odor, "and water acquires a taint unless it is in motion."[30] So also the mind of such people is so divided by manifold misfortunes and anxieties that the fire of the Holy Spirit cannot kindle them, just as scattered wood cannot be easily set on fire. For a man is truly hard-hearted if he abandons his fellow nurslings for strangers and foreigners, that is, the suffering and poverty with which we are born and raised for riches and pleasures.

How wretched and ungrateful are those who always want to receive benefits from the Lord and yet never want to respond to him, like a man

---

30. Ovid, "Ex Ponto," 1.5.6, in S. G. Owen, ed., *P. Ovidi Nasonis Tristium Libri Quinque, Ibis, Ex Ponto Libri Quattuor, Halieutica, Fragmenta* (Oxford, 1915).

who is ashamed of his neighbor. The Lord served us upon the cross such that he said to the hammer and nails fixing him to it as is commonly said: "hold tightly."[31] And yet we do not want to serve him, nor even give straw in exchange for his grain. We run into danger on rivers and nonetheless do not want to cling to the tree which, firmly rooted, is safe from the water's waves. However, he truly has an iron heart who cannot be saved by the nail by which hell itself was emptied, so that the Lord in Jeremiah 5[:3] says: "I called and you refused." We would not dare to transgress the edict of an earthly king, so how do we dare to transgress the edict of the Eternal King? There is hardly a fool or even a child who would not willingly accept what he was given and yet you do not want to accept the remission of sins and heavenly kingdom which is offered to you.

So then, tow is easily lit, that is, paupers who are inclined to every good and to whom the kingdom of heaven belongs. However a rotten tree trunk does nothing except smoke and cannot be set on fire, as Jeremiah 6[:29–30] testifies. "In vain the bellows-blower blows," that is, Christ, who makes a bellows from the skin of his flesh and the wood and nails of the cross and yet these trunks are so full of mud and clay that they cannot be set alight by this bellow nor can they be pierced by the arrows of the Lord's word although they can be sharply pierced by the iron of his nails. Similar to the beautiful falcon called a *leuiers*, which, when summoned, does not want to return to its master's hand but perches on a branch, these kinds of men are also held back by the verdure of temporal things or rather by the corpses of riches. And when Christ says through Isaiah [50:5]: "I did not go back, I did not contradict," these men contradict and go back and scuttle backward like a crab. For this reason, Jeremiah 7[:24] says: "They went backward and not forward." And Christ himself says in Isaiah 50[:6–7]: "I set my face like the hardest rock, I did not avert my face from those insulting and spitting upon me, I surrendered my body to those striking me and my cheeks to those pulling out my beard," or according to the Septuagint: "I bared my back to the whip and my cheeks to blows from him who contradicts me." As if to say, when I accomplished so many and such great things for you, how can you contradict me? You must either suffer for the Lord or you will be required to suffer far more for the Devil.

31. Literally, "to his hammer and to his nail." For the Old French phrase *à son fer et a son clou,* meaning "tightly, securely," see G. di Stef, *Dictionnaire des locutions en moyen française* (Montréal, 1991), 335–336.

The merchant who buys a sack full of straw and rejects a sack full of grain which he could have possessed for an equal or lesser price is foolish. In particular, you who gather to God's word are similar to a hen which is friendly when it is fed and comes to the hand [of its master] but when it ought to be caught runs away. If perhaps you do not believe that this market is a good one, consult the wise merchants who best know costly merchandise, that is, archbishops, bishops, priests, and scholars who flock to this market.

If, however, you pay heed to the Devil's war against you and to your danger, the arms of the cross would not seem so burdensome or heavy to you, similar to a warrior who, when surrounded on every side by enemies, does not pay much heed to the weight of his shield amid such danger, but is pleased with the arms which defend him even though they are heavy. Luke 22[:36]. So then, "those who have a tunic ought to sell it and buy a sword," by abandoning the bodily tunic for the salvation of their souls. Many people until they are healed do not consider how great the usefulness of this pilgrimage is, like the madman who at first mocks his doctor but after he is healed thanks him. Similarly, when they are being taught, boys hate their masters for beating them, but after they reach adulthood they leave their homeland and, with much labor, wander, seeking the schools of masters who can instruct them. If you want to have the sweetness of the cross's fruit you must taste the bitterness of its root. I trust in the Lord that once you have obtained the full indulgence of all your sins, you will pray for me and bless me when you have attained the reward of eternal life. Proverbs 20[:14]: "Every buyer says 'This is no good, this is no good!'" yet in the end "boasts about his purchase." For the true Joshua distributes the promised land with the rope of the cross [Jo 13–21; Ps 77:54].

Now the Lord proved that he will renew the world on many occasions and summoned us many times so that his wine might be poured from vessel to vessel, lest its fullness become sour. You ought to truly fear lest this be the final and peremptory summons. So then, those who want to rest in this world and be great are similar to Lucifer, whose voice is: "I will ascend" and "I will sit" [Is 14:13]. On the other hand, the voice of Christ and true Christians is: I will descend and I will toil.[32] However, he who carries the emperor's seal with him, that is, the cross of Christ by which the Savior's flesh was sealed and imprinted, can safely labor in this

32. Compare "De crucis commendacione," ed. Bird, "Victorines," 24.

pilgrimage. For a lord arms the knights whom he loves most with his own weapons, for just as the banner leads the way in procession and the cross of Christ has its place in it, so we cannot achieve victory without the cross. For just as a warrior without arms is not safe in battle, so without the cross no one can fight against the devil. For this reason, Jerome [says]: "The hand ought to make the sign of the cross in each action and every proceeding."[33]

And the blessed Gregory tells of a certain nun who, omitting the sign of the cross, ate some lettuce and a demon entered into her. When it was forced by a certain holy man to leave her, it replied: "What is my fault? What did I do? Why do you drive me out? I was sitting on the lettuce and she did not make the sign of the cross, and so she ate me along with the lettuce."[34]

In fact, Gregory tells of a certain Jew who, when he was making a journey, turned aside to a certain cemetery next to the temple of Apollo as night fell. When an evil spirit came upon him at night, although because he was a Jew he had no faith in the cross, he signed himself with it from fear. And the devil was not able to harm him and, returning to his companions, said, "I found a vessel which was empty but sealed." Hearing this, the demons fled and having experienced the power of the cross in his liberation, the Jew became a Christian.[35]

We also read of a certain pilgrim that when he grew ill in foreign regions and did not have any consolation from his friends, the Lord sent angels to him to console him and bear off his soul in death without any pain. When the angels returned, they said, "His soul does not want to come out of his body." Then the Lord sent David to sing with his lyre before the pilgrim. And when the soul of the pilgrim heard the modulations of sweet sound, it left his body with rejoicing and delight.[36] Behold how the Lord loves pilgrims and consoles those who for love of him give up the familiar consolation of their blood relatives and relations.

For in the lives of the [desert] fathers we read that there were two brothers, one dedicated to pilgrimage, the other who rested. So then, it happened that the pilgrim died and the angels led his soul to heaven.

33. Jerome, ep. 22, "Ad Eustochium," in I. Hilberg, ed., *Sancti Eusebii Hieronymi Epistulae*, Corpus scriptorum ecclesiasticorum latinorum 54–56 (Vienna, 1996), 54:202, lines 1–2.

34. Crane, *Exempla*, 59, no. 130.

35. Ibid., no. 131.

36. Ibid., no. 132.

However, when the soul ought to enter, a question arose concerning it and the Lord said, "He was a bit negligent, but because he was a pilgrim, open the gates to him." Then after both he and his brother had died, a certain old man who had seen the angels come to the pilgrim did not see any present by his brother and questioned the Lord why it was so, and a divine voice sounded out, replying to him: "That pilgrim received no consolation from his friends and blood relations [so it was necessary for me to console him through angels. However, his brother had consolation from his blood relations and friends]."[37] We find many other examples in the scriptures concerning the consolation of pilgrims and the power of the cross and the merit or reward of those signed with the cross, who dedicate themselves and their possessions to our Lord Jesus Christ, to whom is honor and glory through all ages. Amen.

20. The Rhineland Crusaders, 1220

The value of this text lies in the detail it provides for the first stages of the crusade in northern Europe, particularly the organization of the fleet and the army in the Rhine region. Especially notable are references to the leaders, Counts William of Holland and George of Wied, to the laws that regulated the crusaders, and the fact that the leaders were aware that the emperor Frederick II was not prepared to depart in 1217. The work was written after the capture of Damietta in 1219 by a well-informed cleric, most probably a man who accompanied the fleet. It does not mention the subsequent defeat of the crusaders, finishing on a victorious note. This indicates that its purpose was to celebrate the achievements of the Rhineland crusaders, and it ended with their return home.

On the progress of the fleet

IN THE year of grace, 1217, William, count of Holland, and Gerard [George],[38] count of Wied, joined other crusaders from Germany and Frisia, desiring to set out for the Holy Land, at Vlaardingen.

Therefore, on the fourth of the Calends of June [May 29], these pilgrims, commending themselves and their own to God, joyfully set sail

---

Source: *"Gesta crucigerorum Rhenanorum," in Reinhold Röhricht, ed.,* Quinti belli sacri scriptores minores *(Geneva, 1879; repr., Osnabrück, 1968), 27–34.*

37. Ibid., 59–60, no. 133. The bracketed portion is published in Crane's edition of the *exempla* from James's *Sermones ad status*, although it does not appear in the Douai and Trento manuscripts.

38. The name "Gerard" was added by a later scribe. The count mentioned is actually George of Wied.

with almost three hundred ships, heading to Dartmouth in England. They agreed together to choose William, count of Holland, as the commander of the army, and they decided under him on laws and new rules concerning the observance of peace. On the third of the nones of the same month [June 5], they arrived at the sea off Brittany, where a ship from Monheim was crushed between the rocks hidden in the sea. The rest of the ships, therefore, anchored in the harbor at Saint Matthew and attempted to rescue the shipwrecked men from the rock they had climbed on. Then the ships sailed to the port of Faro in the kingdom of León, and leaving their ships in the port, they sought out the shrine of the glorious Saint James in Compostela.

Likewise, on the martyrdom of Peter and Paul [June 29], they returned to their ships and set sail. When a terrible storm arose, the ships were separated and the count of Holland sought port with several ships in the kingdom of Portugal, at whose entrance three ships were wrecked. But the count of Wied entered a port in the same kingdom with the rest of the ships. Finally about the ides of July [July 15], with the worst over, they entered the port of Lisbon. Lisbon is a very fine city, situated on a hill, where the gold-bearing Tagus joins the western sea.

Ulysses built this city, when he departed Troy after its destruction. But now, the body of Vincent, priest and martyr, is venerated there. And so when the crusaders were staying for some days in this place, waiting for other ships, Severus, bishop of Lisbon, came to them along with Martin, commander of Palmela, the Templars, Hospitallers, and other nobles. They explained their continuous sufferings and vexations from the fact that the Saracens were too close. They stated that there was a fort inhabited by the Saracens that is called Alcazar, that is, the prison of all men, from which long ago Christians were violently expelled and held captive, adding that this fort was required to send the heads of a thousand Christians to the king of Morocco every year. And so they asked that, motivated by their Christian religion, they would agree to help to free them from the inhabitants of this place, since this fort was the key and the center of error in the whole of Spain. The counts, after they had taken counsel with discreet men, left their ships, swearing an oath, that the sea route was closed to them by adverse winds during this season and their presence in the Holy Land was not needed, especially since the king of the Romans[39] and the Romans, along with many German princes, would

39. Frederick II, crowned king of the Romans in 1215, but not yet crowned emperor (1220).

not cross over at this time. They therefore chose in the meantime to labor at the divine task and to invade the territories of the enemies of the faith and, to bring peace to this place rather than lie around at their leisure like useless serfs.

The abbot of Werden [Heribert] and almost all the Frisians and also some others disagreed with this plan, and they withdrew to Lisbon on the sixth feria [July 31] after the feast of Saint James [July 25], with eighty ships or a few more, and just as it resulted, only one of them did not cross over at this time. But many, blinded by an impenetrable fog, landed unwillingly at the port of Alcazar with the others.

On the siege of Alcazar and the battle fought there

ON THE third of the Calends of August [July 30], the fort, which is situated in a land teeming with fish and wild animals, was besieged by the counts. Not long after, the aforementioned bishops arrived with a large contingent, together with the Sword Brothers[40] and other nobles, and after they had filled in the moat, they erected war machines against the walls. The sappers worked to undermine the wall and on their side the Saracens were impeding our efforts. But by the labor of these two groups, one of the towers fell about the feast of Saint Bartholomew [August 24], and still no entrance was opened, because the interior wall remained and it could not be breeched because of its width: eighteen feet. On the Friday [September 9] following the Nativity of the Blessed Mary [September 8], four Saracen kings gathered at the walls in a huge crowd, reckoned at a hundred thousand. They began to set up camp only about a league from the Christians, either to force them to flee or to take them captive. The Christians were reluctant to fight because of their lack of horses. They quickly dug a ditch around themselves and their goods, but Almighty God, who "resisting the proud, gives grace to the humble" [Jas 4:6], brought them aid in the middle of the night in the person of Peter, master of the Templars, fighting for God on this side of the sea.

In the morning, on the feast of Protus and Hyacinth [September 11], in the greatest elation those kings were drawn up for battle on the eastern side. But the Christians, fewer in number, but stronger in merit, drew up their battle lines in proper order on the western side. The Saracens trusted their strength, the Christians, their faith. But Martin, commander of Palmela, though small in body, had the heart of a lion. He

---

40. The Sword Brothers were the knightly military order of Alcantará that was later absorbed into the Castilian Order of Calatrava.

brandished his banner and burst the middle in the line, and he was joined in battle by Peter, the commander of the Knights Templar, and he followed them quickly with a crowd of his men. Here, horse opposed horse; here, swords faced swords. Here, shield met shield; here, overwhelming experience overcame inexperience. Why should we delay more? The divine power humiliated the proud and made the humble victorious, for one of the kings fell in the first attack and the remaining dead were innumerable. The number of captives was infinite. And we must recount that while the captives were being led through the army, they were asking about the signs of the victors, a shining battle line, wearing red crosses, which had forced their army to flee. Also, the galleys they brought from overseas fled, leaving their horses, camels, tents, and all their supplies for us. Then, our forces, always under the leadership of Count Gerard [George], went back to their attacks on the walls, and both Christians and Saracens were killed, the former with stones, the latter with arrows. The Westphalians and Saxons demonstrated their usual courage, and the Rhinelanders, without equal in ingenuity and deeds, flew to the attack with all their might; the white shields of men of Nusse with their red cross were not hesitant in attack. Also, our men, moved by a strong desire, built siege machines, called "hevenho."

Around the feast of the Eleven Thousand Virgins,[41] another tower was undermined by the sappers. The terrified infidels surrendered the fort, handing themselves and their goods over to the pilgrims by an agreement that all Christians should be released from captivity and not killed. But the commander of the fort, called Abur, along with several hostages sought baptism after they agreed to the treaty, and not long afterward he returned to his error. About three thousand persons, men and women, children and older men, were found in the fort and all were sold and divided among the pilgrims. The infant was snatched from the mother's breast, the spouse divided from his bride, as fate dictated. And we do not think we should omit that in fact the Christians, sensing the odor of profit, crossed through the walls, against the prohibition, stealing purple cloth with gold and silver ornaments. But when they were warned under penalty of excommunication, they brought them back and divided them with the community. But, one of them, seduced by the beauty of the material that he had stolen, presumed to violate the laws of obedience,

41. October 21, the feast of Saint Ursula and her eleven thousand companions, martyrs, a feast much celebrated in Cologne.

and when he had taken food, he was immediately suffocated at the first bite, but by the mercy of God, he escaped the danger by confession and after this he restored the things he had stolen.

After the feast of All Saints [November 1], the whole Christian army, when they had handed the fort over to the Sword Brothers, returned to Lisbon, where their chests were filled with all good things. And behold a miracle should be mentioned. For all the regions and places were yielding abundance to the pilgrims, but after their departure shortage followed in each country, but God especially provided for the clergy, for in Lisbon we found a well-educated theologian, who, relieved of temporal cares, was devoted more studiously to contemplation alone, and by his teaching we were given new life in the sweetness of scripture.

21. Oliver of Paderborn, *The Capture of Damietta*, ca. 1217–1222

The *Historia Damiatina*, long known in English translation as *The Capture of Damietta*, is the most extensive and important narrative account of the Fifth Crusade. Its author, Oliver of Paderborn, was an eyewitness and clerical participant in the crusade, had preached extensively on recruiting missions for it, and was closely involved with its organization, policy, and, on a least one occasion, its military strategy.

Oliver was born to a family of lesser nobility in the vicinity of Paderborn, where he first appears in 1196 as a witness in a dispute between the diocese of Paderborn and a nearby monastery. He is referred to as *magister*, a term meaning a learned cleric, and by 1200 he was the *scholasticus*, or schoolmaster, of the diocese of Paderborn. He was called to the same position at Cologne in 1201, in the heyday of the city's prosperity, and he seems to have worked in both Cologne and at the schools of Paris until 1209, when he returned to Cologne and taught until 1213. In 1213 Innocent III issued the letter *Vineam Domini*, the call for the Fourth Lateran Council and the crusade, and Oliver was launched on his career as a crusade preacher/recruiter. Working primarily in the province of Cologne, he preached in Liège, Namur, Brabant, Flanders, Utrecht, and Friesland. In 1215 he served as a representative of the archbishop of Cologne at the Fourth Lateran Council. On April 10, 1216, he is known to have been in Liège, and on June 1, 1217, he sailed from Marseilles and arrived at Acre in July or August.

He seems to have written his history between 1217 and 1222 (the latest date in the history is the call for a council to meet in Verona in November 1222 to consider another crusade). Oliver's history is not only a narrative chronicle of the current campaign but also an explanation of the failure of the Fifth Crusade and a call for a new crusade to be used in recruiting for Frederick II's intended campaign (in which Oliver was heavily involved, not only in preaching but also in attending some of the organizational councils)—hence, his ending with the call to the Council of Verona in 1222.

Oliver also wrote several other works, a description of the Holy Land, a history of Jerusalem (which ends in 1099), and a history of the kings of the Holy Land, as well as a number of letters.

Oliver returned from the East and was preaching the crusade in Cologne in 1222, and in 1223 he was elected bishop of Paderborn. The election was contested, however, and his election was not confirmed by Honorius III (1216–1227) until April 7, 1225. Oliver was preaching the crusade again in 1223, and in 1225 was made the cardinal bishop of Santa Sabina. He died between August 9 and September 18, 1227.

Oliver was thus one of those learned scholar/teachers who came from the schools of Paris in the late twelfth century, among whom were, of course, also Innocent III and James of Vitry, the latter using Oliver's history for his own history of the Holy Land. Thus, Oliver's narrative and worldview are deserving of the same consideration as the events of the crusade.

Oliver's chronicle is a complete eyewitness account of the response of Christendom to the crusading pleas of Pope Innocent III from a very well-placed observer. The crusade marks a major shift in crusade strategy, since it was aimed at Egypt instead of Syria, intending to capture key places in Egypt and then trade them for Jerusalem. The destination of Egypt had already been considered during the organization of the Fourth Crusade, but obviously could not have been effected. Its near success in the Fifth Crusade reflects the soundness of the change in tactics, and its failure stirred even greater concern for another crusade.

On the preaching/recruiting network of Innocent III and Parisian scholars and the wide breadth of Oliver's interests and activities, see Jessalynn Bird, "Oliver of Paderborn," in Christian-Muslim Relations: A Bibliographical History, *vol. 4, ed. David Thomas and Alex Mallett (Leiden, 2012); Jessalynn Bird, "Crusade and Conversion After the Fourth Lateran Council (1215): Oliver of Paderborn's and James of Vitry's Missions to Muslims Reconsidered,"* Essays in Medieval Studies *21 (2004), 23–48.*

HERE begins the history of Damietta whereat Master Oliver, compiler of this work and preacher of the Holy Cross, was undoubtedly present.

Source: *The translation printed here was first published by John J. Gavigan in the* University of Pennsylvania Translations and Reprints from the Original Sources of European History, *3d series, vol. 2 (Philadelphia, 1948). The entire work, except for the editorial apparatus and notes, is reprinted below. For reasons of space, we have omitted most of the scholarly editorial material from the original English translation, but we have retained the full text of Oliver's chronicle and the numbering of chapters. Those interested in the translator's editorial materials and notes should consult* The Capture of Damietta by Oliver of Paderborn, *translated by John J. Gavigan (Philadelphia, 1948; repr., New York, 1980); or Peters,* Christian Society and Crusade, *49–139. Gavigan's translation was based on the edition by Hermann Hoogeweg,* Die Schriften des Kölner Domscholasters, Späteren Bischofs von Paderborn und Kardinal-Bischofs von S. Sabina Oliverus, *Bibliothek des Litterarischen Vereins in Stuttgart, vol. 202 (Tübingen, 1894).*

Foreword

"LET Mount Sion rejoice, and let the daughters of Judah be glad because of Thy judgments, O Lord. Sing ye to the Lord for he has done great things" [Ps 47:12]. Writing and preaching, let them announce the wonders of the Lord [Is. 13:3]. Who has commanded his sanctified ones and has called his strong ones in his wrath, them that exult not in their own strength, "not in the works of justice which they themselves have done" [Ti 3:5], but in the glory of his majesty, who is blessed in all things in eternity. For "the land whence arose the bread that came down from heaven" [Rom 1:25; Jb 28:5; Jn 6:33] in the place of his birth has been cut off by the sword, and by many fortifications which perfidious men occupy. "The stones of this land are the place of sapphires"[Jb 28:6] because it was the possession of the patriarchs, the nursling of the prophets, the teacher of the apostles, the mother of faith. "The clods of it are gold" [Jb 28:6], because the guardians of religion have clung together by charity and have never failed therein. Freed at last after many groans and frequent sighs, it now exults in hope; and trusting in goodness of its deliverer, rejoicing, it will rejoice when "the rod of sinners has been taken away from the lot of the just" [Ps 124:3]. Indeed what we have seen and heard and have truly understood, we write to all who are orthodox without any admixture of falsity, so that whatever merit there is may appear to the praise of God, and in gratitude to him.[42]

Chapter 1

IN THE year 1217, when the truce of the Christians and Saracens had expired, in the first general passage after the Lateran Council a large army of the Lord assembled in Acre, with the three kings of Jerusalem, Hungary, and Cyprus, who, not bearing with them the mystic gifts, offered one not at all worthy of memory.[43] The duke of Austria was there, and

42. Oliver's text is heavy with biblical citations. Gavigan cites the Old Testament from the Douai Version and the New Testament from the edition of the Confraternity of Christian Doctrine (Paterson NJ, 1941). Here as elsewhere in this volume we have not standardized translated scriptural citations.

43. Oliver opens his narrative by asserting the legitimacy of the expedition (a five-year truce established by John of Brienne in 1212 had expired), the high rank of its leaders, the fact that it was a *passagium generale*—that is a large-scale military expedition—and that it followed the Fourth Lateran Council, linking it tightly to *Ad liberandam*. But he also hints at the sinfulness of some of its members, in this case the Bavarians. The three kings were John of Brienne, king of Jerusalem (1210–1225), Andrew II of Hungary (1203–1235), and Hugh of Lusignan, king of Cyprus (1205–1218). Oliver's circumlocution is a reference to the cult of the Three Kings, very important in Cologne, where their remains were said to be located.

the duke of Meran with many companions and men of noble birth, and the great soldiery of the Teutonic king. There were present pilgrim bishops, the archbishops of Nicosia, Raab, Erlau, Hungary, Bayeux, Bamberg, Zeitz, Münster, and Utrecht; with them was a powerful and noble man, Lord Walter of Avesnes, who, returning in the spring crossing, left forty soldiers in the service of the Holy Land, and provided them with funds sufficient for a year. The Bavarians conducted themselves insolently and contrary to the law of pilgrims, by destroying the gardens and orchards of the Christians, even casting religious out of their hospices. When this did not satisfy them, they killed the Christians. The duke of Austria, like a catholic prince, fought for Christ throughout.

Chapter 2

THE PATRIARCH of Jerusalem, with great humility on the part of the clergy and the people, reverently lifted up the wood of the life-giving Cross, and set out from Acre on the sixth day after the feast of All Saints [November 7, 1217] into the camp of the Lord which had moved to Recordane. Now this sweet wood had been preserved up to this time, even after the loss of the Holy Land. When the conflict of the Saracens with the Christians was threatening in the time of Saladin, as we have learned from our ancestors, the Cross was cut in pieces; part was carried into battle and was lost there, and part was preserved, which now is displayed.[44] With such a standard, we advanced in orderly array, through the plain of Faba as far as the fountain of Tubania, toiling much on that day; and when we had sent scouts ahead, seeing the dust that was being stirred up by our enemies, we were uncertain whether they were hastening to attack us or to flee. On the following day we set out through the mountains of Gilboa, which were on our right, with a swamp on the left, to Bethsan where the enemy had pitched camp. But fearing the arrival of the army of the living God, that was so numerous, and that was proceeding in so orderly a way, they broke camp and fled, leaving the land to be devastated by the soldiers of Christ. Thence, crossing the Jordan on the vigil of Saint Martin [November 11], we washed our bodies at leisure in it, and we rested throughout two days in the same place, finding an abundance of food and fodder. Then on the shore of the Sea of Galilee we made three days' rest, wandering through places in which our Savior

44. On the diplomatic importance of the true cross, see below, chap. 31. The reference is to the battle of Hattin, July 4, 1187, which generated *Audita tremendi*, above, No. 1.

deigned to work miracles, and conversed with men in his corporal presence. We looked upon Bethsaida, the city of Andrew and Peter, then reduced to a small *casale*;[45] places were pointed out to us where Christ called his disciples, walked on the sea with dry feet, fed the multitudes in the desert, went up into the mountain alone to pray, and the place where he ate with his disciples after the resurrection. And thus we returned to Acre, carrying our sick and our needy brethren through Capharnaum on beasts of burden.

Chapter 3

IN THE second raid we approached the foot of Mount Tabor, finding first a lack of water, but afterward plenty when we dug for it. Our leaders despaired of the ascent of the mountain until, after a Saracen boy had told them that the camp could be seized, they formed a plan. Indeed, on the first Sunday of the Advent of the Lord [December 3], when the gospel was read—"Go into the town that is over against you " [Mt 21:2]—the patriarch went forward with the sign of the Cross, with bishops and clergy, up the ascent of the mountain, praying and singing psalms. Although the mountain was steep on all sides and high, and apparently impossible to ascend beyond the well-trodden footpath, nevertheless the knights and their attendants, horsemen and foot soldiers, ascended manfully. John, king of Jerusalem, with the army of the Lord, overthrew the chatelain and the emir together in the first attack; he reduced to flight and terror the defenders of the fort, who, to defend the mountain, fearlessly resisted the enemy outside the gates. But the king then lost as much in merit by descending as he had gained by ascending. For in descending on the same Sunday and making others descend, he gave courage to the infidel by the space of time that was granted to them; but we do not know by what judgment of God or by what plan of the leaders the army of the Lord descended then and withdrew ingloriously. This, however, we do know, that the eye of the human mind cannot penetrate the abysses of divine decrees. Now many Templars and Hospitallers and certain seculars were wounded in the second ascent of the mountain when they had received forces from the camp, but few died. We believe that Christ Our Lord reserved this triumph of the mountain for himself alone, since he ascended it with a few disciples, pointing out there the glory of the future resurrection. Furthermore, in the first and second raids, the Christians

45. A *casale* (pl. *casalia*) was a village or hamlet.

carried off with them a very great multitude of captives, men and women, and even children. Now the bishop of Acre baptized the little ones, whom he could win over by a gift or by a prayer, and apportioning them among religious women, he arranged for them to receive instruction.[46]

Chapter 4

ON THE third raid, in which the patriarch, with the sign of the Cross, and the holy pontiffs took no part, we sustained many losses and hardships, as much through highwaymen, as by the severity of the winter, especially on our journey on the vigil of the Nativity of the Lord [December 24], when many poor men and beasts perished from cold, and on the holy night itself, when we endured a severe storm on land, produced by wind and rain in the country of Tyre and Sidon near Sarepta.

Chapter 5

AFTER this, the army of the Lord was divided into four parts. The king of Hungary and the king of Cyprus set out for Tripoli, where the youthful king of Cyprus ended his days. After a short delay, the king of Hungary withdrew, to the great detriment of the Holy Land; he took away with him pilgrims also, and helmets, horses, and beasts of burden, with weapons, although he was repeatedly warned by the patriarch that he should not retreat thus. Finally, being excommunicated, he departed stubbornly with his retinue. Another division of lazy and cowardly pilgrims who, lying down, consumed the abundance of temporal things, remained in Acre. But the king of Jerusalem and the duke of Austria, with the Hospitallers of Saint John and the bishops mentioned above, and certain others, in a short time manfully and faithfully strengthened the fort in Caesarea of Palestine, although the arrival of the enemy was frequently announced. Through this fort, God granting, the city itself will be restored. In the basilica of the Prince of the Apostles, the patriarch with six bishops solemnly celebrated the feast of the Purification [February 1, 1218]. Moreover the Templars with Lord Walter of Avesnes and some pilgrim helpers, and the Hospitallers from the house of the Teutons, began to refortify the Pilgrims' Castle, which was formerly called Destroit.[47] This is located

46. The bishop of Acre referred to here was James of Vitry, a colleague of Oliver. See above, No. 19.

47. 'Atlit, along the coast of Palestine, is southeast of the edge of Mount Carmel. This important fortification was better known as Château Pèlerin (Pilgrim's Castle). Oliver also refers to it as "the Castle of the Son of God.".

in the diocese of Caesarea between Caiphas and Caesarea. Its location is as follows.

Chapter 6

A LARGE and lofty promontory overhangs the sea, naturally fortified by cliffs to the north, the west, and the south; toward the east is a strong tower erected some time ago by the Templars, and held as well in war as in time of truce. Now the tower was placed there originally because of bandits who threatened strangers ascending to Jerusalem along the narrow path, and descending from it; it was not far from the sea, and on account of the narrow path it was called Destroit. When the fort of Caesarea was built and completed, the Templars, digging constantly crosswise through the promontory, and laboring for six weeks, finally came upon the first foundation, where the ancient wall appeared thick and long. Money also was found there in a coinage unknown to modern times, which was conferred by the goodness of the Son of God on his soldiers to alleviate their expenses and labors. Next, while they were digging and carrying out sand in an anterior section, another shorter wall was found, and between the flat surface of the walls fountains of fresh water freely gushed forth. The Lord also supplied an abundance of stones and mortar. Two towers were built at the front of the fort of hewn and fitted stones of such greatness that one stone is with difficulty drawn in a cart by two oxen. Both towers are one hundred feet in length and seventy-four in width. Their thickness encloses two sheds to protect soldiers. Their height rising up much exceeds the height of the promontory. Between the two towers a new and high wall was completed with ramparts; and by a wonderful artifice, armed horsemen can go up and down within. Likewise another wall slightly distant from the towers extends from one side of the sea to the other, having a spring of living water enclosed. The promontory is encircled on both sides by a high new wall, as far as the rocks. The fort contains an oratory with a palace and several houses. The primary advantage of this building is that the assembly of Templars, having been led out of Acre, a sinful city and one filled with all uncleanness, will remain in the garrison of this fort up until the restoration of the walls of Jerusalem. The territory of this fortress abounds in fisheries, salt mines, woods, pastures, fields, and grass. It charms its inhabitants with vines that have been or are to be planted, by gardens and orchards. Between Acre and Jerusalem there is no fortification which the Saracens hold, and therefore the unbelievers are harmed greatly by that new fortress; and with the fear of God pursuing them, they are forced to abandon these cultivated regions. This structure has a naturally good harbor which will be better when aided by artifice; it is six miles away from Mount Tabor. The construction of this castle is presumed to have been the cause of the destruction of the other, because in the long wide plain, which lies between the mountainous districts of this camp and of Mount Tabor, no one could safely plow or sow or reap because of fear of those who lived in it.

Chapter 7

THE BISHOP of Münster fell asleep in the Lord at Caesarea. Master Thomas, a theologian and a good and clear-minded doctor, brought to an end his last day at the castle of the Son of God.

Chapter 8

AFTER this the army of the Lord returned to Acre. The bishops of Germany and many others prepared themselves to cross the sea after having delayed a short time in the Land of Promise. There was expected a second new passage, and especially a fleet coming from the north, which it was hoped would sail through the narrow sea of Carthage. From the beginning of the preaching of the cross of Christ, the province of Cologne, with great zeal and also at enormous expense, prepared almost three hundred ships, some of which survived, but others perished from the force of a storm; but a large part arrived at Acre with great courage on the part of the warriors.[48] Discord arose there when certain ones wished to proceed, and others desired to spend the winter in the siege of that most powerful fort which is called Alcatia.[49] And there the fleet was divided: part spent the winter at Gaeta and Corneto; the other part besieged Alcatia under two leaders, Count William of Holland and Count George of Wied. This fort [Alcatia] was captured by the Germans and the Frisians. Until that time they had carried on the siege against a great multitude of Saracens whom the Templars and the knights of Saint James fought manfully, together with the army of the queen of Portugal. Finally the Saracens

48. The reference is to the account of the Rhineland crusaders; see above, No. 20.
49. Alcazar de Sol, west of Setubal in Portugal. For another version of the siege, see above, No. 20.

were conquered by divine strength; one of their kings was killed, and with him a great many were massacred or led into captivity.

Chapter 9

THE PROVINCE of Cologne was stirred up to the service of the Savior of the world through signs which appeared in heaven.[50] For in the province of Cologne and in the diocese of Münster in a village of Frisia, namely, Bedum, in the month of May on the sixth day before Pentecost [May 16], when the cross was preached there, a triple form appeared in the heavens, one white toward the north, another toward the south of the same color and shape, a third in the middle, tinted with color, having the fork of a cross, and the figure of a man suspended upon it, with arms raised and extended, with the mark of nails in hands and feet, and with bowed head. This middle one was between two others on which there was no likeness of a human body. At another time and in another place, in a village of Frisia, at the time of the preaching of the cross, there appeared alongside of the sun a cross of a blue color; more saw this than saw the former. The third apparition was in the diocese of Utrecht in the village of Dokkum where Saint Boniface was martyred. When on the feast of the same martyr [June 5] many thousands had assembled there for the station of the same martyr, there appeared a large white cross as if one beam had been artificially placed over another.[51]

This sign we all saw. Now it moved gradually from the north to the south. But we believe that the two apparitions were manifested so that all the ambiguity of the first vision might be removed, as the Apostle says about the resurrection of Christ, "that he appeared to Cephas, afterwards to the eleven apostles, and next to more than five hundred brethren" [1 Cor 15:5–6].

Chapter 10

IN THE year of grace 1218, in the month of March, ships began to sail to the port of Acre from the province of Cologne with other small ships from the province of Bremen and Trier. Thus was accomplished that plan formed in the Lateran Council at Rome under the Lord Pope Innocent

---

50. Stories of celestial signs and portents evidently circulated well beyond the localities in which they occurred. Here Oliver incorporates into his history miracles that occurred during his own preaching of the crusade that he had earlier publicized in letters intended for other preachers, which circulated widely and were incorporated into contemporary sermons and chronicles.

51. Compare with above, No. 17.

of good memory, for leading the army of the Christians into the land of Egypt. Therefore in the month of May, after the Ascension of the Lord [May 24], when the ships had been prepared, and the galleys had been equipped with arms, and the other ships had been loaded, there set out from Acre John of Brienne, king of Jerusalem; the patriarch with the bishops of Nicosia, Bethlehem, and Acre; the duke of Austria with the three houses,[52] and a copious multitude of Christians. The fleet was ordered to assemble at the castle of the Son of God, which is called the Castle of the Pilgrims; then with a north wind blowing, when the king, the duke, and the masters of the houses came to the appointed place, the host of the Lord set out under full sail, arriving at the harbor of Damietta on the third day. Now the above-mentioned leaders, since they had made a slight delay at the castle, could not follow after the host until the sixth day after their departure from the harbor of Acre. Many also who had not been prepared and who made some delay at Acre, after those who sailed first, either remained there entirely or were driven back into Acre by the violence of the winds; or, being tossed about for three or four weeks, were delayed on the sea. The archbishop of Reims and the bishop of Limoges remained in Acre because of their advanced years. The bishop of Limoges died there; the archbishop of Reims, having returned on the passage of the Holy Cross [53] perished on the way.

Now upon coming to land at the port of Damietta, they chose the count of Saarbrücken [Sarrebruck] as their leader, and captured the hostile land on the third day [May 29] without any loss of blood, before the king and the aforesaid dukes followed them. For when a few Saracens advanced upon the knights at the harbor, a certain Frisian, with his right knee planted on the ground, turned his shield with his left hand, and brandished and hurled an iron spear with the right. A Saracen horseman watched him, thinking he was playing, when suddenly horse and rider, struck down by the Frisian, perished and fell to the ground. When the others fled, abandoning their baggage, the Christians fixed the boundaries of the camp between the seashore and the bank of the river Nile, to the great admiration of those following when they saw the tents that had been set up. God brought about this wonderful fact, that upon their first

52. That is, the three military orders: Templars, Hospitallers, Teutonic Knights.

53. During the Middle Ages, there were generally two sailing seasons or "passages" across the Mediterranean Sea, one in the spring and one in the autumn. Oliver here refers to the spring passage, which occurred around the feast of the Invention of the Holy Cross (May 3).

arrival the water of the river, though it was joined to the sea and on many occasions afterward was of a salty taste, was drawn up fresh all the way to the *casale* which is almost a mile above Damietta. A short time after the arrival of the Christians there took place an almost complete eclipse of the moon; and although it usually comes from natural causes at the time of full moon, yet because our Savior says, "There shall be signs in the sun and moon" [Lk 21:25], we interpreted this eclipse to the disfavor of the Saracens, as if it portended the failure of the very ones who impute the moon to themselves, putting great strength in the waning or waxing moon. Now it is read in Quintus Curtius that when Alexander the Macedonian, the hammer of the whole world, set out against Darius and Porus from Greece into Asia, and his well-ordered battle lines proceeded on this side and that, there occurred an eclipse of the moon. Alexander, interpreting this in favor of the Greeks against the Medes and the Persians, encouraged his men, fought against Darius, and conquered him.[54]

Chapter 11

A TOWER located in the middle of the river had to be captured before crossing.[55] The Frisians, however, who were impatient of delay, crossed the Nile and carried off the animals of the Saracens. Wishing to pitch camp on the farther shore, they held their ground, fighting against the Saracens who came out of their city to oppose them. They were recalled through obedience because it did not seem wise to our leaders that a tower filled with pagans should be left behind the Christians. Meanwhile the duke of Austria and the Hospitallers of Saint John prepared two ladders on two ships, and the Teutons and Frisians fortified a third ship with bulwarks, setting up a small fortress on the top of the mast without hanging a ladder. Their head, their leader, and their counselor was Count Adolph of Berg, a noble and powerful man, the brother of the archbishop of Cologne. The count died at Damietta before the tower was captured. The ladders of the duke and of the Hospitallers were directed against the tower about the time of the feast of Saint John the Baptist [June 24], with the Saracens defending it manfully. The ladder of the Hospitallers was shattered and crashed with the mast, hurling its warriors headlong;

54. Quintus Curtius Rufus, *History of Alexander the Great* 4.40. This is one of the very few references to a classical writer in the entire work. See chapter 71 below.

55. For the chaintower before Damietta, see Benjamin Z. Kedar, "Prolegomena to a World History of Harbour and River Chains," in *Shipping, Trade and Crusade in the Medieval Mediterranean*, eds. Ruthy Gertwagen and Elizabeth Jeffreys (Farnham, Surrey, 2012), 3–37.

the ladder of the duke, being broken in like manner at almost the same time, sent up to heaven soldiers who were vigorous and well armed, wounded in body to the advantage of their souls, crowned with a glorious martyrdom. The overjoyed Egyptians, mocking us violently, raised their voices, beating drums and sounding sackbuts; gloom and sadness invaded the Christians. But the ship of the Germans and Frisians cast anchor between the tower and the city, causing great losses to the Egyptians through its ballistae, which had been set up within, especially to those who were standing on the bridge that extended between the city and the tower. The ship itself, however, was being quite violently attacked by the warriors of the city, by the javelins of the tower and of the bridge, and by Greek fire. Finally it was seized upon by the fire; and although the Christians feared that it would be entirely destroyed, its defenders bravely extinguished the flames. Likewise pierced by arrows within and without, both in that fortress placed on the top of the mast and even on the ropes of the rigging, the ship, bearing the great honor of Christianity, was brought back to its position. No slight damage was dealt out and endured by one ship of the Templars, fortified by bulwarks which were held alongside of the tower at the time of this assault.

Chapter 12

HOWEVER, we realized that the tower could neither be captured by the blows of petraries or of trebuchets (for this was attempted for many days), nor by bringing the fort closer, because of the depth of the river, nor by starvation, because of the surroundings of the city, nor by undermining, because of the roughness of the water flowing about. With the Lord showing us how and providing an architect, and with the Germans and the Frisians providing supplies and labor, we joined two ships which we bound together sturdily by means of beams and ropes and so prevented (by their closely connected structure) the danger of drifting. We erected four masts and the same number of sailyards, setting up on the summit a strong fortress joined with poles and a network fortification.[56] We covered it with skins about its circumference, as a protection from the attacks of their machine, and over its top as a defense against the Greek fire. Under the fortress was made a ladder, hung by very strong ropes and stretching out thirty cubits beyond the prow. This task having been successfully

56. James of Vitry identifies the engineer as Oliver himself. On the device, see Dominic Francis, "Oliver of Paderborn and His Siege Engine at Damietta," *Nottingham Medieval Studies* 37 (1993), 28–32.

completed in a short time, the leaders of the army were invited to see it, so that if anything was lacking that ought to be supplied by material or by human ingenuity, they would point it out. They replied that such a work of wood had never before been wrought upon the sea. We realized that we must hasten, because, by frequent blows of the machines, the bridge which conveyed the enemies of the faith from the city to the tower in great part had been destroyed. Therefore on the sixth day [August 18] before the feast of Saint Bartholomew [August 24], we made a procession barefoot to the Holy Cross with devotion on the part of our people. After humbly imploring divine assistance that the affair might be free from all envy and empty boasting, we summoned to the execution of this task some men of every nation that was then in the army, although the nation of Germans and Frisians would suffice to fill and direct the ships.

Chapter 13

ON THE feast of Saint Bartholomew [August 24], the sixth day, since the Nile had violently overflowed and the force of the waters greatly hindered our work, with the greatest difficulty and danger this engine was dragged against the current from the place in which it had been made, to the tower.[57] A smaller ship, a companion of this machine, went along spreading its sails. The clergy, barefoot, walked as suppliants on the shore. When they had come to the tower, that twofold arrangement could not be turned around toward the west side, but by moving up it was placed directly toward the northern section. The ropes and anchors were finally made firm, although the force of the flooding waters strove to drive it back. Six or more machines were drawn up on the top of the towers of the city, and were placed there to shatter it. Now one, more dangerous than the others, being destroyed after a few blows, ceased its action; but the others without any intermission cast out stones like hail. And no less a danger did the first ship withstand, located at the foot of the tower. The Greek fire from the tower of the river close at hand came from the city afar like lightning and was able to inspire fear; but by sour liquid and gravel, and other means of extinguishing it, those who were toiling were aided.

The patriarch lay prostrate in the dust before the wood of the Cross; the clergy, standing barefoot, garbed in liturgical robes, cried out to

57. The crusaders' failure here and elsewhere to estimate the unpredictability of the Nile flooding of Lower Egypt and the complex of connecting channels was one of their greatest errors.

heaven. The defenders of the tower with lances extended, smeared the front of the ladder with oil; next they added fire which caused it to burst into flames. And when the Christians who were on it ran to put out the fire, they pressed on the head of the ladder with their weight so much that the movable bridge placed near its edge was made to bend. The standard-bearer of the duke of Austria fell from the ladder, and the Saracens captured the banner of the duke. The Babylonians, thinking that they were victorious, shouted madly, disturbing the air with their clamor. The Christians, descending from their horses, threw themselves down in supplication, beating their hands; their faces streamed with tears of sorrow as they protested the pity they had for those who were enduring peril in the depth of the river, and the loss of all Christendom. In answer to this devotion of the people and the raising of their hands to heaven, divine kindness lifted the ladder, the tears of the faithful extinguished the fire; and thus our men, with renewed vigor, manfully fought with the defenders of the tower by means of swords, pikes, clubs, and other weapons. A certain young knight of the diocese of Liège was the first to ascend the tower; a certain young Frisian, holding a flail by which grain is usually threshed but which was prepared for fighting by an interweaving with chains, lashed out bravely to the right and to the left, knocked down a certain man holding the saffron standard of the sultan and took the banner away from him. One came after another, vanquishing the enemy, who were known to be hard and cruel in their resistance. O ineffable kindness of God! O unexplainable joy of Christians! After lamentation and grief, after weeping and groaning, we saw joy and triumph. "We praise Thee, O God," "Blessed be the Lord God of Israel," and other canticles of thanksgiving to the heavens we sang for joy, our voices being mingled with tears and our praises repeated.[58]

Chapter 14

MEANWHILE the Saracens, who had withdrawn to the inner part of the tower, having put fire under the top part of the tower, burned it; our men, though victorious, retreated over the ladder, not being able to stand the heat. But the bridge, which had been prepared in the lower part of the fortification, was let down to the narrow foot of the tower, with deep waters surging about on all sides. With iron hammers the victors attacked

58. The *Te Deum laudamus* was a prayer of thanksgiving at times of great rejoicing. Since the ninth century it had also been known as the Ambrosian hymn. The second reference is to Lk 1:68–79.

the door while the Saracens who were within defended it. Both fortifications remained impregnable; the rungs of the ladder, in part, and the circuit of the work which was held together by very strong ropes were pierced by blows of the machines. From the ninth hour of the sixth day until the tenth hour of the following Saturday [August 25] this danger lasted. But the netlike arrangement which protected the ladder remained unharmed, along with the fort in which were stationed the ballistae and the petraries, which protected them. Finally, being enclosed in the tower, the Saracens sought a conference, and, under a guarantee that their lives would be spared, they surrendered to the duke of Austria, except those who on the preceding night had thrown themselves headlong through the windows and escaped the narrow bounds of the tower; several of them were drowned in the river and perished. But the captives numbered one hundred men.

Chapter 15

ALTHOUGH from that day the Babylonians were confused and terrified, and, as it was thought, prepared for flight, our leaders fell into idleness and laziness according to their custom. They invented a motive for deferring negotiations, and they did not imitate Judas Maccabeus who "seeing that the time served him" [1 Mc 12:1] gave no rest to the enemy.

Chapter 16

THE SHIPS prepared to withdraw. A great multitude of Frisians and Teutons set out in the next passage of the Holy Cross [August-September, 1218]. In that passage came certain Romans, and after that the [cardinal] bishop of Albano,[59] the delegate of the apostolic see, and with him a Roman prince; next the archbishop of Bordeaux who made a useful delay; the bishops of Angers, Mantua, Humana, and Salpi; next Master Robert of Courson, cardinal bishop of the title of Saint Stephen on Monte Celio; the bishops of Paris, Gerona, Erlau, and Hungary, who died before the crossing of the river on the sand of Damietta, and Cardinal Robert likewise. The count of Nevers came also, who, when danger threatened, retreated, to the scandal of the Christians. The count of La Marche, and the count of Bar and his son, Brother William of Chartres, master of the

59. Pelagius Galvani, cardinal bishop of Albano, 1211–1240, the legate of Honorius III to the crusade. He came from either Spain or Portugal. He had also served Innocent III. His responsibility for the failure of negotiations with the sultan has long been fiercely debated by historians.

army of the Temple, Hervé of Vierzon, Ithier of Toucy, Oliver, son of the king of England, and many others of the knightly order, and common people, ended their days at Damietta. Many martyrs for Christ, more confessors of Christ, being delivered from human cares at Damietta, went to the Lord.

Chapter 17

"He is wise in heart and mighty in strength who doth great things and unsearchable things without number and marvelous. Who judges those that are high, who places the humble on high" [Jb 9:4, 5:9, 5:11]. He alone was magnified in the siege of Damietta. For not as in other expeditions against the Saracens, when various opportunities were arranged through human wisdom or the agency of the warriors, but through himself did he work miraculously through the power of his divinity what man did not presume to seek; giving honor not to kings or other princes or nations, but to his name, that the prophetic promise might be fulfilled in us sinners: "The Lord will fight for you and you will hold your peace" [Ex 14:14].

Chapter 18

After the tower had been captured that was located in the depths of the river Nile, Saphadin,[60] grown old with evil days and sickness, the disinheritor of his cousins and the usurper of the kingdoms of Asia, died and was buried in hell. Afterward on the feast of Saint Denis [October 9] the Saracens, coming unexpectedly with armed galleys and invading the most important of the camps where the Romans had set up tents, were repulsed by a small band of Christians; King John of Jerusalem fought manfully there at the exhortation of the bishop of Bethlehem, when he pursued them as they ran back quickly to their galleys; nevertheless, they were unable to escape the swords of their pursuers and the whirling of the river. Now, like the Egyptians formerly in the raging waters of the Red Sea [Ex 13–14], so in the Nile about one thousand were drowned, as we learned afterward from the Saracens.

60. Al-Malik al'Adil Saif ad-Din, called "Saphadin" by the Christians, brother of Saladin, died on August 31, 1218. His sons, with whom he displaced the sons of Saladin, and who included the Ayyubid caliphs, played prominent roles in Near Eastern affairs for several decades, particularly al-Malik al-Kamil Muhammad (d. 1238), sultan of Egypt, and al-Malik al-Mu'azzam Isa (d. 1227), known as "Coradin" to the Christians, sultan of Damascus. A third son, al-Ashraf (d. 1249), ruled Jazira, northern Syria.

On the feast of Saint Demetrius [October 26], who is said to have been the uterine brother of the blessed Denis, the enemy at dawn invaded the camp of the Templars, and though causing us a slight loss, they were driven away by our alert horsemen, to the bridge which they had built a short distance from us in the upper part of the river; they were killed to the number of five hundred, as we learned from deserters.

Chapter 19

NEXT, since many of the Christian people were pleasing to the Lord, it was necessary that temptation should prove them. Jonah, being cast out into the sea because of the trouble of the tempest, and being shut up in the belly of a fish, returned to dry land when he had been proved. The Apostle escaped when he had been tried by a threefold shipwreck; the people of the Lord deserved to be tried when they had practiced a three-day fast, which the clergy observed obediently on bread and water, and when many processions had been ordered by the venerable Lord Pelagius, the bishop of Albano, legate of the apostolic see. For on the vigil of Saint Andrew the Apostle [November 29], in the middle of the night, the waves of the sea rose, swelling and making a terrible advance even to the camp of the faithful. The river, rushing in from the other direction, took us unaware. The tents floated off, the food supply was destroyed, fishes of the river and of the sea, as though fearing nothing, piled into our sleeping quarters, and we caught them with our hands, delights nevertheless which we were willing to be without. And unless, by the plan of the Holy Ghost, preparations had been made beforehand on the rampart which had been made for other uses, the sea joined with the river would have dragged off to the enemy the men with the animals, and the ships with the weapons and food supplies. This danger, however, four ships, upon which had been erected fortresses to capture the city, did not escape. In one attack, they, along with a fifth ship which was caught in their midst, were driven to the opposite shore by the force of the winds, and were burned before our eyes with Greek fire. The Lord spared the labors of the Frisians and the Germans by whom the tower had been captured. Laden ships which were standing in the port of the sea were lost when their ropes were suddenly broken. This storm lasted for three continuous days. When this had elapsed, the Lord "who consoles his people in every tribulation, comforts in all our afflictions, commanded the wind and the sea to be still, making it cease from raging" [Mt 8:26; 2 Cor 1:4; Jon 1:15].

Chapter 20

BESIDES, many of the army were struck down by a certain plague against which physicians could find no remedy in all their skill.[61] A sudden pain attacked the feet and legs, and at the same time corrupt flesh covered the gums and teeth, taking away the power of chewing; a horrible blackness darkened the shins, and so having been afflicted with a long stretch of illness, very many went to the Lord with much suffering. Certain ones, surviving until spring, escaped, being delivered by the advantage of heat.

Chapter 21

AFTER the aforesaid tempest, the ships were prepared to cross the river; these, going up at great risk between the city and the captured tower, were greatly retarded by Greek fire and javelins. Wherefore it happened that one ship of the Templars, carried away by the violence of the current, was cast over near the side of the city toward the enemy, who for a long time assailed it with barbots[62] and grappling irons, hurling out Greek fire and stones from the towers above; and since they could not prevail on account of the bravery of the defenders, they eagerly climbed up the ship, and throwing themselves headlong into it, descended upon the Templars. When they had fought there for a long time, the ship at last was pierced (whether by the enemy or by our own men we do not know) and sought the depths, drowning Egyptians with Christians, so that the top of the mast scarcely appeared above the water. And as Samson "killed many more at his death than he had killed before in his life" [Jgs 16:30], so also those martyrs dragged into the abyss of the waters along with themselves more than they could have killed with swords. But the citizens of Damietta mourned their bloody victory for almost seven days. Thereupon, while repairing the bridge they left a narrow opening, so that our ships could not go up without danger. But the Germans and the Frisians, fired with the zeal of righteous indignation, having no help except from heaven, manfully attacked the bridge with the smaller ship by whose aid the tower had been captured, and which the Gauls called "Holy Mother." Less than ten men of the above-mentioned nation climbed the bridge in the face of all the hardihood of the Babylonians, with a great

---

61. Crusade expeditions were also epidemiological nightmares, involving reaction to new diets as well as carrying new diseases and becoming vulnerable to local diseases. The disease here may have been scurvy. The best general study is Piers D. Mitchell, *Medicine in the Crusades: Warfare, Wounds, and the Medieval Surgeon* (Cambridge, 2004).

62. A small vessel with a deck protected by a leather covering in the shape of an arch.

multitude of Christians looking on and highly praising this boldness. They broke it down; and thus, with the four ships upon which the bridge had been founded, they returned in triumph, leaving a way free and open for the ships sailing upward.

Chapter 22

WHEN all this had been so accomplished, the Saracens, while awaiting the danger which threatened them, fortified the bank opposite us by means of ramparts and a claylike substance with high wooden defenses, setting up machines and petraries there, taking from us the hope of crossing through that place. But from the *casale*, which is almost a mile away from the city, where this new fortification ended, all across the river they sank ships and fixed stakes in the eddies. Nevertheless the legate of the apostolic see, having the good desire of besieging the city, urged the ships gathered higher up to cross. Wherefore the ships, fortified by defenses and fortresses, and also by armed men with galleys and other ships, Christ being their leader, escaped the sunken ships mentioned above. But the enemy, pretending fear, placed three ranks of armed men opposite the position of our ships: one of foot soldiers above the bank with shields, which they call targes, ranged in lines; the second behind them like the first; the third of horsemen, long and terrible, violently harassing the position of the Christians with showers of stones and weapons.

In addition, on the night of the solemnity of Saint Agatha, virgin and martyr [February 5, 1219],[63] when the people of the faithful assembled who were to cross on the following day, rains and winds added much peril and difficulty to our men. But "God is faithful" and "will not permit you to be tempted beyond your strength" [1 Cor 10:13], and looking at the camp of his servants, he turned into ease and joy a thing which according to less important causes would have been difficult or impossible, renewing the wonders of his power. After the middle of the night he struck such terror into the sultan of Babylon and his satraps that, abandoning the camp unknown even to the Egyptians whom he had ranged for resisting, they placed their hope in flight alone. A certain apostate who, having transgressed the law of the Christians for some time, had fought on the side of the sultan, stood on the bank and cried out in French, "Why do you delay? Why are you afraid? Why do you hesitate?

63. Here as elsewhere, Oliver uses liturgical dating, that is, dating according to the fixed annual feast days of saints or according to the prayers, usually the Introit and Gospel, in the Mass for a particular day.

The sultan has gone away." And having said this he asked to be taken back into a ship so that being put in their power he might give proof to his words. Therefore at early dawn, when the office of the Mass of the feast day had been begun throughout the oratories of the Christians, these words, "Let us all rejoice in the Lord,"[64] were announced to the legate, the king, and the others. And so as the Egyptians fled, our men crossed eagerly and quickly with no hindrance from the enemy and no shedding of blood.

But the land of the enemy was so muddy and so difficult to land upon because of the rather deep waters that the horses, being driven without saddles or riders, could scarcely get up. The Templars, leaders in the ascent of the horses, having put up their banners, hurried to the city in a swift march, throwing down the wicked ones who came boldly from the gates to resist those who were advancing. "The axe shall not boast itself against him that cutteth with it nor shall the saw exalt itself against him by whom it is drawn" [Is 10:15].[65] To what shall we equal or compare this miracle except to that which is read concerning Benadab, king of Syria, who besieged Samaria, reducing it greatly, to whom the Lord sent such terror that he fled abandoning his camp [2 Chr 6:24, 7:3]? And as the flight of the Syrians was announced to the Samaritans by the lepers who were at the entrance of the gate, so the flight of the Egyptians was announced by one who was a leper in his soul, that is to say, the aforesaid apostate; and as the people of the Samaritans gathered up the spoils left in the camp of the Syrians, so our army plundered the tents and booty of those who were fleeing; the victors seized many targes and all the galleys, along with the barbots and other ships, which were found below the *casale* as far as the city, with other spoils. Many warriors, having left their wives and children, fled from Damietta, terrified because of the unexpected crossing. And the city was besieged firmly in a circle, the army being joined together through the arrangement of a bridge touching both banks.

Chapter 23

HOWEVER, through the idleness and laziness of those whose names God knows, it happened that as Coradin arrived with the men of Aleppo and

---

64. These words open the Introit of the Mass of the feast of Saint Agatha and on many feasts associated with the Virgin Mary.

65. Oliver's frequent references to scripture offer a framework for his interpretation of the crusaders' actions.

a great multitude, the enemy with renewed vigor and spirit seized that place [March 3] from which our men had made a miraculous crossing. And thus, as we were besieging the city, they besieged us more danger-ously; and unless by divine counsel the first camp which was between the sea and the river had been held by the Germans and Frisians especially, the port would have been taken from us and the whole business, greatly imperiled, would have wavered. But in order that the miracle of the cross-ing might become more famous, and be unhesitatingly ascribed to Christ alone, the Saracens reached such a point of temerity that at daybreak of the Saturday before "Oculi mei semper" Sunday [March 9],[66] since we did not foresee such a danger, they drew nearer with a great multitude and pressed on as far as the rampart; but by divine assistance they were driven back, with a loss of horsemen and foot soldiers.

Chapter 24

IN THE year of grace 1219, Jerusalem, the queen of cities, which seemed impregnably fortified, was destroyed within and without by Coradin, son of Saphadin [March 19 or 25]. Its walls and towers were reduced to heaps of stones except for the temple of the Lord and the tower of David. The Saracens took counsel about destroying the glorious sepulcher, and they threatened this through letters which they sent across to the citizens of Damietta for their own consolation; but no one presumed to set his hand to this act of boldness because of reverence for the place.[67] For as they had written in the Qur'an, the book of their law, they believe that Jesus Christ Our Lord was conceived and born of the Virgin Mary and they protest that he lived without sin as a prophet and more than a prophet. They firmly assert that he gave sight to the blind, cleansed lepers, and raised the dead; they do not deny the word and the spirit of God, and that he ascended alive into heaven. But they do deny his passion and death, and also that the divine nature is united to the human nature in Christ. They likewise deny the Trinity of Persons. Therefore they ought to be called heretics rather than Saracens, but the use of the false name prevails.

Therefore, at the time of truce, when their wise men went up to Jerusalem, they asked that copies of the Gospels be shown to them. These

---

66. The third Sunday of Lent. The introit of the Mass for the day begins "Oculi mei."
67. The dismantling of the fortifications of Jerusalem in 1219 should be considered both when Frederick II agreed to leave Jerusalem unfortified in 1229 in his treaty with al-Kamil and also when the Khwarizmians later destroyed the city in 1244. See below, Parts IV and VI. Coradin was the Latin name of the brother and frequent rival of al-Kamil.

they kissed and venerated because of the purity of the law which Christ taught, and especially because of the Gospel of Luke: "The Angel Gabriel was sent" [Lk 1:26], which the learned among them often repeat and recall to mind. But their law, which Muhammad, under the dictation of the devil, gave to the Saracens, and which was written in Arabic by the ministry of Sergius, a monk, an apostate, and a heretic, began from the sword, is upheld by the sword, and will be ended in the sword. Muhammad was unlearned, as he himself gives evidence in his Qur'an, and what the forenamed heretic dictated, he promulgated and ordered to be observed through threats. For he was dissolute and warlike, and therefore he laid down a law concerning uncleanness and vanity, which those who live carnally on the side of pleasure carefully observe. And as truth and purity fortify our law, so worldly and human fear and carnal pleasure guard their error most firmly.[68]

Chapter 25

ON PALM Sunday of the aforementioned year [March 31, 1219], our enemies, having made many threats that they would destroy themselves or all of us in one day, collected a fearful and innumerable army of horsemen and foot soldiers and rushed upon us, invading our ramparts on all sides, especially the bridge of the Templars and the duke of Austria, which he was eager to defend with the Germans. The enemy, with picked soldiers, leaped from their horses and fought savagely with the Christians. On this side and that many fell dead and wounded, and finally, climbing the bridge, they burned part of it. The duke of Austria ordered his men that when the bridge had been abandoned they should give approach and entrance to those who were pressing on us; but they did not presume to enter because of our army, which had ranged its lines as an aid to those defending the fortifications. The women fearlessly brought water and stones, wine and bread to the warriors; the priests persisted in prayer, binding up and blessing the wounds of the injured. On that day, we were not given the opportunity of carrying palms other than crossbows, bows, and arrows, lances and swords and shields, so violently did they attack

68. This description of Muslim belief echoes much traditional Christian understanding of Islam, but it also suggests that some Islamic tenets were better understood in the early thirteenth century and that the relationship between the two religions was cast by Christians in terms of the recently articulated concepts of schism and heresy. Both Oliver and James of Vitry were keenly interested in learning about variants in Christian belief in the East and in Islam, and Oliver wrote letters to al-Kamil and the learned scholars of Egypt urging them to convert.

and harass us from sunrise to almost the tenth hour—they who had come to destroy us in the desire of freeing the city; at last they retreated wearily with great losses.

Chapter 26

THE SPRING passage was now imminent. The duke of Austria was going to withdraw, he who for a year and a half had fought faithfully for Christ, full of devotion, humility, obedience, and generosity.

Besides all the other innumerable expenses which he had incurred in the dealings of war and in private alms, he is believed to have bestowed on the house of the Teutons six thousand marks of silver or more, to obtain land; and on the new fort of the Templars fifty marks of gold. To it also the earl of Chester gave fifty marks of silver for the strengthening of its walls and towers.[69]

Chapter 27

ON THE first of May a great multitude of pilgrims began to withdraw, leaving us in the greatest danger. But our kind and merciful Father, our leader and comrade in arms, Jesus Christ, "the protector and defender of those who hope in him, for whom it is easy to save either by many or by few" [Ps 17:13; 1 Kgs 14:6], did not permit the unbelievers to rush in upon us until new and recent pilgrims arrived with abundant aid; a supply of provisions and horses sent over by divine power gladdened the assembly of the faithful. Therefore, on the feast of the Ascension of the Lord [May 16], when the number of the soldiers of Christ was renewed, the untrustworthy enemy, according to their custom, rushed upon us by land and by water. As they could not prevail, though they made many attempts, they challenged our men particularly near the camp, losing and inflicting losses. But on July 31 they brought forward all the power which they could muster, and after many assaults, finally crossed the ramparts against the army of the Temple. Violently bursting the barriers, they put our foot soldiers to flight, to such an extent that the whole army of the Christians was then endangered. The knights and soldiery of France tried

---

69. Ranulf, earl of Chester, one of King John's strongest supporters. He took the cross on Ash Wednesday, 1215, and in 1218 set out for the East. He landed soon after the capture of the chain tower and returned to England at the beginning of August, 1220. Ranulf's and the duke of Austria's arrivals and departures signal the advantages and disadvantages of the practice of rotating leaders and their armies into and out of the theater of combat during any prolonged campaign. They also signal the need to await reinforcements on the part of the crusaders in the field, which Oliver emphasizes often.

three times to drive them farther back beyond the rampart, but were unable to do so. The Saracens, when our wooden fortifications had been shattered, ranged lines of horsemen and foot soldiers within our walls; their shouts arose as they mocked us; the whole multitude prepared its retinue. Fear welled up in the Christians, but the spirit which came upon Gideon animated the Templars. The master of the Temple, with the marshal and other brothers who were then present, made an attack through a narrow approach and manfully put the unbelievers to flight. The house of the Teutons and the counts and other knights of different nations, seeing the army of the Temple placed in such danger, quickly brought aid through entrances opposite them; thus the foot soldiers of the Saracens threw away their shields and were killed, except those whose headlong flight had snatched them from their killers. Our foot soldiers went out after our horsemen. The enemy retreated a short distance, their armed ranks holding out here and there, until evening twilight put an end to the battle. The Saracens went away first. Bodies of massacred wretches lay strewn near our rampart in great numbers, except those who were wounded seriously or slightly, and were brought back to the camp. Thus on that day did God save those who hoped in him through the courage of the Templars and of those who, having worked together with them, committed themselves to the conflict. A few of our men were killed or captured.

Chapter 28

ALMOST all the machines prepared against the city were burned in a many-sided sortie of the defenders of Damietta. The Pisans, the Genoese, and the Venetians stoutly affirmed that they would attack the city by means of four ships upon which ladders hung; "but they were not of the race of those men by whom salvation was brought to Israel" [1 Mc 5:62]; for they wished to make a name for themselves, going forward with trumpets and reed pipes and many standards.[70] The legate of the apostolic see supplied copious funds to them from the common store and the king and others produced ropes and anchors in abundance according as they needed them. And so, attacking the city, they killed and wounded many on the first day; and the more often they made an attack afterward, so

70. The economic interests of these commercial port cities have often been considered by historians to the exclusion of other motives on their part. We have seen this in discussions of the Fourth Crusade as well. Oliver seems to think that the troops of these cities wanted some of the same reputation for bravery and heroism as their knightly and noble companions in arms.

much the more were the walls strengthened by wooden towers and palisades; the defenders resisted the oncoming forces even more vigorously and efficaciously, and thus the ladders, injured by fire and several times repaired, were forced to the bank, and the attempt was fruitless. And so it was truly understood that by divine power alone would Damietta be delivered into the hands of the Christians.

Chapter 29

BUT WE, insensible and unmindful of the benefits and wonderful deeds of God, which he had done, "provoked the eyes of his divine majesty" [Is 3:8] against us through the idleness of the leaders and the complaints of the followers. The foot soldiers reproached the cowardice of the horsemen, the horsemen made light of the risks of the foot soldiers when they went out against the Saracens. Therefore it happened that on the feast of the beheading of Saint John the Baptist [August 29], with our common faults urging us on, although scarcely any were to be found who would remain in the custody of the camp, we led forth a naval and land army and proceeded to the camp of the Babylonians between the sea and the river, where fresh water could not be found to drink. But taking up their tents, they pretended flight; and when our men had advanced to a point where it was clear that our adversaries did not wish to meet us in open combat, our leaders began a long debate whether they should advance or retreat; the feeling among them was divided. Meanwhile the ranks were scattered except for a group of those whom obedience bound in military discipline. The knights of Cyprus, who were on the right flanks, showed their timidity to the Saracens as they made an attack from the side. The Italian foot soldiers fled first, after them horsemen of various nations, and certain Hospitallers of Saint John, while the legate of the Roman see, and the patriarch, who was carrying the Cross, begged them earnestly to stand their ground, but in vain. The heat of the sun was intense, the foot soldiers were burdened with the weight of their arms. The difficulty of the way increased the heat, and those who had brought wine with them drank it unmixed in the distress of their thirst because of the lack of water.[71]

With all these things happening at the same time, those who defended themselves as they stood their ground and turned their backs on those who fled first in their breathless course were wiped out, collapsing without

---

71. Both Oliver and James of Vitry in his sermons to pilgrims and letters on the crusade warned of the dangers of drinking wine unmixed with water.

wounds. But the king, with the Templars, and the house of the Teutons, and the Hospitallers of Saint John, and the counts of Holland, and of Wied, of Saarbrücken and Chester, with Walter of Berthout, several counts of France and of Pisa, and other knights, sustained the attack of the pursuers. The king was almost burned with Greek fire; these men all served as a protection for those who were fleeing. As often as they showed their faces to the enemy, so often did the enemy flee, but as they gradually returned, these men had to sustain the blows and weapons of the enemy.

Captured in that defense of Christianity were the bishop-elect of Beauvais and his brother; the chamberlain of France and his son; the viscount of Belmont and brother of the bishop of Angers; John of Arcis, a noble and vigorous man; Henry of Ülmen; and many others who were massacred or taken into captivity. Thirty-three Templars were captured or killed with the marshal of the Hospital of Saint John, and certain other brothers of the same house. Nor did the house of the Teutons escape without loss. The army of the Temple, which is usually first to assemble, was last to retreat. Therefore, when it arrived last at our ramparts, it stayed without, so that it might bring those who were before it back within the walls as soon as it was possible. Our persecutors finally returned to lead off the captives and to gather their spoils, presenting, as we afterward learned from a Saracen, five hundred heads of Christians to the sultan.

Gloom took possession of our men, but not despair. For we know that this affliction was the punishment of sin, and that there was less in the punishment than our fault demanded, since he tempered the chastisement who says to the soul of the sinner, "Thou hast prostituted thyself to many lovers; nevertheless return to me, and I will receive thee" [Jer 3:1]. But it is clear to us that the unbelievers sustained grievous losses in their own picked army. That day "was the day of our tribulation, and of divine rebuke" [2 Chr 19:3]. Truly the Lord is merciful who "does not forget to show mercy, and in his anger will not shut up his mercies, who in time of tribulation forgiveth sins; who commanded light to shine out of darkness; who turns our mourning into joy" [Ps 76:9; 1 Cor 4:6; Est 13:17], our sorrow into gladness. For the sultan, sending one of our captives, began to negotiate with us concerning peace or a truce, during which negotiation we promptly repaired our ramparts and other fortifications.[72]

72. By setting this disaster into a dense, relevant, and tightly woven context of scriptural references, Oliver here and elsewhere provides a framework for understanding events in a salvation-related cognitive theology of history.

Chapter 30

MEANWHILE the sailors, who were betrayers of Christianity, and with them very many pilgrims whose love of themselves was greater than their compassion for their brethren, before the time of the accustomed passage, left the soldiers of Christ in the greatest danger. Hoisting their sails and leaving port, they afforded dejection to us and courage to the Babylonians.

Interrupting our arrangement of peace on the vigil of Saints Cosmas and Damian and on the following feast day [September 26–28] and even on the next Saturday, with galleys and barbots on the river, and with mangonels, shields, and tree trunks for filling in the ditch on land, they attacked us with their usual barbaric ferocity and violence. But the mighty Warrior, the "Triumpher in Israel" [1 Kgs 15:29], using his customary kindness, defended his camp, sending Savary of Mauléon over the sea with armed galleys and very many warriors in this crisis of distress; and we, crying out to heaven, did not hesitate to rush into battle, but manfully stood our ground, killing, and forcing the enemy, wounded and confused, to withdraw from his three-day attack by the power of him who saves those who trust in him.

Chapter 31

MEANWHILE the city, being grievously afflicted by the long siege, by sword, famine, and pestilence, even more than can be written, placed its hope solely in the peace which the sultan had promised the citizens. For famine had grown so strong in it that desirable foods were lacking, although spoiled foods abounded. For the grain of Egypt is not lasting on account of the soft earth in which it grows, except in the higher lands around Babylon where it is skillfully preserved for years; and as we heard, one fig was sold there for eleven bezants. Because of the distress of the famine, various kinds of diseases harassed them; among the other grievances which they suffered, they were said to see nothing at night, as if struck by blindness, though their eyes were open. The sultan, dissuading them from surrender, deceived the wretched men from day to day by empty promises. Finally, however, they blockaded their gates from within so that no one, coming to us from their number, might tell us how the days of affliction beset them. But any who could escape through the postern gate or down the walls by ropes clearly proved the distress of their people by their swollen and famished condition. The supply of bread and fodder began to diminish even for those who were besieging us from without in the army of the Saracens.

For the Nile, which usually overflows from after the feast of Saint John the Baptist [June 24] until the Exaltation of the Holy Cross [September 14] and irrigates the plains of Egypt, did not rise this year according to its custom to the mark which the Egyptians usually place, but, as we learned, left a great part of the land dry, which could not be plowed or sown at the proper season.[73] Therefore the sultan fearing dearth and famine, and also because of his desire to keep Damietta, offered the Christians a peace with Coradin, his brother, on these terms: that he would give back the Holy Cross which had formerly been captured in the victory of Saladin, along with the holy city and all the captives who could be found alive throughout the kingdom of Babylon and Damascus, and also funds to repair the walls of Jerusalem. In addition he would restore the kingdom of Jerusalem entirely, except Kerak and [Krak de] Montréal, for the possession of which he would offer tribute for as long as the truce would last.[74]

Now these are two places located in Arabia, which have seven very strong fortresses through which merchants of the Saracens and of the pilgrims, going to Mecca or returning from it, usually cross; and whoever holds them in his power can very seriously injure Jerusalem with her fields and vineyards when he wishes. The king and the French and the count of Chester with the leaders of the Germans firmly believed that this arrangement was of advantage to Christianity, and ought to be accepted; and it was not to be marveled at, since they would have been satisfied with the much more insignificant peace which was formerly offered, had they not been opposed by wise counsel. But the legate, with the patriarch, the

73. The fragile ecological balance of Lower Egypt (as well as its complex and sometimes unpredictable hydrology) is evident here. This chapter is a kind of prologue to the horrific conditions that the crusaders discovered in Damietta when the city was finally taken.

74. The offer was diplomatically as well as symbolically substantial. The restoration of Jerusalem to the Christians, the return of all captives, the refortification of the city (reduced by al-Mu'azzam in 1219), and the restoration of the Latin kingdom except for the two key fortresses Krak and Montréal, which guarded the great caravan route between Syria and the south (but with tribute paid for them until the truce expired) were obviously attractive to John of Brienne, Ranulf of Chester, the French, and the Germans, and the ultimate rejection was not immediate. The symbolic importance of the captured part of the True Cross cannot be doubted. Reading the rejection of this offer back from the later defeat is tempting. However, Oliver was broadly informed and considered Pelagius's decision to reject the offer reasonable. It had been made, after all, following consultation with the pope and Frederick II. The debate among historians is long running and often acrimonious.

archbishops and bishops, the Templars and Hospitallers, and all the leaders of Italy and many other prudent men, effectively resisted this arrangement, showing reasonably that Damietta ought to be taken before everything.[75] Difference of opinion produced discord which was quickly settled because of the common need. Meanwhile the sultan secretly sent a great multitude of foot soldiers through the marshy places to the city on the Sunday night after the feast of All Saints [November 2–3]; two hundred and forty of them attacked the palisades while the Christians were sleeping; but the outcry of the sentries roused us, and about two hundred or more, according to our count, were killed or captured.

Chapter 32

ON NOVEMBER 5, in the reign of the Savior of the world, and with Pelagius, bishop of Albano, skillfully and vigilantly executing the office of legate of the apostolic see, Damietta was captured without treachery, without resistance, without violent pillage and tumult, so that the victory may be ascribed to the Son of God alone, who inspired his people to the entrance of Egypt and administered help there. And when the city was captured before the eyes of the king of Babylon, he did not dare, according to his usual custom, to attack through our rampart the soldiers of Christ who were prepared for the attack. At the same time also the river overflowed, filling our ditch with copious water. The sultan himself, in confusion, burned his own camp and fled. But God, who on the third day gathered the waters under the firmament into one place, who himself brought his soldiers through the waters of the sea to the harbor of Damietta on the third day of the month of May, led them over the Nile to besiege the city on the third day of the month of February, and himself captured Damietta located amid the waters, on the third day of the month of November.

We can liken this city, which was overthrown by a third shaking of the earth, to a destroying bull; we call it "bull" because of its wantonness. For because of its fishes, birds, and pastures, grain, gardens, and orchards, it grew rich by trading and by practicing piracy. It has overflowed with delights in its guilt, it has overflowed in hell. "But in one hour has thy judgment come" [Apoc 18:10]. We say "destroying" because its inhabitants perished in the third shaking of the earth, yet it remained unharmed

75. It is clear which side in the debates over al-Kamil's offer Oliver favored, and his support for the legate Pelagius is also clear. See chapter 34 on the crusaders' expectations of Frederick II and reinforcements and Oliver's eulogy of the city and people of Cologne.

itself. It was first besieged by the Greeks and Latins who finally went away from it; next by the Latins under Amalric, king of Jerusalem, who were not successful; but this third time, the "King of kings and Lord of lords" [Apoc 19:16] delivered it to his servants; Jesus Christ, who conquers and reigns and commands, "who for the Egyptians has dried up everything sown by the water, and hath confounded them that wrought in flax and silk, combing and weaving fine cloth" [Is 19:7–9]. With this Leader, the soldiers of Christ, attacking Damietta, found its streets strewn with the bodies of the dead, wasting away from pestilence and famine; very much gold and silver, silk stuffs of the merchants in abundance, various household goods in superabundance. In addition to the natural location of the place, by which it is fortified, this city is surrounded by a triple wall, stoutly protected by many large brick towers; it is the key to all Egypt, and its protection is well located between Raamses and the field of Tanis in the land of Gessen, as we can surmise because there is the pastureland which the sons of Israel sought from Pharaoh at the time of famine [cf. Gn 47].

Chapter 33

DAMIETTA! renowned among kingdoms, very famous in the pride of Babylon, ruler of the sea, plunderer of Christians, seized in the pride of your persecutors by means of a few small ladders, now you are "humbled under the mighty hand of God" [1 Pt 5:6]; and casting out the adulterer whom you kept for a long time, you have returned to your former husband; and you who first brought forth bastards, now shall bear legitimate sons for the faith of the Son of God, being firmly held by the faithful of Christ. The bishop of Acre released from you the first fruits of souls for God by cleansing in the sacramental waters of baptism your little ones, who were found in you, alive by his power, even though they were near death. You have been subjected to manifold punishments because besides those who were taken alive in you, your dead of both sexes from the time of the siege round about you are computed at thirty thousand and more. The Lord struck them down without sword and fire, scorning henceforth to endure the uncleanness committed in you.

Chapter 34

THEREFORE let the universal church rejoice by returning worthy acts of thanksgiving for such a triumph, and not only for Damietta, but for the destruction of the dangerous fortress of Mount Tabor and for our free approach into Jerusalem, that its walls may be rebuilt at the time foreseen by the Most High; besides, for the castle of the Son of God, which the army of the Temple, at great expense, is making useful and impregnable, concerning which we have written more fully above. Rejoice, province of Cologne, exult and give praise, because in ships, instruments of war, warriors and weapons, supplies and money, you have given more aid than the rest of the entire German kingdom! Our illustrious emperor and king of Sicily is being eagerly awaited by the people of God for the happy consummation of the enterprise. Thou, O Cologne, city of saints, who dwellest in the gardens of the roses of martyrs, of the lilies of virgins, of the violets of confessors [Sg 6:1–2], now rejoicing in a temporal peace through our venerable archbishop, because of the devotion of thy daughters, bend the knees of thy heart before the Most High, who has power of life and death. "Be not high minded, but in his sight fear, reprove your ways, lest the wrath of God which hath fallen upon thee" be turned into hail, but . . . since peaceful times have long been granted, serve him with a free mind, to whom is honor and excellence, might and power [Rom 11:20; Jb 13:15; 2 Chr 34:21].[76]

Chapter 35

BEFORE the capture of Damietta there came to our attention a book written in Arabic, in which the author says that he was neither Jew nor Christian nor Saracen. But whoever he was, he predicted the evils which Saladin cruelly brought upon the Christian people in the destruction of Tiberias, and in the victory which he had over the Christians when he took captive the king of Jerusalem and its princes, occupied the holy city, and destroyed Ascalon. It also predicted how he tried to seize Tyre but did not succeed, and many other things which the sins of that time deserved. He also foretold the destruction of the gardens of the palm grove of the city of Damietta, which we saw had been accomplished when we examined this book through an interpreter. He also added that Damietta would be captured by the Christians; he does not use the name of Saladin, but points him out by means of his black eyes and saffron banners. Besides, he predicted that a certain king of the Christian Nubians was to destroy the city of Mecca and cast out the scattered bones of Muhammad, the false prophet, and certain other things which have not

---

76. Five manuscripts of Oliver's work omit the reference to Frederick II's anticipated arrival and substitute the formal address to the city of Cologne to the end of the chapter in its place.

yet come to pass. If they are brought about, however, they will lead to the exaltation of Christianity and the suppression of the Agarenes. We know that certain heathen gentiles had the Holy Spirit on their lips, but not in their heart, and prophesied plainly about Christ; therefore we are not surprised if purer water flows through stone channels.[77]

Besides this, a report, spreading through the whole world, that Damietta had been captured by the Christians, caused a letter of the Georgians to be sent to the camp of the catholics. It said that that nation, angered and roused by shame, decreed and swore, as the king convoked the leaders, that she would besiege some famous city of the Saracens, alleging that she would be ashamed because the Franks, coming from regions across the sea, and from the uttermost bounds of the earth, over a vast ocean full of dangers, had captured so well fortified a city by a long siege, unless they themselves, for whom it was easier to attack the enemy, should capture Damascus, or another specified place, by the strength of their arms. Now the Georgians are believers in Christ, and are neighbors to the Persians, separated from the land of promise by a long stretch of country; their kingdom extends as far as the Caspian Mountains, on which ten tribes enclosed (there) await the time of Antichrist, for then they will burst forth and will cause great destruction. The Georgians are warlike men, having the tonsure on their heads, round for the clergy, and square for the laity. Their women of the noble class are trained for battle. When those men are going to attack the enemy in orderly array, each one drinks a small gourd filled with pure wine, and at once they attack their adversaries courageously.

We do not doubt that it is to be counted among the favors of Christ our protector, that he defended our leaders from the murderers of our persecutors in the siege of Damietta. For the Assassins and their chief, the Old Man of the Mountain, had the custom of casting knives against the Christians to cut off the lives of those who care for the business of Christianity.[78] For at the time of the truce they wantonly killed the son of the

77. The validity of pagan prophecy when permitted by God had long been part of Christian apocalyptic, in the case of the Sybils and others. The legendary attraction of Prester John, an Eastern Christian ruler who was coming to the aid of the Eastern Christians, had circulated since 1145, and an increased knowledge of the peoples of the Near East provided a cognitive context for such prophecies that strengthened the message of scriptural prophecy, hence Oliver's discussion of the Georgians and the legendary confinement of the tribes of Gog and Magog by Alexander the Great, linking prophecies relevant to the immediate present to the long-range prophetic future and the end of the world.

78. The order of the Assassins was a close-knit retinue of Ismaili jihadists who killed their enemies and later became political killers. Their leader was known by Christians as the

count of Tripoli, a fine young man, who was prostrate before the altar in the church of the Blessed Virgin at Tortosa; wherefore the army of the Temple did not cease to pursue them for such a violation of religious liberty, until they were humiliated to the servitude of paying a tribute of three thousand bezants annually to the Templars.

Chapter 36

AT THE time of the siege, Leo, king of Armenia, died at a good old age. Likewise the sultan of Iconium died.[79] He is believed to have been baptized, and was so kindly disposed toward the Christians that when making war on the side of the Saracens he ordered the followers of Christ to be released whom he found in chains in the fortification which he attacked.[80] He gave them their choice of returning into their own country, if they wished, or of receiving money from him and waging war under him if they preferred. So familiar was he with Christians, that he made them guardians of his own person, although his father had been killed by Lascaris the Greek. He also supported Miralis, the disinherited son of Saladin, against the sons of Saphadin, as far as the caliph of Baghdad, pope of his own race, permitted.[81]

Melchiseraph, son of Saphadin, inflicted many losses on the Templars when they were in the siege of Damietta; for he burned the town of Safita, and destroyed its fortified towers. But when he returned to his own land, he was conquered by the Saracens. At the same time Bohemond, count of Tripoli, attacking Antioch, forcibly ejected Rupen, a certain kinsman of his, from the rule of that city, choosing rather to have the pleasure of

---

Old Man of the Mountain and the Assassins were feared throughout the Near East. They resemble the modern Druze in their relations with other Muslims.

79. Leo II the Great (1187–1219) had early successes against Seljuk power, but the end of his reign saw the Armenian loss of Iconium and Isauria. Leo's daughter Stephanie became the second wife of John of Brienne. John's first wife, Marie of Montferrat, had died in 1212. Their daughter Isabella II (d. 1228) became the ruler of the Latin kingdom and later married Frederick II, who then claimed the kingship by virtue of his marriage. See below, Part IV. The sultan of Iconium was 'Izz-al-Din Kaikawus I (r. 1210–1219), who destroyed the Armenian army in 1216. To ransom captives Leo II eventually had to concede all of Isauria.

80. The idea that Muslim rulers sometimes favored Christians to the point of considering conversion themselves was more common in the thirteenth century. Oliver himself wrote a letter in 1221 to the "King of Babylon" and another to the "Doctors of Egypt" urging them to convert to Christianity. Francis of Assisi, of course, famously preached directly to the sultan.

81. "Miralis" was the Christian name for Malik al-Afdal, who succeeded his father, Saladin, in Damascus but was overthrown by his uncle Saphadin in 1196.

a temporal sin than to be afflicted along with the Christian people. Therefore the legate of the apostolic see officially proclaimed the sentence of excommunication and interdict against him and Tripoli and the lands in which he committed the crime.

Chapter 37

"THE LORD hath broken the staff of the wicked. He hath broken the horn of the proud; he who above the sons of men is terrible" [Is 14:5; Ps 74:11, 65:5], has powerfully opened the gate of Damietta. As we were entering it, there met us an intolerable odor, a wretched sight. The dead killed the living. Man and wife, father and son, master and slave, killed each other by their odor. Not only were the streets full of the dead, but in the houses, in the bedrooms, and on the beds lay the corpses. When a husband had perished, a woman, powerless to rise and lacking the help of one to support her, died, not being able to bear the odor; a son near his father or vice versa, a handmaid beside her mistress or vice versa, wasted away with illness and lay dead. "Little ones asked for bread and there was none to break it for them" [Jer 4:4], infants hanging at the breasts of their mothers opened their mouths in the embrace of one dead. Fastidious rich men died of hunger amid piles of wheat, those foods being lacking by which they had been raised; in vain did they desire melons and garlic, onions, fish and fowl, fruits of the tree and herbs. In them was fulfilled the prophecy of the prophet: "Instead of a sweet smell there shall be stench, as rotten carcass shall not have company in burial" [Is 3:24, 14:19–20]. Almost eighty thousand, as we learned from the report of captives, perished in the city from the beginning of the siege to its end; all except those whom we found, healthy or ill, about three thousand in number. Three hundred of these, the more notable ones of both sexes, were kept for the ransom of our captives; some died after the victory, others were sold for a great price, and others were baptized and given to Christ.

Chapter 38

THIS city fortified in degrees had its first wall low for the protection of the ditch, the second one higher, the third loftier than the second. The middle wall has twenty-eight main towers containing two or three tortoises each, which all remained unharmed along with the walls, except one which was considerably shattered by the frequent blows of the trebuchet of the duke of Austria. For our army was so given over to dissipation that the knights devoted themselves to leisure, neglecting the work of God, while the common people turned to the taverns and to fraudulent dealings. Two cats had been made at great expense to fill the ditch. One of them in the custody of the king, the other in the custody of the Romans, were burned when the guardians of the city were still powerful in arms. Two subterranean ditches were made to undermine the foundations of the fortifications; but that labor was frustrated after very much expense. The Lord wished to give the city unharmed, without loss of those capturing it, and that by reason of his power. We all swore in common that the spoils carried off from the city should be given up to be divided among the victors; this also was enjoined under terrible anathema by the legate of the apostolic see. Transgressors will remain to be reckoned in disgrace forever with Achan, who at Jericho took something of what had been anathematized [Jo 7]. Truly the concupiscence of the eyes made many men thieves. Nevertheless we received for the benefit of the state a great part of the luxuries of Egypt, in gold and silver, pearls and apples of amber, golden threads and various fringes, precious silken stuffs, as Isaiah enumerates: "In that day he will take away the ornaments of shoes, and little moons, and chains and necklaces, and bracelets and bonnets, and bodkins and ornaments of the legs, and tablets and sweet balls and earrings, and rings and jewels hanging on the forehead, and changes of apparel, and short cloaks and fine linen and crisping pins, and looking glasses, and lawns and headbands, and fine veils" [Is 3:18–23], which no one could list in full. But we are spending much time in considering them. These things were distributed through the army of the Lord with grain which was found in the city.

Chapter 39

THE LEGATE of the apostolic see joined Damietta, with all her dependents and belongings, to the kingdom of Jerusalem forever. The mosque of Damietta, through the invocation of the holy and undivided Trinity, was converted into a church of the blessed and glorious Virgin Mary. Being built in square form, we can see almost as much of its width as we can of its length. It is supported by one hundred and forty-one marble columns, having seven porticoes, and in the middle a long wide-open space in which a pyramid ascends on high in the manner of a ciborium; beyond the west side a tower rises after the manner of a campanile. Four main altars are built in it: the first under the title of Blessed Mary; the second of Peter, the Prince of the Apostles; the third of the Holy Cross; the fourth of blessed Bartholomew, on whose feast the tower in the river was captured.

In Damietta were found four trebuchets with petraries and many mangonels; very strong ballistae with a lathe; on account of the multitude we do not know the number of hand ballistae and bows. Every kind of equipment for brave men that was found was kept for Christianity. Gold and silver, with pearls and other things easy to move, were divided proportionally not only among clerics and knights, but also among attendants, women, and children. The towers of the city with its homes were distributed among the kingdoms whose warriors had assembled for its capture; one tower was in the first place reserved, as was right and fitting, and was assigned to the Roman Church, with its gate, which formerly was called the Babylonian but now is called the Roman. Another tower also was reserved for the archbishop of Damietta; and as formerly Jerusalem, the holy city of the living God, was captured by the enemy at night, so the Christians obtained Damietta before dawn. The machine by which the tower of the river had been captured, the Germans and Frisians donated in common, and out of it was made a new bridge between the city and the fort which is constructed as a defense of the bank opposite the city. Two small fortresses were placed together for the protection of the bridge, by the same machine. Besides, from other trees on which the ladders hung, a watch place was set up on the summit of the new fort to point out the harbor to those sailing at a distance. An old bridge, which with an island in the middle touched both banks, had been attacked many times by the Saracens at the time of siege, and had been manfully defended by the Christians. Having done its work, it is kept for other uses.

Chapter 40

By no less a miracle, but rather by a greater one did the Lord give to the Christians the fort of Tanis, in the month of November, on the feast of blessed Clement [November 23] who has his dwelling on the sea. For scouts were sent, about a thousand in number, in small ships through the little river which is called the Tanis, so that they might take food supplies for themselves from the *casalia* and carefully explore the location of the aforesaid place. The Saracens, who were in the garrison of the fort, seeing the Christians and thinking that the whole army was arriving, fled after locking the doors. But our men, having Christ alone as their leader there, breaking through the barriers, entered the fort. Returning they declared to us that never had they seen a stronger fort on a plain; it had seven very strong towers, fortified by tortoises, and a breastwork; and besides it was surrounded by a twofold ditch, each part of which is protected by a wall. A lake stretches out in breadth round about to such an extent that approach is impossible to our horsemen in winter, and so difficult in summer that it would never be taken by our army in siege. The lake abounds in fish, and from its fisheries four thousand silver marks were paid annually to the sultan of Babylon, as was told to us by elders; besides, it abounds in birds and saltworks; many *casalia* round about were subject to it.

The city beyond the fort, greater than Damietta, once famous but now in ruins, bears witness to the size of its buildings. This is Tanis, whose field the prophet mentions: "Wonderful things did he do in the sight of their fathers" [Ps 77:12]; and Isaiah: "Many princes of Tanis, the wise counselors of Pharaoh, have given foolish counsel" [Is 19:11]. This is Tanis, in which Jeremiah is said to have been stoned [Jer 52]. For when Jerusalem had been destroyed by the Babylonians, and Godolias had been killed by Ishmael [Jer 41], the rest of the people against the counsel of Jeremiah set out into Egypt, taking with them Jeremiah, who remained with them in Tanis, "and the word of the Lord was made known to Jeremiah in Tanis: 'Take great stones and hide them in the vault that is under the brick wall at the gate of Pharaoh's house,'" etc. [Jer 43:8–9]. Afterward Jeremiah said to them: "Thus sayeth the Lord: I have sworn by my great name . . . that all the men of Judah that are in the land of Egypt shall perish by sword and by famine until they be wholly consumed" [Jer 44:26–27]. And the people rose against Jeremiah, and they stoned him with the stones which had been hidden under the brick wall. But the Egyptians honored the prophet, burying him next to the tomb of their kings, being mindful of the benefits which he had shown to Egypt. For by his words he had driven away the beasts of the waters, which the Greeks call crocodiles. Now Alexander the Macedonian, coming to the tomb of the prophet and being acquainted with the mystery of the place, transferred him to Alexandria and buried him gloriously. But we found and killed crocodiles at Damietta. Now this beast is cruel, devouring men and animals, and it cares for its eggs simply by watching them with its eyes open. Its young, being hatched, flee the parent as an enemy; for in an instant it gulps down and devours whomever it can snatch.[82]

82. The stories of the Egyptians and later Alexander the Great are fictitious. But Oliver's interest in crocodiles shows some powers of observation of the ecology of Lower Egypt besides the focus on warfare and diplomacy.

Tanis is separated from Damietta by a journey of one day over the sea in the direction of the land of promise, so that it is easy to place a garrison there or to send food from Acre or from Damietta, across the sea or over land or by river. It caused many losses to the Christians in the siege of Damietta, when ships approaching us or going away from us were carried there by the force of the winds. For before Tanis, the coast, which is curved and without harbors, makes a wide, full bay; and ships drifting into it cannot withdraw without a wind that is highly favorable to them.

Chapter 41

CORADIN, having returned from Egypt into Palestine, besieged the castle of Caesarea, which was in the custody of the king, and in a short time he captured and destroyed it while its defenders acted negligently; nevertheless they almost all escaped because they had a free entrance and exit over the sea. Next he proceeded to the castle of the Son of God with all his army, and regarding it from every direction, he shrewdly realized that it could not be seized; besides he found the Templars prepared for every danger; for they had reinforced the camp with provisions and with all the equipment of brave men. At the same time the Templars manfully drove back the bandits of the Saracens from Acre by killing some and capturing others. But Coradin demanded help from the Saracens, so that coming from the east they might besiege Acre, a thing which he could not accomplish because of the constant discord of the princes of the land themselves, which was highly favorable to the Christians, and which the caliph, their pope, labored to quiet.

Chapter 42

IN THE year of the Incarnate Word 1220, Coradin, prince of Damascus, destroyed Safita. Now this was the strongest fort of the Templars, which Saladin, the scourge of the Christians, reduced by a long siege to such a point that the defenders, wasting away with hunger, and having obtained the permission of the master of the army of the Temple, surrendered it to the tyrant. What voice, what tongue can repeat for us the benefits of our Savior, multiplied without us? They are benefits of him whom an inherent goodness and natural clemency, and also the continued supplication of the church, have induced to look with a kindly eye upon the camp of the faithful because of the sweetness of their devotion! A plea softens him, a tear forces him, and how can the hand of a writer or the tongue of a speaker be sufficient for him for whose praise a conscience remaining quiet in the heart is not sufficient? However, it is pleasing to heap up and admire the marvels wrought in a short space of time which descended from the Father of Lights. The sons of Israel were at hand, going about with the ark of the Lord, sounding their sackbuts and shouting, on the seventh day, when the walls of Jericho fell, so that the people of the Lord might have free entrance [Jo 6:11–20].

But we slept before Damietta, cowardly and sluggish, benumbed and given ever to idleness; nonetheless, the walls of Jerusalem fell, and those of Mount Tabor, Safita, and the other fortifications opposing in a hostile way; besides, the Most High, against the will of certain false Christians, gave us Damietta. To this, from the treasure of his generosity he added the impregnable fort of Tanis with its supply of provisions in a hostile land—he who rained manna from heaven upon his believers in the desert. It is therefore clear to all, through the evidence of miracle, that this holy pilgrimage is pleasing and acceptable to God. May they blush and be confounded who received the rewards of the supreme king from his church, and, fighting indifferently or retreating before time, corrupted his pilgrimage; they will give an account to the Judge who cannot be either corrupted or deceived. Let the sluggish be aroused, who have not yet carried out their vow. For "it is ruin to a man to devour holy ones, and after vows, to retract" [Prv 20:25]. What excuse will they offer on the day of tribulation and distress, who took away the labors of others, killing souls to which preachers of the truth have given life [Ez 23:29]; who had regard for their own avarice and took the sign of the cross from the shoulders of the wretched, whom they made transgressors of their vow? Let them also return to wisdom whom guilt accuses and conscience convicts of this, that by alleging false reasons of poverty and debility, they have cheated the religion of those who have been examined, because only the judgment of God is according to truth.

But the defrauders of the alms which were collected for the aid of the Holy Land, because they have concealed their fault by lying to the Holy Ghost, shall perish and have their lot with Ananias and Saphira [Acts 5:9]; and with Judas, the most wicked thief and betrayer of his Lord, they shall be punished in hell because, though betrayers of Christianity, they kept for themselves the wages of fighting men, and gave their souls for transitory things. Cupidity has caused their theft and they are unmindful of Jerusalem our mother, who, lying prostrate on the ground, desires to be lifted up from her Babylonian captivity by those who are returning. Be consoled, "city of God, because nations from afar shall come to thee, and bearing gifts, shall adore the Lord in thee; they shall be cursed who despised thee, and they shall be condemned that have blasphemed thee. The blessed that built thee up shall rejoice. But thou shalt rejoice in thy children, and blessed are all they that love thee and that rejoice in thy peace" [Tb 13:10–18].[83]

Chapter 43

IT HAPPENED when the year was changing, when kings usually set out to war [2 Kgs 11:1], that John, king of Jerusalem, left the camp of the faithful. He feigned many reasons for excusing himself and promised a speedy return, but forgetful of the past, he turned to the future.[84] When the Lord opened his hand and filled the port of Damietta with abundance of grain, wine, and oil, and when a numerous band of pilgrims and horses had been added so that there might be no grounds of excuse for setting out upon an affair so happily begun, there arrived in the sixth passage the archbishops of Milan and Crete, the bishops of Faenza and Reggio, and messengers of Frederick the king, bearing letters with golden seals and announcing his arrival. There was present the bishop of Brescia and a copious army of Italy. But the legate considered that by a great privilege of grace and by divine bounty everything had been sufficiently attended to that the process of negotiation required; and he was struck with sorrow because time was passing away uselessly, and such a great opportunity was lost. Therefore, assembling the leaders, he, first of all, and after him the archbishop of Milan, and other bishops likewise, strove to urge an advance against the sultan who had pitched his camp on the Nile one day's journey from Damietta. But the knights, after holding a deliberation, spoke against this exhortation, pretending this reason above all—that the king of Jerusalem was away by voluntary choice, and no other prince was present whom the people of different nations were willing to obey to lead out the people of God—and thus they agreed upon inactivity, from which evils were multiplied in the camp.

---

83. Oliver and other crusade leaders' letters to recruiting centers during the campaign often complained about the lack of men or money, which influenced papal policy on vow redemptions and attempts to get local church leaders to force early departers and renegers to fulfill their vows (with the additional problematic of a campaign to a place other than Jerusalem). Perhaps this is also an attempt to assign blame for and explain the failure of the Fifth Crusade. Compare the problems of Gervase of Prémontré in No. 18.

84. For John's Armenian interests, see chapters 36 and 45.

Chapter 44

IN THE month of July came Count Matthew of Apulia with eight galleys, two of which were corsairs that he had captured as they were threatening the Christians on the sea journey.[85]

Chapter 45

LET the temerity of human presumption blush, which trusts erroneously in its own strength or in the strength of others, and clearly is very often confounded. This appeared in the case of the aforesaid count. A previous report announced his arrival by frequent rumors, and, as if the negotiation would proceed only through him, its progress was hindered by delaying circumstances. But the memory of such great hope perished with a crash. It was not due to the count that the hope was not carried through to its desired consequence, because, as the legate witnessed, his will was prompt and the equipment which he had brought and which he afterward added appeared magnificent to all and in complete accord with military knowledge. Besides he made a sojourn in the army that was useful and suitable to the position of a soldier of Christ. But after he arrived at Damietta, the legate took counsel with any nation that was then in the camp who seemed to have the greatest zeal, and with Count Matthew himself, to whom an advance against the king of Babylon seemed advantageous. Next he called the princes and leaders of the multitude, and in a public address roused to labor a people who were sluggish and given over to idleness.

But the leaders, especially the Franks, spoke against this honorable exhortation, effectively inducing the earl of Arundel, a leader among the English, and the more noble among the Germans, to hinder the proposal of the legate. Among other trifling reasons, the absence of King John was frequently alleged who had acted contrary to the agreement which he had made at Acre when the pilgrims were about to sail into Egypt, that he would not desert them while he was alive and free. Contrary to his solemn agreement he returned to Acre; and not attending to the business of Christianity, he prepared himself and made a journey to Armenia. For having as his wife the daughter of Leo, the deceased king of Armenia, he aimed at the dominion of that region, as it is said; but being frustrated in

85. Matteo Gentile, referred to in a charter of 1229 as "count of Alesina (modern Lesina) and captain of the city and master justiciar of Apulia and the Terra di Lavoro"—that is, a high-ranking representative of Frederick II under whose orders he was participating, thus heightening the crusaders' hopes of the emperor's actual arrival.

his hope, he was not received by the barons of Armenia. At almost the same time the queen died, along with the king's little son. Rupen, prince of Antioch, also sought this kingdom; a catholicos, primate of the aforesaid nation, powerfully besieged him in the city of Tarsus; he was taken and imprisoned, and died there. Now the catholicos favored the younger daughter of King Leo, to whom her father before his death made the princes of his kingdom swear fealty; he died a short time afterward.

Chapter 46

THE LEGATE, after frequent public and private admonitions, grieved that so numerous an army was stationary, and not progressing, and would be going back in the next passage; finally by his example of action, he began to urge others to join the retinue, causing his tents to be pitched in a flat place. However, the opposition of the leaders prevailed to such a degree that even some Gallic and German mercenaries, who had accepted his money, hindered his plan of advancing. Certain of them were excommunicated, and others who were to be excommunicated afterward were disturbed, and were compelled to return the pay that they accepted according to proportion of time. The Italian soldiers by vain hope cheated the religious zeal of the legate, promising assistance for the advance, "but the sons of Ephraim, bending and shooting the bow, have turned back in the day of battle" [Ps 77:9]. For while they were clearly regarding the persistence of the legate and the boldness of the march against the sultan, they agreed with the dissenters mentioned above, and opposed the advance, although the Christians did not lack an abundance of soldiers or attendants. Galleys were in abundance, barbots were prepared, a numerous multitude of archers was present, there was a plentiful supply of provisions, there was a suitable place between the river on the right and the lake on the left, as if the Lord were saying to us: "What is there I ought to do more to my vineyard and I have not done it? Was it that I looked that it should bring forth grapes and it hath brought forth wild grapes?" [Is 5:4]. For besides the other things which were provided by the Lord for the setting out of the expedition, as we learned from our scouts, the king of Babylon then had little aid, and a great multitude of Bedouins had joined us and would have given their wives and children as hostages if they had known that the Christians had undertaken the attempt manfully, as we learned through their letters and messengers. And this seemed probable because they are subject under tribute to the sultan; indeed they formerly ruled in the land of Egypt until they were powerfully oppressed by Saladin and were scattered through the wilderness of the desert.

Chapter 47

THE LEGATE, after much weariness, because he had an unwilling retinue and especially because the river overflowed at that time, withdrew to the previous camp, strongly urging the authors of the delay, in a public sermon, that the work of God, being happily begun, should not be ended and that they should judge themselves, lest they be grievously condemned by the Judge of secret things.

Chapter 48

NO ONE can describe the corruption of our army after Damietta was given us by God, and the fortress of Tanis was added. Lazy and effeminate, the people were contaminated with chamberings and drunkenness, fornications and adulteries, thefts and wicked gains. Afterward, certain of our men set out for a day's march into hostile territory, bringing back captives, oxen, and horses. Then the Templars, with their own special following, advanced in a swift march to a town on the seacoast, which is called Broil, and brought back many spoils—about one hundred camels, the same number of captives, horses, mules, oxen, and asses and goats, clothing and much household furniture, returning unharmed after two days. However, on account of a lack of water, many horses and mules died on the way, although the men themselves returned safe. The Teutonic house, with many others, met them for joy, but when they delayed behind the Templars (it is not fully known for what reason), the swift horsemen of the Turks made an attack on them at the sea. Terrified men from other nations fled from them, but the English, the Flemish, the Teutons, and Robert of Belmont sustained the attack as they came upon them. The preceptor and the marshal of the same house, with many other brothers and about twenty secular knights, were captured. Many horses of those who fled to defend themselves were killed because our men went out, not for battle, but to meet the Templars, and therefore were without crossbowmen and archers.

Chapter 49

IN THE month of August there reached Damietta fourteen galleys equipped and sent at the same time by the doge of Venice, which brought some help to the Christians. At the same time the king of Babylon armed thirty-three galleys which caused us inestimable loss. For they captured the merchant ships, along with the men themselves, which were bringing supplies to Damietta; they even took the pilgrims captive, plundering and burning the ships. Besides, they attacked a large ship which was bringing Count Henry of Schwerin, and other Teutonic nobles who were coming to us. They, however, defended themselves manfully; and having killed and wounded many pirates they fortunately escaped, although they lost one vessel from the Teutonic house, with barley which Greek fire destroyed.

Chapter 50

HERE we are forced to insert the account of an unfortunate mishap. Count Diether of Katzenellenbogen left us before the time of the passage with a great multitude of pilgrims, although he was strongly urged and admonished by the lord legate not to board that ship if he wished to set out for Thessalonica, but to go in a smaller vessel with a few men without diminishing the army. But he, with the master of the ship and many pilgrims, stubbornly took up the journey, and therefore, the legate of the apostolic see excommunicated that accursed ship and all who were sailing on it. Falling among pirates near Cyprus, it was burned. However, the shipwrecked count escaped, swimming away with a few men.

Chapter 51

THE GALLEYS of the Venetians and others being requested to hurry, set out rather belatedly from the port of Damietta, going to Rosetta and Alexandria after we had suffered losses at the hands of the Saracens in the manner mentioned above.

Chapter 52

CORADIN, knowing our inactivity, gathered an army from Syria, and more completely destroyed Jerusalem, the city of the living God, though it had been destroyed before. He scattered the cisterns that had previously been filled, had the city's marble columns carried off to Damascus, and advancing through the mountains and fields of Palestine he laid waste its fruit-bearing trees and vines. The Templars, knowing that he wished to besiege the castle of the Son of God, began to destroy the deserted tower of Destroit in the upper section. But he, coming upon them later, razed it to the ground, cutting down the fruitful garden placed before it; he finally besieged the fort with a multitude of Turks, extending the line of their tents from the river to the saltworks. Now he derived this audacity from the fact that he knew that around the beginning of October the seventh passage had been so small; for we believe that not one hundred soldiers came to our aid then with military weapons and horses. But a great multitude of the people of Acre came to Damietta, being driven from their lands by the pronouncement of the church. From that number those were allowed to return whose poverty could be known to us; others returned without permission to the increase of their destruction; and still others returned to their own lands after extorting permission through fraud. But a few, who had a more rational attitude, remained with us in exile.

Chapter 53

CORADIN, having established the siege, and fearing an attack from the camp, ordered a rampart to be made between the fort and his tents. He set up one trebuchet, three petraries, and four mangonels, and harassed the fortification night and day by blows of the machines. However, he could not move one stone from its place in the new towers and the middle wall. But the trebuchet of the camp, with a petrary and a mangonel placed next to it, battered and broke the trebuchet and the petrary of the enemy. In the residence of the Templars, moreover, four thousand warriors were fed daily, except those who at their own expense had come from Acre to defend us or to sell provisions. But the legate in haste requested the queen of Cyprus and the Christians, and the barons of Syria, through messengers and letters, to aid the fortress of Christianity. The master of the Temple, with a tested army of Templars, was permitted by the legate, because of such a great need, to return to the castle, and prepared to fight with Coradin. The men of Cyprus brought a great supply of soldiers and funds. Bohemond, likewise, and the lord of Beirut, Guy of Gibelet, with other *pullani*,[86] quickly prepared themselves to help. Learning this through scouts and betrayers of the Christians, Coradin was struck with fear and basely withdrew from the siege, suffering great losses at the hands of those holding the castle, both in men and in horses. Like a proud and arrogant man, he had threatened that he would take the castle by a long siege; but divine power forced him to retreat after he burned his own camp around the beginning of November.

Now many of the defenders of the castle were wounded and a few died. May the Most High protect this home, built to the honor of the

---

86. *Pullani* was a name given to Syrian-born Franks; cf. modern French *poulain*.

Son of God, hateful to the Saracens, but lovely to the Christians, the breastwork of the city of Acre, as it were. May the custody of angels be upon its walls "even to the consummation of the world" [Mt 28:20]. Truly, "we have faith in the Lord Jesus" [Eph 3:11–12], since he who began to destroy the enemies of the cross is steadfast in his grace, and will accomplish it at the time of His own good pleasure. For already we perceived a certain proof of divine vengeance; for in the siege of the castle, as we learned from our scouts, and clearly saw, since corpses were strewn through the fields, three emirs were killed there, and two hundred Mamluks most skilled in arms;[87] but there was no count of their archers, and of those who were dragging them along in their machines, and who were destroyed by our crossbowmen, three hundred in number. In one day also were killed one hundred and twenty horses of great value, among which was one, bought for fourteen thousand drachmas, which Seraphus, sultan of Aleppo, sent to a certain emir for a gift; besides, the Saracens also sustained many losses of other horses and camels.[88]

Chapter 54

IN THE month of November, Lord Frederick, son of the emperor Henry, was crowned emperor in Rome under Pope Honorius, in the great harmony of state and priesthood, and in the peace of the Romans.[89] Being signed with the cross, he made ready to go to the assistance of the Holy Land, sending ahead the duke of Bavaria, who came to Damietta in the year 1221 in the eighth passage with the bishop of Passau, the marquis of Baden, Count Guy of Brienne, and other nobles in the month of May. The emperor committed his post to this leader until he should cross the sea in person. Then the legate of the apostolic see, considering the fitness of the time, and the cost of idleness, began to treat with the duke again about the business of war, for the forwarding of which he had remained in Egypt. Besides, the aforesaid duke urged that the multitude of the

87. Mamluks were Turkish slaves purchased for service in the army. The Egyptian dynasties that succeeded the Ayyubids (descendants of Saladin and al-Adil) are generally termed "Mamluk" because their sultans were taken from the enfranchised slaves who made up the court and supplied officers to the army.

88. See the appendix to Oliver's text following chapter 89, probably written by someone else as a conclusion to chapter 53.

89. Frederick II—see below, Part IV. Son of Henry VI and Constance of Sicily and grandson of Frederick Barbarossa, Frederick came from a family long associated with crusading. His rule as both emperor and king of Sicily was the cause of great consternation on the part of popes from Innocent III to Innocent IV. Both of his ruling roles made the crusade important to him.

faithful should attack the camp of the sultan, before the river should take up its usual increase.

Therefore by the common plan of the barons, knights, and the common people we began to arrange tents up the river beyond the camp in the month of June on the feast of the apostles Peter and Paul [June 29]. It was known by the statement of the bishop-elect of Beauvais and of others who are detained in captivity, and by the story of very many, that if the legate had not been hindered by the opposition of those of whom we made mention above but, as he had ordered, had advanced against the sultan before or after the swelling of the river, then Egypt would have fallen to the lot of the Christians. For at that time the leaders of Egypt were disagreeing with the sultan; and like Rahab the harlot, begging the kindness of God for her people, for herself, and for her house [Jo 2], so the Egyptians sent presents and gifts to our captives in Cairo, begging that by means of them, they might find mercy at the hands of the victorious Christians.[90] On the third day of the octave of the apostles [July 6], the legate, beginning with a three-day fast, and assembling the clergy with the archbishops and bishops, carried barefoot the saving banner of the Cross in procession beyond Damietta to the camp located where the river rises. On the next day King John returned to Damietta, bringing a numerous following.

Chapter 55

"I WILL begin and I will make an end," saith the Lord. "Behold I shall make a word, and whosoever shall hear it both his ears shall tingle [1 Kgs 3:11–12]. Mine is the dominion in the kingdoms of men, my counsel shall stand, and all my will shall be done; there is no one who can resist my countenance. There is no wisdom, there is no prudence, there is no counsel against the disposition of my will. For the whole world before me is as the least grain of the balance, and as a drop of the morning dew that falleth down upon the earth. Who shall say to me, 'what hast thou done?' or who shall withstand my judgment? I have found David my servant, with my holy oil I have anointed him [Is 46:10; Jer 49:19; Prv 21:30; Ws 11:23, 12:12; Ps 88:21], king of the Indies, whom I have commanded to avenge my wrongs [Dn 7], to rise against the many-headed beast, to

90. With the forces sent by Frederick II at hand and commanded by the duke of Bavaria and count palatine of the Rhine, Ludwig of Wittelsbach, who was also the representative of the emperor himself, as well as the evidence of dissension in Cairo, and the return of John of Brienne, Pelagius's decision to advance makes considerable strategic sense.

whom I have given victory over the king of the Persians; I have placed a great part of Asia under his feet."

The king of the Persians, being lifted up unto excessive pride, wished to be the monarch of Asia; against him King David, who they say is the son of Prester John, won the first fruits of victory. Then he subjugated other kings and kingdoms to himself, and, as we learned by a report that reached far and wide, there is no power on earth that can resist him. He is believed to be the executor of divine vengeance, the hammer of Asia.

Chapter 56

INDEED after the capture of Damietta, the legate of the apostolic see had a book which was written in Arabic read aloud briefly and by means of an interpreter, in the hearing of the multitude; and as we considered and contemplated the antiquity of its bindings and maps, we discovered we ought to proceed. This book is entitled "The Book of Clement," written as they say, from the lips of the Prince of the Apostles by Clement himself concerning the revelations made known to Peter by the Lord between his resurrection and ascension.[91]

Now this book begins from the creation of the world and ends in the consummation of time; and in it are read the precepts and counsels of salvation. He inserts prophecies, certain of which now clearly appear to have been completed, though some depend upon the future. Among other things, it is said that a watery city would be captured by the Christians along with one city of Egypt. The capture of Alexandria is also added, nor is Damascus omitted, which greatly tortured and is still torturing the servants of God. Besides, mention is made of two kings, one of whom, it is claimed, will come from the East, the other from the West, to Jerusalem in that year when Easter will be on the third of April. This book agrees in many things with the one of which we made mention above. Very many letters written about the victory of King David support this prophecy, along with the story well known among Christians and Saracens. We also see as a proof of this that the Christian captives of this king were freed by messengers of King David in Baghdad; these had been taken in the siege of Damietta, and the king of Babylon had sent them to the caliph as a gift.

---

91. On books of prophecy and the role of the crusade in salvation history, see above, chapter 35. James of Vitry gives the correct title of the prophetic book as *The Revelations of Holy Peter the Apostle to His Disciple Clement Redacted in One Volume.*

Chapter 57

ON JULY 17 the Christian army gathered at Fareskur, a *casale* three miles distant from Damietta, and being suitably drawn up in ranks of horsemen and troops of foot soldiers, they went forward quickly. Indeed estimators of the army enumerated twelve hundred men armed in military fashion, provided with the cavalry equipment necessary to accomplish such an undertaking, not counting the turcopoles[92] and numerous other horsemen. We could not find out the exact count of armed foot soldiers because of their great number; the Saracens compared them to locusts because they occupied a great amount of land. We believe that four thousand archers assembled, almost twenty-five hundred of whom were mercenaries. Among the six hundred and thirty larger and smaller ships we clearly counted three hundred casques with eighteen armed galleys, and besides, there were scalanders,[93] tartans,[94] barbots, corsairs, and barks carrying cargoes with provisions. The number of the enemy was declared by fugitives to have been about seven thousand horsemen. The arrangement of the battle line was as follows:

The river on the right, covered over with ships, afforded protection in the manner of a wall; on the left side, the foot soldiers served as a breastwork, going forward in line and in a procession, as it were, in close formation. The lines of horsemen were stretched out diagonally from the river to the ranks of the foot soldiers, giving them support and receiving it from them. The lancers stayed constantly with the archers, sustaining the attack of the enemy with lances close-packed and leveled, if at any time they presumed to rush into close combat. Thus in the danger of horses and horsemen it was provided by prudent counsel that the pack animals should not be wounded.

The common people, unarmed, proceeded in safety with their bundles at the bank of the river, clerics, foot soldiers, and women carried water to those farther off; those who were more experienced against the snares of the deceitful, cautiously sustained the attacks of the enemy in the fore and rear guard. By public edict severe precaution was taken that no one should presume to go ahead of the foremost ranks or to fall behind the rear line or to break into the line in any wise. The scouts of the enemy regarding our forces from both sides of the river and marveling

92. Natives of mixed origin who fought on horseback, usually as light cavalry or mounted archers. They were found in all the eastern armies from Byzantium to Cairo.

93. A small one-masted ship with a large lateen sail and a foresail.

94. A small single-masted ship with a large lateen sail.

at the order of our military discipline, tried in vain to inflict losses; but such a great multitude of archers resisted them that we learned that on that day none of our men had been captured and none of our men had been wounded, who had stayed constantly with the four-sided battle line. The legate distributed wages with a generous hand to the knights and their attendants, he armed ships, sparing neither his body nor his possessions to accomplish the work, exhibiting all the diligence he could; in company with him King John of Jerusalem and the duke of Bavaria, the archbishops and bishops, and the masters of the houses toiled and labored at the undertaking.

Chapter 58

ON JULY 19 the king of Egypt sent a stronger and greater proof of the might which he then had—four thousand horsemen, it seemed, who encircling the people of God timidly enough from without, at a distance, attacked the outermost lines of foot soldiers with arrows. Our men valiantly resisted them, not breaking their own lines in the least on account of this. On the following day, they besieged us more fiercely and compelled our men to use up quite a few arrows. In these two days the few Christians slightly wounded, and the very few dead, took away from the enemy the hope of winning a victory. Returning to their lord on the third day, they opened a peaceful way for us through Saramsah, burning their *casalia* before us. Nevertheless we found plenty of grain and barley and vegetables, even straw, and the fruits of gardens; the inhabitants with their women and children fled altogether before the face of the power of God.

Chapter 59

ON THE vigil of Saint James [July 24] we pitched camp on a triangular head of an island where the Nile divides in two parts, and separates the former camp of the sultan from ours, and where he had made a delay after the capture of Damietta. In this spot the river of Tanis, withdrawing from the bed which goes to Damietta, forms with it an island. This island, extending twelve miles in length, contains many *casalia* located above the waters. Among those on the farther shore better known than the others and more wealthy, are Symon and Saramsah, in which there were the magnificent palaces of the king. This island has obtained a name, and is called the land of Damietta; the one which is across the river is called the

land of Tanis, but the wider one which is found across the river of Damietta is called Mahalech. Beyond the river of Tanis, less than one day's journey to the east, begins the solitude of the desert, in which, however, water
is found at fixed watering places, sufficient for men and animals if it is
increased by digging. Now it ends at Darum and Gaza. Babylon, being
located in the south, causes the land of Egypt to be called Babylonia. The
plan of this city, divided into three parts, forms a triangle. The city of
Babylon itself, built upon the Nile, is extensive in its length and width,
having narrow streets and dwellings crowded together because of the
great number of people. In it there are very many churches of the Christians, and a numerous multitude of these same people serve the prince of
the land under tribute. In it are set down the wares of traders coming
from Leemannia, Ethiopia, Libya, Persia, and other regions.[95] From the
side opposite Damietta at a distance of almost a mile, Cairo spreads out
in buildings and spacious streets; it has magnificent mansions, in which
the barons of the land and the nobler citizens stay. This city does not
descend entirely to the river as does Babylon, but a space planted with
rushlike roots is found between. At a distance a rather high watchtower,
the royal fort, stands out, plain to see, and well protected by great towers.
The great buildings are arranged in a threefold way after the manner of a
triangle. Now from both sides of the fort the wall comes down, enclosing
Cairo and Babylon, but a sandy stretch lies between these three buildings,
in which a numerous army can remain.

Chapter 60

BETWEEN Cairo and Babylon they point out the church of Blessed Mary
where she is said to have made a pause with the child Jesus, when she fled
into Egypt and the idols of Egypt fell. Cairo is a three-day journey distant
from Damietta. From Cairo to the garden of balsam, there is a distance
of a mile; this garden, which has sandy soil, is enclosed by a wall. There is
a fountain in the middle and from it is derived a tale of the ancient people
which is spread abroad by a famous story, that the glorious Virgin drew
it forth by her prayer, and washed the clothing of the infant Savior in it.
Now this garden is cultivated in the manner of vineyards. A trunk of this

95. Leemania may be Upper Egypt, immediately north of Ethiopia. The name occurs
nowhere else. Chapters 59–70 pause for a survey of the Near East, its peoples, and their
religions. Oliver explains his digression at the beginning of chapter 70. The rest of his history
addresses the defeat, and this pause may well be rhetorical as well. These passages may also
be intended as a guide for the anticipated crusade of Frederick II, since they are careful about
geography and potential allies.

garden has the thickness of a plant; its branches shoot out from the trunk to the height of one cubit in the manner of a willow, and its bark is knotty and lined, and of a whitish color. Its wood is called sirobalsam, its seed, carpobalsam, its sparse and pointed leaf, like the leaf of the licorice, is called filobalsam, and also opobalsam in whose branches the farmers make cuts in certain parts of the bark where the balsam is drawn forth, so that the liquid, collecting by degrees, may run out through them. In autumn the balsam is collected in this way: A branch is twisted and scratched with a nail; through this small opening a drop is caught and kept in dishes; next it is melted for twenty days in the sun, and afterward is skimmed off at the fire; the fluid is poured off into bottles, for of the original substance, very little unmixed balsam remains after the purification. But the sellers and resellers usually mix in pine resin or turpentine and deceive the buyers, and therefore it is rarely found pure at the hands of venders. The sultan usually distributed it in bottles among the princes of the earth as a great gift. The master of this garden is a Christian, having Christian and Saracen servants under him.

Chapter 61

BELOW Cairo an island extends for a stretch of three miles in length and width, where the Nile divides its waters into two parts, touching the bank of Damietta on one side, and of Rosetta on the other. Rosetta was a great city, now in ruins, between Alexandria and Damietta, but much closer to Alexandria, and two days away from Cairo. At Rosetta and above it, the river is wider, the water deeper, the harbor calmer than at Damietta; for it receives heavily laden ships, and it is possible to place a large army on the aforesaid island. When we were at its head in the siege of Damietta, the sultan wished to take the river from us; having tried often but in vain to cause its waters to flow into a channel; after great expense he left its course to nature. From Babylon on the upper side to Leemannia, the culture of the land is hedged in by both sides of the river, having vast solitudes on both sides. Leemannia abounds in a variety of spices which she sends out and which various traders of the kingdom carry away.

Chapter 62

BEYOND Leemannia, Ethiopia holds very broad lands, and has an innumerable Christian population partly under Christian kings and partly under the rule of the Saracens. Here are the Nubians who are joined in the sacrament of the altar, and in other Jacobite divine offices, with this exception: The Nubians are the only ones who imprint upon their little ones with heated iron a threefold character of the cross on the forehead near the eyes on both sides. Nevertheless they do baptize. The former and the latter have the Chaldean writing; they use leavened bread for the Holy Eucharist; they make the sign of the cross with one finger; they say that two natures are united in the one nature of Christ, perhaps using equivocally the name of nature, so that in the second place they take "nature" for "person."[96]

Chapter 63

THE GEORGIANS and the Greeks agree in everything pertaining to divine services, but the Georgians have their own writing. While we were carefully examining their books on the mountain of Saint Simeon on the Pillar, where they have their own church, we learned through an interpreter that they have the same order of Gospels that the Latins have, and the canons of the Gospels on arcuated columns as we do. The order of the Epistles of Saint Paul is exactly the same with them as it is with us; they put the Epistle of Saint Paul to the Romans before all the others.

Chapter 64

THE MARONITES have their patriarchate on the side of Mount Lebanon. These received the plan of their ecclesiastical rites from Pope Innocent in the last Lateran Council, and they observe it insofar as their writing allows, which is Chaldean, or near-Chaldean. To these people on the side of the same mountain are joined the Neophorites who keep their law concealed.[97] They do not explain it to their sons and grandsons until the thirtieth year of their age. It is an evil law that desires to be kept secret and not to appear in the light. When we wished to know, as we were passing through that section, why they never revealed their law to their wives or daughters or sisters except at this age, one of the older men answered that women were made by the devil. And we responded, "When you embrace women of this kind, do you therefore embrace the

96. Jacobites were Monophysite Christians of Syria and Mesopotamia. "Monophysite" is the name given to those Christians who believe in only a single, divine, nature of Christ. Although Monophysitism was condemned in the fifth century, it survives to the present day.

97. The Maronites were (and still are) Arabic-speaking Christians named after the Syrian abbot Saint Maron, who died in 433. They seem to have professed the doctrine of a single will in Christ (monothelitism) but reunited with Rome in 1182, hence the reference to Innocent III and the Fourth Lateran Council. The Neophorites are extremely obscure, probably a sect of Ismailian Shiites, hostile to the Maronites.

devil?" Whereupon he withdrew from us confused. Certainly the Christians are sorry that they have such neighbors.

Chapter 65

THE ARMENIANS have their own writing. In the field their priests set aside the grain from which they wish to make unleavened hosts; they thresh it separately from the common crop; they grind it separately and on the day when they wish to consecrate the Body of the Lord, with the singing of psalms before the altar they prepare the flour and sprinkle it with water for the paschal bread, which is in the shape of the Latins. They celebrate with great devotion. However, they are very much to blame in this, that they do not celebrate the Nativity of the Lord with us; they plow and sow on that day while their women spin and card wool. They call the day of the Epiphany "baptisterium"; on this solemnity they assemble with a great crowd of people. They celebrate the Nativity of the Lord with the Epiphany, saying that the Lord was born on the same day as that on which he was baptized after a few years had elapsed. They say that they are subject to Roman laws and they have a catholicos as primate whom they obey in all things.

Chapter 66

STOPPING at Antioch, we carefully examine the Nestorians, who have their church there, and who say that they believe that two natures are united in the person of Christ. They confess that the Blessed Virgin is the mother of God and of man, and that she bore both God and man, which Nestorius denied. But whether they believe in their hearts as they confess in their lips, God knows.

Chapter 67

THE SYRIANS have the Greek writing, chant, and ritual sacrifice, but the Arabic language in common with the Saracens in the deeds and letters which they draw up.

Chapter 68

THE JACOBITES for the most part throughout Egypt are circumcised, but those who remain among the Medes and Persians are content with baptism.[98]

---

98. Oliver is here referring to Coptic Christians.

Chapter 69

THE RUSSI have their own language, but in divine services they are found to be like the Greeks in everything. These different kinds of Christians are mingled with the Saracens throughout all Asia, and so that perfidious nation cannot excuse herself on the ground of ignorance.

Chapter 70

WE have made this long digression not without reason, so that the location of Egypt and the course of the river as well as the variety of Christian inhabitants who are in Asia may appear more clearly to the faithful.[99] Now, as we return to the order of our history, let us sprinkle this book with tears, weeping and grieving for the loss and disgrace of Christianity.

An advance to the great and famous *casale* of Saramsah, of which we made mention above, was of advantage to the army of Christ. Therefore, after the capture of Damietta, the sultan, prudently looking out for what could happen in the future, destroyed the *casale* as well as his beautiful palace located on the Nile. Beyond that spot the river curves and turns back and a certain little stream, coming from the island of Mahalech, flows into it; taking on depth from the waters which increase as they spread out, it is able to bear galleys and other vessels of moderate size. When our leaders saw it, they scorned it and passed it by, hastening to the head of the island. The people also, in hopes of plunder, because it was falsely announced to them that the sultan was preparing for flight, hurried eagerly like birds to a snare, and fishes to a net. But when the king of Babylon was informed that Saramsah had been abandoned from the rear, he united foot soldiers and horsemen from his own kingdom, from Cairo and Alexandria particularly, in an attack on those who were arriving. Whereupon, our captives, considering the fact that Cairo had been evacuated by its inhabitants, formed a plan to seize the towers at our arrival, and to open them to those who were approaching. But a divine Providence which mercifully "heard the groans of them that were in fetters" [Ps 101:21], and the labors and sorrows of those who were in bondage, released them through our distress.

---

99. What seem to be Oliver's digressions on Egypt and Eastern Christians and Prester John may be not only justifications for the crusade's diversion to Egypt but also information for the planning of the emperor's hoped-for crusade, in which Oliver and James immediately involved themselves.

Chapter 71

WHILE this was taking place in Egypt, Seraphus, king of Edessa, the city of the Medes, with Coradin, lord of Damascus, and the leaders of Hama and Homs with a great multitude of horsemen, gathered from all regions of the east, and assembled at Homs. As a result great fear struck the people of Antioch and Acre, and other cities on the coast whose warriors were absent since they had set out on an expedition. Those in Safita, in the country of Tripoli, were especially concerned about this assemblage.

Long and earnestly did the forenamed princes deliberate whether they should come to the aid of Egypt themselves, or whether they should divide the army of the Christians by besieging some one of their fortresses. The power of King David influenced them, since as victor over the king of the Persians in the lands of the Persians and in those of Baghdad, he was acting powerfully, and on account of him they were afraid to go far from their own lands. They also reflected that the castles of the Hospitallers or the Templars could not easily be captured in a short time. Finally the counsel of those who urged advance into Egypt prevailed, especially because their brother frequently sent messengers on courier camels begging them to come. He added that the Christians had taken up their position in such a place that they could not leave it without danger, or that if they could not prevail against them when they came, they would at least arrange peace with them. The queen of Cyprus wrote to the legate, and the brothers of the Hospital and of the Temple wrote to their masters about these troops and their plan, urging them not to retreat from Damietta; or, if they had gone out, to look out for themselves in safe places. But now just when the sins of us all needed it, sane counsel was far removed from our leaders; like Julius Caesar, repeatedly forewarned, and like Alexander the Macedonian, warned in the silence of the night, they neglected to employ precautions against physical danger.[100] The Lord himself spoke through Moses to the sons of Israel: "Go not up nor fight, for I am not with you, lest you fall before your enemies" [Nm 41:42]. They went up, nonetheless, and they fell conquered.

But King John, reflecting more deeply on the matter, wisely showed that the proposal so often proffered by the enemy ought to be accepted,

---

100. The references seem to be to Suetonius, *Lives of the Twelve Caesars* 1.83, and Quintus Curtius Rufus, *History of Alexander the Great* 10.4. See n. 64 above; these are the only other references to classical Latin texts in Oliver's narrative.

rather than that the people of the faithful, being led forth on a longer march, should be exposed to chance accidents. But the supreme pontiff forbade any agreement without a special decree of the Roman Church; the emperor, through letters sealed with gold, would not permit peace or a treaty to be arranged with the Saracens.[101]

Chapter 72

MEANWHILE we strengthened our fort by a deep ditch; on the other hand our adversaries made a wall of earth and high bulwarks on the opposite banks of both rivers, setting up on them machines, petraries, and ballistae with a lathe, causing serious injury to the men and to the animals which were taken out to drink. The strength of our adversaries increased daily; our gathering, being depleted, proved unfaithful. As the time for passage drew near, timidity increased among those who, going away openly or deceitfully, deserted us in the camp. Many ships also, that went to Damietta to bring food, could not return. For on the eighteenth day of August four of our galleys were captured or sunk in the river; this gave added courage to the enemy. For the sultan had sunk some of his galleys all through the river, of which we made mention above, below our camp through the island of Mahalech at the bank of the river, without our knowledge; this cut off passage for our men, so that they could go neither up nor down. Besides, since a multitude of armed men had wisely been stationed there, a continual guard night and day watched both banks as far as Damietta, so that our people could neither send nor receive messengers.

Chapter 73

FROM the day when we lost the river our men frequently assembled to consult together, and to ponder what would be more expedient: to wait in camp for the galleys promised by the emperor, or to go out, no matter what the loss, because of our dwindling supply of food. The greater number counseled going out, which was more dangerous because of the arrival of the enemy and the decided hindrance of the waters. But a certain one[102] of the lesser members, who saw and heard these things and

101. Pelagius had been instructed to report all diplomatic negotiations to the pope. Honorius III admitted the substantial cost in life, labor, and resources in refusing the terms offered by al-Kamil, but he also expected the momentary intervention of Frederick II, who had vowed to sail to the East. Honorius was also aware of reports concerning Prester John and King David. Frederick himself prohibited the crusaders from accepting al-Kamil's terms.

102. Oliver is here referring to himself, as one of the lesser members in the army. The proposal recorded below is his own.

described them with a crude but truthful pen, proposed David as an example, who having choice among three things, any one of which was hard, chose not a famine of seven years, nor to be conquered by an enemy for three months, but what was the common wish of the king and the poor people: a pestilence of three days. Wherefore he answered, when he was consulted, as did the weak and infirm whom there were not sufficient ships nor animals to carry, that help should be awaited in a fortified place, since the provisions, if they were carefully distributed, could last even for twenty days. Nevertheless this plan was not accepted, but a departure, and that by night, was more favored. In this, the opinion of the bishop of Passau and that of the Bavarians prevailed.

Chapter 74

THEREFORE on August 26, in the first watch of the night, when the tents were taken up, the first men, following the judgment of their own will, and not that of reason, put fire to the tents. Then others also did it eagerly, as if they were announcing their own flight, and inviting the Egyptians, who had already surrendered their bodies to sleep, to follow us. At the same time the Nile had received its full increase, and, as its waters surged even higher than usual, it had flooded the fields. The fore-named kings also came through the desert above the river Tanis at Symon, where a bridge was built, and stopped and encamped. It added greatly to our misfortune that the people were greatly intoxicated that day with wine of which there was such an abundance that it could not be brought along; but being freely exposed, it had overwhelmed the unwary, who remained sound asleep in the camp or prostrate on the road. They were unwilling to be roused, and in great part they left us, being either cut off or captured.

Others came into the overflow of the river in the shadows of night, and struggling wretchedly in the deep mire, stayed behind the others. Others, falling into the ships and pressing them down too much with their weight, were drowned. On the same night we lost camels and mules carrying burdens, including the silver vessels, clothing, and tents of the rich, and what was more disastrous, the arrows of defense. The Templars, bringing up the rear at their own great risk, stayed constantly together as a protection for those who went ahead, as they were prepared with weapons. But those who went ahead, going into different roads, wandered through the darkness of the night like sheep astray. The Egyptians were informed of our flight by the fire and smoke and promptly followed after us. They reached us even more quickly and inflicted on the Christians losses which we cannot describe. No less danger and injury was sustained by those who went down in a ship along the bank. The ship of the legate, carrying a great number of the sick, as well as provisions, was extremely well fortified with armed men and archers, just as if it were a fort, and valiantly protected the galleys which naturally stayed close together. But hurrying too much, perhaps because of the force of the current, and being fatally separated from the land army, it could not supply food to us at the proper time. Furthermore, one of our ships filled with German warriors got too far away from the legate's ship and was surrounded on all sides by galleys of the enemy; while sinking one of them into the deep after a long defense, it caught fire and destroyed the combatants. A scalander of the legate carrying many temporal goods, and one small galley of the Templars in which were fifty ballistae, besides other equipment of brave men, was seized and went out of our possession.

Why do I linger over the enumeration of the losses which that night caused us? "Let a darksome whirlwind seize upon that night, let it not be counted in the days of the year, nor numbered in the months. Let that night be solitary and not worthy of praise" [Jb 3:6–7]. In the beginning of this night the king of Egypt, quickly sending messengers, had the sluices broken (which those people usually call "calig") through which there could be a passage for us. Their own night is memorable to the Egyptians, and to us also. When the banks had been burst to a great extent, the superabundance of water, following the declivity of the reservoirs through conduits, softened the earth, made dry by long drought, into sticky mud which held tight the horses' hooves; it made the open space of the fields quite impassable and greatly hindered horses and riders.

Chapter 75

AROUND the first hour of the following Friday [August 27] there appeared the great and fearful cavalry of the Turks harassing us at the right; annoying galleys went up and down at the left; a phalanx of black Ethiopians going on foot and using the marshy places for a camp pressed upon us savagely from the rear; and also a wedge-shaped formation of enemies, coming from the front, denied us rest. In this contingency King John made an attack on the Turks who were opposite him, and returned to his own battle line. The Templars, with the Hospitallers of Saint John who at that time were united with them, did not tolerate the insolence of the Ethiopians. As they massacred them they made them jump onto the bank like frogs, and even drove them back when they wished to approach the bank on our side. Thus about a thousand of the great multitude, swimming away or suffering wounds, perished. On account of this misfortune our opponents retreated a little.

And since we were not permitted to go forward, the king ordered a few tents, which had stayed behind, to be taken up; nevertheless, through that whole day our adversaries stayed close to us, attacking us fiercely with their archers. We put our foot soldiers against them as a rampart and used them also, for they shot back the arrows directed against us. Our horsemen, laboring under the constant weight of their armor, served as a protection to the foot soldiers. On the following night, whether by the command of the sultan or without his knowledge, the Egyptians broke open the floodgates and made the waters pour in upon the heads of those who were sleeping. Before daybreak, when darkness still covered the earth, the Ethiopian foot soldiers who had escaped the grasp of the river came, desiring to avenge their losses; they swarmed like locusts, and although for the greater part they were naked, they attacked our rear lines. You could see that our knights and their attendants were attempting flight in a closely packed throng; and the common people, being unarmed, displayed manifest timidity, but being blocked on all sides by the waters and the enemy, they had nowhere to flee. However, the marshal of the Temple with his battle line which he was leading, raised his banner, turned upon those who were pursuing, and forced them to halt and retreat.

Chapter 76

AT THIS juncture, distress which gave understanding persuaded the leaders of the multitude to send messengers for terms of peace. But Imbert, a worker of great evil, took with him those whom he could get away, and went over to the enemy, explaining the whole of our distress to the sultan. This Imbert usually took part in the secret councils of the lord legate, and was by far the worst traitor of that time.[103] Nevertheless, the sultan heard the messengers patiently, and, pending a confirmation, ordered his men to cease from disturbing us. And although his brother, and especially the lord of Homs, who was extremely hostile to the name of Christian, tried to dissuade him from an agreement, saying that since the Franks were blocked on all sides by water, they could not escape, he himself, like a

---

103. The identity of Imbert is unknown. Oliver is the only source that mentions him.

wise and mild man, desired an arrangement of peace more than the shedding of blood. Therefore, he held a secret council with his brothers and the great men of his kingdom. He proposed as an example the king of the Persians, who was exceedingly lifted up in mind because of many events, and shook off the yoke of subjection or servitude to the king of Babylon himself and other kings of Asia. King David conquered him on the battlefield, took away Persia, and destroyed its greatest and wealthiest cities. After this, the messengers of peace spoke on both sides, as is usually done in matters of this kind, and protracted the business all through the Saturday and Sunday following, even until evening, settling upon nothing definite.

Chapter 77

On the very day of the Beheading of Saint John the Baptist [August 29], at about the twelfth hour, our side, urged on by the lack of food and fodder, but especially by the great size of the waters, decided that it was more honorable to live happily or to die bravely in war, than to perish infamously in the flood. So when all the Franks had been roused to combat, battle lines were drawn up here and there looking upon each other fiercely and dreadfully. But the Turks realized that he who provokes an enemy is by his own fault bound by a yoke; they retreated a little upon receiving a command from their king, and the arrival of nightfall prevented a battle. Besides, while the treaty of peace was pending, a display of treachery was feared by wise men, if the common good were to be destroyed by a dangerous attack.

Chapter 78

And so on the thirtieth day of August, being forced into a lamentable peace by the perversity of circumstances, we surrendered to the Egyptians and Assyrians, that we might be filled with bread; and thus the flood of waters and the lack of food, not the bow or the sword, humbled us in the land of our enemies. An astonishing thing, an astounding thing, a thing to be handed down to the knowledge of the future: At one and the same time the just judgment of divinity appeared and the moderation of mercy shone clearly in opportune assistance. The enormity of our evil deeds and the vast number of our crimes were compelling the vengeance of divine decision, but the natural fount of goodness, whose property it is always to have mercy and to spare, mitigated the sentence of just severity. For this did we fall into danger, that by the mediation of mercy, a miracle might shine forth. "God will not have his creature to perish, and recalling, intends that he that is cast off should not altogether perish" [2 Kgs 14:14]. The angel of great counsel, speaking for man, as one among thousands appealed for us, announcing the justice of man [Jb 33:23]; for although we may be sinners, nevertheless, carrying his cross we have left homes or parents or wives or brothers or sisters or sons or fields for the sake of him who shows anger placidly, Who judges calmly, Who chastises lovingly, having the blows of a father, but the heart of a mother.

Chapter 79

AND SO when the conditions had been laid down according to the decisions of the sultan, the documents of the contracts were completed by both sides, oaths were sworn, and hostages were named. The sultan, therefore, placing his right hand on a paper which he had signed, swore in this way: "I, Kamil, king of Babylon, from a pure heart and a good will, and without interruption, do swear by the Lord, by the Lord, by the Lord and my law, that I will in good faith observe all the things that this written paper contains which is placed under my hand. If I shall not do this, may I be separated from future judgment and the society of Muhammad, and may I acknowledge the Father, the Son, and the Holy Ghost." In this manner swore Seraphus and Coradin, and their more eminent emirs. Behold under how many mistakes and contradictions is that blind nation laboring; three times they name God, but not knowing the mystery of the Trinity, they are unwilling to distinguish the name of the Father, of the Son, and of the Holy Ghost, to the increase of their own damnation. If they swear in bad faith or with any interruption of the form of the ritual, they say that they are not under obligation.

Now this writing contained an agreement of this kind: that they would restore the True Cross, along with all captives taken any time at all in the kingdom of Babylon, or all Christians held in the power of Coradin; and that when they had received Damietta with all its belongings, they would send us all away free, as well as all our movable goods, and would faithfully keep a truce of eight years. Our leaders swore that they would free all Saracen captives, whom they were holding in the two kingdoms of Egypt and Jerusalem; that they would restore Damietta and would observe the treaty, unless our crowned king who was coming should wish to break it. Besides, twenty-four hostages were given, whom the sultan chose: the legate, the king of Jerusalem, the duke of Bavaria, and three masters of houses, along with eighteen others. On the other hand, the son of the sultan, heir of the kingdom, and one of his brothers of whom there are many, and sons of nobles were given to us until our return to Turo and the port of Damietta.

Chapter 80

LET all posterity know that in view of the critical point of our necessity, we made an excellent bargain, when the wood of our redemption was restored to us in exchange for one city which Christianity could not hold for long, since grain or wheat is spoiled there in less than a year and the master of Egypt himself can scarcely keep it peopled; and when so many thousands of captives, in whose number we counted ourselves, from the greatest to the least, were restored to their own freedom. When the emperor Heraclius entered Persia, he captured it with difficulty after five successive years; and having defeated Chosroes, he carried the Cross of the Lord in triumph and brought the patriarch Zachary back to Jerusalem with his captive people.[104] The sultan had been keeping as captive the patriarch of Alexandria, a man of great piety and perfection of morals; he sent him back to us as we were going up the Nile, released from his chains and free from the squalor of prison. The enemies of the cross declare that they were deceived in this agreement, saying that they had regained their own city of Damietta, that they had destroyed Jerusalem, and other fortresses of this illustrious kingdom, but that the Christians had erected one impregnable fort in Palestine itself, very dangerous to them and without their consent.

Besides, if we had been completely destroyed, or imprisoned after losing all our possessions, and if Damietta had been lost without any recompense, the rest of the land which the worshippers of Christ hold would have wavered on the edge of certain danger. For those who had remained to guard Damietta, when they heard our adverse circumstances, left the city and fled, for the most part. Not only did they flee, but also those who had but recently arrived heard the unfavorable report and returned. The count of Malta reached Damietta around the end of August with forty galleys. Pirates despoiled the Hospitallers of Saint John and the Templars of their goods, killed one noble knight and religious brother of the Temple who was defending what had been entrusted to him, and fatally wounded another brother, a Teutonic knight.

104. Oliver's point is that a piece of the True Cross was worth far more than the meager resources of Damietta.

Chapter 81

BEFORE the restoration of Damietta the sultan began to carry out what he had promised. For he commanded that the bishop-elect of Beauvais and certain other captives be released from chains and brought to their own camp. The master of the army of the Temple and the master of the Teutonic House were sent by the leaders to surrender the city in accordance with the pledge and assurance of their oath.[105] This was done without great difficulty. For among the new pilgrims who were arriving, there was not to be found a man powerful, vigorous, and constant enough to be either willing or able to hold it after the aforementioned happenings.

Chapter 82

"THE BEAST has gone into his covert, and abides in his den" [Jb 37:8]. If it is asked why Damietta returned so quickly to the unbelievers, the reason is clear: It was luxury loving, it was ambitious, it was mutinous; besides, it was exceedingly ungrateful to God and to men. For to pass over other things, when that city had been given to us from on high by heaven in the distribution of the riches that were found in her, not an old woman nor a boy of ten years and over was excluded; to Christ alone, the bestower of the goods, was a share denied, not even a tenth being paid to him. Formerly Roman pagans dedicated a golden vessel to Apollo under the form of tithes; the sons of Israel according to custom assigned to the Lord his share of the spoils of the enemy; the sons of Israel said to Moses when they had conquered the Midianites, "We offer as gifts to the Lord what gold we could find in the booty, in garters, rings, tablets, bracelets, and chains" [Nm 31:50].

In the distribution of towers and dwellings most praise was deservedly given to that obedient and energetic nation, who from the beginning attacked Damietta with great courage, and considered no position either humble or lowly;[106] by the fleet of ships which it brought, the camp of the faithful was supplied with food and weapons, the tower of the river was captured, the crossing to the opposite bank was organized,

---

105. The master of the Teutonic Knights was Hermann von Salza, one of the closest advisers of Frederick II. On the division of the Teutonic Knights with most moving to northern Europe and others remaining in the Holy Land, see Klaus Militzer, "From the Holy Land to Prussia: The Teutonic Knights Between Emperors and Popes and Their Policies Until 1309," in Jürgen Sarnowsky, ed., *Mendicants, Military Orders, and Regionalism in Medieval Europe* (Aldershot UK-Brookfield VT, 1999), 71–81.

106. The Frisians.

the upper and lower bridges were built, the watchtower of Turo was constructed, the walls of the rampart were fortified. It has consolation in the face of such ingratitude since "God will render the inestimable reward" of his slaves "and will conduct them in a wonderful way" [Ws 10:17].

Chapter 83

O LOVER of men, King of glory, Savior of the world, who hast holy knowledge and omnipotence above all power, who dost reprove some and dost console others, thou didst humble our pride by taking away Damietta from the ungrateful and by mercifully preserving Armenia and Antioch against the efforts of wicked men. For those who were in the fortress inflicted great disaster upon Christianity, but those who were then in the valley added irreverence to wickedness; as they presumptuously gathered in defiance of thy goodness, from one side thy justice appeared plainly, and from another the mercy of thy customary goodness clearly shone on those who were willing to open their eyes.

Chapter 84

RUPEN, formerly lord of Antioch, was of very noble stock, but because of a lack of discretion he was unsuitable for the management of great things; with the help of Guérin, master of the Hospital of Saint John, and of those whom he could persuade, he seized Tarsus, attacking the Armenians because of a desire for kingdom. This did not escape the Turcomans of Iconium. They were encouraged by the discord of the Christians, and attacked Armenia with troops. But as the leaders of that kingdom, in making their complaint, affirm and state on peril of their lives, the army of Christians in that region at that time was reduced to about twenty thousand after they counted those who had been killed or captured by the Saracens, and also after many had fled because of the loss of their goods.

Chapter 85

THEREFORE in addition to all thy praise, insofar as I am able and as thou wilt permit, I shall continue by adding the following things.

Chapter 86

IN THE year of grace 1222 in the month of May it happened that there was a great earthquake on Cyprus, in Limassol, Nicosia, and other places of that island, especially in Paphos, to such a degree that the city was completely destroyed along with the fort; human beings of both sexes who were there at the time of the earthquake were completely lost; the harbor was dried up, where afterward waters or fountains burst forth.

Chapter 87

IN THE month of June in that same year Coradin assembled a numerous army from Arabia, Palestine, Idumea, and Syria—ten thousand horsemen, and fifteen thousand foot soldiers—against Guy of Gibelet who, like a vain and wicked man, did not wish to take part in the general truce, nor to return the captive Saracens whom he held. Although he was well enough fortified by the difficult nature of the region and by the help of Christians, nevertheless he submitted to a truce with Coradin that was injurious to him and shameful to the Christian name.

Chapter 88

IN THE month of June in the same year, the boy Philip, son of Bohemond, prince of Antioch, became a knight in Armenia; he married the daughter of Leo, formerly king of Armenia, and was solemnly crowned with her as king of that kingdom. And when the nuptials were being celebrated, and the Armenians were joyfully assembled for the great affair, Turks from Iconium savagely attacked that land with a great multitude, massacring whomever they could find and taking away much plunder with them. At the same time Bohemond, prince of Antioch and count of Tripoli, was present. Although he had only a few Latins with him at the time, since he had not foreseen this mishap, nevertheless, with his son the king he promptly and vigorously pursued the enemy over long, hard roads. Although many of his number were killed, like a vigorous man, and one skilled in arms, he drove them out beyond the boundaries of Armenia. After this, the Armenians recovered a certain well-fortified camp, Siblia by name, located at the boundaries of Armenia and Turkey, which the sultan of Iconium had taken away from them along with other fortresses after the death of Leo.

Chapter 89

MEANWHILE Frederick, emperor of the Romans and king of Sicily, sent four galleys to Acre, summoning the king, the patriarch, and the master of the Hospital of Saint John. They crossed in the month of September, hastening to the Council of Verona, which had been proclaimed by the supreme pontiff and the emperor for the feast of Saint Martin [November

11]. At the same time, along with the aforementioned princes, came Lord Pelagius, bishop of Albano, a legate of the apostolic see. The master of the Temple, with the army of the same house, remained in the land of promise for the protection of Christianity, according to the common advice of the barons, after sending discreet and honorable messengers to the council.[107]

Appendix: Concluding section of the Darmstadt manuscript

In a single manuscript of this work in Darmstadt, this appendix follows chapter 53. It seems to have been written by a different hand, and it is uncertain whether it is the work of Oliver.

WHEN this had been so accomplished, our pilgrims grew sluggish through idleness and riotous living, and, being eager for earthly gain, they provoked the wrath of the Almighty against themselves. When he saw that we were ungrateful for the blessings we had received he judged us unworthy to receive more. Truly, since neither power nor triumph is long-lived without God on account of our sins, which in their different uncleannesses had offended the author of our salvation, certain sons of Belial, under a false pledge of Christian faith, deceitfully suggested to us that we set out against the sultan with all the force of our army which had been stationed in nearby forts with a multitude of pagans as great as the sands of the sea which cannot be numbered. But, hoping that the affair would be accomplished by the Lord our God, in accordance with the common advice of the pilgrims, we set out against the enemies of the faith, unwisely leaving Damietta without defense.

When the sultan, after three days, saw the flight of the pilgrims, he pretended flight on his own part, and deceitfully left his camp to be plundered by us. With the whole strength of Egypt he hurried swiftly to Damietta by another road, and established his camp in a narrow spot below the city and us, so that we could have neither retreat nor intercourse with it. Behold how sudden a change of the right hand of the Most High! Then, with God favorable to us, we reigned mightily in the land of Egypt; now, with him against us, we drift wretchedly between Scylla and Charybdis, between hunger and thirst. For this is that day of which it is written: "That day is a day of wrath" [Zep 1:15], etc. Sorrow and groaning and the moisture of tears do not permit me to describe our

---

107. Oliver thus ends on the hopeful note that a new council at Verona in 1222 will take up where the Fifth Crusade has failed and learn from its strategic and moral mistakes.

tribulations and distresses, and the particular dangers of death. But since nothing was left for us but a wretched death, we all with one voice cried out to heaven to our lord Jesus Christ humbly begging pardon. But he who says in his kindness, "I desire not the death of the wicked but rather that he be converted and live" [Ez 33:11], frequently, when he is angry, is mindful of his mercy and is also just and merciful.

Since he now saw that we had been sufficiently purified by penance and a fountain of tears, he mitigated the cruelty of our enemies to such an extent that they sent messengers to us, who were wasting away with hunger, to treat of peace and concord with us, on these terms: That the sultan might take back his city to be possessed in peace, and that he would give us safe-conduct to it along with complete integrity of our persons and belongings by supplying adequate ships and provisions. But we knew that the delegation had been procured by God, since there was nothing else left for us but death or the everlasting disgrace of slavery; and we willingly embraced it, humbly returning deserved thanks to God. When these agreements had been firmly settled through hostages and oaths, the sultan was moved by such compassion toward us that for many days he freely revived and refreshed our whole multitude. Finally when our affair had been disposed and settled, he procured ships and provisions for a just price, along with safe-conduct. Who could doubt that such kindness, mildness, and mercy proceeded from God?

Those whose parents, sons, and daughters, brothers and sisters we killed with various tortures, whose property we scattered or whom we cast naked from their dwellings, refreshed us with their own food as we were dying of hunger, although we were in their dominion and power. And so with great sorrow and mourning we left the port of Damietta, and according to our different nations, we separated to our everlasting disgrace.

22. A Stirring Lament and Three Letters from the East from the Chronicle of Roger Wendover

The defeat of the Fifth Crusade, after all of the lessons its planners had supposedly learned from earlier failures, the detailed preparations for it, and the extensive commitment to it on the part of all orders of Christian society, is explicable from our own removed perspective, but it proved immensely frustrating to those who experienced it. Oliver of Paderborn, who knew more about the crusade from its origins to its defeat, is probably the best example of the papal/clerical perspective on the disaster. Honorius III himself acknowledged and accepted responsibility for much of the loss. Others were much more hostile to the consequences of clerical leadership. And there was always the argument from crusader and general Christian sinfulness, *peccatis exigentibus*, an argument readily illustrated by several passages in Oliver's narrative. But as James M. Powell has suggested, the lament of Ricardo of San Germano eloquently illustrates both frustration and incomprehension that characterized the aftermath of the failure:

> Damietta, bought by such labors and by so much bloodshed,
> You formerly obeyed Christian princes, now you obey their enemies.
> From you the sound of fame went out: Damietta is not what it was.
> In you the faith of Christ flourished where now the son brings shame
>   on the maidservant.
> The Ismaelites have brought you down, overturned your altars, violated
>   your temples;
> As often as they heap up punishments for you, our sins sprout up.
> Where now is the honor of the church and the flower of Christian
>   knighthood?
> Conquered, the legate, the king, and the duke of Bavaria yielded to the
>   poisons of perfidy.
> O why did these leaders, guided by bad advice, go forth to battle?
> O Damietta, you gave exile to those you favored for almost two years.
> What mass of evil caused it? It touches all our miseries; it is the cause of
>   all our tears
> The whole world and the princes of the world are sharers in this pain;
> We pray you, O Christ, to help us to vindicate your cause.[108]

News traveled quickly, and from various sources. Letters from James of Vitry, Oliver of Paderborn, Pelagius, and others carried news of the campaign and requests for men and money, as did information from rotated crusaders returning home after completion of their terms of service. Many of these also attempted to rationalize defeat and victory for distant European audiences. Communications networks of the religious and military orders also carried news and appeals for aid.

Roger Wendover includes the texts of three letters from the East, two of them from Peter of Montague, grand master of the Templars, the first in 1221 to the bishop of (probably) Elne and the second in 1222 to the preceptor of the Templars in England. Another letter, from Peter of Albany to Ranulf, earl of Chester, also in 1222, offers yet further detail in the aftermath of defeat.

---

108. Cited in Powell, *Anatomy*, 195–196.

Of the condition of the Holy Land after the capture
of Damietta and Tanis, 1221

To OUR reverend brother in Christ N., by the grace of God, bishop of *Elimenum*, Peter de Montague, master of the knights of the Temple, greeting. How we have proceeded in the business of our Lord Jesus Christ since the capture of Damietta and the castle of Tanis, we by these present letters set forth to your holiness. Be it known to you then that, in the first passage after the aforesaid captures, such a number of pilgrims arrived at Damietta that, with the rest of the army which remained, they were sufficient to garrison Damietta and to defend the camp. Our lord the legate and the clergy, desirous to advance the cause of the army of Christ, often and earnestly exhorted the people to make an attack on the infidels, but the nobles of the army, as well those of the transmarine provinces as those on our side of the water, thinking that the army was not sufficient for the defense of the aforesaid cities and castles, and at the same time to proceed further for the advantage of Christianity, would not consent to this plan.

For the sultan of Babylon, with an innumerable host of infidels, had pitched his camp near Damietta, and on each arm of the river had built bridges to obstruct the progress of the Christians, and was there waiting with such an immense army that the crusaders, by proceeding further would incur the greatest danger. Nevertheless we fortified the said city and camp and the coast round with trenches in all directions, expecting to be consoled by the Lord with the assistance of those who were coming to help us. The Saracens, however, seeing our deficiency, armed all their galleys and sent them to sea in the month of September, and these caused great loss among the Christians who were coming to the assistance of the Holy Land. In our army there was such a great deficiency of money that we could not maintain our ships for any length of time. Therefore, knowing that great loss would be incurred by the Christian army by means of these said galleys of the Saracens, we immediately armed our galleys, galliots, and other vessels to oppose them.

Be it also known to you that Coradin, the sultan of Damascus, assembled an immense army of Saracens, and, finding that the cities of Acre and Tyre were not sufficiently supplied with knights and soldiers to oppose him, continually did serious injury to those places both secretly and openly; besides this he often came and pitched his camp before our

Source: Giles, Wendover's Flowers of History, *2:432–439.*

camp which is called the Pilgrims', doing us all kinds of injury; he also besieged and reduced the castle of Caesarea in Palestine, although numbers of pilgrims were staying in Acre. I have also to inform you that Seraphus, a son of Saphadin, and brother of the sultans of Babylon and Damascus, is with a powerful army fighting against the Saracens in the eastern parts, and has prevailed much against the more powerful of his enemies, although not against all, for, by God's favor, he will not be able easily to conquer all of them. For if he could bring that war to a conclusion, the county of Antioch or Tripoli, Acre or Egypt, whichever of them he might turn his attention to, would be in the greatest danger, and if he were to lay siege to any one of our castles, we should in no wise be able to drive him away.

This said dissension among the pagans however gives us pleasure and comfort. Moreover we have long expected the arrival of the emperor and other nobles by whom we hope to be relieved, and on their arrival we hope to bring this business, which has commenced by the hands of many, to a happy termination; but if we are deceived in our hope of this assistance in the ensuing summer, which I hope will not happen, both countries, namely Syria and Egypt, and that which we have lately gained possession of as well as that which we have held for a long time, will be placed in a doubtful position. Besides, we and the other people on our side of the water are oppressed by so many and great expenses in carrying on this crusade, that we shall be unable to meet our necessary expenses, unless by the divine mercy we shortly receive assistance from our fellow Christians. Given at Acre, the twentieth of September.

Of the loss of Damietta, 1222

To HIS worshipful lord and friend R[anulf], earl of Chester and Lincoln, his ever faithful P. de Albeney, health and sincere affection. I have to inform your excellency that on the day of the Assumption of the Virgin Mary [August 15] we sailed from the port of Marseilles, and on the Monday before the Nativity of the same virgin we arrived before Damietta, and there we saw many ships leaving the town, and I spoke with a certain vessel, and made presents to the crew, on which they came to speak to us, and brought us very sad reports. These were that our people at Damietta and the nobles in that city, namely, the king of Jerusalem, the legate, the duke of Bavaria, the Templars and Hospitallers, with many others, amounting to about a thousand crusaders and five thousand other knights with forty thousand foot soldiers, had all gone on an expedition toward Babylon, against the wish of the king of Jerusalem, as was said, having set out on the feast of Saint Peter *ad vincula*;[109] that they had been now absent on that expedition three weeks or more, and were about halfway between Damietta and Babylon. The sultan of Babylon and his brother Coradin then came with all the forces they could muster, and often attacked our people, and often lost some of their own men; and when our people wished to return to Damietta, the river became swollen, and for several days overflowed its banks, and our people were between two branches of the river.

The Saracens then made a canal from one branch to the other in the rear of our army, while the river increased so in height, that our people were in water up to their legs and waists, to their great misery and suffering, and thus might have been either slain or taken prisoners if the sultan of Babylon wished it. In this condition our people agreed to a truce for eight years with the sultan, on the condition that they should give up Damietta and all the prisoners whom they held in captivity. For the due observance of this truce, the king of Jerusalem, the legate, the duke of Bavaria, and other influential people, remained as hostages; and the sultan had given twenty hostages for the due observance of the truce on his part.

When we heard these reports we were much grieved, as all Christians must need be; we therefore thought it best, as we did not wish to be present at the surrender of Damietta, to make our way to Acre, where we arrived on the day after the Nativity of the Virgin Mary; on the day following Damietta was given up to the sultan, and he himself set free all the prisoners in it. I have also to inform you that his majesty the king of Jerusalem is about to go to your country; therefore I beg of you that you afford him assistance according to promises made toward the king and other nobles, for it is difficult to describe his great and admirable merits.

Another letter about the same matters, 1222

BROTHER P. of Montague, humble master of the knights of the Temple, to his well-beloved brother in Christ, A. Martel, holding the office of preceptor in England, greeting.—Although we have from time to time informed you of the prosperity which attended us in the affairs of Jesus Christ, we now by this present letter relate to you in the order they have happened the reverses which we, owing to our sins, have met with in the land of Egypt. The Christian army after the capture of Damietta having remained quietly at that place for a long time, the people of our side of

109. Saint Peter in Chains, August 1.

the water, as well as those of the transmarine provinces, cast reproofs and reproaches on us on that account; and the duke of Bavaria having arrived, as lieutenant of the emperor, explained to the people that he had come for the purpose of attacking the enemies of the Christian faith. A council therefore was held by our lord the legate, the duke of Bavaria, the masters of the Templars and Hospitallers, and the Teutonic order, the earls, barons, and all the rest, at which it was unanimously agreed by all to make an advance. The illustrious king of Jerusalem also, having been sent for, came with his barons, and with a fleet of galleys and armed ships to Damietta, and found the army of the Christians lying in their camp outside the lines.

After the feast of the apostles Peter and Paul, then his majesty the king and the legate, with the whole Christian army, proceeded in order both by land and water, and discovered the sultan with an innumerable host of the enemies of the cross, who however fled before them; and so they proceeded without loss till they arrived at the camp of the sultan. This was surrounded by the river which they were unable to cross; the Christian army therefore pitched its camp on the bank, and constructed bridges to cross over against the sultan, from whose camp we were separated by the river Tanis, which is a branch of the great river Nile. While we made some stay there, great numbers left our army without leave, so that it was decreased by ten thousand men or more. In the meantime the sultan, by means of a trench constructed previously, when the Nile rose, sent galleys and galliots into the river to obstruct our ships, that no supplies might come from Damietta to us, we being then destitute of provisions; for they could not reach us by land, as the Saracens prevented them. The road both by sea and land, by which necessary supplies could reach us, being thus blocked up, the army held council as to returning; but the brothers of the sultan, Seraph and Coradin, the sultans of Aleppo and Damascus, and other sultans, namely, of Camela, Haman, and Coilanbar, with many pagan kings, and a countless host of infidels, who had come to assist them, had cut off our retreat. Our army however departed by night by land and water, but lost all the provisions in the river, besides a great many men; for when the Nile overflowed, the sultan turned the water in different directions by means of hidden streams, canals, and rivulets, which had been made some time before to obstruct the retreat of the Christians.

The army of Christ therefore, after losing among the marshes all its beasts of burden, stores, baggage, carriages, and almost all their necessaries, and being destitute of provisions, could neither advance nor retreat, nor had it any place of refuge, neither could it give battle to the sultan on account of his being surrounded by the river, and it was thus caught in the midst of the waters like a fish in a net.

Being therefore in this strait, they, although unwillingly, agreed to give up to the sultan the city of Damietta, with all the prisoners which could be found in Tyre and Acre, in exchange for the true cross and the Christian prisoners in the kingdoms of Babylon and Damascus. We therefore, in company with other messengers deputed by the army in common, went to Damietta, and told the people of the city the terms which were imposed on us; which greatly displeased the bishop of Acre, the chancellor, and Henry, count of Malta, whom we found there: for they wished to defend the city, which we should also have much approved of, if it could have been done with any advantage, for we had rather been consigned to perpetual imprisonment, than that the city should be given up by us to the infidels to the disgrace of Christianity; we therefore made a careful search throughout the city of all persons and effects, but found neither money nor people wherewith it could be defended. We therefore acquiesced in this agreement, and bound ourselves by oath and by giving hostages, and agreed to a confirmed truce for eight years. The sultan, till the arrangement was made, strictly abided by what he had promised, and supplied our famished army with loaves and flour for about fifteen days. Do you therefore, compassionating our sufferings, assist us as far as you are able. Farewell.

23. Two Crusade Recruiters in Marseilles, 1224

By the time of the Third Crusade, Marseilles had become an important port for maritime traders and crusaders departing for the Holy Land. Like its Italian rivals, Genoa, Pisa, and Venice, Marseilles provided fleets to aid the Christian-occupied coastal cities of Palestine and had been rewarded by various trading privileges. The letter translated here, preserved in incomplete form as a model letter, recounts the success of two crusade preachers in using the crusade as a common project to resolve a conflict that had resulted in the city's excommunication. Peacemaking efforts and jurisdictional wrangles were part and parcel of the crusade preachers' commission. Like Oliver of Cologne/Paderborn, who had publicized the miracles gracing his crusade preaching in a letter to other crusade preachers in 1214, the authors of the letter forwarded news of the Marseillais' reconciliation with their bishop, their zealous involvement in the crusade, and miracles involving the cross to demonstrate the Marseillais' orthodoxy and advertise the port as an ideal place for departing crusaders.

There is a hidden subtext to this letter. Pope Honorius III was organizing recruiting in the province of Arles for the forthcoming expedition of William of Montferrat, which diverted new recruits and crusaders who had failed to fulfill their vows before the fall of Damietta in 1221 from the Holy Land to the aid of the besieged Latin kingdom of Thessalonica. The two preachers appointed to recruit for the new campaign were well aware of the challenges facing them in Marseilles. The citizens' support for the suspected "fosterer" of heretics, Raymond VI of Toulouse, their violence against the clergy and bishop of the city whose political, judicial, and financial power they resented, and their formation of a communal government in an attempt to erode these rights had resulted in the city's excommunication from 1216 to 1219 and again in 1223. The crusade preachers appear to have exploited their role as outsiders and their right to celebrate mass, absolve excommunicates, and offer various spiritual rewards via the various crusading indulgences to present the crusade as a common spiritual project capable of enabling the citizens to clear themselves of the suspicion of heterodoxy and make peace with their bishop without losing face. This peace was short-lived. By 1225 Frederick II had placed the city under imperial ban, and its bishop was dispensed from his crusading vow in order to deal with renewed unrest.

The letter is discussed in Cole, Preaching of the Crusades, *148–149.*

To OUR venerable brothers in Christ, the preachers appointed throughout the kingdom of France on behalf of the Holy Land, greetings in Christ Jesus from Raimond Fouque, provost of Arles and Master R., prior of Saint-Pierre de Meyne in the diocese of Orange, preachers for the aforesaid business in the province of Arles.

From on high, the Risen One has visited the province of Arles in the business of Jesus Christ. Realizing that when we directed our steps to the illustrious city of Marseilles, it had remained bound by the chain of excommunication for so long a time that it appeared to be far removed from every hope of eternal salvation and that it could be said, not undeservedly, that the entire populace, full of dread and lamenting, used to sit alone, prostrate upon the dung heap [Jb 2:8], we nonetheless sowed the word of God among the populace, and the grace of the Holy Spirit

Source: E. Baratier, *"Une prédication de la croisade à Marseille en 1224,"* in Économies et sociétés au Moyen Âge: Mélanges offertes à Edouard Perroy *(Paris, 1973),* 690–699, text 698–699.

descending upon them illuminated their hearts and led them from the shadows back to the light, and the Risen One visited them from on high [cf. Is 9:12; Mt 4:16; Lk 1:78–79].

Indeed, in truth, when we entered the renowned city its neighbors used to prophesy to us that we would labor in vain, sowing our seed among thorns and thistles [Lk 8:4–8], because their hearts were hardened to such an extent that it would be a miracle if we were able to lead back even one from among its thousands to the way of truth. We, however, trusting calmly in divine grace, were not abandoned by it, rather, hastening with willing assent to fulfill a reasonable apostolic injunction, we strove to fulfill the apostolic office entrusted to us by His Holiness. To such a degree we labored, ever more diligently and very repeatedly persuading the populace of Marseilles with medicinal admonitions, that by the inspiration of divine grace, we led the sheep wandering from the path back to the safety of salvation [Lk 15:3–7; Mt 18:12–14].

For in the aforementioned city, in which we tarried profitably for five weeks for the aforesaid business, we signed more than thirty thousand persons, and very few households remained in that place where there was not at least one or more [members] signed with the symbol of the cross. And from the time in which we entered the city hardly a day passed where we did not give the cross to at least one hundred or two hundred persons and so daily [the numbers] grew from hundreds to thousands.

Indeed, let it be known that we very much commend their devotion to the Lord because just as a starving person yearns for food, a thirsty person for drink, and just as the sweetness of honey or a taste of a similar thing whets the appetite and soothes the gullet, so without a doubt their souls were revived in hearing the preaching of the Lord. And since we found them so zealous and so generous in the business of Jesus Christ and since the city itself is indispensable before all others for those crossing in aid of the Holy Land, not only because of its suitable port but also because the men of that place are prepared in arms and full of spirit, zealously placing themselves and their possessions in God's service, we beseech your fraternity in the Lord that you take pains to proclaim the aforesaid Marseillais as men who are catholic and ready for God's service and that in that place a well-prepared passage would be advantageous for all who have taken the cross.

Know in fact that in that very place God showed forth many wondrous things concerning the cross visibly and in visions to those signed with the cross. In truth, during the day, the heavens opened and God appeared to certain persons upon the cross and the dead used to appear in visions to their friends, who had taken the cross for the sake of their souls, and used to say that they were freed from their punishments[110] for the sake of the cross. For fear of her man, a certain woman did not dare to wear the cross which she had taken upon her person and as soon as she placed the cross in a chest, so great a pain weighed upon her shoulder that she could not bear it. Revealing this to her husband, by his permission she took the cross and lifted it up, and at once, through God's grace, she was fully[111] freed. In fact, another woman used to forbid one of her brothers, a nobleman, to take the cross in any manner, and at night it seemed to her that her throat was swollen so much that she wanted to die, and this was through the cross which she had forbidden her brother to receive. And so she lay awake with trembling and [at daybreak] begged her brother to take the cross immediately and he took it. It would take a long time to relate the miracles which in the aforementioned city . . . the entire day concerning the cross and for the sake of the cross. There women rapt in ecstasy used to see many secret things concerning the cross.

Strengthen each other with these words and if such signs should befall you, write to us . . . if it pleases you. And let each one send to the other this letter with its seal, throughout the entire kingdom of France and England and in Germany. And not only were they won over in this manner in the city of Marseilles . . . but in the entire province of Arles, which lies on the sea, and from either part we are commanded that we should go as far as the places where we did not give the cross, knowing that because whenever so great a people . . . ought to be gathered by all means often they used to move more single-mindedly than we could wish for. Know moreover that out of reverence for the Holy Cross these very Marseillais have restored . . . full jurisdiction and all his legal rights to their lord and father,[112] which they had despoiled him of and had held for a long time. . . .[113] Given in Marseilles in the year of Our Lord 1223 in the month of January in the day of the Epiphany of Our Lord.[114] You

110. The Latin term here is *poena*, meaning the penalty owed for a sin, paid either through penance in this life or the sufferings of purgatory or hell in the next.

111. As crusade preachers, the authors play here with the term *plenarie*, often used to describe the complete remission of duly confessed sins accorded by the full, or "plenary," crusading indulgence.

112. The bishop of Marseilles.

113. The letter becomes increasingly fragmentary at this point, but appears to be asking church prelates to consider the Marseillais as absolved from their previous excommunication.

114. This actually means January of 1224.

ought to know also that a certain . . . by the name of William on whose behalf God has wrought and works innumerable miracles; the blind see, the lame walk, the deaf hear.

24. Ibn Wasil on the Frankish Surrender, ca. 1282

Narrative accounts in Arabic are more extensive for this period and later, although a number of them consist largely of compilations from earlier, often lost, accounts. The most detailed account is that of Ibn al-Athir. The present account is that of Ibn Wasil (1207–1298), a servant and administrator of several of the later Ayyubids and early Mamluk sultans. In 1261 he was sent by the great sultan Baibars as an ambassador to Manfred, illegitimate son of Frederick II and king of Sicily. His great work is the *Mufarrij al-Kurub fi akhbar Bani Ayyub* (The Dissipator of Anxieties Concerning the History of the Ayyubids), which is an extensive account of the rulers of Arab territories from the early twelfth century to 1282. That is, he is an important source for the Fifth Crusade (as here), Frederick II's crusade, and the crusade of Saint Louis IX of France. Ibn Wasil seems to conflate the Fifth Crusade with the crusade of Louis IX (Part VII, below).

See Ibn al-Athir, 'Izz al-Din, The Chronicle of Ibn al-Athīr for the Crusading Period from al-Kāmil fī'l-Ta'rīkh, *part 3*, The Years 589–629/1193–1231: The Ayyubids After Saladin and the Mongol Menace, *trans. D. S. Richards (Aldershot UK-Burlington VT, 2008). The writer's dates are 1160–1233. See also Carol Hillenbrand,* The Crusades: Islamic Perspectives *(Chicago, 1999); and R. Stephen Humphreys,* From Saladin to the Mongols: The Ayyubids of Damascus, 1193–1260 *(Albany NY, 1977).*

THE FRANKS sent ambassadors to al-Malik al-Kamil and his two brothers al-Malik al-Mu'azzam and al-Malik al-Ashraf asking for their lives to be spared in exchange for Damietta with no indemnity. Al-Malik al-Kamil consulted the princes of his house about this. Some advised him not to grant them an amnesty but to seize them at once, while they were in his control and made up the majority of the Unbelievers (on Muslim soil). When he had done this he could take Damietta and the parts of Palestine that they held. But the sultan al-Malik al-Kamil disagreed, and said: "There are other Franks; even if we destroy [or detain] them too it will take us a long time and a hard fight to win Damietta. The Franks beyond the sea will hear what has befallen them and will arrive in more than double the numbers of these here, and we will have to face a siege."[115]

Source: *Francesco Gabrieli,* Arab Historians of the Crusades, *trans. E. J. Costello (Berkeley-Los Angeles, 1969), 264–266.*
115. Al-Malik al-Kamil is portrayed here as essentially pragmatic, but he also appears in Latin sources as a moderate, even thoughtful ruler.

At the time the troops were exhausted and tired of fighting, for the Frankish occupation of Egypt had lasted for three years and three months. So they all accepted his decision to grant the Franks their lives in exchange for Damietta. He accepted the Frankish petition on condition that al-Malik al-Kamil held hostages from them until Damietta was handed over. They in their turn asked for one of al-Kamil's sons and a group of his nobles as hostages for the return of their king [John of Brienne]. So an understanding was reached and oaths were taken on 7 rajab 618 [1221].[116] The Frankish hostages were the king of Acre [John of Brienne], the papal legate [Pelagius] who was the representative of the pope in Rome the Great, King Louis and other lords, numbering twenty altogether. Al-Kamil's hostages were his son al-Malik as-Salih Najm ad-Din Ayyub and a group of his nobles. Al-Malik as-Salih was then fifteen, for he was born in 603.[117] When the nobles presented themselves before al-Malik al-Kamil he held audience in great pomp, in the presence of all the kings and princes of his house. The Franks received a vivid impression of his royal power and majesty.[118]

. . . (When Damietta surrendered) the Frankish and Muslim hostages were returned to their respective sides, and the sultan entrusted the government of the city to the emir Shuja ad-Din Jurdik al-Muzaffari an-Nuri, an experienced and worthy man. At the time of the peace the Franks found that they had at Damietta some enormous masts for their ships and they wanted to take these away with them to their own land. Shuja ad-Din refused permission for this, so they sent messages to al-Malik al-Kamil complaining about it and saying that these masts were their own property, and that according to the terms of the treaty they should be free to take them. Al-Malik al-Kamil wrote to Shuja ad-Din commanding him to hand over the masts, but he persisted in his refusal: "The Franks took the pulpit from the Great Mosque of Damietta," he said, "and cut it up and sent a piece to each of their kings: let the sultan command them to return the pulpit, and the masts will be theirs." The sultan did write to the Franks about this, referring them to what Shuja ad-Din said, and the Franks, unable to return the pulpit, gave up their claim to the masts.

116. The Muslim calendar is lunar and slightly shorter than the Christian calendar, thirty-three Muslim years almost equaling thirty-two Christian years, and begins with the year of Muhammad's departure from Mecca. Rajab was the seventh month of the Muslim year. The term means "forbidden" in Arabic.
117. He later ruled Egypt from 1240 to 1249.
118. A little earlier in the same campaign "in the presence of the mighty sultan," Saint Francis of Assisi came forward and preached, evidently in a setting much like this.

PART IV
The Emperor's Crusade, 1227–1229

Behind all the planning and mobilization of the Fifth Crusade was the figure of the emperor Frederick II (1194–1250). After the sudden death of Henry VI in 1197, Frederick's mother, Constance, regarded by the nobles of Sicily as the heiress of Roger II, proved willing to submit the kingdom of Sicily to the pope in order to secure Frederick's succession. She also persuaded Innocent III, who was now acknowledged as ultimate lord of the kingdom, to permit Frederick to succeed to the Sicilian throne, which he did on May 17, 1198. At the death of Constance in November 1198, Innocent III as the lord of the kingdom became the guardian of Frederick II. After the struggle for the imperial crown between Philip of Swabia and Otto IV between 1198 and 1208, the assassination of Philip in 1208, and the troubled reign and excommunication of Otto IV (1209–1211), Frederick was elected and crowned king of the Romans at Aachen on July 23, 1215, four months before the Fourth Lateran Council.

Son and grandson of crusading emperors, Frederick took the cross at his Aachen coronation (with the knowledge and approval of Innocent III) and again at his imperial coronation in Rome on November 22, 1220. Between 1212 and 1216, Frederick made a number of significant promises to protect the interests of the church in Sicily, the most important of which was to separate his Sicilian crown from the imperial crown by having his son Henry elected king of the Romans. The prospect of large numbers of crusaders from Frederick's German kingdom (like the great army led by Frederick Barbarossa on the aborted Third Crusade) and the close interest that Sicily and South Italy had in Mediterranean affairs and the Holy Land made Frederick the ideal crusade leader.

In spite of the considerable and time-consuming difficulties involved in securing his position in Sicily and Germany, which were generally if grudgingly accepted by Innocent's successor Honorius III (1216–1223), Frederick remained the great hope of the crusading forces at Damietta. Even if delayed by local concerns himself, Frederick sent his own high officials with troops to aid the crusade, as Oliver of Paderborn points out, and he may have supported the decision of the legate Pelagius to refuse the truce offers of al-Malik al-Kamil. But revolts and political opposition persisted in delaying Frederick's departure, even to the point of trying the patience of Honorius III, who later bitterly regretted his extensions of Frederick's date of departure.

The surrender of Damietta and the collapse of the Fifth Crusade caused considerable resentment and spread blame to the pope and his legate, but already the planning for a new crusade had begun. The pope and the emperor held meetings in 1222, and in 1223 Frederick, on the advice of his close friend Hermann von

Salza, master of the Teutonic Knights, began proceedings to marry Yolande/
Isabelle, daughter of John of Brienne and heiress to the crown of the kingdom of
Jerusalem. Frederick, whose first wife had died in 1222, then could lay claim to
the crown of Jerusalem by right of his new wife, thus claiming for himself, along
with his crusader's vow, his kingship of Sicily, and his identity as emperor, a status
that no previous crusade leader could claim. Frederick now promised to leave on
crusade in 1225, but a revolt of the Muslim inhabitants of western Sicily in 1224
caused yet further delay.

Finally, Frederick and Honorius agreed, at the Treaty of San Germano in July
1225, that Frederick would deposit one hundred thousand ounces of gold with
Hermann von Salza, master of the Teutonic Knights, provide a thousand knights
for two years service in the Holy Land, and equip one hundred fifty ships for
service in his crusade. Frederick also agreed to undergo excommunication if he did
not depart by August 15, 1227. Frederick, now married to Yolande/Isabella,
indeed launched his army and fleet on August 15, but his own departure was
delayed until September, and an epidemic swept through his armies, killing Ludwig IV of Thuringia among others, and striking Frederick himself, whose ship had
to turn back to port. Although the crusade army sailed off without Frederick, the
new pope, Gregory IX (1227–1241), refused to grant yet another delay and,
invoking the Treaty of San Germano, excommunicated Frederick, using the occasion to negotiate a number of other points of dispute between pope and emperor
and destabilizing Frederick's relations with the northern Italian city-republics.

Shortly after the Fifth Crusade, al-Malik al-Kamil, sultan of Egypt, deeply
worried about his deteriorating relations with his brother al-Mu'azzam, opened
diplomatic communication with Frederick. In June 1228 Frederick sailed to Acre,
began the fortification of Caesarea and Jaffa, and marched his army south to Jaffa.
His ensuing negotiations with al-Kamil resulted in Frederick's acquisition of Jerusalem, Bethlehem, and other sites, and to Frederick's coronation in Jerusalem, and
reforming the government of the kingdom of Jerusalem, after which he returned
to Italy. Although the terms of his agreement with al-Kamil were restrictive, the
excommunicated Frederick had gained access to Jerusalem where others had failed.
Frederick's efforts were variously interpreted, favorably by some, highly unfavor-
ably by others. The following selections offer an alternation of views, two from
chronicles, two from Arabic commentators, one letter from Frederick himself, and
one (probably forged) piece of propaganda.

25. The Crusade of Frederick II: From the Chronicle of Roger Wendover, ca. 1230

Roger Wendover narrates the departure of the first elements of Frederick's
army and Gregory IX's letter to all faithful Christians, the effect of the delay and
then the arrival of Frederick II in 1228, and the treaty with al-Kamil of 1229.

Roger then offers a meditation on the meaning of the loss and regaining of Jerusalem and the moral difficulties of local Christians in dealing with the excommunicated emperor who had regained Jerusalem. Roger was careful to note the signs and portents heralding significant events.

David Abulafia, Frederick II: A Medieval Emperor (Baltimore, 1988; repr., Oxford, 1992); James M. Powell, "Church and Crusade: Frederick II and Louis IX," Catholic Historical Review 93 (2007), 251–264; Jaroslav Folda, Crusader Art in the Holy Land: From the Third Crusade to the Fall of Acre, 1187–1291 (Cambridge, 2005); Christoph Egger and Damian Smith, eds., Pope Gregory IX (1227–1241) (Farnham UK-Burlington VT, 2012).

How a great stir was made at this time to assist in the crusade, 1227

IN THE same year at the end of June, a great stir was made to aid the cross by all the crusaders throughout the world, who were so numerous, that from the kingdom of England alone forty thousand tried men were said to have marched, besides women and old men. This was declared by Master Hubert, one of the preachers in England, who asserted that he had in fact set down as many as that in his roll. All these, and especially the poor, on whom the divine pleasure generally rests, entered upon the crusade with such devotion that they, without doubt, obtained favor with the Almighty, as was shown by manifest indications. For on the night of the Nativity of St. John the Baptist, the Lord showed himself in the sky as when crucified; for on a most shining cross there appeared the body of our Lord pierced with nails and with a lance, and sprinkled with blood, so that the Savior of the world by this showed his faithful followers in the world that he was appeased by the devotion of his people.

This vision was seen by numbers of people, and among others by a trader, who was carrying fish for sale near the town of Uxbridge; being struck with astonishment at the strange apparition, and awed by the brightness of it, he was, as it were, lost in ecstasy and stood in amazement, not knowing what to do. His son, however, who was his only companion, comforted his father, and asked him to stop his cart and give praise to God for having condescended to show them such a vision. On the next day, and indeed every day after, wherever he exposed his fish for sale, he publicly told every one of the heavenly vision he had seen. He added his son's evidence to his own; many put faith in their story, but some disbelieved it, till they were induced to believe it by the number of visions which appeared about the same time to many in various places; and in

Source: Giles, Wendover's Flowers of History, 2:489–494, 511–512, 521, and 524–527.

these the Crucified One himself deigned to open the heavens and to show to the incredulous his wonderful glory with immense splendor. Among others who went from England to join in the crusade were the bishops Peter of Winchester and William of Exeter, who had now fulfilled their vow of pilgrimage for nearly five years.

Of the progress of the crusade at this time, 1227

How the business of the cross prospered in this crusade will plainly appear by the following letter which Pope Gregory sent to all the faithful followers of Christ: "Gregory, bishop, servant of the servants of God, to all faithful Christians, greeting, etc. Be it known to the whole community of you that we have received letters from the country beyond the sea to the following purport:—Gerold, by the divine mercy, patriarch of Jerusalem, P. archbishop of Caesarea, the humble and unworthy legate of the apostolic see, and N. archbishop of Narbonne, P. bishop of Winchester, and W. bishop of Exeter, the masters of the Hospitallers, of the Knights of the Temple, and of the Teutonic order of Hospitallers [the Teutonic Knights], to all to whom these letters may come, health in our Lord Jesus Christ.

"We are compelled to inform the whole community of you of our most urgent necessities, and of our progress in the cause of Jesus Christ, who shed his blood for all of the true faith. It is with much fervor of mind and shedding of tears, that his serene highness the emperor did not, as we all hoped, come into Syria in the month of August last past as he had promised. On this the pilgrims from those districts, hearing that the said emperor had not arrived in the aforesaid passage, amounting to more than forty thousand strong men, returned in the same ships as they had come, putting their trust in man rather than God. After their departure there remained here nearly eight hundred knights, who continued to cry with one consent, 'Either let us break the truce or let us all depart together'; and they have been detained here not without great difficulty, because the duke of Limburg, a man of noble birth, has been appointed to command the army in the place of the emperor. A council was therefore held, especially of the Hospitallers, Templars, and of the German Hospitallers, and it was agreed that the duke aforesaid should act as seemed most expedient for the cause of Christianity and the Holy Land; the duke then, having asked and received advice on these points, appeared on a day specially appointed for the purpose before us and some of the nobles of that country, and there openly declared that he wished to break the truce, and asked the assistance and advice of those present, as to how he could proceed most advantageously in that intention. And when the duke and his councilors were told that it would be dangerous to break the truce, and, as it was confirmed by oath, dishonorable as well, they replied that his holiness the pope had excommunicated all those crusaders who would not join in this crusade, although he knew that the truce was to continue for two years more. And by this they understood that he did not wish the truce to be kept, and, besides this, the pilgrims would not remain there idle. There were also many who said that, if the pilgrims were to go away, the Saracens would, after their departure, attack them, notwithstanding the truce. Some also thought that Coradin was engaged in a fierce war with the rulers of Haman, Camela, and Aleppo, and on that account was more than usually afraid of the truce being broken by the Christians. And if the truce were broken, they thought that Coradin, on seeing himself pressed by war on all sides, would probably offer terms of peace.

"At length after a long discussion on these matters, all unanimously agreed to march to the holy city, which Jesus Christ consecrated with his own blood; and that the approach might be more easy, it was unanimously determined to fortify in the first place Caesarea, and then Jaffa, which they hoped undoubtedly to be able to do before the passage of the ensuing August. And then they would be able in the following winter to set out joyfully for the house of the Lord, under his protection. This determination was made public outside the city of Acre on the feast of the apostles Simon and Jude, in the presence of all the pilgrims, and there they were solemnly enjoined to be ready on the day after All Saints' Day, to set out toward Caesarea. The pilgrims, who did not know of the plan which the army had determined, on hearing this, after strengthening the above-mentioned fortresses, were suddenly seized with such a great desire to proceed to Jerusalem that they wept abundantly, and they felt so strengthened by the grace of the Holy Spirit, that each man felt as if he could overcome a thousand enemies, and two could conquer ten thousand.

"We need not therefore use many entreaties in urging it on you, when such pressing necessity speaks for itself and demands immediate assistance; for delay brings danger, and speed will be productive of the greatest advantages. The blood of Christ calls from this country on each and every one; this small and humble, though devout, army entreats for speedy assistance, hoping and trusting in the Lord that this business, commenced in all humility, may be by his favor brought to a happy termination. Do you therefore, each and all of you, exert yourselves to assist the Holy Land, since this may be considered the common cause both of your faith and of the whole Christian people. And we, under God's care and guidance, will not cease to promote the cause, confidently hoping, that it may prosper in the hands of the faithful who persevere with confidence. Given at the Lateran, the 23rd of December, in the first year of our pontificate."

How the crusade was impeded through the absence of the emperor, 1227

IN THE meantime the emperor Frederick, who with other crusaders had, under penalty of excommunication by the pope in the before-mentioned passage, determined to fulfill his vow of pilgrimage, went to the Mediterranean Sea, and embarked with a small retinue; but after pretending to make for the Holy Land for three days, he said that he was seized with a sudden illness, so that he could not at the risk of his life any longer endure the roughness of the sea and an unhealthy climate, therefore he altered his course, and after three days' sailing landed at the port where he had embarked. On this, the pilgrims from different parts of the world, who had preceded him to the Holy Land in hopes of having him as a leader and protector in fighting the enemies of the cross, were struck with consternation at hearing that the emperor had not come, as he had promised in the passage of August, and therefore, embarking in the ships in which they had sailed to the Holy Land, they returned home to the number of about forty thousand armed men. And this conduct of the emperor redounded much to his disgrace, and to the injury of the whole business of the crusade. It was on this account, in the opinion of many, that the Savior of the world showed himself, as above related, to the Christians, suspended on the cross, pierced with nails and sprinkled with blood, as if laying a complaint before each and every Christian, of the injury inflicted on him by the emperor.

How the emperor Frederick arrived at the Holy Land and promoted the cause of the crusade, 1228

IN THE same year the Roman emperor, Frederick, took ship at the Mediterranean Sea, and on the feast of the Blessed Virgin Mary, landed at Acre, where the clergy and people of that place came to meet him, and received him with the honors due to such a great man; but when they found out that he was excommunicated by the pope they did not confer on him the kiss of peace, nor did they sit at table with him, but they advised him to give satisfaction to the pope and return to the community of the holy church. The Templars and Hospitallers, however, on his arrival, went on their knees and worshipped him, kissing his knees; and the whole of the Christian army which was present there gave praise to God for his arrival, being now in hopes that by this means there would be salvation in Israel. The emperor then complained bitterly to the whole army against the Roman pontiff, that the latter had unjustly pronounced the sentence against him, asserting that he had delayed marching to the assistance of the Holy Land, on account of serious illness.

The sultan of Babylon [al-Kamil], when he heard of the emperor's arrival in Syria, sent him a number of costly presents of gold and silver, silks and jewels, camels and elephants, bears and monkeys, and other wonderful things which are not to be found in western countries.

The emperor, on his arrival at Acre, found the Christian army under the command of the duke of Limburg, the patriarch of Jerusalem, the archbishops of Nazareth, Caesarea, and Narbonne, the English bishops of Winchester and Exeter, the masters of the Hospitallers, Templars, and of the Teutonic order of Hospitallers, who had under their joint command about eight hundred pilgrim knights, and about ten thousand foot soldiers assembled from different parts of the world. All these, inspired with a common feeling of devotion, marched to Caesarea, and had garrisoned some castles there, so that it now only remained for them to restore Joppa and then to march on the holy city. The emperor on learning the condition of the Holy Land, fully approved of the plan of the pilgrims, and, having made all necessary preparations to march forward, they set out preceded by the emperor, and on the 15th of November arrived without obstruction at Jaffa. But as it was impossible for each man to carry by land provisions enough for himself and his horses for several days, as well as his baggage, ships had been procured at Acre for the purpose of bringing provisions to the army. But a sudden storm arose and the sea became so rough that for seven successive days the Christian pilgrims were without provisions. Great alarm then arose among many of them, that the Lord in his anger would destroy his people from the face of the earth; however, the unspeakable mercy of God, which allows no man to be tried beyond endurance, was at length aroused by the lamentations of his faithful people, and he commanded the winds and the sea and there was a calm. Then a great number of ships arrived, under the guidance of the Lord, at Jaffa, loaded with immense quantities of corn and barley, wine, and all kinds of provisions, so that there was always an abundant supply of provisions in the army till the said fortress was rebuilt.

How the Holy Land was restored
to the emperor Frederick, 1229

IN THE same year, our Lord Jesus Christ, the Savior and Consoler of the world, visited his people in his compassion, and in compliance with the prayers of the universal church, restored to the Christian people in general, but to the Roman emperor Frederick in particular, the city of Jerusalem and the whole country which the Lord our Redeemer and Son of God had consecrated by his blood. Such was the goodwill of our Lord to his people, of him who exalts the merciful to eternal life, that he may work vengeance on the nations, and dissension among the tribes of the Saracens. For at that time the sultan of Babylon was so severely harassed by internal wars in all directions, that not being able to attend to more, he was compelled to make a truce of ten years with the emperor, and to give up the Holy Land to the Christians without bloodshed. And thus a good war was sent by the Lord that a bad peace might be broken.

Of the signs preceding the restoration of the Holy Land, 1229[1]

IT SHOULD be remarked concerning this restoration of the land of promise and Jerusalem to the Christians, that as the astronomers of Toledo, before this cause of general rejoicing and exultation among Christians, wrote concerning the concourse of the planets, and of the dreadful storms of wind, so that they would stand together, and at the same time that there would be an earthquake, and an eclipse of the sun as well as the moon, which has been before mentioned among the events of this year, in the same way, before the taking of the Holy Land and the cross of our Lord by that perfidious and cruel man Saladin, some other astronomers

---

1. The following two chapters on the Toledan prophecy were later omitted from Matthew Paris's revision of Roger, probably because they reflected a different attitude toward portents and offered a version of the fall of the Latin kingdom and its causes with which Matthew did not agree. In their place Matthew Paris attaches a description of the great seal appended to Frederick's bull: "The form of the emperor's golden seal was as follows: On one side was the royal figure and around it was written, 'Frederick, by the grace of God, the august emperor of the Romans.' On the same side as the royal figure, over the left shoulder, was written, 'King of Jerusalem'; in another part, over the right shoulder, were the words 'King of Sicily.' On the other side of the seal was engraved a city, representing Rome, and around it was written, 'Rome, the head of the world holds the reins of the round world.' This seal was somewhat larger than the pope's." The events described are the conquest of the kingdom of Jerusalem by Saladin in 1187. The pope is Clement III.

then living in the same city also wrote to Pope Clement as follows: "From the present year, which is the one thousand one hundred and seventy-ninth year of our Lord's incarnation, till the expiration of seven years, in the month of September, the sun being in Libra and the tail of the Dragon, there will be, if God so permit, an assembling of the planets in Libra and the tail of the Dragon, and this is a wonderful signification of a change of immutable events. And there shall follow a dreadful earthquake, and the accustomed places of perdition shall be destroyed by Saturn and Mars, etc. This conjunction of the planets will produce a strong wind, which will thicken and darken the air, and infect it with poison, and the sound of this wind will be dreadful, disturbing the hearts of men. And from sandy regions it shall raise the sand and overwhelm the cities lying nearest to them in the plains, and in the first place the eastern cities of Mecca and Babylon, and all cities lying near to sandy places; not one will escape being overwhelmed with sand and earth. But signs of these events will precede them; in the same year there will be, before the planets assemble in Libra, a total eclipse of the sun, and in the preceding conflict the moon will be totally eclipsed. And the eclipse of the sun will be of a fiery and unsightly color, denoting that there will be a war among chiefs near a river in the east, and likewise in western countries; and a doubtfulness shall fall among the Jews and Saracens, until they shall altogether abandon their synagogues and mosques, and their sect shall at the command of God be entirely destroyed and annihilated. Therefore, when you see the eclipse, know that you are to leave that land with all your followers."

How on account of the sins of man the Holy Land was lost, 1229

AT THAT time there was much evil among men on earth, so that "all flesh almost had corrupted its way before the Lord" [Gn 6:12]; for the practice of sin had burst forth among the people to such a degree, that all, casting aside the veil of shame, everyone inclined to wickedness openly. Too tedious is it to enumerate the slaughters, robberies, adultery, obscenities, lies, treasons, and other crimes, especially so to us, who design to write of the events which occurred. However the old enemy of man after having disseminated the spirit of corruption far and wide in the world, invaded Syria in particular, from which place other nations received their religion in the first place, and from that place they then took the example of all uncleanness. For this reason therefore the Lord and Savior of the world, seeing that the land of his nativity, suffering, and resurrection had fallen into the depths of wickedness, scorned his inheritance, and allowed the rod of his anger, namely Saladin, to vent his rage to the extermination of that obstinate race. For he preferred that the Holy Land should for a short time be a slave to the profane rites of nations, than that those people should any longer flourish, who were not restrained from unlawful actions by any regard to probity.

The approach of the destruction which was to happen was prognosticated by diverse events, namely by a great famine, frequent earthquakes, and eclipses of the sun and moon. But the storm of wind, which the astronomers of Toledo, from an inspection of the stars, had pronounced would come from the assembling of the planets, together with a mortality and foul atmosphere, was without doubt changed to signify this event. For in the spring there was a heavy wind which shook the four quarters of the world, and signified that its different nations would be stirred up to battle and to the destruction of the Holy Land. And the holy city of Jerusalem, with the whole land of promise, and also the life-giving cross of our Lord, remained in the hands of the enemies of Christ for forty-two years up to this present year, which is the one thousand two hundred and twenty-ninth year of our Lord's incarnation. When at length the time arrived for our Lord in his compassion to give heed to the prayers of his humble servants, and to rebuild Sion, to appear in his glory in the place of his holy nativity, suffering, and resurrection, to hear the lamentations of his enslaved people, and to release the sons of the destroyed ones. Truly and without doubt did the Lord hear the groans of his enslaved people at the restoration of the Holy Land, which at that time was brought about by the diligence of the emperor Frederick, with the cooperation of the divine clemency, inasmuch as all the captives who were in the power of the pagans and subjected to the vilest kinds of slavery, were now released from the yoke of bondage and came to the holy city of Jerusalem. There they showed themselves to many and after having paid their devotions in the sacred places of the holy city, returned to their own countries in various parts of the world, praising and blessing God in all things, for they had heard and seen what wonderful works the Lord had done for them and showed to them.

Of the reconciliation of the holy city of Jerusalem and other places, 1229

THE ARMY of the Christians then, as we have said, entered the holy city of Jerusalem, and the patriarch, with the suffragan bishops, purified the temple of the Lord and the church of his holy sepulcher and resurrection, and all the other sacred churches of the city. They washed the pavement and walls with holy water, and forming processions with hymns and psalms they reconciled to God all his places which had been so long defiled by the filth of the pagans. But as long as the emperor, who was excommunicated, remained inside the city, no prelate dared to perform mass in it. However a certain master Walter, a religious, wise, and discreet man, of the Order of Preachers [Dominicans], who had been entrusted by the pope with the duty of preaching in the army of Christ, which duty he had for a long time prosperously fulfilled, performed divine services in the suburban churches, by which he greatly excited the devotion of the Christians. After then the prelates, inferior as well as superior, and all the religious men had had their churches and old possessions restored to them, and had rejoiced in all the heavenly gifts which had been bestowed on them far beyond their expectations, they all set to work in conjunction with the rest of the pilgrims, at great expense and trouble, to rebuild the city, to surround the walls with trenches, and to repair the ramparts of the towers. Not only was this done in the holy city of Jerusalem, but also in all the cities and fortresses of that land, which Jesus Christ had trodden with his holy feet, and consecrated with his sacred blood.

26. The Crusade of Frederick II: From the History of Philip of Novara, ca. 1230

Philip of Novara, in the service of the powerful Syrian-Frankish family of the Ibelins, lords of Beirut, was extremely hostile to Frederick, not so much for Frederick's alleged neglect of his crusader's vow and his subsequent excommunication as for his high-handed treatment of the lords of Ibelin and the king of Jerusalem, John of Brienne. The description is in marked contrast to that of Roger Wendover. See also below, No. 72, "The Templar of Tyre on the Fall of Acre."

The best edition, with a modern Italian translation, is Filippo da Novara, Guerra di Federico II in Oriente (1223–1242), *ed. Silvio Melani, Nuovo Medioevo 46 (Naples, 1994).*

IN THE year 1229 [1228] the emperor came to Syria with all his navy and the king and all his Cypriots with him. The lord of Beirut [John of Ibelin]

Source: Philip de Novare, The Wars of Frederick II Against the Ibelins in Syria and Cyprus, *ed. and trans. John L. La Monte, Records of Civilization, Sources and Studies, no. 25 (New York, 1936), 87–93.*

went to Beirut and was most gladly beheld there, for no lord was ever more dearly loved by his men. He remained only one day, and then at once followed the emperor and joined him at Tyre. The emperor was very well received in Syria and all did homage to him.[2] He left Tyre and went to the city of Acre, and was received there with honor. His fleet, which consisted of seventy galleys and ships, entered the port of Acre, and he [the emperor] was quartered in the castle. Then he had the liegemen assembled and demanded of them that they do homage to him as the bailli [regent] because he had a small son who was called King Conrad [later Conrad IV] and was rightful heir to the kingdom of Jerusalem through his mother [Yolande/Isabella] who was dead. The emperor, his men, and all the men of Syria left Acre to go to Jaffa, and there they made terms of truce with al-Kamil, who was then sultan of Babylon and Damascus and who held Jerusalem and all the country. Thereby were surrendered Jerusalem and Nazareth and Lydda to the emperor.

In the same year [1229], in the midst of all these events, the emperor sent Count Stephen of Cotron to Cyprus, and other Lombards as well, and had all the fortresses and revenues of the crown seized for his use, and he said that he was the bailli and that it was his right. The Cypriots were much frightened as were their women and children, and they placed themselves in the charge of the clergy wherever they were able. Some fled outside of Cyprus; notably Sir John of Ibelin—who later became count of Jaffa and who was at that time a child—with his sister and other gentlefolk fled in the heart of winter, and they encountered such bad weather that they barely escaped drowning. However with the aid of God they reached Tortosa. The emperor held Cyprus; the Cypriots who were in his host were very ill at ease and, if the lord of Beirut would have consented to it, they would have carried off and kidnapped young King Henry and would have deserted the emperor.

The emperor was by now unpopular with all the people of Acre, especially was he disliked by the Templars; and at that time there was a most valiant brother of the Temple, Brother Peter of Montague, who was very brave and noble; and most valiant and wise was also the master of the Teutonic Knights; and the people of the plain were not well inclined toward the emperor. The emperor did much that seemed evil, and he

---

2. News of the emperor's excommunication did not reach Syria until after Frederick's arrival. Afterward, the local clergy, Templars, and Hospitallers estranged themselves from Frederick, but the Teutonic Knights under Hermann von Salza remained loyal, as did many of the Syrian barons.

always kept galleys under arms, with their oars in the locks, even in winter. Many men said that he wished to capture the lord of Beirut, his children, Sir Anceau de Brie, and others of his friends, the master of the Temple and other people, and that he wished to send them to Apulia. On one occasion they said that he wished to kill them at a council to which he had called and summoned them, but they became aware of it and came in such strength that he did not dare to do it. However he made his truce with the Saracens as was desired and went to Jerusalem,[3] and thereafter came to Acre. The lord of Beirut never left him and, though there were those who often advised him to leave, he did not wish to do it.

At Acre the emperor assembled his men and had all the people of the city come there, and there were many Pisans who were very well disposed toward him. He addressed them and stated that which he desired; and in his address he complained much of the Temple.

He laid siege to the house of the Temple; and the house of the Temple was badly damaged, for the convent was all outside, but thereupon many folk came to it both by sea and by land. I do not know how long the siege lasted, but villainously he abandoned it.[4]

The emperor arranged for his passage secretly, and on the first day of May at dawn, without letting it be known by anyone, he got into a galley before the street of the butchers. Whence it happened that the butchers and the old people of the street, who were most ill disposed, ran along beside him and pelted him with tripe and bits of meat most scurrilously.

The lord of Beirut and Sir Eudes de Montbéliard heard talk of this; and they hurried there and drove away with blows those who had been throwing things at him, and they cried to him from the land to where he was on the galley that they commended him to God. The emperor replied in so low a voice that I do not know whether it was well or ill. He said that he was leaving as baillies in his place the lord of Sidon and Garnier l'Aleman. The emperor had very well equipped the castle of Tyre, and he gave it to the lord of Sidon to command and made it appear that he trusted much in him; but King Henry of Cyprus he took with him.

Thus the emperor left Acre; hated, cursed, and vilified. He arrived in Cyprus at Limassol, and there established the aforementioned King

3. This is Philip's only reference to Frederick's coronation in Jerusalem. Cf. Philip's scurrilous account of Frederick's departure, below.

4. The Templars and Hospitallers had come to an agreement to cooperate with the excommunicated emperor by serving as allies under the "ban of Christ," but not under the emperor's command.

Henry and gave him to wife one of his cousins, the daughter of the marquis of Montferrat. There he made the final terms with the five bail-lies, whom you have heard named already, who were of his party, selling them the bailliage of Cyprus and of the land for ten thousand marks, until the majority of the aforesaid king of Cyprus. He had them swear that they would not suffer the lord of Beirut and his partisans to return to Cyprus, and he commanded that they should dispossess them. They accepted this willingly from the emperor, whereat he turned over to them mercenaries, German, Flemish, and Lombard, whom they themselves should pay, and they sought and hired mercenaries in Acre and in other places. Certain men of the king, because of the fact that they [the baillies] had King Henry with them and moved by desire to return to their homes, joined with them and placed themselves under their command; but the castles were not surrendered to them until they had paid the money. The emperor Frederick went on over the sea and left in his place men to receive the money and deliver to them the castles.

27. Letter from Frederick II to Henry III of England, 1229: The Imperial Achievement

Frederick was his own best propagandist, and his account of his crusading triumphs stands in sharp contrast to the previous selection (No. 26). The text of his letter to Henry III of England is from the chronicle of Roger Wendover. Fred-erick's tone in this letter is as ambitious and "imperial" as the description of his great seal by Matthew Paris above. The opening paragraph is a cluster of scriptural citations, including a key traditional crusading verse from Daniel 2:21, "God . . . who changes times and seasons." Psalm 132 is also prominent in Frederick's narra-tive, identifying the Holy Land, via an error in the Latin Vulgate text, as "the place where the feet of Christ trod."

Frederick's relations with Henry III of England as well as England's continental interests in the thirteenth century are astutely discussed in Björn Weiler, Henry III and the Staufen Empire, 1216–1272 *(Woodbridge UK, 2006); Weiler, with I. W. Rowlands,* England and Europe in the Reign of Henry III *(Farnham UK-Burlington VT, 2002); and Weiler, "Greg-ory IX, Frederick II and the Liberation of the Holy Land, 1230–9,"* Studies in Church History *36 (2000), 192–206. On art, see Jaroslav Folda,* Crusader Art in the Holy Land: From the Third Crusade to the Fall of Acre, 1187–1291 *(Cambridge-New York, 2005).*

FREDERICK, by the grace of God, the august emperor of the Romans, king of Jerusalem and Sicily, to his well-beloved friend Henry, king of the English, health and sincere affection.

Source: Giles, Wendover's Flowers of History, *2:522–524.*

Let all rejoice and exult in the Lord, and let those who are correct in heart glorify him, who, to make known his power, does not make boast of horses and chariots, but has now gained glory for himself, in the scarcity of his soldiers, that all may know and understand that he is glorious in his majesty, terrible in his magnificence, and wonderful in his plans on the sons of men, changing seasons at will, and bringing the hearts of different nations together. For in these few days, by a miracle rather than by strength, that business has been brought to a conclusion, which for a length of time past many chiefs and rulers of the world among the multitude of nations, have never been able till now to accomplish by force, however great, nor by fear.

Not, therefore, to keep you in suspense by a long account, we wish to inform your holiness, that we, firmly putting our trust in God, and believing that Jesus Christ, his Son, in whose service we have so devotedly exposed our bodies and lives, would not abandon us in these unknown and distant countries, but would at least give us wholesome advice and assistance for his honor, praise, and glory, boldly in his name set forth from Acre on the fifteenth day of the month of November last past and arrived safely at Jaffa, intending to rebuild the castle at that place with proper strength, that afterward the approach to the holy city of Jerusalem might be not only easier, but also shorter and more safe for us as well as for all Christians. When, therefore, we were, in the confidence of our trust in God, engaged at Jaffa, and superintending the building of the castle and the cause of Christ, as necessity required and as was our duty, and while all our pilgrims were busily engaged in these matters, several messengers often passed to and fro between us and the sultan of Babylon. For he and another sultan, called Xaphat, his brother, were with a large army at the city of Gaza, distant about one day's journey from us. In another direction, in the city of Sichen, which is commonly called Neapolis, and situated in the plains, the sultan of Damascus, his nephew, was staying with an immense number of knights and soldiers also about a day's journey from us and the Christians.

And while the treaty was in progress between the parties on either side of the restoration of the Holy Land, at length Jesus Christ, the Son of God, beholding from on high our devoted endurance and patient devotion to his cause, in his merciful compassion of us, at length brought it about that the sultan of Babylon restored to us the holy city, the place where the feet of Christ trod, and where the true worshippers adore the Father in spirit and in truth. But that we may inform you of the particulars of this surrender each as they happened, be it known to you that not only is the body of the aforesaid city restored to us, but also the whole of the country extending from thence to the seacoast near the castle of Jaffa, so that for the future pilgrims will have free passage and a safe return to and from the sepulcher. It is provided, however, that the Saracens of that part of the country, since they hold the temple in great veneration, may come there as often as they choose in the character of pilgrims, to worship according to their custom. And we shall henceforth permit them to come, however, only as many as we may choose to allow, and without arms, nor are they to dwell in the city, but outside, and as soon as they have paid their devotions they are to depart.

Moreover, the city of Bethlehem is restored to us, and all the country between Jerusalem and that city; as also the city of Nazareth, and all the country between Acre and that city. The whole of the district of Turon, which is very extensive, and very advantageous to the Christians; the city of Sidon, too, is given up to us with the whole plain and its appurtenances, which will be the more acceptable to the Christians the more advantageous it has till now appeared to be to the Saracens, especially as there is a good harbor there. And from there great quantities of arms and necessaries might be carried to the city of Damascus, and often from Damascus to Babylon. According to our treaty we are allowed to rebuild the city of Jerusalem in as good a state as it has ever been, and also the castles of Jaffa, Caesarea, Sidon, and that of Saint Mary of the Teutonic order, which the brothers of that order have begun to build in the mountainous district of Acre, and which it has never been allowed the Christians to do during any former truce. Nevertheless the sultan is not allowed, till the end of the truce between him and us, which is agreed on for ten years, to repair or rebuild any fortresses or castles.

And so on Sunday, the eighteenth day of February last past, which is the day on which Christ, the Son of God, rose from the dead, and which, in memory of his resurrection, is solemnly cherished and kept holy by all Christians in general throughout the world, this treaty of peace was confirmed by oath between us. Truly then on us and on all does that day seem to have shone favorably, in which the angels sing in praise of God, "Glory to God on high, and on earth peace, and good will toward men" [Lk 2:14]. And in acknowledgment of such great kindness and of such an honor, which, beyond our deserts and contrary to the opinion of many, God has mercifully conferred on us, to the lasting renown of his compassion, and that in his holy place we might personally offer to him the burnt offering of our lips, be it known to you that on the seventeenth day of the month of March of this second indiction,[5] we, in company with all the pilgrims who had with us faithfully followed Christ, the Son of God, entered the holy city of Jerusalem, and after worshipping at the holy sepulcher, we, as being a catholic emperor, on the following day, wore the crown, which Almighty God provided for us from the throne of his majesty, when of his special grace, he exalted us on high among the princes of the world. So that while we have supported the honor of this high dignity, which belongs to us by right of sovereignty, it is more and more evident to all that the hand of the Lord hath done all this; and since his mercies are over all his works, let the worshippers of the orthodox faith henceforth know and relate it far and wide throughout the world, that he, who is blessed forever, has visited and redeemed his people, and has raised up the horn of salvation for us in the house of his servant David.

And before we leave the city of Jerusalem, we have determined magnificently to rebuild it, and its towers and walls, and we intend so to arrange matters that, during our absence, there shall be no less care and diligence used in the business, than if we were present in person. In order that this our present letter may be full of exultation throughout, and so a happy end correspond with its happy beginning, and rejoice your royal mind, we wish it be known to you, our ally, that the said sultan is bound to restore to us all those captives whom he did not in accordance with the treaty made between him and the Christians deliver up at the time when he lost Damietta some time since, and also the others who have been since taken.

Given at the holy city of Jerusalem, on the seventeenth day of the month of March, in the year of our Lord one thousand two hundred and twenty-nine.

28. Ibn Wasil (ca. 1282) and Ibn al-Jauzi (ca. 1250) on the Loss of Jerusalem

Al-Kamil had been very cautious in his negotiations with Frederick II, since he needed to keep his brother al-Mu'azzam at a distance and reduce the opportunity for criticism among his own subjects. Al-Mu'azzam died in 1227, reducing

5. That is, March 17, 1229, Easter Sunday. This description of his own coronation as king of Jerusalem invokes King David and is packed with scriptural confirmation of God's favor toward Frederick, a messianic claim that had usually been made by popes on behalf of all Christian society. The indiction was a fifteen-year taxation cycle used in the Roman Empire and implies a distinctly imperial calendar. This letter to Henry III was dispatched on the same day.

part of the threat to al-Kamil. But in order to secure al-Mu'azzam's Damascus and
avoid all-out war even with Frederick's reduced forces, al-Kamil maintained the
diplomatic relations he had begun with Frederick, which had included the earlier
skillful negotiations conducted by his emissary Fakhr al-Din with Frederick in Sicily, during which Frederick had actually knighted the Ayyubid emissary.

The terms of the agreement of 1229 were carefully spelled out, each side
claiming the advantage without demeaning the concessions of the other. The
imperial grandeur of Frederick's letter to Henry III gracefully neglects several key
terms of the treaty. The treaty allowed for a ten-year truce (till 1239) during which
Frederick guaranteed the protection of al-Kamil from all enemies including Christians. Although several key holy places were turned over to Frederick, Muslims
were to retain control over their own holy places in Jerusalem, especially the
Haram as-Sharif,[6] and could freely enter and leave Jerusalem as pilgrims, although
they could not reside there.

As a result of the treaty both Frederick and al-Kamil saw the need to launch
propaganda offensives in both the East and the West. Just as different interests
in the Christian West produced different estimates of Frederick's success or lack
of it, so too did various Muslim accounts. Two contemporary or near-contempo-
rary Arabic accounts by Jamal ad-Din ibn Wasil, later the Mamluk ruler Baibars's
ambassador to the Sicilian court of Frederick's illegitimate son Manfred, and
Sibt ibn al-Jauzi (1186–1256), author of a vast history called *Mir' at az-zaman*
(Mirror of the Times), both recorded Muslim despair over the loss of Jerusalem
but also promoted the image of Frederick II as phil-Islamic and respectful of
local traditions and practices. The following accounts offer insight into the Muslim view.

> On al-Jauzi and Ibn Wasil, see Gabrieli, Arab Historians, *xxxi–xxxii. Other sources in
> Arabic include Ibn al-Athir, The Chronicle of Ibn al-Athir for the Crusading Period from
> al-Kamil fi'l-Tarikh, part 3, The Years 589/629–1193/1231: The Ayyubids After Saladin
> and the Mongol Menace, trans. D. S. Richards (Aldershot UK-Burlington VT, 2008); and
> Ibn al-Furat, Ayyubids, Mamlukes and Crusaders: Selections from the Tarikh al-duwal wa'l
> Muluk, text and trans. U. Lyons and M. C. Lyons, historical intro. and notes by J. S. C. Riley-
> Smith, 2 vols. (Cambridge, 1971).*

Ibn Wasil (ca. 1282): Frederick arrives at Acre

IN 625/1228 the emperor Frederick arrived at Acre with a great company
of Germans and other Franks. We have already described how Fakhr ad-
Din, the son of the sheikh ash-Shuyukh, was sent to the king-emperor

Source: Francesco Gabrieli, Arab Historians of the Crusades, *trans. E. J. Costello
(Berkeley-Los Angeles, 1969), 267–275.*
      6. The Haram as-Sharif, *al-haram al-qudsī as-sharīf* ("The Noble Sanctuary"), was
the Temple Mount, the third holiest site in Islam, and the location of the al-Aqsa mosque
and the Dome of the Rock.

from the sultan al-Malik al-Kamil. This was in the time of al-Malik al-Mu'azzam.[7] The idea of the approaches made to the emperor, the king of the Franks, and of his invitation, was to create difficulties for al-Malik al-Mu'azzam and prevent his availing himself of the help offered to him by the sultan Jalal ad-Din ibn 'Ala ad-Din Khwarizmshah and Muzaffar ad-Din of Arbela, in his quarrel with al-Malik al-Kamil and al-Malik al-Ashraf.

The emperor made his preparations, and arrived with his army on the coast of Syria in the same year and disembarked at Acre. A great number of Franks had preceded him there but they could not move off for fear of al-Malik al-Mu'azzam and so they were waiting for their leader the emperor.[8] This word means in the Frankish language "the king of the princes." His kingdom consisted of the island of Sicily, and Apulia and Lombardy in the Long Country [Italy]. It is the author, Jamal ad-Din ibn Wasil, who speaks: "I saw these parts when I was sent as ambassador of the sultan al-Malik az-Zahir Rukn ad-Din Baibars [d. 1277], of blessed memory, to the emperor's son, Manfred by name. The emperor was a Frankish king, distinguished and gifted, a student of philosophy, logic, and medicine and a friend to Muslims, for his original home was Sicily, where he was educated. His father and his grandfather were kings of the island,[9] but its inhabitants were mostly Muslims."

When the emperor reached Acre, al-Malik al-Kamil found him an embarrassment, for his brother al-Malik al-Mu'azzam, who was the reason why he had asked Frederick for help, had died [1227], and al-Kamil had no further need of the emperor. Nor was it possible to turn him away and attack him because this would have led him to lose the goals on which his heart was set at the time. He therefore made a treaty with Frederick and treated him with great friendship.

Ibn Wasil (ca. 1282): Jerusalem is handed over to the Franks

THEN followed negotiations between al-Malik al-Kamil and the emperor of which the object had been fixed earlier when al-Kamil and the emperor

---

7. Al-Mu'azzam was al-Kamil's brother, the ruler of Damascus, who had come to the aid of al-Kamil at Damietta during the Fifth Crusade. But relations between them deteriorated, and this tension, exacerbated by Jalal ad-Din, the sultan of Khwarizm and the emir of Arbela, had led al-Kamil to approach Frederick with an offer very similar to that made originally at Damietta in 1220.

8. These were the troops who had left Italy in August 1227 and had to await Frederick's arrival in September.

9. Only Henry VI, not Frederick Barbarossa, had ruled Sicily. But Frederick II was also the grandson of Roger II, first Norman king of Sicily.

first met, before the death of al-Malik al-Mu'azzam. The Frankish king
had refused to return home except on the conditions laid down, which
included the surrender of Jerusalem and part of the area conquered by
Saladin, whereas al-Malik al-Kamil was by no means prepared to yield him
these territories. It was finally agreed that he should have Jerusalem on
condition that he did not attempt to rebuild the walls, that nothing outside it should be held by the Franks, and that all the other villages within
its province should be Muslim, with a Muslim governor resident at al-
Bira, actually in the province of Jerusalem. The sacred precincts of the
city, with the Dome of the Rock and the Masjid al-Aqsa were to remain
in Muslim hands, and the Franks were simply to have the right to visit
them, while their administration remained in the hands of those already
employed in it, and Muslim worship was to continue there. The Franks
excepted from the agreement certain small villages on the road from Acre
to Jerusalem, which were to remain in their control unlike the rest of the
province of Jerusalem.

The sultan al-Malik al-Kamil maintained that if he broke with the
emperor and failed to give him full satisfaction the result would be a war
with the Franks in which the Muslims would suffer irreparably, and everything for which they were working would slip from their grasp. So he was
in favor of satisfying the Franks with a disarmed Jerusalem and making a
temporary truce with them. He could seize the concessions back from
them later, when he chose to. The emir Fakhr ad-Din ibn ash-Sheikh
conducted the negotiations for him, and many conversations and discussions took place between them, during which the emperor sent to al-
Malik al-Kamil queries on difficult philosophic, geometric, and mathe-
matical points, to test the men of learning at his court. The sultan passed
the questions on to Sheikh 'Alam ad-Din Qaisar, a master of that art, and
the rest to a group of scholars, who answered them all. Then al-Malik al-
Kamil and the emperor swore to observe the terms of the agreement and
made a truce for a fixed term.[10] In this way they arranged matters between
themselves, and each side felt secure in its relations with the other. I was
told that the emperor said to the emir Fakhr ad-Din: "If I were not afraid
that my prestige among the Franks would be destroyed I should not have
imposed these conditions on the sultan. I have no real ambition to hold
Jerusalem, nor anything else; I simply want to safeguard my reputation
with the Christians."

---

10. Ten years, five months, and forty days from 28 Rabi I 626 (February 24, 1229).

After the truce the sultan sent out a proclamation that the Muslims were to leave Jerusalem and hand it over to the Franks. The Muslims left amid cries and groans and lamentations. The news spread swiftly throughout the Muslim world, which lamented the loss of Jerusalem and disapproved strongly of al-Malik al-Kamil's action as a most dishonorable deed, for the reconquest of that noble city and its recovery from the hand of the infidel had been one of al-Malik an-Nasir Saladin's most notable achievements—God sanctify his spirit!—but al-Malik al-Kamil of noble memory knew that the Muslims could not defend themselves in an unprotected Jerusalem, and that when he had achieved his aim and had the situation well in hand he could purify Jerusalem of the Franks and chase them out. "We have only," he said, "conceded to them some churches and some ruined houses. The sacred precincts, the venerated Rock and all the other sanctuaries to which we make our pilgrimages remain ours as they were; Muslim rites continue to flourish as they did before, and the Muslims have their own governor of the rural provinces and districts."

After the agreement the emperor asked the sultan for permission to visit Jerusalem. This the sultan granted, and ordered the qadi of Nablus, Shams ad-Din of blessed memory, who enjoyed great prestige and favor with the Ayyubid house, to be at the emperor's service during the time of his visit to Jerusalem and his return to Acre. The author Jamal ad-Din ibn Wasil says: "The qadi of Nablus Shams ad-Din of blessed memory told me: 'I took my place beside him as the sultan al-Malik al-Kamil had ordered me to and entered the Sacred Precinct with him, where he inspected the lesser sanctuaries. Then I went with him to al-Aqsa, whose construction he admired, as he did that of the Dome of the Rock. When we came to the mihrab he admired its beauty, and commended the pulpit, which he climbed to the top. When he descended he took my hand and we went out in the direction of al-Aqsa. There he found a priest with the Testament in his hand about to enter al-Aqsa. The emperor called out to him: "What has brought you here? By God, if one of you comes here again without permission I shall, have his eyes put out! We are the slaves and servants of al-Malik al-Kamil. He has handed over this church to me and you as a gracious gift. I do not want any of you exceeding your duties." The priest made off, quaking with fear. Then the king went to the house that had been prepared for him and took up residence there.' The qadi Shams ad-Din said: 'I recommended the muezzins not to give the call to prayer that night, out of respect for the king. In the morning I went to him, and he said: "O qadi, why did the muezzins not give the call to prayer last night in the usual way?" "This humble slave," I replied, "prevented them out of regard and respect for Your Majesty." "You did wrong to do that," he said. "My chief aim in passing the night in Jerusalem was to hear the call to prayer given by the muezzins, and their cries of praise to God during the night." Then he left and returned to Acre.'"

When news of the loss of Jerusalem reached Damascus, al-Malik an-Nasir began to abuse his uncle al-Malik al-Kamil for alienating the people's sympathies, and ordered the preacher sheikh Shams ad-Din Yusuf, the nephew of sheikh Jamal ad-Din ibn al-Jauzi, who was in great public favor as a preacher, to preach a sermon in the Great Mosque in Damascus. He was to recall the history of Jerusalem, the holy traditions and legends associated with it, to make the people grieve for the loss of it, and to speak of the humiliation and disgrace that its loss brought upon the Muslims. By this means al-Malik an-Nasir Dawud proposed to alienate the people from al-Malik al-Kamil and to ensure their loyalty to himself in his contest with his uncle.[11] So Shams ad-Din preached as he was told to, and the people came to hear him. It was a memorable day, one on which there rose up to heaven the cries, sobs, and groans of the crowd. I myself was one of the crowd there, and among the matters to which I heard him refer was a qasida composed by him, rhyming in 't', into which he had inserted a few lines by the poet Di'bil al-Khuza,[12] of which I recall the following:

> In the Sanctuary of the Ascent and of the Rock, which surpasses
>   in glory every other rock in the world.
> There are Qur'anic schools now deprived of the recitations of
>   the sacred verses, and a seat of revelation in the now deserted
>   courtyards.

ON THAT day one saw nothing but weeping men and women. Now that the truce between al-Malik al-Kamil and the emperor had been ratified the latter weighed anchor and returned home.[13]

---

11. An-Nasir was the son and successor of al-Kamil's hostile brother al-Mu'azzam. His design of the sermon and other steps he took were as much for his own political benefit as based on religious outrage.

12. A poet of the eighth and ninth centuries. The preacher has taken a line from one of his laments for the 'Alids and adapted it to the loss of Jerusalem (the second of the two lines quoted here). The subject of Arabic prosody is too complicated to treat here.

13. At the end of Jumada II (May 1229).

Sibt ibn al-Jauzi (ca. 1250): Muslim grief at Damascus; Frederick in Jerusalem

NEWS of the loss of Jerusalem spread to Damascus, and disaster struck all the lands of Islam. It was so great a tragedy that public ceremonies of mourning were instituted. Al-Malik an-Nasir Dawud invited me to preside over a meeting in the Great Mosque of Damascus and to speak of what had occurred in Jerusalem. I could not refuse him, considering obedience to his desire as one of my religious duties and part of my zeal for the cause of Islam. So I ascended (the pulpit) of the Great Mosque of Damascus, in the presence of al-Malik al-Nasir Dawud, at the gate of Mashhad 'Ali. It was a memorable day, for not one of the people of Damascus remained outside. In the course of my oration I said: "The road to Jerusalem is closed to the companies of pious visitors! O desolation for those pious men who live there; how many times have they prostrated themselves there in prayer, how many tears have they shed there! By Allah, if their eyes were living springs they could not pay the whole of their debt of grief; if their hearts burst with grief they could not diminish their anguish! May God burnish the honor of the believers! O shame upon the Muslim rulers! At such an event tears fall, hearts break with sighs, grief rises up on high . . ." and so on through a long discourse. The poets too composed many works on the same subject.

The emperor entered Jerusalem while Damascus was under siege.[14] During his visit curious incidents occurred: one was that when he went into the Dome of the Rock he saw a priest sitting near the imprint of the Holy Foot, and taking some pieces of paper from the Franks.[15] The emperor went up to him as if he wanted to ask a benediction of him, and struck him a blow that knocked him to the ground. "Swine!" he cried. "The sultan has done us the honor of allowing us to visit this place, and you sit here behaving like this! If any of you comes in here again in this way I shall kill him!" The scene was described by one of the custodians of the Dome of the Rock. They said too that the emperor looked at the inscription that runs around the inside of the sanctuary, saying: "Saladin purified this city of Jerusalem of the polytheists . . ." and asked: "Who would these polytheists be?" He also asked the custodians: "What are

14. By al-Kamil and his brother al-Ashraf against their nephew an-Nasir.
15. The nature of the paper is not known. Ibn Wasil (above) says the priest held a Testament.

these nets at the doors of the sanctuary for?" They replied: "So that the little sparrows should not come in." He said: "God brought the giants here instead!"[16] When the time came for the midday prayer and the muezzins' cry rang out, all his pages and valets rose, as well as his tutor, a Sicilian with whom he was reading (Aristotle's) logic in all its chapters, and offered the canonic prayer, for they were all Muslims.

The emperor, as these same custodians recall, had a red skin, and was bald and short-sighted.[17] Had he been a slave he would not have been worth two hundred dirhams. It was clear from what he said that he was a materialist and that his Christianity was simply a game to him. Al-Kamil had ordered the qadi of Nablus, Shams ad-Din, to tell the muezzins that during the emperor's stay in Jerusalem they were not to go up into their minarets and give the call to prayer in the sacred precinct. The qadi forgot to tell the muezzins, and so the muezzin 'Abd al-Karim mounted his minaret at dawn and began to recite the Qur'anic verses about the Christians, such as "God has no son,"[18] referring to Jesus son of Mary, and other such texts. In the morning the qadi called 'Abd al-Karim to him and said: "What have you done? The sultan's command was thus and thus." He replied, "You did not tell me; I am sorry." The second night he did not give the call. The next morning the emperor summoned the qadi, who had come to Jerusalem as his personal adviser and had been responsible for handing the city over to him, and said, "O qadi, where is the man who yesterday climbed the minaret and spoke these words?" The qadi told him of the sultan's orders. "You did wrong, qadi; would you alter your rites and law and faith for my sake? If you were staying in my country, would I order the bells to be silenced for your sake? By God, do not do this; this is the first time we have found fault in you!" Then he distributed a sum of money among the custodians and muezzins and pious men in the sanctuary; ten dinars to each. He spent only two nights in Jerusalem and then returned to Jaffa, for fear of the Templars, who wanted to kill him.

---

16. These exchanges imply a speaking and reading knowledge of Arabic on Frederick's part, in the latter instance probably including the ability to pun.

17. This is one of the very few physical descriptions of Frederick II. It appears to be accurate.

18. Qur'an 23.93

29. Letter from Gerold, Patriarch of Jerusalem, to the Christian Faithful: The Coming of Antichrist, ca. 1230

The circumstances of Frederick II's crusade, especially his status as an excommunicate, his claim to the throne of the Latin kingdom (first on behalf of his wife Isabella and after her death in childbirth in 1228 on behalf of his new son Conrad), his difficult relations with both ecclesiastical and secular powers in the Holy Land, and his relations with the sultan al-Kamil have supported various and often conflicting accounts of Frederick in the East by historians. One difficulty with the problem is the way in which original texts may have been altered or their accounts distorted because of later political conditions. This well-known letter of Gerold of Lausanne, patriarch of Jerusalem, has often been cited as an example of the divided opinion about Frederick. Although Gerold had sent a letter on a similar subject to Pope Gregory IX in March 1229, the present letter, addressed more broadly to the universe of the Christian faithful, is found in the chronicle of Matthew Paris, interpolated into the material of Roger Wendover for 1229.

It seems that the present letter, because of distinctive features of its Latin and its differences from the letter of Gerold to Gregory IX, is a later composition created or modified from an unknown original and intended to serve in the propaganda campaign against Frederick launched in the late 1230s. It suggests that crusade imagery could also be turned to political partisanship.

The most important studies are James M. Powell, "Patriarch Gerold and Frederick II: The Matthew Paris Letter," Journal of Medieval History 25 (1999), 19–26, and "Frederick II and the Muslims: The Making of an Historiographical Tradition," in L. J. Simon, ed., Iberia and the Mediterranean World of the Middle Ages (Leiden, 1995), 261–269, both reprinted in James M. Powell, The Crusades, the Kingdom of Sicily, and the Mediterranean (Aldershot UK-Burlington VT, 2007), VII and III; and Robert E. Lerner, "Frederick II, Alive, Aloft, and Allayed in Franciscan-Joachite Eschatology," in Werner Verbeke, Daniel Verhelst, and Andries Welkenhuysen, eds., The Use and Abuse of Eschatology in the Middle Ages (Leuven, 1988), 359–384.

GEROLD, patriarch of Jerusalem, to all the faithful—greeting.

If it should be fully known how astonishing, nay, rather, deplorable, the conduct of the emperor has been in the eastern lands from beginning to end, to the great detriment of the cause of Jesus Christ and to the great injury of the Christian faith, from the sole of his foot to the top of his head no common sense would be found in him. For he came, excommunicated, without money and followed by scarcely forty knights, and hoped to maintain himself by spoiling the inhabitants of Syria. He first came to

Source: Dana C. Munro, Letters of the Crusaders, Translations and Reprints from the Original Sources of European History, vol. 1, no. 4 (Philadelphia, 1896), 25–29.

Cyprus and there most discourteously seized that nobleman John of Ibelin and his sons, whom he had invited to his table under pretext of speaking of the affairs of the Holy Land. Next he retained almost as a captive the king, whom he had invited to meet him. He thus by violence and fraud got possession of the kingdom.

After these achievements he passed over into Syria. Although in the beginning he promised to do marvels, and although in the presence of the foolish he boasted loudly, he immediately sent to the sultan of Babylon to demand peace. This conduct rendered him despicable in the eyes of the sultan and his subjects, especially after they had discovered that he was not at the head of a numerous army, which might have to some extent added weight to his words. Under the pretext of defending Jaffa, he marched with the Christian army toward that city, in order to be nearer the sultan and in order to be able more easily to treat of peace or obtain a truce. What more shall I say? After long and mysterious conferences, and without having consulted anyone who lived in the country, he suddenly announced one day that he had made peace with the sultan. No one saw the text of the peace or truce when the emperor took the oath to observe the articles which were agreed upon. Moreover, you will be able to see clearly how great the malice was and how fraudulent the tenor of certain articles of the truce which we have decided to send to you. The emperor, for giving credit to his word, wished as a guarantee only the word of the sultan, which he obtained. For he said, among other things, that the holy city was surrendered to him.

He went there with the Christian army on the eve of the Sunday when "Oculi mei" is sung.[19] The Sunday following, without any fitting ceremony and although excommunicated, in the chapel of the sepulcher of our Lord, to the manifest prejudice of his honor and of the imperial dignity, he put the diadem upon his forehead, although the Saracens still held the temple of the Lord and Solomon's temple, and although they proclaimed publicly as before the law of Muhammad—to the great confusion and chagrin of the pilgrims.

This same prince, who had previously very often promised to fortify Jerusalem, departed in secrecy from the city at dawn on the following Monday. The Hospitallers and the Templars promised solemnly and earnestly to aid him with all their forces and their advice, if he wanted to fortify the city, as he had promised. But the emperor, who did not care

---

19. The third Sunday in Lent.

to set affairs right, and who saw that there was no certainty in what had been done, and that the city in the state in which it had been surrendered to him could be neither defended nor fortified, was content with the name of surrender, and on the same day hastened with his family to Jaffa. The pilgrims who had entered Jerusalem with the emperor, witnessing his departure, were unwilling to remain behind.

The following Sunday when "Laetare Jerusalem" is sung he arrived at Acre.[20] There in order to seduce the people and to obtain their favor, he granted them a certain privilege. God knows the motive which made him act thus, and his subsequent conduct will make it known. As, more-over, the passage was near, and as all pilgrims, humble and great, after having visited the Holy Sepulcher, were preparing to withdraw, as if they had accomplished their pilgrimage, because no truce had been concluded with the sultan of Damascus, we, seeing that the Holy Land was already deserted and abandoned by the pilgrims, in our council formed the plan of retaining soldiers, for the common good, by means of the alms given by the king of France of holy memory.[21] When the emperor heard of this, he said to us that he was astonished at this, since he had concluded a truce with the sultan of Babylon. We replied to him that the knife was still in the wound, since there was not a truce or peace with the sultan of Damas-cus, nephew of the aforesaid sultan and opposed to him, adding that even if the sultan of Babylon was unwilling, the former could still do us much harm. The emperor replied, saying that no soldiers ought to be retained in his kingdom without his advice and consent, as he was now king of Jerusalem. We answered to that, that in the matter in question, as well as in all of a similar nature, we were very sorry not to be able, without endan-gering the salvation of our souls, to obey his wishes, because he was excommunicated. The emperor made no response to us, but on the fol-lowing day he caused the pilgrims who inhabited the city to be assembled outside by the public crier, and by special messengers he also convoked the prelates and the monks.

Addressing them in person, he began to complain bitterly of us, by heaping up false accusations. Then turning his remarks to the venerable master of the Templars he publicly attempted to severely tarnish the repu-tation of the latter, by various vain speeches, seeking thus to throw upon others the responsibility for his own faults which were now manifest, and

20. The fourth Sunday in Lent.
21. Philip II Augustus.

adding at last, that we were maintaining troops with the purpose of injuring him. After that he ordered all foreign soldiers, of all nations, if they valued their lives and property, not to remain in the land from that day on, and ordered Count Thomas, whom he intended to leave as bailiff of the country, to punish with whips anyone who was found lingering, in order that the punishment of one might serve as an example to many. After doing all this he withdrew, and would listen to no excuse or answers to the charges which he had so shamefully made. He determined immediately to post some crossbowmen at the gates of the city, ordering them to allow the Templars to go out but not to return. Next he fortified with crossbows the churches and other elevated positions, and especially those which commanded the communications between the Templars and ourselves. And you may be sure that he never showed as much animosity and hatred against Saracens.

For our part, seeing his manifest wickedness, we assembled all the prelates and all the pilgrims, and menaced with excommunication all those who should aid the emperor with their advice or their services against the church, the Templars, the other monks of the Holy Land, or the pilgrims.

The emperor was more and more irritated, and immediately caused all the passages to be guarded more strictly, refused to allow any kind of provisions to be brought to us or to the members of our party, and placed everywhere crossbowmen and archers, who severely attacked us, the Templars, and the pilgrims. Finally to fill the measure of his malice, he caused some Dominicans and Franciscans who had come on Palm Sunday to the proper places to announce the Word of God, to be torn from the pulpit, to be thrown down and dragged along the ground and whipped throughout the city, as if they had been robbers. Then seeing that he did not obtain what he had hoped from the above-mentioned siege, he treated of peace. We replied to him that we would not hear of peace until he sent away the crossbowmen and other troops, until he had returned our property to us, until finally he had restored all things to the condition and freedom in which they were on that day when he entered Jerusalem. He finally ordered what we wanted to be done, but it was not executed. Therefore we placed the city under interdict.

The emperor, realizing that his wickedness could have no success, was unwilling to remain any longer in the country. And, as if he would have liked to ruin everything, he ordered the crossbows and engines of war, which for a long time had been kept at Acre for the defense of the

Holy Land, to be secretly carried onto his vessels. He also sent away several of them to the sultan of Babylon, as his dear friend. He sent a troop of soldiers to Cyprus to levy heavy contributions of money there, and, what appeared to us more astonishing, he destroyed the galleys which he was not able to take with him. Having learned this, we resolved to reproach him with it, but shunning the remonstrance and the correction, he entered a galley secretly, by an obscure way, on the day of the Apostles Saint Philip and Saint James, and hastened to reach the island of Cyprus, without saying adieu to anyone, leaving Jaffa destitute; and may he never return!

Very soon the bailiffs of the above-mentioned sultan shut off all departure from Jerusalem for the Christian poor and the Syrians, and many pilgrims died thus on the road.

This is what the emperor did, to the detriment of the Holy Land and of his own soul, as well as many other things which are known and which we leave to others to relate. May the merciful God deign to soften the results! Farewell.

PART V
The Barons' Crusade, 1234–1245

Honorius III was succeeded in 1227 by Cardinal Hugolino, who took the papal name Gregory IX (1227–1241). Gregory had been protector of the Franciscan order, papal legate in Lombardy for the Fifth Crusade, and was a relative of Innocent III. His complex relations with Frederick II have already been noted, particularly his concerns with Frederick's power over ecclesiastical affairs in Sicily, his fears about Frederick's power in the Latin Kingdom of Jerusalem, and his excommunication of Frederick in 1227. But Gregory's powers were also limited. He could not impose his will on the Roman nobles who dominated the city, and he could not ignore the emperor who had regained Jerusalem, not when other problems emerged in the early 1230s.[1]

The Holy Land itself was protected for ten years by the truce that Frederick II and al-Kamil had made in 1229, but as early as 1234 Gregory had begun to call for a crusade to depart for the Holy Land in 1239. He had already released Frederick II from the ban of excommunication in 1230 and their uneasy cooperation continued for most of the decade. The autocratic assertion of Frederick's authority in the Latin Kingdom of Jerusalem and Cyprus and resistance to Frederick's claims and continuing conflict among the Ayyubid rulers sharpened by the death of al-Kamil in 1238 characterized the situation in the East.

Gregory was also concerned with the unstable fortunes of the Latin Empire of Constantinople and the failure of ecclesiastical unification of the Greek and Latin churches. Gregory even tried as early as 1236 to deflect the Holy Land crusade to Constantinople, although most crusaders rejected his urging, choosing in 1239 to go to Acre instead. The putative date for the departure of the crusaders was also repeatedly changed—Gregory IX originally planned for the crusaders to depart well before the actual date of the expiration of Frederick II's truce with al-Kamil, while Frederick exhorted the participants to wait instead until August 1239, promising them imperial aid if they adhered to the later deadline. Moreover, by March 1239 the papal-imperial conflict had renewed itself. Gregory excommunicated Frederick yet again, and both pope and emperor appealed to crusaders to delay their departures. Such attitudes illustrate the variety of responses to the call for crusade that were possible in the 1230s.

A group of French barons including Thibaut of Champagne, Peter of Dreux, and Amalric of Montfort had taken the cross in France in 1236. Gregory IX had attempted to finance the crusade by levying a tax of one penny per week upon every inhabitant of Western Christendom and through repeated appeals for income

---

1. Björn Weiler, "Gregory IX, Frederick II and the Liberation of the Holy Land, 1230–9," *Studies in Church History* 36 (2000), 192–206.

tax levied upon ecclesiastics, but many of the barons who took the cross were severely impoverished. In the end the majority of French crusaders left for the Holy Land in August 1239. Their first priority was the fortification and defense of the city of Jerusalem, which had been ceded to Frederick under the terms of his treaty with al-Kamil and was now threatened with Muslim recapture. Based initially in the port city of Acre, the crusaders also faced a difficult choice of which threat to the Latin Kingdom of Jerusalem to neutralize—the sultan of Damascus or the sultan of Egypt. While marching south toward Ascalon, part of the crusader army encountered the advance forces of the sultan of Egypt and was defeated at Gaza, with the result that many influential crusaders were taken prisoner. The fate of these prisoners became a matter of later diplomatic negotiation on the part of Richard of Cornwall.

Although the main crusader army managed to beat back the Egyptian forces, the army's leaders, among them Thibaut of Champagne, decided to return to Acre. Shortly thereafter, the forces of an-Nasir Dawud of Kerak, lord of the Transjordan, captured Jerusalem. Despite this grim development, civil war within the Ayyubid political world presented a unique opportunity to the crusaders.

Although Thibaut was ultimately unable to forge an alliance with the lord of Hama, who, under attack from the sultan of Damascus and the lord of Homs, offered to turn his fortresses over to the crusaders and convert to Christianity, he proved luckier when an-Nasir Dawud, lord of Transjordan, and his relative and prisoner as-Salih Ayyub, the deposed lord of Damascus, managed to conquer Egypt and present a viable threat to the new sultan of Damasacus, as-Salih Ismail.

Ismail made a stunning offer to the crusading army. In return for its support against the sultan of Egypt, he would surrender the fortresses of Beaufort, Tiberias, and Safad [Saphet] and eventually the land and fortresses the Franks had lost in Galilee, Jerusalem, and Bethlehem (including a corridor to the coastline), Ascalon, and the region of Gaza with the exception of the city itself (most of which remained to be rewon from the sultan of Egypt). The offer was opposed by the Hospitallers (perhaps because the truce benefited their rivals the Templars) and those who felt that the men recently captured would never be freed. Thibaut and the crusader army were joined by the army of the sultan of Damascus near Jaffa, but the alliance seems to have dissolved, leading the crusaders to retreat to Ascalon.

Despite opposition from the Templars and other parties within the crusader army, Thibaut soon accepted the offer of the sultan of Egypt to release the crusader captives and to confirm the cession of the territories already promised (although not yet won) by the sultan of Damascus. In one fell swoop, despite the festering divisions within the Latin Kingdom of Jerusalem, Thibaut had secured all those lands won by Frederick II in his truce of 1229 with al-Kamil and the equivalent in new territorial gains, restoring the Latin Kingdom of Jerusalem to a position very near to that before Saladin's conquests of 1187. Although the duke of Burgundy and the count of Nevers and some of Thibaut's own followers remained to rebuild the castle at Ascalon, the majority of French crusaders departed before the projected arrival of Richard of Cornwall and the English crusaders.

Richard of Cornwall, the fabulously wealthy brother of Henry III of England, had taken the cross in 1236 together with other English notables, including his brother-in-law Gilbert Marshal, earl of Pembroke (head of the barons opposed to the king, Gilbert took the cross only after Richard promised to reconcile him with Henry III). Although Henry appears to have influenced the pope to suspend the vows of Richard and other noblemen in February of 1238 in order to retain his supporters in England during his struggle with the English barons, two months later Gregory ordered Henry to assist Richard in the fulfillment of his vow. Richard soon also received conflicting imperial and papal instructions regarding the crusade. At one point Gregory IX suggested that Richard redeem his crusade vow by dedicating the money he would have spent on crusade to the defense of the kingdom of Constantinople, although by 1238 he relented and instructed his legate in England to give to Richard to fulfill his Holy Land vow the money raised in England (which he had earlier ordered to be diverted to the crusade in aid of the Latin Kingdom of Constantinople).

However, with the resumption of the papal-imperial conflict in 1239, Gregory was somewhat leery of the English crusaders passing through Italy, because Frederick's current empress was Richard's and Henry's sister Isabella. Richard, for his part, appears to have been eager to steer clear of both the royal-baronial conflict in England (he managed to establish a temporary peace between the king and Gilbert Marshal before leaving on crusade) and the papal-imperial conflict. Ignoring Frederick's invitation to depart on crusade from imperial lands in Italy, he chose instead to depart from Marseilles with the blessing and support of Louis IX.

He arrived at Acre in October 1241 to find Christian division once again rife in the Holy Land. After consulting the heads of the major military orders, the barons of the Latin Kingdom of Jerusalem, and the remaining French crusaders, Richard ignored the Templars' insistence that an alliance with Damascus be renewed and instead confirmed the truce with the sultan of Egypt (following the lead of his brother-in-law Frederick II, who had used similar diplomacy with Egypt in 1229). He then marched to Ascalon to continue refortifying the castle there. Upon its completion he faced the tricky decision of to whom to entrust the castle and urged his brother-in-law's imperial representative, Walter Pennenpié (already installed in Jerusalem), to come and take custody of the new fortification. After overseeing the exchange of prisoners provided for in the treaty, Richard arranged for the proper burial of the French crusaders who had perished near Ascalon and set sail in May of 1241. Although his crusade saw little military action, Richard, following in the footsteps of Thibaut of Champagne and Frederick II, won major territorial concessions for the Latin Kingdom of Jerusalem, which enabled it to survive for decades to come, in spite of the destruction of Jerusalem itself in 1244.

For all the varieties of crusade perception and participation, the Barons' Crusade of 1239–1241 did manage to achieve some success in the Holy Land. The vigor and combat skills of the troops led by Thibaut IV and Richard of Cornwall recovered Galilee and refortified Ascalon. The crusaders profited diplomatically from the Ayyubid internal conflicts after the death of al-Kamil in 1238, and enabled the local Frankish aristocracy to reject Staufer rule in the person of Frederick II's son Conrad IV around 1243.

But the alliance of the son of al-Kamil, al-Salih Ayyub, with Berke Khan, ruler of the fierce army of the Khwarizmians (themselves displaced from the Black Sea coast by the arrival of the Mongols [see below, Part VI]) resulted in the furious sacking of Jerusalem in July 1244 and the shattering defeat of the Frankish army at La Forbie on October 18, a defeat that rivaled that of Hattin nearly six decades earlier. The sack of Jerusalem and the slaughter at La Forbie placed the problem of the Holy Land squarely on the agenda of the First Council of Lyons in 1245.

30. *Rachel suum videns*: Gregory IX Issues a New Call to the Crusade, November 17, 1234

Spurred on by the knowledge that the truce that Frederick II had signed with the sultan al-Kamil would expire in 1239, Gregory IX sent out copies of the bull *Rachel suum videns* in 1234 with instructions to preach the crusade throughout Christendom. His attempts to organize an Eastern crusade resulted in several expeditions to the Holy Land and one to the Latin Kingdom of Constantinople in 1239.

Under Gregory IX, the idea of universal participation in crusading, enhancing the role of crusade throughout all levels of Christian society and creating the opportunity for increasing the financing of crusades became prominent. The bull *Rachel suum videns* of 1234 reversed some of Innocent III's strictures on the taking of the crusade vow by the unfit. It was an expanded version of *Ad liberandam* (see above, No. 16). Next, Gregory turned to the mendicant orders, the Dominicans and Franciscans, for preachers and recruiters. By 1234 the ways in which an individual could be involved in crusading had extended to the financial redemption of vows, ecclesiastical taxation of clergy, alms donated to crusading individuals and armies, special liturgies, individual prayers, and acceptance of papal calls for peace between feuding powers. Some of these expansions of crusade participation generated severe criticism, exemplified here by the scorn of the English chronicler Matthew Paris, who was not alone. On the other hand, the lay spirit of devotion is reflected in the crusade songs written by Thibaut IV.

There are several novel departures in this bull, although it depends upon the Fourth Lateran Council's crusading decree *Ad liberandam* for some of its more specific measures. Gregory would also set other important precedents, including the first systematic commissioning of the mendicant orders as crusade preachers. The new Order of Friars Minor (OFM, Franciscans) and the Order of Preachers (OP, Dominicans) came into their own as unique instruments in papal service during Gregory's pontificate. The friars were to promote the crusade to every level of Christian society. However, the quest for universal participation in the crusading movement (whether on the domestic or on the foreign front) was not entirely new. Innocent III and the reformers he had appointed to preach the crusade had been accused of giving the cross to whoever desired it, regardless of their military expertise. In response to pressure from the episcopate and potential military leaders of the crusade, Innocent III abandoned this policy in *Ad liberandam*, which omitted all mention of indiscriminate signing with the cross and specifically reserved the plenary indulgence for those who participated in the crusade in person, sent substitutes, or served as a substitute. The Innocentian policy did not deter eager preachers and recruiters, as seen in James of Vitry's preaching to the women of Genoa on his way to Acre (see below, No. 65). For Innocent III those who merely contributed to the crusade were to receive a partial indulgence only.

In contrast, Gregory IX's organization of new crusades represents an attempt to utilize giving the cross to all comers and the redemption of the vows of the unsuitable in return for a cash contribution to the crusade as a deliberate and systematic means of ensuring universal participation in the crusading movement while preventing noncombatants from burdening the crusading army. This novel intention of partly funding the crusade through the collection of vow redemption fees influences the imagery employed in Gregory's crusade bull. Rachel, a figure who traditionally represented the contemplative rather than the active life, is used to appeal to means of participation in the crusade movement that could be shared by combatants and noncombatants alike, including crusading liturgies, prayers, lamentation, and financial sacrifice. While much militaristic imagery is still present, the audience is assured that intention is as important as the deed itself, an image crucial to justifying the grant of the plenary indulgence to those who would never journey to the Holy Land. Similarly, while *Ad liberandam* had attempted to distinguish between the categories of participants who would receive the plenary rather than a partial indulgence, *Rachel suum videns* deliberately eliminates the distinction between these categories and officially incorporates indiscriminate signing with the cross into the crusade recruiting process.

Michael Lower, The Barons' Crusade: A Call to Arms and Its Consequences *(Philadelphia, 2005); Christoph Maier,* Preaching the Crusades: Mendicant Friars and the Cross in the Thirteenth Century *(Cambridge-New York, 1994); Björn Weiler,* Henry III and the Staufen Empire, 1216–1272 *(Woodbridge UK, 2006).*

By BEHOLDING her Creator with the knowledge of true faith, that pious mother Rachel, the holy Roman Church, skillfully increased her prosperity and sons. Her grief over the slaughter of her offspring as boundless as the sea, she unleashed her cry of lamentation, wailing and mourning [Jer 31:15; Mt 2:17–18], and continues to unleash it to this day. We are

Source: Carl Rodenberg, ed., Epistolae saeculi XIII e regestis pontificum Romanorum, *selectae G. H. Pertz, 3 vols. (Berlin, 1883–1894), no. 605, 1:491–495.*

devoted to making this heard on high. Therefore, let the eyes of the faithful not be mute but shed the tears of sorrow by day and night, and let them not rest until the Lord shows mercy. For we ought to lament when the abode of the heavenly bread, Mount Sion, from whence the law went forth, the city of the great king, of which so many glorious things were said, that land, which the son of God consecrated with his own blood, shed for our sakes, has lost the best part of its excellence and its territory. We ought to weep, because she who was once free is now enslaved under the yoke of ungodly tyranny. We ought to mourn, because where once the host of the heavenly army celebrated peace through song, now in that very place a shameful throng of the most unclean people has arisen, and also dissensions and schisms. And by renewing the commencement of armed strife the enemy has extended their hand toward her valuables, exiling the order of priests and sacred things, godly laws, and the very laws of nature from the temple of the Lord, and instituting contrary abominations and filthinesses in their stead. And for this very reason, in the midst of her enemies Jerusalem has become soiled, as if polluted by menstrual blood, mocked during her Sabbaths [Lam 1:7, 10].

For although not long ago through our most beloved son in Christ, Frederick, always august emperor of the Romans, illustrious king of Jerusalem and Sicily, the same city was restored with the exception of the Lord's temple, nonetheless because the omnipotent God did not at that time deign to deal more generously with the Christian people, the aforesaid emperor entered into a truce with the sultan. The expiration of that truce is so very near, that it is believed that the intervening time is barely adequate for preparation, unless we hasten to ready whatever is necessary through promptitude, hope, and fervor of faith.

Therefore let no one grow weary of undertaking a pilgrimage in aid of the Holy Land and to fight for one's homeland with hope of victory for the sake of a crown, to die for the sake of life, to endure hardships and disagreeable things for a time for the sake of him who, disgraced by ruin, bespattered with spittle, battered by blows, tormented by scourging, crowned with thorns, suffered himself to be arraigned before Pilate as one guilty of a host of crimes, and at last, after having been crucified and drunk vinegar, after being pierced by a lance, sent forth his spirit with a loud cry for the sake of restoring the human condition, finishing the race of this present life filled with insults. For this is he, who, so that we might seek out higher things, wondrously removed himself from the throne of his father's glory in heaven, and descended to the depths of our mortality.

God did not disdain to become man, the Creator to become the created. The Lord took up the form of a servant [Phil 2:7–8], so that we who could not hope for pardon through our own righteousness, pursued by this unheard-of grace, might on the other hand, as heirs to God, coheirs with Christ, obtain fellowship with divinity, and participation in eternal blessedness.

And although through the blessing of our adoption we might daily accumulate charges of ingratitude, he nonetheless abounds in the riches of parental love. For taking into account differences in dispositions, strengths, and abilities, he offers to those offending him various ways of making satisfaction according to circumstances. And he rouses the weary by restoring them with manifold remedies, when he allows the land in which he chose to be born, to die, and to rise again to be occupied by the infidel for so long for the training of the faithful. For the hand of the Lord does not fall short [Is 59:1] nor is his power in any way diminished. No, on the contrary, just as he created everything from nothing, so he could free it in an instant. But he uses those occasions to seek out compassion and love from mankind, just as he himself first wanted to be despised, abandoned, and condemned by man in order to demonstrate the end of every consummation and the fullness of the law [Mt 5:17]. And so by no means would he have permitted impious hands to be strengthened against the godly until the present time, unless he also foresaw that his own injury would be revenged by our being confounded and our discipline would be preserved by his own victory. Unless this plank had drifted to them, there were very many given over to luxury who would otherwise not be able to make satisfaction for the extent of their offenses and who would have despaired utterly as if shipwrecked in the depths of their wickednesses. For through this opportunity, this shortcut placed before them, they were slain briefly in their souls for Christ's sake and so fulfilled the equivalent of penances requiring many portions of time. In fact, many, longing to discover the place where the Lord's feet once stood, first attained the prize without running the race or afterward achieved the martyr's crown without dying by the sword [cf. 1 Cor 9:24–25; 2 Tm 4:7–8; Apoc 2:10, 4:4, 4:10]. For, when rewarding his soldiers, he regards the intent alone in what is offered.

Therefore, so that on this account the aforementioned faithful might be purified more powerfully and effectually, we, by the mercy of the omnipotent God and the authority of the blessed apostles Peter and Paul entrusted to us—by which, to us, albeit unworthy, the Lord entrusts the power of binding and loosing—grant an indulgence and promise an increase in eternal salvation as the righteous's reward to all who truly undertake this labor with contrite heart and oral confession. However, to those who will have gone to the Holy Land not in their own person, but simply through their expenses we grant an indulgence according to their resources and the quantity of their aid and the state of their devotion, also to all who will have suitably given from their possessions in aid of the same land.

In addition, we receive under our protection and that of Saint Peter the persons and possessions of those individuals, from the time at which they shall have taken the cross. And surely the same individuals shall remain under the protection of the archbishops, bishops, and all the prelates of the church of God, who shall ensure that until their death or return is most certainly established, they shall remain unharmed and continue unmolested. Furthermore, those prelates of the churches who might be negligent in showing justice to those who have taken the cross and their households should know that they will be severely punished. For if anyone should presume the opposite, he ought to be restrained by the prelates of the churches through ecclesiastical censure without right of appeal.[2]

If indeed there are those who are setting out for that place who are tightly bound by an oath to pay interest, we command that their creditors are to be compelled by the same punishment to remit the oath of surety and desist from the exaction of interest. And if anyone will have been coerced by his creditors to pay interest, we order that they be forced by a like censure to restore it to him. In fact we command Jews to be compelled through secular power to remit interest to the same. And until they will have repaid it to them, they are to be utterly denied association with the entire faithful of Christ both in trade and other activities through the sentence of excommunication. Certainly to those who cannot pay their debts to Jews at the present time, secular rulers ought to provide a useful delay in such a manner that, from the point at which they have begun their journey until their death or return is most certainly ascertained, they ought not to incur the losses associated with paying interest. The Jews ought to be constrained to reckon and repay the yields which they have received in the mean time from the crusaders' pledges, after deducting

2. That is, those who breach the rights of *crucesignati* and their households should be restrained by judicial punishments levied by prelates, including excommunication or interdict.

necessary expenses, since a benefit of this kind ought not to seem to have many associated injuries, for the payment is deferred in such a way that it does eat up the debts.[3]

Moreover, so that assistance may be more easily devoted to the Holy Land by being divided into many forms, we implore each and every person through the Father, Son, and Holy Spirit, the one true and eternal God, requesting as Christ's representative on Christ's behalf, from archbishops and bishops, abbots and priors, and the chapters of both cathedral and other conventual churches, and from the clergy as a whole, and from cities, towns, and villages besides, that they speedily send a fitting number of fighters with necessary expenses according to their own resources in aid of the Holy Land. And if any one person does not possess sufficient resources to do this, let many join together as one. Because we believe with certainty that persons will not be lacking if expenses are not wanting, we request this very thing from kings and princes, counts and barons and other magnates, who perhaps will not themselves be personally undertaking the journey overseas in the service of the Crucified. Certainly we call for assistance in the form of seagoing ships from maritime cities. And assuredly we are prepared to grant dispensations to clerics in matters essential to this business. With all opposition ceasing, for the sake of this undertaking they may mortgage the income of their benefices for up to three years as a pledge for a loan, in such a way that those to whom they will have been led to entrust or even mortgage it may receive the income of the aforesaid benefice within the prescribed time in its entirety, as they themselves would have received it if they were personally resident in the churches in which they possessed the revenues.

Surely assistance to the Holy Land would be greatly hindered or delayed if it were necessary to examine everyone before permitting them to take the cross, as to whether they were suited and possessed sufficient resources for fulfilling this kind of vow in person. And so we grant, that

---

3. That is, from the moment that they leave for the Holy Land, crusaders should be granted freedom from interest and a moratorium on repaying the principle of the loan until their return. If they have taken out a loan in the form of a mortgage, the yields or rents from the land, property, herds, and so on, held by the lender should not be withheld from the crusader as a form of interest charged on the loan, but should be repaid to the crusader upon his return (after the deduction of necessary expenses), for just as the principle owed to the lender is not diminished by the moratorium, so the crusader should not lose out on the proceeds of what he has pledged. What Gregory is implying here is that these very proceeds will be essential for the crusader to repay the principal of the debt (as well as financing his/ her participation in the crusade).

with the exception of the regular religious, whosoever desires it may take the sign of the cross, on the condition that if pressing need or manifest usefulness should demand it, their vows may be commuted or redeemed or deferred by papal command. We therefore strictly command all the prelates of the churches, that in their jurisdictions, each one should assiduously admonish and move those who have put down the sign of the cross to resume it, and urge both these and others previously signed with the cross and those who thus far will have happened to be sealed with the sign of the cross to fulfill their vows to the Lord.

Moreover, because corsairs and pirates hinder aid to the Holy Land beyond measure by seizing and plundering those crossing the sea to that land and returning from it, we bind them and their employers, accomplices, and supporters with the chain of excommunication, forbidding under pain of anathema that anyone knowingly associate with them in any contract involving selling or buying, and enjoining the rulers of cities and their territories that they recall and restrain them from this wickedness. Otherwise, because to be unwilling to confound malicious men is nothing other than to support them, nor does one who forbears to oppose a manifest evildoer lack the secret guilt of association, we will take pains to exercise ecclesiastical severity upon their persons and lands, since such men oppose the Christian name no less than the Saracens. In addition, we renew the sentence of excommunication promulgated at the Fourth Lateran Council against those who deliver weapons, iron, and timber suitable for ships to the Saracens, whoever fulfills the office of pilot in the piratical ships of Saracens, or lends them any kind of counsel or aid in constructing war machines or anything else whatsoever to the detriment of the Holy Land. And we publicly decree that if they should be captured, that they be penalized both by the confiscation of their possessions and enslavement to their captors. And we command that sentences of this kind be publicly renewed throughout all maritime cities on Sundays and feast days. And the bosom of the church shall not be opened to men of this ilk, unless they send as assistance to the Holy Land everything which they will have received from such damnable commerce, so that with an equitable sentence they might be punished through that by which they transgressed. For even if perhaps they will not have made complete satisfaction by paying in this manner, others guilty of such things will be chastised, because through the punishment of these persons others will be prohibited from presuming to similar temerity.

Because surely in order to accomplish this business it is particularly necessary that the princes and Christian people observe peace among themselves, we decree and command, according to what was established in the general council,[4] that a peace be generally observed for at least four years throughout the entire Christian world, such that those quarreling with one another are led to inviolably observe a full peace or firm truce through the prelates of the churches. And if, perforce, there are those who refuse to comply, they are to be compelled to observe it most bindingly through excommunication upon their persons and interdict upon their lands, unless the malice of their injurers will have been so great that they ought not to enjoy peace. And if perhaps they should despise ecclesiastical censure, they should, not undeservedly, be afraid, lest through the authority of the church the secular power is invoked against them as disturbers of the business of the Crucified. Therefore let all the sons of divine adoption gird themselves in allegiance to Jesus Christ, transforming discord and strife into covenants of peace and love, in the firm conviction that if they will have been truly contrite and confessed, by the fruitful commerce of their labors, which will quickly pass away, they will purchase eternal rest.

31. Gregory IX to the Mendicant Orders, *Pium et sanctum*, 1234

While individuals from the mendicant orders had received commissions to preach the crusade, Gregory IX took the novel step of entrusting the preaching of many crusades to these orders as a whole, with instructions for them to appoint suitable individuals from among their own ranks. As a cardinal, Gregory had been deeply involved in his predecessors' promotion and protection of the mendicant orders and continued to foster their growth and spread as an antidote to the flaws of traditional religious orders and the inability of the secular clergy to cope with the demand for pastoral care, particularly preaching and confession. Aware that the decade-long truce Frederick II had arranged with al-Kamil of Egypt would expire in 1239, Gregory began preparations for a crusade with the crusade bull *Rachel suum videns* issued in 1234. Shortly afterward he sent out this letter to various leaders within the mendicant orders. Copies survive addressed to the Franciscan minister of Lombardy, the Dominican provincial prior of Tuscany, and the Franciscan minister of the province of Ireland. However, the criticisms of Matthew Paris and other evidence indicate that friars preached the crusade in England and

4. Fourth Lateran Council; see above, Part II.

other regions as well. The mendicant orders also began to provide military chaplains.

David Bachrach, "The Friars Go to War: Mendicant Military Chaplains, 1216–ca. 1300," Catholic Historical Review 90 (2004), 617–633. See also Maier, Preaching the Crusades.

To OUR beloved son, the minister of the province of Friars Minor in Lombardy, greetings and apostolic blessing.

The just and holy plan, which we conceived by divine inspiration concerning assistance for the Holy Land for the sake of general spiritual health and which we strive to bring into effect, you can observe plainly from our general letters. We consider the Franciscans fitting for performing the office of legate in this matter for the sake of Christ; and so we therefore admonish your devotedness, and entreat you in the Lord, commissioning you by strictly ordering you through this papal rescript that whichever two brothers of your order seem to you to be most suited for this business you enjoin on our behalf, that throughout the province of Lombardy they carry the word of the cross in humility of heart and body, and that they might move his faithful to avenge the injury of the Crucified. And they ought to expound assiduously and effectively, with diligent care and solicitous industry and exactness, all those things which pertain to the aid of the Holy Land, just as they are laid out in the general letters. If, however, something is offered to them for the assistance of the Holy Land, they ought to cause it to be carefully deposited in some religious place,[5] and the progress and the success of their care ought to be made known to us in writing at the end of the year; so that we might be able to know to what extent they have made progress in recruiting persons or materials allotted to this salutary business; and we will write back to them at our gracious pleasure.

32. Matthew Paris on Mendicant Preaching the Crusade, 1234–1236

During the early to mid-thirteenth century, those responsible for commuting the vows of the unfit were often not the same individuals involved in recruiting. A tenuous link between the arduous suffering implied in the crusade campaign and

Source: J. H. Sbaralea, ed., Bullarium Franciscanum, 4 vols. (Rome, 1759–1768), here 1:139, no. 146.

5. That is, in a local church or monastery.

the rewards of the plenary indulgence was therefore maintained since all who took the cross were technically liable to fulfill their vow for a considerable period after they took their crusade vows. However the offices of preacher, dispensator, and collector of crusade monies were combined when the mendicant orders were systematically entrusted with preaching the crusade by Gregory IX from 1234 onward, leading the Benedictine chronicler Matthew Paris to paint vitriolic portraits of recruiters who seemed to him intent more on mustering money than saving souls.

Matthew Paris (1200–1259) succeeded Roger Wendover in 1236 in writing the great chronicle of the monastery of Saint Albans, the *Chronica majora*, and other works, including interpolations in the text of Roger. Well-informed by the proximity and interest of the royal court and by visitors to the monastery (and to Matthew personally), as well as by his useful habit of obtaining copies of important documents and including them in the chronicle, Matthew's "chronological encyclopedia," as Richard Vaughan has described the *Chronica majora*, reflects the author's universal curiosity about all kinds of affairs, his suspicion about growing papal authority (especially when it seemed to interfere excessively in English affairs), his defense of the local (particularly his own monastery), his love of gossip and scandalmongering (especially when, as in the section here, it came to the mendicant orders), and his (even if grudging) admiration for some figures, notably the emperor Frederick II, otherwise universally condemned by most of his clerical contemporaries. But writers like Ricardo of San Germano and other Ghibellines of course regarded Frederick quite differently. Matthew was also a talented writer of narrative, skillful at dramatizing scenes, handling direct speech, and depicting believable characters. Although not at all a theorist or abstract thinker, Matthew Paris was remarkably capable of controlling a vast narrative of different kinds of events occurring all across Europe and the Mediterranean and presenting them vividly and memorably. As the cover of this book indicates, Matthew was also a gifted artist who provided his own illustrations to his text.[6]

As a Benedictine monk, Matthew resented the advent of the mendicant orders (their wandering lifestyle was antithetical to Benedictine enclosure) and their popularity as preachers and confessors, which diverted donations from traditional establishments and threatened to erode the spiritual authority and jurisdiction of the more-established monastic orders and diocesan clergy. A well-informed English monk who hotly resented papal intervention in local political and spiritual affairs, Matthew viewed with extreme suspicion any collection of crusade taxes (which seemed to enrich papal coffers rather than fund English crusaders) and papal attempts forcibly to commute crusade vows from one front to another or to convert the intent of personal participation to money donations to the crusade. Although many considered unfit by the leaders of the crusade continued to take

---

6. Björn Weiler, "Matthew Paris on the Writing of History," *Journal of Medieval History* 35 (2009), 254–278; Suzanne Lewis, *The Art of Matthew Paris in the "Chronica Majora"* (Berkeley-Los Angeles, 1987).

the cross and intended to fulfill their vows, the process of recruiting soldiers gradually became divorced from preaching tours intended to raise money through offerings, legacies, and vow redemptions during the mid- to late thirteenth century. Many of the innovations against which Matthew Paris was complaining represented attempts by the papacy to create new forms of taxation and fund-raising to support the crusades as well as to link the crusade to interior devotion. Matthew's real gripe is manifested in the peculiarly insular view of an English Benedictine who resented papal intervention in English affairs and viewed with extreme suspicion papal attempts to collect crusade taxes that did not seem to wind up funding English crusaders. Matthew's account is a good example of the increasingly wide variety of responses to crusading in the thirteenth century that Michael Lower and others see as one of is most prominent and important features.

The best study of Matthew remains that of Richard Vaughan, Matthew Paris *(Cambridge, 1958). See also, especially for Matthew's illustrations, Richard Vaughan, trans. and ed.,* The Illustrated Chronicles of Matthew Paris: Observations of Thirteenth-Century Life *(Cambridge UK-Dover NH, 1993). The standard Latin edition is that of H. R. Luard,* Chronica majora, *7 vols., Rolls Series (London, 1872–1884). The standard English translation (used throughout this book with some editorial revision) is that by J. A. Giles,* Matthew Paris's English History from the Year 1235 to 1273, *3 vols. (London, 1852–1854). On crusade preaching, see the Introduction, above, and the headnotes to Nos. 13 and 19. On the problematic situation regarding crusade financing and the commuting of vows, see Jessalynn Bird, "Innocent III, Peter the Chanter's Circle, and the Crusade Indulgence: Theory, Implementation, and Aftermath," in Andrea Sommerlechner, ed.,* Innocenzo III: Urbs et Orbis *(Rome, 2003), 1:503–524. See also the classic work by W. E. Lunt,* Papal Revenues in the Middle Ages, *2 vols. (New York, 1965). On preaching, see Maier,* Preaching the Crusades.

Matthew Paris describes the impact of *Rachel suum videns* in England, 1234

[MATTHEW Paris complains that both in the West and in the East the Christians were thrown into turmoil.] For the lord pope, seizing upon the pretext of the emperor's aforementioned persecution of him, contriving and multiplying his ingenious extortions, particularly in England, sent out everywhere his legates under the guise of simple nuncios (who nonetheless possessed the powers of legates), who collected money in many ways; now by preaching, now by begging, now by commanding, now by threatening, now by excommunication, now by demanding procurations. Throughout the kingdom of England they rendered countless people homeless and reduced them to beggary. And so that they might more effectively empty everyone's treasuries, and collect money everywhere as if for the assistance of the Holy Land (although in reality they wanted this money for their own), they arranged things so that they were appointed

Source: Matthew Paris, Chronica majora, ed. Luard, 3:279–280, 287–288.

as the dispensers of vows and collectors of money, not, however, in such a manner that the church ever detected their self-promotion. And the lord pope wrote to all the Christian faithful with these most eloquent words, which would have seemed able to pierce the stony hearts of men, except that the events which followed proved otherwise very clearly when viewed by the light of humility and righteousness. . . .

[THE TEXT of *Rachel suum videns* (see above, No. 30) follows.]

THESE things became known to the Christian faithful throughout the regions of Christendom, particularly in England, and especially through the brothers Preacher and Minor, who had been granted the power of signing with the cross and dispensing vows in return for money, so that they themselves signed with the cross many persons, a countless number. But within a short time, the Preachers and Minors became puffed up with such superiority, nay, shall I say arrogance, that they who had chosen voluntary poverty and humility, took pains that they be received in religious houses and cities with solemn processions, with banners, burning candles, and with an array of persons clad in feast-day vestments. And they were granted the ability to confer an indulgence of many days to their audiences, and those they signed with the cross today, tomorrow they absolved from their crusade vow in return for money. Within a short period of time, such a great commutation of vows was made, and so manifold was the exaction of money, that when it could not be discerned into what abyss had sunk such a great sum of money (which was collected by papal procurators), the faithful became indifferent to the business of the cross. Nay, I might rather say that the charity of all grew cold. And for this reason the business of the Holy Land never received productive assistance.

Further consequences, 1236

IN THE same year [1236] by papal order, a solemn preaching was made, both in England and France, by the brethren of the order of Preachers and Minorites and other famous clerks, theologians, and religious men, granting to those who would assume the cross a full remission of the sins of which they truly repented and made confession. These preachers wandered about among cities, castles, and villages, promising to those

Source: Giles, Matthew Paris's English History, *1:37–38.*

who assumed the cross much relief in temporal matters, namely, that interest should not accumulate against them with the Jews, and the protection of his holiness the pope for all their incomes and property given in pledge to procure necessaries for their journey, and thus incited an immense number of people to make a vow of pilgrimage. The pope afterward sent his familiar Master Thomas, a Templar, into England. He was commissioned to absolve those crusaders whom he chose and thought expedient from their vow of pilgrimage, on receiving money from them, which he considered that he could expend advantageously for the promotion of the cause of the Holy Land. When the crusaders saw this, they wondered at the insatiable greediness of the Roman court, and conceived great indignation in their minds, because the Romans endeavored thus impudently to drain their purses by so many devices.

For the preachers added, that if anyone, whether he had assumed the cross or not, should be unable in person to undertake such a toilsome journey, he must not omit to contribute as much of his property as his means permitted, for the assistance of the Holy Land, and thus he would fully enjoy the before-mentioned indulgence. But all these things rendered their hearers suspicious; for they said, "Will our dispenser prove faithful?" And so it turned out; for the pope, conceiving indignation against the people, made war, extorted money, collected a tenth part from all countries, and accumulated an enormous sum of money to defend the church, but peace was soon made, and he and the emperor became friends; the money, however, was never restored, and thus the devotion of many became daily weakened, and their confidence was abated.

33. The Lyrics of Thibaut IV, Count of Champagne and King of Navarre, ca. 1234–1239

Thibaut III died before the birth of his only son and heir, struck down by illness in the midst of preparations for the Fourth Crusade, of which he was expected to be the leader. Thibaut IV (1201–1253) was also an heir to a thriving culture of literary patronage in the court of the counts of Champagne, a culture in which he himself partook, earning himself the nickname of Thibaut le Chansonnier. Thibaut's mother, the widowed yet formidable Blanche of Navarre, placed her children under the protection of Philip Augustus of France, and Thibaut appears to have spent at least part of his youth at the court of the French king. As a powerful nobleman in his own right, Thibaut maintained a rather ambivalent relationship with his contemporary, the crown prince and future Louis VIII. While he participated in Louis VIII's royal crusade against heresy in Languedoc in 1226, Thibaut returned home despite the king's protests, after serving the minimum period of service required to acquit himself of his vow. Louis VIII died shortly thereafter of dysentery, leading to vicious rumors that Thibaut's besottedness with Louis's wife, Blanche of Castile, had led him to poison the king (see above, No. 7).

In fact, Blanche was temporarily alienated from the seemingly disloyal Thibaut, although their reconciliation shortly thereafter and Blanche's position as regent for the future Louis IX ensured that those barons who rebelled against royal authority in 1229 targeted Thibaut's territories in Champagne as well. With royal support, Thibaut managed to regain some semblance of peace in 1234, the year that he acceded to the throne of Navarre (his claim came through his mother, Blanche of Navarre, niece of the king of Navarre). Newly secure politically and financially, Thibaut followed the example of his father in taking the cross in response to Gregory IX's appeal for aid for the Holy Land in 1239. He appears to have composed most of his crusade songs before departing for the crusade from the port city of Marseilles in August of 1239. The Barons' Crusade, as it became known, provided an opportunity for Thibaut and his former rivals to collaborate in a common goal against shared enemies. However, once the expedition reached the Holy Land, divisions resurfaced, sabotaging the military success of the campaign. Thibaut nonetheless visited Jerusalem before returning to France in 1240.

Thibaut left a considerable body of poetic work, including crusade songs (*chansons de croisade*), which combined elements of satirical or political poetry with concepts of courtly love. In them, the call to save the Holy Land, expressed in terms of feudal duty and loyalty, conflicts with the bond of the lover with the beloved, in the tradition of earlier crusade songs. He also composed several songs to the Virgin Mary and a political poem chastising the pope for his struggle against Frederick II and his attempts to divert the participants of the Baron's Crusade from their original project of aiding the Latin Kingdom of Jerusalem to aiding the beleaguered Latin Empire of Constantinople.[7] Thibaut's poems illustrate the interchange of ideas concerning and images of the crusade between the aristocratic and ecclesiastical elites. Just as ecclesiastics including James of Vitry and the other recruiters whose works are included in this volume (see Nos. 13, 19, 70) used feudal imagery and appeals to chivalric (or mercantile) values in their harangues, so too aristocratic appeals in support of the crusade internalized or appropriated "ecclesiastical" motifs such as the image of the pelican (common in sermons) and attacks on clerical vice.

Thibaut's poems are translated in Kathleen J. Brahney, ed. and trans., The Lyrics of Thibaut de Champagne *(New York, 1989). Their place in crusade history has been evaluated by William Chester Jordan, "The Representation of the Crusades in the Songs Attributed to Thibaud, Count Palatine of Champagne,"* Journal of Medieval History *25, no. 1 (1999), 27–34. The best study of the crusade itself is Lower,* The Barons' Crusade. *For other aspects, see*

7. "Dex est ensi conme li pellicanz" (see below).

Michael Routledge, "Songs," in Jonathan Riley-Smith, ed., The Oxford Illustrated History of the Crusades *(Oxford, 1997).*

Seigneurs, sachiez, qui or ne s'en ira

Lords, be informed: anyone who will not go
To the land where God died and lived,
And will not bear the crusade cross,
Will hardly go to paradise.
Anyone who has pity and is mindful
Of the Supreme Lord, ought to seek vengeance
And deliver his land and his country.

All of the lowly will remain behind,
Those who love neither God, love, nor honor;
And each says: "My wife, what will she do?
Nor would I leave my friends at any cost."
Such men have fallen into foolish concerns,
For one has no friend except he who, without fear,
Was placed on the true cross for us.

Now the valiant knights will go forth,
Those who love God and the honor of this world,
And who rightly wish to go to God;
And the sniveling, the cowardly, will remain behind.
They are blind—of this I have no doubt—
Such a man never aids God during his life,
And for so little loses the glory of the world.

God let himself suffer on the cross for us,
And he will tell us on that day, when all men gather,
"You, who helped me carry my cross,
Will go where my angels are;
There you will see me and my mother, Mary.
And you from whom I never received aid,
Will all descend into the depths of hell."

Everyone thinks he will remain healthy
And that ill should never befall him;

Source: *Brahney,* Lyrics, *no. 53, pp. 226–229; no. 55, pp. 234–237; and no. 56, pp. 238–241.*

Thus the enemy and sin take hold of them,
Until they have neither sense, boldness, nor power.
Gracious lord God, take such thoughts from them
And put us in your country
With such holiness that we might see you!

Sweet lady, crowned queen,
Pray for us, Virgin of good fortune,
And henceforth no evil can befall us.

Au tens plain de felonnie

In a time full of wickedness,
Envy, and deceit,
Wrongs and outrage,
Without good or courtesy,
And when our barons
Make the whole world grow worse,
When I see excommunicated
Those who offer the most sense,
I wish to sing a song.

The kingdom of Syria
Cries out to us in a loud voice
That we repent,
For God's sake, for not going there,
For we only do great evil.
God loves fine, upright hearts,
From such men does he wish to receive aid;
They will exalt his name
And win back his house.

I still prefer, above all,
To remain in the Holy Land,
Than to go, a poor coward,
To a place where I would have no solace.
Philip, one must win
Paradise by having discomfort,
Or you will never have, indeed,
The well-being, pastimes, nor the laughter
To which you have become accustomed.

Love has run in search of prey,
And thus takes me, bound,
Into the hostel from which, indeed,
I would never seek issue,
If it were up to me.
Lady, Beauty's heiress,
[I want you to know:]
I shall never leave this prison alive;
Thus I shall die, a loyal *ami*.

Lady, it is fitting that I remain;
I never wish to part from you.
I've never hesitated
To love and serve you;
The love that assaults me so often
Is well worth death.
I await your mercy always,
For no good can come to me
Unless it is through your pleasure.

[Song, go and tell Lorent for me
That he guard himself most carefully
From undertaking the great folly
Of being found to be false.]

Dex est ensi conme li pellicanz

God is like the pelican
Who makes his nest in the highest tree,
And the wicked bird, who is so vile,
Comes from below and kills his offspring;
The father returns, distressed and grieving,
And kills himself with his beak. His sorrowful blood
Forthwith revives the fledglings.
God acted likewise through his passion:
With his noble blood he bought back his children
From the Devil who was of great power.

Recompense is difficult and slow in coming,
For no longer does anyone have goodness, justice, or pity,

Thus pride and deceit have the upper hand,
As well as wickedness, treachery, and debauchery.
Our state is indeed in great peril;
One must not take the example of those
Who love disputes and battles so much,
—To wit, the clerics who have renounced sermon-writing
For murdering and waging war—
Never have such men believed in God.

Our head causes great pain in all our members
And it is indeed fitting that we complain to God about it;
Our leader accuses our barons of great sins
Which he weighs upon them when any wishes to be of worth;
And people find fault with one another
For they know well how to lie and deceive;
They bring misfortune upon each other:
Whoever seeks evil will not fail to receive evil.
He who ardently expels small sins
Will not harbor great ones in his heart.

We should learn from the story
Of the battle of the two dragons
As found in the book of the Bretons,
In which the castle fell to the ground:
It is the world itself which will be overthrown
If God does not put an end to the battle.
One should call upon the powers of Merlin[8]
To divine what the outcome will be.
The Antichrist draws near, it is clear,
Waving the bludgeons of the enemy.

Do you know who the evil birds are
Who murder God and his children?
The *papelards*, whose name is well-suited—
They are indeed cruel, foul-smelling, and evil.
With their wicked words,

8. Thibaut here refers to prophecies associated with the figure of Merlin. Popularized by the widely diffused Latin works of Geoffrey of Monmouth, the figure of Merlin was also incorporated into various vernacular tales.

They slay the simple, God's children.
The *papelards* make the world tremble;
By God the Father, may evil befall them!
They have taken away joy, solace, and peace,
And will carry the burden of it into hell.

[God grant that we might serve him
And the Lady whom one must not forget;
May he always protect us
From the evil birds with venom in their beaks!]

34. Gregory IX to Frederick II, *Considerantes olim*, March 17, 1238

After negotiations for the reunion of the Greek church with Rome failed in 1237, Gregory IX wrote to Frederick II asking for his support for a crusade to bolster the threatened kingdom of Latin Romania. After the fall of Constantinople to the Latin crusaders in 1204, attempts to collect and dispatch money and men to the remnants of the Latin kingdom of Romania alternated with or accompanied negotiations with the Greek potentates whose rival kingdoms threatened its survival throughout the early and mid-thirteenth century. However, the demands of the eastern crusade, political rivalry in Europe, and the papal-imperial struggle prevented much of this aid from reaching the embattled Latin settlers. In 1238 Gregory and Frederick II were still on civil diplomatic terms, but Gregory's request that Frederick allow a crusading army to pass through his Sicilian territories on its way to Constantinople sat ill with memories of Gregory's anti-Frederician military activity in 1228–1229. Following the Greeks' recapture of Constantinople in 1261, negotiations for reunion with the Greek church intensified, leading to a formal, but again temporary, declaration of reunion at the Second Council of Lyons in 1274.

SOME time ago, the church of the Greeks was severed from obedience to its mother, the Apostolic See. From this schism it [the Greek church] appears to have parted with the life of the catholic faith, because it did not fear to be divided from its head, that is, the Roman church in which the Lord fixed the mastery of the faith and the entire ecclesiastical organization. Because no branch survives when it is detached from its root, nor can a member which is severed from the body retain life. And since the

Source: *Rodenberg*, Epistolae saeculi XIII, *1:623–624.*

church, as the spouse of Christ ought to be the one and only church, and there is no doubt that because it was founded upon blessed Peter, the prince of the apostles, any other church whatsoever which is organized outside this church or believes it is possible to be organized outside it, is certainly sundered from the life of the true faith and will fall into the death of heresy. Considering all this, we fear, with prescient deliberations, lest the aforesaid Greeks, whom the flood of schism swept from the church of God into the synagogue of Satan, overwhelmed by its raging fury, will be hurled into the abyss of heretical depravity.

After the example of the highest shepherd, we long to carry back the lost sheep into the Lord's sheepfold upon our own shoulders [Mt 18:12–14; Lk 15:3–7]. And so for this very reason we have sent brothers Preacher and brothers Minor [Dominicans and Franciscans] fully trained in the divine law, to Vatatzes, the so-called patriarch of Nicaea,[9] urging the Greek clergy, with paternal admonitions and entreaties, to rouse themselves from the sleep of death and, fleeing from the coming wrath, enlightened by the light of celestial splendor, reform themselves by rejoining the catholic union. And, as we learned from the truthful account of the same brothers, these very men setting forth various errors against the orthodox faith and stopping up their ears in the manner of vipers, could not be induced by any admonition that they ought to return to the path of ecclesiastical unity.

Troubled by strong sorrow over this, lest the heavenly power of uprooting and planting be entrusted to us to no purpose, against the aforesaid schismatic Vatatzes and his supporters, whose excommunication is pronounced by us once every year, because this kind of medicine cannot heal their wounds, not only for the aid of the Latin Empire of Constantinople but for strengthening and defending the catholic faith in the eastern regions, we caused many princes, barons and knights to be signed with the sign of the cross, following the example of the farmer in the gospel, who at first dug and broadcast manure around the sterile fig tree, yet unless it bore the expected fruit, cut it down the following season [Lk 13:6–9].

For this reason we ask Your Serenity by papal messenger and in writing, that you permit the aforesaid crusaders free passage through your

---

9. John III Doukas Vatatzes (r. 1221–1254) was not actually the patriarch, but rather the Greek emperor of Nicaea. The Greek patriarch of Constantinople, in exile at Nicaea (1223–1240), with whom Gregory IX corresponded in 1232 on attempts at reunion was Germanus II.

lands. However, as we understand, you set against our requests the objection of the difficulty this would involve. And so we are thus led, as if for a second time, to more carefully admonish and invite Your Imperial Highness, that you sagaciously attend to what degree damage will be done to your good reputation among men and to your soul before God by refusing this kind of transit, in that you would appear to foster the error of the aforesaid schismatics, and we ask that you concede to the crusaders seeking to succor the city of Constantinople free and safe passage through the aforementioned land and empire. Otherwise, it behooves you to realize that the church cannot overlook with winking eyes what should happen to be attempted for the overthrow of the catholic faith.

So then, in order to better and more effectively promote this business, we are led to send to your presence our beloved son, our notary and subdeacon Master Gregory, a man particularly prudent and experienced. And we ask more intently that you look upon the same with a fair eye, and that you would acquiesce more to his admonitions or rather to ours, and that you would desire to trust and efficaciously put into effect those things which he will have said to you on our behalf, and that after that you will nonetheless write back to us concerning the pleasure of the imperial will.

35. Matthew Paris: Richard of Cornwell on Crusade, 1245

This and the following two excerpts are taken from Matthew Paris's *Chronica majora*, reedited from the Giles translation. Matthew was an unusually well-informed chronicler, partly because his monastery, Saint Albans, was uniquely located near London and the royal court. Matthew appears to have acquired documents and eyewitness information from Richard of Cornwall personally or from his entourage, as the accounts below and Matthew's own bias against the French barons' crusade (derived largely from Richard of Cornwall, who wished to highlight his own achievements) illustrate.

N. *Denholm-Young*, Richard of Cornwall *(Oxford, 1948); Christopher Tyerman*, England and the Crusades, 1095–1588 *(Chicago, 1988); Lower*, The Barons' Crusade; *Weiler*, Henry III and the Staufen Empire.

Richard of Cornwall takes the cross, 1239

ABOUT the same time, namely on the morrow of Martinmas Day [November 12, 1236], the crusading nobles of England met at Northampton to arrange plans for starting on their expedition to the Holy

Land, and, in order that their honorable vow might not be impeded by
the cavilings of the Roman church, nor be turned aside for the shedding
of Christian blood, to Greece or to Italy, as had been hinted to them was
intended, all swore to set out in that year to the Holy Land, to liberate
the holy church of God. The first among them all to swear was Earl Richard, who took the oath on the great altars in All Saints' church, in the
middle of the city. After him Earl Gilbert Marshal repeated the same oath,
on condition that he should previously become reconciled to the king.[10]
But Earl Richard said to him, "Do not on that account fail to take the
oath, my dear brother-in-law, for the weight of that business I take upon
myself." Next came Richard Seward, and after him Henry de Trubleville,
and a great many nobles too numerous to mention, who all, with one
impulse and one mind, prepared themselves for the service of the cross.

Frederick II writes to Richard of Cornwall, 1238:
Departure and route

FREDERICK, by the grace of God, emperor of the Romans, ever Augustus,
and king of Jerusalem and Sicily, to his beloved brother-in-law Richard,
earl of Cornwall, health and sincere affection.—The general advantage of
the Holy Land, which depends on the exertions of the crusaders, often
induces us, by warnings and entreaties to them, to urge the postponement
of the passage of the crusaders in the kingdom of France and other parts
of the world until the predetermined time of the truce, namely, from the
month of August next ensuing till the end of the following year [1239],
since we think that it will be expedient for assisting the said land, and to
the advantage and honor also of those crossing over to it, that the passage
of such a numerous host should take place at an opportune time, namely,
after the next festival of Saint John the Baptist [June 24] until that same
feast in the following year.

And we ought not to pass over this in silence, since the burden of
the business for the liberation of the said country lies on our shoulders
more than on any other of the princes of the world. And for that purpose

Source: *Giles,* Matthew Paris's English History, *1:239, 117–118, 289–290, 303, 314–*
315, 363–367.

10. Gilbert Marshal was Richard's brother-in-law and one of the most important barons opposing the policies of Henry III during the Barons' Revolt. Richard's response indicates one of the most important domestic functions of crusading—the reconciliation of even
the most severe disputes before starting off.

we are bound to afford assistance and to spend our money. So that by this delay we may fully weigh all the circumstances, without omitting any contingencies by previously taking advice, when they [the princes] themselves are perfectly prepared for the service of Christ. Those persons who have devoted their hearts and bodies to the service of the cross and desire to give advantageous assistance to the Crucified One, having been asked on this matter by our messengers and letters, have prudently and wisely replied to our suggestions that, until the expiration of the before-mentioned truce they would comply with our request. Wherefore, with many thanks we have approved of the wisdom evinced by their reply; wherefore, as we with brotherly affection desire to see you in person and to procure you an honorable passage, we wish and beg of you, if you live, at a convenient time to make your passage through our kingdom of Sicily, because it would not be agreeable to us if you were to take your journey any other way without seeing us, and especially since our kingdom is so situated that a more easy and convenient passage is afforded through it to the transmarine countries.

In 1240 Richard visited the monastery of Saint Albans, then went to London to take leave of his brother the king. He proceeded across the channel to France, where he was welcomed lavishly and guided to the Rhône valley, down which his army sailed through Avignon, Vienne, and Arles. He stopped at Toulouse, where he bestowed an endowment on the Cistercians and asked for their prayers.

Richard is forbidden to depart, 1240

WHEN Earl Richard arrived at Saint Giles's, he was met by a legate and the archbishop of Arles, who forbade him by authority of the pope to set sail. At which the earl was greatly astonished and replied that he once believed in the words of the apostolic see and in the preachers whom it sent. But being greatly vexed at this prohibition, he said, "I have made all the necessary preparations for my passage, I have bidden farewell to my friends, I have sent my money and arms in advance of me, and I have got my ships ready and loaded them with provisions, and now the tone is altered. But as I have arrived at the seacoast and am about to embark, the pope, who is called the successor and vicar of Jesus Christ, who is said never to have broken his word, forbids me to proceed on the service of Christ, although I am now ready for all emergencies."

The legates, then, seeing that they could not prevent his setting sail, advised him to leave the port of Marseilles and to put to sea from the port of Aigues Mortes, which latter place was abhorred by the whole army, owing to its foul and sickly state, and they therefore dissuaded the earl from doing so.[11] He therefore, despite the false and ambiguous arguments of the legates, and detesting the duplicity of the Roman church, with great bitterness of spirit, adhered to his purpose of sailing from Marseilles. He then went, in the first place, to the port of Roche, where he prepared and loaded his ships. He also sent word to the emperor by special messengers, namely, the knight Robert de Twenge and others, informing him of his condition and the pope's cunning devices. And on the week before the octaves of the Nativity of Saint Mary, he put to sea.

The letter from the Templar master Hermann of Perigord: Good news from Damascus in 1240

BROTHER Hermann of Perigord, by the grace of God, humble master of the poor knights of the Temple, to his beloved brother in Christ, Master Robert Sandford, preceptor of the house of the said knights in England, greeting in the Lord.

We have to inform your community that the Christian army had lain for a long time on the sand, weary and inactive, and could not decide what course to hold or what to do, until the Lord, rising on high, has visited it—not owing to the urgency of its merits, but in the clemency of his usual mercy. For the sultan of Damascus, not through fear of the Christians, but by the miraculous intervention of the Lord, has restored to the Christian power the whole of the country entire, from the river Jordan, with this covenant and agreement between the two parties, namely, that the one shall assist the other to the utmost of his power in defending their country against the sultan of Babylon, neither party to make terms with the said sultan without the other's agreeing to it. This agreement was received with unanimous consent. Blessed be God for all things, who has effected this. . . .

THE MESSENGER who brought this good news from the Holy Land met the fleet of Earl Richard making a prosperous voyage. He also announced that the sultan of Damascus most certainly purposed receiving the rites of baptism.

Richard's fleet landed at Acre on October 11, 1240, and was received with great ceremony and exultation. He commanded all crusaders to remain in the Holy

---

11. The name Aigues Mortes means "dead waters," a port avoided by other crusaders as well.

Land, and if they had no money, he himself would pay for their services. Matthew Paris then goes on to describe what he considers to be the psychological collapse of the French crusaders in and out of captivity.

The French barons, confounded, leave for home, 1240

ABOUT the end of the year [1240], the innate nobility of mind of the French declined and degenerated; for the king of Aragón, the count of Brittany, and some others of the French nobles in the Holy Land were indignant at the increasing fame of Earl Richard, while they became, as it were, a broken army and the relics of an already dispersed multitude. They were stirred up by stings of envy, and they despised the earl's youth, as well as his English birth, inexperience, and effeminacy. They therefore went secretly to the Saracen chiefs, without the knowledge of the army in general, and on receipt of a large sum of money from them granted them a truce for ten years. And then they secretly packed up their baggage, and, with their packsaddles filled with gold, went to the port of Jaffa and thus dishonorably left the Holy Land.

Richard of Cornwall sends home news, 1241

RICHARD, earl of Cornwall, and count of Poitou, to the noble, venerable, and well-beloved masters in Christ, Baldwin de Rivers, earl of Devon, the abbot of Beaulieu, and Robert, clerk, health and every good wish, with sincere affection.[12]

Of the great desolation and grief of which the Holy Land has long been the seat, and how difficult a matter has been its reparation and relief since the catastrophe of Gaza, wise men are sensible. And experience of the truth has reached those dwelling near, and report has carried to those at a distance. But since the present letter might disclose our secret if it is opened on the way to you, and might also give occasion to a sinister interpretation, many things would be explained in it which now sleep and lie concealed in the bottom of our heart. From the time when kings and kingdoms turned aside from Jerusalem, owing to its being divided and held by unjust possessors, we have been consumed with no small grief, and cannot altogether be silent, but must loose our tongue in bitter complaint, since there is no pleasant matter to occupy it. For the sword of compassion has pierced to our soul, so as not to be able to contain itself.

---

12. There is another translation of this and another relevant letter in Barber and Bate, *Letters from the East,* 135–140.

For some time past, indeed, in the Holy Land, discord has reigned instead of peace, schism instead of union, hatred instead of affection, and justice has been totally excluded. Of such seed there have been many planters in that land, and many have become collectors of fruit springing from it, but I hope they are now eradicated. And there is no one among all its beloved ones to console it. For twin brothers disagreeing in the bosom of their mother, whose business it was to defend her, becoming proud in their affluence, have nourished and fomented these humors at the roots and caused the branches of it to spread far and wide. For an abundance of good things produces such an itching after mutual contention, that the reprimands of the father who presides over the see of Peter are encountered with the utmost indifference, provided that the stronger party dazzle the world with their renown.

To the pacification of these discordant parties we have applied no small portion of care, but as yet the footsteps of peace leave no impression, inasmuch as the followers of discord do not acquiesce in the words of peace. Those who have money easily allure others to them as long as the money lasts, but when the time for vindicating the modesty of their mother arrives, they leave the peacemakers, and, feigning secret impediments, show no regard to bring consolation to their mother. From this cause, and the great number of the Gallic cavalry, almost twice as numerous as the Saracens, but utterly prostrated by evil habits, the enemies of the cross were so unexpectedly encouraged that a small body of them thought little or nothing of our numbers. Owing to this, on our first arrival here the nobles who were thought likely to help us were taking their departure, and it appeared to be a serious and difficult matter to relieve the country.[13] Yet, the divine clemency, when it wills it, allows injuries to be without their remedies, and sorrow to be without means of consolation.

For when we were expecting our arrival here, in conjunction with the rest of the Christians, to the utmost of our power, as was incumbent upon us, according to our vow, to revenge the insults offered to the cross on the enemies of that cross, by attacking their territory and afterward occupying and restoring them to good condition, behold the king of Navarre, the then head and chief of the army, and the count of Brittany,[14] although aware of our approach for fifteen days before we arrived at Acre,

---

13. So far this letter in its extraordinary circumlocutions simply repeats Matthew Paris's blunt and insulting accusations in the preceding text.

14. That is, Thibaut of Champagne, the poet and king of Navarre, and Peter of Dreux.

took their departure with an immense host. Before they left, however, in order that they might appear to have done at least something, they made a kind of truce with an-Nasir, the lord of Kerak,[15] by which it was agreed that he should give up all the prisoners taken at Gaza, whom he had in his custody or power, together with some lands contained in the conditions of the truce, as security for which he gave his son and brothers as hostages, fixing on a term of forty days for fulfilling the terms of the truce.

Before that period, however, had elapsed, the said king and count departed, paying no heed to the time agreed on or to the terms of the truce. Within this said period, namely on Saint Dionysius's eve [October 8], we, as we have before informed you, arrived at Acre. And by the general advice of all, we at once sent to the aforesaid Nasir to ask him if he could observe toward us the truce he had made with the said king.[16] We received word in reply that he would willingly do so if possible, owing to his respect for the said king of Navarre, although he should gain little by it. We, therefore, by the advice of the nobles, awaited the completion of the term fixed on to see the result. At the expiration of the term, however, we received another message from him, stating that he could on no account abide by the aforesaid agreement. On hearing this, by the common consent of all, we betook ourselves to Jaffa to improve with all possible caution the condition of the Holy Land, which had deteriorated from the aforesaid causes.

At this place a man of rank and power came to us from the sultan of Babylon and told us that his lord was willing to enter into a truce with us if we pleased. After hearing and perfectly understanding what was to be set forth to us by him, and having with all sincerity invoked the grace of God, we, by the advice of the duke of Burgundy, Count Walter of Brienne, the master of the Hospitallers, and other nobles, in fact, the chief part of the army, agreed to the terms of truce. Although at our first arrival this appeared to be a difficult matter to accomplish, it is yet a praiseworthy one, and productive of advantage to the Holy Land, since it is a source of delight and security to the poor people and to travelers, advantageous and agreeable to the middle classes of the inhabitants, and useful and honorable to the rich and to religious men. Nor did it appear to us, on looking at the melancholy condition of surrounding events, that we could then employ ourselves more advantageously than in releasing

15. An-Nasir Dawud of Kerak, lord of the Transjordan.
16. Thibaut of Navarre/Champagne.

the wretched prisoners from captivity, since there was a deficiency of men and matériel (although we alone still had money about us), and profiting by the time of truce to strengthen and fortify against the Saracens the cities and castles that had fallen into ruin.

Richard recounts the fortification of Ascalon and the voyage home, 1241

As SOON as the aforesaid truce was arranged, we took our way to Ascalon, and that the time might not hang idly on our hands, by the advice of all the Christian chiefs, we began to fortify a large castle. From that place we sent messengers to the sultan of Babylon, to make him swear to observe the same truce, if he would do so, and at the same time to send the aforesaid prisoners.[17] The sultan, however, for what reason we do not know, detained our messengers, without giving us any reply, from Saint Andrew's Day [November 30] until the Thursday after Candlemas Day [February 2]. But during this time, as we afterward found by his letters, he, by the advice of his nobles, swore to keep the same truce. During all this time, we remained at Ascalon, assiduously intent on building the aforesaid castle, which, by God's favor has in a short time progressed so far that at the time of dispatching this letter, it is already adorned and entirely surrounded by a double wall with lofty towers and ramparts, with four square stones and carved marble columns, and everything which pertains to a castle, except a fosse round it which will, God willing, be completed without fail within a month from Easter Day.[18]

And this was not done without good reason. As we could not be certain that the truce would be confirmed, we thought it best to employ our time in building and fortifying this castle, so that, if the truce should be broken by any casualty, we might have, in the march and in the very entrance of their territory, this place, which was formerly under their dominion, as a safe and strong place of refuge if it were necessary for us to retreat there. And those who remained therein would have no occasion to fear the result of a siege. For although the besiegers could cut off all

17. The prisoners from the battle at Gaza. Richard also notes that he used part of the time to bury the bodies of slain crusaders at Gaza in a cemetery in Ascalon and endowed a daily mass for their souls. He counts the freed prisoners at "thirty-three . . . nobles, five hundred knights and pilgrims of the middle rank, and a great many knights and retainers of the Templars and Hospitallers."

18. On crusader castles and "everything which pertains to a castle," see Roni Ellenblum, *Crusader Castles and Modern Histories* (Cambridge-New York, 2007); and Hugh Kennedy, *Crusader Castles* (Cambridge, 1994, repr. 2001).

assistance and provisions from them by land, yet all the necessaries could reach them by sea. In times of peace, too, we believed that this castle would not be without its advantages, since it is the key and safeguard, both by land and sea, of the kingdom of Jerusalem, but will be a source of destruction and ruin to Babylon and the other parts of the country. On Saint George's day [April 23], then, after peace had been sworn to be observed on both sides, and after the truce had been confirmed, we received, according to the terms of the truce, all the Christian captives whom we had been so long expecting. After duly completing all these matters, we took leave of the Holy Land in peace, and on the festival of the Finding of the Holy Cross [August 18], we embarked at Acre to return home. But owing to the fair wind failing us on the voyage, and being much fatigued, we landed at Trapani in Sicily in the octaves of Saint John the Baptist [September 8].

36. Matthew Paris on Vow Redemptions in 1241

Here Matthew Paris complains about the common practice of assigning the crusade taxes and vow redemptions collected from a certain area to a noble crusader, who was expected to use them to fund either poor crusaders or an entourage of trained soldiers. In this instance, Richard of Cornwall, one of the wealthiest men in England, was collecting such funds long after his return from a crusade to the Holy Land.

AT THIS time [1241], in order that the wretched country of England might be robbed and despoiled of its wealth by a thousand devices, the Preacher and Minorite brethren, supported by a papal commission, in their preaching granted full remission of sins to all who should assume the cross for the liberation of the Holy Land. And immediately, or at least two or three days after they had prevailed on many to assume the cross, they absolved them from their vow on condition that they should contribute a large amount of money for the assistance of the Holy Land, each as far as his means would permit. And in order to render the English more ready and willing to accede to their demands, they declared that the money was to be sent to Earl Richard of Cornwall, and moreover, they showed a letter of his, for better security. They also granted the same indulgence to old men and invalids, women, imbeciles, and children, who

Source: Giles, Matthew Paris's English History, 1:359.

took the cross or purposed taking it, receiving money, however, from them beforehand for this indulgence, and showed letters testimonial from Earl Richard concerning this matter, which had been obtained from the Roman court. By this method of draining the purses of the English, an immense sum of money was obtained, owing to the favor in which Earl Richard was held. But we would here ask, who was to be a faithful guardian and dispenser of this money? For we do not know.

37. Matthew Paris: The Sack of Jerusalem, 1244

The crusades of Thibaut of Navarre/Champagne and Richard of Cornwall had helped to stabilize the remnants of the Latin kingdom of Jerusalem, but their efforts could not bring about a lasting solution to the bitter factions (pro-imperial, pro-Ibelin, and moderates) struggling to control its remaining territories (consisting largely of a narrow portion of the coast from Beirut to Ascalon, with the addition of Galilee, the county of Tripoli, and the principality of Antioch). Although Frederick II's son Conrad was technically heir to the throne of the Latin kingdom of Jerusalem, rivals within the kingdom united in using his coming to legal majority in 1243 to disregard the mandates of the imperial representatives ruling in his stead and entrust the care of the kingdom to a succession of local regents until Conrad should come in person to claim the throne.

Initially united in their opposition to Frederick II, the Templars and Hospitallers, backed by competing Italian commercial colonies, supported rivals within the Latin kingdom (the Ibelins versus the Filangieri) and pursued incompatible alliances with adjoining powers (the Hospitallers favored Egypt, the Templars Damascus). With the triumph of the anti-imperialists, the Templars took advantage of divisions within the Ayyubid political world. By pursuing an alliance with as-Salih Ismail, the sultan of Damascus, and his cousin an-Nasir Dawud of Kerak, they gained the restoration of Jerusalem to the order's control, a concession soon confirmed by as-Salih Ayyub, sultan of Egypt.

However, when war broke out between the rival sultans in 1244, the Latin Kingdom of Jerusalem, which had chosen to support Ismail of Damascus in return for a share of Egypt when it was conquered, was invaded by Khwarizmian mercenaries, who, after losing their leader Jalal ad-Din and territories in Persia to the Mongols, had entered the service of the sultan of Egypt. After a bloody, destructive, and successful march along the coast of Syria and Palestine, the Khwarizmians burst into the city of Jerusalem in the summer of 1244, while most of the Frankish army was away mustering in the vicinity of Acre.

The threat of advancing forces sent by the Franks' ally, an-Nasir, sultan of Kerak, allowed the Christian garrison of the citadel of Jerusalem to surrender in return for a promised safe passage to Jaffa, but the majority fell prey to bandits along the coastal roads. The walls of Jerusalem had been taken down in 1219, but the Khwarizmian forces virtually leveled the entire city. While the holy city was being sacked by its Khwarizmian invaders, a combined army of forces from Ayyubid Damascus, Homs, and an-Nasir joined with contingents from the Latin Kingdom of Jerusalem, advancing to meet the Khwarizmians and the Egyptian army at the village of Harbiya (La Forbie) near Gaza. The joint Ayyubid-Frankish army was roundly defeated by the Egyptian-Khwarizmian forces led by Rukn ad-Din Baibars, and shortly after, Damascus and then Ascalon and eastern Galilee fell to Ayyub's armies.

Matthew Paris includes in his chronicle a long, politically polemical letter from Frederick II to his brother-in-law and erstwhile crusader Richard of Cornwall, blaming the destruction of Jerusalem and the disaster at La Forbie on his political enemies and blaming the pope for failing to act in retaliation. But perhaps the letter of Brother Gerald of Newcastle, master of the Hospitallers, to M. de Merlaye offers a less partisan account.

Several of the letters translated here, as well as others from the period and occasion, are translated in Barber and Bate, Letters from the East, nos. 66–68, pp. 136–146.

To THE most potent lord M. de Merlaye, brother G., of Newcastle, by the grace of God, humble master of the holy house at Jerusalem and guardian of the poor followers of Christ, greeting:

From the information contained in our letters, which we have sent to you on each passage, you can see plainly enough how ill the business of the Holy Land has proceeded on account of the opposition which for a long time existed, at the time of making the truce respecting the espousing of the cause of the Damascenes against the sultan of Babylon. Now, wishing your excellency to be informed of other events since transpired, we have thought it worth our while to inform you that, about the beginning of the summer last past, the sultan of Damascus and Ismail Seisser, sultan of Cracy,[19] who were formerly enemies, made peace and entered into a treaty with the Christians, on the following conditions: namely, that they should restore to the Christians the whole of the kingdom of Jerusalem and the territory which had been in the possession of the Christians near the river Jordan, besides some villages which they retained possession of in the mountains, and that the Christians were faithfully to give them all the assistance in their power in attacking the sultan of Babylon. The terms of this treaty having been agreed to by both parties, the Christians began to take up their abode in the holy city, while their army remained at Gazara in company with that of the aforesaid sultan's, to harass the sultan of Babylon.

After they had for some time been engaged in that undertaking, the patriarch of Jerusalem landed from the transmarine provinces. After taking some slight bodily rest, he was inspired with a longing to visit the sepulcher of our Lord, and he set out on that pilgrimage on which we also accompanied him. After our vow of pilgrimage was fulfilled, we heard in the holy city that a countless multitude of that barbarous and perverse race, called Khwarizmians had, at the summons and order of the sultan of Babylon, occupied the whole surface of the country in the furthest part of our territories adjoining Jerusalem and had put every living soul to death by fire and sword. A council was held on this by Christians living in Jerusalem, and, since they did not have the power to resist these people, it was prudently arranged that all the inhabitants of the holy city, of both sexes and of every age, should proceed under escort of a battalion of our knights to Jaffa as a place of safety and refuge.

On that same night, after finishing our deliberations, we led the people cautiously out of the city, and had proceeded confidently half the distance to Jaffa, when, owing to the intervention of our old and wily enemy the Devil, a most destructive obstacle presented itself to us. For the Khwarizmians raised on the walls of the city some Christian banners which they found left behind by the fugitives, in order by these means to recall the unwary, by making them believe that the Christians who had remained behind had defeated their adversaries. Some of our fellow Christians hurried after us to recall us, comforting us with pleased countenance and declaring that the banners of the Christians, which they well recognized, were raised on the walls of Jerusalem in token that they had defeated the enemy. And they, having been thus deceived, deceived us also. We, therefore, in our exultation, returned confidently into the holy city, thinking to dwell there safely. And many others from feelings of devotion, and others in hopes of obtaining and retaining possession of their inheritances, rashly and incautiously returned, either into the city itself or into the suburbs. We, however, endeavored to dissuade them from this altogether, fearing treachery from these perfidious people, and so we went away from them.

Not long after our departure, these perfidious Khwarizmians came in great force and surrounded the Christians in the holy city, making violent assaults on them daily, cutting off all means of entry and exit to and from the city, and harassing them in various ways, so that, owing to these attacks, hunger, and grief, they fell into despair. All by common consent exposed themselves to the chances and risk of death by the hands of the enemy. They therefore left the city by night and wandered about in the trackless and desert parts of the mountains until they came at last to a narrow pass, and there they fall into an ambuscade of the enemy, who, surrounding them on all sides, attacked them with swords, arrows, stones, and other weapons, slew and cut to pieces, according to a correct computation, about seven thousand men and women and caused such a massacre that the blood of those of the faith, with sorrow I say it, ran down the sides of the mountains like water. Young men and virgins they carried off with them into captivity and retired into the holy city, where they cut the throats of the nuns and aged and infirm men like sheep doomed to the slaughter. These, unable to endure the toils of the journey and flight, had fled to the church of the Holy Sepulcher and to Calvary, a place consecrated by the blood of our Lord, thus perpetrating in his holy sanctuary such a crime as the eyes of men had never seen since the commencement of the world.

At length, as the intolerable atrocity of this great crime aroused the devotion of all the Christians to avenge the insult offered to their Creator, it was agreed, by the common consent of all, after asking assistance from heaven, to arrange ourselves in order and give battle to these treacherous people.[20] We accordingly attacked them and fought without resting from early in the morning till the close of the day, when darkness prevented us from distinguishing our own people from our enemies. Immense numbers fell on our side, but four times as many of our adversaries were slain, as was found out after the battle. On the following Saint Luke the Evangelist's Day [October 18], the Knights Templars and Hospitallers, having recovered breath and invoked assistance from above, together with all the religious men devoted to this war, and their forces and the whole army of the Christians in the Holy Land assembled by proclamation under the patriarch and engaged in a most bloody conflict with the aforesaid Khwarizmians and five thousand Saracen knights who had recently fought under the sultan of Babylon and who now joined these Khwarizmians. A fierce attack was made on both sides, since we could not avoid them, for there was a powerful and numerous army on both sides of us. At length, however, we were unable to stand up against such a multitude, for fresh and uninjured troops of the enemy continued to come upon us, since they

20. That is, the battle at La Forbie.

were ten times as numerous as we. And we, weary and wounded, and still feeling the effects of the recent battle, were compelled to give way, abandoning the field to them, with a bloody and dearly bought victory, since greater numbers fell on their side than on ours.

We were so assisted by him who is the Savior of souls that not a hundred of us escaped by flight, but, as long as we were able to stand, we mutually exhorted and comforted one another in Christ, and we fought so unweariedly and bravely to the astonishment of our enemies. We were at length taken prisoner, which, however, we much tried to avoid, or fell slain. Hence the enemy afterward said in admiration to their prisoners, "You voluntarily threw yourselves in the way of death. Why was this?" To which the prisoners replied, "We would rather die in battle, and with the death of our bodies obtain glorification for our souls, than basely give way and take to flight. Such people indeed are greatly to be feared." In the said battle, then, the power of the Christians was crushed, and the number of slain on both sides was incalculable. The masters of the Templars and Hospitallers were slain, as also the masters of other orders, with their brethren and followers. Walter, count of Brienne, and the lord Philip of Montfort, and those who fought under the patriarch were cut to pieces. Of the Templars, only eighteen escaped, and sixteen of the Hospitallers, who were afterward sorry that they had saved themselves. Farewell.

38. On Help for the Empire of Constantinople, from the First Council of Lyons, 1245

Pope Gregory IX died in 1241, by then locked in implacable hostility with Frederick II. He was succeeded by the short-lived Celestine IV (October–November 1241). After a nearly two-year delay partly caused by Frederick's opposition, Celestine IV was succeeded by the Genoese canon lawyer Sinibaldo Fieschi, who took the papal name Innocent IV (1243–1254). Embroiled in the conflict with Frederick II and appalled by the news of the destruction of Jerusalem by the Khwarizmians and the slaughter at La Forbie in 1244, Innocent had to deal also with the problem of the Mongols (see below, Part VI) and the Latin empire of Romania as well. After much difficulty, he called for a church council to assemble at Lyons in 1245. The canons of the First Council of Lyons include the formal deposition of Frederick II, but they also attend to other important matters like the infinite detail of crusade recruiting and financing illustrated here.

On the apocalyptic literature and its association with the Mongols, see Bernard Hamilton and C. F. Beckingham, Prester John: The Mongols and the Ten Lost Tribes *(Aldershot UK-Burlington VT, 1996).*

Canon 2: Concerning aid for the empire of Constantinople

ALTHOUGH our mind is engrossed with difficult affairs and distracted by competing concerns, yet among other things to which our attentive eye ought to pay heed, it particularly focuses the pupil of its consideration upon the liberation of the empire of Constantinople. It longs for this with burning desire and is busied with the burden of planning in this respect. Yet although the Apostolic See ardently pursued this very thing by exerting great diligence and applying the remedy of varied forms of assistance, and for a long time catholics have striven for this (not without grievous hardships and burdensome expenses and troublesome toils and with the outpouring of bloodshed), the right hand of such great assistance (impeded by its sins), has not been able to rescue entirely that same empire from the bonds of its enemies. And on account of this we are stirred up, not without good reason.

However, from the loss of the aforementioned empire, the body of the church would incur the brand of shameful deformity on account of a missing member, and would endure the affliction of painful debility. If it were deprived of the suffrages of the faithful and abandoned for its enemies to openly overpower it, this disaster could be attributed rightly to our inactivity and that of the church itself. And so we resolve with powerful purpose to assist the same empire with effectual and swift aid, so that the church rising up zealously to relieve it and extending a protecting hand, it might simultaneously be able to wrest that same empire from the tyranny of its enemies and by the Lord's power lead it back to the unity of the same ecclesiastical body. After the crushing hammer of its enemies it might feel the comforting right hand of the mother church, and after the blindness of mistaken assertion, might recover its sight by possession of the catholic faith. And so for this reason it is appropriate that the prelates of churches and other ecclesiastics appear more vigilant and attentive in freeing this empire and set an example both in service and material assistance. In addition they are bound to attend to the increase of the same faith and ecclesiastical liberty which may chiefly be achieved through

Source: J. Alberigo et al., eds., Conciliorum oecumenicorum decreta, *3d ed. (Bologna, 1973), 295–296.*

a liberation of this sort; particularly since when the aforesaid empire is aided, assistance is given to the Holy Land as a consequence.

Certainly so that there might be speedy and useful relief for the afore-mentioned empire, we decree with the universal approval of the council, that half of all incomes be devoted to the aid of the same empire, both from dignities and parsonages and also ecclesiastical prebends and other benefices of those ecclesiastics who do not personally reside in them for at least six months of the year, whether they should possess one of them or many (with the exception of those who are occupied in serving us or our brothers or their prelates, or are engaged in pilgrimage or studying at the schools or attending to the affairs of their churches by the command of the same, or have taken or will take the sign of the cross for the afore-said Holy Land, or should personally depart in aid of the same empire). And if any of these same excepted, apart from those who have taken the cross and those setting out in person, should receive from their ecclesiasti-cal incomes more than the value of one hundred marks of silver, a third part of the remainder ought to be collected annually for the assistance of the same empire, through those persons who have been appointed by apostolic foresight for this task. And after having estimated honestly the sum to be collected for up to three years, you ought to confirm it by oath or some other form of surety, notwithstanding certain customs or statutes of local churches or whatever exemptions were granted to those churches or persons by the Apostolic See. And if perhaps anyone should deliber-ately practice deception in this matter, they shall incur the sentence of excommunication.

Certainly, from the revenues of the Roman church, having first deducted from them the tenth dedicated to the aforesaid Holy Land, we allot a full tenth for the assistance of the aforementioned empire. More-over, since if the same empire is helped, it furnishes the most useful aid to the Holy Land itself, and the recovery of the same is particularly pur-sued when the freedom of the same empire is worked for, by the mercy of the omnipotent God and the authority he entrusted to his blessed apostles Peter and Paul, from which is bestowed upon us, albeit unwor-thy, the power of binding and loosing, we grant to everyone assisting the same empire the pardon of their sins, and we wish the same persons to enjoy those privileges and immunities which are granted to those going in aid of the aforesaid Holy Land.

Canon 3: Admonition to be made by the prelates
to the persons entrusted to them

WE recognize that for the preservation of the enduring homeland [that is, Latin Romania], and on the other hand for the sake of redeeming that land which the son of God made holy by the shedding of his own blood [that is, the Holy Land], the entirety of the sons of the church have lavished for a long time not only innumerable expenses but an incalculable abundance of blood. And so for that very reason we are burdened with a sorrowful heart, by all that has for a long time befallen those who are opposing the impious fighting against the faithful in regions overseas.

Certainly on account of this the Holy See ought to exercise a most powerful vow. And so that by it the fulfillment of universal longing concerning the redemption of the Holy Land might be achieved by appeasing God, we are taking proper precautions to pray for the divine favor by rousing you to this business with our letters. Therefore we incite all of you and beseech you, exhorting you in the name of the Lord Jesus Christ, that to the extent you are able each of you ought to persuade by means of conscientious admonitions the faithful people entrusted to your care, either through your preaching or when you enjoin penance on them that in their wills (which they will have made according to their circumstances) they should leave something for the assistance of the Holy Land or the empire of Romania for the remission of their sins, granting for this a special indulgence, as seems expedient to you. And you ought to make very clear the provision that the money these persons will have given for aid of this nature is to be kept under your seals in predetermined places, preserving regard for due reverence of the Crucified, and that you diligently record in writing those things which will have been bequeathed for this in other forms. For you ought to more assiduously busy yourself in this work of piety, in which only the business of God is sought and the salvation of the faithful is procured, so that you might await untroubled the reward of heavenly glory from the hand of the celestial judge at the end of time.

PART VI
The Mongol Crusades, 1241–1262

The Mongol Empire and its expansion into China, eastern Europe, and the eastern Islamicate in the twelfth and thirteenth centuries turned the geopolitical world of Eurasia upside down. Assembled by a talented chieftain named Temujin (d. 1227), who overcame and absorbed neighboring peoples until in 1206 he was acclaimed Chinggis Khan, the empire expanded enormously under his sons and successors. His claim to world rule was based on earlier imperial nomadic steppe practices, but his highly selective adaptation of his various subjects' linguistic and administrative practices made his empire far more complex than earlier nomadic empires. Military rivalry with a neighboring people brought Chinggis Khan's generals across the Caucasus and into Georgia in 1223, crushed the Cumans and their Kievan allies, and brought the Mongols dramatically to the attention of both eastern Europeans and the Muslim world. Chinggis was succeeded by his son Ögödei (1229–1241), whose armies returned to the western steppes in 1235 and destroyed armies of Ukrainians, Poles, Hungarians, and others at Kiev in 1240 and at Liegnitz in 1241. Hungary, the Balkans, and Poland fell, and Gregory IX proclaimed a crusade against the Mongols in 1241 when again they withdrew eastward to the steppes.

The growing intensity of the conflict between Frederick II and the popes prevented the formation of any organized resistance to Mongol expansion, and for much of the central decades of the thirteenth century the Mongols shaped Western discussions of the crusade movement.

The letters and eyewitness accounts translated here represent but a fraction of the sources used by Matthew Paris and others for the fullest European chronicle accounts of the Mongols. Matthew's and others' impression of the Tartars was also heavily influenced by reports submitted by mendicant missionaries to the council of Lyons (1245), a letter purporting to be from the "king" of the Tartars, and correspondence from exiled prelates, monks, and friars forwarding news of the invaders and seeking spiritual and material assistance from Western ecclesiastics and secular magnates. Matthew Paris's descriptions of the Tartars were even accompanied by his own drawings, which emphasized their bestial and savage behavior, and his at times near hysterical tone indicates the terror their advent inspired in many in Western Christendom and the Latin kingdoms in the East. His and many contemporaries' conceptions and expectations of the Tartars were shaped by descriptions of the wondrous peoples and animals said to inhabit the Near and Far East (common in classical authors and medieval versions of the Alexander legend), including the monstrous races (identified with the biblical Gog and Magog) said to have been shut up by Alexander the Great behind the Caspian Gates. Their unleashing would initiate the harrowing of the earth in its final days prior to the advent of the Antichrist himself.

A competing and more optimistic legend was that of the Christian king Prester John, who, from the mid-twelfth century onward, was rumored to dwell to the east of Muslim-occupied territories and to desire to ally with Western Christendom in their annihilation.[1] In fact, the first reports of the activities of the Mongols to reach the West came in the form of prophecies regarding the aid expected from a mysterious "King David," which surfaced among the armies of the Fifth Crusade. They were publicized by James of Vitry and Oliver of Paderborn, among others present in the crusader camp, to Rome, England, France, and other regions in Western Christendom, and they influenced the army's disastrous decision to proceed toward Cairo. These accounts actually mixed components of the legendary Prester John with a composite of the recent conquests of the Christian Naiman king Küchlüg and/or Chinggis Khan (who had successfully attacked the Kara-Khitai and the Khwarizmian Empire as he assembled his own Mongol Empire), and ignited Western hopes for potential alliances with a Far Eastern power against the Muslims.

However, as further news regarding the Mongols' activities reached the West, doubts arose concerning their formerly assumed Christianity and their potential as allies against Islam. From the early thirteenth century onward, Hungary had attempted to come to terms with the Cumans on its borders by sending missions to evangelize them and by persuading some of their chiefs to swear fealty to the king of Hungary, to effectively serve as a buffer between Hungary and threats farther east. With the rise of Ögödei to power, the Mongols once again began their western advance, attacking western Asia, particularly the Volga River valley. From 1237 to 1238 a Mongol army under the general Batu attacked the Bulgars, Russians, and Cumans, forcing many to join their army, while others escaped to Hungary and joined with King Bela IV. By 1240, the Mongols had sacked Kiev, leading some Kievan princes to flee to Hungary and Poland with news of the Mongol conquests. Further attacks on Poland, Hungary, and eastern Germany in 1241 led to a growing realization that the Mongol threat must be checked, something stressed in a flood of letters from secular and religious authorities whose countries had been invaded or were threatened.

News of the Mongol people also began to trickle back via Dominican missions, including that of Friar Julian of Hungary, who traveled east toward the Mongol court as a representative of King Bela IV in 1234–1235 and 1237. The message he brought back from Batu's envoys was an ominous one: the Mongols were intent on conquering the world and bore a letter intended for Bela IV that accused him of harboring fugitive Cumans and detaining Mongol emissaries. Bela quickly forwarded the threats to various ecclesiastical and secular authorities, as did Julian, who brought news of his mission to Rome. However, although both Frederick II and Gregory IX knew of the Tartars by 1237 and had received pleas

---

1. F. Schmieder, "*Nota sectam maometicam atterendam a tartaris et christianis.* The Mongols as Non-believing Apocalyptic Friends Around the Year 1260," *Journal of Millennial Studies* 1 (1998), 1–11.

for aid from Queen Rusudan of Georgia (1239) and the Ismaili Assassins (1238) and promises from the Jacobites and Nestorians of reunion with the Roman Catholic Church in return for protection, the papal-imperial struggle prevented the muster of any effective aid. While Thibaut IV of Champagne, Richard of Cornwall, and other French and English barons were occupied in the Holy Land during the Barons' Crusade of 1239–1241, the Mongols invaded Poland, Bohemia, Saxony, Meissen, Moravia, and finally Hungary, defeating Bela IV's field army in the spring of 1241 and sacking the capital city of Buda. Pleas for assistance from Bela, Henry Raspe, landgrave of Thuringia, and the mendicant orders were quickly dispersed throughout Christendom, leading Frederick II and Gregory IX to publish public manifestos in which each blamed the other for the success of the Tartar invasion and the failure to mount an effective resistance. By 1242, the Mongols had crossed the Danube and had led raids across the Austrian border; only a lack of pasturage and the death of Ögödei (which led to a succession struggle within the Mongol world) resulted in the withdrawal of the Mongols' western armies and a brief respite for Latin Christendom.

Innocent IV called for an ecumenical council to assemble at Lyons in 1245. Its agenda included the papal-imperial struggle, the Mongols (perhaps ethnically related to a people known as "Tatars," and called in western Europe "Tartars"), and a crusade in aid of the Holy Land. In order to gather information about the Tartars and the state of the East before and immediately after the council, Innocent IV turned to the mendicant orders used by his predecessor Gregory IX in missionary efforts and negotiations with Eastern Christians to make contact with the Mongol world. He sent out John of Plano Carpini and Lawrence of Portugal (to approach the Mongols via eastern Europe), and Ascelino of Cremona, Simon of Saint Quentin, and Andrew of Longjumeau (to approach via the Near East), equipping them with letters both missionizing and diplomatic (intended for both the Mongols and other Christian churches in the East whom Innocent hoped to reunite with the Roman church). The Mongols promptly rejected the papal letters' invitation to convert and adopt a nonaggressive stance toward Christians. Because they believed in the universal sovereignty of the Great Khan, they instead issued ultimatums demanding the speedy submission of the pope and Christian magnates. Similar ultimatums delivered to the prince of Antioch and king of Armenia in 1244 (demanding tribute and slaves, among other harsh conditions) led the second to submit to Mongol overlordship (in part to escape Turkish domination) and the first to withhold his own forces from the Latin army protecting the Holy Land against the invading Khwarizmians.

Undeterred by the somewhat ominous reports from the early missions, Innocent IV sent out further mendicant missions to the Mongols. While engaged on his first crusade (1248; see below, Part VII), Louis IX had also been approached by Nestorian Christian emissaries from the Mongols with a letter from Eljigidei, praying for his success against the Muslims (which lacked the usual demand for personal submission), combined with an oral message stating that Eljigidei planned to besiege Baghdad the following spring in revenge for the attacks of the

Khwarizmians and hoped that the Franks would attack Egypt and prevent its forces from aiding the caliph of Baghdad. The emissaries also sought to link Güyük and Eljigidei to the legend of the Christian Prester John by stressing their conversion to Christianity and by pledging to help Western Christians free Jerusalem. Louis sent a return mission with gifts and letters led by Andrew of Longjumeau, but was shocked at the reply his legation received at the court of the regent Oghul Qaimish, widow of the recently deceased Güyük. Treating Louis's letter as an act of submission to bolster her uncertain rule, she sent the embassy back to Louis with a letter demanding Louis's personal submission and yearly tribute. Eljigidei may have been eager to ensure that the Westerners' crusades did not become directed toward previously Frankish territory that was currently under Mongol rulership (Louis had already sent troops to aid the prince of Antioch against the Turks, some of whom had gone into Cilician Armenia). Although further missionary (rather than diplomatic) envoys were sent out, notably one under William of Rubruck (who wrote a report to Louis IX circa 1255), the reports they carried back only worked to further undermine any lingering aura of the Prester John legend and eastern aid against the Muslims.

The prolongation of the papal-imperial struggle in the West continued to prevent any united response to the worsening situation in the Near East, where the Mongols had made gains in western Asia and Mesopotamia. The diplomatic reality which faced Western Christendom and the Latin settlements in the East was a difficult choice between allying with the various Muslim powers against the relatively unknown nature of Mongol ambitions, or chancing an alliance with the Mongols against the various powers of the Muslim world. Was a known enemy a better ally than an unknown force that potentially strove for world domination? Appointed head of armies in the Near East by his brother Möngke, the fourth Great Khan of the Mongol Empire (r. 1251–1259), Hülagü expelled the Assassins from Persia in 1256/7 and by 1258 had put an end to the Abbasid caliphate in Baghdad, which he captured and sacked with the aid of Eastern Christian allies, including Hetoum of Armenia and his son-in-law, Bohemond VI of Antioch. Hülagü's execution of the Ayyubid caliph of Baghdad, Hülagü's own devout Nestorian wife, and the fact that many of his court were Nestorian Christians, including his general Kitbuqa, may have kindled aspirations among some Christians regarding Mongol aid against the Muslims, particularly since he had promised toleration for Eastern Christians in Asia Minor and had pledged to return any holy places conquered to Christian control. However the vast majority of Latin settlers in the Near East appear to have regarded the advent of the Mongols with dread rather than hope.

Möngke's unexpected death in 1259 led Hülagü to withdraw to Persia, leaving behind only a small army under Kitbuqa. With the splintering of the Mongol Empire, the Ilkhans of Persia became increasingly caught between the hostile rulers of the Golden Horde in the East and the Mamluks in Egypt. They soon began to court Christian powers by promising conversion to Christianity and the reinstallation of Christian rulership in Jerusalem, hoping to piggyback on a Western crusade to wrest Syria from the Mamluks. Despite the Mamluks' rise to power in

Egypt, Latin settlers concerned by the Mongol's increasing advances in the Near East (including the formal submission of the crusader states of Antioch and Tripoli to Mongol overlordship and the Mongols' openly stated goal of conquering Syria and Egypt) refused to ally with the Mongols against the Mamluks, leading to the defeat of Kitbuqa's army by the Mamluks at 'Ain Jalut in 1261.

With the accession of the powerful Mamluk Baibars (r. 1260–1277), the Mamluks soon regained control of former Ayyubid dominions in Syria and began to dislodge Latin settlers from their few remaining outposts in a bid to check the Mongol advance and secure Palestine as a Mamluk possession.[2] Meanwhile, the Mamluks allied with Batu's Muslim brother Berke, khan of the Golden Horde and open opponent of the Christian Hülagü after the disaster of 'Ain Jalut. Caught between these two powers, Hülagü approached the West and Eastern Christians for alliances, although the Mongol invasions of eastern Europe and open designs on the Near East had led the papacy and other authorities to mistrust the Mongols, such that when Hülagü entered Syria in 1257, Pope Alexander IV urged all Latin Christians to oppose him and condemned Christian leaders who aided his advance, with the result that some crusaders arrived in the Holy Land in 1260 to defend it against the Mongols.

However, in 1263–1264, Hülagü continued overtures toward Pope Urban IV and the kings of Europe, proposing a united front against the Mamluks, as did his son Abagha (r. 1265–1282). Despite the fact that the Mongols' weakened position made them amenable to something closer to a true alliance and led them even to hint at conversion to Christianity, their previously open claims to world domination meant that their embassies were met with skepticism, despite Baibars's victories in Syria and Lesser Armenia. Among the plans mooted was that of uniting a Western-led crusade with a Mongol offensive in the Euphrates valley to split the Mamluk forces into two fronts, with the cession of the Holy Land to Frankish forces should it be conquered. Such a program was sketched by Abagha in letters of 1267 and 1268. Yet when Latins responded favorably to the invitation in 1269, Abagha found himself unable to spare troops to aid the crusaders, including those participating in the anti-Mamluk crusade of Prince Edward (later Edward I, king of England) of 1271–1272 (see below, Part X). Negotiations continued with Gregory X in preparation for his planned Eastern crusade, although Western interest in an alliance effectively died with the pope and his crusade in 1277.

See especially Charles Burnett and Patrick Gautier Dalché, "Attitudes Towards the Mongols in Medieval Literature: The XXII Kings of Gog and Magog from the Court of Frederick II to Jean de Mandeville," Viator 22 (1991), 153–167; Peter Jackson, "The Crusade Against the Mongols (1241)," Journal of Ecclesiastical History 42, no. 1 (1991), 1–18; Peter Jackson, "The Crisis in the Holy Land in 1260," English Historical Review 376 (1980), 481–513; Peter Jackson, "The Mongols and Europe," in David Abulafia, ed., New Cambridge Medieval

2. Robert Irwin, *The Middle East in the Middle Ages: The Early Mamluk Sultanate, 1250–1382* (London, 1986); Irwin, *Mamluks and Crusaders: Men of the Sword and Men of the Pen* (Farnham UK-Burlington VT, 2010).

History, *vol. 5, c. 1199–c. 1300 (Cambridge, 1999), 703–719; Sophia Menache, "Tartars, Jews, Saracens, and the Jewish-Mongol 'Plot' of 1241,"* History 263 (1996), 319–342; *Peter Jackson,* Studies on the Mongol Empire and Early Muslim India *(Farnham UK-Burlington VT, 2009); Paul Meyvaert, "An Unknown Letter of Hülagü, Il-Khan of Persia, to King Louis IX of France,"* Viator 11 (1980), 245–259; D. O. Morgan, *The Mongols (Oxford, 1986); Reuven Amitai-Preiss and David O. Morgan, eds.,* The Mongol Empire and Its Legacy *(Leiden-Boston, 1999). On the intense and shifting devotional matrix into which the Mongols were fitted, see Gary Dickson, "The Flagellants of 1260 and the Crusades,"* Journal of Medieval History 15 (1989), 227–267; *and Hamilton and Beckingham,* Prester John; *James M. Muldoon, ed.,* Travellers, Intellectuals and the World Beyond Europe *(Farnham UK-Burlington VT, 2010). On the role of the Mongols in Christian prophecy well into the early modern period, see Robert E. Lerner,* The Powers of Prophecy: The Cedar of Lebanon Vision from the Mongol Onslaught to the Dawn of the Enlightenment *(Berkeley-Los Angeles, 1983). On the role of the Mongols in the formation of Christian thought concerning infidels, see James M. Muldoon,* Popes, Lawyers, and Infidels: The Church and the Non-Christian World *(Philadelphia, 1979); and F. Schmieder, "Cum hora undecima: The Incorporation of Asia into the Orbis Christianus," in G. Armstrong and I. N. Wood, eds.,* Christianizing Peoples and Converting Individuals *(Turnhout, 2000), 259–265.*

39. Henry of Saxony to the Duke of Brabant, 1241

Before his description of the Tartar invasions of eastern Europe in 1241, Matthew Paris also depicted various other crises that came to a head in the same year. The emperor Frederick II and his son Henry were leading armies and attacking cities in Lombardy that had refused to acknowledge his authority, including Faenza and Genoa. His son Conrad, heir to the kingdom of Jerusalem, was leading another army from Germany and adjacent lands against the Tartars with the dukes of Austria, Saxony, and Bavaria and many other prelates and magnates who had taken the cross against the Tartars. As part of the papal-imperial struggle, another army was led by Frederick's ally Theobald of Apulia, podestà of Padua, in the march of Treviso in Italy, and another in the march of Ancona. Led by Frederick II's marshal, to whom Count Richard of Cornwall had entrusted the lands recently conquered by him, yet another army was engaged in the Holy Land. To Matthew Paris's mind, the Tartar terror was a threat perhaps outweighing all the others in its urgency.

DURING all this time that inhuman and brutal, outlawed, barbarous, and untameable people, the Tartars, in their rash and cruel violence, visited the northern provinces of the Christians with dreadful devastation and destruction, and struck great fear and terror into all Christendom. Already with unheard-of tyranny, they had in a great measure reduced to a wasteland the countries of Frisia, Gothland, Poland, Bohemia, and both divisions of Hungary [that is, on both sides of the Danube], slaying or putting to flight princes, prelates, citizens, and rustics. This occurrence is

Source: Giles, Matthew Paris's English History, *1:338–341.*

evidently testified by the following letter, which was sent into these parts [that is, England].

A letter from Henry, count of Lorraine, to the duke of Brabant (1241)

HENRY, by the grace of God, count of Lorraine, palatine of Saxony,[3] to his well-beloved and always to be beloved lord and father-in-law, the illustrious duke of Brabant,[4] goodwill in his service whenever he shall demand it.—Owing to our sins, the dangers foretold in the Scriptures in times of old, are now springing up and breaking out. For a cruel and countless horde of people, lawless and wild, is now invading and taking possession of the territories adjoining ours, and has now, after roving through many other countries and exterminating their inhabitants, extended their incursions as far as the Polish territory. Of these matters we have been fully informed by our own messengers as well as by the letters of our beloved cousin the king of Bohemia,[5] and have been called on to prepare ourselves with all haste to proceed to his assistance and the defense of the Christians.

For we are truly and plainly informed by him that this said race of people, the Tartars, will cruelly and impetuously invade the Bohemian territory about the octaves of Easter. And if seasonable assistance is not given to the Bohemians, an unheard-of slaughter will take place. And as the house adjoining our own is already on fire, and as the neighboring country is open to devastation, while some countries are even now being ravaged, we, on behalf of the church universal, anxiously invoke and beg assistance and advice from God and our neighboring brother princes. And as delay is pregnant with danger, we beg of you, with all possible diligence, to take arms and to hasten to our aid, for the sake of our freedom as well as for that of your own, and to use strenuous endeavors to prepare a powerful force, by arousing the powerful and brave nobles with people subject to them, to hold them ready and prepared until we again send our messengers to you.

---

3. Perhaps Henry III, margrave of Meissen, whom Frederick II rewarded with the duchy of Saxony in 1242. Broadly, see Archibald R. Lewis, *Nomads and Crusaders,* A.D. 1000–1368 (Bloomington IN, 1988).

4. Henry II, duke of Brabant (1235–1248). He later supported his sister's son, William of Holland, in his bid to become king of Germany.

5. King Wenceslaus of Bohemia (1230–1253) successfully repelled Mongol raids against his kingdom in 1241.

We have now, by the instrumentality of our prelates and the Preacher and Minorite brethren, called a general crusade (for it is a matter connected with Christ) to be preached, prayer and fasting to be enjoined, and our territory in general to be roused to war for the sake of Jesus Christ. To this we may add that a large horde of this detestable race of people, in conjunction with another army allied with them, is ravaging Hungary with unheard-of cruelty, to such an extent that the king is said to retain only a very small portion for himself. To sum up the matter in a few words, the church and the people in the northern countries are so oppressed and overwhelmed with so many and such great troubles and difficulties that they have never suffered so severely from any scourge since the beginning of the world. Written in the year of grace 1241, on the day when "Let Jerusalem rejoice" is chanted.

LETTERS of similar purport were also sent by the duke of Brabant to the bishop of Paris, and the archbishop of Cologne[6] also wrote to the king of England. . . .[7]

Wherefore, to heal this severe infliction and to settle the disputes which had arisen between the pope and the emperor, fasting and prayer, with bountiful almsgiving, were enjoined on the people of the various countries, that the Lord, the mighty subduer of his enemies, who fights with few or with many, might become pacified toward his people and crush the pride of these Tartars.

40. Frederick II to All the Christian Princes, July 3, 1241

This letter was but one of many appeals for aid copied by Matthew Paris for the year 1241. He follows it with a report of the conspiracy rumors circulating concerning Frederick II's role in the Mongol invasion. Frederick II's son Conrad took the cross against the Mongols and appealed to secular rulers to publicize the crusade in their territories by May of 1241, which appears to have led other prelates and rulers to muster contingents. However, although Conrad ordered the army to advance, its progress appears to have stalled and it achieved nothing, leading some chroniclers to blame the absence of a definitive leader, others the cooling fervor and charity of leaders and followers alike. The real reason for the lack of an effective crusade lay in the ongoing struggle between Frederick II and Gregory IX

6. Conrad of Hochstadt (1238–1261). He played a key role in the papal-imperial conflict in Germany.
7. Matthew Paris copied several other letters that clearly influenced his perception of the nature of the Mongol threat, all reproduced in Giles's translation (3:449–455).

and their supporters; Conrad's army disintegrated by the autumn of 1241, and he soon was drawn into a protracted struggle with German ecclesiastical magnates who used the papal-imperial war as an occasion for rebellion against imperial authority.

Frederick offered even less aid to Bela IV of Hungary than the beleaguered Gregory IX, despite Bela's desperate offer to become the emperor's vassal. Frederick's lack of assistance led contemporaries to accuse him of engineering the Mongol invasion for his own dubious ends. Although he had not precipitated the crisis, Frederick did attempt to take advantage of it to obtain papal absolution from his excommunicate state and guarantees that his kingdom would not be invaded if he joined the anti-Mongol crusade. He also exhorted fellow monarchs to take up the anti-Mongol cause, ordered German magnates to aid him when he should come north to oppose this new threat, and urged Bela to collaborate with his son Conrad. However, the German forces had little intention of fighting in Hungary, but rather seem to have been intent upon preventing Mongol advances into their own lands. Mongol forces continued to ravage Hungary, despite Bela's resistance with a motley force composed of various troops and members of the military orders. Hungary was saved only when Mongol forces precipitously withdrew in the spring of 1242, probably due to political crises within the Mongol Empire and a lack of fodder for their horses.

ON hearing these things, the emperor [Frederick II] wrote to the Christian princes, and especially to [his brother-in-law] the king of England [Henry III],[8] as follows. . . .

We cannot be silent on a matter which concerns not only the Roman Empire, whose office it is to propagate the Gospel, but also all the kingdoms of the world that practice Christian worship and threatens general destruction to the whole of Christianity. We therefore hasten to bring it to your knowledge, although the true facts of the matter have but lately come to ours.

Some time ago a people of a barbarous race and mode of life, from what place or origin I know not, called Tartars, has lately emerged from the regions of the south, where it had long lain hid, burnt up by the sun of the torrid zone. And marching toward the northern parts, they took forcible possession of the country there, and remaining for a time, multiplied like locusts, and have now come forth, not without the premeditated judgment of God, but not, I hope, reserved to these latter times for the ruin of the whole of Christianity.

Source: Giles, Matthew Paris's English History, *1:341–348.*
8. Frederick II had married Henry III's sister Isabella in 1235.

Their arrival was followed by a general slaughter, a universal desolation of kingdoms and by utter ruin to the fertile territory, which this impious horde of people roved through, sparing neither sex, age, nor rank. For they confidently hope to destroy the rest of the human race and are endeavoring to rule and lord it alone, trusting to their immense power and unlimited numbers.

Frederick II details the Mongol victory over the Cumans, the Ruthenians (including the sack of Kiev), and the unprepared Hungarians.

AT THIS very moment they are ravaging the largest and finest part of Hungary, beyond the river Danube, harassing the inhabitants with fire and sword, and threaten to involve the rest in the same destruction, as we have been informed by the venerable bishop of Vatzen, the aforementioned king of Hungary's ambassador to our court, afterward sent to that of Rome, who, passing through our territory first, bore testimony to what he had seen. . . . We have also been fully informed of these events by letters from our beloved son Conrad, king elect of the Romans, heir to the kingdom of Jerusalem and king of Bohemia and from the dukes of Austria and Bohemia, as also by the word of mouth of messengers, who have been practically made certain of the enemy's proximity. And we have heard all this with great perturbation of mind.

As we have been informed, and as the rumor of their proceedings, going in advance of them, declares, their innumerable army is divided into three ill-omened portions. . . . One of these has been sent through the Prussian territory and entered Poland, where . . . the whole of that country has been devastated by them. A second portion has entered the Bohemian territory, where it is brought to a stand, having been attacked by the king of that country, who has bravely met it with all the forces at his command. And the third portion of it is overrunning [that part of] Hungary adjacent to the Austrian territories.

Hence fear and trembling have arisen among us, owing to the fury of these impetuous invaders, which arouses and calls upon us to arm. Necessity . . . urges us to oppose them, and the certainty of the general ruin of the whole world, especially of Christendom, calls for hasty assistance and succor. For this race of people is wild, lawless, and ignorant of the laws of humanity. They follow and have for their lord one whom they worship and reverence with all obedience and call the god of the earth.[9] The men themselves are small and of short stature in regard to height, but compact, stout, and bulky, resolute, strong, and courageous, and ready at the nod of their leader to rush into any undertaking of difficulty. They have large faces, scowling looks and utter horrible shouts, suited to their hearts. They wear raw hides of bullocks, asses, and horses, and for armor they are protected by pieces of iron stitched to them, which they have made use of till now. But now, and we cannot say it without sorrow, they are providing themselves with more suitable weapons from the spoils of the conquered Christians, that through God's anger we might be the more basely slain with our own arms. Moreover, they are supplied with better horses, live on richer food, and adorn themselves with more handsome clothes than formerly. They are incomparable archers and carry skins artificially made in which they cross lakes and the most rapid rivers without danger. When fodder fails them, their horses are said to be satisfied with the bark and leaves of tree and the roots of herbs, which the men bring to them. And yet they always find them very swift and strong in a case of necessity.

We have, however, by some means or another, been forewarned of and foreseen all these events, and have by letters and messengers frequently requested of Your Majesty as well as other Christian princes, and earnestly advised and entreated of you, to allow unanimity, affection, and peace to flourish among those who hold supreme authority, to settle all dissensions, which frequently bring harm on the commonwealth of Christ, and to rise with alacrity and unanimously to oppose those lately emerged savages, inasmuch as weapons foreseen are less apt to wound, so that the common enemies of us all may not have cause to rejoice, in furtherance of their progress, that discord is shooting forth among the Christian princes.

O God! How much and how often have we been willing to humiliate ourselves, giving vent to every kind of good feeling, in order to prevail on the Roman pontiff to desist from giving cause of scandal throughout the world, by his enmity against us, and place the bounds of moderation upon his ill-advised violence in order that we might be able to pacify our lawful subjects and govern them in a state of peace, and not to protect those

9. Frederick here refers to the Mongols' belief that the world had been granted to them by heaven and that all rulers were destined to become subjects of their own ruler, the Great Khan. This meant that all diplomatic contacts tended to be viewed as preliminaries to capitulation and letters sent to Western authorities typically demanded compliance to Mongol plans of world domination, formal submission, tribute, and military service.

who kick against our authority, a large portion of whom are still favored and assisted by him. Thus by peaceably settling matters and by reforming our rebellious subjects, against whom we have expended a large amount of money and exhausted our strength, our power would increase and rise in greater force against the common enemy. But will is law with him, for he does not rule the deceitful discourse of his tongue. And he has refused to abstain from the manifold quarrels which he has sought against us. And he has ordered a crusade to be published against me, who am an arm and advocate of the church, which it was his duty and would have become him better to have put into practice against the tyranny of the Tartars or the Saracens invading and occupying the Holy Land. And he exults in the rebellion of our subjects, who are conspiring against our honor and fame, and as it is our most urgent business to free ourselves from enemies at home, how shall we repel these barbarians as well?

For by their spies, which they have sent out in all directions, these people, although governed without any regard to divine law, yet well-skilled in the devices of war, have discovered this public discord and have found out the unprotected and weaker parts of the country. And hearing of the animosity of kings and the clashing of kingdoms, they are inspirited and rise against us with greater eagerness. How much does exulting courage add to strength! Therefore we have turned our attention to both matters, and, with the help of God's providence, will apply our strength and industry to avert the scandal to the church caused on one side by our enemies at home and on the other by these savages. And so we have expressly sent our beloved son Conrad and other chiefs of our empire to meet and check the attacks and violence of these barbarians with a strong force.

And we most sincerely adjure Your Majesty in the name of the Lord Jesus Christ, the author of our Christian faith, with the most careful solicitude and by prudent deliberation to take precautions for the protection of yourself and your kingdom, which may God keep in a state of prosperity, and to prepare as soon as possible a complete army of brave knights and soldiers and a good supply of arms. And this we beg of you by the blood of Christ shed for us and by the ties of relationship which connect us. And let them prepare themselves to fight bravely and prudently in conjunction with us, for the freedom of Christianity, so that by a union of our forces against these enemies who are now purposing to enter the boundaries of Germany, which is the door of Christendom, as it were, the victory may be gained to the honor and renown of the Lord of Hosts. And may it please Your Majesty not to pass these matters by unnoticed or to delay giving your attention to them. For if, God forbid, they invade the German territory and meet with no opposition, the rest of the world will then feel the thunder of the suddenly coming tempest, which we believe to have arisen from a divine judgment, as the world is defiled by the infection of various sins, as charity begins to grow cold in many by whom the true faith ought to be preached and upheld, and their pernicious example pollutes the world with usury and divers kinds of simony and ambition.

May it please Your Majesty, therefore, to provide for this emergency, and while these enemies of us all in common are venting their fury in the neighboring countries, do you by prudent counsels make preparations to resist them. For they have left their own country, heedless of danger to their own lives, with the intention of subduing the whole of the West and of ruining and uprooting the faith and name of Christ; God forbid its being carried into effect. And owing to the unexpected victories which they have hitherto gained by God's permission, they have arrived at such a pitch of insanity that they consider they have already gained possession of all the kingdoms of the world and may subdue and bind the prostrate kings and princes to their own vile service as they please. But we hope in our Lord Jesus Christ, under whom as a leader and guide we have hitherto released ourselves from and triumphed over our enemies, that these also, who have burst forth from the abodes of Tartarus, may find their pride humbled, and after experiencing the strength of the West, be thrust back to their own Tartarus.

Frederick ends by calling upon all the regions of Latin Christendom for assistance.

. . . . "[MAY they] send forth their chosen ornaments preceded by the symbol of the life-giving cross, at which, not only rebellious subjects, but even opposing demons, are struck with terror and dismay. Written on our retreat, after the surrender and depopulation of Faenza, on the third day of July [1241].

Matthew Paris notes that similar letters were written to other magnates by the emperor, who warned the French king that the pope was aspiring, in his insatiable ambition and avarice, to bring all Christian kingdoms to subjection to himself.

AND a difference of opinion arose among many different people entertaining different thoughts on these matters. There were some who said that the emperor had, of his own accord, plotted this infliction of the Tartars and that by this clever letter he basely cloaked his nefarious crime, and that in his grasping ambition he was, like Lucifer or Antichrist, conspiring against the monarchy of the whole world to the utter ruin of the Christian faith.

41. Gregory IX to Bela IV of Hungary on the Mongol Threat, *Vocem in excelso*, June 16, 1241

Several months before writing this letter, Gregory IX had commissioned the preaching of the anti-imperial crusade in Hungary, authorizing the commutation of even Holy Land crusading vows to this effort. Increasingly besieged (Frederick II had intercepted many prelates and cardinals called to the general council Gregory had summoned with the intent of deposing the emperor), Gregory IX assured Bela IV and all who took the cross to defend Hungary that they would receive the same indulgences and privileges as the crusaders currently occupied in the Holy Land. Although he went so far as to permit the commutation of vows for the crusade to the Holy Land or elsewhere to the crusade against the Mongols, the demands of disparate campaigns meant that neither the papacy nor Frederick II could assure the new crusade of the manpower it needed. Gregory IX even told Bela that aid for Hungary could only come when Frederick II submitted. The papacy did help indirectly in the respect that the mendicant orders traditionally pressed into service to promote the crusades played a crucial role in recruitment for the anti-Mongol crusade. Mendicants fleeing westward from Hungary and Poland and friars local to the region appear also to have promoted the crusade, leading to an extraordinary response, both in vows to personally fight the Mongol threat and in commutations of crusade vows to donations to the cause.

On the history of southeastern Europe, see Florin Curta, Southeastern Europe in the Middle Ages, 500–1250 *(Cambridge, 2006); Nora Berend,* At the Gate of Christendom: Jews, Muslims and "Pagans" in Medieval Hungary, c. 1000–c. 1300 *(Cambridge-New York, 2001); James Ross Sweeney, "Hungary in the Crusades, 1169–1218,"* International History Review 3 (1981), 467–481.

To BELA [IV], illustrious king of Hungary. We have heard a voice of lamentation and weeping from on high [Jer 31:15], and, filled with bitterness with manifold sufferings, we lament, because through the judgment pronounced by heaven the Christian people are everywhere laid waste, because on one hand the sword of the faithful is directed injuriously upon the faithful and on the other, the edged weapon of the pagans fiercely rages against the followers of Christ. For the numerous clamor of the crimes of the human race ascending to the ears of the creator of all things himself, he who as if unseeing passed over such things, who like a

Source: *Rodenberg,* Epistolae saeculi XIII, *1:721–722, no. 821.*

tolerant person, waited for the correction of his people, has been forced
to exercise his sword to avenge these injustices and to cleanse the abomi-
nation of [such] disgraceful acts from the eyes of his patience, and thus
brought grievous vengeance upon sinners.

For this very reason, it is fitting that all whose hearts have been
touched by the fear of God implore divine mercy by donning sackcloth
and sprinkling [themselves] with ashes with weeping and sighing, so that
he who shows himself always exceedingly ready to forgive, who is accustomed to be exalted over evil [Jl 2:3] at all times, might command the
brandished sword to return to its sheath, and pouring out his wrath upon
the peoples who do not acknowledge him, might deign to have mercy
upon the people marked with the seal of his son.[10]

However, we trust that even if our God has begun to condemn us
with harsh rebukes, that nonetheless he does not intend to erase from his
presence those kingdoms which call upon his name. Nay, on the contrary,
he takes pains to deliver sinners from eternal punishment by those very
temporal punishments which he diligently applies as a gift for the correction of our kind, because even though the sons of Israel [were subjected
to] the danger of death in the desert whenever he struck them, nonetheless the Lord's wrath did not endure for very long.

Certainly, although we ought to be deeply disturbed by the oppression of all the faithful, our heart is filled with particular and a very great
sorrow on account of the suffering of the kingdom of Hungary, the
majority of which has been invaded and occupied by the Tartars (which
we discovered through reading your letters, not without shedding many
tears). For we have found in the same kingdom the signs of purer devotion to God and the Apostolic See, and we know that your ancestors of
celebrated memory were and [your own] distinguished court is ever ready
to fulfill the wishes of the church.

We fix our hope firmly in him, who although he permitted Senna-
cherib, the king of the Assyrians, free entry into the land of Israel, nonetheless [was] aroused by the contrition of Ezekiel [and] wiped out the
enemy host in one night. And we exhort and urge Your Serenity more
assiduously and entreat [you] in the [name of] the Lord Jesus Christ, that
trusting in him, who keeps a humble people safe and humbles the haughty
eye, you gird yourself vigorously and manfully, as befits your royal greatness, to the defense of the aforesaid realm and of the catholic faith (which

---

10. That is, Christians signed with the cross.

is understood to be particularly besieged by the same Tartars). And you ought take care to show yourself more zealous and assiduous in attacking them, by those [means] you will have discerned [how best] to attend to [your kingdom] more powerfully, to the exaltation of your name and your reputation.

For we will take care to impart effectual counsel and aid to you and the aforementioned realm, whom we neither can nor ought to neglect in so great a hinge of necessity. With divine approval, we take both your person and household under the protection of the Apostolic See, and in order to advance the defense of the aforementioned realm, we grant that [same] privilege and enlarge with that indulgence which was conceded to those aiding the Holy Land in the general council. . . . Written in the same manner to the illustrious king Coloman [of Halych] and to the duke of Slavonia.[11]

42. Gregory IX to the Abbot of Heiligenkreuz, *Vocem in excelso*, June 19, 1241

Notified that the Mongols were potentially threatening Bohemia, Germany, and Austria as well, Gregory IX commissioned the abbot of Heiligenkreuz and the Dominican prior at Vienna to preach the crusade for the defense of these regions, enabling them to commute vows from other crusades to the war against the Mongols. In 1188, Leopold V, duke of Austria, had gifted Heiligenkreuz with a relic of the True Cross obtained from King Baldwin IV of Jerusalem. This donation, the monastery's patronage by leading families of the region (including the dukes of Austria), and its membership in the tightly organized Cistercian order ensured that its members were soon commissioned to recruit for the crusades. The letter's other recipients were the more recently established mendicant orders who were becoming central to crusade organization.

Aware that speedy help and organization might not be forthcoming from the emperor or the pope, churches of the regions invaded or threatened had quickly taken matters into their own hands, organizing a crusade prior to imperial or papal approval. At least two months prior to Gregory's letters, Siegfried, archbishop of Mainz, regent for Frederick II's son Conrad IV, convened a council at Erfurt that produced a comprehensive series of decrees for a crusade against the Mongols. These included prayers, processions and fasting, provisions for compelling persons to attend crusade sermons, enumeration of privileges, and authority for friars to

11. Gregory here refers to the brother of Bela IV, Coloman of Lodoveria (1208–1241), who married the daughter of Duke Leszek of Poland and was made titular king of Halych. He became duke of Slavonia in 1226, and died of wounds inflicted by Mongol forces at the battle of Mohi (April 11, 1241).

absolve excommunicates and commute any previous vow to a crusade vow against the Mongols. He and his suffragan bishops also appear to have quickly implemented these decrees, and although they infringed upon papal prerogatives in issuing crusade indulgences, they protected themselves by being vague as to what specific spiritual benefits were being granted. Multiple chronicles report that the preaching met with an enthusiastic response and large sums of money were collected.

See Maier, Preaching the Crusades, *38, 59–63, 84–5, 104, 172, and Maier,* Crusade Propaganda, *144–51 for sermons against the Mongols.*

GREGORY IX to the abbot of Heiligenkreuz, [a monastery] of the Cistercian order in the diocese of Passau. . . . [The letter begins with the first two paragraphs of No. 41 above.]

Consequently, we are deeply disturbed by the universal oppression of the faithful, although in these days a particular and powerful grief fills our heart, because, as we have learned through reading the letters of those noble men . . . [Frederick II] of Austria and . . . [Bernhard II], duke of Carinthia, not without shedding many tears, the Tartars, after invading and occupying the majority of the kingdom of Hungary, slaked their swords with the blood of all whom they could lay hands on, without regard for age or sex, [and] now endeavor to invade the kingdoms of Bohemia and *Teutonia* [Germany], desiring to lay waste the entire land of the Christians and destroy their faith.

Fixing our hope firmly in him, etc., as above until:[12] we commission you by strictly enjoining you in the virtue of obedience, that through neighboring regions to what extent [you can] you publicize the word of the cross according to the prudence given to you by God, through [both] yourselves and others whom you know to be suited [to this task]. And you ought not to neglect to persuade catholic men with salutary admonitions, that [they ought to] consider that just as the aforementioned Tartars seek the destruction of the entire Christian people, so through attacking them the salvation of everyone is procured and that they ought to take the sign of the cross and gird themselves powerfully and manfully to the defense of the kingdoms mentioned above against the aforesaid

Source: *Rodenberg,* Epistolae saeculi XIII, *1:722–723, no. 822.*
12. To save parchment, the scribe has omitted a paragraph nearly identical to that mentioning Sennacharib in No. 41 above.

Tartars, trusting in him who keeps a humble people safe and humbles the haughty eye.

For we to all, etc., as above, until is granted [to them].[13] In fact, if [some] of those signed with the cross are bound by the chain of excommunication because they laid violent hands upon ecclesiastical persons or because of arson, provided that they make suitable satisfaction for injuries and damages suffered according to your discretion, and their transgressions are not so weighty and outrageous that on account of it they deserve to be sent to the Apostolic See,[14] we grant to you full powers for applying the blessing of absolution according to the form of the church, and in addition the [power] to commute the vows of those who [plan to] depart in aid of the Holy Land or vowed another pilgrimage for the remedy of their sins to [the crusade] against the aforementioned Tartars.

. . . In the same manner . . . [to] the prior of the brothers Preacher [Dominicans] in *Teutonia* [Germany]. In the same manner . . . to the prior of the brothers preacher in Vienna. In the same manner to . . . the provincial minister of the brothers Minor [Franciscans] in *Teutonia* [Germany].

43. *Continuatio Sancrucensis,* 1234–1266

The monastery of Heiligenkreuz's connections with local notables, including the dukes of Austria, ensured that it was the recipient of news concerning the Tartars, probably as part of appeals for its members to intercede liturgically on behalf of Christendom and to involve itself in the promotion of the anti-Mongol crusade. The tone of the entry may reflect the kind of propaganda the monastery publicized in response to Gregory IX's commission to preach the crusade and/or the concerns of its informants.

1242 [1241]. The Cumans, that cursed and aforementioned people, crossed the borders of Hungary, and on the sacred day of Easter, entered the city of Rodna, whose inhabitants were feasting and drinking and

Source: Continuatio Sancrucensis, 1234–1266, *ed. D. Wilhelmus Wattenbach,* MGH SS, *vol. 9 (1851), 640–641.*

13. The scribe here refers to the paragraph in No. 41 above that describes the crusade indulgence and privileges offered to those who took the cross against the Mongols.

14. That is, forced to journey to Rome for the imposition of penance and absolution because their crime was one reserved to papal penitentiaries.

dwelling free from care, and they killed everyone, religious and irreligious, young men and virgins, the old with the young, sparing no one. Afterward, they swarmed through the entirety of that province like locusts, thirsting after the blood of men, which they poured out like water.

In fact, those who first seized that land to dwell in, joined themselves to them and created an innumerable horde. Their king, by the name of Gutan,[15] killed himself after first slaying his two queens and others who were gathered with him in his household, out of fear of the duke of Austria[16] who was attacking that very house and finally seized it. On the other hand, the king of Hungary, having mustered together a numerous host of one hundred thousand men, as it was said, went to attack them in the vicinity of Pest. While they were resting in their camp, the Cumans came upon them unexpectedly at first dawn. And after first burning the camp, they then slew all the bishops, counts, men young and old, with no one resisting them, such that out of such a great multitude only a few escaped, together with the king himself.

Once they had accomplished these things, they were followed by another people who are called Tartars, arriving from the rising of the sun [that is, the East], and they destroyed many kingdoms, cities, and castles [including], of course, Russia [and] Poland with its duke Henry,[17] because they were so innumerable that no one dared to oppose them. Heretics and false Christians joined them so that they might work their malice upon Christians and erase their name from the earth. This people subjected the Cumans to themselves, such that they subdued them in all respects. Consequently, from that time onward, their wickedness was multiplied upon the earth, such that they spared no one, and although they would sometimes make peace with those asking for it, they never kept it. Their king used to declare that he alone was lord upon the earth, and for that reason he would receive neither [military] assistance nor counsel nor legation unless the person in question was willing to follow his law, which was to deny the omnipotent God and slay men. He demanded this very thing from the duke of Austria via his messengers, but the latter would not consent. Part of their army entered the boundaries of Bohemia and Austria, and after killing many, they returned to their own lands. The persons responsible for all these wicked deeds were officials

15. That is, Butan.
16. Frederick II, duke of Austria and Styria (1230–1246).
17. Probably Henry II, duke of Lower Silesia, who with Conrad, duke of Mazovia, was defeated by Mongol forces in February of 1241.

[*comites*] who killed the mother of the king because her son had removed them from their positions. There was neither people nor kingdom who did not dread the sound of their name. For when Pope Gregory [IX] comprehended this evil, stricken with sorrow, he devoted himself to aiding the holy church. Reeling, but not failing [his charge], he sent out his legates to preach and give the cross for the remission of all sins, which many received with rejoicing—kings, dukes, bishops, counts, nobles and the ignoble, the old with the young, and they prepared to wreak vengeance upon the sons of diffidence. But the lord emperor [Frederick II] forbade this to be done, with the result that the king of Hungary refused to come when summoned by him and to speak with him. Unreconciled to the emperor, the lord pope Gregory died [in this year, 1241].

1243 [1242]. The Tartars and Cumans, with no one resisting or opposing them, withdrew from Hungary with limitless spoils of gold and silver, clothing and animals, and furthermore they led away many captives of either sex to the disgrace of [all] Christians. Entering Greece, they depopulated that entire land with the exception of castles and strongly fortified towns. In fact, when the king of Constantinople, named Baldwin [II], encountered them in battle, on the first occasion he defeated them, but on the second encounter he was vanquished by them. Meanwhile a horrible and unheard of famine invaded the land of Hungary and more perished from hunger than [had been slain] before by the pagans. . . . Meanwhile the Roman church lacked a high priest and the lord emperor subjugated to himself the cities and castles of the Roman church and was either bargaining with or acting indulgently toward others who surrendered to him; for the Longobards [that is, Lombards] were not yet made subject to him.

44. A Thirteenth-Century English Liturgical Response to the Mongol Invasions

The surviving prayers, translated below, survive untitled and undated in a late thirteenth-century manuscript. They may date to a council held at Oxford in 1241, which the Dunstable annalist claims legislated public fasting and prayers, probably in response to the Tartar invasions of eastern Europe in 1240 and 1241. Or they may have been produced in connection with the Council of Lambeth, held in 1261 in response to Alexander IV's appeal of November 15, 1260, or to another later council entirely. The prayers are a fascinating example of how images of the Mongol threat were transmitted to the populace.

An ordinance for processions and prayers

So THAT the scourge of divine anger which was kindled for vengeance and came upon us because of our sins [might be lifted], that is to say, the savagery of the Tartars who spared no one, let us oppose [to them] appropriate remedies pleasing to God. We [now] take care to return to prayers and fasting and works of piety through which, if they are offered to the Lord in a spirit of humility and with a contrite spirit, we trust that the populace will be freed in body and mind from their enemies with the cessation of divine displeasure. On this account we are led to provide, with the approval of the present council, that in all cathedral and collegiate churches, whether secular or regular or parochial, in cities, fortified places, and towns, that on the fourth and sixth day of each week processions ought to be made with the eight penitential psalms and the litany before the greater mass, such that those who participate in the procession should proceed with bare feet and without linen undershirts. In fact, after the litany, these three prayers ought to be said, that is: "O God, to you your own," etc.; "O Lord, your church laments," etc.; "God to whom holy petition," etc. Indeed, in churches outside [population centers], because of the dispersion of the populace occupied in the cultivation of the land, let processions of this sort be made whenever the parishioners gather on Sundays and feast days; and let the laypersons be exhorted that in procession they ought to say seven Lord's Prayers with the same number of salutations of the Blessed Virgin. Certainly in the great mass, after the second "through all things," first let the "Peace of the Lord" be said, and then these two psalms ought to be said daily, that is: "O God, [come] to [our] aid" [Ps 69:2] and "O God, [the peoples] have come [into thy inheritance]"[Ps 78:1], with the prayer which is said on Good Friday: "Omnipotent God in whose hand are all powers."

Moreover, we command that the parish priests should preach to their parishioners the cruelty of the Tartars, that is, that their swords spare no one, that they lay waste and burn cities and villages, and leave the lands which they occupy desolate, so that stricken with fear, their devotion might be aroused. Certainly concerning the fasts we regulate them in such a manner that both the clerks and prelates and those subject to them ought to keep a fast on the fourth and sixth days of the week, abstaining

Source: *Christopher R. Cheney and Frederick M. Powicke,* Councils and Synods, with Other Documents Relating to the English Church, *vol. 2, pt. 1,* A.D. 1205–1265 *(Oxford, 1964), 339–340.*

from eating flesh on the fourth day. However, [priests and prelates] should also urge their parishioners that they ought to take pains to watch over themselves in a similar manner, taking precautions that they do not neglect to persuade them to make frequent confessions, and if they should find anyone in discord, they ought to give assistance and take effectual action to recall them to mutual charity and concord. Toward this [end], their parishioners ought to be exhorted with every diligence and care to give alms to the poor according to their resources . . . according to the counsel of Tobias "If you have much, give abundantly: if you have little, take care even so to bestow willingly a little" [Tb 4:9].

45. Matthew Paris: Archbishop Peter on the Mongols in 1244

In addition to letters, news of the Tartars was transmitted to the West via refugees from newly Mongol-occupied territories, including dispossessed clerics and regular religious, who sought shelter in religious houses in western Europe and made their pleas for aid to various magnates. "Archbishop" Peter may have fled to the West with the former prince of Kiev, Mikhail of Chernigov, when the city was granted by its Mongol occupiers to a new prince, the grand duke Vladimir. Peter was presented as a metropolitan possessing significant authority within the Russian church, earning him entrée into the Council of Lyons (1245).

A CERTAIN archbishop from Russia named Peter, an honorable, devout, and trustworthy man as far as could be judged, was driven from his territory and his archbishopric by the Tartars, and came into the Cisalpine provinces to obtain advice and assistance and comfort in his trouble, if, by the gift of God, the Roman church and the kind favor of the princes of those parts could assist him. On his being asked about the conduct of the Tartars, as far as he had experienced, he thus replied: "I believe that they are the remains of the Midianites, who fled from before the face of Gideon to the most remote parts of the east and the north and took refuge in that place of horror and vast solitude which is called Etren." They had twelve leaders, the chief of whom was called the Tartar Khan, and from him they derive the name of Tartars, though some say they are so called from Tarrachonta, from whom descended Chiarthan, who had three sons, the eldest named Thesir Khan, the second Churi Khan, and

Source: Giles, Matthew Paris's English History, 2:28–31.

the third Bathatar Khan,[18] who all, although they were born and brought up among the most lofty, and, as it were, impenetrable mountains, rude, lawless, and inhuman beings, and educated in caverns and dens, after expelling lions and serpents therefrom, were nevertheless aroused to the allurements of the world.

The father and sons, therefore, came forth from their solitudes, armed in their own way, and accompanied by countless hosts of warriors and laying siege to a city called Ernac, took possession of it, and seized the governor of the city, whom they immediately put to death, and his nephew Cutzeusa, who took to flight, they pursued through several provinces, ravaging the territories of all who harbored him; among others, about twenty-six years ago, they devastated a great part of Russia;[19] where they became for a long time shepherds over the flocks they had carried off, and after conquering the neighboring shepherds, they either slew them or reduced them to subjection to themselves. Thus they multiplied and became more powerful, and appointing leaders among them, they aspired at higher things and reduced cities to subjection to them, after conquering the inhabitants. Thesir Khan proceeded against the Babylonians; Churi Khan against the Turks; and Bathatar Khan remained at Ernac, and sent his chiefs against Russia, Poland, Hungary, and several other kingdoms. And [these] three, with their numerous armies, are now presumptuously invading the neighboring provinces of Syria. Twenty-four years, they say, have now elapsed since the time when they first came forth from the desert of Etren.

The archbishop, when asked as to their mode of belief, replied that they believed there was one ruler of the world; and, when they sent a messenger to the Muscovites, they commenced it in these words, "God and his Son in heaven and Chiar Khan on earth." As to their manner of living, he said, "they eat the flesh of horses, dogs, and other abominable meats, and in times of necessity, even human flesh, not raw, however, but cooked. They drink blood, water, and milk. They punish crimes severely, and fornication, theft, lying, and murder with death. They do not abominate polygamy, and each man has one or more wives. They do not admit

18. This may be a garbled reference to Chinggis Khan, who had four sons by his first wife. To Ögödei, who succeeded him as Great Khan, he gave his lands in eastern Asia (including China); to Chagatai, Central Asia and northern Iran; and to his eldest son, Jochi, the newly conquered lands of Russia and Ruthenia. Because Jochi predeceased his father, his lands were divided among his sons, among them Batu, who invaded Russia, Poland, and Hungary before being recalled to eastern Asia after Ögödei's death.

19. This perhaps refers to the Mongols' devastation of Azerbaijan and Georgia and their defeat of the Cumans (along with their Russian allies) on the river Kalka in 1223.

people of other nations to familiar intercourse with them or to discuss matters of business or to their secret councils. They pitch their camp apart by themselves and if any foreigner dares to come to it, he is at once slain." With respect to their rites and superstitions, he said, "Every morning they raise their hands toward heaven, worshipping their Creator; when they take their meals, they throw the first morsel into the air, and when about to drink, they first pour a portion of the liquor on the ground, in worship of the Creator. They say, also that they have John the Baptist for a leader, and they rejoice and observe solemnities at the time of the new moon.

"They are stronger and more nimble than we are, and better able to endure hardships, as also are their horses and flocks and herds. The women are warlike and, above all, are very skillful in the use of bows and arrows. They wear armor made of hides for their protection, which is scarcely penetrable, and they used poisoned iron weapons of offense. They have a great variety of engines, which hurl missiles with great force and straight to the mark. They take their rest in the open air and care nothing for the inclemency of the weather.

"They have already enticed numbers of all nations and sects to them, and intend to subjugate the whole world. And they say that it has been intimated to them from heaven that they are to ravage the whole world for thirty-nine years, asserting that the Divine vengeance formerly purged the world by a deluge, and now it will be purified by a general depopulation and devastation which they themselves will put into execution. They think and even say that they will have a severe struggle with the Romans, and they call all the Latins Romans. They fear the miracles wrought by the church and that the sentence of future condemnation may be passed against them. They declare that, if they can conquer them, they will at once become lords over the whole world. They pay proper respect to treaties in the cases of those who voluntarily give themselves up to them and serve them, selecting the best soldiers from among them, whom, when they are fighting, they always station in front of them. In the same way also they retain among them the various workmen. They show no mercy to those who rebel against them, reject the yoke of their domination, or oppose them in the field. They receive messengers with kindness, expedite their business, and send them back again."

The said archbishop was finally asked as to their method of crossing rivers and seas, to which he replied that they cross rivers on horseback or on skins made for that purpose, and that in three places on the seacoast they build ships. He also said that one of the said Tartars named Kalaladin,

son-in-law of Chiar Khan, who was discovered to have told a lie, was
banished to Russia, his life having been spared by the Tartar chiefs out of
kindness to his wife.

46. The First Council of Lyons on the Tartars, 1245

Although the papal-imperial struggle and the death of Gregory IX in 1241
had prevented the formation of an effective crusade against the Tartars, and there
is evidence that Gregory's successor Innocent IV was reluctant to call a crusade,
further information of their attacks in Russia and eastern Europe continued to
reach Europe in the form of letters and refugees. After the sack of Jerusalem by
the Khwarizmians in 1244, Innocent IV summoned an ecumenical council to meet
at Lyons in 1245 to deal with the issues of the papal-imperial struggle, the embattled Latin Empire of Constantinople, the mustering of aid for the Latin kingdom
of Jerusalem, and the Tartar threat.

In addition to the council's resolution printed below, Innocent IV dispatched
a mission to the Mongols' Great Khan, composed of two Franciscan friars, Lawrence of Portugal and John of Plano Carpini. Upon their return, further missions
were sent, including one made up of several Dominicans charged with averting
hostilities against Christendom. Among these new missionaries was the Franciscan
William of Rubruck (ca. 1210–ca. 1270), whose account was the first detailed
and generally accurate description of central Asia.[20] Although initially Innocent IV
appears to have viewed the Mongols as an enemy more threatening even than
Frederick II, within a few years the papal-imperial struggle eclipsed all other
efforts. However, in 1247, rumors of a fresh Mongol invasion led Innocent to
promise Bela IV that as soon as a Mongol attack materialized, he would commute
the vows of all those who had taken the cross for other crusades to his aid. Fortunately for Bela, the invasion never materialized, but the Mongol presence in Syria
from 1244 onward meant that they continued to be viewed as a potential threat
to the Holy Land and any crusades being planned for that region.

Canon 4: On the Tartars

DESIRING above all things that the cult of the Christian religion might
be spread farther and more widely throughout the world, we are pierced
with a dagger of incalculable sorrow whenever anyone opposes our ardent

---

Source: J. Alberigo et al., eds., Conciliorum oecumenicorum decreta, *3d ed. (Bologna,
1973), 297.*

20. The reports of both missions have been published. See Christopher Dawson, *Mission to Asia*, Medieval Academy Reprints for Teaching 8 (Toronto-Buffalo NY-London,
1980). For an updated translation of William of Rubruck's mission, and a fuller description
of the Mongol missions, see Peter Jackson and David Morgan, *The Mission of Friar William
of Rubruck: His Journey to the Court of the Great Khan Mongke, 1253–1255* (London, 1990),
esp. pp. 1–55.

desire in this matter, with a hostile desire and action, such that they strive to completely wipe out that same cult from the surface of the earth with complete zeal and all their power. Certainly the impious people of the Tartars, hungering to subjugate to themselves or rather destroy the Christian populace, having already not long ago collected under themselves the forces of [various] nations, invaded Poland, Russia, Hungary, and other Christian territories. And these marauders so savaged these regions that their sword spared neither age nor sex, but with dreadful barbarity they raged against all indifferently, and laid waste [those lands] with unheard-of destruction, and with uninterrupted advance [acquired] for themselves the kingdoms of others. Unable to rest their swords in their sheaths, they forced submission [to themselves] with ceaseless pursuit.

And so in consequence they may be able to exert their savagery more fully upon even stronger Christian armies, attacking them with vigor, and thus after they have denuded the world of the faithful (which God forbid!), faith may turn aside [its face], when it weeps over what its followers have endured from the ferocity of that people.

Therefore lest the greatly to be detested purpose of the same people be able to be accomplished, but rather that it might fail and by divine intervention be brought to a contrary end, by all the Christian faithful there ought to be careful contemplation in planning and procuring with assiduous exertion, so that in this manner their progress might be checked, so that [their ability] to cross through [Christian lands] any further whenever [they wish] might be denied to them by the power of their armored arms. And for that reason, following the advice of the holy council, we admonish, beseech, and urge all of you, intently commanding that insofar as it is possible, you most carefully investigate the ways and approaches by which this people can enter into our lands, and that you take care to protect them with such ditches and walls or other devices or fortifications as seem fitting, so that the same people will be unable to obtain easy entry into your lands. But if you can, you ought first to announce their advent to the Apostolic See, so that we might direct the assistance of the faithful to you, and so that, with God as your helper, you might be able to be safe from the attempts and attacks of this people.

For toward such necessary and useful expenses which you make for that reason, we shall contribute generously, and we will cause to be contributed toward by all the Christian regions in [due] proportion, since through this a shared danger is counteracted. Nevertheless, in addition to all these things, we shall send letters similar to the present [statute] to all the Christian faithful into whose regions the aforesaid people might have entry.

47. The Master of the Temple to the Preceptor of Templar Houses in England, 1261

In response to the appeal below or another like it, Alexander IV wrote letters reiterating the dangers of the Tartars' ambitions in the Near East and eastern Europe (they had already invaded Hungary) and called for provincial councils to be held and attended by ecclesiastics, secular leaders, and the populace at large to address ways of countering these threats. In England, the archbishop of Canterbury, assisted by the papal nuncio Walter de Rogatis, convened a provincial council in London in the spring of 1261 and sent proctors to Rome with the council's proposals for aid. In response, Henry III wrote a letter intended for Alexander IV, which, while swearing his intention to aid the anti-Tartar efforts, protested the fact that the council had not included royal or noble representatives and had legislated many things that undermined the laws, liberties, and customs of his realm. The letter may never have been sent (in any case, the pope was dead by the time it would have reached Rome), but it suggests one of the elements that prevented the mustering of effective countermeasures to the Tartar threat in western Europe. The letter, Henry III's proposed response to Rome, and Alexander IV's letter (below, No. 48) all illustrate how popes and other parties responded to appeals from the East, which virtually forced Alexander IV to respond and perhaps also sparked liturgical appeals like the one above (No. 44). The letter also balances the overture of Hülagü (below, No. 49), offsetting the Il-Khan's[21] proposals for an alliance by displaying the military orders' panic at the Mongol advance and its subjugation of other Latin princes in the region.

BROTHER Thomas Bernard, by divine grace, humble master of the poor militia of the Temple, to his dear, pious, and prudent brother Amadeus, great preceptor of the houses of the Temple in England, greetings and his sincere esteem.

Although in many preceding years we have often announced to you beforehand in our accustomed style, the dread and terrible advent of the little-known Tartars, now there is no further place for hiding their exploits

Source: The Annals of Burton, *in* H. R. *Luard, ed.,* Annales monastici, *5 vols., Rolls Series 36 (London, 1866–1869), 1:491–495.*
    21. Il'khan was an honorific term meaning ruler.

under a bushel basket [cf. Mt 5:15; Lk 11:33], because those once out-side presently hammer at the gates.[22] We ought rather to demonstrate visibly their astounding and wondrous deeds, through which Christendom overseas is battered forcibly from without, and from within is disordered by excessive fears and anguish and is harrowed by the sword.

Hence it is that these same men are bolstered by so great and such an incredible numerousness and power and subject provinces to their rule without distinction with such great ease, that no none is able to oppose their forces. Perhaps this was permitted by the Lord, who is wont to purge his people, placed in the evil position of a pestilence of this sort, with scourges, so that perhaps they might be restored to heart, since according to the prophet David, the Lord's judgments are an abyss to many [Ps 35:7]. But after subjugating the Persians, Medes, Assyrians, Chaldeans, Turks, Armenians, Georgians, and other infinite nations, and by means of an unexpected opportunity,[23] having unexpectedly subjugated Baghdad, that great and most powerful city, they have moreover savagely devoured with the mouth of their sword the flesh of the caliph, that is the pope of the Saracens, and the lords and leaders of the same, together with their children and immeasurable households and others living in that same city.

Afterward, in addition, in the county called Rochas, they most powerfully subjugated to themselves Haman, la Chamele [Camela], Caesarea majora, and various cities, fortifications, and provinces and lands of the Old Man of the Mountain, Harran, Hassar and other fortifications from this place, and recently fiercely besieged the county of the lord of Aleppo near Ephesus. For this reason the people of Antioch, fearing lest sudden disaster fall upon them, particularly since the city of Antioch could by no means be held because of the unsuitability of its defenses, by the will and authority of the lord H., its noble prince,[24] they sent illustrious messengers to the Mongols with various gifts of great value, that is, Preachers, Minorites, Jacobites, Greeks, and religious men, his bailiff and constable, so that at least by sparing their blood their leader might allow them to wretchedly exist under tribute and the servitude of subjection. Their war

22. Thomas's point here seems to be that he is not conveying general information as he might otherwise do, but rather an urgent news bulletin that requires an immediate response.

23. The phrase "unexpected opportunity" can also be read as "sudden overthrow" or "misfortune," reflecting the Latin settlers' ambiguous feelings regarding the downfall of Baghdad and the death of the last Ayyubid caliph. The actual circumstances of the Mongol triumph in this case derived from a series of unforeseen contingencies.

24. Despite the erroneous initial "H.," this refers to Bohemond V, prince of Antioch (1233–1252).

leader and lord Halan[25] gave kind audience and assent to their petitions. It was nonetheless feared that, on the contrary, the worshippers of Christ might be allotted to others under him—may it not be so.

As a matter of fact, after the expedition of the aforesaid messengers, Halan commanded that the city of Aleppo be surrounded by his men and that it be assailed both by various kinds of machines and through mines and cats and other things necessary in such business, so that within five days they broke into the same city with violence, not without an immense slaughter of the Saracens. And on account of their great number, in one day the city's walls were completely demolished by their army, and with their army and machines they dreadfully assaulted the castle situated in that same city.

However, the sultan of Aleppo and Damascus[26] had reinforced the garrison with a hundred and fifty mounted warriors in order to resist the Mongols, and hearing of the unexpected fall of his city, terrified and conquered by fear alone, withdrew from Damascus with swift flight, and made the crossing with some men near our castle which is called Saphet [Safad], and from there directed his steps toward Gaza, not without danger.

As a matter of fact, on account of that situation others were plunged into desolation and terror. The entire populace of that same city and land, having witnessed their lord and captain fleeing with no one in pursuit, with no one terrifying them as yet or throwing them into a panic, were vanquished without combat. Abandoning their own, they took sudden and deranged flight in so great a throng that no one turned their eyes toward another: not parents to children, husbands to their wives, brother to brother, the humble to the lofty, the powerful to the powerless and conversely. Nor could anyone be found who would administer alleviation or assistance to the falling, since they believed that no place could be reached in which they could find any comfort from so great a dread and terror. And so the nobility of Damascus were left defenseless in subjugation to the Tartars.

Moreover, as public report testifies, on the advice of the king of Armenia [Hetoum I], the aforesaid prince of Antioch made an arrangement with the lord of the Tartars [Hülagü] concerning Tripoli and the rest of his land according to the form of the city and land of Antioch. And

25. That is, Hülagü.
26. An-Nasir Yusuf, ruler of Aleppo (1236–1260), Damascus (1250–1260), and Baalbek. For his fate, see document No. 49 below.

as that truthful assertion proposed, in the preparation of those present terms, there was the proposition of the prince visiting the same lord of the Tartars personally, or at least through distinguished messengers, carrying with them costly gifts. Certainly, as you know, in the regions on this side of the sea the cities of Acre and Tyre, and altogether seven of our houses and three castles—two in Antioch and one castle of the house of the Teutons in Apolitana, and in the province of Jerusalem two, and in the hospital of Saint John two, in the land of Tripoli one castle of the house of the Teutons—were fortified in order to resist the same Tartars according to the power granted to us by the Lord, and with the help of God we resolve to manfully preserve the same for the work of Christendom all the way to the very last intermission.

However, because of the Christians' small number and impotence, we do not see how other lands and places can be held, unless they are mercifully passed over by the Lord. However much, solicitously and assiduously, we may follow up on this matter, it will manifest itself according to the means of the times and malice of the times. Moreover, we are completely ignorant of what kind of scourges, tribulations, difficulties, and pressures of what measure the eye has not seen nor the ears heard, we will be obligated to endure. And since for the sake of so great a business one does not brook delay, before the appropriate season, in a certain galley which could not, as befitted the matter, hold a host of messengers, we were led to send personally our beloved brothers—our brother Stephen to the parts of Spain, and a certain Hospitaller to the parts of France, and a third lord of the Teutons to the parts of *Alemannia*.[27] They bore letters from ourselves and the lord legate and the community of Christians overseas, in which we inform Your Excellence more fully, and seeking more intently and imploring with humble prayers and conjuring in many ways by the shedding of the blood of Jesus Christ, so that directing the eyes of piety and compassion toward the land specially consecrated by his own blood, and having heard the letters and those things set forth through the aforesaid brothers and messengers, you might be eager to give speedy and fit advice upon so great a business, to the extent that the Lord will have granted to you, understanding as a certainty, that unless from these very regions we are swiftly aided, to such a degree that we can withstand the assault and whirlwind of so great a horde, there will be indeed no middle ground. All Christendom overseas will be subjected to their rule.

27. That is, the German-speaking regions of Europe.

To this end, Your Prudence ought to know that . . . in addition to the fortification of our castles and the city of Acre, our house, which answers in the service of greater causes, has and is shouldering such grievous burdens of expenses that it is known to remain in a condition so perilous that, unless through your precaution and that of other faithful persons it is assisted with timely and suitable aid, it will become necessary for us, resulting in no mean injury and scandal to our house, to either desist from the defense of the Holy Land altogether or to alienate some of the possessions and alms of our house in the transmarine region in no small quantity.

For such is the evil of the times in these very parts in these days (because of the same pestilence and the absence of the Genoese and other merchants from Acre) that it is not possible to obtain a loan of money at interest or through securities. On the contrary, for the sake of the aforesaid defenses it is necessary for us to shoulder expenses four times larger than usual. For hired men cannot be had unless they also receive their livelihood, and what price can equal the danger of their death?[28] For is there in the world any prince who without considerable sacrifice could keep seven key castles defensible and well fortified on one and the same day against this incredible horde and shoulder the accumulation of expenses due to those things done for the defense of as great a city as Acre, which for the greater part falls upon us, a city to which all Christendom on this side of the sea recurs as to a solitary refuge? Certainly we do not believe so.[29]

And, O, that merchants and other lenders could be found who through the mortgaging of church ornaments, that is, crosses, chalices, thuribles, and everything else in our houses, would hand over money to us. For in this kind of emergency by no means do we endeavor to spare our own body. On the contrary, we and our honorable religious house rather stand firm in our great desire to pay the debt of nature in regard to the defense of the Christian faith. May the Lord in his mercy spare our souls: we are not anxious about temporal things. Moreover, with great entreaty of prayers we are begging the lord king of England and also the

28. As well as the overwrought and urgent language of this appeal, there is the distinct sense that the author is quite aware of the extremely complex financial conditions and their causes in his lands and the difficulty of hiring mercenaries, as well as the risks for them.

29. The several mentions of Acre in the letter are ominous, and the author's estimation is accurate. The city held out for thirty years after this letter was written. See below, Part X.

queen, that she would implore the king herself,[30] that in order to relieve our house of the lack of ten thousand marks of silver, he ought to aid us mercifully through a loan made out in his name. For this reason we command you to steadfastly solicit the king as solicitously and assiduously as you are able, until you have secured this kind of favor from him, writing back to us your will on this and other matters.

Written in Acre, the fourth day of the month of March, in the year of the Lord 1261.

48. Pope Alexander IV on the Tartar Threat, *Clamat in auribus,* 1261

Alexander IV (1254–1264) issued a number of letters throughout Christendom concerning the Mongol threat. The letter translated here, however, is one of the last papal letters concerning the Mongols, although it is no less apprehensive than earlier letters. It illustrates the general papal perception of the Mongol threat. Similar papal letters on the Mongol threat were sent to Prince Edward of England and many other addressees.

See Reuven Amitai-Preiss, Mongols and Mamluks: The Mamluk-Ilkhanid War, 1260– 1281 *(Cambridge, 1995).*

BISHOP Alexander [IV], servant of the servants of God, to our venerable brothers the archbishop of Canterbury and his suffragans, and also to our beloved sons the abbots, priors, deans, provosts, archdeacons, and other prelates of the churches, to chapters and religious houses of every order in the province of Canterbury, greetings and the apostolic blessing.

The dread trumpet of the public crier calls to the ears of everyone and rouses those whom torpor of soul has not stupefied to vigilance of attentiveness and growing stronger by the credibility of confirming events, with so true a sound it announces beforehand wars leading to general disaster, the scourge of heavenly wrath, of inhuman Tartars bursting forth as if from hidden places of hell, who pull down cities and destroy the face of the earth, so that now it should not be necessary for the ears of the Christian people to be roused to learn of these things by the recital of more certain [facts], as if [matters] were still uncertain, but [rather] that they be admonished to prudently resist this openly violent and hastily approaching danger.

Source: Annals of Burton, *495–499.*
30. Henry III of England and his wife Eleanor of Provence.

For in fact these Tartars, saying that the God of heaven has handed over the entire earth to be occupied by them (which they understood not at all), already have occupied all the eastern regions and have trodden down its inhabitants. Already the hardness of the Saracens which occasioned and produced the wars of many periods, [has been] shattered by the utmost punishment, the desolation of exile. Already the foremost of their cities—Baghdad, Damascus, and Aleppo—have been hostilely seized and destroyed by the same [Tartars] together with many other renowned regions and moreover, the caliph, the head of their infidelity, and a very large host of his people, as it is said, were slain after their surrender had been accepted. And they [the Mongols] reached the boundaries of the kingdom of Jerusalem and attacked by invading it, subjecting the Christian region of Armenia and the illustrious cities of the Christians, Antioch and Tripoli, to their name. Ah the shame of it! And since from the northern region through Hungary and Poland, which border upon the Roman Empire [and] where already—Oh, the mortification!—they have already shed not a little of Christian blood, they may yet attempt a hostile entrance into Europe with a mighty orgy of massacre upon the inhabitants of those regions. For they plan to annihilate the mighty heads of Christendom, and after overthrowing the thrones of kings and seats of powerful rulers, secure the sole rulership of the entire globe. It is for that reason preferable to think of opportune remedies in the face of such a near and pressing danger, than to demand a more swift or more grave enunciation of them.

For this very reason all inactivity arising from unconcern or cowardly sluggishness [ought to be banished, since] it prepares and sets up the improvident for the risk of destruction. And it is fitting that in particular those who lead be roused to attentiveness with the most urgent of goads, lest a sudden defeat at their hands fall upon stupefied men paralyzed through negligence, because the ruin at first menacing evil men occasionally is overcome through diligence of care should they be vigilant. [Yet this did not happen in the case of] the aforementioned Saracens and innumerable other peoples, who deprived of the counsel of prudence and unworthy of heavenly aid, were assailed by the oppression of the Tartars, as is known to have happened. For it is well known that the bane of pestilence and a more ruinous plague infects those who are secure and at peace. And he tests God who when danger menaces neglects to counteract it with remedies provided by human foresight in presumptuous confidence upon heavenly assistance.

For this reason, considering that the scourge of divine ire rages against the sins of the human race through the hand of the same Tartars, nonetheless toward the faithful he demonstrates great evidence of devotion. For he does not wish that [danger] to menace us unforeseen, but that by the antidote of divine propitiation and the counsel of prudence that which was long before foreseen might be successfully prevented. Trusting in the mercy of the compassionate God, that if he should visit the rod upon their iniquities and the blows of discipline upon their sins, in the end he will not hide his mercy from them, we deliberated with [our] brothers in what way our special pastoral office demands from us (to whom it is granted, albeit undeservedly to command) to order useful [and] salutary remedies against this same scourge.

Certainly it seems that in the face of such a hinge of universal necessity a general council ought to be convoked not only of ecclesiastics (for it is evident that the men of the church alone cannot suffice) but also of secular princes and of peoples of the faith, so that general deliberation may be held concerning the universal danger to everyone, with the attentive observations of each individual for the provision of fitting remedies. For in this situation, most common to everyone and most peculiar to each individual, no one takes the lead. Although it should particularly concern the very powerful, who before all else are accustomed to organizing the response, what should happen if they are killed at the beginning of whatever kind of desolation, so that the others might be more easily, like leaderless men, taken captive and scattered to their harm?

Anything concerning the whole touches each one in particular, binding together the ruin and position, death and life of each individual. For among those same Tartars no one was protected by patronage, condition of rank or weakness of sex or compassion for age or respect for rank. They undertook the ruin and destruction not of certain groups but of everyone. They observe no pact or pledge of faith, which in fact the infidels cannot make.[31] For this very reason when they pretend that they have the intention of private affection for Christians, this snare of theirs ought rather to be guarded against by Christians as a cunning ruse, cloaked under the cover of this kind of pretense, by which they will endeavor to trip them up with more subtle deceits, which they trust in and devise for contending against stronger peoples.

---

31. A similar observation on the incapacity of the Mongols, or infidels generally, to make treaties is expressed by Humbert of Romans; see No. 70 below.

In fact, because these Tartars are persisting vigilantly in their wicked plans, this kind of matter does not bear the cost of long delay. Because of injuries to persons and losses to properties it would be of no value for us to assemble the whole world with us in a council after a long stretch of time. And so, according to the necessity by which the general body is burdened, by the advice of the aforementioned brothers, we were led to recommend this present expedient: that in every single kingdom and province the faithful ought to be exhorted to consider those particular causes, on account of which the Saracens and other peoples are clearly provoking divine judgment against themselves, since the displeasure of our God has inflicted them with the plague of the Tartar desolation, and their faithlessness is now subject to a faithless nation. In addition to the failure of human foresight, they were buried by their dilatoriness and inactivity and turned asunder from each other by various quarrels, and so they deprived themselves of the timely remedies of defense. As far as possible, after absorbing a warning for themselves from the dangers facing foreigners, the faithful ought to preserve themselves from the evils threatening them by applying contrary remedies.

We therefore admonish, urge, and invite the whole of you, commanding you through apostolic writings, [and] strictly enjoining that according to the virtue of obedience to the extent that you are able, that you, brother archbishop, through yourself and through those to whom you entrust this matter, convoke to a provincial council, and, if it should prove necessary, bind through ecclesiastical censure, the prelates of your province, both regulars and seculars and equally the exempt. . . . [And we urge] you to swiftly and suitably arrange in one universal provision how through the word of exhortation the people subject to you might be effectually led to reconcile themselves to God and God to the same through fitting fruits of penance, and indeed to reform in themselves the fellowship of mutual peace. Let the wrath of divine punishment, inflamed by the iniquity of those sinning, be appeased by the devout humility of those doing penance and crying out to God in heaven. For no enemy opposition will harm those who do not allow themselves to be mastered by any depravity of vices or dissension among themselves.

Then you ought to take care to premeditate with well-considered weighing of deliberation by what means and by what remedies and subsidies both ecclesiastical and secular the same Tartars may be resisted, both in the Holy Land which they are assaulting and invading, and in the kingdom of Hungary and in the land of Poland. For in these and other [regions], they endeavor to gain entrance by force in order to occupy other kingdoms of the Christians, and the forces of the Christian people ought to unite together as one. For the resources of one king or realm are not sufficient for containing the incursions of a horde so great and so indomitable.[32] We ought also to ascertain what penalties and what spiritual censures and compulsions may be necessary to restrain Christians of whatever exalted rank or condition from entering into alliances with the same Tartars, lest they make void the faith which they ought to keep with God and their neighbors of the catholic religion and attempt anything to the injury and damage of the Christian name and people.

Moreover, they ought to be held to aid these regions against the same Tartars either in person or through other measures or other men. Indeed as war leaders or captains they ought to take command of the army of the faithful in the battle of the Lord that will be advancing against the satellites of the infidels. In particular ecclesiastics and the Christian people ought to be led to make gifts and other things suited to support and assistance on behalf of those accomplishing these things.

You ought no less to ponder—according to the prudence given to you by God and with opportune foresight—about the remaining intercessions and deliberate upon matters pertaining to so great and well-known a business, keeping God and the collective danger before your eyes. And you ought to engage in careful deliberation on all these things until the next octaves of the feast of the apostles Peter and Paul to come (because having considered the urgency of necessity, assuredly that space of time ought to seem brief to no one). Afterward, you ought to send to the apostolic seat some of your number or otherwise your messengers. These men ought to be suitable and discreet and sufficiently instructed and possessed of a full mandate from you pertaining to the accomplishing of all the matters mentioned above (which you would have the power to accomplish if personally present), through whom your wishes and counsel regarding the aforementioned matters might be made known to us. And once their advice has been communicated to us, the aforesaid apostolic seat may with provident deliberation decree, arrange, and order those things which the service of the public welfare of Christendom demands in such an arduous affair.

For we resolutely trust in the Lord and in the might of his power that if all these measures are prepared together with fitting order, the

---

32. Or, "so impious."

Tartars might find the Christians readied to withstand the Tartars' savagery and fortified beforehand with the assistance of divine favor and the
stratagems of human foresight. We hope that with these there might be
experienced among them the dread of a host of vicious events, fictitious
wonders, the deceits of trickery and schism of discord, that those
unprovided-for means through which they have thus far prevailed over
foreign peoples might benefit them little. And in fact that rather with
God's favor they [the Christians] will demonstrate to them how much
the name of Christ is worth to those faithfully and worthily calling upon it
in the war of the faithful against the perfidious. If, however, you, brother
archbishop, should be absent or neglectful (may this not be so), you
ought to see to it all these things are carried out by your son, the chapter
of Canterbury, supported by apostolic authority.

The annalist notes that Pope Alexander died this same year.

49. A Letter from Hülagü, Il-Khan of Persia, to Louis IX of France, 1262

The letter translated below appears to have been one of many carried by an
embassy sent by Hülagü, the il-khan of Persia, to Louis IX, Urban IV (1261–
1264), and other Western rulers in 1262. A later legation sent by Hülagü's son
and successor Abagha to the Second Council of Lyons (1274) mentioned this
earlier attempt to make an alliance but claimed that its messengers had been intercepted by Manfred, the illegitimate son of Frederick II. However, it appears that
at least one messenger, John the Hungarian, did reach Urban IV with an official
letter and accompanying oral messages. A copy of the letter intended for Louis IX,
preserved by a fourteenth-century scribe, is translated below. Although we cannot
say with absolute certainty that it reached its intended audience, some scholars
believe that the Mongol embassy did reach Louis in Paris.

Written not long after the battle of 'Ain Jalut, the letter uses a curious blend
of blandishment and intimidation to urge Louis to lend naval assistance and block
the Mamluks' retreat from a planned Mongol land offensive. The editor of the
letter convincingly suggests that it was composed in Latin (rather than being translated into Latin from the Mongolian) by Richard, a trusted notary of Hülagü and
his successor Abagha. A European who entered the service of the Mongol court,
Richard drafted other letters intended for Western audiences and was mentioned
in a document presented to the Second Council of Lyons in 1274.

Source: Paul Meyvaert, *"An Unknown Letter of Hülagü, Il-Khan of Persia, to King
Louis IX of France,"* Viator 11 (1980), 245–259, text 252–259.

A formal greeting to Louis IX, the intended recipient of the letter, appears to have been omitted by the scribe who copied the letter.

SOME time ago God spoke to our forefathers through prophets concerning these last days variously and in many ways. He spoke to our grandfather Chinggis Khan through his blood relative Teb Tngri (a name which is interpreted as "prophet of God"), miraculously revealing to him events of future times, signifying by making known to the said Teb Tngri: "In the heavens I alone am the omnipotent God, and I appoint you ruler over all peoples and kingdoms, and you will become king of the entire globe, so that you will 'uproot and demolish, scatter and destroy, build up and plant' [Jer 1:10]. I therefore proclaim to you that you ought to make known my commission to you to every generation and tongue and tribe of the north, south, east, and west. And you ought to declare it to every single region of the entire globe in which rulers or kings reign, governors govern, lordship is exercised and wherever horses' hooves may tread, ships may sail, messengers may arrive, and letters be heard, so that those with ears might hear, those hearing might comprehend, those comprehending might believe. In fact, anyone who does not believe in my divine commission ought to consider how those who do not believe in my mandates may be humbled afterward."

We, however, in the Might of the Everlasting Heaven (that is, of the living God) Hülagü Khan, commander of the army of the Mongols, zealous devastator of the faithless people of the Saracens, benevolent exalter of the Christian faith, vigorous conqueror of enemies, and assuredly the loyal friend of his allies the illustrious king of the Franks Louis and also the princes, dukes, counts, barons, knights, and others, send our greetings to each and every person in the entire kingdom of France in the mercy of God. We made these things known to you by announcing the aforementioned revelation so that you might choose to ally with us without hesitation. For we are fulfilling the mandate of the living God, which if you reflected upon it attentively (as you ought), you would see that our power was conferred by the Lord Messiah himself (that is, the living God). However, lest we perhaps have caused a message of this nature to be written to you in vain, we will explain succinctly a few of the many things which in our times not long ago befell those of our opponents who did not believe in our mandates, or rather those of the living God.

For it pleased our majesty to begin by announcing the divine command to the kings and rulers of the East, that is: the king of the Kästimi, the king of the Naiman, the king of the Merkid, the king of Kirgis, the king of the Nangyaz, the king of the Kitai, the king of the Kangut, the king of the Töbed, the king of the Uihur, the king of Quamul, the king of Ulbäri, the leader of the Quarasan, the sultan of the Persians, the leaders of the Cumans, and in addition to the kings and sultans, princes and leaders of the southern region (that is, those ruling India and the surrounding areas), and also to the rest and countless others, whose names it would breed disgust to enumerate in writing.[33] Contrary to the divine edict, they contemptuously resisted the lordship conferred upon us by God, and in their pride, trusting in their own armed forces, they were not the least bit afraid to draw up their battle lines against us in combat. And so that we might summarily pass over these matters, we caused these noxious pests to be destroyed by slaughter. We vigorously attacked their kingdoms, possessions, cities, and fortresses, laying waste each and every one of them as we pleased. However, some of their more prominent men, bolstered by our kindness, allied themselves to our excellency in a friendly manner. And we spared them with all those who looked to them for leadership, and the more prominent of them rejoiced that without hesitation on our part they were permitted to remain there.

And in the other intervening years, the might of the living God leading the way toward the eastern zone, we sent a resolution first to the sultan of the Assassins, that is, the murderer of the circumcised. And we intimated to him that after previously reflecting upon the nature of our authority, he ought speedily to make himself subject to us. However, applauding their fortresses situated on the peaks of the loftiest mountains, and believing himself to possess a vast army and sufficiency of supplies, he instead rashly desired to do battle with us. But we erased the name of Rukn-ad-din [Khurshah] from this earth together with all of his generation, and also his most mighty fortresses, that is, the fortress of Maimundiz, the fortress of Alamut, and each and every fortress we razed to the foundations, nearly one hundred and fifty.[34]

    33. On the lists of Mongol conquests, see George D. Painter, "The Tartar Relation," Excursus B, in R. A. Skelton, T. E. Marston, G. D. Painter, eds., *The Vinland Map and the Tartar Relation* (New Haven CT, 1965), esp. 104–106.
    34. The Assassins, an Ismailite sect with adherents in northern Syria and Palestine, were said by Matthew Paris to have sent ambassadors to western European leaders requesting aid against the Mongols. After Latin settlers established themselves in the Near East they became alternately targets for "assassination" and potential allies with the Assassins against other competing powers in the region. The Latin imagination was captivated by the Assassins, and they quickly became the stuff of legend, particularly the leader of the Syrian branch, who became known as "the Old Man of the Mountain." The Assassins came under threat

And once this was accomplished, we sent the foresaid mandate to the kings and princes of the circumcised, and fourteen kings and princes who were reported to be disobedient to us we caused to be destroyed with all their men in the same manner. In fact, when these things were completed, after some time had passed, it pleased us to send the original mandate, as described above, to the caliph of Baghdad. Contemptibly boasting of himself, he by no means hesitated to swear most firmly that he was assuredly the pope, head of the world for the race of the aforementioned Muhammad, that most wicked pseudo-prophet, and that he himself was the all-powerful creator for the aforesaid Muhammad and his entire race, that he had created the heaven and the earth and everything contained in them. And so trusting in his noble eminence and boundless riches, countless fortresses, and the most powerful hosts of his armies, he chose rather to battle against us than graciously to submit to our mandate. However, so that by publicly fighting against him we might subdue other rebels, by the power of the omnipotent God we slew from his forces by our reckoning two thousand of thousands fighters, omitting others, of whom there was a countless multitude. We commanded that a certain patriarch of the Nestorians dwelling in the aforementioned city of Baghdad with his bishops, monks, priests, clerics, and all of the same Christians be separated out from the Saracens one by one and that they be granted enlarged possessions and be permitted to reside in that city quietly and without molestation of their possessions.

After we hanged the sultan of Aleppo and Damascus, his terror-stricken son conveyed to us his wish to become our subject. Pleased by his submission, we sent officials to the same [ruler] throughout his lands and privileges written upon golden tablets, which were a sign of fuller preferment. However, after a little while, incited by the instigation of fate, he reneged on his solemn promise and contrary to himself, proved himself hostile to us. Therefore, when the same person fled, we vigorously assaulted his lands and fortresses and destroyed the cities of Aleppo and

---

from the Mongols when the latter began to expand into Asia Minor, and the Assassins, as Muslim "heretics," could expect little help from other Muslim powers in the Near East. The Mongol general Hülagü captured the Assassin "headquarters" in the fortress of Alamut in Persia and other strongholds in 1256, while the Syrian branch lost its main castle of Masyad to the Mongols in 1260 and its remaining holdings to the sultan Baibars in 1272. Matthew's account is in Giles, *Matthew Paris's English History*, 1:131–132, 312–314; 3:449–552. See also J. J. Saunders, "Matthew Paris and the Mongols," in T. A. Sandquist and M. R. Powicke, eds., *Essays in Medieval History Presented to Bertie Wilkinson* (Toronto, 1969), 116–132; Farhad Daftary, *The Assassin Legends: Myths of the Isma'ilis* (London, 1994).

Damascus, Haman and Haniz, Baalbek, Harran and Baya.[35] After capturing him in flight, we commanded his head to be hung above the gate of
the city of Tabriz as an example to other traitors.

We understood without a doubt through John of Hungary that certain Latin slaves had come to the Holy Land for the sake of devotion,
against the infidels on behalf of the holy city of Jerusalem. And we do not
believe that we ought to conceal from your lordship that through the
same John we caused them to be restored to their former liberty. Moreover, you ought to recognize that our excellency is not unacquainted
with the fact that, although there are ever so many kings of the western
Christians, you nonetheless are distinguished before all others by the
splendor of your exceptional zeal, such that, of everyone who is reckoned
worthy of the Christian name you are the most assiduously intent upon
salvation. For although we had not already sent to you our messengers,
as a sign of our particular friendship in honor of the most omnipotent
and living God, you took pains to dispatch to our predecessor Güyük
through your trustworthy messengers a portable chapel dedicated to the
divine name as a special refreshment.[36]

If at that time, as we said, you were not yet intent whatsoever upon
these things which were signified by us, you were much more so intent
concerning the rest, since not only by letters, but also by our trusty messengers we have taken care to visit Your Majesty. And touched previously
by your friendship, we do not fail to believe that you wish to renew such
an alliance with us by reforging a stronger bond between us. Moreover,
we wished to reveal ourselves in a friendly manner to your lordship. And
at first we believed the highest priest, the pope, to be the king of the
Franks or the emperor. But after making a more careful investigation, we
realized that he was a holy man praying devotedly to God on behalf of all
peoples, taking the place upon earth of the Lord Messiah himself, son of
the living God, and that he was the head of all those believing in Christ
and calling upon him. And once we understood these things we commanded that the holy city of Jerusalem, detained for so long by sacrile-
gious men, be given back to him, with all the other things pertaining to

35. The Hebrew chronicler Bar Hebraeus mentions Harran, Baklash, Hama, B'elbek
(Baalbek?)-Harim as among the cities conquered by Hülagü in 1260. E. A. Wallis Budge,
trans., *The Chronography of Gregory Abu'l Faraj, the Son of Aaron, the Hebrew Physician,
Commonly Known as Bar Hebraeus* (London, 1932).

36. When Louis IX landed at Cyprus in 1248, he received messengers from the
Mongol commander Eljigidei, who hoped to ally with him against the Muslims. The envoys
reported that Güyük had become a Christian, and so in 1249 Louis had sent a return

that entire kingdom, through our faithful and devoted servant John the Hungarian, follower of the aforesaid Christian faith. And we believe without a doubt that this news has already resounded in your ears at various times.

However, because we are accustomed to retire more gladly to the cooler places of the snowy mountains during the summer heat, after the aforementioned cities of Aleppo and Damascus had been laid waste, and both provisions and forage were for the most part consumed, it pleased us to withdraw to the mountains of Greater Armenia for a little while. And we dispatched a few of our men to the aforesaid places in order to destroy the remnants of the Assassins' fortresses, in which they were stealthily hiding after contemplating the scarcity of their surviving numbers, and our men fell upon those Babylonian dogs when they crept out of their holes like mice. Yet some of our men, as their offenses deserved, were gnawed to pieces by the aforementioned mice, because they had been deceitful about obeying our commands by invading the possessions of the Franks.[37] Although the vengeance wreaked upon those faithless men was not entirely displeasing to us, nor did it even inflict detectable damage upon us, nonetheless our intention is to fulfill utterly and in a short period our plan against the aforesaid Babylonian dogs of the infidel race, just as we also plan against other rebels. Because, however, if they are attacked by land they might find a refuge by the waters of the sea, as we understand it, we have taken pains to inspire Your Eminence so that you might exert your power from the opposite quarter upon the shores of the sea. For through your assiduous precaution with armed vessels in the sea you might check the aforesaid infidel dogs, enemies to us and to yourself equally, and you might take care to obstruct the aforesaid refuge, lest due to a lack of sea defenses they might be able to escape our assaults in any respect.

May you prosper in the Lord Messiah, that is, in the living God, eternally without end. If it pleases you, make known your intentions upon these and other matters with timely dispatch, through your special messengers together with ours. Given in the city of Maragheh in the tenth year of Hülagü's reign, in the Year of the Dog, on the tenth day of the month of April.

---

embassy to the Great Khan. Led by Andrew of Longjumeau, it carried among its gifts a portable chapel made of scarlet cloth.

    37. Perhaps an allusion to the Mongol general Kitbuqa's sack of Sidon and his ensuing defeat by a Mamluk army in September 1260, at 'Ain Jalut.

PART VII
The Saint's Crusades, 1248–1270

Like Frederick II and other thirteenth-century crusaders, Louis IX of France came from a distinguished crusading dynasty. His great-grandfather Louis VII had been one of the leaders of the Second Crusade, his grandfather Philip II Augustus one of the leaders of the Third Crusade, and his father Louis VIII had died on the Albigensian Crusade. This family legacy and the ominous events of the 1230s and early 1240s—the Mongol threat, the destruction of Jerusalem and the slaughter at La Forbie in 1244, the papal call for a crusade against Frederick II in 1239 and again in 1244, and the optimism created by the apparent successes of the Barons' Crusade—certainly sharpened Louis's sense of devotion and crusading obligation. In 1238 Louis had purchased the Crown of Thorns from the Latin emperor of Constantinople, Baldwin, and began construction of the Sainte Chapelle to house it and other relics. Over the winter of 1244 Louis was overtaken by a life-threatening illness, and on his recovery, he took the cross.

Louis and his three brothers—Robert of Artois, Alphonse of Poitiers, and Charles of Anjou—and many of his subjects attended the great assembly in Paris in 1245, which was followed by the most detailed planning of any crusade. As William C. Jordan, Caroline Smith, Peter Jackson, and others have pointed out, Louis examined virtually every facet of royal governance, rights, and resources in the entire kingdom. Louis used mendicants as inquirers into every corner of the kingdom, and he appointed his mother Blanche of Castile as regent during his absence. Louis designated Cyprus as the main staging area, and for two years Cyprus was stocked with substantial amounts of every conceivable crusading need, from food (and wine) to weapons and other resources. The immense cost of the crusade—around two million livres tournois—amounted to eight times the annual royal income and was raised also through a tax of one-twentieth on all ecclesiastical incomes and for three years a tax of one-tenth on the French clergy. Louis formally took up his pilgrim's scrip and staff as well as the oriflamme, the banner of the kings of France at war, in Paris on June 12, 1248.

The army of twenty to twenty-five thousand troops sailed to Cyprus, planning, like the Fifth Crusade, an attack on Egypt. The army landed on the Egyptian coast and moved swiftly south, finding Damietta deserted, and encountered the forces of the sultan as-Salih under the command of Fakhr ad-Din at Mansura on February 8, 1250. Again, the crusader forces were defeated by the strength and skill of as-Salih's army, greatly increased by the slave-soldiers known as Mamluks, the treacherous hydrology of Nilotic northern Egypt, and several tactical errors on the part of Christian leaders. Louis himself was captured and released in exchange for Damietta, a ten-year truce was agreed upon, and other nobles were ransomed for the sum of 800,000 gold bezants (around 400,000 livres tournois).

Louis and much of the surviving army sailed to Palestine, where they spent four years refortifying the defenses and extracting their captured comrades from captivity. In April 1254, Louis returned to France.

In 1266 Pope Clement IV planned a small crusade in conjunction with Abagha of Persia and the Byzantine emperor Michael VIII Palaeologus. But delays on the part of Clement and his allies permitted the new Mamluk sultan Baibars to retake Antioch in 1268. Clement IV died in the same year, and there was no papal election until 1271. But Louis IX once more took up the cross, and in July 1270 he sailed for North Africa again, this time to Tunis, where he became seriously ill and died in August 1270. His remains were carried back to France with great mourning.

The sources for Louis's internal reforms in France and for his first crusade are abundant. The most widely known of them is the *Life of Saint Louis* written by the seneschal of the county of Champagne, Jean de Joinville (below, No. 50). There also survive several letters from this crusade sent back to inform the kingdom of the early triumphs on the way to Mansura (below, No. 51), and a long letter from Louis himself to his subjects concerning the defeat (below, No. 53). There are also several Arabic accounts of Louis's defeat and captivity (below, No. 52). The bitter resentment on the part of many of Louis's subjects over the defeat and captivity of their king as well as resentment at the diversion of papal and imperial resources in the papal-imperial conflict triggered a popular reform movement that came to be known as the Crusade of the Shepherds (*Pastoureaux*) in 1251 (below, No. 54). The temper of much of France around the time of Louis's second crusade is illustrated by the poems of Rutebeuf (below, No. 56), while excerpts from the register of Eudes, archbishop of Rouen manifest the complexities facing a conscientious prelate responsible for promoting multiple crusades (below, No. 55)

M. Cecilia Gaposchkin, The Making of Saint Louis: Kingship, Sanctity, and Crusade in the Later Middle Ages *(Ithaca NY, 2008); Gaposchkin, "The Place of the Crusades in the Sanctification of St. Louis," in Thomas F. Madden, James L. Naus, and Vincent Ryan, eds.,* Crusades—Medieval Worlds in Conflict *(Farnham UK-Burlington VT, 2012), 195–209; Peter Jackson,* The Seventh Crusade, 1244–1254 *(Aldershot UK-Burlington VT, 2007); William C. Jordan,* Louis IX and the Challenge of Crusade: A Study in Rulership *(Princeton NJ, 1979); Jean Richard,* Saint Louis, Crusader King of France *(Cambridge, 1992); Caroline Smith,* Crusading in the Age of Joinville *(Aldershot UK-Burlington VT, 2006); Janet Shirley,* Crusader Syria in the Thirteenth Century: The Rothelin Continuation of the History of William of Tyre with Part of the Eracles or Acre Text *(Aldershot UK-Burlington VT, 1999); Jacques Le Goff,* Saint Louis, *trans. Gareth Evan Gollrad (Notre Dame IN, 2009); William C. Jordan, "The Rituals of War: Departure for Crusade in Thirteenth-Century France," in William Noel and Daniel Weiss, eds.,* The Book of Kings: Art, War, and the Morgan Library's Picture Bible *(Baltimore, 2002), 98–105; Daniel H. Weiss,* Art and Crusade in the Age of Saint Louis *(Cambridge-New York, 1998); Daniel H. Weiss and Lisa Mahoney,* France and the Holy Land: Frankish Culture at the End of the Crusades *(Baltimore, 2004); Madden, Naus, and Ryan,* Crusades—Medieval Worlds in Conflict.

50. Jean de Joinville's Description of His Crusade Preparations, 1248

Jean de Joinville was born around 1225 and educated in the court of his lord, Thibaut IV of Champagne, himself the scion of a crusading family and a well-known poet (see above, No. 33). Only recently named to the seneschalsy of Champagne and lordship of Joinville while in his early twenties, and with a young family to support, Joinville nonetheless joined the crusade of Louis IX in 1248, despite the fact that no direct pressure from the king or his lord was exerted upon him to take the cross. In fact, Joinville pointedly stated that he was not Louis's vassal, and he may have been more influenced by family traditions of crusading (a Joinville had participated in every major crusade between 1147 and 1248). Although he quickly ran out of funds to support himself and his men, Joinville was soon retained by Louis IX and became the king's close associate during the crusade in Egypt and during the king's extended stay in the Holy Land. Despite being rewarded for his loyal service overseas and subjected to direct pressure both from Thibaut of Champagne and Louis himself, Jean refused to participate in Louis IX's second doomed venture. He may have done so because he believed that it was his duty to prevent the harm his estates and men had suffered during his prior absence on crusade. Certainly by the 1260s, Jean appears to have suffered financial losses resulting from the costs of his prior crusade, but he also acquired new assets that required delicate management in order to provide for his dependents and would have been endangered by any prolonged absence.

Recent scholarship suggests that what became Joinville's *Life of Saint Louis* was written in two distinct phases. The first draft appears to have been largely intended as an account of Joinville's experiences on crusade which he wrote in the 1270s or 1280s and which contained a more "human" portrait of his king and friend Louis IX. In response to the request of Jeanne de Navarre, wife of Louis's grandson Philip (IV) the Fair, for a depiction of Louis the saint, Joinville later framed his crusading text with a presentation of Louis that reflects his own attempt, as a noble layman, to reconcile the values that he considered saintly with those typically portrayed in hagiography and the canonization proceedings. These sections were written after 1297, probably in the early years of the fourteenth century. Joinville's memoirs seem to have been intimately related to the testimony he gave at the inquests held to gather information for Louis IX's canonization in 1282–1283 and to the failings he perceived in the court of Louis's grandson, Philip the Fair. For Joinville and Louis's other biographers, the crusade provided a context for Louis to demonstrate key traits of sainthood familiar from hagiographical texts but also enabled him to epitomize certain chivalric and religious values shared by knightly circles in France and elsewhere. Louis embraced the crusade with zeal, used the crusade as a context for pious works and the demonstration of personal bravery, kept his word, his honor, and his faith during his captivity, and proved himself a true king in exercising justice and refusing to abandon his people after defeat.

Joinville's memoirs and other evidence seem to indicate that, like Louis IX, he viewed his crusade not only as participation in a military expedition but as a personal religious and penitential pilgrimage undertaken in imitation of his illustrious ancestors, something signified by his reception of the tokens of a pilgrim, the local pilgrimages he undertook before his departure on crusade, and his collection of relics both sacred and secular in the Holy Land (including the shield of his crusading ancestor Geoffrey V). Possessed of a highly limited income and a young family, Joinville mortgaged substantial portions of his lands to support himself and his followers on crusade and, as a good crusader should, made reparations to all and numerous gifts to religious houses to ensure the material and spiritual safety of himself and his family. His account of his own preparations is virtually a model of how a crusader should act. His emotional portrait of his departure on crusade was almost certainly influenced by epic poetry and crusade songs (written by his lord Thibaut IV of Champagne among others) which dwelled upon the sufferings of lovers and families parted by the crusade, although strangely enough, Joinville made no mention of his wife (despite his careful provision for her spiritual welfare in various charitable donations). Perhaps he did so because of his indebtedness to another source: crusade sermons that exhorted crusaders to view their emotional suffering as part of their sacrifice for Christ while refusing to let the tears (and often reproaches) of their spouses keep them from taking and fulfilling their crusade vows.

Smith, Crusading in the Age of Joinville; *Edward Peters, "There and Back Again: Crusaders in Motion, 1095–1291,"* Crusades *5 (2006), 157–171; Caroline Smith, "Saints and Sinners at Sea on the First Crusade of Saint Louis," in Madden, Naus, and Ryan,* Crusades, *161–172; Jordan, "Rituals of War"; John H. Pryor, "Transportation of Horses by Sea During the Era of the Crusades: Eighth Century to 1285 A.D.,"* Mariner's Mirror *68 (1982), 9–27, 103–125.*

FOLLOWING the events just described it happened that God's will was that King Louis should be taken seriously ill at Paris.[1] It was said that he was so unwell that one of the women attending him wanted to draw the sheet over his face, maintaining that he was dead. But another woman, on the other side of the bed, would not allow her to do this. She said his soul was still in his body. As the king listened to the two argue Our Lord

Source: Caroline Smith, trans., Joinville and Villehardouin: Chronicles of the Crusades *(London-New York, 2008), 173–174, 176–177.*

1. Joinville has just described Louis's successful confrontations with rebellious barons in 1226–1242. The king fell ill at Pointoise, not Paris.

worked in him, and restored him immediately to health, for he had been struck dumb and unable to speak. He asked for someone to give him the cross, and they did. When the queen, his mother, was told that he had regained the power of speech, she displayed the greatest possible joy, but when she was told by the king himself that he had taken the cross, she demonstrated grief as profound as if she had seen him dead.

After he had taken the cross, so did the king's three brothers: Robert, count of Artois, Alphonse, count of Poitiers, and Charles, count of Anjou, who later became king of Sicily. Hugh, duke of Burgundy, took the cross and so did William, count of Flanders (the brother of count Guy of Flanders who died recently), the good Hugh, count of Saint-Pol, and his nephew my lord Walter, who conducted himself very well overseas and would have been a most worthy man had he lived. Along with them were the count of La Marche and his son Hugues le Brun, and the count of Sarrebruck and his brother my lord Gobert d'Apremont. It was in the count of Sarrebruck's company that I, Jean, lord of Joinville, crossed the sea in a ship we had hired together because we were cousins. We were twenty knights in all on that crossing, nine of them with him and nine with me.

At Easter, in the year of grace 1248, I summoned my men and my vassals to Joinville. On the eve of Easter, when all the people I had summoned had arrived, my son Jean, lord of Ancerville, was born of my first wife, who was the count of Grandpré's sister. All that week we feasted and danced, for my brother, the lord of Vaucouleurs, and the other rich men present took it in turns to provide a meal on the Monday, Tuesday, Wednesday, and Thursday. On Friday I said to them: "My lords, I am going away overseas and I do not know if I will return. So if I have done you any wrong, come forward, and I will right it for each of you in turn, as I would usually do for anyone who has a claim to make against me or my people." I settled these claims on the advice of all the men of my lands, and, so that I might not exert any undue influence, I withdrew from the meeting and followed all their recommendations unquestioningly.

As I did not wish to take any money with me that was not rightfully mine, I went to Metz in Lorraine, to leave a large portion of my lands in pledge. You should know that on the day I left our country to go to the Holy Land, I had not 1,000 livres-worth of lands, for the lady my mother was still alive.[2] And so I left with nine other knights; three of us were bannerets. I mention these things to you because if God, who has never let me down, had not helped me, I would scarcely have been able to support myself for so long a time as the six years I spent in the Holy Land.

As I was preparing to leave, John, lord of Apremont, count of Sarrebruck by right of his wife, sent word to me informing me that he had made preparations to go overseas as the head of a group of ten knights. He said that, if I wished, he and I might share the hire of a ship. I agreed, and his people and mine hired a ship at Marseilles.

The king summoned all his barons to Paris and had them swear an oath that they would offer faith and loyalty to his children should anything happen to him during the expedition. He asked this of me, but I was unwilling to swear an oath because I was not his man.[3] . . .

Joinville goes to Paris and while there, sees a clerk who had killed three sergeants who had robbed him and was sentenced by the king to accompany him on crusade in his service.

I RETURNED to our own country after these events. The lord of Sarrebruck and I made preparations to send our equipment to Auxonne in carts, where it would be put on the River Saône and taken as far as Arles, via the Saône and the Rhône.

On the day I left Joinville I sent for the abbot of Cheminon, who was said to be the greatest *preudomme* of the white order. . . .[4]

This same abbot of Cheminon gave me my staff and purse. And then I left Joinville, not to enter my castle again until my return. I was on foot, barelegged and wearing a hairshirt. I went thus to Blécourt, Saint-Urbain, and other shrines thereabout. As I made my way to Blécourt and Saint-Urbain, I did not want to cast my eyes back toward Joinville at all, fearful that my heart would melt for the fine castle and two children I was leaving behind.

2. The income from Joinville's lands was less than 1,000 livres per year. While his mother, Beatrice, was alive she continued to receive the profits of the land she had brought to the Joinville family as her dowry; they passed to her son after her death in 1261.

3. Joinville was not a vassal of the king in 1248, but became one during the crusade in 1252.

4. The Cistercians. *Preudomme* was a term in increasingly common use in the thirteenth century, denoting an admirable man who was an ideal person in both his internal disposition and outward conduct. It could be applied to laymen and clerics alike. There is a discussion in Joinville's text in Smith, *Chronicles,* 284.

I and my companions ate at Fontaine-l'Archevêque, near Donjeux, and there Abbot Adam of Saint-Urbain—may God absolve him—gave a great quantity of fine jewels to me and my knights. From there we went to Auxonne, and from there to Lyons. All our equipment had been loaded on to boats and was taken down the River Saône [to Lyons]. The large warhorses were led along beside the boats. At Lyons we entered the river Rhône to go to Arles-le-Blanc. On the Rhône we came across a castle called Roche-de-Glun, which the king had had torn down because Roger, its lord, was accused of robbing pilgrims and merchants.

In the month of August [1248] we embarked on our ships at the Rock of Marseilles. On the day we embarked, the door on the ship was opened, and all the horses we had to take overseas were placed inside before the door was closed again and well caulked—as you would seal a barrel—because when the ship is on the high seas the whole door is underwater.

When the horses were inside, our master mariner called to his sailors who were in the prow of the ship, and said to them, "Are you ready?" They replied, "Yes, sir, you can let the clerks and priests come forward." As soon as they had come, the master mariner called to them, to them, "In God's name, sing!" And they all chanted with one voice *Veni Creator Spiritus*. The master mariner called to his sailors, "In God's name, set sail!" And so they did. Before long the wind had filled the sails and taken us out of sight of land, so that we could see nothing but sky and water. Each day the wind took us farther away from the lands where we were born. I am describing these events to you to show how foolhardy is he who dares place himself in such peril, when he is in possession of another person's property or is in a state of mortal sin, because seafarers go to sleep in the evening not knowing whether they will find themselves at the bottom of the sea the next morning.

51. John Sarrasin, Chamberlain of the King of France, Describes the Capture of Damietta, 1249

This was one of several letters written by members of the king's household, perhaps as part of a royal propaganda campaign to spread the news of Louis's achievement in the capture of Damietta. Of these, three letters survive and are particularly valuable as accounts written from laypersons' (rather than clerical) perspective, but John Sarrasin's letter stands out as the only one written in the vernacular, with express instructions to its recipient to circulate it widely. It seems that

Nicholas Arrode abided by these instructions; the author of the Rothelin continuation of William of Tyre possessed and effectively used a copy of the letter.

Jeanette M. A. Beer, "The Letter of Jean Sarrasin, Crusader," in Barbara N. Sargent-Baur, ed., Journeys Toward God: Pilgrimage and Crusade *(Kalamazoo MI, 1992), 135–155.*

To MY Lord Nicholas Arrode, from John Sarrasin, Chamberlain to the King of France, greeting and kind love.

This is to tell you that the king and queen, and the count of Anjou[5] and his wife, and I are safe and sound in the city of Damietta, which God in his mercy and pity and by his miraculous power, restored to Christendom on the second Sunday after Pentecost.

Next, I must tell you how this happened. After the king and the Christian army had embarked at Aigues Mortes, we sailed on the feast of Saint Augustine and were off the island of Cyprus a fortnight before the feast of Saint Remy, that is, on Saint Lambert's Day. The count of Angers landed at the city of Limassol. The king and those of us who were with him in his ship (it was called the *Montjoy*) landed early the next morning, and the count of Artois[6] at about nine o'clock at the same port. There were very few of us on the island and we spent until Ascension Day waiting for the fleet, which had not arrived.

The Christmas before, one of the great princes of the Tartars, called Eltheltay,[7] who was a Christian, had sent his ambassadors to the king of France at Nicosia in Cyprus. The king sent Brother Andrew, of the Order of Saint James, to the ambassadors. They had not known to whom they should address themselves, but they understood Brother Andrew as well as we understand one another, and he them. The king had the ambassadors brought before him and they spoke at length in their own language. Brother Andrew translated their message into French for the king, to the effect that on the feast of the Epiphany the supreme prince of the Tartars had become a Christian, and many of his people with him, in particular some of their greatest lords. They said also that with his whole army of Tartars Eltheltay would help the king of France and the Christian forces against the caliph of Baghdad and the Saracens because he wished to

Source: René Hague, trans., The Life of Saint Louis *(New York, 1955), 241–246.*

5. Charles, count of Anjou, was Louis IX's brother. Blanche of Castile, Louis's mother, was named regent of the kingdom in her son's absence.

6. Robert, count of Artois, also Louis IX's brother.

7. That is, Eljigidei. For this embassy, see Part VI above on the Mongols.

avenge the great and shameful injuries the Khwarizmians and other Saracens had inflicted on our lord Jesus Christ and on Christendom.[8] They said that their master also urged the king to cross to Egypt in the spring and attack the sultan of Babylon while the Tartars would at the same time invade the territory of the caliph of Baghdad. Their enemies would thus be unable to help one another.

The king of France decided to send his own ambassadors back with them to their master, Eltheltay, and to the supreme lord of the Tartars, whose name was Quioquan,[9] to verify the truth of the message. They told him that it was a good six-month journey to the place where Quioquan lived, but that their master Eltheltay and the Tartar army were not very far away; they were in Persia, which they had completely overrun and made subject to the Tartars. They stressed again the good will of the Tartars to the king and to Christendom.

A fortnight after Candlemas Day, the Tartar ambassadors left in company with the king's envoy, that is, brother Andrew of Saint James,[10] and a brother of his, Master John Goderiche, another clerk from Poissy, Herbert the Sommelier, and Gerbert of Sens. At mid-Lent the king had news of them; under the protection of the banner of the Tartar chief, they were crossing the territory of the infidels; respect for his ambassadors obtained for them anything they wanted.

After this the king and his whole expedition, which he reckoned at a good twenty-five hundred knights, five thousand crossbowmen, and a large number of other persons, mounted and on foot embarked at Limassol and other ports in Cyprus and set sail for the city of Damietta. This was on Ascension Day, which that year was the thirteenth of May. It was only a three-day journey to Cyprus, but we had many setbacks and difficulties at sea, and the crossing took us twenty-two days.

At about nine o'clock in the morning on the Friday after Trinity Sunday, we were off Damietta with a large part but by no means all of our fleet. We were about three leagues from the shore. The king gave the

---

8. That is, the Khwarizmian sack of Jerusalem and other cities in 1244 and the defeat of the army of the Latin Kingdom of Jerusalem at La Forbie by a Khwarizmian and Ayyubid alliance in the same year, developments that undid the gains of the crusades of Frederick II and the French and English barons in 1239–1241. Letters beseeching aid in the aftermath of the Khwarizmian invasion had led Louis IX and others to plan the current campaign.

9. The Great Khan Güyük (1246–1248).

10. Better known as Andrew of Longjumeau. Andrew's embassy joined others including that of John of Plano Carpini, who was sent to the Mongols from the Council of Lyons in 1245.

word to anchor and summoned all the barons who were with the fleet. They assembled on board the *Montjoy*, the king's ship, and agreed to land very early the next morning in spite of any resistance the enemy might dare to make. Orders were given to prepare all the galleys and small vessels in the fleet, and for all who could to embark in them early in the morning. Everyone was urged to go to confession, prepare himself, make his will, and settle his affairs in readiness for death, should it so please Our Lord Jesus Christ.

Early the next morning, the king attended Divine Office and heard the Mass for travelers by sea, armed himself, and gave orders for all men to arm and embark in the small vessels. He himself embarked in a Normandy lighter with us and our companions and the legate, who held the True Cross and blessed the armed men who had entered the boats for the landing. The king had my lords John of Beaumont, Matthew of Marly, and Geoffrey of Sargines go into the ship's barge, and with them he put the standard of my lord Saint Denis.[11] This barge took the lead, all the other vessels following behind it after the standard. The lighter in which were the king with the legate at this side holding the holy True Cross and us went in the rear.

As we approached to within crossbow range of the land, a large number of well-armed Turkish infantry and cavalry who were facing us on the shore opened a heavy fire, which we returned. As we grounded, several thousand of the cavalry and many of the infantry dashed right into the sea in the face of our men. When our men in the boats who were well armed saw this, particularly the knights, they would not wait for the standard of my lord Saint Denis, but jumped into the sea, fully armed as they were and on foot. The sea was deeper in some parts than in others, so that some went in deeper than others, one man going in up to his chest and another right up to the armpits. Many of our men got their horses out of the boats, a dangerous and difficult task which called for great bravery. Meanwhile our crossbowmen were working hard and kept up a galling and almost incredibly heavy fire. Finally our people made good their landing and held it.

When the Turks saw what we had done, they rallied in a body, chattering in their own language, and then attacked our men so furiously and ferociously that they seemed certain to cut them to pieces. However, our

11. The oriflamme, the banner of Saint Denis borne by French kings in battle and by Louis IX's predecessors on crusade.

men stood firm on the shore and fought back with such vigor that you would never have thought that they had been suffering the confinement and discomforts and miseries of a sea voyage. And this was through the grace of Jesus Christ and of the holy True Cross which the legate held aloft over his head in the face of the infidels.

When the king saw the others jump down into the sea, he wished to follow them. They tried to stop him, but in spite of them he jumped down and went into the sea up to his waist, and all of us with him. The battle went on for a long time after the king had jumped into the sea, but when it had lasted on the shore and in the water from morning till midday, the Turks withdrew into the city of Damietta. The king, with the whole Christian army, was left in command of the shore. Few or none of the Christians were killed in this battle, but the Turks lost at least five hundred men and many of their horses. Le Roux, who had been their commander at the battle in which the counts of Bar and Montfort were defeated near Gaza, was killed. He was, it was said, the most important man in Egypt after the sultan, a good knight, brave and skilled in the arts of war.[12]

On the morning of the next day, that is on the Sunday after the octave of Pentecost, a Saracen came to the king and told him that all the Saracens had left Damietta, and that they might hang him if what he said was not true. The king had him put under guard and sent men to discover the truth. Before three o'clock in the afternoon he had certain news that many of our people were already in the city and that the royal banner was displayed on a high tower.

When our people heard the news, they praised Our Lord heartily and thanked him for his great kindness to the Christians, for the city of Damietta was so strongly fortified with walls and ditches, with numbers of strong and tall towers, with battlements and barbicans, countless engines, quantities of arms and provisions and whatever is needed for a city's defense, that it was difficult for anyone to see how human strength could capture it except at enormous cost and labor. Our people found that it was amply furnished with everything needful.

Imprisoned in the city were found fifty-four Christian slaves, who had been there for twenty-two years, so they said. They were released and brought to the king. They said that the Saracens had fled on the Saturday

12. Jean is referring to the disastrous defeat of Amalric of Montfort and the count of Bar in 1239. The emir in question may be an-Nasir Dawud (1206–1261), cousin to the sultan of Egypt, then lord of Kerak (1229–1248).

night, saying one to another that the swine had arrived. Numbers of Syrian Christians were also found, who lived there as subjects of the Saracens. When these saw the Christians entering the city, they safeguarded themselves by finding crosses to carry. After they had spoken to the king and the legate, they were allowed to keep their houses and their contents.

The king and the army struck their camp and encamped opposite the city. The day after the feast of Saint Barnabas the Apostle, the king made his first entry into Damietta. He had all the mosques in the city destroyed, including the chief one, and made them into churches dedicated in honor of Jesus Christ.

We are pretty certain that we shall not leave the city until the feast of All Saints, because of the flooding of the river of Paradise, called the Nile, which flows by it; for it is impossible to go to Alexandria or Babylon or Cairo when the river floods the whole countryside, and we are told that it will not subside before All Saints.

We have no news, I should add, of the sultan of Babylon, but the king has been given to understand that some other sultans are at war with him. I must tell you, though, that ever since God gave the city into our hands, we see no one near our camp except Bedouin Saracens who sometimes come within a couple of leagues of it. When our crossbowmen open fire on them, they run. These same Bedouins lurk around the camp at night to steal horses and human heads; the sultan is said to give ten bezants for every Christian head brought to him. It is said that they similarly cut off the heads of men who have been hanged and dig up the corpses buried in the ground to get their heads to take to the sultan. A Bedouin who got in by himself was captured and is still under guard. They can do this thieves' work without difficulty because, although the king has the queen his wife inside the city of Damietta and some of his equipment in the palace and fortress of the sultan of Babylon (the legate has his in the house and fortress of the king who was killed in battle when we landed, and each of the barons also has his own fine big lodging in the city according to his station), nevertheless the Christian army, the king, and the legate are lodged outside. The work of these Bedouin thieves has obliged the Christians to begin making good ditches all round their camp, wide and deep; but these are not yet finished.

So it was that in his mercy, Our Lord Jesus Christ restored the noble and very strong city of Damietta to Christendom in the year of the Incarnation twelve hundred and forty-nine, on the Sunday after the octave of

Pentecost, that is on the sixth day of the month of June, which fell on a Sunday.

This was thirty years after the Christians, with great pain and labor, had won it from the Saracens and lost it again within the same year when they marched to besiege Cairo and the river rose and spread all around them so that they could neither advance nor go back. It is for that reason that we think the army should not leave Damietta until the river has subsided and returned to its normal channels.

Pass on to all our friends the news in this letter. It was written in the city of Damietta on the vigil of the Nativity of my lord Saint John the Baptist, which was in this same month.

52. Ibn Wasil (ca. 1282) and al-Maqrizi (ca. 1440) on Louis's Defeat

Jamal ad-Din ibn Wasil (604/1207–697/1298) held a number of offices in the service of the later Ayyubids (the descendants of Saladin) and the early Mamluks, including the great Baibars, who sent him in 1261 on a diplomatic mission to Manfred, the son of Frederick II (below, Nos. 57–59). The work of his quoted here is *The Dissipator of Anxieties Concerning the History of the Ayyubids*, which deals with late Ayyubid and early Mamluk history up to 680/1282.

Taqi ad-Din al-Maqrizi (776/1364–845/1442) was a learned scholar and antiquarian in Cairo. His work cited here, largely a compilation from earlier writers, is *The Book of Proceeding to the Knowledge of the History of the Kings*, which deals with the period 577/1181 to 840/1436. He deals with both Frankish expeditions to Egypt (the Fifth Crusade and the first crusade of Louis IX) and the Mamluks' conquest of all of al-Sahil, "the Coast," the Frankish Levantine mainland that ended with the fall of Acre in 1291. Another translated source from Arabic is Ibn al-Furat, Muhammad ibn 'Abd al-Rahim, *Ayyubids, Mamlukes and Crusaders: Selections from the Tarikh al-duwal wa'l Muluk, text and translation by U. and M. C. Lyons, historical introduction and notes by J. S. C. Riley-Smith (Cambridge, 1971)*.

Ibn Wasil on Louis's defeat and captivity

ON THE night before Wednesday, 3 Muharram 648 [April 7, 1250], the resplendent night that had disclosed a great victory and a stupendous triumph, the Franks marched out with all their forces toward Damietta,

Source: Francesco Gabrieli, Arab Historians of the Crusades, *trans. E. J. Costello (Berkeley-Los Angeles, 1969), 293–295, 298–302.*

which they counted on to defend them, and their ships began to move downstream in convoy. When the Muslims heard the news they set out after them, crossed to the Frankish bank of the river and were soon at their heels. As Wednesday dawned the Muslims had surrounded the Franks and were slaughtering them, dealing out death and captivity. Not one escaped. It is said that the dead numbered 30,000. In the battle the Bahrite mamluks of al-Malik as-Salih distinguished themselves by their courage and audacity: they caused the Franks terrible losses and played the major part in the victory. They fought furiously: it was they who flung themselves into the pursuit of the enemy; they were Islam's Templars.

The accursed king of France and the great Frankish princes retreated to the hill of Munya, where they surrendered and begged for their lives. They were given assurances by the eunuch Jamal ad-Din Muhsin as-Salihi, on the strength of which they surrendered. They were all taken to Mansura, where chains were put on the feet of the king of France and his companions. They were imprisoned in the house where the secretary Fakhr ad-Din ibn Luqman was living, and the eunuch Sabih al-Mu'az-zami, a servant of al-Malik al-Mu'azzam Turanshah, son of al-Malik as-Salih Najm ad-Din Ayyub, was set to guard them; he had come with his master from Hisn Kaifa and had been promoted and shown great honor.

Referring to this episode, the imprisonment of the king of France in Fakhr ad-Din ibn Luqman's house, and the appointment of the eunuch Sabih to look after him, Jamal ad-Din ibn Yahya ibn Matruh wrote:

> Speak to the Frenchman, if you visit him, a true word from a
>   good counselor:
> "God requite you for what has happened, the slaughter of the
>   Messiah's adorers!
> You came to the East boasting of conquest, believing our martial
>   drumroll to be a mere breath of wind.
> And your stupidity has brought you to a place where your eyes
>   can no longer see in the broad plain any way of escape.
> And of all your company, whom you commanded so well that
>   you led them into the tomb's embrace,
> Of fifty thousand not one can be seen that is not dead, or
>   wounded and a prisoner.
> God help you to other similar adventures: who knows that in
>   the end Jesus will not breathe freely (of your impious
>   worship)!

If your pope is content with this, how often is a statesman guilty
of deceit!"
And say to them, if they ever think of returning to take their
revenge, or for any other reason:
"The house of Ibn Luqman is always ready here, and the chain
and the eunuch Sabih are still here."

AFTER this al-Malik al-Mu'azzam and the victorious army advanced to
Damietta and camped at Fariskur in the province of Damietta. The sultan's tent was erected, and beside it a wooden tower which from time to
time al-Malik al-Mu'azzam would climb to while away the time, putting
off the capture of Damietta. If he had surrounded it and had entered it
quickly and forced the king of France to surrender all his possessions, he
would have taken it very quickly. But the evil conduct to which he abandoned himself deterred him, and indeed his fate was already sealed.

                              *   *   *

WHEN the emirs and the army had taken oaths of loyalty and affairs were
settled as we have described, the surrender of Damietta was discussed
with the king of France. The man who conducted the negotiations was
the emir Husam ad-Din ibn Abi 'Ali, for everyone agreed to rely on his
advice and opinion because of his reputation for wisdom and experience,
and because of the trust that al-Malik as-Salih had in him. So he and the
king of France held a series of conversations and finally agreed that
Damietta should surrender and that the king should go free. The qadi
Jamal ad-Din ibn Wasil, the author of this history, says

> The emir Husam ad-Din told me: "The king of France was
> an extremely wise and intelligent man. In one of our conversa-
> tions I said to him: 'How did Your Majesty ever conceive the
> idea, a man of your character and wisdom and good sense, of
> going on board ship and riding the back of this sea and coming
> to a land so full of Muslims and soldiers, thinking that you could
> conquer it and become its ruler? This undertaking is the greatest
> risk to which you could possibly expose yourself and your sub-
> jects.' The king laughed but did not reply. 'In our land,' I
> added, 'when a man travels by sea on several occasions, exposing
> himself and his possessions to such a risk, his testimony is not

accepted as evidence by a court of law.' 'Why not?' 'Because such behavior suggests to us that he lacks sense, and a man who lacks sense is not fit to give evidence.' The king laughed and said: 'By God, whoever said that was right, and whoever made that ruling did not err.'"

*   *   *

When agreement was reached between the king of France and the Muslims on the surrender of Damietta, the king sent to order his henchmen in Damietta to hand the city over. They, after objections, and the messengers coming and going between them and the king, finally obeyed, and handed the city over to the Muslims. The sultan's standards entered the city on Friday, 3 Safar 648 [May 1250], and were raised on the walls, proclaiming once again the rule of Islam. The king of France was set free and went, with the remains of his army, over to the western shore. The next day, Saturday, he went aboard and set sail for Acre. He stayed some time in Palestine and then returned home. So God purified Egypt of them, and this victory was many times greater than the first [in the Fifth Crusade], because of the large number of the enemy killed and captured; so many that the prisons of Cairo were full of Franks. The joyful news spread to all the other countries, and the public manifestations of joy and happiness were seen.

After the king of France left, the army marched straight to Cairo and entered the city. There, for many days on end, rolls of drums announced the glad tidings of the Muslim victory over the Franks and the recovery of the province of Damietta, pearl of Islam and frontier of Egypt. This was the second time that the infidels had taken it and lost it again and had fled in defeat and disarray.

Al-Maqrizi on Louis's crusade

DISEMBARKING in Egypt the king of France sent a letter to the sultan al-Malik as-Salih. After the introductory heretical phrases,[13] he continued:

You will be aware that I am the head of the Christian community, as I acknowledge that you are the head of the Muslim community. You know also that the (Muslim) population of

---

13. That is, formal Christian greetings and protocols.

Andalusia pays tribute to us and gives us gifts, and we drive them before us like a herd of cattle, killing the men, widowing the women, capturing their daughters and infants, emptying their houses. I have given you sufficient demonstration (of our strength), and the best advice I can offer. Even if you were to promise me anything on oath and to appear before the priests and monks and carry a candle before me as an act of obedience to the cross, it would not deter me from attacking you and fighting you on the land that is dearest to you. If this country falls into my hands, it will be mine as a gift. If you keep it by a victory over me, you may do as you will with me. I have told you about the armies obedient to me, filling the mountains and the plains, numerous as the stones of the earth, and poised against you like the sword of destiny. I put you on your guard against them.

WHEN this letter arrived and was read to the sultan his eyes filled with tears and he exclaimed: "We belong to God, and to him we return!" Then he had a reply composed by the qadi Baha' ad-Din Zuháir, head of Chancellery. After an introductory formula with the name of God and benedictions on God's apostle Muhammad, his family and companions, the letter went on:

Your letter has reached us in which you threaten us with the size of your armies and the number of your warriors. Now we are a warlike race; never is one of our champions cut down without being replaced; never has an enemy attacked us without being destroyed. Fool! If your eyes had seen the points of our swords and the enormity of our devastations, the forts and shores which we have taken (from you) and the lands that we have sacked in the past and present, you would gnaw your fingers in repentance! The outcome of the events you are precipitating is inevitable; the day will dawn to our advantage and end in your destruction. Then you will curse yourself: "and the wicked shall know the fate that awaits them" [Qur'an 26:228]. When you read my letter let your response comply with the Sura of the Bees: "You shall see God's command brought about; do not hurry it" [Qur'an 16:1]. (Remember) too the Sura of *Sad*: "You shall know what this signifies after some time" [Qur'an 38:88].

We have recourse to God's word, for he declares most truthfully: "How many times has a small band defeated a large army, with God's support! For God is with the patient" [Qur'an 2:250], and to the words of the wise, according to whom: "The man of might is brought down in the end": so your might will finally be brought down, and will bring catastrophe upon you. Greetings.

[AFTER the victory at Mansura the sultan Turanshah] wrote to the emir Jamal ad-Din ibn Yaghmur, his commander in Damascus, a letter in his own hand which said:

> Praise is due to God, who has lifted our sorrow from us! Victory comes from God alone. On that day the faithful will rejoice in the help of God. Speak of the grace received from your Lord! If you wish to count God's graces, you will not be able to number them [Qur'an 35:31, 3:121, 30:3, 93:11, 6:18].
>
> We inform His Excellency Jamal ad-Din and all Islam of the victory bestowed by God over the enemies of the Faith. Their threat grew and grew, their evil was already established in the land, and the believers despaired of the fate of their country, their wives and their children. "But do not despair of God's aid" [Qur'an 12:87]. On Monday, the first day of this blessed year, God poured out his blessing on Islam's behalf. We opened our treasures, scattered wealth, distributed arms and summoned the desert Arabs, the volunteers and a multitude of whose number God alone knows, from every deep valley and distant place. On the Tuesday night the enemy abandoned their tents, their possessions and their baggage and fled to Damietta, pursued all night by our swords, beyond shame, crying out in anguish. When Wednesday morning dawned we had killed 30,000, apart from those who cast themselves into the waves. As for the prisoners, it is impossible to count them. The Franks took refuge in al-Munya and begged for their lives, and this was granted them. We made them our prisoners, treated them honorably, and recovered Damietta with God's help and assistance, his majesty and highness. . . .

and so on at length.

With the letter the sultan sent the king of France's mantle, and the emir Jamal ad-Din ibn Yaghmur put it on. It was of scarlet red, trimmed with ermine. Sheikh Najm ad-Din ibn Isra'il said of it: "The mantle of the Frenchman, sent in homage to the Prince of Emirs was white as paper, but our swords have stained it the color of blood."

And also:

> Lord of all the Kings of this time, you have seen fulfilled the divine promises of victory.
> May our Lord always triumph over his enemies, and clothe his servants in a king's booty!

53. Louis IX Writes to France Explaining the Failure of His Crusade, 1250

Louis appears to have intended this letter to be circulated widely as part of a campaign to recruit individuals to join his crusade. He faced the difficult task of explaining the disastrous defeat of the crusaders (which would appear to indicate divine displeasure with his crusade) and drumming up further financial aid from a heavily taxed French church and his loyal subjects in order to finance further military efforts in the Holy Land and the staggering ransom imposed by his captors.

While ecclesiastics in this period seemed to be increasingly cautious in ubiquitously imposing the title "martyr" upon deceased crusaders (aware that not all crusaders died in a proper state of devotion), Louis attempts to comfort the relatives of those crusaders executed in captivity for defending their faith (who fit the most stringent definition of martyr) and of those who died upon the battlefield, including his brother, Robert of Artois, by labeling the deceased as true martyrs (something that his hagiographers would fail to officially earn for Robert of Artois and for Louis himself, who was classified instead by the papal inquest as a slightly less illustrious confessor). Louis's appeal for aid utilizes many of the themes common to both crusading sermons and crusading songs and epics: crusading as an act of loyalty to one's heavenly and earthly lord (with the worldly and spiritual rewards this implied); imitation of one's illustrious crusading ancestors; and vengeance for the blasphemies and cruelties visited upon holy places, fellow crusaders, and Christ himself.

Penny J. Cole, David L. D'Avray, and Jonathan Riley-Smith, "Application of Theology to Current Affairs: Memorial Sermons on the Dead of Mansurah and on Innocent IV," Bulletin of the Institute of Historical Research 63 (1990), 227–47; Smith, Crusading in the Age of Joinville.

LOUIS, by the grace of God, king of the French, to his dear and faithful prelates, lords, knights, citizens, burgesses, and to all else who live in his kingdom to whom these letters shall come, greeting.

For the honor and glory of the name of Our Lord, and with the desire to forward with all our energy the work of the crusade, we have thought it well to tell you all that after the capture of Damietta (which Our Lord Jesus Christ, by his extreme mercy, delivered, as we believe you know, in an almost miraculous manner that surpassed all human powers, into Christian hands), we left the town on the twentieth of last November. Marshaling our naval and land forces, we marched against those of the Saracens, which were collected and encamped in a place commonly known as Massoria.[14] During our march we had to face the attack of our enemies, whose losses were considerable. On one particular day a detachment of the Egyptian army which had attacked us was wiped out. While we were on the road, we heard that the sultan of Cairo had just ended his miserable life but that it was commonly reported that before his death he had sent for his son, who was in the east, to come to Egypt. He had made all the principal officers of his army take an oath of loyalty to the son and had left the command of all his forces to one of his emirs called Farchardin.[15] When we arrived at Massoria, which was on the Tuesday before Christmas Day, we found that the news was true.

At first we were unable to engage the Saracens, as the two armies were separated by a branch of the river, called the Thaneos, which at that point leaves the main stream of the Nile. Between these two streams we encamped, our camp extending from the larger to the smaller. There we fought several engagements with the Saracens, a number of whom fell to our swords. But many more were drowned in the deep and swift current.

As the depth of the water and height of the banks made it impossible for us to ford the Thaneos, we began to build a causeway which would enable the Christian army to cross. For some days we worked with great pain and labor at this costly and dangerous task, while the Saracens did their utmost to hinder us. They set up engines of war to silence those we had set up, and smashed with stones or burnt with Greek fire the wooden castle we had built on the causeway. We had lost all hope of crossing by

Source: Hague, Life of Saint Louis, *247–254.*

14. That is, Mansura.

15. In actuality, the sultan's widow Shajar-ad-Durr conspired with several high officials to conceal the sultan's death, meanwhile forging an appointment of the emir Fakhr ad-Din as general of the Egyptian army and sending letters for the sultan's heir, Turanshah, to return to Egypt.

this means when a Saracen deserter told us of a ford by which the army might cross. On the Monday before Ash Wednesday we consulted our barons and the chief men in the army and decided that on the next day, Shrove Tuesday, we would set out early in the morning and cross the river at the spot he pointed out, leaving a detachment to guard the camp.

So then, on the Tuesday we drew up our forces in battle order and marched down to the ford. We crossed the stream, but it was a most dangerous task, for the ford was deeper and more difficult than we had been told. Our horses were obliged to swim and it was no easy matter to climb the high and muddy bank on the farther side. After crossing, we pushed on as far as the place where the Saracen engines had been set up. Our advance guard fell on the enemy and killed a great number of them, sparing neither age nor sex. Among the slain were their commander and several other emirs. Our men then scattered; some of them crossed the Saracen camp and reached a town called Massoria, cutting down any of the enemy they met on the way. The Saracens, however, realized the folly of this advance, rallied, and fell upon our men, who were surrounded and overwhelmed. Our barons and knights, both of the military orders and others, suffered heavy and grievous losses. There, we lost our brother, the count of Artois, of dear memory. It is with sorrow and bitterness of heart that we speak of this, though indeed we ought rather to rejoice, for we believe and hope that, crowned as a martyr, he has gone to his heavenly home and that there he will have everlasting joy in the company of the holy martyrs.

That same day the Saracens attacked us from all sides, pouring showers of arrows on us. Until about three o'clock in the afternoon, we had to withstand their attacks without any support from our own engines. In the end, after we had had many men and horses killed and wounded, we managed, by God's help, to hold our position, rallied our men, and encamped close to the captured enemy engines. There we remained with a small body of our men, having first made a pontoon bridge by which those on the other side of the stream could cross to us. The next day a number came over by our orders and encamped by us. As the Saracen engines had been destroyed, we built barricades to protect the approach to the bridge and there was nothing then to hinder traffic to and fro.

The following Friday, the children of perdition assembled on all sides of us with the intention of wiping out the Christian army; swarms of them attacked our lines with a ferocity that has never, many said, been equaled on that coast. By God's help, we held together and beat them off all along the line, causing them heavy losses.

Some days later, the sultan's son arrived at Massoria from the east. The Egyptians received him as their monarch with a great display of joy. His arrival greatly improved their morale, but at the same time, we know not by what decision of God, everything began to turn out ill for us. Fatal epidemics attacked men and horses, so that there were very few of us who had not to mourn lost comrades or nurse those close to death. In a short time our numbers were greatly reduced. Provisions were so scarce that many died from hunger and want. The enemy had carried boats overland and launched them in the river; these pirates had cut the river and prevented our vessels from delivering the stores they carried. They captured some of our ships, taking two convoys in succession laden with food and stores and killing many of the crews and passengers.

The complete lack of food and fodder for the horses made nearly everyone lose heart, and combined with the losses we had already suffered, obliged us to leave our position and retreat—should God permit us—to Damietta. But as man's ways are not in himself but in him who directs all men's steps and disposes all things according to his will [Jer 10:23], while we were on the road, that is on the fifth of April, the Saracens gathered all their forces and attacked the Christian army in overpowering numbers. And by God's permission and as a result of our own sins, we fell into their hands.

We and our dear brothers, the counts of Poitiers and Anjou, and almost all the rest of those who retreated by land were captured, not before there had been great slaughter and shedding of Christian blood. In addition, the greater part of those who were returning by river were captured or killed, and the ships they were in were burnt, with the unfortunate sick [still] on board.

Some days after our capture, the sultan proposed a truce. Backed with threats and hard words, he insisted on the immediate surrender of Damietta and all its contents, with an indemnity to cover all his expenses and losses since the Christians entered the town. After several conferences, we concluded a year's truce on the following terms.

The sultan was to release, with freedom to go wherever we liked, us and all the prisoners taken by the Saracens since our arrival in Egypt, together with all other Christians of whatever nationality taken since the time when the Sultan Kyemel had concluded a treaty with the emperor.[16] The Christians were to keep all the territory they held in the kingdom of Jerusalem at the time of our arrival.

On our side, we were to surrender Damietta to the sultan and pay 800,000 Saracen bezants for the release of the prisoners and the indemnity and expenses of which we have just spoken (of this we have already paid 400,000), and to release all Saracen prisoners taken by Christians since our arrival, as well as those taken in the kingdom of Jerusalem since the truce between the same emperor and sultan. All our equipment and that of all the others left in Damietta after our departure was to be kept in safety and taken in the charge and under the protection of the sultan, and removed to Christian territory when the opportunity should arise. All Christians who were sick or who remained in Damietta to sell their belongings were to have a similar surety and to leave by sea or land when they wished, without harm or hindrance. The sultan was to give a safe-conduct to Christian territory to all who should wish to leave by land.

This truce concluded with the sultan had been sworn to on both sides and the sultan had already left for Damietta to carry out the agreed conditions, when, by the judgment of God, some of his own troops—no doubt with the connivance of the greater part of the army—attacked him as he rose from table in the morning and severely wounded him. He nonetheless managed to get out of his tent, hoping to find safety in flight, but they cut him down with their swords in full view of nearly all the emirs and a mob of other Saracens. Some of them, in the first flush of their rage, came sword in hand to our tent as though they meant, as some of us feared, to wreak their fury upon us and the other Christians.[17]

The divine mercy, however, calmed their ferocity, and they pressed us to carry out the conditions of the truce made with the sultan and to hasten the surrender of Damietta. Although their words were accompanied by violent threats, we finally by the will of God, who is the Father of Mercy, the consoler of the afflicted and who heeds the laments of his bondsmen, confirmed with a new oath the former truce. From each and all of the emirs we received a similar oath, framed according to the

16. The sultan of Egypt, al-Kamil and the emperor Frederick II had concluded a ten-year treaty in 1229.

17. This assassination and the effective end of Ayyubid dynasty was plotted by a group of dissatisfied Mamluks which included the future sultan Baibars. Another Mamluk, Aybeg, assumed command of the army, legitimizing his rule by marrying the former sultan's widow, Shaja-ad-Durr and appointing a young member of the Ayyubid dynasty as titular co-sultan.

requirements of their faith, to observe the conditions of the truce, and a day was fixed for the surrender of Damietta and the release of prisoners on both sides.

It was with difficulty that we decided to come to an agreement with the sultan about the surrender of the town, and we had the same difficulty with the emirs. From what we heard from those who came back to us from Damietta and knew how things stood, it was apparent that there was no hope of holding the town. We accordingly decided that it would be more to the interest of Christendom that we and the other prisoners should be released on the terms of the truce we have described, than that we should completely lose Damietta with the remainder of its Christian inhabitants and at the same time should ourselves, with the other prisoners, be still subject to all the dangers of captivity.

So then, on the appointed day, the emirs took over the town of Damietta, after which they released us and our brothers, the counts of Brittany, Flanders, Soissons, and many other barons and knights of the kingdom of France, Jerusalem, and Cyprus. We were confident, then, that, as they had released us and these others, they would hand over all the other Christians and respect their oaths in accordance with the treaty's terms.

We then left Egypt, leaving trustworthy persons charged to receive the prisoners from the Saracens and to look after what we had been obliged to leave behind for lack of shipping. The task of recovering the prisoners is very close to our heart, and we afterward again sent ships and ambassadors to Egypt for that purpose, and to bring back the equipment, such as engines and arms, tents, some horses, and other things which we had left behind. Our ambassadors pressed for the return of these in accordance with the terms of the treaty, but the emirs kept them in Cairo for a long time in the hope of obtaining all they demanded. At length, after daily expectation of receiving all the prisoners the emirs had pledged to release, amounting to more than twelve thousand, some being recent captives and some having been taken earlier, they handed over to our ambassadors only four hundred, and of these some were released only after the payment of money. The emirs also refused to surrender any of the rest of our property.

But what is more detestable is that after the conclusion of the truce, according to one ambassador's report and that of trustworthy prisoners who have returned from Egypt, they have picked out young people from the prisoners and forced them at sword's point, like lambs led to the slaughter, to abjure the catholic faith and embrace that of Muhammad. Some have been weak enough to succumb, but others rooted in their faith and constant in their firm resolution could not be shaken by the enemy's threats and blows and have received the bloodied crown of martyrdom. We do not doubt that their blood will cry out to Our Lord on behalf of the Christian people; in the court of heaven they will be our advocates before the sovereign judge and in that heavenly home they will be more useful to us in our fight against the enemies of the faith than they would be if they shared our life in this world. The emirs also massacred some of the sick left behind in Damietta. And although, as we are still prepared to do, we had observed the conditions of the treaty, we have no certainty of seeing the prisoners released or our property returned.

After the truce and our own release, we were confident that the part of the Holy Land occupied by the Christians would be at peace until the truce expired, and had intended and planned to return to France. We were already preparing our passage when we realized from what we have been telling you that the emirs were openly violating the truce and, in spite of their oaths, did not shrink from deluding us and Christendom. We accordingly summoned an assembly of the barons of France, of the Temple, of the Hospital of Saint John, of the Teutonic Order of Saint Mary, and the barons of the kingdom of Jerusalem, and consulted with them as to what we should do.

The majority thought that if we were obliged to return at this moment, we should be leaving the country exposed to complete loss. It was now unhappily reduced to a miserable state of weakness and our departure would leave it open to the Saracens. We should also have to count as lost the Christian prisoners who were in the enemy's hands, and give up all hope of their release. On the other hand, if we stayed in Palestine, there was hope that time might bring some improvement, the release of the prisoners, the retaining of castles and fortresses in the kingdom of Jerusalem, and other advantages for Christendom, especially since trouble has arisen between the sultan of Aleppo and the rulers of Cairo. Already this sultan has collected his forces and has seized Damascus and some castles belonging to Cairo. It is said that he is to invade Egypt in order to avenge the death of the sultan whom the emirs killed, and make himself master of the whole country if he can.

Although many dissuaded us from prolonging our stay overseas, these considerations, our pity for the miseries and sufferings of the Holy Land we had come to help, and our compassion for the hard lot of our prisoners in captivity determined us to delay our return and stay some time longer in the kingdom of Syria rather than entirely to abandon the cause of Christ and leave our prisoners exposed to such dangers.

However, we have decided to send back to France our very dear brothers, the counts of Poitiers and Anjou, that they may comfort our very dear mother[18] and the whole kingdom. As all who bear the name of Christ should be full of zeal for the task we have undertaken, and in particular you men of the church, who are descended from the blood of these whom Our Lord chose as a special people for the deliverance of the Holy Land, which you should count your own by right of conquest, we summon you all to the service of him who served us and shed his blood for your redemption on the cross, that your hearts may be in Christ Jesus.

For this vile people, not content with the blasphemies it vomited against the Creator in the presence of Christian men, beat the cross with rods, spat on it and trod it underfoot in hatred of the Christian faith. Come then, knights of Christ, own soldiers of the pope of the living God, take up your arms and be strong to avenge these outrages and insults. Imitate the example of your ancestors, who of all nations were distinguished by their devotion to the exaltation of the faith and their loyal obedience to their worldly masters and filled the world with the report of their high deeds. We have led the way for you in God's service. Do you follow us, and although you come later you will receive with us from the Lord the reward which the husbandman in the Gospel gave equally to those who came at the end of the day to work in his vineyard and to those who came at the beginning. Those who come or send effective help to us or rather to the Holy Land while we are still here, will earn, besides the indulgences promised to those who take the cross, the respect and gratitude of God and men.

Hasten then, and let those whom the power of the Most High shall inspire to come in person or send help, be ready to cross the sea in this coming April or May. As for those who cannot be ready for this first passage, let them at all events be ready for the Saint John's day passage. The nature of the task calls for speed and every delay will be fatal. Do you, prelates and other loyal servants of Christ, help us with the Most High by the fervor of your prayers. Order them to be said everywhere in your jurisdiction, that your prayers and those of other good men may obtain for us from the divine mercy the graces of which our own sins make us unworthy.

18. Blanche of Castile.

Written at Acre, in the year of Our Lord 1250, in the month of August.

54. The *Pastoureaux*, 1251

While attempts had been made since the later twelfth century to diminish the number of commoners accompanying crusading armies, the ideal of personal participation remained strong throughout the thirteenth century, despite a gradual increase in the practice of voluntary or, in some instances, forced commutation of vows to donations to the crusade cause. The arrival of Louis IX's letter concerning the defeat at Mansura would combine with frustration at the diversion of money and men from Louis IX's crusade to the anti-Staufer crusade in Italy to spark a popular crusade in 1251 that became known as the Crusade of the Shepherds (*Pastoureaux*). Its participants' identification with the welfare of Louis IX and his crusade testifies to the way in which the inquests into injustices Louis had ordered as part of the preparations for the crusade persuaded many in France that their interests were tied intimately to those of the king. The participants' anticlerical sentiment and attacks against the mendicant orders may also have expressed their opinion that the widespread redemption of vows had actually undermined rather than aided Louis IX's crusade in Egypt.

Similar to the crusade of the *pueri* in 1212, that of the *Pastoureaux* was composed of a mélange of groups denied personal participation in the crusade. One band led by a demagogue calling himself the Master of Hungary proceeded to Paris, where Queen Blanche, acting as Louis's regent, welcomed them as a source of potential aid for her son in the East. However, after the movement's participants committed acts of violence against laymen and clerics who they claimed had sabotaged the king's crusade, Blanche disowned them. The Master of Hungary appears to have been killed by the citizens of Bourges after violently persecuting the Jews in their city. After his death, the various bands broke up, vanishing like smoke, in the words of one chronicler.

Of the accounts printed below, the most extensive and retrospectively analytical account comes from Matthew Paris, who also recorded many letters describing events during Louis IX's crusade, particularly the exploits of the English who fought alongside the French in Egypt. However, his conspiracy theories were shared by others, and Matthew did base his account on eyewitness reports from Thomas of Sherborne, an English monk temporarily imprisoned by the insurgents, and from the archbishop of Canterbury, among others. An eyewitness account written by a member of the Franciscan house in Paris decrying the *Pastoureaux*'s activities (the mendicant orders were one of their particular targets) also reached England and was preserved in the annals of the English monastery of Burton. The two remaining accounts come from a biographer of Louis IX and a house of canons regular in Saint-Lô in the archdiocese of Rouen (one of the regions directly affected by the *Pastoureaux*).

Malcolm Barber, "The Crusade of the Shepherds in 1251," in J. F. Sweets, ed., Proceedings of the Tenth Annual Meeting of the Western Society for French History *(Lawrence KS, 1984), 1–23, reprinted in Barber,* Crusaders and Heretics, 12th–14th Centuries *(Aldershot UK-Brookfield VT, 1995); Gary Dickson, "The Advent of the* Pastores *(1250)," Revue Belge de Philologie et d'Histoire 66 (1988), 249–267, reprinted in Dickson,* Religious Enthusiasm in the Medieval West *(Aldershot UK-Burlington VT, 2000).*

Guillaume de Nangis's *Gesta sanctae memoriae Ludovici regis Franciae*

IN THE year of our Lord 1251 many youths [*pueri*] and shepherds took the cross. Some of them were pretending that they had seen visions and worked miracles, and had been sent by God to avenge the king of France, Louis [IX]. Among those going astray were some who called themselves masters, and according to the custom of bishops they consecrated holy water even in the city of Paris itself. They joined persons in marriage, and dissolved [marriages] at their whim, and perpetrated many outrages and murders upon the [regular] religious and clergymen and laypersons, such that there was no one who would resist them. They gave the cross to and uncrossed many according to their own inclination. In fact, while their leader and master, whom they called the "Master of Hungary," was passing through Orléans with a considerable retinue, they slew clerics. And committing many other wicked deeds he came to Bourges, destroying the books of the Jews, and despoiling them of their possessions unrightfully. When he left Bourges, he was killed by the citizens of Bourges, who had been following him, between a village called Mortemer and Villeneuve-sur-Cher. However, many more of them were killed or hanged in various locales because of their wicked deeds. All of them were scattered and vanished like smoke.

From the chronicle of Saint-Lô of Rouen

IN THE year 1251, there occurred an unfortunate uprising of shepherds who claimed that they were setting out for the Holy Land. For there was among them some who acted as if they were masters and imposed the cross upon others; and they mendaciously asserted that they worked signs and omens. For in order to dupe the simple, the leaders of these brigands pretended to have seen visions of angels and that the Blessed Virgin Mary had appeared to them and had commanded them to take the cross and to gather the shepherds and other simple folk, whom God had chosen, into

Source for Guillaume de Nangis: RHGF 20:382.
Source for Saint-Lô: RHGF 23:395–396.

an army in order to aid the Holy Land and King Louis, who was then staying in that very place. And so, when the aforesaid bandits crossed through villages and fields throughout Flanders and Picardy, they used to lead astray shepherds and simple people with their deceitful exhortations. When, however, they came into France, they had already grown such that they were nearly one hundred thousand [strong], like an army; and whenever they passed through rural areas, shepherds used to abandon their animals without the consent of their relations.[19] However, whenever they crossed through villages and cities they used to brandish swords and axes and other weapons, so that they were dreaded by the populace and by those possessing the powers of justice. In fact, their error grew to such an extent that they used to create marriages, they signed individuals with the cross and absolved them from their sins. And yet they had also so deceived the populace that many used to believe that food and other things set before them did not diminish when they ate and drank them, but were increased. Yet because the clergy wanted to speak out against error of this sort, they incurred the strong hatred of the same, which grew so great that they slew many clerics whom they came upon in the country.

However, the queen Blanche, then regent for the realm, used to believe that through them help might come to her son King Louis in the Holy Land, and so she permitted them to cross through the city of Paris without opposition: and for this reason the boldness of their errors grew so very great that when they came to the city of Orléans with thievery and plundering, a fight broke out with the clerics of the university, and they killed many of them, and many of them [the *Pastoureaux*] were also slain. Then they traveled to the city of Bourges, and there their prince and leader, whom they used to call the "Master of Hungary," entered the synagogue of the Jews, and destroyed their books and carried off their possessions. But when he left the city with his followers, the citizens of Bourges, well-prepared and armed, pursued them vigorously, and they slew the aforesaid master with many of his associates, and caused a great slaughter. However, from its inception, their error had grown so great, that they expelled the archbishop of Rouen[20] from the church in Rouen

19. The veneration of the Virgin Mary and the apparent route south into Flanders and Picardy and then "France" (= Île de France) suggests that the chronicler thought that their origin was in the Low Countries.

20. That is, Eudes, or Odo, Rigaud of Rouen. He played a considerable role in promoting Louis IX's failed crusade and may have been viewed as somehow contributing to its failure in Egypt. His register has been translated into English: *The Register of Eudes of Rouen*, trans. Sydney M. Brown; ed. with introduction, notes, and appendix by Jeremiah F. O'Sullivan (New York, 1964), excerpted below, No. 55.

during the Pentecostal synod, with all the priests there gathered in synod. However, after the aforementioned slaying, they were scattered through various places. Some of them were killed or hanged on account of their wicked deeds, others perished by shipwreck, others returned to their own [lands]; and thus they came to nothing.

A Franciscan from Paris reports on the *Pastoureaux*

To HIS venerable brothers in Christ, to Adam de Marisco, and to the Brothers Minor[21] in Oxford, Brother [name missing in text] . . . appointed guardian of the order of the Brothers Minor in Paris, greetings. Not long ago, during the feast of the Resurrection, when we were hoping that at last peace was restored to the holy church, and the hammer of every land might be worn out,[22] an unexpected evil arose. There came a certain heretic or pagan, distinguished in his mores and teaching and in false prophecies, in his hypocrisy like a wolf not entering the sheepfold through the doorway, and yet clad in the pelt of a sheep. Under the pretext of signing with the cross and the appearance of piety, he made himself leader of the shepherds [cf. Mt 7:15; Jn 10:18–21]. He swore that revelations had been made to him by God, that he would transport himself across the sea to fight with the Saracens, [and] with Christian shepherds he would wear a sword for fighting. And in combination with I know not what, in spite of this God permitted that so great a folly grew so strong, that everywhere shepherds from various parts of the world, gathered into a throng in a very short period of time, and followed that incorrigible man himself. But in addition the favor of the common people grew so very powerful toward him and his accomplices, that they were able to say and do whatever they liked. And so that corrupt man, seeing himself surrounded by so great a mob, and the favor of the people, could not longer contain the venom he harbored. In fact he began to profane ecclesiastical authority by execrating the sacraments, by blessing the people, by preaching, by giving the cross, by consecrating [the holy] water for sprinkling in an unheard of manner, by pretending [to perform] miracles, moreover, in attacking and slaughtering men of the church.

Finally, after his arrival in Paris and that of his forerunners and followers, such a powerful agitation of the populace against the clergy was produced that within a few days many clergymen were slain, others were

Source: Annals of Burton, *in Luard,* Annales monastici, *1:290–293.*
21. That is, the Franciscans.
22. Probably Emperor Frederick II, who had recently died (1250).

thrown into the river [Seine], but even more were injured: even a parish priest celebrating mass was stripped of his chasuble and crowned with roses, was ridiculed. And this wickedness grew so very great, that unless the mercy of the Savior had intervened, they would have eradicated the university from Paris, with shedding of ecclesiastical blood and to the disgrace of Christianity. At Rouen, they destroyed the church and the archbishop's house. Moreover, in Orléans they killed many clergymen, and the community of clergymen, which had already resided in that place for a long time, they forced to depart. At Tours, among other things, the school of the house of the Preachers[23] was attacked by a powerful mob which wounded some [brothers] and others they dragged after them like captives without the decency of their habits, and they deprived the same of the victuals and other things which Christian piety had granted to them throughout the city. But what is dreadful to hear and to relate, but even more dreadful to witness, when they entered the church where the very inviolate and most holy sacrament of the body of Christ lay respectfully on the altar, they shamefully threw it [down upon the floor], and broke off the nose of the image of the glorious Virgin, and gouged out its eyes, and those things which pleased them they stole with impious hands. And at length those things which God had given to our brothers, they carried off while [committing] further outrages. For breaking into the little house of our brothers by force, they drove out the brothers, shaken by their injuries, in terror and sorrow. But alas! All these events did not trouble the French. What more? It does not suffice to narrate the blasphemies of these criminals, and the contempt of the people for the divine word of God, the injuries inflicted upon religious persons and clergymen; and among other things, the madness of the commoners in bringing forward the sick for healing to such men, that is, homicides, brigands, and murderers. And [even] when they were not cured, or did not get any better, they [still] preached the virtues of those wretched men.

Nevertheless, God arranged, from the superabundance of his goodness, not because of our merits, that this son of perdition should come to a fitting end. When he reached Bourges, he began to spread the poison he had conceived more widely, and began to say that all those standing near him ought not to believe those things which were spoken by clergymen, since their teaching deviated from their life, and for that reason he added that everything [they said] was worthless. At these words a kind of

---

23. That is, the Dominicans, known as Brothers Preacher.

solitary phoenix, filled with zeal for the Most High, began to resist this man with powerful and wise words, declaring that those things which were spoken by the clergy and religious, albeit in some instances their teaching did not match their life, possessed a solidity and strength through [their confirmation by] the writings of the Old and New Testaments. However, the words of that man possessed completely no support. Hearing this, the son of perdition, unable to restrain his proud mind, attacked the man of Christ and struck him with a sword, such that he killed him. When they saw this, the fellow citizens of the deceased ran to arms, with not a few deaths among their own ranks (the son of perdition defending himself, and calling upon Muhammad, as it was said), they slew him together with his accomplices, cutting him to pieces in their anger, and put the others to flight.

It was said, however, that this was their scheme, that first they would extirpate the clergy from the earth, second, wipe out the regular religious, and finally attack knights [*milites*] and noble persons, so that with the land thus deprived of any defense, it might be more easily laid open to the errors and attacks of the pagans. Which seemed close to the truth; particularly since a certain host of unknown knights [*milites*] garbed in white began to manifest themselves in parts of Germany. These things to this day we have heard and [consider] worthy of belief, thus matters stand. Written in Paris, in the year of our Lord 1251.

Matthew Paris on the *pastores*

ABOUT this time, the enemy of the human race, conceiving confident hopes that the Jordan would flow into his mouth, as he had already drunk from it by means of the sultan of Babylon, and seeing that even in sweet France the Christian faith was tottering and ready to fall, employed himself in originating a new kind of false doctrine. A certain person, a Hungarian by birth, who was now sixty years old, and had since his early years been an apostate from the Christian religion, who had copiously imbibed the falsehoods and cunning emanating from the sulfurous pit, and was become a servant and disciple of Muhammad, had faithfully promised the sultan of Babylon, whose servant he was, that he would present an immense number of Christians to him as prisoners, that France, being thus destitute of people and deprived of its king, the means of entering the country of the Christians would be more easy to the Saracens.

Source: Giles, Matthew Paris's English History, *2:451–458.*

This said impostor, then, who knew the French, German, and Latin tongues, without any authority from the pope or the patronage of any prelate, wandered hither and thither, preaching, and mendaciously asserting that he had received orders from Saint Mary, the mother of our Lord, to assemble the shepherds and keepers of other animals, to whom, as he stated, was granted by heaven the power, in their humility and simplicity, to rescue the Holy Land, together with all the prisoners, from the hands of the infidels; for, as he said, the pride of the French soldiery was displeasing to God. His eloquence confirmed his words, as also did the clasping of his inseparable hands, in which he falsely stated that he held a paper containing the order of the Blessed Virgin. He summoned all shepherds to join him, and they, abandoning their flocks, herds, and horses, and without consulting their lords or their relations, followed him on foot, caring naught about food. For this man practiced that chief of devices which was formerly adopted by a beardless youth in France, who about forty years back had infatuated the French people, and convoked an immense host of boys, who followed his footsteps, singing; and, what was wonderful, could not be restrained by bolts or bars, nor recalled by the commands, entreaties, or presents of their fathers and mothers.[24]

By the same deceitful devices, Robert le Bougre, a false brother of the Order of Preachers, was said to have infatuated countless numbers of people, to have consigned these deluded harmless people to the flames, and assisted by the secular power of the French king, whom he inclined to his purpose, to have caused enormous ruin: but these matters are fully related elsewhere.[25]

The aforesaid lying impostor, as well as all who followed him, bore the sign of the cross; and there were many who showed them favor and gave them assistance, saying that "God frequently chooses the weak portions of the world to confound the stronger ones; neither is the Almighty well pleased with a man's legs, nor are those acceptable to him who presume on their skill and bravery in war." The Lady Blanche, too, the queen and regent of the French, in hopes that they would obtain possession of the Holy Land and avenge her sons, granted them her favor and showed

24. Matthew Paris here refers to the crusade of the *pueri* of 1212.
25. In the early 1230s the Dominican Robert le Bougre, said by many to be a converted heretic, had obtained papal authority to conduct inquests against heresy in France and neighboring regions and at first received support from secular authorities in sentencing condemned heretics. Punishments he meted out to repentant heretics included the wearing of yellow crosses, which perhaps aligns him with others signed with the cross in Matthew Paris's mind.

them kindness. They therefore multiplied to such a degree that they were reckoned to amount to a hundred thousand and more; and they made standards for themselves to fight under, and on that of their leader was painted the figure of a lamb—this symbol being in token of their humility and innocence, and the standard bearing the cross as a token of victory.

About the feast of Saint Barnabas, the archbishop of Canterbury arrived in England, testifying the truth of the above matters, and stated that this annoyance commenced in the aforesaid kingdom after Easter. Besides this, he added that the pope, after having excommunicated Frederick's son Conrad and all his adherents, on the day of the [Last] Supper, set out on the Friday in Easter week, under the conduct and protection of Philip, bishop elect of Lyons. . . . The departure of the pope and his absence inspired the shepherds, who multiplied in France, with confidence and boldness, and they increased in number and strength.

There now flocked to join their band thieves, exiles, fugitives, and excommunicated persons (all of whom are commonly called ribalds in France), so that they collected a most numerous army, and had five hundred standards similar to that of their master and chief. They carried swords, axes, darts, daggers, and long knives; so that they seemed to cherish the thoughts of war more than of Christ. Madly raving, they contracted unlawful marriages; and their leaders and instructors, who, although laymen, presumed to preach, enormously strayed in their preachings from the articles of the Christian faith and the evident rules of truth. And if anyone contradicted or opposed them, they attacked him with arms, and not by reasoning or force of argument. When their chief leader preached, he was surrounded by armed followers, and condemned all orders excepting their own conventicles, but especially those of the Preachers and Minorites, whom he called vagrants and hypocrites; the monks of the Cistercian order he declared to be most avaricious lovers of flocks and lands; the black monks [Benedictines], he affirmed, were gluttonous and proud; the canons, he said, were half-secular and meat-eaters; and the bishops and their officials were only money-hunters, and affluent in all kinds of enjoyments. Of the Roman court he made many unmentionable statements; so that from his statements they appeared to be heretics and schismatics. The people, out of hatred and contempt of the clergy, applauded these ravings of his, and listened favorably to his dangerous doctrines.

On Saint Barnabas's day, these shepherds reached Orléans in great pomp and strength, and against the wish of the bishop and all the clergy—

although the citizens were well pleased at their arrival—they entered the city, and their chief, like a prophet powerful in miracles, by the voice of a herald gave notice, or rather issued an edict like a king, of his intention to preach; whereupon the people flocked to him in endless numbers. The bishop of the city, in great fear at this ruinous peril, forbade any clerk, under penalty of anathema, to listen to their discourses, or to follow in their steps, declaring that all these proceedings were the snares of the devil; for the laymen already despised his threats and commands. Some of the clerical scholars, however, transgressing the bishop's prohibition, could not refrain from lending a longing ear to such extraordinary new doctrines, not, however, designing to follow their errors, but only to witness their insolence. Strange, indeed, it was, and absurd, that a layman, and indeed a commoner, despising the authority of the pope, should so boldly preach in public in a city where the scholastic community was in its vigor, and should incline the ears and hearts of so many people to his impostures. They carried with them five hundred standards, at which the clerks of sounder understanding firmly bolted and barred their doors and concealed themselves in perturbation and fear in their houses.

Their said master then rose to preach to the people, and without prefacing his discourse by a text, began to burst forth in loud tones with much unmentionable abuse, when suddenly one of the scholars, who was standing at a distance, boldly forced his way near, and broke forth in the following speech: "Base heretic and enemy to the truth, you lie on your own head; you are deceiving these innocent people by your false and deceitful arguments." Scarcely, however, had he uttered these words, when one of those vagrants rushed upon him, and raising a beaked axe, clove his head in two parts, so that the wounded man did not speak a word more. A tumult then arose, and the people whom we have called pastors, but who now deserve the name of impostors and forerunners of the Antichrist, armed themselves against the clergy of Orléans in general, and rushed on the unarmed citizens, carried off their beloved children, and broke all the doors and windows of the houses, and set the houses themselves on fire, on January 13. With the connivance, or more properly speaking, the consent of the people of the city (who therefore deservedly obtained the appellation of a set of hounds), they cut to pieces many of the citizens, drowned many in the [river] Loire, and those who escaped death, were wounded and robbed of their property. Those who had remained concealed in their houses, on seeing these proceedings, fled in crowds from the city by night. The whole community was thrown into confusion, and it was afterward discovered that about twenty-five clerks had perished, besides numbers who were wounded and injured in diverse ways. The bishop and his followers also, who had hidden themselves to avoid being involved in a similar calamity, underwent many insults, and suffered much injury.

After this the shepherds took their departure, fearing lest the citizens should rise against and attack them; and the bishop, that he might not appear like a dog unable to bark, laid the city under an interdict, because the inhabitants of it had rendered themselves culpable and infamous by permitting such proceedings, and even consenting to and cooperating in them. The cry of complaint at length reached the ears of the Lady Blanche and the nobles and prelates, on hearing which that queen modestly replied, "As the Lord knows, I believed that they in their simplicity and sanctity would gain possession of the entire Holy Land; but since they are deceivers, let them be excommunicated, seized, and destroyed." All these villains were therefore excommunicated and denounced as such; but before the sentence was made public, they went with treacherous designs to Bourges, the gates of which city were thrown open to them by the consent of the citizens, who would not listen to the prohibition of their archbishop. And the greater part of them entered the city, the remainder staying in the vineyards outside the city; for they were so numerous that no city could conveniently receive them all, and their hosts were divided throughout several cities, and even Paris suffered perceptible injury from them. The chief of these deluded men, having announced his intention of preaching a sermon in public, and having promised to work some astounding miracles, an immense multitude of people flocked together from all quarters to hear things hitherto unheard of, and to see things which they had never before seen. When this deceiver gave utterance to some raving speeches, and the miracles he had promised were found to be mere trickery, one of the people, a butcher, bearing an axe, struck him on the head, and sent him brainless to hell. His body was thrown on a crossway and left to rot unburied.

And as the reports spread abroad that these shepherds and their abettors, and all who listened to them, were excommunicated, they dispersed, and were dispatched like mad dogs. At Bordeaux, also, when some of their assemblages approached that city, the gates were locked by order of Simon, earl of Leicester, and they were not allowed to enter. And on their demanding admission, the earl, in reply, asked them: "By whose authority do you act thus?" To which they answered: "We do not plead the authority of pope or bishop, but that of the Omnipotent God, and the Blessed Mary, his mother, which is greater than theirs." When the earl heard this reply, considering such a speech frivolous, he sent back the following message: "Depart all of you, as speedily as possible, or I will assemble all my troops, as well as the . . . inhabitants of this city, and will attack you and cut you to pieces."

These deluded wretches were astounded at hearing these words, and becoming like sand without lime, dispersed in all directions; and as each of them consulted his own safety by flight, they were exposed to peril in many shapes. Their chief and master secretly took flight, and taking ship, endeavored to make his way with all speed to the land of the pagans, whence he had come. But the sailors, finding that he was a traitor and companion of the aforesaid Hungarians, who had been slain by the people of Bourges, bound him hand and foot and threw the wretched vagrant into the Garonne; and thus in his endeavors to escape Scylla he fell into Charybdis. Among his baggage, besides a large sum of money, were found several papers written in Arabic and Chaldean letters, as well as some other strange and unknown characters, and some deleterious powders for making various kinds of poisons. The purport of some of the letters, as was afterward found out, was, that "the sultan earnestly exhorted him to proceed in his undertaking, in expectation of large rewards"; others of the letters were to the effect that "he, the said preacher, would give innumerable people to the sultan." Thus two magi were ensnared in the toils of Satan and perished.

A third preacher presumed to come to England, and, landing at Shoreham, induced more than five hundred people to follow him, consisting of shepherds, plowmen, swineherds, neatherds, and such people. But when it was spread abroad that they were excommunicated, that the Hungarian, their principal teacher, and his companion, had been slain, and their followers dispersed, their condition was much altered for the worse. Their chief, on arriving at Montreuil, attempted to preach there. But as he began to give utterance to foolish, or rather raving assertions, his hearers rose against him, and on their taking to arms, he fled to a wood, but being soon caught, he was put to death, being torn not only limb from limb, but into small particles, and his body was left as a meal for the birds of prey.

Then, indeed, many of their followers found that they had been led astray, and discovering their wretched state, accepted the penance enjoined on them, and laid aside the crosses they had received from the hands of these deceivers, and reassuming the sign of the cross from the hands of good men, duly proceeded on their pilgrimage. And setting out for the Holy Land, they entered the service of the French king after his release from the power of the Saracens, as will be stated in the ensuing narrative. For they said that they had learned from their master that they would liberate the king of the French, wherefore they had all vied with one another in assuming the sign of the cross. One Master Thomas, a native of Normandy and a monk of Sherborne, a discreet and eloquent man who was sent at that time to the continent to transact some urgent and arduous business for the king, was made prisoner by the above-mentioned shepherds, and was detained by them for eight days, and as he would not lend a favorable ear to their arguments, he was severely beaten. With some difficulty, he, however, at length escaped by night, and making his way to the king at Winchester, gave a full account of all their proceedings and deceitful tricks to the king, in the hearing of the writer of this work, who faithfully and fully noted down all that he heard from the mouth of the narrator, as he was a credible person.

55. The Register of Eudes Rigaud, Archbishop of Rouen, 1260–1269

Eudes, or Odo, Rigaud appears to have joined the Franciscan order while studying theology in Paris. After his election as archbishop of Rouen (1247–1275), Eudes zealously visited the dioceses under his authority, recording the results of his visitations in a lengthy and highly informative register. He became close to Louis IX as a master of theology in Paris and aided the king in organizing his second crusade. Eudes was greatly persecuted by the *Pastoureaux*, who seem to have blamed him for some of Louis IX's defeat in Egypt. Eudes later presided over the Second Council of Lyons (1274) in Gregory X's absence (below, No. 71). His register offers a valuable view of what might be termed the home front of thirteenth-century crusading.

The period represented by the excerpts from Odo's register printed below (1260–1269) was marked by numerous appeals for financial contributions and/or recruits for numerous crusades. The projects included aid for political crusades in Italy and the ailing Latin kingdom of Romania (whose capital, Constantinople, fell in 1261 to the Greeks), and an attempt to muster a crusade in response to the ingress of the Mongols into the Middle East (ca. 1260). In addition, after Urban IV gained French royal support for his anti-Manfred crusade, recruiting efforts in

France in support of Charles of Anjou's conquest of Manfred in South Italy competed with recruitment for a Holy Land crusade from circa 1264–1265 (below, No. 59). Despite the Mamluks' capture of Haifa and Arsuf in 1265 and of Antioch in 1268, the efforts of Egidius, archbishop of Tyre, to preach and collect a crusading tax from the French clergy were sabotaged by Clement IV and his legate in France, Simon, cardinal priest of Saint Cecilia. Simon had been commissioned to preach the anti-Manfred crusade and allow crusaders in the kingdom of France to commute their vow for the crusade to the Holy Land to pledges of support for Charles of Anjou. Despite earlier commissions to preach a crusade against the Mamluk Baibars, and the continuing recruitment activities of Egidius and his agents, Odo and other prelates were soon commanded to step up their preaching for the anti-Manfred crusade. The West's failure to muster a crusade soon meant that the few Latin strongholds remaining in the Holy Land were endangered by further Mamluk offensives, and by May 1266 Clement urged his legate Simon to shift his efforts toward quickly mustering a Holy Land crusade in France. Despite Louis IX's adoption of the cross, the failure of his first crusade meant a lukewarm response from his realm's overtaxed and overrecruited clergymen and nobles. Complaints about the collection of revenues for the crusade were abundant, and the following excerpts from the register of Eudes of Rouen illustrate the difficulties that faced even one of the most prominent churchmen in France in supporting on the home front the second crusade of Louis IX.

Williel R. Thomson, Friars in the Cathedral: The First Franciscan Bishops, 1226–1261 *(Toronto, 1975), 78–89; Adam J. Davis,* The Holy Bureaucrat: Eudes Rigaud and Religious Reform in Thirteenth-Century Normandy *(Ithaca NY, 2006); Michael Lower, "Louis IX, Charles of Anjou, and the Tunis Crusade of 1270," in Madden, Naus, and Ryan,* Crusades, *173–194.*

In January of 1260, Odo (Eudes) of Rouen held a council for the archdiocese of Rouen with the bishops under his authority. The statutes passed during the council including the following resolution.

[JANUARY 12, 1260.] Since it is a work of charity to weep with the weeping, and to open the bowels of compassion for those who are afflicted, we, moved by fraternal affection for our brethren who are dwelling in lands overseas, in Constantinople, and in the Morea, and are oppressed by grievous burdens, decree that throughout the entire province there shall be sung before the Lord, once a day, at the Mass of the day, and just before the *Pax Domini,* the psalm *Deus venerunt gentes* [Ps. 78] with the Lord's Prayer, versicles, and usual prayers for the Holy Land.

Source: The Register of Eudes of Rouen, *trans. Sydney M. Brown, ed. Jeremiah F. O'Sullivan (New York, 1964), 442–443, 463, 500–503, 576, 658, 669, 687, 724.*

[September 2, 1261.] This day we received a letter from the cardinals concerning the business of the Tartars, on which the proctors had gone to the Roman curia. The letter was brought by Master John of Neuilly-en-Thelle and his colleague who had just returned from the curia.

[August 20, 1262.] At Paris . . . we celebrated the Mass of the Holy Spirit at our chapel, and then we went to the sacred council, called by the venerable father, the bishop of Agen, the pope's legate. The father began by preaching a sermon in which he brought out the need which the church of Rome had for financial assistance, not only for repairing the damages which have already been suffered, that is, in recovering the land belonging to Constantinople, which has already been lost; but also to avoid dangers which threaten, that is, to preserve the land of Acre, which was in peril of being lost; and if this were lost, then Christians, according to the father, would no longer have access to the Holy Land. These matters being presented and demonstrated, the father concluded by stating that he had been appointed an apostolic legate to deal with this matter, and that, having called together and in one place all the prelates of the realm of France, he would beseech them to grant a worthy subsidy for the alleviation or avoidance of the above-mentioned perils. Indeed, he revealed an apostolic letter in which he was given authority to do this and to make such a plea. However, with the consent of the said legate, the answer of the prelates to this was postponed until the morrow.

[August 31, 1262.] We convened at the bishop's hall . . . to give our response to the legate. After we had taken counsel among ourselves and then with the proctors of the chapters, we gave our reply through the Reverend Father G. [Vincent], archbishop of Tours. He pointed out that the church in Gaul had been long oppressed with burdens because of the subsidies which it had made in response to papal request for the recovery of the Holy Land, namely, a tenth and a twelfth, which it had paid for a long time. Because of certain other special subsidies which it had paid to the pope on occasion, together with other subsidies for the land of Constantinople, with the common consent of all, he replied that, at present, we were not able to help that land. On this same day we caused to be read a letter which had been sent from the apostolic see to us and to the venerable man Eudes of Lorris, canon of Beauvais, concerning the collection of a hundredth for the relief of the Holy Land.

[September 1, 1262.] The proctors of the . . . archbishops and bishops noted below appeared before us and that venerable man, Eudes of Lorris, canon of Beauvais, and tendered to us the following letter. . . .

"We, the proctors of the archbishops of Bourges, Reims, Sens, and Tours, and of G[irard], the bishop of Autun, G[ilbert], the bishop of Limoges, and J[ohn], bishop of Mâcon, in their behalf and that of their suffragans, subjects, and adherents, [appeal] to you, the lord archbishop of Rouen and to your colleague, Master Eudes [of Lorris], who consider yourselves officially deputized by the Holy See in the matter of a subsidy levied against them [the prelates], their subjects, and their churches to the extent of a hundredth to be exacted from them and their subjects for the succor of the Holy Land. They have many sound reasons why they should not be compelled to pay this at all, and they are prepared to demonstrate these reasons at the proper time and place: first, because for a long time, or for many years, they have been burdened and oppressed by heavy subsidies for the Holy Land, so much so in fact that because of the aforementioned subsidies, they, their subjects, and their churches are still under many obligations of debt; second, by reason of the bad harvest there has been a lack of good crops, and the greatest cost of provisions has resulted; third, real danger does not threaten, nor are preparations set for a general passage overseas, nor has any prince or equally powerful man assumed this task for which a subsidy should be extorted from them; fourth, since truces have for a long time been in effect between the Saracens and the Christians overseas, the subsidy is not necessary, and it may be that when the pope sent the letter to you, there were no truces, or if there were, perchance he was not aware of them.

"For these and other reasons, to be presented and demonstrated in their time and place, we beseech and supplicate you not to proceed with the matter of this subsidy so far as they and their subjects are concerned. Lest you should so proceed notwithstanding the aforementioned reasons and the others to be presented and proved in time and place, and without giving us a copy of the apostolic letter which is said to have been sent to you, we appeal in writing to the Apostolic See, requesting you that, referring to such an appeal, you will give us *apostoli* about this; which if you refuse to do, we, aggrieved, appeal in writing to the Apostolic See."

[December 22, 1264]. . . . On the Sunday before Christmas, we were present while the archbishop of Tyre [Egidius] preached the crusade in the vestibule of the cathedral in Rouen. He spent this night . . . with us at our manor at Rouen.

[March 25, 1266]. . . . On the feast of the Annunciation of Our Lady [in Paris] . . . the king of France and three of his children, that is, my lords Philip, John, and Peter, together with many nobles of the realm of France, counts, barons, and also the countess of Flanders, took the cross.

[June 5, 1267]. On Pentecost [in Paris] . . . by God's grace, Sir Philip, the eldest son of the king of France, together with many nobles of the kingdom of France were girded with the sword of knighthood. We, the king of Navarre, the count of Dreux, the lord of Harcourt, and many other nobles took the cross, with God's aid, from the lord legate on the island of Notre-Dame, where we preached before the king, the said legate, many prelates and barons of France, a multitude of the clergy, and a great gathering of the people.

[March 18, 1269]. . . . Mid-Lent Sunday. With God's grace we preached the crusade at the Halls of the Old Tower, and thence we translated, with great veneration and procession, relics of Saint Mary Magdalene, which the king had sent through us to the prior and convent of the Hôtel-Dieu in Rouen. We celebrated high mass in the cathedral.

The papal legate Ralph, cardinal bishop of Albano, joined Eudes at Gaillon on June 22, 1269, and continued to travel with him for some time.

[JUNE 30, 1269]. With God's aid, we preached the crusade in the presence of the legate, to the people who had gathered after a procession at the atrium of Saint-Gervaise. We had the legate at our manor in Rouen, at our expense.

56. Rutebeuf's "Lament of the Holy Land," ca. 1266

Rutebeuf is one of the most important vernacular French poets of the thirteenth century. Of the fifty-six poems commonly attributed to him, eleven deal directly with crusading matters relating to the Holy Land or Apulia, chiefly in the form of praise of individuals or calls to action. It is generally accepted that the present poem, "The Lament of the Holy Land,"[26] was written some time after Pope Clement IV's letter of July 1265, in which he called for a holy war in the East to be preached in France, perhaps after his call in April 1266 for the cessation of preaching of the crusade in Sicily in favor of one in the Holy Land; the call to Louis IX to participate in the crusade indicates that the text predates Louis's taking of the cross in March 1267. The poem itself combines satirical criticism of general

26. The original title is "*La complainte d'outre-mer*." The literal sense of outremer is "overseas"; by extension, this became synonymous with the Holy Land, as a part of Christendom, which happened to be located overseas.

contemporary laxity and indifference with an exhortation to emulate the great crusading deeds of emblematic forebears. What a conscientious Franciscan archbishop like Odo of Rouen could not easily say about the difficulties of recruiting for a Holy Land crusade in the 1260s could be said bluntly by a gifted poet.

The text is transmitted in four manuscripts. This translation is based on the text contained in MS Paris, Bibliothèque nationale, fonds français 837, which serves as the base manuscript for the edition of Edmond Faral and Julia Bastin, Œuvres complètes de Rutebeuf, *2 vols. (Paris: Picard, 1959–1960). The original poem is composed in octosyllabic rhyming couplets. This verse form is so common in Old French that the closest equivalent in modern English is unbroken prose. The translation has been separated into paragraphs corresponding to the large initials provided in the manuscript. The best general introduction remains the general introduction in Faral and Bastin's edition (1:82–93) and their notes introducing and accompanying their editions of the individual texts (1:411–516). Also worthy of note are Nancy Freeman Regalado,* Poetic Patterns in Rutebeuf: A Study in Noncourtly Poetic Modes of the Thirteenth Century *(New Haven CT-London, 1970), 39–54; Arié Serper,* Rutebeuf, poète satirique *(Paris, 1969); D. A. Trotter,* Medieval French Literature and the Crusades (1100–1300) *(Geneva, 1988), 226.*

EMPERORS and kings and counts and dukes and princes, for whose entertainment we perform a range of tales about those who used in the past to fight for the sake of the Holy Church, pray tell me through what service you believe that you will find a place in heaven. In the past, those men of whom you hear these stories told earned it through the pain and through the martyrdom that their bodies suffered on earth. Now is the time when God comes to beseech you, with his arms outstretched and covered in his blood; through him, the fires of hell and purgatory will be extinguished for you. You must take the lead in a new epic tale: serve God with all your noble heart, for he is showing you the path to his kingdom and his marches, which the unrighteous are trampling underfoot. This is why you should devote your efforts to avenging and defending the promised land, which is in tribulation and will be lost unless God turns his attention to it and unless it receives support as soon as possible. Remember God our Father who sent his son to earth to suffer a terrible death. Now the very land where he died and lived stands in great danger. I do not know what else to say to you: if anybody does not help in this time of need or shirks his responsibility, I shall have little respect for whatever else he does, no matter how pious an appearance he might be able to present. Rather, from this day on I shall say day and night: "All that glisters is not gold."

Oh, King of France, King of France! Religion, faith, and belief are all standing on the brink. Why should I keep hiding this from you? Now

Source: *Edmond Faral and Julia Bastin, eds.,* Œuvres complètes de Rutebeuf, *2 vols. (Paris: Picard, 1959–1960), 2:440–450, trans and ed. Daron Burrows, Manchester University.*

it is essential that you, the count of Poitiers,[27] and the other barons come together to rescue them. Do not tarry so long that death takes your soul from you, by God, my lords! Rather, may anybody who wants to have honor[28] in heaven earn it; I cannot offer any other advice. Jesus Christ says in the Gospel, which contains no lies or half-truths: "He should not reach heaven who does not leave his wife and children and belongings for the sake of the love of him who in the end will be his judge."[29]

Many people are full of sorrow because Roland[30] was betrayed, and shed tears out of false pity, even as they see with their eyes the love shown to us by God, who created us, and who cried to the Jews on the holy cross that he was dying of thirst. This was not so that he might drink for the pleasure of it, but rather because he was thirsty to redeem us. We should fear and revere him; we should cry for such a lord who let himself be tortured in this way and had his side pierced to save us from the realm of evil. From his side flowed blood and water which clean and wash his friends.[31]

King of France, who put your wealth and your friends and even yourself in prison for the sake of God,[32] it will be a terrible mistake if you fail the Holy Land. Now is the time that you must go there or send people there, without skimping on gold or silver, in order to lay claim to the rights of God. God does not wish to wait any longer for his friends to pay what is due to him, or keep them on too loose a leash;[33] rather he wants to stake his claim, and wants those who wish to sit at his right hand to go and see him.

Alas! Prelates of the Holy Church, who do not wish to attend matins in order to keep themselves from the cold air, my lord Geoffrey of Sargines[34] is calling out to you from over the seas. But I shall say this: he acts

27. Alphonse of Poitiers (1220–1271), brother of Louis IX.

28. The Old French honor has further connotations, including wealth, good fortune, and a fief.

29. Cf. Mt 10:37; Lk 14:26–27.

30. A famous hero of the Old French epic, best known to us through the Chanson de Roland.

31. Cf. Jn 19:34.

32. An allusion to Louis IX's imprisonment during the Seventh Crusade.

33. The pun cannot be adequately captured. The speaker says that God will not grant longer *giez*: on the one hand, delays in payment of a tax, and on the other, the bands fastened around the legs of a bird of a prey to which a leash is attached.

34. Geoffrey accompanied Louis IX on the Seventh Crusade and remained after his departure, leading a campaign of resistance from his base at Jaffa before becoming seneschal of Jerusalem. His reputation for bravery is reflected by Joinville, William of Nangis, and, prior to the present poem, by Rutebeuf in his "*Complainte de monseigneur Geoffroi de Ser-*

dishonorably who asks of you nothing more than fine wines and good food and that the pepper should be spicy. This is your war and the extent of your efforts, this is your God, this is your wealth: your Father is treated as nothing more than a dung-bearer![35] Rutebeuf, who hides nothing, says that a little bit of cloth[36] will be enough for you, unless your bellies are too fat. And what will your weary souls do? They will go to that place that I dare not name: God will be the judge in this matter. May you send to Jesus Christ the tenth of the tithe which is rightly his; do at least this much goodness unto him, since he has raised you so high!

Alas! Great clerics and holders of great prebends, who place so much importance on what your tables hold and turn your bellies into God, tell me precisely on what terms you will share in the kingdom of God, you who are so wicked that you will not read a single psalm from your Psalter, except for the one which only contains two lines, which you read after eating.[37] God wants you to go and avenge him without inventing any more excuses, or that you should relinquish the patrimony which belongs to the Crucified One. You keep it badly, I can assure you. If you serve God in church, God returns your service in another form, for he gives you food in your house: it is quite rightly a mutual exchange. But if you are interested in the abode which offers joy without end, you must buy it, because God is selling it. For he certainly needs buyers, and those who do not make the transaction now are cheating themselves, for the time will come when they will want to have this abode, but they will not be able to acquire it by any material wealth.

Tourneyers, what will you say when you come to the Day of Judgment? What answer will you be able to give when facing God? For at that moment neither clergy nor laity will be able to hide themselves, and God will show you his wounds. If he demands of you the land in which he was prepared to suffer death for your sake, what will you say? I cannot imagine. The bravest will be so docile that one could lead them away by the hand; and we do not have a tomorrow, for the hour when death will close our mouths is inexorably approaching.

---

gines." Baibars's violation of the truce in 1263 had elicited frequent calls to support Geoffrey.

35. The precise interpretation of the preceding two sentences has eluded editors. This translation leans in favor of reading it as more of the criticism of prelates, which predominates in this section.

36. That is, a funeral shroud.

37. That is, Ps 116.

Oh, Antioch! Holy Land! How painful and lamentable it is that that you no longer have any Godfreys![38] The fire of charity has gone cold in every Christian heart; no men, be they young or old, can be bothered to fight for God. The Dominicans and Franciscans could struggle for a long time to find any Angeliers, Tancreds, or Baldwins.[39] Instead, they will allow the Bedouins[40] to hold the Holy Land, which has been taken from us through our failings, and already God has suffered that it has been burnt from one side. From the other the Tartars are coming, and then Khwarizmians and Canaanites[41] will come to destroy everything: there will not be anybody to defend it. If my lord Geoffrey asks for help, may he look well for somebody who might give it to him, for I see no other recourse. If I were to talk any longer, the situation would only get worse. This world is coming to its end: anybody who does the right thing will find it rewarded after his death.

38. Godfrey of Bouillon, a leader of the First Crusade, and by the thirteenth-century a figure of heroic, legendary proportions.

39. Tancred and Baldwin are two of the most renowned participants in the triumphant First Crusade. By contrast, Angelier of Gascony, as one learns in the Chanson de Roland, is one of the twelve peers of Charlemagne, felled at the battle of Roncevaux—a fine example of the blurring of historical and mythical heroism.

40. Here, a general term denoting Saracens.

41. The Tartars, having merged with the Mongols, attained particular notoriety in Europe subsequent to their incursions into Russia, Hungary, and Poland (cf., e.g., Council of Lyons, 1245, canon 4, translated as No. 46 above), while the Khwarizmians took Jerusalem in 1244. "Canaanites" (*Chenillier*) is a generic term denoting Saracens.

PART VIII
The Italian Crusades, 1241–1268

Crusades launched by popes against European Christian opponents have often been called (and criticized as) "political crusades," as if they were devoid of religious significance and could only be understood as conflicts between worldly popes and their purely political enemies. To be sure, the exclusive papal authority to call a crusade for any purpose or destination was universally recognized (if not always universally observed, and in the course of the thirteenth century popes consistently lost control over crusades once they began to move). But the popes also had several distinctive spheres of responsibility and influence—territorial Christendom as a whole, the Holy Land, the Greek and Eastern Christian world, certain kingdoms and principalities that had been given by their rulers to Saint Peter (for example, England, Sicily, Hungary, Aragón), and the lands of Saint Peter, the city of Rome and its surrounding territories (generally termed the "Papal States"), as these had been negotiated with Christian rulers and local powers since the eighth century and became in the thirteenth century a matter of considerable importance and conflict as a consequence of rapid demographic, economic, and political change. No thirteenth-century pope could afford to neglect any of these spheres, nor could any pope cease to be pope while dealing with one or another of them, no matter how purely secular a conflict might appear.

On the global level the pope was responsible for Christian relations with non-Christians, on the legitimacy of infidel rule over Christians, and on the alternatives of conquest and conversion—that is, diplomatic relations, crusade, and mission. On the European level the pope was responsible for the spiritual and moral condition of Christian society and especially relations with the emperors, primary defenders of the church, who came to be called, under Innocent III, "vicars of the pope" and "the secular arm" of the church. The twelfth century had witnessed active conflicts between the papally protected city-republics of northern Italy and the emperor Frederick Barbarossa, who attempted to assert imperial rights in Italy over them. After the marriage between Henry VI and Constance of Sicily, the popes had to attend closely to their borders with the kingdom of Sicily, since the inextricable connection between imperial affairs and those of the kingdom had to be balanced with the rights and claims of the church, which had been given Sicily in 1059 by its Norman ruler Robert Guiscard. Finally, the popes were also the temporal rulers of Rome and its environs, whose particular patron and lord was Saint Peter, and they had to deal with the local nobility as well as imperial/royal powers along its borders.

They had limited resources for carrying out these obligations. In theory the popes wielded only the spiritual sword—sacramental powers and ecclesiastical discipline, such as denunciation, liturgical opposition, the giving or withholding of privileges, malediction, interdict, jurisdiction over reserved sins, the right to hear universal appeals, and excommunication—while lay powers wielded the material sword—property, wealth, criminal law, and the legitimate use of force, including the shedding of blood.[1] Again in theory, popes might invoke lay protection for the church, and laymen were obliged to give it. Theorists debated whether lay powers received their validation exclusively from the church or independently from God. Even theorists who argued that the church alone authorized lay power allowed that the pope could not personally wield the temporal power himself but had to confer it on a lay ruler, retaining only supervisory legal rights and judging the effectiveness of such a ruler's activities.[2] One of the few exceptions to this rule was the Papal States, where the pope was anomalously both spiritual and temporal lord (in the latter case acting as the vicar of Saint Peter, the actual lord).[3] Thus, popes and their supporters justified the crusades (and other specific invocations of material force) on the grounds that the popes were obligated to protect the spiritual needs of the Christian community and to offer opportunities for penitential activities in certain circumstances. The crusaders' taking up the cross of Christ and following in his footsteps was regarded as a literal instance of this papal responsibility and a prospect of the rewards it could offer.

Although several popes had called secular powers into their service since the ninth century—Pope Leo IX had even personally led an army into battle with Norman Christians at Civitate in 1053, having promised his troops salvation if they fell in battle, and Gregory VII had proposed the creation of a *militia sancti Petri,* a militia of Saint Peter—after the late eleventh century the elaboration of programs for ecclesiastical reform, the increasing complexity of theological argument, and the formation of classical canon law with its emphasis on papal authority expressed these relationships with far greater precision to a society that had become much larger and far more complex than the Europe of 1053 or 1095. New difficulties could trouble established practices.

One such new difficulty was the growing practice in the city-republics of northern and central Italy for competing groups of political elites to profess alliance with either the papal or the imperial cause. Those who favored the imperial cause are usually called Ghibellines, and those who favored the papal cause Guelfs. Although in some cities Guelfs and Ghibellines lived together in a state of political

1. On the thirteenth century, see J. A. Watt, "The Papacy," in Abulafia, *New Cambridge Medieval History,* 5:107–163. For malediction, Lester K. Little, *Benedictine Maledictions: Liturgical Cursing in Romanesque France* (Ithaca NY, 1993); for excommunication, Elizabeth Vodola, *Excommunication in the Middle Ages* (Berkeley-Los Angeles, 1986); for interdict, Peter D. Clark, *The Interdict in the Thirteenth Century: A Question of Collective Guilt* (Oxford-New York, 2007). For other forms of ecclesiastical discipline, see Richard Helmholz, *The Spirit of Classical Canon Law* (Athens GA, 1996).

2. The classic collection of translated texts on this topic is Brian Tierney, *The Crisis of Church and State, 1050–1300* (1964; repr., Toronto, 1988).

3. On this complex of territories, see Peter Partner, *The Lands of St. Peter* (Berkeley-Los Angeles, 1972); Daniel P. Waley, *The Papal State in the Thirteenth Century* (London, 1961).

tension, in most cases one group, rising to power because of external circumstances, would often exile the other, sending its members to other cities which shared their political sympathies, where they would usually plot their return to drive out their enemies or negotiate some form of return under strict and often unbearable conditions. Such events as the deposition and death of Frederick II meant a temporary weakening of imperial sympathies and the growth of papal alliances within a number of cities. But imperial or papal alliances often played subordinate roles in the internal political lives of individual cities, whose growth and increasing wealth was a marked phenomenon of the thirteenth century.

When Innocent III became pope in January 1198, he found that he had to establish order in central and southern Italy because the nobles who had served the late king-emperor Henry VI were encroaching on ecclesiastical privileges and papal territories. Lacking other resources, in 1199 Innocent threatened one of these pop-up princes, Markward of Anweiler, with a crusade, but solved the crisis diplomatically in 1204. In Markward's case, the threat of a crusade was a papal last resort. Innocent frequently and bitterly criticized the diversion of the Fourth Crusade to warfare with the Christian East, as did many of the crusaders, including those who left the crusade before Constantinople and went on to the East themselves. The Albigensian Crusade resulted from Innocent's frustration with local conditions in the south of France, the French king's reluctance to act, Innocent's fear of the corrupting power of obstinate, publicly demonstrated, heretical activity in the very heart of western Europe, and the murder of the papal legate in 1208. Innocent also discovered the terrible consequences: the diversion of men and finances from the Holy Land and Iberia, the alienation of many otherwise devout Christians, and the difficulty of periodically suspending the Albigensian Crusade in favor of crusading efforts elsewhere—chiefly in Iberia and the Holy Land in anticipation of the Fourth Lateran Council and the Fifth Crusade.

These crusading efforts were indeed a precedent, but not a very satisfactory one. Nor were the circumstances that created them sufficiently similar as to lay out a general theory. But the troubled relations between Gregory IX and Frederick II after 1239 and the chaos into which both the empire and the kingdom of Sicily plunged after Frederick's death in 1250 turned the popes once again to the crusade as the only instrument available to defend the church in the heartland of Italy. Gregory IX had already called a crusade to invade the kingdom during Frederick's absence in the Holy Land in 1229. Gregory's invocation of a crusade against Frederick II in 1239 and Innocent IV's in 1244 did not succeed, although they contributed to the war of polemic that swept across Europe, nor did Innocent IV's urging in 1244 of Louis IX to delay his own crusade until Italy was pacified.

At the death of Gregory IX in August 1241, Celestine IV was elected, but reigned for only three weeks. The cardinals having been widely dispersed, Innocent IV was not elected until June 25, 1243, the papal vacancy aiding Frederick II's military campaigns. Innocent's decision to call a general council at Lyons in 1245 was made more difficult by Frederick's military successes against the pro-papal Guelf city-republics in northern Italy and his capture of several of the ecclesiastical officials en route to Lyons.

Innocent's deposition of Frederick at Lyons declared open war. The continuation of Staufer power in Germany and Italy in the persons of Conrad IV and Manfred provided stiff opposition. Innocent IV proclaimed crusades against Conrad IV (1250–1254) and Manfred (1255), and in 1255–1260 Alexander IV (r. 1254–1261) called crusades against Alberigo and Ezzelino da Romano, Frederick's servants in northern Italy. In 1261 Alexander IV preached crusades against Manfred and to the Holy Land, signaling once again the problem of diverting men and money from one crusade front to another, greatly influencing public opinion, preaching efforts, and the response to them, which in turn influenced the crusade ethos. In 1264 Pope Urban IV proclaimed a crusade against Staufer power in Italy on behalf of Charles of Anjou and in 1267–1268 against Conradin, son of Conrad IV. Charles of Anjou finally destroyed Staufer power in the kingdom with the public trial and execution of Conradin following his defeat at the battle of Tagliacozzo in 1268. From 1239 to 1268, the "political crusades" dominated both papal and imperial affairs.

The best studies of the crusades against Christians in Italy are those by Norman Housley, The Italian Crusades: The Papal-Angevin Alliance and the Crusades Against Christian Lay Powers, 1254–1343 *(Oxford, 1982); Housley, "Crusades Against Christians," reprinted in Housley,* Crusading and Warfare in Medieval and Renaissance Europe *(Aldershot UK-Burlington VT, 2001), I; and Jean Dunbabin,* Charles I of Anjou: Power, Kingship and State-Making in Thirteenth-Century Europe *(New York, 1998). See also John T. Gilchrist, "The Lord's War as the Proving Ground of Faith: Pope Innocent III and the Propagation of Violence (1198–1216)," in Maya Shatzmiller, ed.,* Crusaders and Muslims in Twelfth-Century Syria *(Leiden, 1993), 65–83. For the general history of the political conflicts in Italy, see Abulafia,* New Cambridge Medieval History, *vol. 5, chaps. 15 and 16.*

57. Gregory IX Writes to His Legate, the Papal Chaplain and Subdeacon John of Civitella in Hungary, *Cum tibi duxerimus*, 1241

Gregory IX had excommunicated Frederick II for failing to depart on crusade in 1227, and during Frederick's absence in the Holy Land, Gregory had mustered a papal army to attack Frederick's supporters in regions of Italy adjoining the papal territories. After severe military reversals, the pope made peace with Frederick II in 1230, even suggesting another crusade for Frederick in 1238 (see above, No. 34), but the papal-imperial conflict was soon revived. By 1240 Gregory was preaching an anti-imperial crusade against Frederick, whose armies were closing in on the papal territories in Rome. Besieged in Rome and thus deprived of the traditional papal retreat into the hills to escape the oppressive summer heat, the aged Gregory died while rallying Rome's citizens against the imperial invasion of papal Italy in 1241. Frederick was deposed by Innocent IV at the Council of Lyons in 1245 and died in 1250, but the papal-imperial struggle continued for decades, diverting recruits and resources from the crusades to the Holy Land and providing occasions for political conflict within many Italian city-republics. In the course of renewed papal-imperial hostility, the crusade became a papal instrument in its defense against Frederick II and his successors.

SINCE we were led to enjoin you to proclaim the word of the cross in the kingdom of Hungary against Frederick, called emperor, son of perdition, some in the aforementioned kingdom have taken the sign of the cross in aid of the Holy Land, which as you have reported, has produced a not inconsiderable impediment. And we consider that it would be far more salutary to aid the apostolic see in this matter, all the more so because when the mother and head of the faith itself is assailed Christendom is greatly endangered. And so we grant to your devotion the power to commute the vows of those signed with the cross in defense of the church against the same Frederick if their consent is obtained for this. By the authority of this present letter, we concede to you the unrestricted ability to grant that pardon of sins which is given to those succoring the aforesaid land in the general council to these and the remainder redeeming their vows, provided that they entrust the expenses which they were going to assume in journeying to the aforesaid land, in dwelling in that place and returning from it, into your hands and those of our beloved son the abbot of Pöls of the Cistercian order and Benedict, canon of Gran, be devoted to this kind of defense [that is, of the apostolic see].

58. Matthew Paris on the Popes and Staufer Italy, 1245–1269

Matthew Paris's great interest in the conflict between Frederick II and his successors and several popes (and his strong opinions about both sides) led to his inclusion of a substantial number of documents and narrative accounts of these matters in his chronicle. It is interesting and illuminating to contrast Matthew's views, those of a Benedictine monk in distant England who admired much about Frederick and Manfred and disapproved of what he considered excessive papal interference in the affairs of kings and peoples, with those of the Franciscan Salimbene (below, No. 60), an anti-imperialist and great supporter of the popes.

For the literature, see the headnote to this part above. For the Muslim colony at Lucera, see Julie Taylor, Muslims in Medieval Italy: The Colony at Lucera *(Lanham MD, 2003); and for a superb study contrasting the ecclesiastical contexts of Matthew and Salimbene, Robert Brentano,* Two Churches: England and Italy in the Thirteenth Century *(Princeton NJ, 1968). Matthew reproduces a commonly held, utterly fictitious account of the life of Muhammad*

Source for Gregory IX: *Rodenberg,* Epistolae Saeculi XIII, *1:706–707.*

and the early organization of Islam in Giles, Matthew Paris's English History, *1:14–28; see James M. Powell, "Matthew Paris, the Lives of Muhammad, and the Dominicans," reprinted in Powell,* The Crusades, the Kingdom of Sicily, and the Mediterranean *(Aldershot UK-Burlington, VT, 2007), VIII.*

ABOUT mid-Lent of this same year [1245], the pope's messengers came into England for the purpose of convoking a general council, and were the bearers of the following papal mandate:

"Innocent [IV], bishop, servant of the servants of God, to his well-beloved sons the abbots and priors throughout all England, health and apostolic blessing. . . . We have become anxious at heart that the fierceness of the tempest by which the church is disturbed and the Christian religion shaken to its foundations, should, with the favoring affection of heaven, be averted by the help of our arrangements. For this reason we have determined to convoke the kings of the earth, the prelates of the churches, and other magnates of the world in general, in order that the church itself may, by the wholesome counsel and beneficial aid of all true Christians, receive all due honor; that assistance may be speedily afforded to the Holy Land in its deplorable peril, and to the afflicted Roman Empire,[4] and that we may find relief against the Tartars and other despisers of the faith and persecutors of the Christian people; and also to determine the matters in dispute between the church and the emperor. We also beg of and exhort you in your devotion, and by these apostolic letters command you, laying aside all pretexts and excuses, to appear in person in our presence at the next festival of Saint John the Baptist,[5] in order that the church may conceive spiritual joy by the honor of your visitation and profitable counsel from our industry. We also have to inform you that we have in our preaching cited the aforesaid emperor to appear in person, or by his messengers, at the council about to be held, there to answer to us and to others who may set forth anything against him, and to give proper satisfaction for the same. . . . Given at Lyons, this thirtieth of January, in the second year of our pontificate."

. . . . [Then] Walleran, bishop of Beirut, who had endured the troubles of a long journey . . . to bring word of the calamities of the Holy Land and to ask counsel and assistance, now ordered Arnulph, one of the Preacher brethren, to publicly read the letters which the nobles left in the

Source: *Giles,* Matthew Paris's English History, *2:48–49, 67, 84–86, 102–103, 174–175, 218, 298, 302–304, 306–7, 313; 3:102–103, 122–124, 143, 307–308, 332–333, 337, 358, 373.*
4. That is, the Latin Empire of Constantinople.
5. June 24.

Holy Land had sent to all the Christians of the West. These letters have been inserted in a former part of this work and their mournful contents now excited all who heard them to tears, and not without good reason.

Matthew then goes on to narrate the dramatic events at the First Council of Lyons, including decrees for the relief of the Holy Land (2:86–94), culminating in Innocent IV's reading aloud to the council the remarkable letter deposing Frederick II, Ad apostolicae sedis. *We excerpt here only those parts of the letter dealing with Frederick and crusading matters.*

"BESIDES, he is united by a detestable alliance with the Saracens—has often sent messages and presents to them, and in turn received the same from them with respect and alacrity; he embraces their customs, notoriously keeping them with him in his daily service, and, after their fashion, he shamelessly appoints as guards over his wives, whom he has received from the descendants of a royal race, certain eunuchs, especially those whom he has lately caused to be castrated. And what is a more execrable offense, when formerly in the country beyond the sea, he made a kind of arrangement or rather collusion with the sultan, and allowed the name of Muhammad to be publicly proclaimed in the temple of the Lord day and night; and lately, in the case of the sultan of Babylon, who, by his own hands and through his agents, had done irreparable mischief and injury to the Holy Land and its Christian inhabitants, he caused that sultan's ambassadors, in compliment of their master, as is said, to be honorably received and nobly entertained in his kingdom of Sicily.[6]

"He also, in opposition to the Christians, abuses the pernicious and horrid rites of other infidels, and entering into an alliance of friendship with those who wickedly pay little respect to and despise the Apostolic See, and have seceded from the unity of the church, laying aside all respect to the Christian religion, he caused, as is positively asserted, the duke of Bavaria, of illustrious memory, a special and devoted ally of the Roman Church, to be murdered by the Assassins. He has also given his daughter [Constance] in marriage to Battacius,[7] an enemy of God and the church, who together with his helpers, counselors, and abettors, was solemnly expelled from the communion of the Christians by sentence of excommunication. Rejecting the proceedings and customs of catholic princes,

---

6. Including Ibn Wasil.
7. John III Ducas Vatatzes, Greek emperor of Nicaea (1222–1254), one of the Latin emperor of Constantinople's prime rivals in the region of the former Byzantine Empire.

neglecting his own salvation and the purity of his fame, he does not employ himself in works of piety; and what is more (to be silent on his wicked and dissolute practices), although he has learned to practice oppression to such a degree, he does not trouble himself to relieve those oppressed by injuries, by extending his hand, as a Christian prince ought, to bestow alms, although he has been eagerly aiming at the destruction of the churches and has crushed religious men and other ecclesiastical persons with the burden and persecution of his yoke. . . .

"We therefore, having maturely and carefully deliberated with our brother cardinals and the holy council on the above-named and other nefarious deeds of his, seeing that we, undeserving as we are, hold on earth the authority of our Lord Jesus Christ, who said to us in the person of Saint Peter, 'Whatever ye shall bind on earth shall be bound also in heaven, etc.' [Mt 16:19, 18:18], do hereby declare the above-named prince, who has rendered himself unworthy of the honors of sovereignty, and for his crimes has been deposed from his throne by God, to be bound by his sins and cast off by the Lord, and deprived of all his honors, and we do hereby sentence and deprive him, and all who are in any way bound to him by an oath of allegiance, we forever absolve and release from that oath, and, by the apostolic authority, strictly forbid anyone from obeying him or in any way whatever attempting to obey him as an emperor or king; and we decree that any who shall henceforth give him assistance or advice or show favor to him as an emperor or king shall be excommunicated ipso facto. And those in the empire on whom the election of an emperor devolves may freely elect a successor in his place. With respect to the aforesaid kingdom of Sicily, we, with the advice of our brother cardinals, will make such provision for it as may seem expedient to us. Given at Lyons, the sixteenth of July, in the third year of our pontificate [1245]."

When this letter was published in open council, it struck terror into all who heard it, as if it were flashing lightning. . . . But the pope and the prelates sitting round him in council, with lighted tapers, thundered forth dreadful sentences of excommunication against the emperor Frederick, while his agents retreated in confusion.

The pope, being full of anxiety for the relief of the Holy Land, and concerning the affairs of the cross, made the following decrees in those matters . . .

Matthew Paris here inserts the council's decree for a planned crusade, which repeats many of the provisions found in Ad liberandam *(see above, No. 16), including*

a three-year ecclesiastical income tax of one-twentieth. The full text is in Giles, Mat-
thew Paris's English History, 2:86–91. Matthew then considers other activities of the
council, returning to the crusade in the following passage.

WHEN these statutes were made known to the assembly, they gave satisfaction to all the wise part of the community, and in this matter indeed
the pope deservedly obtained the thanks and favor of all in common.[8] Yet
some statutes were made before the council, some during it, and some
after it; and some decrees were wisely and prudently made at the council
concerning the matter of the crusade; but when mention was made of a
contribution of money, the pope was refused to his face. . . . For many
times and in manifold ways have the faithful followers of the church complained that they had been cheated by the Roman Church of the money
which they had contributed for the assistance of the Holy Land. But the
other decrees, which were wisely ordained and gave satisfaction to the
hearts and ears of the Christians, were written word for word according
to those made by Pope Gregory [IX] in the year of our Lord one thousand two hundred and thirty-four; under which date will also be found a
most eloquent sermon composed by Pope Gregory; and that same sermon was now repeated at this council by Pope Innocent IV as if it were a
new one. . . .

In [1246], mournful news from the Holy Land flew through the
Christian countries, filling them with fear and sorrow; which was that
the said Holy Land was now almost entirely in the occupation of the
Khwarizmians and the Babylonians [Mamluks]. The citizens of Acre, too,
now either fearing, or not choosing, or being unable to leave their city,
were in expectation of being besieged or compelled to surrender their
city, for they endured such a scarcity of provisions that they pined away
among themselves, nor were they held up by any hopes of release. Frederick, too, who was now become a formidable hammer of the church,
would not allow any provisions or assistance in the way of troops to be
transported to them, declaring that the Roman Church had never had
such effectual grounds for extorting money from the Christians, on which
it had fattened and grown proud, as on the plea of the Holy Land and on
the sophistical preaching of the crusade for its liberation.

Ascalon also, about the fortifying of which such expensive, laborious,
and long-protracted time and labors were devoted by Earl Richard [of
Cornwall] and many other nobles, now endured the most fierce attacks

8. For the canons of the First Council of Lyons, see Nos. 38 and 46.

from the enemy, and could scarcely be defended against them. Other castles, too, which appeared to be impregnable, for instance, Krak [des Chevaliers] and the Pilgrims' Castle, at once cities and fortresses, to the sorrow and fear of those who inhabit them, seemed to them, as they had no hopes of succor, to be prisons rather than places of protection, a source of fear rather than confidence. On all sides the Christians were hemmed in by their enemies, who roved about at will, indulging in pillage. . . .

On hearing of these events, the pope was overcome with grief, and sent four cardinals, as special legates, through the four quarters of Christendom, for the purpose of defaming the said Frederick and his son Conrad, for having dared to attempt such proceedings, and to encourage all Christians, in remission of their sins, to attack and harass the said Frederick, and, if possible, to crush him; and also to endeavor, by all the modes in which the Roman court was usually well skilled, by cunning avarice and avaricious cunning, to extort money for the purpose of subduing the hateful Frederick. One [legate], therefore, he sent into Germany, another into Italy, a third into Spain, and the fourth into Norway, besides certain other specious legates, invested with great power, whom he underhandedly sent into England, without their insignia, that he might not seem to infringe the king's privilege. Among others, the Preacher and Minorite brethren, whom, not without injury and scandal to their order, he made tax-collectors and beadles. The legate who was sent into Norway, was [William] the [cardinal] bishop of [Saint] Sabina, who was also sent to anoint and crown Haco [Haakon], king of Norway, and perform the functions of legate in that country and in Sweden, to the injury of the aforesaid Frederick, and not without great expectations of gain. . . .

Since the pontificate of Gregory IX, the campaign against Frederick II was conducted at the most violent level of polemic, an excellent example of which is the letter from Gregory IX to the province of Canterbury in 1239 (Giles, Matthew Paris's English History, 2:213–239). On occasion Matthew reproduced some of the most vituperative and evidently effective anti-imperial texts, as he did in the following letter of Cardinal Reinier in 1249. Full text is in Giles, Matthew Paris's English History, 2:298–304; excerpt here, 298, 302–304.

ABOUT the same time [1249] the name of Frederick became so notorious in different parts of the world that he was worse than Herod, Judas, or Nero. For the deadly stench exhaling from his deeds, as mentioned in the following letter, provoked the ears and hearts of Christians, and filled them with astonishment and grief. . . .

"Alas! How has the fear of God gone to sleep in Christian princes, and how entirely lukewarm has the love of the Savior become. Some time ago, in the time of the Gentiles, if any demon who gave replies in idolatrous countries was denied worship by anyone, that person was torn to pieces and killed by many tortures. And now faith is despised, heretics begin to prevail and are protected by this impious man. Heresies are preached in the dominions of this wicked wretch, apostates increase there, the enemies of the Lord are protected, the sacraments and keys of the church are despised, ecclesiastical liberty is trampled upon, and no care is taken of souls. Some time since, when the Christian army, which was intent on the capture of Babylon, was cut off from retreat by the overflowing waters, was it not, by the kindness of the sultan, supplied with provisions, preserved in safety, and sent back home without injury? And with that army were the bishops of Albano [Pelagius] and Acre [James of Vitry], of illustrious memory, some other bishops and prelates, and John of Brienne, king of Jerusalem of illustrious memory. Was not John of Colonna of illustrious memory, the cardinal priest who had gone to Greece with the [Latin] emperor of Constantinople to recover possession of that country and was made prisoner by Theodore Comnenus, was not he, I say, respectfully treated and set at liberty?

"See how the madness of this most cruel enemy, not content with these evil deeds, has caused the churches to be profaned by Saracens, the altars to be overthrown, the sacred relics to be dispersed, and Christian virgins, widows, and married women to be violated in the holy places. Moreover, by his order, the Minorite brethren and other religious men who were traveling about among the Christian troops to assign penances and to bury the bodies of the slain, were slain by the swords of his impious followers. Besides this, that the anger of the Lord might kindle more fiercely against this wicked man, the Saracens lately, at Harnia, in the sight of the multitude, dragged about at the ass's tail the images of the Crucified One, the blessed Mary, and other saints. They afterward cut off the legs and arms of the image of Christ and fitted it and other images to their shields, that the Christians might be obliged to pierce them with their spears and arrows in battle.

"Why, then, did the crusaders, paying no heed to these insane acts, plow the rivers with their arms or cross the sea to attack the Saracens or Tartars, who vent their fury at a distance, when their cruelty is considered much less than these proceedings of his? This villainy of the Saracens should be first exterminated, together with their leaders and abettors, and afterward let them proceed to others, as the cause is at home, which is sought for abroad, and now the pagan persecution is carried on in the very bowels of the church, in the cloisters of the Christians, and within the bounds of Christianity. It seems expedient that the perpetrators of such great crimes should be first expelled from Italy lest the serpent should be cherished in the bosom, the mouse in the sack, and fire in the womb, and they should then proceed to farther extremities. For the Lord has not chosen his people with regard to place, but rather the reverse, as appears from Saint Peter and the other apostles leaving Jerusalem and passing to the nations.

"Consider, therefore, if there is anyone of understanding, if there is anyone who grieves for his death, if there is anyone who looks into the injuries done to his ministers, that the Lord looks down from heaven and sees the sons of men [Pss 52:3, 13:2, 32:13]. Let each Christian consider, too, that at the last judgment he will have to answer to the Lord if he passes by such crimes. Prosecute, therefore, the cause of the Son of the Most High God, that you may bring your own to a good result. Protect his spouse by the right hand of your power, that at the Judgment Day the just Judge may place you at his right hand to be introduced to eternal glory."

This dreadful letter, on coming to the knowledge of the public, pierced the hearts of many and would have encouraged them to take part against Frederick, had it not been that the papal enemies of his were polluted by the stains of avarice, simony, usury, and other vices. Among other acts of madness, they shamelessly harassed the crusaders, urging them under penalty of excommunication at one time to send assistance to the Holy Land, at another, to the empire of Romania, and at another, hinting to them that they should rise against the emperor Frederick. And, what was considered more detestable, making the Preachers and Minorites their tax-collectors, they, on some pretext or other, extorted the necessary supplies for the journey from those who had assumed the cross. Wherefore, although the tyrant Frederick committed disgraceful crimes, yet, to the disgrace of the Romans, he found a great many open as well as secret abettors and companions in crime. . . .

About the same time [1249], the French king [Louis IX], who was passing the winter in Cyprus and suffered much from want of provisions . . . [sent messengers to the Venetians, who] freely sent six large ships laden with corn, wine, and other kinds of provisions, and also a reinforcement of troops and numbers who had assumed the cross. Some other cities and islands, too, from whom he had asked assistance, sent him various supplies, Frederick not only allowing this but even kindly persuading them to it. He himself, that he might not show himself inferior to others, sent him a large supply of different kinds of food, by which the French king obtained an abundance, and, after returning thanks to him, wrote to the pope, begging him to receive Frederick into his favor and no longer to make war on or defame such a great friend and benefactor of the church, by whom the whole Christian army was released from imminent peril of famine . . . [His mother Blanche] also wrote to the pope, entreating him to mitigate the rancor he had conceived against the said Frederick. His holiness, however, rejected all these entreaties and harassed Frederick more and more every day, but everywhere got the worst of the matter. . . .

About the same time, too, [in 1249], Peter Capoccio, a clerk and influential friend of the pope's, was sent by him as a legate into Apulia, and armed with great power to remit sins, in order that he might crush Frederick and his friends. This man, then, with increased strength, which he had gained, in all quarters, by giving money and granting full indulgence from sins, did much injury to Frederick, and recalled many nobles from their allegiance to him.

Frederick II died in 1250, leaving a legitimate son, Conrad IV, a grandson, Conradin, and his natural son Manfred, who essentially ruled the Regno and was crowned king in 1258. After the death of Conrad IV, Manfred succeeded his father as the prime target of papal opposition to the Staufer. Frederick's eldest son Henry had predeceased him, and another son, Enzo, had been captured and imprisoned for life in Bologna.

[IN 1254], Pope Innocent IV being taken from among us, another man was appointed in his stead. . . . He was bishop of Ostia and nephew of Pope Gregory [IX], lately deceased, who had advanced him to his bishopric, and he now took the name of Alexander IV [1254–1261]. . . . By the advice of some persons in whom he reposed heartfelt trust and confidence, and on the persuasions of his predecessor Pope Innocent IV, who at the point of death had urged his cardinals to it, he vigorously continued the war commenced against the partisans of Frederick, and especially against Manfred, the natural though legitimate son of Frederick . . . especially as they told him that it would be absurd and manifestly contrary to the religion of the church to allow in Christian territories a city inhabited by and crammed full of Saracens, which Frederick had founded.[9] The pope was determined by this specious pretext, as well as by another course of reasoning, which was that it would be inhuman to balk the king of England in his hope, conceived by the church's promise, of obtaining the kingdom of Sicily, for the sake of which he had already expended an endless amount of money.[10]

When some time ago the city referred to above, called Lucera, was built by the emperor Frederick, as stated above, and was peopled by infidels, it was, as it were, a house of refuge and a place of trust to him. And he was bitterly reproached for his act and accused of polluting the Christian religion. To this he replied . . . that he preferred to expose such people as those to the risks of wars which might arise in the kingdom or the empire rather than Christians for the shedding of whose blood he should have to give a strict account before the awful tribunal of the Supreme Judge. The church therefore allowed it and connived at it. But because in later times it became a place of refuge and a source of trust and confidence to the lately deceased Conrad, and now, in like manner a place of refuge and succor to Manfred, it became a sort of thorn in the side of the Roman Church. The citizens dwelling in Lucera were infidels, and among them were about sixty thousand soldiers ready to engage in war, who were feared the more because it was the custom of the Saracens in war to use poisoned spears, Greek fire, and other nefarious warlike instruments. . . .

About this time [1255], Pope Alexander [IV] . . . sent Cardinal Octavian with a large army, consisting of sixty thousand armed men, to utterly destroy the city of Lucera, together with Manfred who was hidden there and all its inhabitants. . . . The papal army was numerous and formidable, receiving large amounts in daily pay from the coffers of the king of England. . . . Such had been the orders and arrangements of Pope Innocent [IV], lately deceased; and all these proceedings took their rise with him and were carried out by the cardinals. . . .

Matthew describes how a stalemate arose where neither the besieged nor besiegers dared to attack each other.

9. The city referred to just above was the Muslim colony of Lucera, the only place in Christian Europe in which Muslims, chiefly warriors and administrators loyal to Frederick II and Manfred, were permitted to practice their own religion—an added charge of faithlessness against the Staufer.

10. Henry III had hoped to acquire the kingdom of Sicily for his son Edmund.

MANFRED thereupon sallied forth from the city, attended by his followers and all the citizens armed to the teeth, and . . . approached the papal troops with the rapidity of a whirlwind. But while they were indulging in the hope of seizing all their enemies like birds caught in a net, at that very time [the cardinal] Octavian was warned by some friend of what was about to take place and made his escape, although with difficulty; while his army, with the exception of the marquis's followers and friends, were slain, or made prisoners, or scattered. After this triumph, Manfred began to prosper day after day, to the great confusion of the church.

Meanwhile, the pope and the whole Roman Church were overwhelmed with grief at the news, particularly because the church had promised the kingdom of Sicily and Apulia to the king of England for the benefit of his son Edmund, to whom the pope had transmitted the ring of investiture by the bishop of Boulogne, and because his advisers had thrown the money of England into a pit. . . .

At this time [1255], Master Rustand also issued orders to all zealous supporters of the holy church to publicly preach a crusade, first at London and afterward at other places, against Manfred, the son of Frederick, late emperor of the Romans, as being an enemy to God, the church of Rome, and the king of England, an ally, abettor, and protector of the Saracens, and as unjustly occupying the kingdom of another. And to those who should join in that expedition, a promise was made of obtaining the fullest remission of their sins, as though they went on a pilgrimage to the Holy Land. When true Christians heard this announcement, they were astonished that they were promised the same for shedding the blood of Christians as they formerly were for [shedding] that of infidels, and the versatility of the preachers excited laughter and derision. At one place, when Master Rustand was preaching, he added at the end of his sermon: "Become the sons of obedience, pledge yourselves to such and such a merchant for such an amount of money": and this among religious men in their chapter, when no previous rumor of such a proceeding had ever disturbed them.

Finding that the pope cared little for the liberation for the Holy Land which our Lord himself consecrated by his presence and finally by his blood, the inhabitants of the Holy Land entered into a truce with the sultan of Babylon [Egypt], who was at war with the sultan of Damascus, and prolonged the said truce for the space of ten years. . . .

[In 1258], too, the Roman court began to fall into low repute, for the prelates and nobles of Apulia, contrary to the pope's wish, elected and crowned as their king the emperor Frederick's son Manfred, who with his whole family was held in great contempt by the pope and the whole court of Rome. Moreover, the king of Apulia created bishops and archbishops without asking the pope's consent, and even against his wish, and all of them were unanimous, despite the papal prohibition, in showing greater obedience and in paying more honor and respect to the said king than to the pope. The nobles also made no mention of Edmund, son of the king of England . . . but had done homage and sworn allegiance to this same Manfred. In consequence of this, the king of England complained, and with good reason, of the pope . . . yet he . . . received with all honor the papal messengers who were sent to England . . . who had come as proctors for the purposes of expediting the business of his son Edmund in the matter of the kingdom of Apulia. . . .

[In 1259] . . . Manfred, son of Frederick, caused himself to be crowned king of Sicily, on receipt of the false report of the death of his nephew Conradin. Pope Alexander [IV] therefore excommunicated him as an invader of the kingdom and a favorer of the Saracens, and by a judicial sentence deprived him of all honors and dignities.

. . . In [the] year [1261] Pope Alexander died and was succeeded by Urban IV [1261–1264], formerly patriarch of Jerusalem. After his coronation, with the aid of the crusaders, he put to flight an army of Romans, which Manfred had forcibly introduced into the patrimony of Saint Peter. He gave the kingdom of Sicily to the French king's brother Charles [of Anjou], but on the condition that he should drive Manfred from the kingdom. . . .

In this year [1261], Baldwin, emperor of the Greeks, with the French and Latins, was expelled by the Greeks with the assistance of the Genoese and Venetians. Thus having recovered their kingdom, the Greeks appointed as their emperor one from among themselves, named [Michael VIII] Palaeologus. Baldwin took flight, and remained an exile in France.

In [the] year [1266], Ottobuono, cardinal deacon of the title of Saint Adrian, was sent by Pope Clement [IV] to England as a legate. The French king's brother Charles [of Anjou] made a voyage to Rome and was crowned king of Sicily by Pope Clement. A large number of Frenchmen who had taken the cross against Manfred arrived in Rome, under the command of Guy, bishop of Auxerre, Robert, son of the count of Flanders, and Boucard, count of Vendôme, to render assistance to Charles. . . .

At this time [1269], Conradin, the grandson of the former emperor Frederick on the side of his son Conrad [IV], aspired to the sovereignty

of Sicily, as his uncle Manfred was dead, and made his way to Rome with
the assistance of the Germans and a host of Lombards and Tuscans who
had joined them.[11] At that city he was received with all the solemnities
due to the emperor, and joined by the senator of the city, Henry, the
brother of the king of Castile, and a great number of the Romans, he
entered Apulia with a strong force against King Charles. After a severe
pitched battle, however, Conradin's army turned in flight and he himself
was taken prisoner and was decapitated by order of King Charles,
together with several nobles of his family. The king of Castile's brother
Henry fled from the battle to the castle of Cassino, but was afterward
given up to Charles and committed to prison.

59. Urban IV to Louis IX Against Manfred, *Ecce fili carissime*, 1264

Urban IV wrote this appeal when organizing a crusade against the imperial
party and its allies in southern Italy and Sicily, led by Frederick II's bastard son
Manfred, who had been crowned king of Sicily. The church party's forces were to
be led by Louis IX's brother, Charles of Anjou.

On the popes and the Staufer, see Jean Dunbabin, Charles I of Anjou; *and Dunbabin,*
The French in the Kingdom of Sicily, 1266–1306 *(Cambridge UK-New York, 2011).*

SEE, most beloved son, how Manfred, once prince of Taranto, not content with the innumerable injuries and vexations with which he has so far
damaged the Roman Church, assails the church herself more roughly and
more harshly than usual with continuous attacks, using as a pretext the
business of the kingdom of Sicily which is engaging us and our beloved
son the nobleman Charles, count of Anjou and Provence, your brother.
He strikes her with unremitting persecution, divides her with tyrannical
frenzy and incessantly afflicts her with various other kinds of tribulation
to such an extent that the same church . . . can scarcely breathe under
oppressions of this kind. For this Manfred, who has embraced the rites of

Source: Urban IV, Registres, *ed. J. Guiraud (Paris, 1901), 2:395–396. Trans. Louise
Riley-Smith and Jonathan Riley-Smith,* The Crusades: Idea and Reality, 1095–1274 *(London, 1981), 86–89.*
11. Manfred had been killed at the battle of Benevento in 1266, sealing the triumph
of Charles of Anjou and the papal party. Conradin was beheaded by Charles of Anjou in
1268 after the battle of Tagliacozzo. Matthew's dates, even years, are often a year or two off.

the Saracens and adheres to them particularly in his daily prayers, and to the dishonor of the catholic faith, gives them precedence over Christian rites, attacks the church, especially helped by the advice, aid, and favor of these Saracens.[12] He also detains, or damnably has detained and occupied, archbishoprics, bishoprics, and other churches and monasteries of the kingdom of Sicily by forcing into some of them false and pernicious ministers or by wickedly cherishing those already forced upon them, by actually commandeering some of them for his pleasure and converting their revenues most dangerously to his own uses.

On account of these things heresies crop up nearly everywhere in Italy, the worship of God is diminished, the orthodox faith is borne down, the state of the faithful is thoroughly depressed and oppressed, the liberties of the church are enslaved and the rights of the church are trampled upon. And prelates and other men who hold distinguished positions in the clerical army are forced to undergo the penalties of exile, are seized and treated ignominiously and are thrust into dreadful prisons and condemned to most shameful deaths. Sacred and holy places, whether in the hands of religious or others, are despoiled of their possessions and other goods and, although they are dedicated to divine worship, are given over to illicit and profane uses, are despised and are defiled by abominable practices. Several clerics are also forced to celebrate divine services in places on which an ecclesiastical interdict has been imposed, in contempt of the keys of the church, and to give the church's sacraments to wicked, excommunicated, and impious persons. Episcopal authority and power is counted for little, ecclesiastical censure is despised, souls perish, bodies are slaughtered, cities are burned, castles are destroyed, the security of the roads is disrupted, travelers are robbed, Saracens and schismatics are set over orthodox Christians, heretics are defended to such an extent that in several places we dare not take action against them. In fact in some lands those who preach the truth of the gospel are forbidden to put the word of God to the faithful and in certain places heresies are publicly preached.

Very many other detestable and abominable things are committed, moreover, which offend the eyes of divine majesty, generate scandal in the church and weaken and abuse the dread force of ecclesiastical censure. Since the forces of this persecutor have grown strong, the church herself cannot employ a suitable remedy for these things, especially because

12. The rulers of Sicily, including Frederick II and his successors, had allowed conquered Muslims to continue living and practicing their religion in Sicily and later in Lucera and used them in their armies.

recently this Manfred, putting savage hands into her vitals, presumed to send certain Germans, the particular agents of his persecution, into the patrimony of Blessed Peter in Tuscany, where we reside with all our curia, to the disgrace of ourselves and the church herself, the disorder of the province and the injury of the faithful in it. He has also arranged to send other large forces of knights into the duchy of Spoleto so that, confining us and the aforesaid church as if in a net, he is so pressing in on the roads from all sides and fencing in the passes that no one can reach us nor can we send out any men from our curia.

Because by the counsel of heaven on high the liberation of the aforesaid church has been reserved for you and your most Christian house and it appears to be God's desire that the yoke of the same church's burden and the dominion of her taskmaster should be surmounted by means of the power of your kingdom, you should know that we, with the advice of our brothers, send our beloved son Simon, cardinal priest of the title of Saint Cecilia, to whom we have given fully the office of legation, to your most Christian kingdom to promote under the Lord's guarantee the business of the said kingdom of Sicily—it is in fact this kingdom which is the source of all the evil afflicting the same church and is the cause of such great perils—and to treat with the person of the said count to whom we have looked, having weighed the merits of his devotion and vigor.

And so we think that Your Serenity ought to be asked most carefully and encouraged—and we urge you no less for the remission of your sins—to assist that cardinal with all diligence and the ready giving of counsel and favor, out of reverence for the Holy See and ourselves receiving with royal kindness the cardinal who is assuredly relying on your benevolence. And you ought to treat with him on the serious matters which concern the honor of the church and the more willingly entrust him with the promotion of those necessary arrangements for the same business which its nature requires. . . . And so, most Christian prince, we ask you to show powerfully and willingly the feeling of this your compassion in the advancement of this business, by means of which we hope, with the favor of the Lord, to liberate the church from her enemies who surround her.

60. Salimbene of Parma on Staufer Italy, ca. 1285

Born in Parma in 1221 to a wealthy family and christened after his godfather Balian of Sidon, Salimbene de Adam, as he became known, entered the Franciscan order as a young man. Salimbene was the religious name he took as a Franciscan.

He tells us that his own father had gone on crusade. Well-traveled and gregarious, Salimbene wrote a garrulous and rambling chronicle before his death circa 1289. Salimbene is particularly informative about some of the allies of Frederick II, particularly the da Romano brothers, Alberigo and Ezzelino, who became and remained legends of ferocity for many decades. It is also important to note the levels of devotion in the northern Italian city-republics: the emergence of local spiritual associations, like the one formed at Parma by John Barisello and later subsumed into the Society of the Cross of Charles of Anjou, or the sudden and unexpected appearance of charismatic leaders like the Franciscan friar Clarello.

One of the striking differences between Salimbene and Matthew Paris is that the former seems to have been everywhere, knew everybody, and saw everything "with [his] own eyes," while the latter made only one extensive journey (briefly, to Norway) and keeps himself pretty much out of his narrative. Another is Salimbene's extraordinary use of scriptural quotations throughout his narrative. These two works, with Joinville, virtually span the possibilities of historical narrative in the thirteenth century.

The broad civic devotional context of the period is described in Augustine Thompson, Cities of God: The Religion of the Italian Communes, 1125–1325 (*University Park PA, 2005); and for one significant episode, see Thompson,* Revival Preachers and Politics in Thirteenth-Century Italy: The Great Devotion of 1233 (*Oxford-New York, 1992*). *A good general history is John Larner,* Italy in the Age of Dante and Petrarch, 1216–1380 (*London-New York, 1980*). *The literature on Salimbene is summed up in the English translation by Joseph Baird, with Giuseppe Baglivi, and John Robert Kane,* The Chronicle of Salimbene de Adam, Medieval and Renaissance Texts and Studies, vol. 40 (*Binghamton NY, 1986*).

SEEING Frederick as the great persecutor of the church . . . and fearing not a little for his own person, the pope [Innocent IV] sent his legate to the king of France [Louis IX] requesting him to delay his crusade until he should discover what God would finally do with Frederick. To further his request, moreover, he alleged that there were also in Italy a huge number of men who had become infidels and worse, violent, perverse men . . . needy men and robbers, who followed Frederick as their prince and were destroying church property.

What more can one say? The pope labored in vain, for he could not change the king's mind about going to the Holy Land, since all preparations had already been made: all expenses had been laid out and everybody had been given the sign of the cross. And so the king wrote Innocent saying that he should commit the problem of Frederick to Divine Judgment. . . . With a firm determined mind and devout spirit

Source: Baird, Baglivi, and Kane, Chronicle of Salimbene, *201–202, 365–370, 373–377, 396–399, 442–443, 478–482.*

King Louis of France planned to go abroad and bring help as quickly as possible to the Holy Land. . . .

In Treviso, Alberigo da Romano ruled for many years, and his reign was cruel and harsh, as those who experienced it know very well. This man was the very limb of the devil himself and the son of iniquity, but eventually he perished by a wretched death, along with his wife and sons and daughters. For those who killed them pulled the arms and legs off the children while they were still alive in the presence of Alberigo and his wife and struck them in the mouth with these limbs. Then they tied the mother and daughters to stakes and burned them. Yet these daughters were young and beautiful virgins and were guilty of nothing. But their slayers showed no mercy to innocence and beauty on account of the great hatred they had for the mother and father. For they were horrible in their evil treatment of the people of Treviso. Thus in the public square of the city they came at Alberigo with pinchers and tore the flesh piecemeal from his body while he was still alive, and so they tore his body to pieces amid jeers, and insults, and heavy torments. For Alberigo had killed their kinsmen: their brothers, and fathers, and sons. And he had laid such heavy taxes and fines on the land that the citizens had to tear down their houses and send the materials of which they were constructed . . . on ships to [sell in] Ferrara in order to get the money to meet these obligations. I saw these things with my own eyes. Moreover, Alberigo pretended to be at war with his own blood brother Ezzelino da Romano so that he could be the more secure in doing his evil deeds, and he did not spare his own citizens and subjects in the slaughter. . . .

Alberigo had had twenty-five civic leaders of Treviso hanged on a single day, and they had neither offended nor harmed him in any way. But because he was afraid that they would perhaps do him harm, he had them revoked from before his face and shamefully hanged. And he required thirty noble women—their mothers, wives, daughters and sisters—to come and watch the execution. He wanted also to cut off the noses of these women, but by the happy intervention of a man who was falsely said to be Alberigo's bastard son, this was not done. Furthermore, he had their clothes cut off from their breasts down so that with bodies all naked they stood before the eyes of the men who were to be hanged. Moreover, he had the men hanged very near the ground and then forced the women to walk between their legs so that the men kicked them in the face as they were dying in bitterness of spirit. And the women had to endure the horror and pain of such base mockery. To see such things was the greatest kind of misery and cruelty, the like of which has never been heard. Then Alberigo had these women carried off beyond the river Sial or Sile to go wherever they could. And with the pieces of garments they had about their breasts, the women made coverings for their genitals . . . and then walked the whole day for fifteen miles with bare feet and nude bodies through wild fields, bitten by flies, and torn by thorns and briars and nettles and burrs and thistles. And they went weeping, for they had cause for weeping and they had nothing to eat. . . .

These women arrived late in the day at the Venetian lagoons, and behold, suddenly they saw a lone fisherman in his little boat, and they called out to him. . . . And when they had told him all their terrible misfortunes, he said to them, "I have great pity for you, and I will not leave you until God does well by you. But since my boat is so small that it will hold only one of you, I will row you across one at a time until I have transported all of you to the safety of solid ground. For if you remain here during the night the wolves might devour you. Tomorrow, however, very early in the morning, I will get a larger boat and carry all of you to the church of San Marco, where I trust God will comfort you." What more? After he had transported them all except one, he took this last one to his poor fisherman's home and fed her well, and treated her with the utmost kindness, courtesy, humanity, and love. The next day he dutifully fulfilled all that he had promised.

Then after he had taken them to San Marco he went to Lord Ottavio, the cardinal and papal legate in Lombardy, who was living at the time in Venice, and told him the story of these ladies and their great misfortunes, and where they were now lodged. When he heard this story, the cardinal immediately went to them and had food prepared for them. Then he sent a messenger throughout the city asking the citizens to hasten to him without delay, to San Marco, both men and women, small and great. . . . For he had things to tell them and show them such as they had never heard or seen. What more? The message circulated very quickly, and all the citizens of Venice gathered together in the square of San Marco, and Lord Ottavio recounted to them the entire story given above. And in order to anger the people more against Alberigo and make them pity these ladies more, the cardinal also did the following: he had the women come forth in that same shameful and nude condition that the wicked Alberigo had reduced them to.

And when the Venetians had heard this entire story and looked upon the nude women, they cried out in loud voices, "Let him die, let that evil

man die! Burn him and his wife alive! And destroy all his progeny from
the face of the earth!" Then the cardinal said, "Holy Scripture totally
agrees with you, for it likewise curses the wicked man, [Eccl 8:13]: 'But
let it not be well with the wicked, neither let his days be prolonged, but
as a shadow let them pass away that fear not the face of the Lord.' This is
'a perverse and exasperating generation. A generation that set not their
heart aright: and whose spirit was not faithful to God' [Ps 77:8]. This is
'a generation that for teeth hath swords, and grindeth with their jaw
teeth, to devour the needy from off the earth, and the poor from among
men' [Prv 30:14]. 'May there be none to help him: nor none to pity his
fatherless offspring. May his posterity be cut off; in one generation may
his name be blotted out. May the iniquity of his fathers be remembered
in the sight of the Lord: and let not the sin of his mother be blotted out.
May they be before the Lord continually, and let the memory of them
perish from the earth: because he remembered not to show mercy' [Ps
108:12–16]. See also Job 18[:17–19]: 'Let the memory of him perish
from the earth, and let not his name be renowned in the streets. He shall
drive him out of light into darkness, and shall remove him out of the
world. His seed shall not subsist, nor his offspring among his people, nor
any remnants in his country.' 'Let them be blotted out of the book of the
living; and with the just let them not be written'" [Ps 68:29].[13]

Then they all cried out, "So be it! So be it!"[14] After this, by the will
of the entire city, both men and women, the cardinal preached a crusade
against the accursed Alberigo: whoever would take up the cross and go
to destroy him—or send someone in his place, paying all expenses—
would receive plenary indulgence for all his sins. And he confirmed that
indulgence fully for all men by the authority of the omnipotent God and
his blessed apostles Peter and Paul, as well as by his authority as legate
vested in him by the apostolic chair. Thus excited by the cardinal's preaching, they all took the cross, "small and great" [1 Kgs 5:9], "man and
woman" [Jo 6:21]. And they did so for the following reasons: because
it was offered by a man of high authority, because of Alberigo's great
wickedness, because those noble men had been hanged so unjustly,
because they saw the shameful dishonor that those ladies had suffered, as

13. These biblical citations had long been used in the formal process of cursing those
guilty of great offenses. The liturgy of ecclesiastical cursing was formidable and made a profound impression on those who witnessed it.

14. A cry eerily and perhaps deliberately reminiscent of the cry of those who took the
cross for the First Crusade at Clermont, "God wills it!"

well as because of the plenary indulgence they would receive. And the cardinal legate had further incited them to this action by citing the example of the Levite woman whose shameful abuse and murder, the Jewish people, by divine will, avenged so harshly that they destroyed almost an entire tribe of their own people [Jgs 19:20].

These people then marched unanimously against Alberigo and did him great harm, although they did not totally destroy him. Only a short time after the cross was taken up against him, however, he was completely destroyed along with all his offspring, and he was subjected to all the abuse, torments, and misfortunes described above—all of which he thoroughly deserved. For, once, when he lost his falcon, he pulled down his pants and turned his arse up to the heavens in mockery and insult to God himself, thinking in this way to avenge himself on God for his loss. And when he got home he went into the church and defecated on the very altar itself, in the place where the body of the Lord is consecrated. Moreover, his wife called noble ladies and matrons whores and prostitutes and neither did her husband rebuke her at any time, saying: " 'Why hast thou done this' " [cf. 1 Chr 1:6]. Nay, rather, he gave the protection which permitted her to do such things with impunity. Thus, rightly were the people of Treviso avenged on these two, in fulfillment of the Lord's words in Luke 6[:38]: "For with the same measure that you shall mete withal, it shall be measured to you again."

After his sermon, the cardinal recommended these ladies to the Venetians to care for as they would his own person. And they gladly provided them with food and clothing. It should be noted that the people of Treviso spared the man on whose insistence the noses of these ladies had been saved; they permitted him to live and indeed gave him many goods, of which he was well worthy. For he had often restrained Alberigo and his wife from many wicked deeds that they would otherwise have committed.

The brother of this Alberigo, Lord Ezzelino da Romano, ruled in the other marches, that is, in Padua, Vicenza, and Verona. This man was the very limb of the devil himself and a son of iniquity. For, once, in Saint George field in Verona—and I have been in that very place—he had eleven thousand Paduans burned to death in a large house where he had them chained up as prisoners. And while they were burning, Ezzelino rode about the house singing and playing war games with his knights. For he was the worst man in the world, and, truly, I do not believe there has been a more evil man from the beginning of the world up to our own days. Everybody trembled in his presence like a reed in water—and not without reason, for a man might be totally secure in his position one day; the next, put to death. For a father would kill his son, a son his father, another man his relative—all merely to please Ezzelino.

In the March of Treviso, indeed, Ezzelino destroyed all of the chief and best men, the powerful, rich, and noble; and he used to mutilate women and cast them in prison, along with their sons and daughters, where they perished from hunger and misery. He also killed many men in religious orders or imprisoned them for a long time. . . . And not even those worst men in the world in their time—Nero, Decius, Diocletian, Maximian, Herod, Antiochus—could approach him in wicked maliciousness. Truly the two brothers were veritable demons of hell. . . .

At his death, however, Alberigo was fully repentant. But Ezzelino never returned to God. . . . In Alberigo's repentance the great mercy of God may be seen, in that he received such a man at his death. A certain man named Mastino succeeded Ezzelino as ruler of Verona, but, after a time, he was killed by assassins. But the rightful ruler of Verona, the count of Saint Boniface, was an exile traveling about the country, as I myself saw, and he was totally devoted to the church party—a good, holy, wise, and honorable man, a man proved in arms and experienced in war. . . .

The great problem of reconciling exiled political groups who were permitted to return to their cities is shown by Salimbene in the case of Parma, which permitted its pro-imperial exiles to return after the death of Frederick II. But the disaffected imperial party began to conspire with Uberto Pellavicino, ruler of Cremona, against the pro-church party of Parma, and the Parmese greatly feared conquest.

In Parma itself, behold, suddenly a man arose . . . called John Barisello; he was a tailor and the son of a tenant farmer. . . . And John Barisello took the cross and the text of the gospel in his hands, and he went throughout Parma to the houses of the men of the imperial party whom he suspected of betraying the city to Pellavicino, and made them swear allegiance to the pope and to the church party. He had five hundred armed men with him who had made him their captain and "followed him as their prince" [Jgs 11:3] and leader. Many men, therefore, swore to uphold the pope and the church party, partly voluntarily, partly from fear, because they saw the men of arms. But those who would not agree to swear were escorted out of Parma unceremoniously, and went to live in Borgo San Donnino. . . .

When John Barisello was going through Parma requiring an oath of all men under suspicion, he came to the house of Lord Roland Guido Bo, who lived in Cò de Ponte near the church of Saint Gervase. And calling him out of his house, John informed him that he had to swear an oath of allegiance to the church party without delay if he wanted to live in peace; otherwise, he would have to leave Parma. For this Lord Roland Guido Bo was of the imperial party, and he had received many appointments as podestà from the emperor. But seeing so large a group gathered together, threatening him and requiring such things . . . he swore the following oath, "I swear to stand by the Roman pontiff and obey his commands, and to adhere to the church party for the entire term of my life to the shame of the most miserable and shitty party under heaven." He used these words about his own party, that is, the imperial party, because they had allowed themselves to be trodden underfoot shamefully by such men. The Parmese of the church party loved him for these words, and it was not considered disgraceful for him to have sworn such an oath.

[The Parmese made John Barisello] a rich man, whereas before he was a pauper. Second, they gave him a wife from a noble family. . . . Third, they made him a lifetime member of the council without the requirement of election, for he had a natural sense and ability in politics. Fourth, they allowed him to gather together a company of men, named for himself, to accompany him everywhere, providing that it was for the honor and benefit of the city of Parma. And this company lasted for many years. It was finally dispersed, however, by a Modenese podestà of Parma named Lord Manfredino de Rosa . . . [who] commanded John Barisello to mind his own business and his own household, to dismiss his company of men and to strip himself of all his pompous trappings, because he himself meant to rule Parma since he was the podestà of Parma. John obeyed humbly. . . . Yet the Parmese always loved John Barisello, and he always had prestige and a high reputation in Parma.

Later, however, hearing that the Parmese were great warriors and his friends who were always ready to come to the aid of the church, King Charles [of Anjou], brother of the king of France (who went to the Holy Land twice on crusade), commanded them to create a society in honor of God and the holy Roman Church, and give it the name of the Society of the Cross. He himself wished to be a member of this society, and he desired that all other societies be incorporated into this one, so that they might always be prepared to come to the aid of the church when need arose. And the Parmese did indeed create this group and called it the Society of the Cross. And they wrote the name of King Charles in golden letters at the beginning of the register to signify that this prince, duke, count, king, and magnificent conqueror was the captain and leader of this society. And whenever someone in Parma who is not a member of the society offends someone who is, all the members defend each other like bees, and they all run immediately and tear down the offender's house. . . . And this is a source of fear to the citizens, for they must either tread lightly or join the society. Thus this society grew marvelously. . . .

"And it came to pass . . . at the time when kings go forth to war" [2 Kgs 11:1], Lord Philip, archbishop of Ravenna and papal legate, came to Ferrara . . . and he called together all the citizens of the city, along with all the Paduans who were guests there, and made a speech to them at the door of Saint George Cathedral. . . . And all the men of religion gathered there and all the common people from the highest to the lowest. For they expected to hear great things of God. I too was there near the archbishop, and Bonusdies Judeus, who was a friend of mine, sat next to me in order to hear. Then standing "in the gate of the house of the Lord" [Jer 7:2], the legate began to speak out in a loud voice, and he preached to the people, but only a brief sermon, for the words should be short and to the point if they are to move the audience to action. And he laid out clearly how he had been made legate by the pope in opposition to Ezzelino da Romano and how he wished to organize a crusading army for the purpose of recovering Padua, so that the exiled Paduans could return to their city. And whoever would join the army in that expedition, he made clear, would have the indulgence and remission and absolution of all their sins.

"And let nobody say: 'It is impossible for us to fight against so devilish a man, whom even the demons fear,' because it is not impossible to God, who will fight for us. Thus we read that Judas Maccabeus said to his troops when he prepared to engage the enemy [1 Mc 3:18–19]: 'It is an easy matter for many to be shut up in the hands of a few: and there is no difference in the sight of the God of heaven to deliver with a great multitude or with a small company: For the success of war is not in the multitude of the army, but strength cometh from heaven.'" Then the legate added, "In honor and praise of the omnipotent God, of his blessed apostles Peter and Paul, and not least of Saint Anthony, whose body is venerated in Padua, I say to you that if I had in my army only the orphans, school boys, widows, and others afflicted by Ezzelino, I would still expect to have the victory over that limb of the devil and son of iniquity. For now the 'cry' of his evil ascends 'up to heaven' [1 Mc 5:31] and will thus battle against him from heaven. For Holy Scripture says, [Ecclus 35:16–19, 21–23]: 'The Lord will not accept any person against a poor man, and he will hear the prayer of him that is wronged. He will not despise the prayers of the fatherless; nor the widow, when she poureth out her complaint. Do not the widow's tears run down the cheek, and her cry against him that causeth them to fall? From the cheek they go up even to heaven, and the Lord that heareth will not be delighted with them. The prayer of him that humbleth himself shall pierce the clouds: . . . And the Lord will not be slack, but will judge for the just, and will do judgment: and the Almighty will not have patience with them, that he may crush their back: And he will repay vengeance to the Gentiles, till he have taken away the multitude of the proud and broken the scepters of the unjust.' "

And when the legate had ended his exhortation, the audience was overjoyed. Then with his army thus gathered he went at the proper time to do battle against Padua, which Ezzelino had strongly fortified with fifteen hundred knights, all powerful men experienced in war. Ezzelino, however, was living elsewhere, for he feared the fall of Padua as little as God fears that the heavens will fall, especially since he had fortified the city with three walls and had moats both inside and out, not to mention a host of knights and people. . . .

In this army there was a lay brother of the Order of the Friars Minor, a Paduan whose name was Clarello, and I knew him very well. He was a man of great courage, and his highest desire was for the Paduans who had been exiled from the city for a long time to be able to return home. Seeing "that the time served him" [1 Mc 12:1] and knowing that "the weak things of the world hath God chosen, that he may confound the strong" [1 Cor 1:27], this man made himself the standard-bearer of this army. For he wished to discover whether God, who had once given victory to his people through Jonathan and his standard-bearer, would give salvation through his hand. He marched at the head of this army, and coming upon a farmer with three mares, he took one of them away from him by force. Then he mounted the horse and holding in his hand a long pole like a lance, he rode back and forth crying out loudly, "Eia, soldiers of Christ! Eia, soldiers of Saint Peter! Eia, soldiers of Saint Anthony! Cast off your fear, 'be strengthened in the Lord, and in the might of his power' [Eph 6:10], for the Lord 'is strong and mighty: the Lord mighty in battle' [Ps 23:8]. 'Do ye manfully, and let your heart be strengthened' [Ps 30:25], because the Lord 'will give power and strength to his people. Blessed be God' [Ps 67:36]. 'The Lord will give strength to his people: the Lord will bless his people with peace' " [Ps 28:11].

What more? The army, excited and comforted by this man's cries, was ready to follow him wherever he went. And Brother Clarello added, "Let's go, let's go! Get them, Get them! 'Salvation is of the Lord: and thy blessing is upon the people' [Ps 3:9]. 'Let God arise, and let his enemies be scattered: and let them that hate him flee from before his face' [Ps 67:2]. Now the words of the Scripture, [Lev 26:7–9] must be fulfilled: 'You shall pursue your enemies, and they shall fall before you. Five of yours shall pursue a hundred others, and a hundred of you ten thousand: your enemies shall fall before you by the sword. I will look on you and make you increase: you shall be multiplied and I will establish my covenant with you.'" Therefore, the army followed this herald and standard-bearer and laid siege to the city. And the Lord laid fear on the hearts of those inside, so that they did not dare to resist.

There was another lay brother in this army, a holy man devoted to God, and when this man was still a secular he had served as Ezzelino's master engineer in charge of making war machines—catapults and battering rams—all used to capture cities and castles. And so the legate commanded him, on his love of the order, to divest himself of the robe of the brothers and to put on a simple white garment and employ himself in constructing a battering ram by which the city could be taken suddenly. This brother humbly obeyed, and very quickly he built a battering ram, in the front part of which there was fire and in the rear, armed men. And so the city was quickly captured. When the men of the church party entered the city, however, they sought to injure no one: they neither killed nor captured nor took spoils nor laid waste, but they spared everyone and allowed them to leave freely. . . .

Salimbene goes on to drive the point home, contrasting the new conquerors' fairness to the "destroyers and wasters" who had previously occupied the city.

BECAUSE the Paduans recaptured their city and gained the victory on the octave of Saint Anthony, they now celebrate this day even more splendidly than they did in the past. . . .

Later a certain chaplain was sent as papal legate who sought to enlist soldiers from every city to help King Charles in his war with Manfred, son of Frederick. And Lombardy and Romagna responded well, providing a fixed contingent of soldiers, and fighting with Charles and the French army, they won the victory over Manfred. And when this legate came to Faenza seeking soldiers, the Friars Minor and the Preachers gathered together in the bishop of Faenza's palace, where the bishop was also present with his canons. I was there and I heard what the papal legate had to say. He explained everything in a few words in the manner of the French, unlike the Cremonese who love to expound at large. In our presence he condemned and roundly criticized Manfred. Then he told us that the French army was already on its way. . . . Third, he said that the battle would soon be over with the victory in their hands. And so it turned out, although some in the audience said jeeringly, "Ver, ver, cum bon baton," which is to say, "The French will win the victory with good sticks!". . . .

In 1262 . . . Pope Urban IV was elected. And he accomplished two notable things: through crusaders he put the army of the Saracens to flight which had been sent by Manfred, son of Frederick sometime emperor, into the territories of the church; and he gave the kingdom of Sicily to Count Charles of Provence, brother of the king of France on condition that he recover it from Manfred. . . .

In 1265 . . . Lord Charles, brother of the king of France, came to Rome and was confirmed as king of Apulia and Sicily. . . . Then going into Apulia, he deprived Manfred of both life and kingdom in a battle. And in that same year the papal legate came into Lombardy to enlist soldiers to help Charles in the war against Manfred. . . . In that year, near Christmas, the French came in great numbers to help Charles, brother of the king of France, who was in Rome. And I myself saw them arriving when I traveled from Faenza to San Proculo. . . . And they went into Apulia to fight against Manfred, son of Frederick, the late emperor. And they killed him near Easter in the year of the Lord 1266, and carried off all that he possessed. In the year that they came a great miracle took place, because there was neither cold weather, nor frost, nor ice, nor snow, nor rain and mud—so that the roads were in fine shape, safe and excellent, as if it were May. And this was the work of the Lord, because the French had come to succor the church by exterminating that accursed Manfred, who merited such a death by his iniquities. For he had committed many evil deeds, if indeed, as they say, he had killed his own brother Conrad. . . .

In the year 1266 King Charles crossed the bridge of Ceprano with his army in opposition to King Manfred, prince of Apulia and Sicily. . . . And in that year he defeated Lord Manfred with his army at Benevento. And Manfred was killed there along with three thousand soldiers . . . and Manfred was buried at a bridge near Benevento on Friday, February 26. And Manfred's wife and two children were captured, along with all his treasure in the city called Manfredonia, which city Manfred himself had built and given his own name. This city was built near the city of Siponto, which is situated two miles from it. And if the prince had lived a few more years, Manfredonia would have been one of the most beautiful cities in the world. . . . But King Charles hates it exceedingly, so much so that no one is allowed to call it by its rightful name. Rather King Charles wishes it to be called New Siponto. . . . Manfred had some good qualities which I have fully described in the treatise which I wrote on Pope Gregory X. For a historian should be a fair man and not give just the bad qualities of a person and keep silent about the good. . . . And note that King Charles had a large number of men who claimed to be Manfred killed one after another. For these men pretended to be Manfred in order to gain money, and thus exposed themselves to the danger of death. . . .

Also, in 1266 a huge number of Saracens from Apulia crossed the straits into Spain and joined the Saracens already there, and they struck a heavy blow against the Christians, intending to recover Spain which they had lost. But the Christians of that country joined by crusaders from many countries won the victory over the Saracens, though with heavy losses among the Christians.

61. The Chronicle of Pedro III of Aragón (r. 1276–1285)

The chronicler of the exploits of King Pedro III of Aragón was interested in the case of Manfred, the illegitimate son of Frederick II who had claimed the crown of Sicily in 1258 against the will of Pope Alexander IV, largely because Pedro had married Manfred's daughter Constance in 1260 and therefore had a claim to the Sicilian succession. The name Constance had been associated with the ruling dynasty of Sicily since the mother of Frederick II. There is another useful account in *The Chronicle of San Juan de la Peña: A Fourteenth-Century History of the Crown of Aragon*, trans. Lynn H. Nelson (Philadelphia, 1991), 68–86. See also Jaume Aurell, *Authoring the Past: History, Autobiography, and Politics in Medieval Catalonia* (Chicago, 2012), esp. 55–71, and *Thomas M. Bisson, The Medieval Crown of Aragon: A Short History* (Oxford, 1986).

IT CAME to pass that in those days [1263] there was a pope at Rome [Urban IV] who was a great friend of Count Charles, he that was count of Anjou and of Provence and brother of the king of France, the one who died at Tunis [Louis IX]. And the pope set down King Manfred from his

Source: *Bernat Desclot, Chronicle of the Reign of King Pedro III of Aragon, trans. F. L. Critchlow, 2 vols. (Princeton NJ, 1928–1934), 1:153–154, 161–163, 179–182.*

throne and gave his kingdom [of Sicily] to Count Charles. But this gift brought great evil upon all Christendom. Count Charles made ready in Provence and gathered a great host of men to go against the land of King Manfred. And he was in no wise supplied with as much treasure as he needed, but he pledged and bartered whatsoever he was able. . . .

When the day came [in 1266] on which Count Charles crossed the border and entered into the kingdom of Sicily with his horsemen fully armed and arrayed for battle, King Manfred was ready . . . the armies on both sides were drawn up for battle . . . and when King Manfred perceived his horsemen fleeing and when he knew that he had been forsaken and betrayed, he spurred his horse and in full armor as he was and with his shield before him and his lance at rest, rode headlong against the press of the French, crying out that he would rather die a king than live as an exile. . . . [Later] King Manfred was found dead and with him six thousand horsemen of both armies. And King Charles caused King Manfred to be buried with great honor, which when he had done, he marched forward and entered into the land of King Manfred without hindrance. And he cast into irons many counts and barons that had turned traitor to the king and who had thought thereby to gain great reward from King Charles, but they were all put to death at his hands. . . .

The chronicler goes on to describe how Charles's treatment of the Sicilians soon earned him their hatred.

THEN the count of Pisa and divers barons of the kingdom of Sicily sent a messenger to Conrad, who was the nephew of King Manfred and at that time in Alamayn [Bavaria], entreating him to come to them and saying that they would pay the cost of all things needful and would aid him with all their power by land and by sea to regain the realm of Sicily. When Conradin received this message, he and the son of the duke of Estalrich [Austria] set forth with five hundred horsemen from Alamayn and went by way of Lombardia as far as the coast of Genoa. And they came to a haven called Vada which is near Savona, and from there they went by sea to Pisa. . . .

When the people of Rome learned that Conradin was come to Pisa, they were filled with great joy, as were also the people of Romania and of all the country round about and of all Tuscany, inasmuch as they were greatly angered by the rule of Charles and borne upon heavily by him. And so they sent an envoy to Conradin praying him to come without any fear whatsoever, as they would establish him in Rome and aid him against Charles. . . .

Conradin is joined by others opposed to Charles, including Enrico of Castile.

. . . IN THE space of a few days, all were armed for war and Conradin with all his host set forth from Rome and marched toward the land of Apulia. And when Charles learned that Conradin was coming upon him to take his land, he assembled his army and marched into the region of the land of Llavor, hard by the bridge of Ceprano, and he there arrayed his men. . . .

A battle ensued, and despite the temporary victory of Conradin's forces, an ambush by Charles forced Conradin to flee. His men advised him to go in disguise to Terracina, from which they could take ship to Pisa and gather reinforcements, but they were discovered and betrayed to Charles.

Now it is well known that all the land which Charles possessed was aforetime the realm of the grandfather and father of Conradin [Frederick II and Conrad IV]. Wherefore, it was not to be marveled at that Conradin laid claim thereto and waged war with Charles, for the land was his by right. So when Charles held Conradin in his power, he desired much to destroy him and sought out judges who wished him harm. And he caused him to be condemned like a felon at Naples in the marketplace before all the people. And there he caused him to be beheaded and with him also the son of the duke of Estalrich and Count Galvano [di Lancia] and his son.[15]

But Charles had not heard or read of the Gospel of Saint Matthew which tells of a certain king that forgave his servant who owed him ten thousand talents [Mt 18:23–35]. . . . If Charles had been mindful of the time when the Saracens of Babylonia took captive both him and his brethren who had gone into the land of the Saracens to destroy them and to lay waste their domain, albeit they let them and their followers go free, safe and unharmed, he would have been righteous and merciful when he seized Conradin as a prisoner who came to seek his land by lawful claim, not to have dealt despitefully with him nor to have put him to death. And even as Charles had found mercy at the hands of the Saracens who were not of his faith, so much the more should Conradin, who was a Christian

---

15. Galvano was actually beheaded in Palestrina, a month before Conradin and his kinsman Frederick of Austria were beheaded in Naples.

and of like faith with him, have found mercy at the hands of Charles. . . . Thus Charles ruled harshly over the people of Apulia and of the kingdom of Sicily, insomuch as they were filled with anger against him.

This King Charles had so great a name throughout all the world that all peoples feared him and held him in awe. And he begat a son by his first wife, who was daughter of the count of Provence. And to this son the prince of Morea gave his daughter to wife and all Morea and, by reason of this land of Morea, King Charles thought to gain Romania. And so when the son became prince of Morea, Charles put to death the Greek Christians. But God, who hateth pride and evil, did so thwart him that he could not fulfill his purpose. And Charles caused a mighty fleet of armed ships and barges and other vessels to be made ready, to the end that he might cross over to Romania. And all this great armada perished most miserably, according to the will of God, as you shall hear of further in this book.[16]

Moreover, Charles had dethroned and despoiled of his realm a king that was in Jerusalem and who was king of Egypt and had possessed the land for twelve years. And this king of Egypt was victorious over the Saracens and would have seized Acre and all the country round about, had he not tarried there and wasted all his treasure in horsemen and men on foot in defending the land against the Saracens who came thither each year with great armies.

Now a space of five years had scarce gone by when Charles sent to Acre with the aid of the Temple a knight from Apulia named Roger de Saint Severin, who held the land in the name of Charles. But the king of Cyprus remained in Cyprus and the land of Acre and of Syria fell into great confusion, so that Charles reaped no other profit or gain therefrom than war and suffering and famine. And in the end, Count Roger was forced to abandon Acre and the sovereignty thereof and return to Apulia in great distress and need.[17]

16. The author refers to the outbreak of the Sicilian Vespers, which prevented Charles's plan to reclaim the Latin emperorship of Constantinople, recently captured by Michael VIII Palaeologus in 1261. See Stephen Runciman, *The Sicilian Vespers: A History of the Mediterranean World in the Later Thirteenth Century* (Cambridge, 1958; repr., 1992).

17. Charles had bought the rights of Maria, queen of Antioch, to the kingdom of Jerusalem and had sent Roger to Acre in 1278 to act as his bailiff.

PART IX
Living and Dying on Crusade

Crusades did not consist solely of preaching, recruiting, and fighting in distant lands. They also involved planning, local arrangements, and travel across great distances. Those distances were originally crossed overland, but as early as 1125 the idea of maritime expeditions with Egypt as the primary target became more common, and by the end of the twelfth century the Atlantic and Mediterranean seas had become the crusaders' roadways. One of the emerging themes of crusade historiography is the actual experience of those who went on crusade, from leaving home and parting with family and friends to obtaining transportation, making agreements, expecting agreements to be kept, and providing for the future. The texts in this section reflect a number of facets of the crusade experience that characterize the entire period treated in this book.

Mediterranean seaports played a key role in trade in the Mediterranean and in the transport of passengers and crusaders to the East. The relative cheapness of sea travel made the crusade affordable even to artisans and merchants, who could hope to supplement their funds and perhaps combine their pilgrimage with profit-making by practicing their trades in the crusader camp. Those who did not find passage in ships hired or even built to order by great magnates or kings had to book their own passage and appear to have occasionally formed consortia for their own protection.

The size of thirteenth-century ships could be surprisingly large: the largest could carry one hundred horses in addition to crusaders and their attendants, and in ordinary voyages could carry up to one thousand passengers or more in cramped quarters (a place represented little more than the space needed to lie down and was often marked out by chalk) in addition to its crew and supplies. When merchants chartered a vessel for a trading voyage, they often tried to limit or ban the amount of livestock or pilgrims allowed on board in order to preserve space for themselves and their merchandise. Female pilgrims were considered particularly undesirable, perhaps because their need for privacy consumed further valuable space, and they represented sexual temptation to the crew and passengers. However, as the case involving the passengers of *Saint Victor* attests (No. 64), this did not deter many women from making the sea voyage, including some who participated in Louis IX's first crusade.

On Mediterranean trade and the crusades in general, see Ruthy Gertwagen and Eliza-beth Jeffreys, eds., Shipping, Trade and Crusade in the Medieval Mediterranean *(Farnham Surrey, 2012). For shipping contracts and the* Saint Victor *case, see Robert S. Lopez and Irving W. Raymond, ed. and trans.,* Medieval Trade in the Mediterranean World: Illustrative Documents *(New York, 2001), 240–241; Benjamin Z. Kedar, "The Passenger List of a Crusader*

Ship, 1250: Towards the History of the Popular Element on the Seventh Crusade, Studi Medievali, *3d ser., 13, no. 1 (1972), 267–279; Eugene H. Byrne,* Genoese Shipping in the Twelfth and Thirteenth Centuries *(Cambridge MA, 1930), 8–10, 85–87, 91–97, 99–102, 106–112, 114–118. On women travelers, see James M. Powell, "The Role of Women in the Fifth Crusade," reprinted in Powell,* The Crusades, the Kingdom of Sicily, and the Mediterranean *(Aldershot UK-Burlington VT, 2007), IV; Susan Edgington and Sarah Lambert, eds.,* Gendering the Crusades *(Cardiff, 2001); Natasha R. Hodgson,* Women, Crusading and the Holy Land in Historical Narrative *(Woodbridge UK-Rochester NY, 2007).*

62. Ticket-Scalping on a Crusade Ship, 1248

Round-trip or single fares to the East were becoming increasingly affordable in this period. As Benjamin Kedar notes, in preparation for Louis IX's crusade, the syndics of Marseilles set the various fares of the first-, second-, and third-class places on the ships Louis IX ordered at four pounds (*livres, librae*), sixty shillings (*solidi*), and forty shillings of Tours. When Master Garnier made this contract in June 20, 1248, the prices were higher, but still affordable. Even if Garnier made a 25 percent profit, the resulting price of fifty-six shillings per place would have been affordable for a cook or tailor earning from ten to thirty deniers (*denarii*) per day.[1]

WE, William de Cadenet, Hugh Quillan, and William Sansier, citizens of Marseilles, in good faith and without any deception lease or charter to you, Master Garnier Marignino, two hundred places on a certain *buzze,*[2] our ship called the *Saint Leonard,* that is, on the three decks[3] of the commonly called ship, excepting from this [agreement] places beneath the bridge [*pontus*] and places in the *paraviso*[4] and castle.[5] We lease or charter the aforesaid two hundred places to you for the price or wage or freight charge of forty-five shillings of Tours for each place. We confirm the price which we ought to have and receive from you for the aforesaid places as thirty-three pounds of Tours. . . . We likewise promise to you through a

Source: Louis Blancard, Documents indits sur le commerce de Marseille au Moyen Age, *2 vols. (Marseilles, 1884–1885), doc. 914, 2:248–249.*

1. See preceding note.

2. A common but poorly described type of medieval ship.

3. This was unusual. Normally the first, or upper, deck was reserved for wealthy passengers, the second and third decks (with less light and fresh air) for cheaper fares. The naming of ships after saints became widespread during the thirteenth century.

4. More commonly spelled *paradiso* (the same word as Paradise), this was a large chamber on the upper deck.

5. All these exceptions were desirable quarters normally reserved for wealthy passengers—fresh air and light came at a premium. For example, one contract from Marseilles specifies places in and under the castle, in the *paradisi* and bridge and under the bridge, as costing four livres tournois, whereas places on the upper and middle decks were only sixty solidi. The lower deck, or "steerage" class, was only forty solidi.

formal agreement and we make a pact with you that we will not allow any cargo [to be loaded] on the said ship [with the exception of what] you are bound to provide toward the prepaid rations for the pilgrims or Romans [*romeis*], in the aforementioned two hundred places not [*sic*] in loading the cargo of the pilgrims in said ship,[6] binding both ourselves and all our possessions, both present and future in entirety to yourself and yours, on behalf of all the things laid forth above; renouncing to the benefit of the new agreement the two conditions [*reis*] and stay of twenty days and four months and every other delay and legal right and exception through which we could go against the aforesaid agreement.

And I, the said master Garnier, agreeing to all of the compacts and covenants mentioned above, promise to you, the masters or shareholders of said ship through a [formal] stipulation, to give and pay to you the remainder of the price or freight charge for the aforesaid two hundred places, in the middle of the month of the next coming August or meanwhile at whatever time I charter or sell the said places to pilgrims. I likewise promise to you through a [formal] stipulation to faithfully and attentively be careful in seeking out and obtaining pilgrims for the remainder of the said ship [both] through myself and my partners and [thus acquire] every profit and gain by whatever means I can for you and your partners in the ship. And thus I therefore pledge to you in my guarantee and in good faith before God; binding all my possessions present and future to you and yours for all of the aforesaid matters, renouncing the stays of twenty days and four months and every other delay and legal right and exception through which I could go against the aforesaid [contract].

Drawn up in Marseilles, in the house of William Sansier. Witnesses: John Brignoes, John Dantignac, Nicholas Roche, John Sans, John Prouvins.

63. Adam of Jesmond's Contract of Service with Lord Edward of England, July 20, 1270

In addition to employing professional mercenaries, rulers and cities commonly subsidized knights otherwise unable to participate in the crusade to serve under them. Jean de Joinville initially funded a small company of knights, which

6. That is, no cargo apart from pilgrims and their victuals and baggage.

he took with him on Louis IX's first crusade, but after running short of money, Joinville was himself retained by Louis IX to prevent his leaving the crusade campaign. Just as Louis IX used contracts to outline the expectations of both parties regarding obligations and funding, so Lord Edward used them to recruit the core of the force he led on crusade in 1270–1272, having been inspired by Louis IX, ensuring that he possessed a group of knights under his direct command with proven loyalties. Many of these followers were important noblemen with long-standing ties of service to Henry III and his family and were duly rewarded for their service on crusade (as were Jean de Joinville and other participants in the crusades of Louis IX). In addition to this contract, Adam of Jesmond obtained the royal privileges of holding a weekly market and annual fair on his lands before his departure on Lord Edward's crusade.

See Simon Lloyd, English Society and the Crusade, 1216–1307 *(Oxford, 1988), esp. 113–153; Michael Prestwich*, Edward I *(New Haven CT-London, 1997), esp. 66–86; James M. Powell, "Crusading by Royal Command: Monarchy and Crusade in the Kingdom of Sicily," in Powell*, The Crusades, the Kingdom of Sicily, and the Mediterranean, X.

To ALL those who shall see or hear this writing Adam of Jesmond wishes salvation in Our Lord. Know that I have agreed with my lord Edward, the eldest son of the king of England, to go with him to the Holy Land, accompanied by four knights, and to remain in his service for a whole year to commence at the coming voyage of September. And in return he has given me, to cover all expenses, six hundred marks in money and transport, that is to say, the hire of a ship and water for as many persons and horses as are appropriate for knights. And should it happen that I am detained by sickness or any other accident, which God forbid, a knight in my place and my knights aforesaid will undertake his service fully for the year or else I will return to him, as much money as shall be necessary to complete the period which is lacking from the year, and this shall be at my choice. And if it should by chance happen that God's will shall be that my aforesaid lord, Sir Edward, shall die, I shall be bound to him, whom my lord shall leave or send in his place, as to himself, according to the form above written. And in witness hereof I have caused my seal to be set in this writing. Given at Westminster the twentieth day of July in the fifty-fourth year from the coronation of our lord King Henry, son of King John.

Source: *H. G. Richardson and G. O. Sayles*, The Governance of Mediaeval England from the Conquest to Magna Carta *(Edinburgh, 1963), 465.*

64. A Verdict from Judges in Messina Concerning a Lawsuit for Breach of Contract Lodged by a Group of Passengers Against the Masters of the Ship *Saint Victor*, July 30, 1250

The following case illustrates the way in which the relatively inexpensive sea journey to the Holy Land made popular participation in the crusade possible well into the thirteenth century. A group of independently funded crusaders of all classes and both sexes are represented by several of their number in a case against the masters of the ship *Saint Victor* from Marseilles, which they had hired to take them to Damietta, the intended goal of Louis IX's crusade, or to any eastern port or wherever the king might be. When the ship arrived at Messina, news of the loss of Damietta and the arrival of King Louis in Acre meant that the passengers demanded to be taken to Acre. When the ship owners refused to do so, the pilgrims lodged an expensive and lengthy case against them in Messina and eventually were awarded all legal expenses and free passage to the destination of their choice by the judges at Messina, subjects of Frederick II, a strong supporter of Louis IX's crusade.

The document represents some of the earliest evidence into the composition of a shipload of some 453 crusaders. The passengers included various knights and their followers and retainers, some Templars and a Hospitaller, seven clerics, and some 342 commoners. Of the commoners, 42, or more than 9 percent, were women traveling with their husbands, male relatives, or, surprisingly, on their own—this despite clerics', crusade organizers', and sailors' objections to women traveling with men on crusade expeditions. There were also craftsmen on board, who may have intended to settle in the lands conquered by Louis IX in Egypt. Others may have had the cross imposed on them as a punishment or penance. Sometimes a passenger might take the cross to atone for a previous criminal sin, even to the point of redeeming himself politically and spiritually by a distinguished crusading career.[7]

. . . . THE PILGRIMS Terric Theotonicus, Peter de Latigniaco, John de Ala, and Richard Anglicus, on their own behalf and as agents or proctors appointed by the pilgrims whose names are written below, set forth [a lawsuit] against William Mayus and Peter Constantinus, masters and shareholders of the ship *Saint Victor*, saying that the aforesaid masters of the ship, contracted on their own behalf and through the other owners and shareholders of the aforesaid ship . . . to rent to them the aforesaid ship and their services for a fixed price set and paid in [coins of] Tours

Source: *J. de Laborde et al., eds.,* Layettes du Trésor des Chartes, *vol. 3 (Paris, 1875; repr., Nendeln, 1977), no. 3883, pp. 103–106.*
7. See Kedar, "Passenger List."

and in other silver coin [and promised] that they would transport them to regions overseas for the sake of completing their pilgrimage. And they agreed and promised through a solemn contract to carry them in the aforesaid ship on an overseas voyage to Damietta or wherever the aforesaid ship was able to go through the sea and make port in the aforesaid regions overseas, or to where the king of France would be. And for this reason, when the aforesaid masters of the ship together with the aforesaid ship could have gone in this manner into the aforesaid regions, that is, to Acre, and could have made port there, and particularly since the king of France was there, as it was publicly said, they petition on behalf of themselves and in the name of those they represent that the faith, promised compact, and appropriate law in the said contract be kept by them, according to what was said, and they seek damages and expenses.

The names of the aforesaid pilgrims are . . .

An extensive list of passengers follows, including men and women of all social classes traveling in small groups according to blood relation or regional affiliation or by themselves.

THE ACCUSED, contesting the lawsuit [put forward against them], admit that they are the owners and shareholders of the aforesaid ship and that the aforementioned Peter, the accused, together with John Madio, father of William Mayus, the [other] aforementioned accused, leased the same ship to the aforesaid Terric Theotonicus, John de Ala, and Richard Anglicus, [acting] on behalf of themselves and certain other pilgrims whose names are designated above, at the established price written above, in order to carry them to Damietta. The other things which were declared [above], they deny, maintaining their restrictions [in the contract]. An oath against false witness was furnished by each of the parties. And after the contesting of the lawsuit occurred, succeeded by the oath against perjury, articles were presented to the court on the part of the plaintiffs and on the part of the accused with exceptions, [each] on their own day, and then questioning on these things occurred on either side, as is lawful, and each side obtained a deadline for proving, before which deadline each side produced its witnesses. When the deadline arrived, according to the wish of the parties, the witnesses were made public in court, [and] a formal disputation followed upon the efficacy of the witnesses [presented] by either party, [and] by the common wish of them [both parties] it was broken off and ended, and both sides requested with urgency that a sentence be imposed.[8]

Therefore we, having diligently reviewed the merits of and challenges to the case, with scrupulous consultation and deliberation upon the things mentioned before, because the intention is fully established of Terric Theotonicus, Peter de Latigniaco, John de Ala, and Richard Anglicus, both for themselves and also as agents and procurators and representatives in the complaint of the pilgrims contending against William Mayus and Peter Constantinus, masters and shareholders of the ship *Saint Victor*, albeit the intention was broken down through the exceptions of the aforesaid masters, nonetheless, because the aforesaid exceptions were broken down and excluded through the replications of the pilgrims, we condemn the aforesaid William and Peter Constantinus in the form of a judicial sentence to transport them to regions overseas, to wherever the king of France may be. And because both ancient and new laws demand that the vanquished ought to be forced to pay the victor's expenses, we officially sentence the aforesaid guilty in name [to pay] the expenses of the aforesaid representatives, both on behalf of themselves and on behalf of the part of the pilgrims contending in the complaint, in one hundred tremisses of gold, vouched for by oath by the same and surpassing our estimation. Whence, for future memory and as a warranty for the aforesaid pilgrims, the sentence was written down by the public instrument then present, [that is] by the hand of Perronus de Calvarosa, imperial magistrate of Messina and notary of the acts of the court of the same city, and fortified by the signatures of ourselves and the same notary. . . .

65. Traveling in Style and at Risk, October 1216–March 1217

Elected bishop of Acre, the famed crusade preacher James of Vitry traveled to Perugia for his consecration and then took ship from Genoa for the Holy Land, bent on reforming its inhabitants (especially those in the notorious port city of Acre) in preparation for the crusaders' arrival as part of the Fifth Crusade. He described his preparations in letters addressed to his acquaintances (many of them involved in the organization of the crusade) in the dioceses of Liège and Paris, whose prayers he requested for his own safety and the favorable outcome of the

8. This paragraph is an excellent illustration of the formal legal procedure known as the accusatorial process, at the end of which the party against whom a verdict is declared must pay for the costs of the procedure as well as any award given to those in whose favor the verdict was found.

crusade. His description of his travels shows the hazards and frustrations that faced a relatively wealthy crusader who financed an entourage that traveled with him overseas, both to serve him as bishop of Acre and to participate with him in the Fifth Crusade. His deliberate targeting of the Genoese for recruitment illustrates the important role that the naval powers of Italy played in Mediterranean trade and in providing shipping and provisions for the crusades.

Gervase of Prémontré had nominated James as a potential replacement for his longtime colleague Robert Courson, whose commission as legate for the crusade in France had terminated with the Fourth Lateran Council (1215), but Honorius III seems to have thought that James would prove more useful overseas. Robert himself departed from Genoa in 1218 with a contingent of crusaders from France and joined James in the crusader army before Damietta, dying of disease there. James collaborated with Oliver of Paderborn and other clerics in the crusader army before Damietta in preaching sermons, offering (often unsolicited) military and spiritual advice, interpreting prophecies, drafting army regulations, sending letters meant to inform audiences in Europe of the course of the crusade and to summon aid, and writing histories of previous crusades and the current campaign.

See Maier, Crusade Propaganda and Ideology; *Powell*, Anatomy; *Jessalynn Bird, "James of Vitry's and Oliver of Paderborn's Missions to Muslims Reconsidered," in* Essays in Medieval Studies: Proceedings of the Illinois Medieval Association *21 (2004), 23–47; Jessalynn Bird, "The* Historia Orientalis *of Jacques de Vitry: Visual and Written Commentaries as Evidence of a Text's Audience, Reception and Utilization," in* Essays in Medieval Studies: Proceedings of the Illinois Medieval Association *20 (2003), 56–74. On the voyage, see John Pryor, "The Voyage of Jacques de Vitry from Genoa to Acre, 1216: Juridical and Economical Problems in Medieval Navigation," in M. Peláez, ed.,* Derecho de la navegación in Europa *(Barcelona, 1987), 1689–1714.*

IT HAPPENED that when I entered Lombardy, the Devil upset and threw overboard my weapons, that is, my books, with which I was resolved to subdue the Devil himself, with the other things necessary for my expenses, into a violently rushing and terrifyingly bottomless river, which from the melting of the snow forcefully grew beyond bounds and was carrying with it bridges and boulders. One of my baskets full of books was carried off among the flood's surges, another, in which I had placed the finger of my [spiritual] mother, Mary of Oignies,[9] sustained my mule

Source: James of Vitry, Lettres, *ed. R. B. C. Huygens (Leiden, 1960), nos. 1–2, pp. 72, 76–78, 80–83.*

9. James refers to a finger of Mary encased in a silver reliquary. This relic was particularly special to James since he had had a close spiritual relationship with the recently deceased Mary of Oignies, one of the holy women overseen by James and other reformers and crusade recruiters working in the diocese of Liège. James had recently written her hagiographical *vita* at the request of another crusade recruiter, Fulk, bishop of Toulouse, who viewed Mary's example as the perfect orthodox antidote to the allure of the heretical "good women" of his

so that it was not entirely overwhelmed. However, when [it seemed] that
scarcely one out of a thousand would be able to escape [Eccl 6:6], my
mule came safely to the riverbank with the basket, while another basket
was later miraculously recovered after snagging in some trees. What is
more miraculous yet, although my books were a trifle blurred, I am still
able to read them all. In fact, after this I came to a certain city known as
Milan, which was a pit of heretics . . . after this I came to a city called
Perugia. . . .[10]

When I left the aforesaid city [Perugia], I took the road toward
Genoa, which is a noble city in the confines of Tuscany and Lombardy
situated on the ocean. However, when I was but three days journey from
the city, I found the road difficult and mountainous, and so put out to
sea with my companions in a certain small ship toward the city of Genoa,
which has an excellent port, and arrived there by ship. Since we sailed
by night and day among the ocean's swells, often our little ship was so
continually prone to sinking from the battering of the waves that the force
of the waves would sometimes enter the ship. Nonetheless we had one
remedy—that our sails were opposing the waves. Indeed, after we had
been brought to Genoa, the citizens of that city, although they received
me kindly, in the end led my horses with them to the siege of a certain
fortification, whether I wished it or not. For this was the custom of the
city, that whenever they go to war, wherever they find horses and whoever's they may be, they take them with them. . . .

*James stays in Genoa and converts many of the women and others left behind to
the crusade effort.*

So THEN, after the citizens returned from their battle, they gave me back
my horses. . . . However, I tarried in the city of Genoa throughout the
entire month of September and frequently pronounced the word of
preaching to the city's people on Sundays and feast days; even though I
did not know their dialect, still many thousands of people were converted
to God, receiving the sign of the cross. Now these men are wealthy and
powerful and bellicose and vigorous in war, possessing an abundance of
ships and of the finest galleys and seasoned sailors who know the route

region. James probably intended for this miracle to contribute to the case for Mary's official
recognition as a saint.

10. At Perugia James saw the abandoned and despoiled corpse of Innocent III, who
had died there the day before. The experience forced James to contemplate the relation
between earthly greatness and the leveling experience of death.

on the ocean and often venture into the land of the Saracens for the sake of obtaining various merchandise. And so I do not believe that there is another city which would be able to help so much toward the succor of the Holy Land. And because they returned from battle, in the month of October,[11] around the feast of Saint Michael [September 29, 1216], I put out to sea with my companions, entrusting myself to God and to the winter sea and [its] tempestuous waves. . . .

For the men of that city own very seaworthy ships and a great quantity of them, and for this reason they customarily cross the sea in the winter time, because during this season the victuals in the ships do not spoil as easily nor does the water on the ship putrefy as it does during the summer, nor is it necessary for them to be delayed for a long time at sea on account of a lack of winds and becalmedness of the sea. So then, I hired a newly built ship which had never crossed the sea for the price of a thousand pounds, for a bad ship, so I heard, had been bought for the price of five hundred pounds. I prepared five rooms for myself and my possessions, that is, the fourth part of the upper castle, in which I would eat and study my books and would remain during the day unless there was a storm at sea. I hired another room, in which I would sleep at night with my companions, and another room in which I stored my vestments and kept the victuals necessary for myself throughout the week. I rented another room in which my servants would sleep and prepare food for me and procured another place where my horses, which I arranged to cross the sea with me, would be kept. In fact, I caused to be gathered together in the ship's hold my wine and biscuit and [preserved] meats and other things sufficient for my sustenance for nearly three months. And I boarded the ship safe and sound with my associates and my possessions uninjured. So then, pray urgently for me and for mine, that God will lead us to the port of the city of Acre and from there to the port of eternal blessedness.

In a second letter to his friends, James describes the perils of his voyage.

By DIVINE favor I and all who are with me are safe and sound through God's grace and I hope to hear the same of you. So then, after we left the port of the city of Genoa in order to cross the sea, we labored for five weeks upon the ocean and endured many adversities in various places.

11. Traditionally two voyages were made to the East in the spring and autumn in order to avoid the summer heat and winter storms that plagued the Mediterranean.

James describes how after passing an island near Sardinia, they were driven back to it and exchanged bread, oil, and clothing with a hermit there in return for fresh meat and water.

HOWEVER, not long after this there fell upon us a great and truly fearful danger. For by a certain great impetus a ship was lifted above our ship, drawing near as if it were going to collide. We were hardly able to avoid it without one or the other of us being broken up, nor could we turn aside in the opposite direction on account of a projecting rock;[12] in the end, it was necessary to either bear the impact of the other ship or dash our ship against the rock. Then all raised a great outcry and the tears of the wailing and people confessing their sins could be heard in either ship. And people were leaping from one of the ships to the other in turn, because one man believed one boat to be stronger and another the other. Others stripped off their clothing and tied what they possessed in gold and silver [coin] to themselves in case they might be able to escape by swimming. However, some of the sailors, having compassion on me and deferring to me, tried to persuade me to enter the small boat which was tied to the larger ship. But I would by no means acquiesce because of the bad example [it would set], but wanted to undergo the common danger with the others. Yet the Lord regarded my affliction [cf. Gn 3:42; Ex 4:31], for we repelled the ship pressing upon our ship with lances and staves, so that neither ship was broken up, although they collided with each other. However, from the force of the collision our ship twisted a little to the left side and so drew away from the rock on its right side. In fact, although the ship remained in the vicinity of the rock and should already have been dashed to pieces and sunk, yet when the sails were dropped and the anchors thrown overboard, it stood firm and as if by a miracle we avoided being crushed by the grace of God. Now certain men from the aforesaid ship had thrown their silver and gold into our ship.

And when we sailed from that place we met with a strongly contrary wind, yet we reached as well as we were able, a port next to another island, where we were delayed for nearly fifteen days. Since we had continually contrary weather and winter was quickly approaching, we were already nearly despairing of making the crossing, very much afraid lest we be forced to winter on another island. Moreover, the master of our ship wanted to expel all the poor from our ship and abandon them on the island because he did not have sufficient provisions. In fact, I vehemently

12. This could alternatively read: "looming cliff."

implored him not to expose the poor to the danger of death, since up until now he had been dependent upon God's mercy. However, although he by no means wanted to acquiesce, the Lord sent to us a sudden tempest so strong that the fifteen anchors which we threw into the sea could hardly hold our ship—why then did we not perish? For the ship's prow was now lifted to the heights, now plunged into the depths.

In fact, these storms lasted continuously for two days and two nights, so that some of us could hardly withstand the force of the winds (for slamming down the castle of our ship, they broke it to pieces) while others neither ate nor drank for fear of death. In fact, I ate nothing cooked, for no one dared to light a fire on our ship. And when I drank, I would hold the cup in one hand while holding tight with the other, lest I fall or the cup spill. And yet, since we were afraid that our water would run out, we stretched out our clothing under the rain so that we obtained a double benefit: while we washed out our clothing, we drank the washing water.

However, these storms expelled the storm of sins from the minds of many. In fact, many who had persisted in their sins for many years tearfully came to confession. Moreover, merchants and powerful men took the sign of the cross from my hand, and after we cried out to the Lord [cf. Pss 3:5, 76:2, 141:2], he sent a peaceful sky and favorable winds to us, [winds blowing] from behind [our sails]. He bestowed aid after tribulation [cf. Pss 59:13, 107:13], such that within a few days we were sailing near to Sicily and Crete. Passing to the left side Scylla and Charybdis, to the right side the island of Melitus where the blessed Paul, shipwrecked, wintered and a serpent bit him while he was gathering branches [Acts 28:1–6], we hailed the island of Cyprus, where enormous fish,[13] who followed and preceded our ship, leapt around it while disporting themselves, signaling to the sailors that we were not far from land. So then, on the sixth day after the feast of All Saints [November 7, 1216] we arrived at the port of the city of Acre.

66. The Last Will and Testament of Barzella Merxadrus, December 9, 1219

Written shortly after the crusading army's capture of Damietta, Barzella's will sheds light on the concerns and resources of a crusader and his wife from the Italian city-republic of Bologna. From the description of his equipment, Barzella

13. That is, dolphins. A number of crusade narratives make a point of seeing dolphins for the first time.

appears to have fought, along with his companions, as a well-equipped foot soldier, perhaps trained through membership in a city militia or confraternity. Part of a Bolognese contingent of crusaders later assigned a portion of the city of Damietta and its walls, Barzella's companions and his wife would have expected their due share of real estate and spoils, which had yet to be divided among the crusaders.

In addition to providing for his soul, wife, and companions, Barzella's will illustrates the way in which the property of deceased crusaders was redistributed among the needy army through donations to his circle of acquaintances (probably fellow citizens), a common mess perhaps maintained by the Bolognese, the military orders, and the army's communal chest. It also demonstrates that even those putatively assured of a plenary indulgence for their confessed sins remained uneasy concerning the ultimate fate of their souls and chose to muster as many spiritual intercessions as they could in order to ease their entry into heaven. This included the subsidy of other crusaders in order to earn the indulgences offered to those who enabled others to serve in the crusade army. Barzella's bequeathing to his wife only those possessions he already possessed or expected to acquire in the army before Damietta suggests that he and his wife envisioned settling down in Damietta (as part of a newly enlarged Latin kingdom of Jerusalem) or selling up to others.

See W. S. Morris, "A Crusader's Testament," Speculum 27 (1952), 197–198. On skilled physicians maintained by the Bolognese, see Piers D. Mitchell, Medicine in the Crusades (Cambridge, 2004), 26–28. On the Bolognese contingent, Powell, Anatomy, 69, 74, 81, 94. On settlement and related topics, Judith Herrin and Guillaume Saint-Guillain, eds., Identities and Allegiances in the Eastern Mediterranean After 1204 (Farnham UK-Burlington VT, 2011).

IN THE year of the Lord 1219, on the ninth day of December, in the seventh indiction, Barzella Merxadrus, a citizen of Bologna signed with the cross [*crucesignatus*] having become gravely ill in the army of the Christians before Damietta, drew up his will in this manner. First, for the sake of his soul he bequeathed five bezants to be spent for his funeral and burial and for singing masses; by his executors, the lord priest Giles and his wife Guiletta and his uncle Rainald Maldinarus. To the hospital of the Germans in Jerusalem [the Teutonic Order], where he wishes to be buried, he bequeaths all his weapons and armor and his hauberk with one arm guard and a coif. Similarly for the sake of his soul he bequeaths from those possessions which he had in the aforesaid army to one person who will remain overseas in it until the next feast of Saint Michael two sacks of biscuit, two measures of flour, two measures [*corbae*] of wine, and the

Source: Ludovico Vittorio Savioli, ed., Annali Bolognesi, 3 vols. in 6 (Bassano, 1784–1795), 2.2:419–420, no. 480.

fourth part of one *mezzina*[14] of wheat, one set of breeches, one shirt, and six bezants for accompaniments to bread and wine.

He bequeaths to the priest Giles one bezant for singing masses; to Rainald Maldinarus, two bezants; to Conrad of Pontecchio, five small imperial solidi. He leaves three bezants to all his companions and a share of the tent and its furnishings to the same companions and his wife Guiletta as below mentioned. His companions are not to cause any injury to his aforementioned wife in regard to the same tent and its furnishings for as long as she shall continue to dwell fully and peacefully in the same tent just as she has dwelled in it up to the present, for as long as she shall remain in that same army. To the notary James of Ugine he leaves two bezants. To the Hospital of Saint Lawrence, one bezant. To the common chest of the commune of the army, one bezant. To the temple of the Lord, one bezant. To the Hospital of Saint John, one bezant. Also to the aforesaid priest Giles he leaves five bezants for his soul.

For all other of his goods, movable and immovable, legal rights, and actions which he should hold overseas in the army and in the portion which might fall to him from the spoils discovered in the city of Damietta and from the city itself, he appoints as heir his wife, the aforesaid Guiletta. However, for all his other possessions which he should hold in Bologna and its district he appoints as his heirs his mother Bertha and his brother-in-law Lord Blaise. And this is his final testament, and if it should not prove valid according to the law of testaments, at least it should be valid by the law of codicils and as his free and final wishes. Drawn up in the Christian army before Damietta, having been made in the tent of the testator and his companions. In the aforementioned seventh indiction by the command of testator I have written this, his last will. There were present the lord priest Giles of Sancta T[h]ecla, Lord Tibertinus Rainerius de Spiularia, Bolnisius, nephew of Bonbaronus, Bonbaronus Merxadrus, Rainald Maldinarus, Conrad [of Pontecchio], Ottonellus de Roffeno, Ubertellus de Corvaria, Zagni of the bishop's camp, of all the aforesaid witnesses they were bound by oath by the testator. I, James of Ugine, notary of the emperor Otto,[15] was present and witnessed the seals. I, William of Sanguinetta, notary of the sacred palace, wrote and copied according to what I saw in the authentic instrument written by the hand

14. A medieval Italian unit of measurement that has no precise modern equivalent.
15. That is, Otto IV, deposed in 1210 but whose notarial and some other appointments remained valid.

of James of Ugine, notary of the emperor Otto, nor did I fraudulently add or subtract anything, but prenotarized what I added in writing.

67. Count Henry of Rodez Adds a Codicil to an Existing Will, Acre, October 16–31, 1222

While members of the Italian city-states sought support among themselves, forming confraternity-like organizations, other crusaders turned to monastic or military orders for financial and spiritual assistance. Before departing from their homelands, many crusaders sought to settle disputes over lands and various rights with local religious houses in return for spiritual benefits and increased security for their families during their absence or death. These settlements often resulted in crusaders ceding lands or disputed rights to religious houses in return for prayers and/or burial and legal and financial benefits for themselves and their families in the form of hard cash, gifts of horses or pack animals, and entry into the house as a full regular religious or pensioner.

The military orders' devotion to defending Christendom and the network of houses throughout Europe and, in many instances, the Near East meant that they were viewed as particularly efficacious means of spiritual and financial support. Their combination of monastic rigor, military discipline, and material resources (including ships equipped to navigate the Mediterranean, knowledge of local circumstances, and ability to transfer material and monies over long distances) meant that many crusaders sought to affiliate themselves with military orders while fulfilling their crusading vows. The practice became so common that some military orders soon offered formal terms by which crusaders could attach themselves temporarily to a military order for a set period without taking the monastic vows necessary for permanent entry—the *ad terminem* contract. The Italian Barzella had sought the spiritual intercessions of the military orders (including burial) by leaving money to all three military orders present in the crusader camp. Here, Henry's indebtedness to the Templar and Hospitaller orders, accrued while serving in the crusader army, results in generous donations and favorable legal settlements to clear his financial debts. The codicil also illustrates the stresses in the form of loss of important revenues and potential legal battles that awaited his wife and heir, who were managing his estates in his absence.

Henry had been recruited for the Fifth Crusade by the legate Robert Courson and, together with other noblemen, had requested Robert's appointment as legate for a substantial French contingent that departed from Genoa for the East in 1218. Henry may well have originally taken the crusade vow in part to protect his lands and family from the armies of antiheretical crusaders active in his region, armies led by Simon de Montfort. Accused of harboring lawless mercenaries and standing to lose his territories if he resisted the crusaders, Henry had initially attempted to avoid doing homage to Simon for his lands by claiming to be a vassal of John, king of England. However, as the result of negotiations with local prelates, Simon de Montfort, and Robert Courson (who had formally granted to Simon all lands in the Agenais, Quercy, Albigeoise, and the county of Rodez conquered by the crusaders), Henry and the city of Rodez finally acknowledged Simon as their overlord. Henry's crusade vow may have been partly a means of protecting himself from any further incursions on his territories, as he would have been able to claim local ecclesiastical and papal protection of himself, his family, and his lands. In fact, shortly after giving Henry the crusader's cross, Robert Courson formally took him under legatine protection. Henry was one of the very few southerners to go on the Fifth Crusade, and he appears to have made his will at the famed hospital in Acre, where the majority of crusaders withdrew after their defeat by al-Kamil.

See Corliss K. Slack, ed., and Hugh B. Feiss, trans., Crusade Charters, 1138–1270, *Medieval and Renaissance Texts and Studies 197 (Tempe AZ, 2001); Claire Taylor, "Pope Innocent III, John of England and the Albigensian Crusade (1209–1216)," in Moore,* Pope Innocent III and His World, *205–227.*

IN THE year of our Lord 1222, in the ninth indiction, in the calends of November, let it be evident to all that I, Henry, count of Rodez, gripped by a severe infirmity, yet possessed of a good sound mind and the power to order these matters, wish and command that the will, which I made in my own lands, should be considered firm and effective, and that I wish to confirm as correct all those things which are contained in it according to the law governing wills. Moreover, I add and wish that I bequeath my body to the Hospital of Saint John[16] as a brother of the same house; and I bequeath and gift to the same Hospital, for love of God and for the redemption of the sins of myself and my predecessors and successors, my village of Canet with all its appurtenances, just as it belonged and shall belong to myself and mine; and I bequeath to the same Hospital all my *mansi*[17] at Frontignan; and in addition I will to the same Hospital whatever I possess and ought to possess in La Bastide-Pradines, such that from now on the Hospital shall possess it freely and peacefully, without any contestation. And I furthermore bequeath to the same Hospital the men which I possess in that very place and the *mansi*, which I have in that place nearby the same and surrounding La Bastide. And I leave to the same Hospital all my *mansi*, which are nearby and around Canabières and

Source: *J. Delaville le Roulx, ed.,* Cartulaire général de l'ordre des Hospitaliers de S. Jean de Jérusalem (1100–1310), *4 vols. (Paris, 1894–1906), 2:308–309.*

16. That is the Hospitaller Order, also known as the Hospital of Saint John after their original headquarters in Jerusalem.

17. The word *mansi* could designate various things, including units of land, buildings, or households.

all my *mansi* which are nearby and around Bouloc, and nearby and adjoining La Bastide. In addition I bequeath to the same Hospital half of all the land which I purchased from Hugh of Launhac, and the entire vineyard which I purchased from the same person.

Moreover, I bequeath to the house of the [Order of the] Temple[18] one of my horses, that is, the same horse which used to belong to William of Roquelaure, and the grain which he owes me. And concerning the dispute which I used to have with the Temple over the matter of Badalecum, I want Brother John of Fontaine's word to be trusted concerning the entire matter and Miron of La Roche to be appointed to settle that dispute according to the wishes of the Temple. And I leave to the same house of the Temple the allod and grazing rights which I have around and bordering Saint-Martin-de-Limouze. In addition I desire that the countess and my son and all my successors should understand that I very much commend the house of the Temple, in that it was of great assistance to me in these parts; and for that reason I ask the lady countess and the boy and all my successors and descendants to guide, defend, protect, and guard the house of the Temple as much as they are able to. . . .

Moreover, I gift to the house of the [Order of the] Hospital [of Saint John] all my possessions and horses, and everything else which I have here [in the army], and the master of the Hospital shall make a repayment for this aforesaid gift to all my household through his representatives, as was arranged beforehand; and if my possessions should not suffice in value, I wish and urge the master of the Hospital to repay from the possessions of the house of the Hospital the aforesaid sum to my household, as was arranged. And regarding all losses and expenses which the house of the Hospital made on my behalf and in paying my household, I wish that it be repaid completely and entirely from my lands and from all my revenues, and from the settlement of the case concerning Alverasa. And I ask and command the lady countess and my son to make full repayment in all the aforesaid matters to the house of the Hospital for the great services and honors which they conferred upon me in the region of Syria, that is, in messengers and in all their expenses and outlays, which they made on my behalf and that of my household. I approve of this present document and wish it to be considered binding and to be valid in perpetuity according to the law of codicils; and if it should not be valid according to the

18. The Order of the Temple was another name for the Templars, whose original headquarters were on the Temple Mount in Jerusalem.

law of codicils, I wish that it should be valid according to whatever other law can validate it. Drawn up in Acre in the house of the Hospital [of Saint John]. These were the sworn witnesses called upon for this matter: Master Bertrand, Master Peter Maurinus, the physician, Brother Pontius, draper of the house of the Hospital, Brother Marsilius, and Brother Stephen de Malavilla and Bertrand de Masserebolis, and Gilbert de Boi and Mirus de Rupe, knights; and Bernardonus and Berardus and Peter Cornutus and Gerard, servants of the lord count, and the venerable William, archbishop of Bourges, who was present in his own person.[19] I, Bernard de Villa Franca, public notary of the imperial court, was there, and when asked I wrote out the will, and at the command of the aforesaid count, I firmly validated it with both of his personal seals.

68. Ignoble Pilgrims: Entries from the Register of Walter Giffard, Archbishop of York, 1275

These entries from an archiepiscopal register in England illustrate the increasing commonness of commuting the vows of even the militarily capable into money donations to the crusade by the mid- to late thirteenth century. When Innocent III and his successors removed the stipulation that individuals be assessed as to their capability of fulfilling the crusade vow before they undertook it, the floodgates to recruitment were flung open, and many who voluntarily took the crusader's cross later found themselves unwilling or unable to fulfill the duties implied by this legally and spiritually binding action. There were several remedies open to them provided they petitioned the appropriate authorities (although, theoretically, dispensation from crusade vows was reserved to the pope and his designated agents, some obtained dispensations from fraudulent operators or bishops, abbots, or other spiritual authorities who believed themselves capable of offering dispensations from such serious vows). Those trapped by crusade vows could seek a delay (typically granted in cases of temporary disability such as illness or a sudden drop in cash flow), a commutation (this changed the obligation of the vow into an alternative obligation, which tended in practice to be less onerous), or a redemption (normally the payment of a donation to the crusade or another charitable cause equivalent to the sum the individual would have spent in fulfilling a vow).

19. Master Bertrand and Master Peter Maurinus were physicians who may have been in the count's service and survived the campaign of the Fifth Crusade (many of the campaign's survivors headed to Acre to recover), or they could have been physicians practicing in Acre, either working for the Hospital of Saint John or called in important cases to minister to sick notables. Both men witnessed the will of Henry, count of Rodez (1214–1227), dated October 18, 1221 as he lay sick in the house of the Hospitallers in Acre. Master Peter may perhaps be identified with the same Master Peter who was *medicus* for the princess Isabella, daughter of John of Brienne. See Mitchell, *Medicine in the Crusades*, 18–19.

There was also a long and venerable tradition of ecclesiastical and royal authorities' imposing mandatory penitential pilgrimages on various categories of criminals and sinners (including adulterers, converted heretics, those who committed violence against ecclesiastics, homicides, and arsonists) as an alternative to other potentially harsher or less honorable legal or spiritual penalties (such as humiliating public penances, fines, mutilation, or the death penalty). The crusader's cross and its financial obligations quickly became offered or imposed upon various categories of criminals by ecclesiastical and secular courts, thus preserving a modicum of respectability for the offender and helping to restore a good reputation. While reformers complained of unregenerates corrupting the Holy Land or crusading armies, there was a long tradition of criminals, repentant or otherwise, taking the cross as a more honorable means of exculpating themselves than painfully humiliating public penances or legal penalties. With the potential of death and certitude of expense and temporary exile, the crusade punished offenders while protecting them from an irate community or victim's family. Those unable or unwilling to fulfill the obligations of their vow (voluntary or imposed) often passed its obligations to their heirs, who were forced to fulfill it in person, send a substitute, or pay a stiff fine. Drawn from the registers of Walter Giffard, archbishop of York (1266–1279), the cases printed here illustrate how various social, legal, and religious factors impacted an individual's decision to take the cross, and whether or not their vow was personally fulfilled or dispensed. The first case cited shows how one individual took advantage of the ability to absolve from excommunication imposed for serious offenses (which normally required a journey to Rome for absolution) commonly granted to those preaching the cross and organizing the crusade.

See Jessalynn Bird, "Vows," in Murray, The Crusades, 4:1233–1236; Michael R. Evans, "The Commutation of Crusade Vows: Some Examples from the English Midlands," in Alan V. Murray, ed., From Clermont to Jerusalem: The Crusades and Crusader Societies, 1095–1500 (Turnhout, 1998), 219–229; Mary Mansfield, The Humiliation of Sinners: Public Penance in Thirteenth-Century France (Ithaca NY, 1995); Maureen Purcell, Papal Crusading Policy.

Walter writes to the parish priest of Driffield, August 5, 1275.

. . . . WILLIAM of Driffield deserved to be signed with the character of the cross by us. Because of this, by the apostolic [papal] authority specially entrusted to us we were led to absolve him according to the form of the law from the sentence of excommunication which he incurred because he had rashly laid violent hands upon the clerics Simon Orre and Robert of Langtoft, since the injuries were not grave or enormous, and since he had

Source: William Brown, ed., The Register of Walter Giffard, Lord Archbishop of York, 1266–1279, Publications of the Surtees Society, vol. 109 (Durham, 1904), 280–282.

made competent satisfaction to the victims for the injuries suffered.[20] And we enjoined upon the same [William of Driffield] that he go personally to the Holy Land in the general passage, or that he donate half of all his possessions in aid to the said land if he is led to choose this option. And so we command that you cause the same to be publicly pronounced absolved of excommunication on these terms. . .

Walter, archbishop of York, writes to Helewysae Palmer and her daughter Isabella, September 2, 1275

. . . As WE gather from your account, at some point you uttered a vow to personally visit the threshold of the shrine of Saint James of Compostela. However, because you cannot fulfill the aforesaid vow by reason of your poverty, at your request we are led to convert that vow by apostolic [papal] authority to aid for the Holy Land by conferring the sign of the cross upon you. We enjoin you to pay two silver solidi in subsidy to the aforementioned Holy Land, when you are required to do so through the collectors specially deputed for this.

Walter writes to the dean of Herthil, 1275

. . . That in the octave of the Blessed Virgin Mary, in the year of grace 1275, at Skeffling [*Skelling'*] the nobleman, S., called Constable, a knight, appeared in our presence . . . and confessed with humble and contrite spirit that he carnally transgressed with Katherine wife of the knight John Danthorpe. While touching holy things [relics], he completely abjured her and any association with her and all suspect places, and bound himself at our decision . . . to aid the Holy Land with one hundred pounds sterling if he should relapse with the same woman. And weighing in our heart his contrition and mitigating the rigor of the sentence on account of his strengths, we entrusted to him the sign of the cross in that very place, such that he should go to the Holy Land in his own person or send a fitting warrior there at his own expense on account of the offense he committed.

---

20. That is, Walter informs William's parish priest of the lifting of the sentence of excommunication and the terms William must meet.

PART X
The Road to Acre, 1265–1291

Between 1198 and 1291 both Christendom and crusade underwent a number of substantial changes. Considering crusade, we can see that earlier military expeditions between 1096 and 1204 tended to be responses by various popes to particular crises in the Holy Land and their armies to be composed of aristocratic warriors (either kings or great lords) and their followers drawn broadly from across Christian Europe, regularly as pilgrims and individual warriors but after the establishment of the Latin Kingdom of Jerusalem in 1100 only on specific occasions as crusaders. After 1198 popes and jurists sharpened the definition of crusader status, and the components of crusade to the Holy Land and elsewhere—the papal or papal/conciliar invocation, appointing of preachers and preaching tours, recruitment, privileges, dispensations, and commutations—became more precisely identified, as did crusaders' obligations, responsibilities, methods of recruitment, military strategy, and purpose. During this same period, popes reached out to a broader Christian public, partly for financial support in the forms of contributions, dispensations, commutations, legacies, and donations, but also for devotional commitment to the crusade and its spiritual benefits—through preaching, confessions, forms of penance, processions, images, liturgies, indulgences, and vernacular literature. And Christendom made the crusade its own, as it had not yet done in the twelfth century.

Failure and defeat, which had ended the twelfth century with the loss at Hattin and the surrender of Jerusalem in 1187 and occurred in later crusades—the Fifth Crusade, for example, and the two crusades of Louis IX in 1248–1254 and 1270—did not turn Christendom away from the crusade ideal. Not even the fall of Constantinople to the Greeks in 1261, the failure of the crusade against Aragón in 1285, or the systematic Mamluk conquest of the last outposts in the Levant, culminating in the loss of Acre in 1291, could dislodge crusade from its now-integral place in Christendom. As before, critics might complain about some aspects of the planning, execution, or delay of a crusade or emphasize missionary activity or small-scale crusades over large military expeditions of the type of *passagium generale*, but crusade itself survived in papal ambitions, crusading plans, in the devotional ethos of chivalry, in the commitment of a number of territorial monarchs, and in the spiritual ideals of much of Christian society.[1] Christendom itself was now more firmly organized into parochial and diocesan structures managed by a more closely supervised clergy, reform-minded bishops, and aided by the extraordinary versatility and activity of the mendicant orders.

---

1. See the splendid study by Richard Kaeuper, *Holy Warriors: The Religious Ideology of Chivalry* (Philadelphia, 2009).

Yet for all the highly developed and increasingly articulated apparatus of crusade and the continued commitment to its ideals, after 1250 a number of structural features of crusading Europe underwent considerable transformation as a result of events that often had little to do with crusading but a great deal to do with sheer contingency. After midcentury, the role of the popes was largely reduced to the theological function of issuing spiritual and material privileges at the request of secular lords and the political role of urging secular participation. The last major expedition called out and organized by a pope was the Fifth Crusade; the last major attempt at asserting papal centrality was the canon *Constitutiones pro zelo fidei* issued by the crusade-minded Pope Gregory X (1271–1276) at the Second Council of Lyons in 1274 (below, No. 71). But no *passagium generale* could be assembled to follow it, nor did one follow the loss of Acre in 1291. Thus, we have to consider not only the place of crusade in Christendom during the thirteenth century and the changing nature of crusade itself, but also the particular historical circumstances that stimulated or limited crusade activity and determined various crusade components.

On September 1, 1271, after a vacancy in the papal office from 1268 to 1271, the cardinal-electors finally agreed on Tedaldo Visconti, archdeacon of Liège, who had taken the cross in London in 1267, traveled to the Holy Land, and was in the Holy Land with Lord Edward of England in 1270–1271 when he was elected. At his coronation in Rome on March 27, 1272, he took the papal name Gregory X (1271–1276). Within a week of his coronation, on March 31, 1272, Gregory issued the papal letter *Salvator noster*, calling for a general council to meet at Lyons in May 1274, a lead time comparable to that fixed by Innocent III for the Fourth Lateran Council. Its agenda consisted of church reform, reunion of the Latin and Greek churches, and the problem of the Holy Land. The text of *Salvator noster* left no uncertainty about the importance of crusade to the Holy Land. Invoking a theme long used in papal letters, Gregory cited Psalm 115:2, "And why will the heathen [Muslims] cry 'Where is their god?'" Like Innocent III in 1213, Gregory also asked for advice from some recipients. In Gregory's case a greater number of texts of advice, some of them extensive, have survived.[2]

Selections from the treatises of Gilbert of Tournai, a noted Franciscan, and Humbert of Romans, former minister general of the Order of Preachers are included below (Nos. 69–70). The council assembled on May 7, 1274, and adjourned on July 17, 1274, having sat longer than any of its predecessors. In attendance were three hundred bishops, sixty abbots, the ministers general of the major religious orders, many other prelates, and a single king, James I of Aragón,

2. There is an extensive discussion of these and a list in Sylvia Schein, *Fideles crucis: The Papacy, the West, and the Recovery of the Holy Land, 1274–1314* (Oxford, 1991), 269–270. In addition, see Kedar, *Crusade and Mission;* Anthony Leopold, *How to Recover the Holy Land: The Crusade Proposals of the Late Thirteenth and Early Fourteenth Centuries* (Aldershot UK-Burlington VT, 2000); Jacques Paviot, *Projets de croisade (v. 1290–v. 1330)* (Paris, 2008).

a ruler long interested in crusading.[3] Prominent theologians were on hand to advise the pope. Saint Bonaventure, OFM, was present and with Peter of Tarentaise, OP (who became Pope Innocent V for five months in 1276), was a major adviser to Gregory at the council, but Thomas Aquinas, OP, had died at Fossanova while en route to Lyons.

In many respects the council ended on an optimistic note. Gregory was already negotiating with Michael VIII Palaeologus, not only for the reunion of the Latin and Greek churches, but also for Byzantine military aid to a crusade, and the kings of France, England, Aragón, and Sicily had agreed to participate. On July 4, 1274, Gregory received Mongol ambassadors. On September 24, 1274, Gregory recognized the election of Rudolf of Habsburg as emperor. Furthermore, the council had done considerable work. It made provision for taxation of the clergy, including the pope and cardinals. It maintained collection points in churches. It demanded of all laity the donation of the local equivalent of one sterling or tournois with an additional yearly tax. It condemned pirates and traders of weapons with Muslims. In the canon *Ubi periculum* it set a rule for the election of popes that with very few changes is still in effect. Its great crusade canon, *Constitutiones pro zelo fidei* (below, No. 71), drew heavily on Innocent III's *Ad liberandam* and the First Council of Lyons' crusade canon.[4]

In addition, contingencies that reduced the opportunities for a crusade might change—in 1274 there was an emperor again, a committed pope, and a widely publicized and productive church council. Earlier Muslim regimes, notably the Ayyubids, had failed. Might not the Mamluks fail too? There still existed a substantial network of Mediterranean bases from which expeditions might be launched—Rhodes, Cyprus, Sicily, Aragón, even Constantinople. Europe retained maritime superiority in the Mediterranean. The Mongols, for a while, remained a potential ally. The memory of earlier crusade victories and heroism survived in chronicles and poetry. Finally, there was the promise of eschatology—that God on the eve of the end-time would preserve the Holy Land for his people.

Gradually a new program for crusading took shape. Some of the advice given to Gregory X appeared in crusade proposals in the following decades. The idea of shifting to a largely mercenary army, staffing permanent garrisons in the East; the combining of the military orders into a single superorder; the launching of small expeditions regularly (a perpetual phased crusade); a blockade of Egypt; more effective papal peacemaking efforts in Europe; the regular taxation of both clergy and laity; the responsibility of individual territorial monarchs—all of these begin to characterize the crusade movement in the early fourteenth century. But they could not be activated in the years immediately following 1274.

3. Damian J. Smith and Helena Buffery, *The Book of Deeds of James I of Aragon: A Translation of the Medieval Catalan Llibre dels fets*, Crusade Texts in Translation 10 (Aldershot UK-Burlington VT, 2003). James's *Llibre* is the first autobiography of a medieval monarch.

4. Parallel Latin texts of the 1215 and 1245 canons are printed in Purcell, *Papal Crusading Policy*, 196–199, with the 1274 canon.

Following the death of Gregory X in 1276, a series of short-lived popes and several periods when papal elections became impossible for longer than usual contributed to the restricted role of the papacy and the long delay in reviving Gregory's project. The pontificates of Gregory's immediate successors, Innocent V (January–June 1276), Hadrian V (July–August 1276), John XXI (September 1276–May 1277), Nicholas III (1277–1280), Martin IV (1281–1285), Honorius IV (1285–1287), and Nicholas IV (1288–1292) were all far too brief to organize a crusade, even though Innocent V, Nicholas III, and Nicholas IV were eager to do so, and Martin IV occupied himself with the crusade against Aragon on behalf of France and Angevin Italy. When Acre fell on May 28, 1291, Nicholas IV issued several papal calls in response, including the letter *Dirum amaritudinis* on August 13 and another on August 18, but he died a few months later, and the ensuing three-year papal interregnum prevented any response resembling that to *Audita tremendi* between 1187 and 1198. After the death of Nicholas IV rival interests among the cardinal-electors resulted in a vacancy in the papal office from April 4, 1292, until July 5, 1294, followed by the six-month pontificate of the saintly hermit Celestine V (July–December 1294), his astonishing resignation of the papal office, the highly controversial election of Boniface VIII (1294–1303) and the well-known ensuing chaos in papal diplomacy and rule and the accidental (but greatly influential) papal move to Avignon in 1308.

Nor did imperial affairs appear more promising. The deaths of Conrad IV in 1254 and those of Manfred in 1266 and Conradin in 1268 were the final acts in the disintegration of the Staufer territories and networks of Ghibelline allies in Italy and Germany. The interregnum between 1254 and the election of Rudolf of Habsburg in 1273 occupied the empire so that it, like the papacy, was essentially disabled from leading a crusade. Contending candidates for the imperial crown— William of Holland (d. 1256), Richard of Cornwall (d. 1272), and Alfonso X of Castile (d. 1275), the latter two elected by different groups of electors in the double election of 1257—and the vigorous efforts at internal pacification in Germany signaled by the establishment of the Rhine League in 1254 occupied German affairs until well after the end of the century. The turbulent conflicts of the northern Italian city-republics in the wake of imperial collapse and papal conflict exacerbating internal urban disputes temporarily removed these cities from crusade activity. The Greek conquest of Constantinople in 1261 meant that negotiations with the Byzantines were to be conducted on an entirely different plane, and not to the advantage of the Latins.

The initial success of Charles of Anjou and the Angevin dynasty in South Italy and Sicily after 1264, which included the initial geopolitical concern with the Byzantine Empire and Mediterranean interests, meant that the Angevin presence in Italy threatened to dominate papal policy nearly as much as had that of the Staufer—and stymied papal efforts at reuniting the Latin and Greek churches. With the revolt against Angevin rule in Palermo in 1282, known as the Sicilian Vespers, Sicilians called in the king of Aragón, Pedro III, who had married Constance, daughter of Manfred. The dispute led Pope Martin IV to call out a crusade

against Aragón, ultimately unsuccessful, and the issue was not settled until the
treaty of Caltabelotta in 1302.[5]

Nor was the organization of Christian power in Cyprus and the kingdom of
Jerusalem amenable to focused crusade activity. After the deposition of Conradin
as king of Jerusalem by Clement IV in 1268, the power of any king of Jerusalem
was continuously weakened by the fractious nobility. The military orders pursued
independent military and political policies and offered little cooperation with other
powers, and the mercantile colonies from Italy and elsewhere pursued their own
self-interest, especially when crusade proposals entailed an embargo of trade with
Muslims. The sheer economic dynamism of the Mediterranean as a trade empo-
rium was often in conflict with geopolitical concerns on the part of Western rulers
and popes. Not even the heroic and intelligent policies of Louis IX as overlord of
Outremer from 1250 to 1254, increasing the strength of coastal defenses, establishing a garrison at Acre, and personally negotiating successfully with contending
forces within the kingdom had significant lasting effects. But it also proved that a
king was needed who could rule strongly. Such were the rulers of the territorial
monarchies of Europe, but not the kingdom of Jerusalem.

On the other hand, of course, was the sheer political and military power of
Mamluk Egypt under Baibars, Qalawun, and their successors. The old problems
of Muslim rule—the Damascus-Cairo rivalry, the Mongol threat, and occasionally
effective or at least threatening European military enterprises—were transformed
after 1260. The prestige of the Mamluk victory over the Mongols at 'Ain Jalut in
1260 only grew greater as Baibars united northern Syria (conquering Damascus
and Aleppo) and shaped a highly militarized society that made him the sultan of
the Muslim world. Professing himself, like Saladin, but even more effectively, to
be a *mujahid* and a patron of religion, Baibars ruled autocratically, organized state
finances, and established a communications network throughout his empire that
rivaled any in the world. He rebuilt fortifications and encouraged the recruitment
of troops, while at the same time encouraging the technical development of siege
weapons and military/political intelligence. In terms of siege craft, numerical superiority, and technological achievement, he proved far too formidable an enemy for
the unorganized powers of the European world and of Outremer.

In 1265 his forces took Arsuf, Caesarea, and Jaffa. In 1266 he took the great
Templar inland fortress of Safad. In 1268 he took Antioch. In 1271 he gained the
surrender by the Knights Hospitaller of the great castle of Krak des Chevaliers and

---

5. Runciman, *The Sicilian Vespers*, needs to be used with caution. Norman Housley,
Documents on the Later Crusades, 1274–1580 (London-New York, 1996), translates the bull
of Martin IV of April 5, 1284, proclaiming the crusade against Peter of Aragón (25–27) as
well as a list of French expenses for the crusade (27–28). The work of David Abulafia is of
considerable value, especially *Italy, Sicily, and the Mediterranean, 1100–1400* (Aldershot
UK-Burlington VT, 1987); *Commerce and Conquest in the Mediterranean, 1100–1500*
(Aldershot UK-Brookfield VT, 1993), and *Mediterranean Encounters: Economic, Religious,
Political, 1100–1550* (Aldershot UK-Burlington VT, 2000); see also Powell, *The Crusades,
the Kingdom of Sicily, and the Mediterranean.*

in the same year the Teutonic Knights' fortress of Montfort. One by one the coastal cities fell to Baibars, who died in 1277. His successors Qalawun (1279–1290) and al-Ashraf Khalil took the castle at Marqab in 1285 and Latakia in 1287. Although the arrival and effectiveness of Lord Edward (later Edward I, 1272–1307) delayed the siege of Tripoli, the city nonetheless fell to al-Ashraf Khalil in 1289. Finally, the greatest of the coastal cities, Acre, fell in May 1291. The rest was mopping up: Tyre fell in May 1291, Sidon in June 1291, Beirut, Château Pélerin, and Tortosa in July 1291. The kingdom of Jerusalem settled in Cyprus and the military orders in Malta and Rhodes until the sixteenth century. The other great threat to the Mamluks, the Ilkhanate of Persia, was finally defeated at the battle of Homs on October 29, 1281. From 1260 to 1291 the Mamluks had achieved far more than the Ayyubids, and their vast Muslim state survived into the sixteenth century.

The years 1198–1291 bracket a particular part of crusade history. The role of crusade and its place in Christian society is one dominant feature of this part. Most of the treatises of advice requested by Gregory X and most of the subsequent proposals over the next several decades regarding crusade had a variation of the title "On the Recovery of the Holy Land." None of them indicated that such a goal was impossible. The recovery of the Holy Land remained high on the agenda of all of Christendom.

The best studies remain Sylvia Schein, Fideles crucis: The Papacy, the West, and the Recovery of the Holy Land, 1274–1314 *(Oxford, 1991); and Norman Housley,* The Later Crusades, 1274–1580: From Lyons to Alcazar *(Oxford, 1992); and Housley's collection of translated texts,* Documents on the Later Crusades, 1274–1580 *(London-New York, 1996). In the latter volume Housley shrewdly observes that the apparent homogeneity of crusade components after the late thirteenth century "has led some commentators to see the later crusades as essentially ossified and homogeneous. But this was far from the case. Much of the vitality which historians are increasingly identifying was facilitated by the malleability of crusading's essential features. They were building blocks which could be put together in a number of different ways"* (Documents, 2–3). *See also James M. Powell, "Church and Crusade: Frederick II and Louis IX," Catholic Historical Review 93 (2007), 251–264, and Powell's parallel essay, "A Vacuum of Leadership: 1291 Revisited," in Balard,* La Papauté et les croisades, *165–171. On Baibars and the early Mamluk sultanate, see Peter Thorau,* The Lion of Egypt: Sultan Baybars and the Near East in the Thirteenth Century, *trans. P. M. Holt (London-New York, 1992); Robert Irwin,* The Middle East in the Middle Ages: The Early Mamluk Sultanate, 1250–1382 *(London, 1986); Robert Irwin,* Mamluks and Crusaders: Men of the Sword and Men of the Pen *(Farnham UK-Burlington VT, 2010).*

69. Gilbert of Tournai on Reform and Crusade, ca. 1272–1274

The treatise *Collectio de scandalis ecclesiae* was written by the Franciscan Gilbert of Tournai in response to Gregory X's call for proposals for the Second Council of Lyons (1274). Largely devoted to issues of the reform of the clergy, the regular religious, and the laity, all of which were deemed essential for the recovery of the Holy Land, Gilbert's treatise was based partly on the criticisms made by earlier writers, including James of Vitry. The section translated here deals directly with crusade as a component of larger reform. Gilbert was minister general of his order, which, with the Dominicans, was responsible for most of the promotion of the crusades. He knew Louis IX well and may have preached Louis's first crusade. Some of his suggestions, notably that of a general tax, were adopted at the Second Council of Lyons, while others, notably the permanent presence of mercenary armies in the Holy Land, became a prevalent theme among later writers of crusade treatises that sought to address the failure of popes and secular rulers to organize the massive coordinated departures that had marked previous crusades. Some of Gilbert's criticisms of crusade financing are echoed in the register of his fellow Franciscan, Eudes Rigaud, archbishop of Rouen, who played a considerable role in promoting Louis IX's failed crusade of 1270 and also presided over the Second Council of Lyons during the absence of Gregory X (see above, No. 55).

See A. Stroick, "Verfasser und Quellen der Collectio de scandalis ecclesiae *(Reform-schrift des Fr. Gilbert von Tournay, OFM, zum II. Konzil von Lyon, 1274),"* Archivum francis-canum historicum *23 (1930), 3–41, 273–299, 433–466; Anthony Leopold,* How to Recover the Holy Land: The Crusade Proposals of the Late Thirteenth and Early Fourteenth Centu-ries *(Aldershot UK-Burlington VT, 2000), 13–14; and the work of Palmer Throop,* Criticism of the Crusade, *69–104 (the best English summary of Gilbert's treatise for the Second Council of Lyons); Siberry,* Criticism of Crusading; *and Schein,* Fideles crucis; *Cole,* Preaching, *194–202; Maier,* Crusade Propaganda and Ideology, *176–209, 250–263. For further criticism of financing, see Housley,* Documents, *21–25.*

ALREADY our inheritance has been handed over to strangers, our home to foreigners [Lam 5:2]; for we have lost that land which the Lord conse-crated with his own blood. Nor has one sealed with the sign of the cross delivered it. Already as the price for our sins the Christian people have often been infused with shame. The enemies of the cross of Christ, who loathe the Lord, lift up their head [Ps 82:3] and those who hate Sion [Ps 128:5] frequently boast, saying in their hearts: we will cause the name of Christ to fall quiet, and we will abolish his temple and his people from this land. Certainly it is necessary that the Muhammadan sect should fall and that the scarlet beast should rush to its ruin. But let him who has knowledge reckon the number of the beast [Apoc 13:17, 17:1–7]. Yet a remedy ought to be applied, that is, let a pilgrimage [crusade] or another form of assistance not be accomplished from the sweat of the poor, from the despoliation of churches. Just as on account of these and very similar things and a manifold enormity of sin the sons of Ephraim aiming and

*Source: Gilbert of Tournai, "*Collectio de scandalis ecclesiae: Nova Editio," *ed. A. Stroick,* Archivum franciscanum historicum *24 (1931), 33–62.*

loosing their bows were routed on the day of battle [Ps 77:9], so we did not succeed in our pilgrimages, for from days of old strife was poured out upon the princes [Ps 106:40], so that they do not enjoy success, and it disunites the church. The Lord allowed them to perish in vain, because the inheritance was wrested profitlessly from the children by a stranger, nor is Christ therefore set free when a Christian is injured. But when the Hebrews were plundered, the Egyptians were enriched.

Another confusion results from the redemption of vows through certain men who rate the sums paid for redemption, who with a foolish fist beat down the feeble and disabled and those who have taken the cross under predetermined conditions with secular justice and ecclesiastical censures, and wring more money from them by threatening them with judicial sentences and new, undue, and increasing valuations. This scandal has redounded upon the heads of those preaching the crusade. If they preached the indulgence of the cross anew, it is not certain that they would make progress; but it is certain that they would suffer various insults. So then, let the church devote itself to public prayers, let there be a general contribution, let stipendiary troops be hired, who renewed against the succeeding vicissitudes will be bound to remain in that land and pursue the Lord's war and the business of the church; and with those the salaries of the prayers of the universal church ought to be established so that through the raising of hands in prayer, Moses might vanquish Amalek fighting against Israel, and the walls of Jericho might fall before the priests' clamorings [Ex 17:8–13; Jo 6:1–27]. Papal legates ought not to perform the collection of monies. They ought to be motivated not by an eye for profit but by the glory of Christ, the honor of the church, and the salvation of the people.

70. Humbert of Romans, *Opusculum tripartitum*, ca. 1272–1274

Humbert of Romans, formerly master general of the Order of Preachers (1254–1263), wrote several works on preaching, including one called *On Preaching the Holy Cross Against the Saracens*. His *Opusculum tripartitum*, like Gilbert of Tournai's treatise above, was written in response to Gregory X's appeal for advice on matters that faced the Second Council of Lyons. Humbert focused on crusade, reunion of the Latin and Greek churches, and overall ecclesiastical reform.

As master general of his order, Humbert of Romans had overseen the involvement of the Dominican order in missions and the promotion of various crusades. In addition to the treatise written for the crusade preachers of his order, Humbert wrote another full of suggestions for the agenda of the Second Council of Lyons (1274). Although it shares the reforming fervor of Gilbert's treatise, Humbert became more specific in his recommendations for the difficulties facing the organization of a new crusade. Humbert's advice takes the typical form of an academic treatise, which lists by number arguments and counterarguments bolstered by recourse to authorities, including logic, the sacred scriptures, and canon law.

After recounting what he and many others perceived as past and present threats facing Christianity, including the "barbarians" opposing the Roman Empire, the Tartars, Jews, and heretics, and the "pagans" in the Baltic, Humbert presented Islam as the most potent of them all. Countering those such as William of Tripoli, OP, who argued eloquently for missionizing rather than military crusading, Humbert argued that what he viewed as the specious appeal of Islam made its adherents virtually impossible to convert.[6] He then proceeded to counter various criticisms of the crusade and to offer suggestions for its organization. These suggestions were followed by lengthy treatments of the origin and proposed remedy for the schism between the Greek and Latin churches, and the reform of the clergy, including tirades against abuses associated with the crusades. It could be argued that Humbert's treatise was perhaps the most influential of those submitted in shaping the agenda for the Second Council of Lyons. Many of his suggestions, including that of the creation of a perpetual and permanently funded body of professional warriors in service of the Holy Land, were adopted by later writers of crusade treatises.

Edward Tracy Brett, Humbert of Romans: His Life and Views of Thirteenth-Century Society *(Toronto, 1984); Throop,* Criticism, *147–213, 261; James A. Brundage, "Humbert of Romans and the Legitimacy of Crusader Conquests," in B. Z. Kedar, ed.,* The Horns of Hattin *(Jerusalem-London, 1992), 302–313. On Humbert's treatise on preaching the cross, see Cole,* Preaching, *202–217; Humbert's own crusade sermons are in Maier,* Crusade Propaganda and Ideology, *210–229.*

Humbert's text argues in great detail for the reasons that ought to move Christians to attack Saracens, providing an arsenal of arguments from canon law and theology to justify the crusade as a holy and just war, to assert that if Christianity had not opposed the military might of various Muslim powers by the sword, it would

6. William of Tripoli, Notitia de Machometo: De statu Sarracenorum: *Kommentierte lateinisch-deutsche Textausgabe,* ed. Peter Engels (Würzburg, 1992); Thomas F. O'Meara, "The Theology and Times of William of Tripoli, OP: A Different View of Islam," *Theological Studies* 69 (2008), 80–98; R. I. Burns, SJ, "Christian-Islamic Confrontation in the West: The Thirteenth-Century Dream of Conversion," *American Historical Review* 76 (1971), 1386–1405; *Les dominicains et les mondes musulmans* (Paris, 2002). For another important figure, Ricoldo da Montecroce, OP (ca. 1242–1320), *Pérégrination en Terre Sainte et au Proche Orient: Texte latin et traduction: Lettres sur la chute de Saint-Jean d'Acre,* trans. René Kappler (Paris, 1997).

have been conquered completely, and to stress that Christians who died in what he carefully defines as defensive just wars were martyrs pleasing to God.[7] Humbert emphasizes that Christians have a just cause and, unless their sins alienate them, possess God, the saints, and angels as their allies and therefore can overcome any adverse material circumstances. To fail to oppose the Muslims is comparable to the effects of heresy. Above all, Christians are not to despair. Any tepidness regarding the crusade results in a lack of manly advice, begrudging assistance for the crusade project, discouragement of others, endangerment of Christendom's defense and encouragement of its adversaries. To contravene this, he suggests the following remedies.

. . . IT OUGHT to be noted, that it would be very profitable if in the church of God there were some upright and wise men who would be fired up regarding the promotion of this particular project. And so that this might be understood more clearly, it ought to be noted that the world was at one time converted to Christ partly through preaching, partly through miracles, and in part through the examples of holiness which were seen in those preaching. But the Saracens cut themselves off from the way of preaching, because according to their law they behead every man who would want to preach to them anything against the law or sect of Muhammad. Likewise the time of miracles is not at present, because God does not go forth at this time through our strengths. Moreover, Christians' examples of holiness do not move the Saracens, because they prefer their prayers, their fasting, their almsgiving, their pilgrimages, and similar things to ours: in fact, what is even more absurd, they prefer their incontinence to our continence, calling the continence of Christians superstition, as is clear in the letter of a certain Saracen which urges a certain Christian, his friend, to accept the law of Muhammad.[8]

Therefore, missions to them ought to be abandoned, because there is no longer any hope for their conversion according to the customary course. And for this reason it follows, that as long as they remain in the world, they will multiply without measure unless they are destroyed by some Christian or barbarian power. For this reason it is customarily said that just as Muhammad conquered the world through the sword, so

Source: Humbert of Romans, Opusculum tripartitum, *185–229, here 188–189, 191–201, 204–206, 227.*

7. A number of key texts from canon law are translated by James M. Muldoon in *Fighting Words: Competing Voices from the Crusades*, ed. Andrew Holt and James Muldoon (Oxford-Westport CT, 2008), 259–273.

8. Humbert appears to be referring to one of the centerpieces of the repertoire of anti-Islamic treatises used by Western writers—the *Risalat* of al-Kindi, which Peter the Venerable had translated into Latin in the twelfth century.

through the sword he would be destroyed, in accordance with that authority: "He who lives by the sword will perish by the sword" [Mt 26:52]. Moreover, it ought to be noted that, as is written in the transmarine history of Master James of Vitry,[9] the Lord appeared to Peter the Hermit in a dream when he was keeping vigil in the church of the Lord's resurrection and enjoined a legation upon him, that he should go to Pope Urban and to the Western princes so that they might lend aid to the Christians in the Holy Land trampled upon by the Saracens.[10] Similarly Turpin says in a letter concerning the acts of Charles [Charlemagne] in Spain, that Saint James appeared to Charles in his dreams, exhorting him three times, that just as he had conquered many other lands, so he ought to go into Spain and free his country from the Saracens, so that a way would be provided for the faithful to visit him in perpetuity.[11] From these it is clear that it is pleasing to God and to the saints that the Christian faithful purify countries from the Saracens through warfare. For formerly God similarly wanted the sons of Israel to expel the gentiles from the promised land through warfare, so that where previously dreadful things hateful to God were done, the worship of God might be established.

Nonetheless, it ought to be noted that this kind of project is extremely difficult for Christians both because of the remoteness of places and on account of the perils of the sea and many other things, and for that reason many are very lukewarm regarding that project. However, because there is no hope, according to human judgments, that the Saracens will ever be converted from their error, and it is the will of God and the saints that they be expunged through warfare, and on account of the trouble facing those engaged in this project, there will be many Christians who are extremely lukewarm toward it, [and] it would be very profitable for some upright men who would be fired up about it to spur on other tepid persons, so that this very scandal might be removed from the world

9. See Jacques de Vitry, *Historia orientalis*. For a partial English translation of this history, see Jacques de Vitry, *History of Jerusalem: A.D. 1180*, trans. Aubrey Stewart, Palestine Pilgrims Text Society, vol. 11 (London, 1896; repr., New York, 1971). For a new edition and French translation, see Jean Donnadieu, ed. and trans., *Jacques de Vitry: Histoire orientale/Historia orientalis* (Turnhout, 2008).

10. Humbert here follows the emphasis on Peter the Hermit's role in launching the First Crusade that was contained in the *historia* of Albert of Aachen and taken up by William of Tyre.

11. That is, at Saint James's shrine in Compostela. Humbert here refers to the twelfth-century Pseudo-Turpin chronicle [*Historia Caroli Magni*], which together with the *Song of Roland* and other vernacular accounts spread the legend of Charlemagne's exploits against the Moors in Spain and were frequently invoked in crusade propaganda.

through human power with the assistance of God and the worship of God might be enlarged in their lands. O the disgrace of our times! Formerly one poor hermit, that is, Peter of Amiens, roaming throughout Christian lands, stirred up and set almost all Christendom on fire regarding this very project. And yet in our times hardly any great man can be found who would spur on others, and even those roused could hardly be kindled to considerable fervor regarding entertaining this project. . . .

After urging the pope to promote a new crusade through publicizing indulgences and appointing preachers and other measures enshrined in the decree Ad liberandam *of the Fourth Lateran Council (1215), Humbert draws on his prior treatise on preaching the crusade for a stock of arguments to be used in promoting the crusade.*

FOR CHRISTENDOM is downcast at heart, and yet it would not be of noble and burning spirit to desist from a just war on account of previous disastrous results, particularly when it is acceptable to God. For this very reason upright warriors are accustomed after an occurrence of this sort to devise novel stratagems for pursuing that undertaking. However there are three special reasons, among others, why we ought not to desist. One is the salvation of Christians. For countless persons have been and will be saved in the prosecution of this business, who perhaps otherwise would never have died in a state of salvation. Another matter is the repression of the Saracens. For unless they had been checked through this kind of struggle, they would perhaps have already seized virtually all of Christendom. Third is the hope of triumphing in the end. For Christians ought never to despair, for truly they will finally obtain victory over the Saracens, even if the Lord, for the sake of certain reasons known only to him, until the present has postponed it and has often permitted us to be beaten and slaughtered by them.

On the other hand, there are many examples, both in ancient histories and in our own, for confirming Christians in this hope. Throughout the entire book of Judges we read that the enemies of Israel often prevailed against them, but when they used to cry out to the Lord, he would unexpectedly send to them certain men, through whose hands they would triumph over their enemies. Similarly, when the sons of Israel were completely overcome by the men of Ai during their entry into the promised land and many were slain, after they humiliated themselves before the Lord and performed penance for the offense of Achan, when they returned against that city, and assailed it through various ruses at the

Lord's command, they obtained victory and razed the city after killing everyone in it [Jo 7]. Furthermore, the sons of Israel, after being beaten twice by the sons of Benjamin, returned to battle after prayers and fasting and weeping and burnt sacrifices and conquered them [Jgs 20]. Moreover, in the book of the Maccabees, we read that Antiochus rose up against the Jews and profaned the temple and burned their books and plagued them with countless cruelties and desiring to abolish their law, introduced the law of the gentiles among them. But when Matthias and Judas his son and his brothers opposed him, we read concerning them that afterward they often obtained glorious victories [1 Mc]. There are also many other similar things in the old law regarding the triumphs achieved by the Jews over the gentiles who had often vanquished them.

So then, if anyone would want to know in what way our men, who were defeated many times by the Saracens, afterward often obtained glorious victories over them, let him read the history of the acts of Charles [the Great] in Spain. Let him also read the Antiochene history, and also the transmarine history.[12] And let him also peruse other histories, of which there are many, which testify concerning the same things. And he will discover how there are certain senseless people in our time, who on account of disastrous results think that we ought to desist from the struggle with the Saracens. At the time when these very same Saracens used to occupy Sicily, they also took Sardinia and pillaged Genoa, that most noble of cities, and also attacked various locations on the seacoast and laid waste to many more in Italy, Provence, Catalonia, and Spain. They also occupied all of Spain. Reaching as far as the Aquitaine, they captured many cities and killed countless Christians without mercy. But through the mercy of God, through Christian might they were expelled from all these regions, except for [one] corner of Spain. [And] in this province, albeit recently, throughout the kingdom of Aragón, the city of Valencia, and the kingdom of Majorca, and throughout the kingdom of Castile, particularly in the city of Seville, [these regions] were rewon from them.

Nor do they now dare to attack any of our places anywhere along the coast, because their power upon the sea is reckoned as nothing in comparison to our sea power. Why therefore ought one to despair, nay on the contrary why ought one not to hope that God, who gave to his

12. By Humbert's day, these literary works and others were widely known, and Humbert moves without hesitation from Old Testament stories to more recent Christian stories. He refers here to the Pseudo-Turpin's *Historia Caroli Magni*, probably the *Historia Antiochena* of Fulcher of Chartres, and the *Historia orientalis* of James of Vitry.

Christians such a great victory over them, will not bring his work to completion at an opportune time, hidden to us, but known to himself alone? Since God is powerful indeed, either through the death of sultans, just as through the death of Holofernes he gave victory over his enemies [Jdt 10–14], or through striking them with terror, as at one time he did to the Syrians [2 Kgs 6:8–24], or through a divinely sent plague, as he once did in the camps of the Assyrians [2 Kgs 19:35], or through countless other means known to himself alone, and proceeding according to his own desire, he will lead the Christian conception concerning eradicating the Saracens to a successful conclusion, to his honor and glory.

. . . In order to laudably accomplish this project, I believe that prayers, deliberations, and consultations with those associated with it will be necessary. . . . Since it will be project common to Christendom, public prayers ought to be conducted. And because God does not listen to sinners, greater corrections than usual ought to be enforced everywhere, lest sin impede these prayers. And because it does not suffice to absolve from sin unless satisfaction is made for past offenses, amends ought to be made through communal repentance through some fasts and almsgiving and communal processions and other things of this sort which customarily appease God's anger. For examples and authorities, both from the Bible and from other sources, teach how much power these practices possess, and to how great an extent they are customarily performed in similar cases.

Regarding deliberations, it ought to be noted that as pertains to the desire to efficaciously promote this project, one ought to frequently and for a long time ponder the same business with much deliberation and ought not to suddenly dispose anything. And because talking together customarily contributes much to prudent deliberation, one ought often to confer about this with men suitable for this. And because, once more, the knowledge of our forebearers contributes much to discussions of this kind, one ought to diligently examine ancient histories and [accounts of] deeds pertaining to this put into writing by our forebearers, because through these kinds of former exploits current deliberation is instructed in many things which ought to be accomplished in the future. So then, for confirming this there are many authorities and examples which can be easily found by those who are interested in things of this sort. . . . But one ought to note that there are three kinds of persons who are not suitable for [giving] this kind of advice. One is the inexperienced. For what can they advise concerning accomplishing anything whatsoever, who never learned about these things from experience? Another is the unwilling. For those who have no heart for this business will never give spirited advice concerning it. Third is wicked persons. For these do not possess the spirit of God within themselves. And for this reason there is no hope that the spirit of God, from whom every befitting plan flows, will speak through their mouths. And so for giving counsel concerning this project one ought to choose not indifferently any person whatsoever, but rather the experienced and those devoted to this project, and men whom it is believed possess the spirit of God.

. . . What the general opinion of men is concerning the promotion of this business ought to be noted. Some believe that it ought to be arranged that to those men who are overseas and are fit for battle, both the regular religious[13] and other men, ought to be added a great host of fighters, both mounted men and foot soldiers, who could remain continually in that army, because then it could be plausibly hoped that our men would be able to prevail against the Saracens at all times. However, for this task, men ought to be chosen who are equal to labors of this sort and of a good life, and of such a kind as would not only have eyes for their stipends, as mercenaries do, but would possess zeal for the faith. And whenever any of them died, or were expelled from this kind of fellowship because of a wicked way of life, others should always be appointed in their place. . . . For it is likely that because of the small number of our men, or because of the discontinuation of the war, or because of the weakness of persons, or because of the evil lives of the many, or because of the lack of zeal for the project, this business has been less than successful up to this moment.

If, however, it is asked from what place can such great and continuous stipends necessary for fighters of this kind be procured, it can be said that such great riches exist in Christendom that unless both inclination and shrewdness were lacking to Christians in attending to it, they could be procured readily and without much inconvenience. For even if we were to remain altogether silent concerning the assistance of kings and princes and counts and laypersons, and held a discussion concerning only those ecclesiastical persons who are subject to the pope, what harm would there be to the faith of the churches . . . [if the] gold and silver and precious stones, which are encrusted upon superfluous vessels and crosses and things of this sort which exist in every single diocese, were sold to provide

13. That is, the military orders.

revenue to be applied to this kind of perpetual project? Moreover, what damage would occur if in the cathedral churches and other wealthy chapters where there are many canons, their number were diminished to some extent, and the incomes of the prebends subtracted in this manner were likewise devoted to this very use? On the other hand, what harm would it be if from the priories of the regular religious, which are spread throughout the world without number, and in which the religious living in a very lax manner cause scandal to those living in the world, many were devoted to the same use? And likewise the same thing ought to be done with ruined abbeys, concerning which there is no hope that they can ever be successfully reformed. Similarly, what harm would it be to the faith if some part of vacant and rich benefices were devoted to this same project for one or more years?

However, there are also many other things pertaining to ecclesiastical persons and laypersons which worldly wisdom would better know how to devise, which would ascend beyond human appraisal, if they were brought to effect and would forever strengthen this business. And from certain movable possessions pertaining to this, perpetual revenues could be bought, forever deputed to this business, and everything deputed to this would be rewarded by indulgences and ecclesiastical protection. But because the wisdom of this world would be very much afraid that once that particular time had elapsed these funds would be transferred through the Roman Church to other uses, lest by this occasion progress be impeded in this manner, it would be advantageous to find a suitable remedy against this, so that as the sacred council draws near,[14] this very project might be promoted to the glory of Christ and the exaltation of the Christian faith and the salvation of souls. And if, perchance, permanent remedies cannot be procured, they ought at least to be procured for as long a time as can be obtained.

. . . It ought to be noted, that before the gathering of the council certain things ought to be set in motion which are able to have great influence upon the advancing of this project. One is that all efficacious arguments which can stir the hearts of Christians to aid Christendom against the Saracens ought to be set down in writing in suitable and short words, so that they can be shown at the proper time to those men to whom it will seem useful. For there are many, not only from the laity, but also from the clergy, who know virtually nothing of Muhammad and of

14. What would become the Second Council of Lyons (1274).

the Saracens, except that they hear that there are certain infidels who do not believe in Christ and think that these Saracens view Muhammad as their God, which, however is false.

Another thing is that with the counsel of wise men, both of the learned and of laymen as well, and particularly of noblemen who might cherish this project in their hearts, and with assiduous examination every kind of aid ought to be devised which can be requested whether from the prelates, or from the clergymen, or from the regular religious, or from princes, or from communes on behalf of this project: and let these be put into writing in a short form and with some arguments, so that these things can be shown at the appropriate time either together or separately to those to whom it seems beneficial. . . .

Before the council, from every single country or province ought to be convoked some prelates and men of such a nature, who it is hoped might cherish this project in their hearts and prove suitable for persuading others. And these distinguished men ought to be solicited by the lord pope and effectually induced by the same to personally promote this project before the other prelates of their country or provinces, so that through this kind of advance preparation they might give better advice at the council.[15] At regular intervals the lord pope ought to send official messengers to kings and princes, who would seem to benefit from this with letters including the aforementioned arguments. They ought to diligently explain this business to them and to those noblemen whom they can engage and lead them to lend assistance to this project. And these messengers ought to be accompanied by some noblemen, who might hold this project in their hearts, and would know how, with the aforesaid messengers, to persuade these magnates. For there are many things which ought to move magnates to this business, in addition to the arguments which pertain to everyone in common.

One is the power entrusted to them by God. For every person is bound to serve his lord from the fief which he holds from him. And so, just as clerks are obligated to serve God by the knowledge which they have from God and rich men by the wealth which they have from God, so too powerful men from the power which they hold, since they hold it from God alone. Another is the examples of the Old Testament. For it is found there that kings and magnates always fought against the Philistines

15. That is, at the Second Council of Lyons (1274).

and other enemies of that people. However the prophets were not accustomed to fight, equally the priests. But the prophets used to exhort and the priests offered up sacrifices and prayers on their behalf.

Another is the example of the New Testament, in which is found that magnates always prosecuted that very occupation against the Saracens, as is clear in the case of Charles [Charlemagne], who at the urging of Saint James, who appeared to him, twice went into Spain to expel the Saracens from that place, and so that he might have many of his men with him in his host, he granted many privileges to the Franks on this account. The same behavior is manifest in many other kings and countless magnates, who for the sake of this project tendered themselves and their possessions and their men, crossing the sea.

Another is the necessity of penance, which those who sin inevitably have to accomplish. However, how could they accomplish a more glorious penance than to serve God with their weapons, which they cannot customarily carry during fasts and afflictions of this sort? Another is office. For these men are ministers of the King of kings, according to that which the apostle intimates, saying of such "[for he is] a minister of God [for you for the good. However, if you do evil you ought to fear him, not without reason, for he carries the sword of God]," etc. [Rom 13:4]. And so, just as it pertains in the highest degree to the bailiffs of the king to resist the enemies of their king, so also it pertains in the extreme to those magnates to resist the spiritual enemies of God, that is, the Saracens. Another is nobility. For when there is warfare between two kingdoms, it pertains more to noblemen than to others to fight. And on that account, when the Saracens attack Christendom, this war pertains more to noble Christians than to others. Another is shame. For every nobleman, if he were inside some besieged castle, would consider himself put to shame, unless he resisted more than others on behalf of his men. How great a disgrace it therefore is for the noblemen who are among Christendom, unless they resist more than any other the Saracens besieging it, for the sake of their men? And there are many other things which can stir men up if they are investigated industriously.

71. Gregory X at the Second Council of Lyons, 1274

The Second Council of Lyons, discussed extensively in the headnote to this chapter, was announced by Gregory X (1271–1276) in the letter *Salvator noster* within a week of his coronation at Rome on March 27, 1272. Gregory, who had attended the First Council of Lyons in 1245, had been elected following a vacancy in the papal succession of two years and nine months and had been in the Holy Land in 1270–1271 when he was elected pope. There was much local work for a new pope in these circumstances to do, and the curia was not very interested in long-range crusading prospects. But Gregory firmly put Holy Land crusade at the head of his conciliar agenda, along with the reunion of the Greek and Latin churches and moral reform. The similarity with the Fourth Lateran Council of 1215 was striking, and Gregory opened the Second Council of Lyons on May 7, 1274, with a sermon on the same text that Innocent III had used on the earlier occasion. The crusade constitution *Zelus fidei*, promulgated at the second session, echoed the constitution *Ad liberandam* of the Fourth Lateran Council. Unlike Innocent III, however, Gregory had seen for himself the situation in the Holy Land, the suffering of Christians, and the need for liberation. And Gregory wanted crusaders suitable for battle. Others might share in crusade spiritual benefits, but only fighters were to go, financed by clergy and laity alike.

But for all of Gregory's dedication and energy, both the crusade plan and the union with the Greeks collapsed, and only some of the ecclesiological work of the council survived. The crusade collapsed when Gregory's successors failed to gain the support of England and France and turned their attention instead to the conflict between Pedro III of Aragón and Charles of Anjou over the matter of Sicily and Charles's concern to reestablish a Latin Empire in Constantinople, further alienating the Greeks. *Zelus fidei* had been a clarion call to recover the Holy Land as resonant as *Ad liberandam*. But there were few to answer it. And the circumstances of the later thirteenth and early fourteenth century meant that the cause of the Holy Land had to be considered in new ways.

THE HEARTS of the faithful ought to be aroused by zeal for the faith, ardent devotion, and compassionate affection, such that all who take pride in the Christian name, touched inwardly by heartfelt sorrow [cf. Gn 6:6] from the injury done to their Redeemer, might openly and mightily rise up for God's sake for the defense and assistance of the Holy Land. Who, imbued with the light of the true faith, and meditating with devout consideration upon the extraordinary blessings which our Savior bestowed upon humankind in the Holy Land, which is the rope [measuring out] the Lord's inheritance [Ps 104:11], would not be moved to compassionate love in their innermost parts and with their entire being? Whose heart would not melt with compassion for that very land where by our Creator so great a love was manifested by proofs? But alas, for shame! That very land in which the Lord saw fit to work our salvation [Ps 73:12],

---

Source: J. Alberigo et al., eds., Conciliorum oecumenicorum decreta *(Bologna, 1973), const. 1(a–d), pp. 309–314.*

and so that he might redeem mankind by the price of his death, he consecrated with his own blood, has been for a long time invaded by the most impious enemies of the Christian name, the blasphemous and faithless Saracens, who moved by their temerity, have for a long time kept it in [a state of] fear and undauntedly laid it waste. The Christian people have been savagely butchered in that land, both to the more grievous affront to the Creator and to the injury and affliction of all who profess the catholic faith. Where is the God of the Christians? [Ps 41:11] They have mocked [us] with many taunts, insulting the worshippers of Christ.

These very things and other things which neither our soul suffices to fully comprehend or our tongue to relate aroused our heart and awakened our soul so that we, who not only heard in the aforementioned regions overseas but saw with our own eyes and touched with our own hands [1 Jn 1:1], might rise up, as far as our ability lies, to avenge the insult to the Crucified, with the intervening assistance of those consumed by zeal and devotion for the faith. And because the liberation of the aforementioned land ought to affect all who profess the catholic faith, we have ordered a council to be convoked, so that after having consulted with prelates, kings, and princes, and other experienced men in it, we might arrange and enact in Christ those things through which the liberation of the aforesaid land might be achieved; and, no less, that the Greek people, who have endeavored with insolent necks to rend the seamless tunic of the Lord [cf. Jn 19:23] to some degree, and have withdrawn themselves from allegiance and obedience to the Apostolic See, might be returned to unity with the [Latin] church; and to reform morals, which have so greatly deteriorated among both ecclesiastics and people on account of our sins. In all the aforesaid matters may he [God] direct our actions and deliberations, he for whom nothing is impossible [Lk 1:37], but who, when he wishes, makes troublesome matters easy and the difficult and crooked straight and level by his power [Is 40:4; Lk 3:5].

Certainly so that the aforementioned plans might be more freely brought to fruition, and mindful of the hazards of wars and perils of the way which those whom we are led to summon to the same council might have to undergo, and we and our brothers not shirking but rather willingly embracing hardships so that we might prepare rest for others, burdened with manifold dangers and diverse inconveniences and considerable risks, we entered with our brothers and our curia the city of Lyons. In it we believed those summoned to the council might assemble with less onerous hardship and expenses. In that place all those summoned met for the same council both in person and through fitting representatives, and we deliberated assiduously with them about assistance for the aforementioned land and they, aroused to avenge the injury to their Savior, as they should, gave advice and insights concerning assistance for the same land, recommending from experience the most worthy ways [to help it].

Now [after] listening to their advice, we deservedly commend the praiseworthy resolution and devotion which they demonstrated concerning the liberation of the aforesaid land. But lest we appear to place upon the shoulders of men heavy and insupportable burdens while not wishing to lift a finger [Mt 23:4], we begin with ourselves. For we freely acknowledge that all those things which we have we possess from the only begotten son of God, Jesus Christ, by whose gift we live, by whose support we are sustained, yes, indeed, by whose blood we were redeemed. For the next six years running, we and our brothers, the cardinals of the holy Roman Church, shall pay a full tenth from all our ecclesiastical revenues, fruits, and incomes in aid of the aforesaid land, and with the consent of this sacred council, we decree and order that for the same aforementioned six years, to be reckoned continuously from the next approaching feast of the Nativity of Saint John the Baptist, all ecclesiastical persons, no matter with whatever rank or preeminence they are distinguished, or whatever position or order or religious estate, are to pay a tenth from all their ecclesiastical revenues, fruits, and incomes in each year, within the limits set, that is a half at the feast of the Nativity of our Lord and another half on the feast of the blessed Saint John the Baptist, without fraud and without any kind of diminution. And we will not honor any privilege or exemption [from taxation] granted to them or their churches, no matter what its nature or expression in words [might be], rather, those which were already conceded to them we annul entirely.

And so that we might more mindfully uphold due veneration for the person of him whose business we undertake and for his saints and particularly for the glorious Virgin, whose intercessions we depend upon for this and other matters, and so that there might be fuller assistance for the aforesaid land, the constitution which our predecessor Pope Gregory of blessed memory pronounced against blasphemers we command to be observed without violation. And the monetary penalties of that very statute are to be collected by the authorities of the regions in which the blasphemy is committed, and by others who might exercise temporal jurisdiction in those places. And if it should prove necessary, their diocesan and other local [church] ordinaries are to assist in forcing them to pay the aforementioned aids [fines] in full and they ought to be entrusted to collectors to be converted into assistance for the same [land]. Moreover, we strictly command confessors hearing confessions both under ordinary jurisdiction and by special privilege that they enjoin upon those confessing to them and prompt them to devote the aforementioned money to the same land as full satisfaction [for their sins]; and that they lead those making known their final wishes to bequeath something in their wills from their possessions for the aid of the Holy Land according to their abilities.

Moreover, we order that in every church there be placed an empty chest locked by three keys, the first to be kept in the possession of the bishop, the second in the possession of the priest of the church, the third in the possession of some scrupulous layperson, and all the faithful ought to be instructed to place their alms in it for the remission of their sins, according to how the Lord should inspire them in their minds. And in those very churches for the remission of these sorts of sins and particularly for those offering alms, a mass ought to be sung publicly once per week on a set day which the priest ought to announce to the people beforehand. In addition to this, so that the Holy Land might be more fully assisted, we urge and endeavor to sway with admonishments and exhortations kings and princes, marquises, counts and barons, podestàs, governors [*capitaneos*], and other leaders of various lands that they see to it that in whatever lands fall under their jurisdiction, every single faithful pays one coin to the worth of one tournois or one sterling in accordance with the custom and conditions of the region. And they should impose [an additional] modest [tax] presenting no burden [to anyone] for the remission of sins, to be paid every year for the aid of the same land, such that no one may excuse themselves, because they are obliged to have compassion for the wretched condition of the Holy Land, nor may they be able to refuse to aid it or be prevented from acquiring merit [in this manner]. In fact, lest what was prudently ordered for the assistance of the aforesaid land happen to be impeded through anyone's deceit or armed force or cunning, we excommunicate and anathematize anyone and everyone who should happen to knowingly be responsible for hindering, directly or indirectly, publicly or secretly, the collection of the tenth in aid of the aforementioned land, as was outlined above.

Moreover, since corsairs and pirates greatly hinder those crossing to that land and returning from it by capturing and despoiling them, we bind them and their chief aiders and abettors with the chain of excommunication, and forbid anyone, under threat of anathema, to wittingly communicate with them in any kind of contract involving buying and selling. Indeed, we urge the rulers of cities and [other] places to restrain and check them from this iniquity, otherwise we wish the prelates of the [local] churches to exercise ecclesiastical penalties in the same lands. In addition, we excommunicate and anathematize those false and impious Christians who against Christ and the Christian people transport weapons and iron and wood for building galleys and other sailing vessels [to the Saracens] with which they [the Saracens] attack Christians, and moreover those who sell them galleys or ships, and also those who are employed in the function of helmsman in piratical Saracen ships or in [building] machines for them or in anything else whatsoever lend them aid or counsel to the detriment of Christians, particularly those of the Holy Land. [And] we sentence them to be penalized by the loss of their possessions and they are to become the slaves of their captors. We command that through all the maritime cities on Sundays and feast days this sort of sentence be announced anew in public and that the bosom of the church should not be accessible to men of that ilk, unless everything which they should have received from such a condemnable commerce and moreover a similar amount from their own possessions be sent in aid of the Holy Land, such that they suffer a punishment equal to their transgression. And if perhaps the guilty will not have been [punished] by paying, then they ought to be restrained by other means of such a nature that their punishment might deter the temerity of others daring similar things. In addition we forbid all Christians and prohibit them under anathema to send or take their ships into the lands of the Saracens who live in the eastern regions for the next six years, so that by this a greater abundance of ships might be made available for those wishing to cross in aid of the Holy Land and so that the not inconsiderable assistance which the Saracens customarily receive from this is denied to them.

And since for the pursuit of this business it is particularly necessary that Christian rulers and the Christian populace keep the peace with one another, we therefore command with the approval of this sacred and general council that in the entire world a general peace ought to be upheld between Christians such that those in conflict might be led through the prelates of the churches to a full settlement [*plena concordia*] or peace or firm truce to be inviolably observed for six years. And those who perhaps should refuse to agree to this ought to be most strictly compelled to do so through the sentence of excommunication upon their persons and an interdict upon their lands, unless the malice of those committing the injuries is so great that such men ought not to enjoy peace. And if perhaps they should despise ecclesiastical censures, they ought not undeservedly to fear lest the secular power be invoked against them through ecclesiastical authority as disturbers of the business of the Crucified.

We, therefore, by the mercy of the omnipotent God and the authority entrusted to the blessed Peter and Paul, through which to us, albeit unworthy, God bestowed the power of binding and loosing, grant to all who should undertake personally the labor and the expense of departing for the protection of the Holy Land pardon from the penalty for their sins for which they have truthfully felt contrition in their heart and have orally confessed, and we promise the increase of eternal welfare as the recompense of the righteous. Moreover, to those who cannot personally travel to that place but at least send suitable persons [in their place] at their own expense according to their means and condition, and likewise to those who albeit at others' expense should nonetheless travel there in person, we concede the full pardon of their sins. In addition we wish to be participants in this kind of remission and grant it to all who, according to the nature of their assistance and the sincerity of their devotion, give suitably from their possessions for the aid of the same land or should lend helpful counsel and assistance to the aforementioned [land] and in addition to all those who for the support of the Holy Land offer their own ships or to those who undertake to build ships for the sake of this work. Also, this general council makes participants in the spiritual benefits of its prayers and blessings all who devoutly promote this sacred and holy work, such that it might worthily contribute to their salvation.

Let us give glory and honor to God and not to ourselves [Ps 113:1], and let us give him thanks that at such a sacred council there assembled in response to our summons a numerous host of patriarchs, primates, archbishops, bishops, abbots, priors, provosts, deans, archdeacons, and other prelates of churches both through themselves and through fitting procurators, and also the procurators of chapters, colleges, and convents. Certainly although for the successful promotion of so important a business their counsel is very useful and we are pleased by the presence of the same like that of beloved sons and we are abounding in a certain way in spiritual rejoicing, nonetheless on the other hand because of the diverse inconveniences which their numbers inflict upon many of them, and lest on account of excessive crowding they should suffer any longer and their absence should prove injurious to themselves and their churches, moved by a certain provident affection, with the advice of our brother [cardinals] upon this matter, we determined to take beneficial precautions, such that the prosecution of this business, which we are pursuing with a zealous spirit and indefatigable solicitude, is in no way diminished by the troubles which they might meet. So, therefore, we decree that all patriarchs, primates, archbishops, bishops, abbots, and priors specifically summoned by us by name are thus to remain, such that they ought not to depart before the end of the council without special permission from us. Certainly we compassionately grant, with the blessing of God and ourselves, permission to leave to the remaining nonmitered abbots and priors and other abbots and priors who were not summoned specifically and by name by us, and in addition the provosts, deans, archdeacons, and other prelates of churches and the procurators of any prelates, chapters, colleges, and convents. We command that all who are leaving in such a manner first should send adequate procurators, as described below, for receiving our mandates and those matters which, as the Lord inspires, will be arranged in our present council and may happen to be arranged in the future. That is, those leaving in such a manner should send adequate procurators [in these numbers]: four from the realm of France, four from the realm of England, four from the realms of Spain, four from the realm of Germany [*Alemannia*], one from the realm of Scotland, two from realm of Sicily, two from Lombardy, one from Tuscany, one from lands of the church, one from the realm of Norway, one from the realm of Sweden, one from the realm of Hungary, one from the realm of Dacia, one from the realm of Bohemia, and one from the duchy of Poland.

Moreover, it has become known to us through the reports of certain individuals that not a few archbishops and bishops and other prelates, on the pretext that we had commanded them to be summoned to this council, demanded from their subjects an excessive aid and extorted many things from them, imposing onerous tallages upon the same. Some of these prelates, albeit they exacted many things from their subjects, did not even come to the council. However, since it never was nor ever will be our intention that prelates, in coming to the council, should associate the virtue of obedience with the oppression of their subjects, we warn each and every prelate, firmly instructing them that none of them should dare to burden their subjects with tallages or exactions on the aforementioned pretext. If in fact anyone should not come to the council and should exact anything from their subjects on this pretext, we demand and specifically command that they restitute to them without delay those things which they will have received from them on that pretext. Moreover, those who have injured their subjects by demanding excessive subsidies from them should arrange to make satisfaction to them without [posing] any kind of difficulty, and our command ought to be fulfilled in such a way that it should not prove necessary for us to apply a remedy for this matter by our authority.

72. The Templar of Tyre on the Fall of Acre, 1291

The narrative by the "Templar of Tyre" is the third part of a composite work that has been called since the nineteenth century the *Gestes des Chiprois,* or the "Deeds of the Cypriots." The first part of the work is a version of the Latin text known as the *Annals of the Holy Land,* treating the years 1132–1218. The second part is the memoirs of Philip of Novara, with additions, recounting the wars between Frederick II and the Ibelins (above, No. 26), dealing with the period 1219–1243. The Templar of Tyre deals with the period 1243–1309, and his narrative is the only surviving Christian eyewitness account of the siege and conquest of Acre in 1291.

The unknown author had been born probably in Cyprus around 1255 and had lived in Tyre between 1269 and 1283, although there is no evidence that he was a Templar. He says that he served as a scribe for William of Beaujeu, master of the Templars, and lived in Acre during most of the siege of 1291. He seems to have been of knightly rank and a close and trusted adviser of the Templar master over several years. He knew Arabic and writes in a distinctive Old French, with Arabic and Greek terms included, and his evidence, where it can be checked in this and other instances, is usually reliable. His name, which he never gives, is assumed to have been Gérard de Montréal, based on a later history of Cyprus that used his narrative.

Besides the Templar of Tyre and the Arabic sources considered below, the main Latin sources for the fall of Acre have been edited by R. B. C. Huygens, Excidii Aconis gestorum collectio; Magister Thadeus civis Neapolitanus, Ystoria de desolatione et conculcatione civitatis Acconensis et tocius Terre Sanctae, with contributions by A. Forey and D. C. Nicolle, *Corpus Christianorum Continuatio Mediaevalis 202 (Turnhout, 2004). The remarkable letters of Ricoldo da Montecroce, the widely traveled Franciscan missionary and Arabist, have been edited and translated into French by René Kappler in Ricoldo da Montecroce,* Pérégrination en Terre Sainte et au Proche Orient *(Paris, 1997). The Templar of Tyre has been edited and translated into Italian by Laura Minervini,* Cronaca del Templare di Tiro (1243–1314): La caduta degli Stati Crociati nel racconto di un testimone oculare *(Naples, 2000); and into*

English by Paul Crawford, The "Templar of Tyre": Part III of the "Deeds of the Cypriots," *Crusade Texts in Translation 6 (Aldershot UK-Burlington VT, 2003).*

Now I will tell you the way and the reason why Acre was taken by the Saracens. . . .

> *The rulers of Acre and the military orders had made a ten-year truce with Qalawun in 1289. Under its terms, Muslim peasants and merchants could safely trade in the city. But at some point—the Old French and Arabic sources differ, but agree on this important fact—newly arrived Christian soldiers, probably from the twenty Venetian galleys sent to Acre by Pope Nicholas IV, attacked and killed a number of defenseless Muslims and even some bearded Christian Syrians whom they thought were Muslims.*
>
> *News of the killing and the blood-stained clothing of the victims were carried to the sultan, who protested to the Akkans[16] and received unsatisfactory answers from them. The sultan decided on revenge, found a phrase in the truce treaty that justified his proposed action, and mobilized an army.[17] But Qalawun died suddenly, and his successor al-Malik al-Ashraf quickly established himself as the successor and, contrary to the Akkans' expectations, took up the leadership of his father's immense army, and set off for Acre. The Templar gives the figures as 70,000 horsemen and over 150,000 foot soldiers—in contrast, the entire population of Acre consisted of 30–40,000 inhabitants, including 700–800 horsemen and about 13,000 foot soldiers. As the Akkans attempted negotiations, al-Ashraf sent them the following letter, translated from Arabic by the Templar of Tyre.*

487 [251] "The Sultan of Sultans, King of Kings, Lord of Lords, al-Malik al-Ashraf, the Powerful, the Dreadful, the Scourge of Rebels, Hunter of Franks and Tartars, and Armenians, Snatcher of Castles from the Hands of Miscreants, Lord of the Two Seas, Guardian of the Two Pilgrim Sites, Khalil al-Salihi, to the noble master of the Temple the true and wise:

"Greetings and our good will! Because you have been a true man, so we send you advance notice of our intentions, and give you to understand that we are coming into your parts to right the wrongs that have been done. Therefore, we do not want the community of Acre to send us any letters or presents [regarding this matter], for we will by no means receive them."

Source: *Crawford,* The "Templar of Tyre," *101, 104–117. In each segment, the initial unbracketed number indicates the section number of the entire three-part text used by Crawford, and the lower bracketed number indicates the numbering of the Templar of Tyre text in Minervini's edition.*

16. Akkan here refers to the inhabitants of Acre (Akko/Akka).

17. On treaties, P. M. Holt, *Early Mamluk Diplomacy (1260–1290): Treaties of Baybars and Qalawun with Christian Rulers* (Leiden, 1995).

488 [252] Such was the command and the tenor of the letter of the sultan, as you have heard. Notwithstanding this, they did not leave off sending him messengers, as I have told you; they were arrested and thrown into prison in Babylon, where they later perished miserably.

489 [253] The sultan came before Acre and besieged it on Thursday the fifth of April, in the year 1291 of the Incarnation of Christ, and he took it on the eighteenth day of May in the same year. Now you will learn how it happened.

490 [254] The sultan pitched his tents very close together, from Toron all the way up to as-Sumairiya, so that the whole plain was covered with tents. The tent of the sultan himself, which is called the *dehlis,* was on a small hill, where there was a lovely tower and gardens and vineyards of the Temple.[18] This *dehlis* was entirely red, and its door opened facing the city of Acre. It was a custom of the sultans that everyone would know that the direction in which the door of the *dehlis* opened would be the direction in which he would take the road. They remained for eight days before Acre, doing nothing besides engaging in the occasional clash between our forces and theirs, in which a few were killed on either side.

At the end of the eight days, they brought up and emplaced their siege engines, and the stones that they threw weighed a *quintar* each.[19] One of these engines was called *Haveben,* that is to say "Furious," and it was set up in front of the Templars' section.[20] Another, which fired on the Pisans' section, was called al-Mansuri, that is to say, "Victory."[21] Yet another, very large, whose name I do not know, fired on the Hospitallers' section, and a fourth engine fired on a great tower called the Accursed Tower, which is at the second wall and was in the custody of the king.[22]

18. The term *dehlis* is Arabic, one of several Arabic terms that the author uses competently. It refers to a particular kind of tent used by sultans on campaign.

19. A *quintar* was about one hundred pounds.

20. Each order and social group had responsibility for defending a particular section of the city walls. *Haveben* attempts to render the Arabic word *Ghadban,* which means "wrathful, furious."

21. Abu l-Fida', quoted below (No. 73), mentions the same catapult and its name, which the Hama contingent, of which he was a part, brought with immense effort from Krak des Chevaliers to Acre.

22. This tower was at an exposed corner of the walls, looking toward the fields. Acre was defended by two lines of walls; by "second wall" the author presumably means the inner wall. On the still unresolved question of the archaeology of Acre at this period, see Benjamin Kedar, "The Outer Walls of Frankish Acre," *Atiqot* 31 (1997), 157–180.

491 [255] They set up great barricades and wicker screens, ringing the walls with them the first night, and the second night they moved them further in, and the third night further still, and they brought them so far forward that they came up to the lip of the fosse. Behind these screens the armed men dismounted from their horses, bows in hand. And if you are wondering how they were allowed to draw so near, the answer is that they could not be stopped, as I shall now explain.

These people had their horsemen fully armed, on armored horses, and they stretched from one side of the city to the other, that is to say, from the beach on one side to the beach on the other. There were more than 15,000 of them, and they worked in four shifts a day, so that no one was overworked. None of our men went out against those who were behind the screens, for if they had, those who were behind [the first enemy line] would have defended them and barred the way, and so if it had happened that our men had gone out against them, the men on horseback would have defended them.

So in the end the Muslims advanced to the edge of the fosse, as I have told you, and the men on horseback each carried four or five *buches*[23] on the necks of their horses, and threw them down behind the screens. And when night came, they put them in front of the screens, and bound a cord on top, and the pile became like a wall that no engine could harm, though some of our medium engines shot and battered at it without effect. The stones merely rebounded into the fosse.

After this the enemy brought up their *carabohas*, small, hand-operated Turkish devices with a high rate of fire which did more damage to our men than the larger engines did, since in the places where the *carabohas* were firing, no one dared to come out into the open. In front of the *carabohas* they had made the rampart so strong and so high that no one could strike or shoot at those who were firing [the *carabohas*]. And this situation lasted as long as they were mining, because a great emir named Sanjar al-Shuja'i commanded the enemy sector opposite a new little tower at the first walls in front of the Accursed Tower, which was called the Tower of the King.[24] This Sanjar al-Shuja'i mined out toward the tower, and also mined one of the walls, called the King's Wall. They pressed so hard against it that our men set it on fire and made it collapse. The Saracens also made another mine against the Tower of the Countess

23. *Buches* were bundles of various kinds of wood used to set up defenses for troops or siege engines.
24. Sanjar al-Shuja'i took over the government of Syria after the fall of Acre.

of Blois (which she had made when she came to this side of the sea for her soul's sake),[25] and our men countermined against it, and fought back fiercely. But the Saracens brought fresh men each day, because they had so many troops.

One day our men took counsel and decided to make a general sally on all sides with horse and foot, to burn the *buches.* So my lord the master of the Temple and his men, and Sir John [of Grailly and Sir Otto] of Grandson and other knights went out one night from the Templars' sector (which ran from the seaside to the Gate of Saint Lazarus), and the master ordered a Provençal, who was viscount of the bourg of Acre, to set fire to the wooden *buches* of the great engine of the sultan. [26] They went out that night, and came up to these *buches,* but the man who was supposed to hurl the Greek fire was afraid when he threw it, and it fell short and landed on the ground, where it burned out. The Saracens who were there were all killed, horsemen and footmen. But our men, both brethren and secular knights, went so far in among the tents that their horses got their legs tangled in the tent ropes and went sprawling, where-upon the Saracens slew them. In this way we lost eighteen horsemen that night, both brethren of the Temple and secular knights, though they did capture a number of Saracen shields and bucklers and trumpets and drums. Then my lord and his men turned back toward Acre.

On the way, they ran into a number of Saracens lying in ambush, all of whom they killed, for the moonlight was bright as day and they could see them clearly. As I have already told you, the lord of Hama was in that sector, and he rallied his troops to him and hit us on the seashore with showers of javelins, wounding some of our men.[27] But they dared not close with our men. You should know that they seemed to have close to two thousand mounted men [in this skirmish], but our side had—including knights and other horsemen, and brethren of the military orders and *valés* and turcopoles—scarcely three hundred.

On the other sectors where action had been ordered, nothing was done, because the Saracens perceived the activity and were on guard, and

25. Jeanne of Châtillon, who came to Acre in 1287 on pilgrimage and returned to France in 1290, where she died in 1292.

26. On the topography of Acre, in addition to the study by Kedar, cited above, see the studies of David Jacoby in *Studies on the Crusader States and on Venetian Expansion* (Aldershot UK-Brookfield VT, 1989). Excavations by the Israeli Antiquities Authority are ongoing.

27. Abu l-Fida', below (No. 73), confirms the placement of the Hama troops.

attacked the Christians so fiercely that they turned back without accomplishing anything.

492 [256] Later on it was decided that all the lords and the forces of Acre should make a sortie in the middle of the night from the Gate of Saint Anthony, to fall suddenly on the Saracens. This was decided so secretly that no one knew of it until the command, "To horse!" was given. At the same time when our men mounted up and sallied forth from the Gate of Saint Anthony, the moon was not shining at all, but was obscured. The Saracens were forewarned, and illuminated the scene with torches so that it seemed to be day along their lines. A division so large that it contained well-nigh 10,000 men came against our men and raked them so fiercely with javelins that it seemed to be raining. Our men could not endure this and so withdrew into the city, many of the horsemen being wounded.

Our people in the city of Acre were thus in a sorry condition. But they received news that King Henry was about to come from Cyprus with significant assistance, and they looked for him daily.[28]

493 [257] The king had summoned his men in Cyprus, and assembled them and left from Famagusta, and arrived at Acre on the fourth of May. The city was in dire straits because, as I have told you, the [outer] wall was mined and the tower which had been mined had been burned.

But all the same they took great comfort in the arrival of these men, and that of the king a few days later, so they sent messengers to the sultan: Sir William of Villiers, a knight, and William of Caffran, a man from the household of the master of the Temple. The sultan came out from his *dehlis* before the gate of the city known as the Gate of the Legate, and there was a ceasefire on both sides. The messengers went out unarmed, and they came before the sultan, who was within a small tent.

When the messengers had thrice saluted him on their knees, he approached them and said, "Have you brought me the keys of the city, then?" The messengers replied that the city could not be surrendered so easily, but that they had come to him to ask for some measure of mercy for the poor people.

At this the sultan said to them, "I will give you this much grace, that you cede me the bare stones [of the city] alone, and carry off everything

28. Henry II, king of Cyprus and Jerusalem (1285–1324), who ruled from Cyprus, although Acre was the capital of the kingdom of Jerusalem at the time.

else, and go forth and leave the place. I will do this for your king, who has come here and who is a youth, just as I might have been. But I will do nothing more for you."

Then the messengers said to him that this could not be, "because the people overseas would hold us to be traitors," at which he said, "Then you should go away, for I shall offer nothing more."

As he spoke these words, there was a siege engine which the crusaders were working from the Gate of the Legate, and it fired by I know not what accident, and the stone came so near the tent where the sultan and the messengers were, that the sultan (in an act of youthful bravado, not meaning serious harm) leaped to his feet, and laying his hand on his sword, he drew it out a palm's length, and said, "Ah! You filthy swine, what prevents me from striking off your heads?"

At this, Sanjar al-Shuja'i said to him, "Sir, God forbid that you should foul the iron of your sword with the blood of these pigs! Those who fired the siege engine are traitors, but you should let these men go, for they are here with you." And so the messengers returned to Acre, and thereupon the two sides began again their labors, firing mangonels at one another, and doing the things that are usually done between enemies.

494 [258] The new tower, which they called the Tower of the King, was so badly undermined that the front face fell in a heap into the fosse, so that it was impossible to pass over the top of the stones. Seeing this, the Saracens made small sacks of hemp cloth and filled them with sand. Every man carried one of these sacks on the neck of his horse and tossed it to the Saracens who were there behind the *buches* at that point. Then when night fell, they took the sacks and spread them across the top of the stones, and smoothed them out like a roadway, and the next day (Wednesday) they came across on the sacks at Vespers, and took the tower. Half of the vault was still intact and in one piece on the side of the town, and there were a great many of our men defending the tower, but the defense was all for nothing, because the Saracens took the tower anyway, and planted the ensign of the sultan on it. At this, we loaded the siege engines and aimed them at the tower and fired, and killed some of the Saracens, but not enough to drive them back.

When our men saw that the tower was taken, they built a structure out of leather-covered wood, called a *chat,* and put men inside it, so that the Saracens who had taken the tower might not advance further.

495 [259] When the tower had thus fallen, as I have explained, everyone was thoroughly demoralized, and began increasingly to send their women and children down to the ships. But on the next day, Thursday, the weather was very bad, and the sea ran so high that the women and children who had boarded the ships were unable to stay there, and they disembarked and returned to their homes.

496 [260] Before dawn on the next day, Friday, a drum began a powerful stroke, and at the sound of this drum, which had a horrible and mighty voice, the Saracens assailed the city of Acre upon all sides. The place where they entered first was by the Accursed Tower, which they had already taken. I shall tell you the way in which they came.

497 [261] They came on afoot, so many that they were without number. In the van came men carrying great tall shields, and after them came men who cast Greek fire, and after them came men who hurled javelins and shot feathered arrows in such a thick cloud that they seemed to fall like rain from the heavens. Our men who were inside the *chat* abandoned it. At this the Saracens, whom I have mentioned, took two routes, since they were between the two walls of the city—that is to say, between the first walls and the ditches, which were called the barbican, and the great [inner] walls and ditches of the city proper. Some of them entered by a gate of that great tower called the Accursed Tower, and moved toward San Romano, where the Pisans had their great engines. The others kept to the road, going to Saint Anthony's Gate.

498 [262] When the master of the Temple, who was at his auberge with the men who were defending it, heard the drum beating, he realized that the Saracens were launching some assault. The master gathered ten or twelve brethren and his own household troops and headed for the Saint Anthony Gate, right between the two walls.

On the way he passed the Hospitaller sector, and he summoned the master of the Hospital to join him. The Hospitaller master in turn collected some of his brethren, and some knights of Cyprus and of the Holy Land and some footmen. They moved toward the Saint Anthony Gate, where they found the Saracens coming in on foot, and they counterattacked them.

But it was all to no effect, as I have explained, for there were too many Saracens. When the two masters of the Temple and the Hospital arrived there and went into combat, it seemed as if they hurled themselves against a stone wall. Those of the enemy who were hurling Greek fire hurled it so often and so thickly that there was so much smoke that one man could scarcely see another. Among the smoke, archers shot feathered arrows so densely that our men and mounts were terribly hurt.

It happened that one poor English *valé* was so badly hit by the Greek fire which the Saracens were hurling that his surcoat burst into flames. There was no one to help him, and so his face was burned, and then his whole body, and he burned as if he had been a cauldron of pitch, and he died there. He was on foot when this happened, because his mount had been slain under him.[29]

The Saracens hung back for a bit, and then raised their shields and moved forward a little way, and when men charged down on them, they straightaway fixed their shields and drew up. They did not cease from their work of hurling javelins and casting Greek fire all day. This conflict, this [particular] confused struggle, lasted up until midmorning.

In this place a great misfortune befell, by which those Saracens who had come into the city, as I have said, were able to enter more easily and quickly, and by which our people were greatly disheartened. The occasion was this: a javelin came at the master of the Temple, just as he raised his left hand. He had no shield save his spear in his right hand. The javelin struck him under the armpit, and the shaft sank into his body a palm's length; it came in through the gap where the plates of the armor were not joined. This was not his proper armor, but rather light armor for putting on hastily at an alarm.

When he felt himself mortally wounded, he turned to go. Some of the defenders thought that he was retiring because he wanted to save himself. The standard-bearer saw him go, and fell in behind him, and then all of his household followed as well. After he had gone some way, twenty crusaders from the Vallo di Spoleto saw him withdrawing, and they called to him, "Oh for God's sake, Sir, don't leave, or the city will fall at once!" And he cried out to them in a loud voice, so that everyone could hear him: "My lords, I can do no more, for I am killed; see the wound here!"

And then we saw the javelin stuck in his body, and as he spoke he dropped the spear on the ground, and his head slumped to one side. He

---

29. This is one of a number of references that indicate that the author himself had been an eyewitness.

started to fall from his horse, but those of his household sprang down from their horses and supported him and took him off, and laid him on a shield that they found cast off there, a tall, broad buckler. They carried him off toward the Saint Anthony Gate, but found it closed; instead, they found a small door which had a bridge leading from the fosse into the residence of the Lady Maria of Antioch, which had previously belonged to Sir James of La Mandelée.

There his household removed his armor, cutting his cuirass off at the shoulders, for they could do nothing else because of the wound he had taken. Then they put him, still in his épaulières, under a blanket, and took him toward the seashore, which is to say, on the beach which is between the abattoir where they slaughter beasts and the house of the lord of Tyre. There they heard a cry from in front of the Tower of the Legate, that the Saracens were there, so some of the household leapt into the sea to try to reach two barks that were there—there were only those two, because the sea was so stormy and the waves were so great that the barks were unable to cope with them—and many of the men were lost because of this. Other members of his household carried him to the Temple fortress with the aid of other men, and they laid him within the house—not going in by the gate, which they did not want to open, but taking him by way of a court-yard where they piled manure.

He lived all that day without saying a word, for since he had been taken down from his horse he had not spoken, save only a word to those in the Temple; when he heard the clamor of men fleeing death, he wanted to know what was happening. They told him that men were fighting, and he commanded that they should leave him in peace.

He did not speak again, but gave up his soul to God. He was buried before his tabernacle, which was the altar where they said Mass. And God has his soul—but what great harm was caused by his death!

499 [263] Now I will tell you what happened next.

As men learned what had happened, and saw the master carried off, they began one by one to abandon their posts and flee. For the Saracens, as I have said, had come through the Accursed Tower, and went straight through San Romano, and set fire to the great engine of the Pisans, and went down the straight road to the Germans, and took Saint Leonard, and everyone they encountered they put to the sword. Other Saracens assaulted the Tower of the Legate, which was on the sea. From the edge of the sea to the foot of the tower, the Saracens prized off a latticework which had bars and points sticking out so that horses could not get through there. Then a great number of mounted Saracens came in. Sir John of Grailly and Sir Otto of Grandson and the men of the king of France put up a fierce defense, so that there were a great many wounded and dead. But Sir John of Grailly and Sir Otto of Grandson were unable to withstand the Saracen pressure, and they withdrew from the place and saved themselves, Sir John of Grailly being [badly] wounded.

500 [264] When Henry, king of Jerusalem and Cyprus, saw this disaster, he came to the master of the Hospital, and they perceived plainly that neither counsel nor reinforcement were of any further value, and so they saved themselves and boarded their galleys.

501 [265] Know that that day was terrible to behold. The ladies and the burgesses and the cloistered maidens and other lesser folk came fleeing through the streets, their children in their arms, weeping and despairing, and fleeing to the sailors to save them from death. And when the Saracens came across them, one seized the mother and another the child, and carried them from place to place, and separated them from each other. Once there was a quarrel between two Saracens over a woman and she was killed by them; and another time a woman was led away captive, and the infant at her breast was thrown to the ground where the horses trampled on it, slaying it thus. There were some women who were pregnant and who were caught up in the press of the flight and suffocated and died, and the life in her [sic] womb died with her [sic]. And there were some women whose husband or child was lying ill or wounded by an arrow at their lodging; they left them alone and fled, and the Saracens slew them all.

You should know that the Saracens set fire to the siege engines and to the *garites*,[30] so that the whole land was lit up by the flames. The greater part of the people, men and women and children, more than ten thousand persons, sought refuge within the Temple [compound], for it was the strongest place in the city.

The Templar goes on to describe the Templar possessions in the city, then (502/ 266) those of the Hospital and of the Teutonic Knights (503/267).

30. A moveable defensive shelter or siege tower made of wood.

AND now I want to go back to complete my story.

Everyone who could manage to do so came to the Temple, gathering inside. The king and the others who had retreated onto the galleys and other ships moved off and set sail, as did the *tarides* and *nefs*[31] of the Venetian squadron. The good *preudomme*, the patriarch and legate, Brother Nicholas, withdrew to a *nef* of the Venetians. A sailor seized him by the hand, but he slipped and fell into the sea and was drowned. No one knows if he who took him by the hand let him go because he had put his valuables on that ship, or if he slipped from his hand because he could not hold onto him, but however it happened, the *preudomme* was drowned, as I said.

When all the *leins*[32] had put on sail, those of the Temple who had gathered there gave a great cry, and the ships cast off and made for Cyprus, and those good men who were then come into the Temple were left to their fate, as you have heard. You should know that there were six armed *leins* of the church, and royal galleys, and two Genoese galleys (who did much good as everyone knows, for they collected the men from the seashore and put them on the *nefs* and on the other *leins)*. The commander of these two galleys was a Genoese named Andrea Peleau.

504 [268] Now let me tell you of the fate of the city of Tyre, which was one of the strongest cities in the world. In it there was a bailli named Sir Adam of Caffran, acting on behalf of the king. As soon as he saw the sailing ships that had left Acre, he and all the other knights and the wealthy people cleared out and abandoned the city of Tyre. The poor people remained behind and were taken prisoner, men and women and children who had no ships on which they might withdraw.

505 [269] Now we shall tell you about the people who were within the Temple. There was the marshal, Peter of Sevrey, and some brethren of the Templars, and some other brethren who lay wounded within, and some secular knights, and women and burgesses and many other people. Among those who fell back on the Temple that day was Brother Matthew of Clermont, marshal of the Hospital of Saint John. He saw the master of the Temple, who was dead, as I have told you, and then returned to the

---

31. *Tarides* were large barge-like ships designed for the transport of horses. *Nefs* were single-masted ships commonly used for both military and commercial transport. In general, see Susan Rose, *Medieval Naval Warfare, 1000–1500* (London-New York, 2002).

32. A type of ship smaller than a galley.

battle, gathering around him all his brethren, for he would not abandon any of them, and some of the Templars went with him, and they came to a square of the Genoese quarter, which was empty of houses, and there Matthew plunged into combat. He and his companions slew many Saracens, but in the end he was slain, him and the others, like true knights and valiant and good Christians. May God preserve their souls.

506 [270] Know, fair lords, that no one could adequately recount the tears and grief of that day. The pitiful sight of the little children, tumbled about and disemboweled as the horses trampled upon them . . . ! There is no man in the world who has so very hard a heart that he would not have wept to see the slaughter. And I am sure that all Christian people who saw these things that day wept, because even some of the Saracens, as we learned afterward, had pity on these victims and wept.[33]

507 [271] The Temple held out for ten days [after the fall of the city itself]. The sultan parlayed with those who were in the Temple, to see if they wished to surrender themselves to his safe-conduct, and they sent word back that they would surrender if he should undertake to conduct them to safety wherever they wished to go. The sultan sent a message back agreeing, and dispatched an emir to those in the Temple. The emir brought four hundred horsemen inside the compound with him; these men saw the great number of refugees, and desired to seize the women who pleased them, to dishonor them.[34] But the Christians found this conduct intolerable, drew their weapons and flung themselves upon the Saracens, slaying them all and beheading them, so that none escaped alive. Then the Christians set themselves determinedly to defend their bodies to the death.

The sultan was most displeased by this turn of events, but he did not show it. He sent again, saying that he knew quite well that the folly of his men had been [the cause of] their deaths, because of the outrages they had committed, that he did not hold this against the Christians, and that they could come out securely, trusting in his word. The marshal of the Temple, a great *preudomme* from Burgundy, whose name was Peter of

---

33. See the exculpatory remarks of Abu l-Mahasin, below (No. 73).

34. Other Latin and Arab sources agree on the nature of the sexual molestation of both women and boys. See Donald P. Little, "The Fall of 'Akka in 690/1291: The Muslim Version," in M. Sharon, ed., *Studies in Islamic History and Civilization in Honour of Professor David Ayalon* (Jerusalem-Leiden, 1986), 159–181; and Huygens, ed., *Excidii Aconis gestorum collectio*.

Sevrey (whom I have mentioned above to you), trusted the sultan, and came out to him. Some wounded brethren remained in the tower.

508 [272] Therefore, when the sultan had the marshal and the men of the Temple in his power, he had the heads of all the brethren and all the other men cut off. When the brethren who were still within the tower, who were not so ill as to be unable to fight, heard that the marshal and the others had been beheaded, they set themselves to resist.

At this the Saracens began to mine the tower—they dug a mine and then shored it up. Thereupon those within the tower surrendered, but the Saracens entered the tower with so many men that the supports in the mine gave way, and the tower collapsed, and those brethren of the Temple and the Saracens who were inside were killed. Moreover, when the tower collapsed, it fell outward toward the street, and crushed more than two thousand mounted Turks.

And so this city of Acre was taken, abandoned, on Friday, the eighteenth day of May in the said year [of 1291], and the Temple compound ten days later, in the manner which I have described to you.[35]

73. Abu l-Fida' and Abu l-Mahasin on the Fall of Acre, 1291

Two of the best-informed Arab chroniclers of the siege and fall of Acre were both soldiers and scholars. Abu l-Fida' (ca. 672/1273–732/1331) was an Ayyubid lord of Hama who participated personally as a young man in the siege of Acre and included a description in his *Historical Compendium of the Human Race*, a work that, like the *Shining Stars Concerning the Kings of Egypt and Cairo* of Abu l-Mahasin (813/1411–874/1469), consists largely of earlier accounts, now lost and preserved only in anthologies such as these. After the fall of the Ayyubids, Abu l-Fida' managed to retain the lordship of Hama under the Mamluks. As Gabrieli points out, he resembles another earlier soldier and man of letters from the turn of the twelfth century, Usama ibn Munqidh, whose early twelfth-century *Book of Contemplation* has been newly translated.[36] In the case of Abu l-Fida', the author's inclusion of events in his own lifetime makes this part of his text particularly useful.

Abu l-Mahasin was a fifteenth-century soldier and man of letters whose work was also largely an anthology of earlier writers. His account of the siege of Acre,

---

35. It seems likely that the Templar of Tyre managed to escape from the city on or shortly after May 18 with a detachment of Templars who managed to get to Cyprus (509 [273]). His information for May 18–28 seems not to be that of an eyewitness any longer.

36. Usama ibn Munqidh, *The Book of Contemplation: Islam and the Crusades*, trans. with intro. by Paul M. Cobb (London-New York, 2008).

however, derived from an eyewitness account, and together with the account of Abu l-Fida' constitutes a remarkable Arabic perspective on the campaign of al-Ashraf.

The most exhaustive analysis of the historiography in Arabic of the siege and fall of Acre is that by Donald P. Little, "The Fall of 'Akka in 690/1291: The Muslim Version," in M. Sharon, ed., Studies in Islamic History and Civilization in Honour of Professor David Ayalon *(Jerusalem-Leiden, 1986), 159–181. Little offers a superbly reconstructed account of the Arabic versions of the conquest from all narrative sources, 165–181. On Abu l-Fida', see P. M. Holt, trans., with intro.,* The Memoirs of a Syrian Prince: Abu l-Fida', Sultan of Hama *(Wiesbaden, 1983). During the siege of Acre Abu l-Fida' was roughly the equivalent of a modern platoon leader.*

Abu l-Fida' on the fall of Acre

IN 690/1291 the sultan al-Malik al-Ashraf marched on Acre with his Egyptian troops and sent word to the Syrian army to join up with him and to bring the siege engines. The ruler of Hama, al-Malik al-Muzaffar, set out with his uncle, al-Malik al-Afdal[37] and the whole of Hama's army for Hisn al-Akrad, where we collected a huge catapult called "the Victorious"; a hundred wagons were needed to transport it. (It was dismantled and the pieces) distributed through the army. The part consigned to me was only one wagonload, since at the time I was an "emir of ten." It was the end of the winter when we marched off with the wagons; rain and snowstorms struck us between Hisn al-Akrad and Damascus, causing great hardship, for the wagons were heavy and the oxen weak and dying of cold. Because of the wagons it took us a month to march from Hisn al-Akrad to Acre, usually an eight-day ride. The sultan ordered all the other fortresses to send catapults and siege-engines to Acre, and in this way a great number of large and small artillery concentrated under its walls, more than had ever before been assembled in one place.

The Muslim troops mustered at Acre in the first days of Jumada I 690/beginning of May 1291, and the battle raged furiously. The Franks did not close most of the gates; in fact, they left them wide open and fought in front of them in their defense. The Hama army was in its usual position on the extreme right wing. This meant that we were on the seashore, with the sea on our right when we faced Acre. We were attacked by troops landing from boats protected by wood-faced frames covered with buffalo hides, from which they shot at us with bows and ballistas. Thus we found ourselves fighting on two fronts, the city and the sea. A

Source: Gabrieli, Arab Historians of the Crusades, *344–350.*
37. The two men were the author's cousin and father.

ship came up with a catapult mounted on it that battered us and our tents from the sea. We were severely hindered by it, but one night when a fierce wind blew up, the ship was buffeted on the waves and the catapult broke up and was not rebuilt.

One night during the siege the Franks made a sortie, put the outposts to flight and reached the tents, where they became tangled up with the guy ropes. One knight fell into the latrine trench of one of the emir's detachments and was killed. Our troops turned out in overwhelming numbers and the Franks turned tail and fled back to the city, leaving a number of dead accounted for by the Hama army. The next morning al-Malik al-Muzaffar, lord of Hama, had a number of Frankish heads attached to the necks of horses we had captured and presented them to the sultan al-Malik al-Ashraf.

The blockade was continually reinforced, until God granted to the attackers victory over the city on Friday, 10 Jumada II [June 17, 1291]. As the Muslims stormed the city some of the citizens took to the sea in boats. Within the city was a number of well-fortified towers, and some Franks shut themselves inside them and defended them. The Muslims killed vast numbers of people and gathered immense booty. The sultan forced all those in the towers to surrender, and they submitted to the last man, and to the last man were decapitated outside the city walls.[38] At the sultan's command the city was razed to the ground.

An amazing coincidence occurred: the Franks seized Acre from Saladin at midday on 17 Jumada II 587 [July 12, 1191], and captured and then killed all the Muslims therein; and God, in his prescience destined that this year it should be reconquered at the hand of another Saladin, the sultan al-Malik al-Ashraf.[39]

After the conquest of Acre God put despair into the hearts of the other Franks left in Palestine; they abandoned Sidon and Beirut, which (the emir) ash-Shuja 'i took over at the end of Rajab [end of July]. The population of Tyre also abandoned the city and the sultan sent troops to occupy it. They received the surrender of 'Atlit on the first of Shaban [July 30], and that of Tortosa on fifth of Shaban of the same year. So this sultan had the good fortune, granted to none other, to conquer without effort and without striking a blow these great, well-fortified cities, all of which were at his command demolished.

38. Abu l-Fida' does not mention the sultan's grant of a guarantee of safety, which this massacre violated. However, see Abu l-Mahasin's account, below.

39. Al-Ashraf bore, like his famous predecessor, the title Salah ad-Din.

With these conquests the whole of Palestine was now in Muslim hands, a result that no one would have dared to hope for or to desire. Thus the whole of Syria and the coastal zones were purified of the Franks, who had once been on the point of conquering Egypt and subduing Damascus and other cities. Praise be to God!

Abu l-Mahasin on the fall of Acre

AT THE beginning of 690 [1291] al-Malik al-Ashraf began preparations for his departure for Syria. He called up his troops, assembled siege engines, and employed craftsmen to put them all in order. Then on 3 Rabi I [March 1291] he left Egypt, and began his siege of Acre, on 4 Rabi II [April 5]. A vast army concentrated at Acre, of which more soldiers were volunteers than were regular troops or members of the sultan's private army. There were also fifteen great "Frankish" catapults, capable of throwing a load weighing a Damascene quintal or more,[40] and other, lighter machines as well as a good number of "devils" and the like. Some tunnels were dug for mines. The king of Cyprus himself came to help the people of Acre, who on the night of his arrival lit great fires, greater than were ever seen before, as a sign of their joy. But he stayed only three days before returning home, for he realized their desperate position and the disaster looming over them.

The city was besieged and vigorously attacked until the defenders' morale began to crumble and weakness destroyed their unity. There was fighting every day and a certain number of Muslims fell as martyrs for the faith. At dawn on Friday, 17 Jumada II, the sultan and his troops, mounted on their horses, moved in to attack before sunrise. They beat their drums, creating a terrible, terrifying noise, and the army massed under the walls. The Franks fled and the city was taken by storm. Not three hours of the day had passed before the Muslims entered Acre and made themselves masters of it, while the Franks cast themselves into the sea, trampled on by the Muslim troops who killed and captured them. Only a few escaped. The Muslims took all the booty they could find, goods, treasure, and arms, and the population was killed or taken prisoner. Templars, Hospitallers, and Teutonic Hospitallers made a last stand in four lofty towers in the middle of the city, where they were besieged.

On Saturday, the nineteenth of the month, two days after the fall of the city, regular troops and others attacked the house and tower where

---

40. A Damascene quintal is about one hundred pounds.

the Templars were.[41] The Templars begged for their lives, which the sultan granted them. He sent them a standard which they accepted and raised over the tower. The door was opened and a horde of regulars and others swarmed in. When they came face to face with the defenders some of the soldiers began to pillage and to lay hands on the women and children who were with them, whereupon the Franks shut the door and attacked them, killing a number of Muslims. They hauled down the standard and stiffened their resistance. The siege continued.

On the same day the Teutonic Hospitallers asked for an amnesty and this was granted to them and their women by the sultan, by the hand of the emir Zain ad-Din Kitbugha al-Mansuri. The battle against the Templars' tower continued until Sunday, 20 Jumada II, when they and the defenders of the other two towers sued for their lives. The sultan granted them permission to go where they liked, but when they came out he killed more than two thousand of them, took an equal number prisoners and sent the women and children as slaves to the gate of the sultan's pavilion. One reason for the sultan's wrath against them, apart from their other crimes, was that when the emir Kitbugha al-Mansuri had gone up (to receive their surrender) they had seized and killed him. They had also hamstrung their horses and destroyed everything they could, which increased the sultan's wrath against them. The army and volunteers made a vast haul of prisoners and booty.

When the remaining Franks realized what had happened to their companions they decided to keep up their resistance to the end. They rejected the assurances offered them and fought desperately, and when they captured five Muslims threw them down from the top of the tower. One alone escaped; the other four died. On Tuesday, the eighteenth of the same month of Jumada, the last of the towers to keep up a resistance was taken. The defenders abandoned it in return for their lives, for the tower had been mined from all sides. When the Franks had come out and most of the contents had been removed the tower collapsed on a group of sightseers and on the looters within, killing them all. After that the sultan set the women and children apart and decapitated all the men, of whom there was a great number. . . .

When the sultan had taken Acre, he sent a body of troops under the emir 'Alam ad-Din Sanjar as-Sawabi al-Jashnighir in the direction of Tyre

---

41. Gabrieli's dates are no longer precise because of the defective copy of the source he was using.

to patrol the roads, collect information, and blockade the city. While they were doing this, the ships fleeing from Acre arrived and tried to enter the harbor at Tyre. The emir prevented them, and the people of Tyre asked for an amnesty and were granted security for themselves and their possessions. So they surrendered the city, which is among the best situated and fortified. It was not taken by the sultan Saladin as one of his conquests in Palestine; when he took a town and granted the inhabitants their lives, he sent them to Tyre because of the strength of its fortifications. But now God filled the hearts of its inhabitants with despair and they surrendered it without a battle or a siege of any sort, whereas al-Malik al-Ashraf had in fact had no intention of attacking it. When he received the surrender he sent men to organize its demolition, to pull down the walls and buildings, and he gained from this a good quantity of marble and salvage. With Tyre so easily taken al-Malik al-Ashraf confirmed his intention to proceed with the conquest of all the remaining (Frankish territories).[42]

42. That is, Beirut, Sidon, 'Atlit, and Tortosa, all of which surrendered or were abandoned without a fight in the summer of the same year. The small island of Ruad facing Tortosa remained in the Templars' hands until 1303.

Index

Acknowledgments

We are grateful to the scholars and institutions who have contributed to this book in various ways, all helpful: Alfred J. Andrea, Nicole Bériou, Brenda Bolton, Leonard E. Boyle, OP[†], Kathleen Brahney, Daron Burrows, Gary Dickson, Jean Flori, Benjamin Z. Kedar, Robert Lerner, Jean Longère, Michael Lower, Thomas Madden, John C. Moore, Carolyn Muessig, James Muldoon, Ken Pennington, Jonathan Riley-Smith, Jay Carter Rubenstein, and Christopher Tyerman. We also thank the Bibliothèque Municipale in Douai, the Bibliothèque Nationale in Paris, the Bodleian Library, Oxford, the DePaul University Library, the Newberry Library, the Northwestern University Library, the Parker Library of Corpus Christi College (University of Cambridge), the Vatican Library, the Archivio Segreto Vaticano, the Van Pelt Library Center of the University of Pennsylvania, the Wheaton College Library, Yale University Libraries, and the Free Library of Guilford, Connecticut. Jessalynn Bird acknowledges and thanks the Thouron and Fulbright scholarships.

We gratefully acknowledge the superb and generous technical assistance of Michael Powell. At a critical moment, his information technology skills saved a good portion of the text of the book and converted it to workable files. Michael did so cheerily and quickly, in spite of a serious bout of illness. He also assembled the next-to-final text of this book. We also greatly appreciate the perceptive and very helpful advice of an anonymous reader for the University of Pennsylvania Press. And we are grateful for many other kinds of crucial assistance by Dr. Corin Pitcher.

To our great sorrow, our dear friend, collaborator, and adviser Jim Powell died unexpectedly as the result of an automobile accident in January 2011, after having printed out a hard copy of the manuscript of this book and correcting it by hand a month earlier. His contribution to it is inestimable, his learned affection greatly missed, and we dedicate the book to his memory.

Permissions

The editors and the University of Pennsylvania Press have done their best to determine the possession of rights to the use of the material printed here. We have attempted to make copyright clearance for all texts, although a number of presumed rights holders have not been traceable or have not responded to correspondence. Should any other party assert that its rights have been infringed, we are willing to make all accommodations necessary.

The following items, listed in the order of their appearance in the Table of Contents, depend on reprint rights that we have in every case attempted to obtain.

Nos. 3 and 6: Permission to reprint courtesy of the Catholic University of America Press.

No. 4 is translated with the acknowledgement of Prof. Kenneth Pennington.

No. 5: Originally published by Thomas Nelson, London; rights remain in the estate of Prof. Christopher R. Cheney.

No. 9: Permission to reprint granted by Aris & Phillips, an imprint of Oxbow Books LTD, to reproduce material from *Christians and Moors in Spain*, vol. 1 (pp. 139–141) and vol. 2 (pp. 14–25), edited and translated by Colin Smith, 1988–1989.

Nos. 24, 28, 52, and 73: Permission to reprint granted by the University of California Press, from Francesco Gabrieli, *Arab Historians of the Crusades*, pp. 264–266, 267–275, 293–295, 298–302, 344–350.

No. 26: Permission to reprint granted by the Columbia University Press. E-rights for John LaMonte, *The Wars of Frederick II against the Ibelins in Syria and Cyprus* remain in the estate of Prof. John LaMonte.

No. 33: Permission to reprint granted by Dr. Kathleen Brahney.

No. 50: Permission to reprint granted by Penguin Books Ltd, London, UK.

Nos. 51 and 53: Permission to reprint material from René Hague, *The Life of St. Louis* (Sheed and Ward, 1995), pp. 241–246, 247–254, granted by Continuum International Publishing Group.

No. 55: From *The Register of Eudes Rigaud of Rouen*, translated by Sydney M. Brown, edited by Jeremiah O'Sullivan. Copyright © Columbia University Press. Reprinted by permission of the publisher.

No. 58: Permission to reprint granted by Prof. Jonathan Riley-Smith.

No. 60: Permission to reprint granted by The Arizona Center for Medieval and Renaissance Studies.

No. 61: Permission to reprint granted by Princeton University Press.

No. 63: Rights remain in the estates of Mr. H. G. Richardson and Mr. G. O. Sayles.

No. 72: Permission to excerpt and reprint granted by the Publishers from *The Templar of Tyre*, ed. Paul F. Crawford (Farnham: Ashgate, 2003), pp. 104–114, 115–117. Copyright © 2003.